People of
the Earth

An Indian couple eating, painted by John White in the late sixteenth century. Thomas Hariot wrote of the Indians, "They are verye sober in their eating and trinkinge, and consequently verye longe lived because they doe not oppress nature. . . . I would to God we would followe their exemple."

SIXTH EDITION

People of the Earth

An Introduction to World Prehistory

Brian M. Fagan
University of California, Santa Barbara

SCOTT, FORESMAN AND COMPANY
Glenview, Illinois   Boston   London

TO All the dozens of archaeologists and students who have read and used this book in its various editions and sent me their comments and criticisms. This is the only way I can thank them all and expose them for what they are — honest and unmerciful critics. I am deeply grateful.

And, as usual, to our cats, who disapprove of authors in general and my writing efforts in particular. Their contribution was to tread on the manuscript — with muddy paws, of course.

Library of Congress Cataloging-in-Publication Data

Fagan, Brian M.
    People of the earth.

    Includes bibliographies and index.
    1. Man, Prehistoric.   2. Civilization, Ancient.
I. Title.
GN740.F33   1989   930   88–6467
ISBN 0–673–39908–7

2 3 4 5 6 7 8 9 10 — MVN — 94 93 92 91 90 89

Printed in the United States of America

Cover

Cueva de los Caballos, Spain. From J. G. D. Clark, *Prehistoric Europe*, 1952. Courtesy of Philosophical Library, Inc.

Credits

Frontispiece: Reproduced by courtesy of the Trustees of The British Museum.

CHAPTER 1

Photo Essay

Page 6, top left: Reprinted courtesy of James A. Brown, Northwestern University. *Middle left:* Reprinted courtesy of Stewart Struever. *Bottom left:* Reprinted courtesy of The Colonial Williamsburg Foundation. *Bottom right:* Reprinted courtesy of the Center for American Archaeology. *Page 7, top left:* Reprinted courtesy of The University of California/W. Swalling photographer. *Top right:* Reprinted courtesy of The University Museum, University of Pennsylvania/Nick Hartman photographer. *Bottom left:* Photo by Herb Greer. *Bottom right:* Photo by D.C. Ochsner, © UCLA Institute of Archaeology and JoAnne Van Tilburg, Director Moai Documentation Project, Easter Island 1984.

(Continued on page 609)

To the Reader

People of the Earth is an attempt at a straightforward narrative of human history from the origins of humankind up to the beginnings of literate civilization. To make the book accessible to those who have not previously studied archaeology, I keep technical terms to a minimum and define them where they do occur.

Anyone who takes on a task having the magnitude of a world prehistory must make several difficult decisions. One such decision was to gloss over many heated archaeological controversies and sometimes to give only one side of an academic argument. But the Bibliography of Archaeology at the back of the book is designed to lead you into the more technical literature and the morass of agreement and disagreement that characterizes world prehistory. The essential point is that much of what we know about prehistoric times is still based on very inadequate data. The important truth about archaeology, as with any other science, is that it deals not with absolute truth but with successive approximations of the truth.

The structure of *People of the Earth* is comparatively straightforward. Part I deals with general principles of archaeology, theoretical views of the past, and the climatic background. The remainder of the book is devoted to the story of human prehistory. All measurements are given in both English and metric units. Chronological tables are provided at the beginning of most chapters, putting cultural names, sites, dates, and other subdivisions of prehistory into a framework. Key dates and terms appear in the margins to give you a sense of chronological direction throughout the text. I would draw your special attention to the note below, which is fundamental to your understanding of the chronology of world prehistory.

Chronological Note

All dates cited in the text earlier than about 1000 B.C. (Before Christ) are expressed in years before present (B.P.), *present* being defined as A.D. 1950, the conventional year taken to reflect modern times. We switch to B.C./A.D. dating after about 1000 B.C. as this appears to be conventional usage, and people are more familiar with such a chronology when talking about, say, the Assyrians or the Maya.

To the Instructor

People of the Earth has been part of my archaeological life for fifteen years, years that have seen momentous changes in our understanding of world prehistory. This edition of the book, the sixth, bears little resemblance to the first, written at a time when archaeology was still a much less sophisticated discipline than it is today. Successive editions have reflected this increasing complexity, and the multidisciplinary nature of research into the prehistoric past. To my surprise, the book is used as a text in courses as varied as archaeology, physical anthropology and archaeology, world history, and, of course, world prehistory. *People* is used in Australia, in New Zealand, at European universities, and even in Africa. I am flattered to have had correspondence from Chinese colleagues, who have consulted and critiqued its pages. They are only a few of the many correspondents from near and far who take the touble to write and tell me about their varied researches. As a result, I have learned about archaeological field work that I otherwise would never have discovered. This book now reflects not only my own firsthand archaeological experience but the insights, advice, and research of hundreds of instructors, research archaeologists, and thousands of students. It is flattering, too, to meet occasional colleagues who remember reading *People* as a first undergraduate text—and to hear that it got them interested in archaeology. All of this makes the monotonous and seemingly never-ending task of revision a unique opportunity to look at the world of archaeology on the broadest possible canvas.

Like its predecessors, the sixth edition aims to communicate the work of scientific archaeologists to the widest possible audience. There are still some people who believe that modern archaeology is all an elaborate folderol and a hoax. Archaeologists are under attack from religious fundamentalists who believe that the scriptures offer the only true account of human history as well as from those who believe with the same religious fervor that their theories about the settlement of the Americas or the origins of civilization are the only possible truth. This book is based on scientific research, not religious belief or wild speculation. Its purpose is to provide the student with a straightforward account of human prehistory from the earliest times up to the advent of literate civilization. As such, *People* provides an answer to the critics of our discipline, for its pages show that we know much more about human prehistory than our critics suspect, or want to believe. What this book does *not* attempt is a frontal attack on either creationists or diffusionists. Not only is this a fruitless pastime, for you cannot shake people's sincerely held beliefs, but also I believe that instructors should tailor their courses to suit their audiences. All *People* can do is provide some theoretical background and basic data as a framework for teaching. It is up to you to defend archaeology against its critics, however ignorant they may be. To my mind, one of the best defenses is a well-taught undergraduate course based on good data. And this is what *People* attempts to provide.

I have revised over half the book for this edition, with the greatest changes coming in the Paleolithic (Old Stone Age) chapters. I have recast much of Chapter 2 to reflect new advances and current controversies in approaches to world prehistory. Chapter 3 has been revised extensively, in response to advances in deep sea core research. New theoretical approaches to paleoanthropology, many of them incorporating formulations from evolutionary biology, have led to a quantum jump in our understanding of early prehistory, as have meticulous researches into such esoteric subjects as tool edge wear and bone fracturing. Chapters 4 and 5, origins, *Homo erectus,* and the emergence of *Homo sapiens,* have been completely rewritten to take into account the dramatic advances and new discoveries of the last five years. For the first time, we are acquiring insights into such major developments in world prehistory as the spread of *Homo erectus* and *Homo sapiens sapiens* on a truly global scale. The revised text reflects these insights. Clive Gamble's *The Palaeolithic Settlement of Europe* (Cambridge: Cambridge University Press, 1986) is one of the most important studies of a major issue in world prehistory to appear in a generation. For the first time, it enables us to glimpse the full potential of anthropological archaeology for the study of early prehistory. As much a basis for discussion as a monograph, *The Palaeolithic Settlement* is a provocative look at new directions in prehistoric research. It formed the basis for my complete rewriting of the chapters on the archaeology of *Homo sapiens* in this edition.

Throughout the book I have updated and refined the text and illustrations, changing chronologies here, adding new sites there, and updating references throughout. The chapter on the first Americans has been updated and refined, new theoretical material on the origins of agriculture and civilization added to the chapters on those topics. I have taken into account recent research into European agriculture with a new chapter, and have included the major advances in our understanding of Maya civilization as a result of decipherment. For all these many changes, some chapters have stood the test of time well. Some of the latest research in areas such as Mexico or Sumer is so detailed that it has little impact on a basic text such as this, except, perhaps, in the addition of a reference, a few sentences, or a brief paragraph. The publication of many highly important pieces of research, foreshadowed in preliminary reports cited in earlier editions, has been noted.

There is no question that the basic formula for *People* has worked well. Almost all users have supported the broad geographic coverage of the book, so this remains a feature of the sixth edition. All too often, we teach students about the Americas, Europe, and the Near East, and forget that insights from less well known areas can often illuminate problems nearer to home. One only has to look at the research on early Australian aboriginal adaptive patterns or living archaeology in the Kalahari Desert in southern Africa to get the point. If I have sometimes skimped on detailed coverage of well-known areas, I am unrepentant. The omissions are more than outweighed by the interests of balanced coverage. Talking to many instructors over the years, I have found that they use the text as a basis for making their own comparative analyses of, say, Mesopotamian and Mesoamerican civilization, or of the emergence of food production in China and Peru. This is the purpose for which it is designed—to give both student and instructor a narrative basis for a comprehensive course on the prehistory of humankind.

Anyone writing a book on world prehistory is poised on the horns of a sharp-pointed academic dilemma. Should the book be heavy on theory, perhaps encased in a specific theoretical framework? Or is it better to compile a basic culture history of the world with relatively little emphasis on theory? Most reviewers and colleagues seem to feel we have achieved a realistic balance. *People* is written without an overriding theoretical framework, and with plenty of descriptive passages, in the knowledge that different instructors use the book in different ways, each bringing his or her theoretical bias to the material. If there is a pervasive theoretical theme for the book, it is the gradual progress of humankind as a member of the world ecological community. If there are three overriding developments in world prehistory in recent decades, they are a massive expansion of field research to all parts of the world, the widespread adoption of scientific and quantitative methods, and a much greater concern with theoretical models. *People* navigates between these developments with sedulous care, and tries to avoid excesses of scientific and theoretical bias. Presently, archaeologists seem intoxicated with science, sometimes to the extent that they forget they are studying human beings with all their complex motivations and thought processes. Perhaps the greatest message of world prehistory is not that we humans are different but that our behavior is so strikingly similar. You only have to compare the archaeological record from Mexico and Egypt to see what I mean. And this is a theme which I feel should pervade our world prehistory courses, a theme far more important than the latest nuances of archaeological theory or excavation technique.

Everyone working with students who are new to archaeology has to balance strict scientific accuracy and terminological precision against the dangers of misinformation and overstatement. I have tried to avoid a catalog and have deliberately erred on the side of overstatement. After all, the objective in a first course is to introduce students to a fascinating and complex subject. Overstatement is more likely to stick in their minds and can always be qualified at a more advanced level. The complexities of academic debate will be left to more specialized syntheses and to advanced courses.

As always, the new edition has benefited greatly from the detailed criticisms and frank advice of dozens of colleagues. I owe a particular debt to Professor Katharina Schreiber of the University of California, Santa Barbara, who critiqued the Peruvian chapters for me. Professors Mary Douglas of Portland Community College, Charles McNutt of Memphis State University, Donald Proulx of the University of Massachusetts, Amherst, Irvin Rovner of North Carolina State University, and James Sackett of the University of California, Los Angeles, kindly provided insightful reviews of the text during revision. I am grateful to them all, and have used most, if not all, of their comments in some way.

Last, a word of thanks to Billie Ingram, Paul Santoro, and Maryanne Zoll of the production staff at Scott, Foresman, and to Brad Gray and his editorial staff. They have made the revision of this book a (comparative) pleasure.

Contents

5 Toward Modern Humanity   123

PART III   *Homo Sapiens* and Hunter-Gatherers   165

PART I

Prehistory

We are concerned here with methodical digging for systematic information, not with the upturning of earth in a hunt for the bones of saints and giants or the armory of heroes, or just plainly for treasure.

—Sir Mortimer Wheeler

Part I contains the essential background about the study of archaeology needed for any examination of human prehistory. We make no attempt to give a comprehensive summary of all the methods and theoretical approaches used by archaeologists. Rather, Part I touches some of the high points and basic principles behind archaeologists' excavations and laboratory research. Our narrative is, in the final analysis, based on the systematic application of these principles. Chapter 3 gives some all-important background on the great climatic changes that form the backdrop to human prehistory.

Archaeology

Preview

- The systematic study of world prehistory started in the late nineteenth century as anthropologists began to study human diversity. At the same time biologists and social scientists were exploring the implications of biological and social evolution.

- Archaeology is the study of past human societies and is an integral part of anthropology. Archaeologists have three objectives: the study of culture history, the reconstruction of past lifeways, and the explanation of cultural process.

- Culture is a theoretical concept formulated by anthropologists to define the adaptive systems unique to humanity, for culture is the means by which we humans adapt to the challenges of the world's diverse environments.

- A culture is a complex system, a set of interacting variables that serve to maintain the population in equilibrium with its environment. No cultural system is ever static. It is always changing in ways that can be studied in the archaeological record.

- The archaeological record is the data amassed from archaeological survey and excavation. Preservation factors play an important part in the amount of information that can be obtained from the archaeological record.

- Every archaeological find, be it an artifact, a site, or food remains, has a context in space and time. The study of patterns of artifacts in space depends on the Law of Association, the notion that an object is contemporary with the other objects found in the same archaeological level.

- Relative chronology is based on the Law of Superposition, which holds that the lowest occupation level on a site is older than those that have accumulated on top of it. Chronometric chronology involves dates in years and is developed by a number of methods, including potassium argon dating, radiocarbon dating, obsidian hydration, dendrochronology, and cross-dating using objects of known age.

- Archaeological survey and excavation are carried out using carefully formulated research designs. Excavation methods vary with the type of site being investigated.

■ Archaeologists have developed sophisticated classification methods to describe artifacts and other finds; the classifications provide the basis for theorizing about archaeological cultures.

INTRODUCTION

The two men paused in front of the doorway bearing the seals of the long-dead pharaoh. They had waited six long years, from 1917 to 1922, for this moment. Silently, Howard Carter pried a hole through the ancient plaster. Hot air rushed out of the small cavity and massaged his face. Carter shone a flashlight through the hole and peered into the tomb. Gold objects swam in front of his eyes, and he was struck dumb with amazement.

Lord Carnarvon moved impatiently behind him as Carter remained silent. "What do you see?" he asked, hoarse with excitement.

"Wonderful things," whispered Carter as he stepped back from the doorway.

The door was soon broken down. In a daze of wonderment, the discoverers wandered through the antechamber of Tutankhamun's tomb. They fingered golden funerary beds, admired beautifully inlaid chests, and examined the pharaoh's chariots stacked against the wall. Gold was everywhere — on wooden statues, inlaid on thrones and boxes, in jewelry, even on children's stools. Soon Tutankhamun was known as the golden pharaoh, and archaeology as the domain of buried treasure and royal sepulchers.

Gold, silver, lost civilizations, unsolved mysteries, grinning skeletons . . . all are part of the romantic world of archaeology in most people's minds. Archaeologists seem like romantic adventurers, digging into pyramids and finding long-forgotten inscriptions in remote places. Like Indiana Jones of movie fame, we come across as students of sunken continents and great migrations, as experts on epic journeys and powerful civilizations. A century ago, many archaeologists were indeed adventurers. Today, however, archaeology has become a complex and demanding scientific pastime that studies over 2.5 million years of human existence. On the face of it, modern scientific archaeology may seem dull and highly technical, but the fascination of great adventure has been replaced by all the excitement of the detective story. Fictional detectives take a handful of clues and solve apparently insoluble murders. Archaeologists take a multitude of small and apparently trivial archaeological finds and use them to answer basic questions about ancient societies.

Even as late as the 1870s, you could go out digging in the Near East and find a long-lost civilization. German businessman-turned-archaeologist Heinrich Schliemann was convinced that Homer's Troy had actually existed. Armed with a copy of the *Iliad*, he went out to Turkey and cut great trenches into the ancient mounds at Hissarlik. Schliemann found the remains of nine cities stratified one above the other and announced that the seventh was Homer's Troy (Ceram, 1953; Fagan, 1985). His discoveries caused an international sensation. So did Frenchman Emil de Sarzec when he unearthed Sumer in desolate southern Mesopotamia, a civilization that soon turned out to be one of the earliest in the world, and the society where the Flood legend in Genesis probably originated (Fagan, 1979).

The twentieth century has seen archaeology turn from a casual treasure hunt into a science. There have been dramatic discoveries by the dozens — Tutankhamun's tomb in 1922, the royal cemetery at Ur of the Chaldees in Iraq in 1928, the spectacular early human fossils discovered by the Leakey family in East Africa during the last quarter century, and, in the 1980s, magnificent royal burials in China and Guatemala. While these finds have stirred the popular imagination, archaeologists have been engaged in a less conspicuous but just as fascinating adventure of discovery — through 2.5 million years of prehistoric times.

In the 1840s, most scientists assumed that humankind was only a few thousand years old, perhaps no more than the 6000 years allowed for by the biblical account of the Creation in Genesis (Grayson, 1983). By the late nineteenth century, archaeologists believed that the first human beings had lived on earth some tens of thousands of years ago, perhaps as many as 100,000 years before the present. Modern scientific archaeology, with its elaborate dating methods and close ties to the natural sciences, has drawn back the curtains on a much longer prehistoric stage. Thanks to radiocarbon and potassium argon dating techniques, we know that the first humans emerged in East Africa at least 2.5 million years ago. For more than a million years, our early ancestors lived on wild vegetable foods and by scavenging meat from predator kills. Then, about 1.5 million years ago, the first true humans emerged, hunters and gatherers who spread from the savanna regions of Africa into more temperate latitudes. These larger-brained people were apparently capable of articulate speech and gave way some 400,000 years ago to the immediate ancestors of modern human beings, *Homo sapiens.*

For most of the past 2.5 million years, the rate of human biological and cultural evolution was glacially slow at best, but about 40,000 years ago, the evolutionary pace quickened with the emergence of the first fully modern people. *Homo sapiens sapiens* settled in all parts of the world, in the extremes of arctic and tropical climates. Modern people crossed into the New World from Siberia, settled in the deserts of Australia, and developed the first artistic traditions. Far from being only big-game hunters, many of them specialized in gathering wild vegetable foods, fishing, or collecting shellfish. And, more than 10,000 years ago, some of them began to cultivate the soil and domesticate sheep, goats, and other animals — a true revolution in human existence.

The new economies took off like wildfire. It took only 8000 years for most of the world to turn to food production. Agriculture and stock raising were well established throughout the Near East by 9500 years ago and had spread to Europe a millennium later. The Chinese were cultivating by 8000 years ago, the New Guinea highlanders by about the same time, perhaps much earlier. Only in game-rich Africa and isolated Australasia did hunter-gatherer economies survive into recent times. The inhabitants of much of sub-Saharan Africa started growing crops and herding about only 2000 years ago. The native Americans took to food production by 7000 years ago, domesticating wild cereal grasses and beans, as well as root crops like the sweet potato. Food production was probably the most significant watershed in human prehistory, for it enabled the development of much more complex societies, and, ultimately, our own industrial civilization.

We live in cities with populations in the millions. Yet, only 10,000 years ago, most humans lived in tiny camps or small sedentary villages. The inexorable cultural forces of the agricultural revolution soon led to the emergence of literate, urban civilizations, first in Mesopotamia and Egypt, then in the Indus Valley, the Aegean, and the Far East. The great civilizations of the Americas subsisted on maize and bean cultivation — the Olmec and Maya of Mesoamerica, the coastal and highland civilizations of Peru. And, in the Old World, small-scale city-states and valley civilizations were followed by the imperial civilizations of Persia, Greece, and Rome, which linked many diverse cultures into much larger hegemonies. While the preindustrial civilizations relied on abundant cheap humanpower for their prosperity, the industrial civilization of today evolved from a preindustrial base, propelled to ever greater technological complexity by the use of fossil fuels, the advances of science, and the industrial revolution.

The fascinating chronicle of world prehistory has been written from the testimony of millions of chipped stones, animal bone fragments, and potsherds, from Sumerian clay tablets, pollen grains from Scandinavian bogs, and ancient Peruvian textiles. Archaeology is, as more than one author has reminded us, the science of rubbish (Fagan, 1988b). The data may seem trivial, but the results are not. World prehistory is of vital concern to everyone, for it records the collective cultural heritage of all humankind.

Scientific archaeology developed out of treasure hunting. It is a process of careful research design, site survey, excavation, laboratory analysis, and interpretation. In fact, it is no coincidence that the first scientific excavations were conducted by a retired British general and German archaeologists who came from a strongly military cultural tradition. It was they who imposed the first discipline on archaeological excavation, a discipline that continues to this day. To most people, archaeology *is* excavation — trenches, careful troweling and shoveling, and the clearance of burials with paintbrushes and dental picks. However, as the accompanying picture essay shows, modern archaeology is far more, involving everything from walking the countryside to sophisticated remote-sensing techniques and many months of quiet laboratory analysis. Archaeology is a complicated form of teamwork, involving not only experts but also volunteers from every walk of life. Many college students go on an excavation as part of their learning experience. If you are lucky, you will find an unusual artifact or help the archaeologists interpret a complicated sequence of long-collapsed buildings. You can spend your spare hours sorting shellfish and bone fragments from Indian shell middens, become an expert on a particular prehistoric pottery, or operate a computer program that holds the data from months of field work. Your work may seem trivial, sometimes even dull, but the results are another tiny part of the great jigsaw of world prehistory. None of our attempts to explain the rise of civilization, or the origins of humanity, would mean anything unless they were based on scientifically recovered archaeological data.

People of the Earth takes you on a 2.5-million-year journey through prehistory, from the very earliest times up to the emergence of the first urban civiliza-

Above, left. A general view of excavations at the Koster site, near Kampsville, Illinois. Excavated levels are covered with plastic sheets to protect them against the weather.

Left. A student excavator cleaning a human burial dating from about 5000 years ago. Brushes and dental picks are normally used for this delicate work. The bones are cleaned, then photographed and recorded before being lifted from the grave.

Below, left. An exemplary excavation of an eighteenth-century kitchen at Colonial Williamsburg, Virginia. Large tree roots had damaged the north foundation. Behind it lies the H-shaped foundation for the chimney.

Below. Students at the Koster site surveying the area that has been excavated.

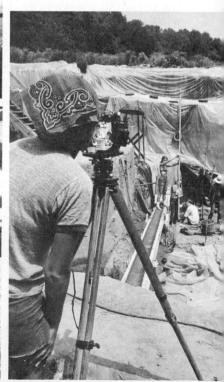

Above. A student archaeologist doing laboratory work; she is sorting through midden debris for small bones and artifacts.

Above, right. A technician working in a radiocarbon laboratory; he is dating archaeological samples from 500 to 70,000 years old.

Below. An archaeologist equipped with scuba gear records features of a Bronze Age shipwreck from Cape Gelidonya, Turkey, dating to about 1200 B.C.

Below, right. Field crew at work measuring a prehistoric Easter Island statue for the Rock Art Archive of the Institute of Archaeology, Los Angeles, California.

tions. However, we begin by explaining some of the basic principles, methods, and theories of archaeology so that you will be better equipped both to understand prehistory and to participate in archaeology yourself as a volunteer if you so desire. Good luck with your adventures in the past!

WHY STUDY WORLD PREHISTORY?

Before starting our journey, we deal with another fundamental point. Why study world prehistory at all? Some people believe that any form of archaeology is a harmless luxury, a low priority in a world beset by inflation, famine, and geopolitics. Why look to the past, they ask, when all our energies should be devoted to preparing for an uncertain future? How can one look at the future, though, without an understanding of the past and, above all, of our own behavior? Whether we like it or not, we live with the legacy of the recent and remote past. Our civilization derives many of its most cherished institutions from Classical Greece, while city life was developed between the Euphrates and Tigris rivers in Iraq more than 5000 years ago. Famine, slavery, warfare, and poverty are nothing new; they were familiar phenomena to the Ancient Egyptians, the Chinese, and the Sumerians. In reality, we live with the consequences of decisions and actions that were enacted centuries or even millennia ago. The study of prehistory gives us a balanced perspective on our behavior and on our responses to pressing problems that are not new, even though they threaten us on a larger scale.

Western civilization has a written chronicle that extends back to Sumerian times, more than 5000 years ago. However, many of the world's societies have very limited historical records, known to us only through scattered folk memories or archaeological excavations. The Aztec people of Mexico first came into contact with the Spanish in 1519. Within a few years their civilization was in ruins, their written chronicles burned by zealous missionaries. As a result, our knowledge of Aztec history is a patchwork of incomplete data from dozens of sources, yet a knowledge of this history is vital not only for fostering a sense of identity among the surviving Aztec people and for nation building in Mexico but also for understanding the ways in which the pre-Columbians solved the problems of living (Fagan, 1984a). It is no coincidence that many African nations have active archaeological programs, designed to reconstruct a national history from a morass of obscure tribal histories and excavations at archaeological sites. Likewise, many American Indian groups have become involved in archaeological research (Kirk, 1975). In prehistoric times, most societies focused on living in equilibrium with their environment, existing in a world that was assumed to have been the same in the past and that would remain unchanged in the future. Today industrial civilization, with its concern with cultural roots and cultural identity, dominates the world, so there are compelling reasons for every society to have at least some sense of its cultural origins. In many cases, archaeology provides the only way of gaining this insight.

We live in a biologically and culturally diverse world, a world that is shrinking rapidly in this age of the jetliner, the satellite, and instant communications.

Even half a century ago the world was a large place. Today the world, in all its bewildering diversity, comes right into our living rooms. We can contact Peru within seconds and watch wars on the other side of the globe as they are being fought. Confronting this diversity often is an uncomfortable experience, especially since we tend to perceive the differences between various societies as much greater than they really are. By looking back over the long millennia of prehistory we obtain a quite different perspective of a world in which people have worked out solutions to extremely challenging problems with brilliant success, problems such as food shortages, rapidly growing populations, and catastrophic environmental changes. Very often the solutions of various societies, although they are separated by thousands of miles, have been remarkably similar: the advent of writing, the development of cities, or the formation of a state-organized society. What is striking is not the diversity of humankind but the remarkably similar ways in which we respond to external challenges. Societies may wax and wane, civilizations rise and fall, but something new always arises in their place. To look back at prehistory is to acquire a faith in humanity's ability to innovate and respond to changing circumstances. We are surrounded by doomsday prophets, by people who forecast the imminent demise of civilization, of humanity itself. Any serious student of prehistory can have no doubt that humankind will rise to the challenges of the twentieth century. We shall survive.

A final compelling reason to study world prehistory is simply for the fun of it. We can look back at an extraordinary landscape of biological and cultural evolution, at our very origins among the nonhuman primates, at the first migrants to the New World more than 25,000 years ago, and at remarkable civilizations as widely separated as Peru and the Indus Valley. We are surrounded by awesome ruins that have survived the centuries to enlighten our own age: the pyramids of Giza erected more than 4500 years ago, the brooding stone circles of Stonehenge in southern Britain, and the vast plazas and temples of the ancient city of Teotihuacán, Mexico. Most of us contrive to visit at least one major archaeological site during our lifetimes, to marvel at the achievements of our predecessors on this planet. An understanding of world prehistory enables us not only to better appreciate these monuments but also to recognize them for what they are, an integral part of the cultural heritage of all humanity.

In the pages that follow the prehistory of humankind from the earliest times is recounted, using scientifically collected data from all over the world. This account is founded on the basic assumption that the theory of biological evolution and natural selection provides a viable framework for the study of world prehistory.

ANTHROPOLOGY

Anthropology encompasses the whole range of human cultures, both Western and non-Western (Pelto, 1966; Penniman, 1965). As the study of humanity, anthropology is a holistic discipline that uses comparative methods to examine the variations in economic, political, religious, and other institutions and customs throughout every human society. Anthropologists are interested in comparisons between different cultures, and in biological and cultural evolution. The comparative and evolutionary aspects of anthropology make it unique among the social sciences.

Archaeology

Archaeology is the study of the lives and cultures of ancient peoples. Archaeologists study and interpret the material evidence of past human activity. The archaeologist is a special type of anthropologist who uses the static evidence of the archaeological record (artifacts, sites, food remains, and so on) to study once-living peoples. Archaeology has three main objectives, all of which involve interpreting the data of the archaeological record using sophisticated analytic techniques, the natural processes that created the data, and controlled experiments and analogies from present-day societies. These objectives are the study of culture history, a reconstruction of past lifeways, and an explanation of cultural process. There are many types of archaeologists, each having distinctive objectives, methods, techniques, and theoretical approaches. *Classical archaeologists* study Greek and Roman civilization; *historical archaeologists* study relatively recent sites such as Colonial American towns or medieval cities. *Anthropological archaeologists* (prehistorians) are concerned with sites of all ages, but they tend to concentrate their research efforts primarily on prehistoric settlements. *Paleoanthropologists* study the earliest human cultures of all.

Physical
anthropology

Physical anthropologists study the emergence and later evolution of humankind and why human populations vary one from another (Weiss and Mann, 1988). Early human evolution is documented by fossil human and prehuman remains found in archaeological sites and geological levels. Physical anthropologists are deeply involved in modern human biology, trying to find out why different human populations have adapted physically to widely differing natural environments. *Primatologists* are physical anthropologists who are experts on ape and monkey behavior. Their work provides information relevant to the study of early human behavior.

History

History is the study of our past through written records; such records extend back only 5000 years, and then only in Mesopotamia and Egypt. *Prehistory*, the millennia before documentary history, goes back at least 2.5 million years.

HUMAN CULTURE

Culture

Culture is a term we will use again and again in these pages. Anthropologists study human cultures, and all of us live within a culture. Most cultural descriptions can be qualified by one or more labels, such as *middle-class, American, mountain-dwelling,* or *Masai.* This qualification often becomes associated in our minds with certain behavior patterns or features that are typical of the culture so labeled. One such attribute for "middle-class Americans," for example, might be the hamburger.

Culture is a concept developed by anthropologists to describe the distinctive adaptive systems used by human beings (Jochim, 1981). The great Victorian anthropologist Edward Tylor (1871) called culture "that complex whole which includes knowledge, belief, art, morals, law, custom, and any other capabilities and habits acquired by man as a member of society." To that definition modern anthropologists would add that culture is our primary way of adapting to our environment.

Until the emergence of humanity, all animals adapted to their environments through biological evolution. If an animal was well adapted to its environment, it prospered. If it was not, it evolved into a new species, moved away, or became extinct. The forces of biological evolution gave the polar bear a thick coat and layers of fat to protect it from the arctic cold, but Eskimos, the human occupants of the Arctic, do not possess layers of fur. They wear warm clothing and make snow houses to shield themselves from the environment. Their tools and dwellings are part of their culture — their adaptive system that coincides with the polar bear's fur.

Ordinarily, when animals die their experience dies with them. However, humans, once biological evolution had led to the development of speech, were able to communicate their feelings and experiences from one generation to the next. They could share ideas, which in turn became behavior patterns that were repeated again and again. We see abundant traces of this development throughout prehistory, when the same types of tools and sites are found, almost unchanged, over millennia of prehistory. A good example of this phenomenon is the stone hand ax, a multipurpose tool that remained in use for more than one million years (Figure 5.8, p. 138).

Human beings use the symbolic system of language to transmit ideas and their culture. Culture is learned by intentional teaching as well as trial and error and simple imitation. Since people share ideas by teaching, the same artifacts and behavior continue from one generation to the next. Culture is an ongoing phenomenon that changes gradually over time.

Unlike biological adaptation, culture is nongenetic and it provides a much quicker way to share ideas that enable people to cope with their environment. It is the adaptive nature of culture that allows archaeologists to assume that artifacts found in archaeological sites are patterned adaptations to the environment.

A culture is a complex system, a set of interacting variables — tools, burial customs, ways of getting food, religious beliefs, social organization, and so on — that function to maintain a community in a state of equilibrium with its environment. When one element in the system changes, say hunting practices as a result of a prolonged drought, then reacting adjustments will occur in many other elements, so that the system stays in a state as closely approximating the original system as possible. It follows that no cultural system is ever static. It is always changing in big and small ways, some of which can be studied in archaeological sites.

Cultural system

Archaeologists tend to think of culture as possessing two broad components:

- The individual's own version of his or her culture, the diversified individual behavior that makes up the myriad strains of a culture.
- Shared culture, where elements of a culture are shared by everyone. These can include cultural activities like hunting or farming, or any shared human activity, as well as the body of rules and prescriptions that go to make up the whole of the culture. Shared culture is the system of behavior in which every

individual *participates.* Not only do you share it with other members of society but you participate in the cultural system as well. Both sharing and participation, however, could not take place without language as a vehicle of communication.

Culture, then, can be viewed as either a blend of shared traits or a system that permits a society to interact with its environment. In order to accomplish more than merely working out chronological sequences, however, the archaeologist has to view culture as a complex set of interacting components. Unless the processes that actually operate the system are carefully defined, these components would remain static, which is why archaeologists are deeply concerned with what is called *cultural process,* the processes by which human societies changed in the past.

Cultural changes take place through time, most being gradual and cumulative. Inventions and design improvements result in dozens of minor alterations in the ways people live. Generally, culture evolution was gradual in prehistoric times, although there are cases of sudden change, such as the Roman conquest of Gaul. Dramatic cultural modification can result from the diffusion from neighboring areas of a new idea or invention, such as the plow (Chapter 2). Culture change is proceeding at a dizzying pace in our own society, to the extent that we have problems adjusting to its constancy.

The cumulative effects of long-term culture change are easily seen. A comparison of the simple flaked stone tools of the earliest humans and the sophisticated contents of the Egyptian pharaoh Tutankhamun's tomb will help one to understand the power of cumulative change over thousands of years.

Modern archaeology swirls with controversy about the goals of research. Earlier archaeologists often were content just to collect and classify their finds into long sequences of human cultures. They described changing cultures but made no effort to explain *why* change took place and *what* changes meant. Today's archaeologist is concerned with explanation as well as description of ancient cultures, with processes of cultural change through time. The term *process* is used in archaeology to refer to mechanisms by which cultures change. These processes of culture change are studied by looking at variables in cultural systems that could lead to cultural change (Chapter 2). Then there is the archaeological record itself. Just trying to understand how it came into being is a far less obvious process than might be apparent (Binford, 1983).

THE ARCHAEOLOGICAL RECORD

Archaeologists study human cultures of the past and have to be content, for the most part, with the surviving, more durable evidence of prehistoric culture (Deetz, 1967; Fagan, 1988a). Any excavator is like a detective piecing together events from fragmentary clues.

What we can find out about the past is severely limited by soil conditions. Stone and baked clay are among the most lasting substances, surviving under almost all conditions. Wood, bone, leather, and metals are much less durable and seldom remain for the archaeologist to find. In the Arctic, however, whole sites have been found frozen, preserving highly perishable wooden tools or, in Siberia, complete carcasses of extinct mammoths (J. D. G. Clark, 1965). Water-logged bogs in Denmark have preserved long-dead victims of human sacrifice, and wooden tools survive well in such sites too. Everyone has heard of the remarkable tomb of Egyptian pharaoh Tutankhamun, whose astonishing treasure survived almost intact in the dry climate of the Nile Valley for more than 3000 years (Romer, 1981). Still, in most archaeological sites only a few durable materials survive, and reconstructing the past from these finds often is difficult.

The *archaeological record* is the data amassed from survey and excavation: we might think of it as the archival raw materials of world prehistory.

Archaeological record

The inevitable result of having only durable remains to study is that many prehistoric cultures are interpreted solely on the basis of such imperishable tools as stone axes or clay potsherds. The only way archaeologists can combat this emphasis is by meticulous study of sites where preservation conditions are outstanding; through careful examination of the arrangement of artifacts in the soil, archaeologists may discover a clue about the activities or social status of the artifacts' owners.

Until recently, most archaeologists simply accepted the limitations of the archaeological record. They made little effort to understand the ways in which the record was formed. Consider for a moment a newly abandoned hunter-gatherer campsite in the Illinois Valley of the Midwest. The inhabitants leave collapsing houses, newly extinguished hearths, broken-up bones, acorn husks, and all manner of domestic debris as well as worn-out artifacts behind them. The years pass. Rain and wind destroy the houses, and they become a scatter of foundation stones and postholes. The acorn husks and bones decay and vanish. Soon the site is covered with dense woodland and grass, soils accumulate, and there are no surface traces of the site left. Once buried, the surviving structures, hearths, and artifacts undergo still further change as a result of processes resulting from the distinctive soil chemistry on the site. Hundreds, if not thousands, of years later some archaeologists come along and dig up the site. All that they will unearth are the surviving remnants of generations of decay processes. These processes vary from site to site and are little understood (Chapter 2).

Since our understanding of these processes is very much in its infancy, most archaeologists still rely heavily on sites where preservation conditions are exceptional and on the assistance of scholars from other disciplines. Botanists and zoologists can identify seeds and bone fragments from ancient living sites to reconstruct prehistoric diets. Geologists study lake beds, gravels, and caves for the many tools from early millennia. Paleontologists and paleobotanists specialize in the evolution of mammals and plants, studying bones from extinct animals and pollens from long-vanished plants. They help reconstruct ancient climates, which have fluctuated greatly through our long history. Chemists and physicists employ radioactive methods of dating for volcanic rocks and organic substances such as bone and charcoal. These techniques have produced a rough chronological framework for more than 2.5 million years of human life. Modern archaeology is truly a multidisciplinary team effort, depending on scientists from many fields of inquiry. In one afternoon, an excavator may call on a glass expert, an authority on seashells, an earthworm specialist, and a soil scientist. Each has a piece to fit into the archaeological puzzle.

THE FINITE ARCHAEOLOGICAL RECORD AND CULTURAL RESOURCE MANAGEMENT

The records of written history are preserved in manuscripts, in books, and on clay tablets or papyrus — archives of the past that can be photocopied, transcribed, and traced. The archives of world prehistory are the sites, artifacts, and other material remains of human behavior that make up the archaeological record. This record is finite, an intricate association of individual archaeological phenomena and geological or occupation layers, the context in time and space in which they occur. Every time someone picks up an artifact, or excavates a site, or constructs a highway through an ancient Indian village, the archives of the prehistoric past are destroyed, at best modified. The archaeological record is quite different from a forest. Trees can regerminate, forests be reseeded. But once disturbed the archaeological record is gone forever. Prehistory is nonrenewable.

Many of the fine artifacts displayed in museums can be admired as magnificent examples of prehistoric technological skill. But most have been wrenched from their sites without regard for their archaeological context, the information they could yield about prehistoric times. The archives of the past consist of far more than fine artifacts in public museums. They consist of archaeological sites and the information, as well as the artifacts, within them. Once disturbed, these cannot be replaced.

Prehistory is under siege — from unscrupulous art dealers and amateur "pot hunters," from industrial activity, road construction, and urban sprawl, from deep plowing and strip mining. Every month, hundreds more sites vanish under the bulldozer or plow, scattered into historical oblivion. Some experts believe that there will be virtually no undisturbed archaeological sites in Europe, parts of Mesoamerica, and North America by the end of this century (McGimsey, 1973).

Many archaeologists are now engaged full-time in a frantic scramble to save sites from destruction. These activities — environmental impact studies and field projects, salvage excavations and complex regional surveys — are called *cultural resource management*, the process of managing archaeological sites and other cultural resources as nonrenewable parts of the landscape. Cultural resource management involves complicated legal and management decisions, some of which can conflict directly with the purely academic task of studying prehistoric times (D. D. Fowler, 1986; Knudsen, 1986), but the mass of information being acquired from such activity shows promise of transforming our knowledge of North American prehistory.

Cultural resource management

The future of the past depends, however, not only on archaeologists but on the public at large. Many people still think of archaeology as a glorified treasure hunt, of archaeological sites as potential treasure troves. But for a significant part of the archaeological record to survive in the twenty-first century there must be concerted effort not only by professionals but by every member of the public. You can do your bit by reporting all archaeological finds to responsible authorities, never collecting prehistoric artifacts or digging into sites, and respecting native American burial grounds.

The future of world prehistory depends on all of us!

ARTIFACTS, SITES, AND CONTEXT

World prehistory is recorded in thousands of archaeological sites and artifacts, each of which has a precise place in space and time, that is, in its context. Some knowledge of the ways in which archaeologists study the dimensions of space and time is essential to an understanding of prehistory (Dunnell, 1971).

Archaeological context is the culturally significant location of a find spot of any object in an archaeological site (Fagan, 1988b). *Cultural context* is a subcategory that represents the position of an object; was it found in a pit, in a room, on a surface? Metric data are used to define the position of the object uniquely. The time component of the context is the date of the object in years or its position in the layers of an archaeological site relative to other artifacts and layers. The time and space context of an archaeological find provides the basis for building up long sequences of archaeological sites in time and space.

Context

An *artifact* is "anything which exhibits any physical attributes that can be assumed to be the results of human activity" (Dunnell, 1971). The term *artifact* covers every form of archaeological find — from stones axes to clay pots, butchered animal bones, and manifestations of human behavior found in archaeological sites.

Artifact

Archaeological sites are places where traces of ancient human activity are to be found. The Great Pyramid of Giza is an archaeological site; so is a tiny scatter of hunter-gatherer artifacts found on the surface of the Utah desert. There are millions of sites in the world, many still undiscovered. They are limited in number and variety only by preservation conditions and the activities of the people who lived on them. Some, like the early bone caches at Olduvai Gorge, Tanzania, were used for only short periods of time (M. D. Leakey, 1971). Others, like the great Mesopotamian city mounds or *tells*, like Ur of the Chaldees, were occupied for thousands of years (Lloyd, 1963; Woolley, 1934). Archaeological sites often are classified according to the activities that took place upon them — living sites, kill sites, burial sites, religious sites, art sites, and so on. Many archaeological sites contain evidence of different activities: those of individual households, of entire communities, perhaps even of a single craftsperson like a potter, whose artifacts lie in a pattern as they were abandoned.

Site

Features are humanly manufactured structures found in archaeological sites, and they can take many forms. These include hut foundations, temples, humble storage pits, graves, fences, and fortifications.

Features

SPACE

The archaeological context of space can run from a simple spatial relationship between two artifacts to the distance between several households, or even to the relationships between an entire regional network of communities (Flannery, 1976). Context in space is closely tied to cultural behavior. Archaeologists infer behavior from artifacts and their associations, from the patterning (spatial arrangement) of tools around, say, an abandoned bison carcass. A single projectile point dug up out of context at this particular site would allow us nothing more than the reasonable inference that it was part of a weapon. However, the patterning of many such weapon points in association with the butchered remains of the bison can tell us much about how the animal was killed and cut up. The relationships between the carcass and the tools in the ground are our primary source of information on human behavior there.

Association

The *Law of Association* is based on the principle that an object is contemporary with the other objects found in the precise archaeological level in which it is found (Figure 1.1). The study of space is the study of associations between artifacts within their archaeological cultures. It also involves the study of the distribution of human settlements against a background of the ancient environment in which they flourished.

FIGURE 1.1 The Law of Association. (a) A skeleton associated with a single dagger; (b) a pot and a stone ax, separated by a stratigraphic break, not in association; (c) two contemporary household clusters associated with each other; (d) an association of two communities that are contemporary.

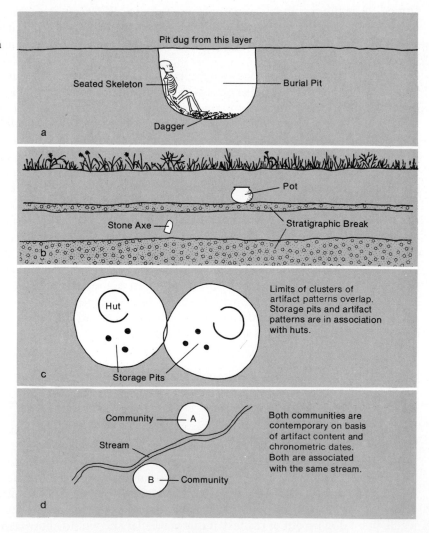

TIME

World prehistory extends through at least 2.5 million years of gradually accelerating cultural change. The measurement of this enormous time scale has been a preoccupation of archaeologists for years.

Relative Chronology

At the end of the eighteenth century, people began to realize that the earth's rocks were stratified, or laid down in layers, one after another. The notion of geological stratification was soon applied to archaeological sites and is now a cornerstone of *relative chronology*, the correlation of prehistoric sites or cultures with one another by their relative age.

Stratification is based on the *Law of Superposition*, which says that the lowest occupation level on a site is older than those accumulated on top of it. The principle can be readily understood if you place a book on a flat surface. Then place a second book on top of the first. Obviously, the first book was put on the table earlier than the second that lies upon it. Unless you took a stopwatch and timed the exact interval in minutes and seconds between the time you placed the first and second books on the surface, you have no idea how much time separated the two events. All you know is that the second book was placed on the first at a *relatively later* moment. Figure 1.2 illustrates the principle of superposition in archaeological practice.

Superposition

Superpositions are established by careful excavation and observation of archaeological layers. These layers are excavated with great care, and the artifacts associated with them are carefully studied relative to the stratigraphy of the site. We have stated that artifact styles change slowly though time. Every artifact style, however elaborate or simple, has a period of maximum popularity. This can be a few short months in the case of a dress fashion or tens of thousands of years for a stone tool type. By careful study of artifacts such as pottery found in the successive layers of several archaeological sites in a single region, it is possible to develop a relative chronology of changing artifact styles that is based on the assumption that the period of maximum popularity of a particular pottery type, or series, is the one when it is most frequently found (see Figure 1.3). By using these plots of artifact frequencies, one can develop a relative chronology that later can be used to place isolated sites into the sequence on the basis of their artifact content. This type of ordered or *seriated* relative chronology is not expressed in years unless it can be checked by some dating method that provides dates in years (Deetz, 1967; Marquardt, 1978).

Seriation

These ordered sequences of sites and layers can be expanded very effectively by a technique known as *cross-dating*. This requires a well-studied sequence of different artifacts whose development through time has been established by excavation, seriation of the artifacts, and stratigraphic observations. In the Tehuacán Valley in Mexico, Richard MacNeish was able to assign a relative date to isolated settlements by careful analysis of their pottery (MacNeish, 1970). (For a Peruvian example, see Menzel and others, 1964.) He counted the different vessel forms and decorative motifs at each site, then simply placed them in chronological order by matching the percentages of forms and motifs at undated sites

Cross-dating

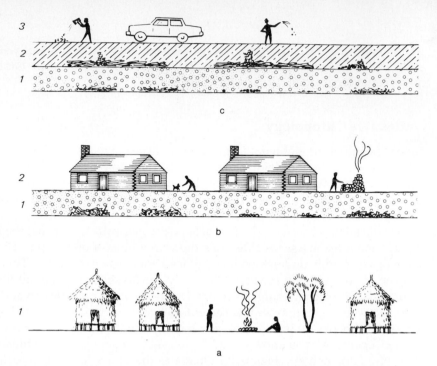

FIGURE 1.2 Superposition and stratigraphy. (a) A farming village built on virgin subsoil. After a time, the village is abandoned and the huts fall into disrepair. Their ruins are covered by accumulating soil and vegetation. (b) After an interval, a second village is built on the same site, with different architectural styles. This in turn is abandoned; the houses collapse into piles of rubble and are covered by accumulating soil. (c) Twentieth-century people park their cars on top of both village sites and drop litter and coins, which, when uncovered, reveal to the archaeologist that the top layer is modern.

An archaeologist digging this site would find that the modern layer is underlain by two prehistoric occupation levels, that square houses were in use in the upper of the two, which is the later (Law of Superposition), and that round huts are stratigraphically earlier than square ones here. Therefore, Village 1 is earlier than Village 2, but when either was occupied or how many years separate Village 1 from Village 2 cannot be known without further data.

with those in a dated sequence nearby. For example, a site with 60 percent red painted bowls is dated to 150 B.C., so it is a reasonable supposition that an undated comparable settlement with the same proportion of similar vessels (and, of course, comparable percentages of other features) is of approximately the same date. Cross-dating like this has been used over wide areas of Mexico to compare sites in different valleys and environments.

Another type of cross-dating has proved useful in European and American sites. The early civilizations of the Near East traded extensively with the Minoan and Mycenaean civilizations of Greece and Crete as well as with Barbarian Europe (Childe, 1958; C. Renfrew, 1972). They exchanged luxuries such as semiprecious stones and ornaments with the illiterate Europeans for copper, salt, and other raw materials. Some of these luxuries can be dated very precisely in their home countries, so much so that their discovery on an archaeological

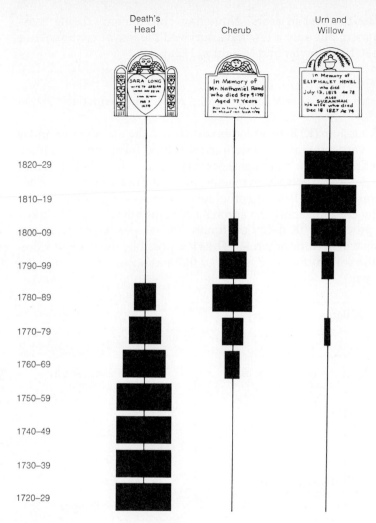

FIGURE 1.3 Seriation. The changing styles of New England gravestones from Stoneham, Massachusetts, between 1720 and 1829, seriated in three different styles. Notice how each style rises to a peak of maximum popularity and then declines as another comes into fashion.

site in central Europe enables one to say that the level in which the dated foreign object was found dates to the time of the import or later. Since the date of the artifact is known at its source, the settlement in which it is found can be relatively dated to a period contemporary with, or younger than, the exotic object of known age. For instance, a Roman coin minted the year Julius Caesar invaded Britain found in an undated French village would date that settlement to a year no earlier than 55 B.C.

Chronometric (Absolute) Chronology

Chronometric dates are dates in calendar years. Prehistoric chronologies cover long periods of time, millennia or centuries as opposed to days or minutes. Some idea of the scale of prehistoric time can be gained by piling up one hundred quarters. If the whole pile represents the entire time that humans and their culture have been on earth, the length of time covered by historical records would equal considerably less than the thickness of one quarter.

How do we date the past in years? Numerous chronometric dating techniques have been tried, but only a few have survived the test of continual use (Table 1.1) (Michels, 1973; Taylor and Meighan, 1978).

Potassium argon dating

TIME SPAN: From the origins of humankind down to approximately 20,000 years ago.

PRINCIPLES: Potassium (K) is an abundant element in the earth's crust and is present in nearly every mineral. Potassium in its natural form contains only a small proportion of radioactive ^{40}K atoms. For every one hundred ^{40}K atoms that decay, 11 percent become argon 40, an inactive gas that can easily escape from its material by diffusion when lava and other igneous rocks are formed. As volcanic rock forms by crystallization, the argon 40 concentration drops to almost nothing, but the process of ^{40}K decay continues, and 11 percent of every one hundred ^{40}K atoms will become argon 40. Thus it is possible, using a spectrometer, to measure the concentration of argon 40 that has accumulated since the volcanic rock formed.

TABLE 1.1   Methods of dating in prehistory.

Date B.P.	Method	Major events
Modern times (after A.D. 1)	Historical documents; dendrochronology; imported objects most useful	European settlement of New World; Roman Empire
4,500 B.P.		Origins of cities
		Origins of agriculture
	Radiocarbon dating (organic materials)	First Americans
		Homo sapiens sapiens
70,000 B.P.	Obsidian hydration	*Homo sapiens neanderthalensis*
500,000 B.P.		*Homo erectus*
	Potassium argon dating (volcanic materials)	*Homo Australopithecus*
5,000,000 B.P.		

These conventions have been used in the tables throughout this book:

——————   A continuous line means the chronology is firmly established.

————▶   A line terminating in an arrow means the time span continues beyond the arrow.

————┤   A line terminating with a horizontal bar means the limit of chronology is firmly established.

— — — —   A broken line means the chronology is doubtful.

?Escale   A question mark beside the name of a site means its date is not firmly established.

APPLICATIONS: We are fortunate that many of the world's earliest archaeological sites occur in volcanically active areas. Human tools are found in direct association with cooled lava fragments from contemporary eruptions. Potassium argon has been used to date Olduvai Gorge and other famous early sites (Chapter 4) (Dalrymple and Lamphere, 1970).

Radiocarbon dating (C14)

TIME SPAN: Approximately 70,000 years ago to A.D. 1500.

PRINCIPLES: The radiocarbon (C14) dating method, developed by physicists J. R. Arnold and W. F. Libby in 1949, puts to use the knowledge that living organisms build up their own organic matter by photosynthesis and by using atmospheric carbon dioxide. The percentage of radiocarbon in the organism is equal to that in the atmosphere. When the organism dies, the carbon 14 (C14) atoms disintegrate at a known rate. It is possible then to calculate the age of an organic object by measuring the amount of C14 left in the sample. The initial quantity in a sample is low, so the limit of detectability is soon reached, although efforts are being made to extend the limit beyond 70,000 years (Grootes, 1978).

Radiocarbon dating is most effective for sites dating between 50,000 and about 500 years before the present (B.P.). Dates can be taken from many types of organic material, including charcoal, shell, wood, or hair. When a date is received from a C14 dating laboratory, it bears a statistical plus or minus factor; for example, 3621 ± 180 years (180 years represents one standard deviation), meaning that chances are two out of three that the reading is between the span of 3441 and 3801. If we double the deviation, chances are nineteen out of twenty that the span (3261 to 3981) is correct. Most dates in the book are derived from C14 dated samples and should be recognized for what they are — statistical approximations (Fagan, 1988b; Sharer and Ashmore, 1987).

The conventional radiocarbon date relies on measurements of a beta ray decay rate. A number of laboratories are experimenting with an ultrasensitive mass spectrometer to count the individual carbon 14 atoms in a sample instead. This faster, accelerator approach allows one to date much smaller samples, as small as a fragment of straw in a potsherd, and the results are more accurate than a conventional reading. Accelerator dates will become increasingly important in future research (Gowlett, 1987).

CALIBRATION: Radiocarbon dating was at first hailed as the solution to archaeologists' dating problems. Later research has shown this enthusiasm to be a little too optimistic (C. Renfrew, 1973). Unfortunately, the rate at which C14 is produced in the atmosphere has fluctuated considerably because of changes in the strength of the earth's magnetic field and alterations in solar activity. By working with tree-ring chronologies from the long-lived California bristlecone pine and European oaks, a number of C14 laboratories have agreed on correction tables for C14 dates between approximately 7200 years ago and A.D. 1950. The discrepancies between radiocarbon and calibrated dates differ widely, but a typical adjustment is that for 10 B.C. ± 30, which has a calibrated interval of 145 B.C. to A.D. 210. We summarize the agreed correction tables at the end of this book (J. Klein et al., 1982).

APPLICATIONS: Radiocarbon dating has been used to establish most of the chronologies described in this book for sites dating to between about 70,000 years ago and A.D. 1500. It has been used to date early agriculture in both the New and Old worlds, the beginnings of metallurgy, and the first settlement of the Americas. Without the C14 method, world prehistory would be almost entirely undated.

Obsidian hydration

TIME SPAN: Recent times to about 800,000 years ago.

PRINCIPLES: Obsidian is a natural glass substance often formed by volcanic activity. It has long been prized by humankind for its sharp edges and excellent qualities for toolmaking. A new dating method takes advantage of the fact that a freshly made surface of obsidian will absorb water from its surroundings, which forms a measurable hydration layer that increases with the passage of time. Thus, the depth of hydration on the fractured surface of a stone tool represents the time since the artifact was manufactured or used. Hydration is observed with the aid of microscopically thin sections of obsidian from artifacts that are ground down to about .003 inches. The thickness of the layer is measured through the microscope in units of microns. Although there are still some problems with such unknown variables as temperature changes and their effects on hydration, the method holds great promise for the future.

APPLICATIONS: Obsidian hydration is a useful way of ordering large numbers of artifacts in relative series, simply by using their micron readings as they increase with age. It can also be used for dating sites, provided one has some other form of chronology, like tree rings, to check the results. Some of the world's earliest sites have yielded obsidian, and this method has been tried experimentally with settlements as early as 780,000 years ago. Once the bugs are worked out, obsidian hydration may be more useful than radiocarbon dating.

Dendrochronology

TIME SPAN: Present day to sites dating to 59 B.C. in the American Southwest.

PRINCIPLES: Many years ago Dr. A. E. Douglass of the University of Arizona used the annual growth rings of trees in the southwestern United States to develop a nonarchaeological chronology for this area that extends back 8200 years (Bannister and Robinson, 1975). Douglass studied the sequoia and other slow-growing trees to develop a long master series of annual rings that he used to date fragments of wooden beams found in Indian pueblos. By analyzing cycles of rings from dry and wet series of years, he was able to set up an archaeological chronology for the Southwest that extends back to 322 B.C. Dendrochronology has been used in other areas of the world as well — in Alaska and the American Southeast, and with great success in Greece, Ireland, and Germany. European experts have linked rings from living oak trees to prehistoric trunks found in bogs and archaeological sites. A tree ring sequence in northern Ireland goes back 7272 years, another from Germany 6000 years.

APPLICATIONS: The chronology of southwestern archaeology described in Chapter 14 is developed from dendrochronology. Tree ring chronologies are used to calibrate radiocarbon dates from Europe as far back as 7200 years ago.

Tree rings have been used to date Roman sites in Germany and even the oak boards that formed the backings for paintings by old Dutch masters (Baillie, 1982)!

Historical records (present day to 5000 years ago)

Historical records can be used to date the past only as far back as the beginnings of writing and written records. The Sumerian King Lists of Mesopotamia are some of the first attempts to record past events (Kramer, 1963). Many areas of the world, such as New Guinea or tropical Africa, entered the realms of recorded history only in the last century, while continual historical documentation began in the Americas with Christopher Columbus.

Experimental methods

A number of newly developed dating methods promise to amplify both potassium argon and radiocarbon techniques.

Fission track dating uses the principle that minerals and natural glasses contain uranium atoms that decay by spontaneous fission (Fagan, 1988b; Fleischer, 1975). The decay rate can be measured in volcanic rocks and has been used to date some samples from Olduvai Gorge. Fission track dating may have applications for sites between a million and 100,000 years old.

Thermoluminescence dating involves measuring the radioactive properties of baked clay vessels. Sudden and violent heating of the vessel allows the scientist to study stored energy and radioactive impurities in the clay. Thermoluminescence may one day provide a means of dating clay vessels as old as 10,000 years, but the method is still under development (Aitken, 1985).

None of these experimental methods has yet played a major part in the development of the chronology of world prehistory.

However effective and accurate a chronometric method, it is useless unless the dated sample — be it a fragment of a wooden beam, a handful of charcoal, or a lump of cooled lava — is interpreted correctly. For instance, a lump of lava associated with an early stone tool does not date the tool, it dates the moment at which the lava cooled. It is up to the archaeologist to establish that the tool is contemporary with the lava. Beams may be used years after their parent tree was cut down. All these factors have to be taken into account when interpreting chronometric dates.

ARCHAEOLOGICAL SURVEY AND EXCAVATION

How do archaeologists find sites? Many large sites, such as the pyramids of Giza in Egypt or Teotihuacán in Mexico, have been known for centuries. Evidence for less conspicuous sites may be accidentally exposed by water or wind erosion, earthquakes, and other natural phenomena. Burrowing animals may bring bones or stone tools to the surface on ancient settlements. Farmers plow up thousands of finds. Road makers and land developers move massive quantities of earth.

Survey

Most archaeological sites are discovered as a result of careful field survey and thorough examination of the countryside for both conspicuous and inconspicuous traces of the past (Crawford, 1953; Schiffer and House, 1977). A survey can cover a single city lot or an entire river basin, a reconnaissance that could extend over several years. The theoretical ideal is to locate all sites in the survey area, but this is impossible, for many sites leave few traces above ground and the best that one can hope for is a sample of what is in the area. The most intensive surveys are made on foot, with field workers spaced out at regular intervals so that as little as possible is missed. Surface finds from newly discovered sites can provide clues about the identity of the occupants, although even scientifically collected surface finds are no substitute for excavation. Surface sampling is of great use not only in site location but as a way of making decisions about modifying research designs for sites that are already being excavated (Redman, 1987).

Originally, archaeologists looked for individual sites, which they then excavated on a large scale. Today, the environmental context of a site is often as important as the settlement itself, so much so that regional surveys of prehistoric sites and their settlement patterns are as important as excavation. *Settlement patterns* are distributions of prehistoric occupation on the landscape. Establishing such patterns requires a large investment of time and money. It took William Sanders and his colleagues a decade to survey the evolving settlement pattern in the Basin of Mexico over the millennia that preceded the emergence of Aztec civilization in the fifteenth century A.D. (Sanders, Parsons, and Santley, 1979). They relied heavily on remote-sensing methods, among them aerial photography. This approach has long been used to plot more conspicuous sites; it works well with prehistoric agricultural systems, Roman road networks, and other large-scale archaeological phenomena.

The days of uncontrolled archaeological excavations are long gone. Yet the destruction of archaeological sites proceeds at a breathtaking pace. Since the archaeological record is being destroyed faster than it can be conserved, archaeologists are more and more avoiding destructive excavation where at all possible and turning to side-scan radar, satellite imagery, and other sophisticated remote-sensing devices to study the past without digging. Remote sensing enables us to look at ancient landscapes, and peoples' imprints upon them, and through computerized data bases to begin to predict densities of archaeological sites in different landscapes. As the number of undisturbed archaeological sites dwindles, we can expect all forms of remote sensing to assume much greater importance than conventional excavation. All kinds of new approaches to site survey are being developed, among them sophisticated computer simulations that help predict where sites will be located. Other computer programs are used to create "site profiles" that aid in the recognition of actual sites in the field.

Excavation

Archaeological excavation has developed from a form of treasure hunting into an exact and precise discipline. The fundamental premise of excavation is that all digging is destruction, even that done by the experts. The archaeologist's primary responsibility, therefore, is to record a site for posterity as it is dug because there are no second chances.

Every excavation is undertaken to answer specific questions, according to a formal *research design* that is worked out beforehand. The research design can ask questions about the chronology of the site, the layout of the settlement it contains, or changing artifact styles within the levels to be excavated (Binford, 1964; Mueller, 1975). By meticulous digging and careful sampling of the archaeological deposits, the excavator implements the research design and digs up and records the data that are used to test the hypotheses developed as part of that research design. Most archaeologists distinguish between two basic excavation methods (Figure 1.4) (Barker, 1983; Joukowsky, 1981; Wheeler, 1954): Research design

1. *Area or horizontal excavation,* in which the objective is to uncover large areas of ground in search of houses or entire settlement layouts. This type of digging is on a relatively large scale and is designed to uncover household and other activities that are normally discoverable only by digging over an extensive area. Area excavation

2. *Vertical excavation or trenching,* designed to uncover stratigraphic information or a sequence of occupation layers on a small scale. This type of excavation often is practiced when chronology or artifact samples are a primary concern. Vertical excavation

The numerous archaeological sites described in this book fall into several broad categories, each of which presents special excavation problems. The most common are *living sites,* the places where people have lived and carried out a multitude of activities. Living sites

Much of our knowledge of the earliest hunters and gatherers is found by excavating abandoned living sites. These people favored lakeside camps or convenient rock overhangs for protection from predators and the weather, availability of abundant water, and ready access to herds of game and vegetable foods. Olduvai Gorge in Tanzania is renowned for its prehistoric sites, small lakeside bone caches used by early humans for a few days or weeks before they moved on in their constant search for game, vegetable foods, and fish (see Figure 4.10, p. 99) (Hill, 1984; M. D. Leakey, 1971).

Fortunately for archaeologists, these people abandoned food bones and tools where they were dropped. Crude windbreaks were left and might have been burned down by the next brush fire or blown away by the wind. In Olduvai, the gently rising waters of a prehistoric lake slowly covered the bone caches and preserved them for posterity with the tools lying where they were dropped. Other people lived by the banks of large rivers. Their tools are found in profusion in river gravels that were subsequently jumbled and re-sorted by floodwater, leaving a confused mass of artifacts, not undisturbed living floors, for the archaeologist to uncover (Oakley, 1964).

Caves already occupied more than half a million years ago were reoccupied again and again as people returned to preferred spots. Many natural caves and rock shelters contain deep occupation deposits that can be removed by meticulous excavation with a dental pick, trowel, and brush. The sequence of occupa-

FIGURE 1.4   Area (horizontal) and vertical excavations. Although archaeologists excavate in many ways and sometimes use sampling techniques, there is a basic distinction between area *(left)* and vertical *(right)* methods.

Left: An area excavation of a stone circle at Strichen, Scotland, is designed to expose large segments of ground on a site so that buildings, all other structures, and even the layout of the entire settlement can be traced over a much larger area than would be uncovered in a vertical excavation. Area excavation is widely used when budget is not a problem and the archaeologist is looking for settlement patterns.

Right: A vertical excavation of Maiden Castle, Dorset, England, shows how a narrow trench is cut through successive layers of an earth rampart. Notice that only a small portion of the layers in the trench walls has been exposed. The objective of this excavation was to obtain information on the sequence of layers on the outer edge of the earthwork and in the ditch that originally lay on its exterior side. Only a narrow trench was needed to record layers, the finds from them, and the dating evidence.

tion layers can be uncovered almost undisturbed from the day of abandonment (Deacon, 1979; Movius, 1977).

In contrast, farmers usually live in larger settlements than hunters, for they are tied to their herds and gardens and move less often. Higher population densities and more lasting settlements left more conspicuous archaeological sites from later millennia of human history. In the Near East and many parts of the New World, farming sites were occupied time after time over several thousand years, forming deep mounds of refuse, house foundations, and other occupa-

Tells

tion debris. These *tells* require large excavations and extensive earthmoving if anything is to be understood about how towns and settlements were laid out.

Kill sites

Kill sites are places where hunter-gatherers killed large mammals, then camped around the carcass for several days as they butchered their prey. The most famous kill sites are in the American Great Plains, at which entire bison herds have been found trapped in narrow defiles where they were driven to their death (see Figure 7.5, p. 220) (Wheat, 1972). The stone projectile heads, scraping tools, and butchering artifacts used by the hunters have been found

around the carcasses. *Ceremonial sites* may or may not be part of a living site Ceremonial sites
(Weaver, 1981). Mesopotamian temples formed the focus of a city, while Maya
ceremonial centers, such as Tikal in Guatemala, were an integral part of a scattered settlement pattern of towns and villages in the countryside (Figure 22.9, p.
521). Some structures, such as the Cahokia mounds in Illinois or Stonehenge in
England (Figures 14.12, p. 372, and 20.6, p. 480) (Chippindale, 1983), were
sites that served the religious needs of a king or of a wider community around
them.

Burial sites can yield important data from periods later than 70,000 years Burial sites
ago, the time when the first deliberate burials were made (J. E. Anderson, 1969;
Brothwell, 1985). Skeletons and their accompanying grave goods give us a
rather one-sided view of the past — funerary rites (Figure 17.5, p. 426). Among
the most famous prehistoric burials are those of the royal kings deposited at Ur
of the Chaldees in Mesopotamia during the second millennium B.C. (Chapter
16) (Woolley, 1934), as well as the Shang graves in China, where charioteers
and many retainers accompanied the royal dead (Figure 21.5, p. 498) (Chang,
1980). The celebrated mounds of Pazyryk in Siberia show us other spectacular
burial customs (Chapter 20) (Rudenko, 1970). Important people were buried
with their chariots and steeds, the latter wearing elaborate harness trappings
preserved by ice that formed when water entered the tombs and froze.

STUDYING THE FINDS

Archaeological finds take many forms. They may include fragmentary bones
from game or domesticated animals (Binford, 1981). Vegetable foods such as
edible nuts or cultivated seeds sometimes are found in archaeological sites
where preservation conditions are good (Ford, 1985; J. Renfrew, 1973). Pottery,
stone implements, iron artifacts, and, occasionally, bone and wooden tools all
build up a picture of early technical achievements.

Archaeologists have developed elaborate classification systems that set
down certain criteria for their finds. They also apply sophisticated analytic
techniques for both classifying and comparing human artifacts (Watson, Le-
Blanc, and Redman, 1984). They use collections of stone tools, pottery, or other
artifacts like swords and brooches for studying human culture and its development. Whatever the classificatory techniques used, however, the objective of
analyzing bones, pottery, and other material remains is the study of prehistoric
culture and of cultural change in the past. We classify the remains into arbitrary
groups either by their shape or design or by their use, the latter a difficult task
(Figure 1.5). We fit them together to form a picture of a human culture.

From time to time we shall refer to archaeological groupings like the Acheulian culture or the Magdalenian culture, which consist of the material remains
of human culture preserved at a specific space and time at several sites; these
finds are the concrete expressions of the common social traditions that bind a
culture. When we speak of the Magdalenian culture, we mean the *archaeologi-* Archaeological culture
cal culture representing a prehistoric social system, defined in a context of time and

FIGURE 1.5 Inference from an artifact. This Chumash Indian parching tray from southern California shows how inferences can be made from an archaeological find. Clearly, the range of inferences that can be made from artifacts alone is limited, especially when the find has no context in a site.

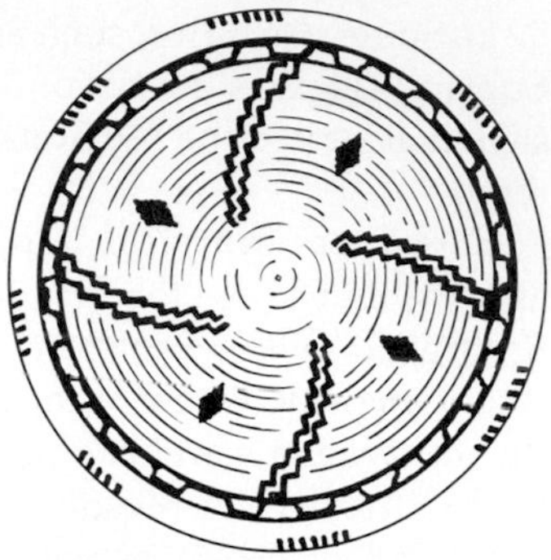

Context

The archaeological context of the tray is defined by its position in a site and what it is associated with, level, square, etc.; its relationship to other features, such as houses, is also recorded. Unless this information is known, the tray is an isolated specimen devoid of a cultural context or even a date. Context cannot be inferred from an artifact alone.

Construction and materials

The tray was made of reed, its red-brown color determined by the reed, known from modern observations to be the best material available. The steplike decoration on the tray was dictated by sewing and weaving techniques of basketry. The diamond patterns were probably added as a personal touch by the craftsperson who made it. The shape and decoration of the tray are repeated in many others that have been found and are evidently part of a well-established Chumash basketry tradition. More information about an artifact's construction and materials can be learned than about any other category of inference.

Function

The flat, round shape of the tray is determined by its function, for such trays were used to roast seeds by tossing them with embers in the tray. The function of a tray normally cannot be inferred from its shape, but identical modern versions have been found that are used for parching. We employ the technique of analogy, inferring that the archaeological find had the same function as the modern tray.

Behavior

The parching tray reveals something about the cooking techniques of the Chumash, but again only by analogy.

space, which has come down to us in the form of tools or other durable objects. The description *Magdalenian* is quite arbitrary, derived from the cave site at La Madeleine, France, where the tools of the culture were first discovered. Such labels as Magdalenian are devised by archaeologists for their convenience.

The geographic extent or content of any archaeological culture is also defined somewhat arbitrarily but as precisely as possible, so that an archaeological word has an exact implication for other scholars. Much of the archaeological data summarized in this book consists of carefully compiled chronological sequences of archaeological cultures often extending over thousands of prehistoric years. The workings of archaeological research compare one collection of artifacts with assemblages from different layers in the same sites or other sites near or far away from the original find. Our record of human activity consists of innumerable classified and cataloged archaeological finds whose relationships determined much of the story of human culture that follows in these pages.

EXPLANATION AND INTERPRETATION

Anthropological archaeology is much more than inference and induction from the archaeological record, for our ultimate aim is to explain the past, not simply describe it. Until recently, most archaeologists concentrated on descriptions of sites and artifacts. They accumulated the minute chronological and spatial frameworks of archaeological data that provide a basis for observing *how* particular cultures changed and evolved through prehistoric times. Many scholars felt constrained by poor preservation conditions from making inferences about anything other than the material remains of ancient human behavior. They were unable to explain *why* the cultures they had studied had changed.

Recent years have seen a rapid change in archaeological approaches. Computers have become commonplace, more and more scientific methods have been applied to raw archaeological data, and there has been an explosion of field research all over the world. There has also been a theoretical revolution, one that places major emphasis on explaining the past and on exploring the processes by which human cultures changed through prehistoric times. Using both advanced data collection methods and new theoretical models, some archaeologists of the 1980s are seeking to apply theories of anthropology to archaeological evidence to arrive at new laws of cultural process. Others are primarily interested in the history of culture, viewing each society as a unique phenomenon (Binford, 1983; Redman, 1973). In recent years, the archaeological record itself has received greater attention. How were sites formed, and what decay processes have been at work over the centuries, even millennia, that separate the archaeological site from the present? A whole new body of archaeological theory is being developed to explore these links between past and present. In Chapter 2 we consider these and other approaches to world prehistory.

GUIDE TO FURTHER READING

Binford, Lewis R. *In Pursuit of the Past.* New York: Thames and Hudson, 1983.
   A personal account of developing ideas in archaeology that is a marvelous introduction to archaeological reasoning. You may not agree with everything Binford says, but he makes you think!

Ceram, C. W. *Gods, Graves and Scholars.* New York: Knopf, 1953.
   This probably is the best-known book on archaeology ever written. A classic account of early archaeologists and the discovery of the early civilizations written for a popular audience.

Fagan, Brian M. *Archaeology: A Brief Introduction* (3d ed.). Boston: Scott, Foresman/Little, Brown, 1988.
   A widely ranging brief introduction, with major coverage of subsistence and settlement patterns.

Fagan, Brian M. *In the Beginning* (6th ed.). Boston: Scott, Foresman/Little, Brown, 1988. A comprehensive survey of method and theory in archaeology that covers everything from stratigraphy to cultural resource management.

Sharer, Robert, and Ashmore, Wendy. *Archaeology: Discovering the Past.* Palo Alto, Calif: Mayfield, 1987. Another detailed introduction to anthropological archaeology that is especially strong on American examples. Excellent bibliography.

CHAPTER 2

Approaches to World Prehistory

Preview

■ Although biological evolution resulted in the emergence of humankind, cultural evolution assumed the dominant role in our prehistory. It became humankind's unique means of adapting to the natural environment.

■ Early archaeologists confronted with the problem of classifying and dating the past were at a loss until Christian Jurgensen Thomsen developed the Three Age subdivision for prehistory. This scheme was verified by excavation and widely adopted during the nineteenth century.

■ The social scientist Herbert Spencer developed the notion of cultural and social evolution. Along with Edward Tylor and Lewis Morgan, Spencer believed in unilinear cultural evolution, under which all humankind progressed from a state of simple savagery to civilization.

■ Later scholars showed that these schemes were too simplistic when tested against data from archaeological excavations. We describe the primary cultural processes — invention, diffusion, and migration — and give examples of their application.

■ Franz Boas and V. Gordon Childe fostered detailed studies of sites, peoples, and artifacts that placed scientific archaeology on a new footing. Boas collected minute details of dozens of societies. Childe believed in cultural evolution in which technology played a major role. He ignored the importance of environmental adaptation in world prehistory.

■ Anthropologists Julian Steward and Leslie White played an important role in showing cultural evolution to be a major cornerstone of world prehistory. Steward demonstrated that all human cultures interact with their natural environments and stressed the importance of constantly changing adaptations. White conceived of cultures as complex systems whose various parts interact with each other and with the natural environment.

■ From these researches developed two concepts — cultural ecology and diverse cultural evolution — both based on the notion that each human culture evolved independently and as a result of changing adaptations to its ever-changing environment.

■ Recent interpretations of early prehistory have come to rely heavily on several new approaches: experimental archaeology, replicating ancient technology and lifeways under controlled conditions; ethnoarchaeology, the study of living hunter-gatherer and agricultural societies; and a new body of middle range theory designed to bridge the gap between the dynamic present and the static archaeological record. All these approaches enable us to derive general theories about the relationship between human behavior and archaeological debris.

■ Elman Service, Morton Fried, and others developed four stages of sociopolitical evolution, which are widely used to classify groups: bands, tribes, chiefdoms, and state-organized societies.

■ Our narrative of world prehistory is based on gradual, multilinear cultural evolution and on increasingly effective adaptations to the natural environment that have led to the dangerous overexploitation of resources commonplace today.

"Descended from apes! My dear, let us hope that this is not so, but if it is, that it does not become known." The worthy Victorian minister's wife who uttered these words more than a century ago would be horrified by the literature of world prehistory today. She would discover that important implications of Charles Darwin's theory of evolution and natural selection have become cornerstones of anthropology and archaeology (Campbell, 1985; Foley, 1984b). Darwin's theories offer an explanation for the biological evolution of human kind. They provide the framework of the evolutionary story of world prehistory, of a pattern of gradual change that can be traced in the archaeological and paleontological record of more than 2 million years.

The antiquity of humankind, sequences of fossils and stone tools, different species of hominids and early humans — these are the familiar landmarks of this story, many of them easily described. But what do these changes mean? How can we explain and analyze this provocative chronicle in meaningful terms? Why did human beings originate in tropical Africa? Why did they spread into other continents and adapt to much colder environments during the later Ice Age? Why, eventually, did human beings start cultivating the soil and living in cities? These are the questions of world prehistory, the questions that scholars have been trying to answer for more than a century, using a variety of theoretical approaches described in this chapter. As we shall see, the devout Victorian minister's spouse would probably be relieved to find out that neo-Darwinian evolutionary theory has still had surprisingly little impact on their researches.

One general statement is obvious. We modern people do differ from our predecessors; we have adapted successfully to the world's many environments as a result of our superior intelligence, gradually acquired during biological evolution. The evolutionary process of *adaptive radiation*, whereby animal species branch off from a common ancestral form, has led to an order of primates, and a family of *Hominidae*, of which modern people (*Homo sapiens*, the wise human being) are only one member and the sole survivors. (For the basics of human biological evolution, see Lewin, 1988a; Weiss and Mann, 1988.)

Humankind is unique in its use of culture as a means of adapting to the natural environment, and our culture has evolved to great levels of complexity since the appearance of the first human beings more than 2 million years ago. The study of world prehistory is the study not only of biological evolution but also primarily of cultural evolution and the ways in which people have adapted to their natural environment. The cultural diversity of humankind is truly amazing and extremely difficult to explain. Ever since scholars first began to study world prehistory, they have tried to explain this diversity and to account for its origins and for the reasons some societies achieved a much greater cultural complexity than others. Why, for instance, did the Australian aborigines never take up agriculture but develop a highly complex social life? Why did their contemporaries, the Ancient Egyptians, enjoy a literate civilization that lasted for thousands of years? The explanations for cultural diversity must come from anthropological archaeology, the primary source of data on early human history.

In Chapter 1 we described the three basic objectives of anthropological archaeology:

- Studying culture history, a descriptive process that involves analyzing archaeological sites and artifacts in time and space
- Reconstructing ancient lifeways, ways in which people adapted to and exploited their natural environment
- Explaining cultural process, how human cultures have changed in the past.

All these goals require interpreting the archaeological record with reference to the processes that created it — site formation processes.

Much of the prehistory recounted in these pages is fundamental culture history, based on hundreds of sites, cultural sequences, and millions of individual artifacts. These culture histories from all areas of the world have been constructed using the basic principles mentioned in Chapter 1. Culture history alone, however, does not explain culture change, nor does it provide information on the ways in which people have adapted to or exploited the natural environment. It is only in recent years that archaeologists have attacked the complex problems of reconstructing past lifeways and studying cultural process, with the aid of digital computers, sophisticated statistical methods, and enormous new bodies of excavated data from all over the world. A whole new battery of analytic approaches have been brought to bear on the archaeological record, approaches that rely heavily on detailed theoretical models, some derived from evolutionary theory (Binford, 1983; Fagan, 1988b).

Today's theoretical models and methodology cannot be considered in isolation from earlier attempts at interpreting world prehistory. Our approaches to the past are cumulative in the sense that they are based on the contributions of many earlier scholars, who worked with inadequate data and much less sophisticated models than those of today. We must, therefore, first examine the intellectual debt we owe our predecessors.

PROGRESS AND CULTURAL DEVELOPMENT

If there is one persistent theme that runs through all theories about world pre-history it is the explicit, or implicit, assumption that human cultures have pro-gressed through the millennia, from very primitive beginnings to the lofty pinnacle of industrial civilization. How can one account for this progress, and for the obvious fact that by no means all human beings live in highly complex, urban societies?

Archaeology in the modern sense really began in the eighteenth century, when curious landowners dug into European burial mounds and ancient settle-ments with such frenzy that they acquired an enormous mass of miscellaneous artifacts that defied classification into any semblance of chronological order. This horrendous jumble made no sense at all until Christian Jurgensen Thom-sen, curator of Denmark's National Museum in Copenhagen, rearranged the

Three Ages prehistoric galleries of the museum in 1807. Boldly he laid out the exhibits to represent three great ages of prehistoric time: a Stone Age, when metals were unknown, a Bronze Age, and an Iron Age. Thomsen worked strictly with tools, each of his three ages in fact representing a stage of technological development in prehistoric times. His Three Age system soon was adopted widely through-out Europe, and its broad labels still are used as convenient terms (Daniel, 1981; Grayson, 1983).

Thomsen concerned himself with how level of technology affected the evo-lution of cultures. The essential validity of his theory of cultural development was proved not long after he proposed it by excavations all over Europe. These early-nineteenth-century digs raised a whole new set of questions about the Three Ages. The Three Age system implied that all humankind had passed through comparable broad stages of technological development, but what

Economic model about economic development? In 1838 another Dane, zoologist Sven Nilsson, invented an economic model for the past, arguing that humankind had devel-oped through a series of stages — from a state of savagery to one of herder-agri-culturalist, and on to a final phase, civilization. He based his economic model on both archaeological and anthropological observations. Nilsson's model was not in conflict with Thomsen's theory; it merely addressed a different aspect of the fact of evolution. What Nilsson did was to concentrate not on technology but on how in different societies lifeways always seemed to change in the same direction.

Archaeology and "The European Century"

The later development of archaeology as an intellectual discipline was part of a much wider movement that also saw the foundation of geology and evolu-tionary studies. Archaeology, and prehistoric archaeology in particular, gained respectability during a period of widespread and fundamental social change during the nineteenth century. Clive Gamble (1986b) points out that archaeol-ogy developed during what some historians call "The European Century [1815–1914]," a time that saw the culmination of three long-term historical processes stemming from the industrial revolution: the development of a world economy, the creation of the administrative and political apparatus of the modern state, and the rise of science. Science, and archaeology as part of it, developed because of a radical shift in the way people conceived of nature, investigated it, and used it.

These three historical processes had a profound effect on the development of archaeology. The nineteenth century was a time of rising wealth, of unprecedented exploitation of natural resources and intensification of agriculture to feed mushrooming European populations. The industrial revolution spawned public works, railroad and canal building, and massive disturbance of the modern land surface. Vast quantities of prehistoric artifacts came to light under the picks and shovels of the manual workers who transformed the landscape. Inevitably, in societies where a newly emergent middle class was on the social ascendancy, these finds began to arouse far more than idle curiosity — they began to acquire a significance in the natural order of things.

In a real sense, prehistory was not "discovered" but was a conceptual framework developed to meet the needs of the emerging middle class (Gamble, 1986b). The Three Age system and the stone artifacts found in ancient river gravels reinforced the ideologies of progress and nationalism that were so much a part of nineteenth-century middle-class identity. The Victorians lived in rapidly changing times, when progress was a natural condition. It was comforting to them to find that change had also taken place in remote prehistory. Progress was inevitable, an integral part of civilization. The middle-class Danes used prehistoric archaeology to provide a link between themselves and the cultural heritage of the nation (Kristiansen, 1981). Nationalism, national identity, and progress were the very essence of nineteenth-century ideology. Age and antiquity became a way in which social value was to be given to contemporary change, by showing they had profound roots in older traditions.

Cultural Evolution

Prehistory, then, was seen as a scientific study of progress in prehistoric times (Trigger, 1981). In the decades following the acceptance of the antiquity of humankind in 1859, biological evolutionary theory was distorted into a simplistic, ordered way of charting human progress. Gabriel de Mortillet, an expert on French Stone Age caves, classified different prehistoric cultures into rigid geological layers that he implied were to be found all over the world. "It is no longer possible to doubt the great law of the progress of man," he wrote in 1867 (Daniel, 1981). Inevitably, this corruption of biological theory led to ethnocentric value judgments that linked levels of cultural development to ideas about racial inferiority and lesser intelligence among technologically unsophisticated non-Western societies like the Tasmanians and Australian aborigines. According to many nineteenth-century archaeologists, progress in prehistory was achieved by advances in human intellect that could be detected by changes in fossil skulls and, above all, by changing designs of stone tools (Gamble, 1986b).

Ideas of inevitable progress were also popular among pioneer social scientists of the day, scholars like Herbert Spencer (1820–1903). Spencer (1855) hailed Victorian civilization as the pinnacle of human achievement, a state to which all humankind aspired. He and his contemporaries wondered whether human culture had evolved just as our bodies had. They developed the notion of *cultural evolution* — the idea that human societies evolved from simple hunter-gatherers to complex civilizations, but along a single evolutionary line. Theoretically, then, every society could achieve the highest reach of civilization. This form of cultural evolution provided not only a rationale for ideas of racial superiority but also grounds for thinking of early prehistory as a mirror of the contemporary world, as remote eras when long-vanished peoples enjoying much the same level of culture as, say, the Tasmanians or Inuit lived on earth. The more complex these prehistoric societies, the more advanced they were — the dead equivalents of specific, still existing non-Western societies. These ideas reached their extreme in the work of William Sollas, an early-twentieth-century geologist turned prehistorian, who called the San of Africa and the Inuit of the Arctic living examples of Upper Paleolithic peoples (Sollas, 1910).

Tylor, Morgan, and Marx

This ethnocentric view of the past had its roots not only in ideas of progress but in the writings about human diversity of two early anthropologists. Sir Edward Tylor (1832–1917) was a gentleman of leisure who became interested in anthropology during a visit to Mexico in the 1850s (Hatch, 1973). He was the first to attempt a chronicle of the full extent of human diversity. He argued that human beings had behaved in a commonsense and rational way since the earliest times. This rational behavior led to cultural evolution over time, while processes of selection, akin to those of natural selection in biological evolution, had made human institutions more efficient and complex. Tylor (1871) proposed three broad stages of human development akin to those of Sven Nilsson — savagery, barbarism, and civilization. His evolutionist view was far too simplistic, but he based his work on two research methods that are still widely used today:

- He used living non-Western peoples at the same general level of cultural development to throw light on imperfectly known prehistoric societies — *ethnographic analogy.*
- He developed techniques for sampling the culture of dozens of different peoples — the *comparative method.*

The American anthropologist Lewis Morgan (1818–1881) was another ardent social evolutionist; he thought that social evolution occurred as a result of human societies adapting to the stresses of their various environments (M. Harris, 1968). Morgan identified no fewer than seven stages of social evolution in his classic work *Ancient Society* (1877), beginning with "Lower Status of Savagery," a stage of simple food gathering, and culminating in "Civilization," when a society developed writing.

Morgan's ideas on cultural evolution had a profound influence on Karl Marx (1818–1883). Marx used Morgan's seven stages but argued that each stage was brought on by economic factors. Changes in material production, and also in the control of the means of production, were *the* forces that determined social, political, and legal aspects of society. This is historical materialism, which regarded economic developments as the prime movers of social evolution. Marx's ideas persist in some archaeological theories to this day.

Neither Morgan's nor Tylor's linear and universal evolutionary schemes have stood up against the sheer complexity of human cultural diversity as we know it today. Their work, and that of other nineteenth-century pioneers, made one lasting contribution to world prehistory — the assumption that human cultures did, in general, proceed from the simple to the complex. The issue that has preoccupied archaeologists since is, of course, how and why they did so.

"PRIMARY CULTURAL PROCESSES": INVENTION, DIFFUSION, AND MIGRATION

Spencer, Tylor, and Morgan may have believed in human progress, in universal schemes of cultural evolution, but their contemporaries were already pondering one of the fundamental questions of archaeology: by what processes did cultural change take place? How, for example, did humankind first acquire bronze weapons? Did one people invent metal tools and then spread their innovation to other parts of the world? Or did metallurgy develop in many widely separated areas? Did culture change result from the invention of the same idea in many different places, through gradual, parallel evolutions? Or did it stem from the diffusion of ideas, or from actual migrations of people carrying new cultures with them?

Two Scandinavian scholars, J. J. A. Worsaae and Oscar Montelius, were among the first to study these processes, which are now called *primary cultural processes* — invention, diffusion, and migration (Worsaae, 1849). They used minute differences in bronze pins, swords, and other artifacts to trace artifact changes from southeast Europe into Scandinavia. Modern culture history studies stemmed in part from their work. Both the comparative method and increased use of ethnographic analogy played an important part in the refinement of the study of the primary cultural processes (Trigger, 1968).

Invention involves creating a new idea and transforming it — in archaeological contexts — into an artifact or other tangible innovation that has survived. An invention implies either modifying an old idea or series of ideas or creating a completely new concept. It can be made by accident or by intentional research. Inventions are adopted by others if they are useful; if sufficiently important, they spread rapidly. The transistor, for example, is in almost universal use because it is an effective advance in electronic technology.

Invention

There is a tendency to think of inventions as dramatic discoveries, the products of a moment of inspiration. In practice though, most inventions in prehistory were the result of prolonged experimentation, a logical extension of the use and refinement of an existing technology or else a response to changes in the surrounding environment.

People once searched for the site where the first solitary genius planted grain and invented agriculture. Today's archaeologists are still investigating the origins of food production, but they are finding dozens of major and minor changes in peoples' lifeways that cumulatively resulted in a shift from hunting and gathering to agriculture and animal domestication. The toolkits and subsistence activities that archaeologists have found show evidence of changes over a long period. In the Tehuacán Valley of Mexico, for example, people experimented for thousands of years with maize cultivation, and their toolkits reflect an increasing dependence on cereal agriculture (MacNeish, 1970), but the old hunter-gatherer tools and practices still appear in the archaeological record long after maize cultivation had become commonplace.

Culture change is cumulative — that is, people learn the behavior patterns of their society. Inevitably some minor differences in learned behavior will appear from generation to generation; minor in themselves, they do accumulate over time, especially among isolated populations. This snowballing effect of slow-moving cultural evolution can be detected in dozens of prehistoric societies, among them the coastal people of Peru, who relied heavily on fishing and maritime resources and gradually developed complex societies based largely on fishing and gathering (Moseley, 1975b).

Diffusion

Diffusion is the label for those processes by which new ideas or cultural traits spread from one person to another or from one group to another, often over long distances. These ideas are socially transmitted from individual to individual and ultimately from group to group, but the physical movement of many people is not involved. Instances of diffusion are legion in prehistory, cases in which ideas or technologies have spread widely from their place of origin. A classic modern example is tobacco smoking, a favorite pleasure of the North American Indians adopted by Elizabethan colonists in the sixteenth century. Within a few generations, tens of thousands of Europeans were smoking pipes and enjoying the calming effect of American tobacco. Tobacco smoking soon reached every corner of the Old World, carried there not by thousands of people migrating from America to Europe but by small numbers of seamen and traveling merchants, by word of mouth, and through the human habit of adopting new, fashionable ideas. Smoking became socially accceptable and remains so to this day in many societies (although not necessarily in ours). There are numerous examples of the diffusion of religious beliefs in prehistory, transmitted through trading contacts and simply by the spread of ideas.

Migration

Migration involves the movement of a people and is based on a deliberate decision to enter new areas and leave the old. English settlers moved to North America, taking their own culture with them; the Spanish occupied Mexico. Such population movements result not only in the diffusion of ideas but in mass shifts of people and in social and cultural changes over a wide front. Migration implies a complete, or at least an almost complete, transformation in culture. Perhaps the classic instance of migration in prehistory is that of the Polynesians; they settled the remote islands of the Pacific in consequence of deliberate explorations of the open ocean by their skilled navigators (Bellwood, 1978; Jennings, 1979). These superb seamen learned the lore of the heavens and made long-distance voyages of discovery, whereby they found such remote islands as Hawaii and Easter Island. In most cases, they returned safely to their homelands with detailed sailing directions that could be followed by later colonists. No one knows why the Polynesians set out on voyages to the unknown. Perhaps population pressure and political considerations played their part. Undoubtedly, many long voyages of exploration were undertaken simply because the navigators were curious to learn what lay over the horizon.

The early students of diffusion and migration often carried their ideas to ridiculous extremes, claiming, for example, that all civilization originated among the Ancient Egyptians and then spread over the globe in a series of great voyaging adventures. Soon the experts reacted violently against these simplistic notions with much more sophisticated research projects. One such expert was Franz Boas (1858–1942), an anthropologist of German birth who immigrated to the United States and became a professor at Columbia University. Boas attacked those who sought general comparisons between non-Western societies; he helped to establish anthropology as a form of science, applying more precise methods of collection and classification of minute details of human cultures, especially those of North America. He and his students sought explanations of the past based on meticulous studies of individual artifacts and customs. Boas instilled respect for the notion that data should not be subordinated to elaborate theoretical schemes. The myriad data provided by Boas and others gave great emphasis to the use of the comparative method and ethnographic analogy in archaeology (Hatch, 1973).

Boas on data

THE COMPARATIVE METHOD

Artifact comparisons were used by pioneer anthropologists like Morgan and Tylor, as well as by early European prehistorians like Worsaae and Montelius in the nineteenth century (Daniel, 1981). But the real proponent of the method was Boas, who devoted a long career to studying and comparing hundreds of American Indian societies. His preoccupation with the minute details of artifacts (as well as other, less tangible aspects of human society) strongly influenced archaeologists of the 1930s and 1940s. Even today, archaeologists spend a great deal of time in comparative studies of artifacts, settlement patterns, and art styles in different archaeological cultures. The comparative method in archaeology is closely tied to the classification and analysis of artifacts such as pottery and stone tools. Much of what we know of the prehistory of Bronze Age Europe is based on the study of swords, brooches, and pins, for example. Archaeologists of the American Southwest rely heavily on changing styles and distributions of painted pottery to construct the culture history of the region. Until the advent of radiocarbon dating in the 1950s, European archaeologists made great use of comparative studies of pottery and metal artifacts to refine their cross-datings of cultures far from the Mediterranean civilizations in which such artifacts had their origin.

V. Gordon Childe

Perhaps one of the best-known experts on the comparative method was an Australian-born archaeologist named Vere Gordon Childe (1892–1957) (Childe, 1958; Trigger, 1980; Tringham, 1983). Childe was a brilliant linguist who made his life's work the study of the diffusion of civilization throughout prehistoric Europe. He became familiar with even the most trivial sites and artifact assemblages, and with obscure central European journals that few English-speaking archaeologists read. He used his encyclopedic knowledge to develop a thesis that Europe was a province of the Near East, an area that had received agriculture, metallurgy, and other major inventions by diffusion from the East. He traced these traits from one end of Europe to the other by comparing cultural sequences and artifact distributions from area to area. Childe combined cultural evolution and diffusionist ideas into unexpected notions of human prehistory. He believed, for instance, that farming was introduced into Europe from the Near East; local cultures developed their own distinctive economies and social institutions in later millennia, he thought.

Childe on cultures

Childe's aim was to distill from archaeological remains "a pre-literate substitute for conventional history with cultures instead of statesmen as actors and migrations instead of battles" (Childe, 1942). He drew together approaches to the past from various schools, including the Marxists (he was a self-professed Marxist). He was convinced that humanity had made rational, intelligent progress from its earliest development. Childe was a brilliant and articulate popular writer whose syntheses of prehistoric times were — and still are — widely read by archaeologists as well as the general public.

Such was Childe's influence on world prehistory that it is only recently that his methods can be seen in historical perspective (Tringham, 1983). He was a consummate synthesizer, someone whose ideas were embraced totally or condemned out of hand. Childe was an idealist, a dreamer, whose theoretical models of the past were far ahead of his time, and of the ability of archaeologists of the day to test them. His historical models, with their strong grounding in anthropology, have been of benefit to American archaeologists, while the scientific rigor of contemporary North American archaeology has brought greater credibility to some of the social, economic, and environmental models that have superseded Childe's visions of prehistory. Above all, today's archaeologists allow for one variable that Childe downplayed — the natural environment. In his day, the necessary scientific methods for reconstructing prehistoric environments barely existed.

American archaeologists adopted the comparative method as a result of Boas's work and developed their own elaborate classification systems for New World prehistory that correlated local cultural sequences over thousands of miles (Willey and Sabloff, 1980). Between 1930 and 1960, they constructed hundreds upon hundreds of local sequences of culture history based on pottery styles and other artifacts. Their concern was with classification and chronology rather than the explanation of culture change or reconstruction of past lifeways. Once again, the natural environment and any notion of cultural adaptation entered but little into archaeological research.

To berate Childe and his contemporaries of the 1930s to 1950s for ignoring the environment as a factor in human history is to miss the point. They worked at a time when the science of ecology was hardly born, when much less was known about prehistory anywhere. Their view of the past was based on long-held ideas about the condition of early human beings, well expressed by Lewis Morgan in 1877: "Mankind commenced their career at the bottom of the scale and worked their way up from savagery to civilization through the slow accumulation of experimental knowledge." This statement was a good basis for understanding the nature of human evolution, the belief that progress was slow and inevitable, culminating in civilization. In a way, it was as if evolution had its own internal driving motor. The limitations of human mental capacity acted as a brake on evolutionary progress. Evolution's motor was believed to be such that archaeologists had no incentive to investigate the forces of selection that acted on human culture and biology (Gamble, 1986b). Archaeology, then, was a way of reconstructing a timetable of technological innovations — toolmaking, fire, housing, burials, art, and metallurgy. This timetable was outlined regionally — in southwest France, in Europe, the Near East, and North America — within a broad and flexible framework of slow progress. The Victorians were concerned with what happened when, not with the forces that caused prehistoric peoples to settle in different areas. It is to Childe's credit that he began to grapple with a far more fundamental and often ignored problem — why did people change and colonize new regions?

CULTURE AS ADAPTATION

Culture history, the kind of archaeology that characterized world prehistory before the 1960s, was basically the study of regional cultural sequences, using refined dating methods and stratigraphic observations. Comparisons between different regions and sites were based on artifact analyses and assemblage composition. Many parts of this book are still based on culture historical sequences from all parts of the world, for there are many areas where data are still thin, and research has hardly begun. But, as the archaeologists of the 1950s began to realize, culture history is narrowly focused on minute details of artifacts and artifact styles. The archaeological record was thought of in tidy, economical terms, as something orderly and simple, archaeology as basically an atheoretical discipline.

Childe, Boas, and their contemporaries were concerned for the most part with precisely this type of culture history, the material remains of human behavior. They paid relatively little attention to prehistoric lifeways. Although Danish archaeologists were identifying animal bones from coastal shell middens as early as the 1840s, and Californian scholars examined seasonality using bird remains in San Francisco shell middens during the 1920s (Fagan, 1988b), it was not until the 1950s that some archaeologists turned from culture history toward ecology and the study of prehistoric lifeways.

The British prehistorian Grahame Clark applied pollen analysis to a 10,000-year-old hunter-gatherer site in northeast Britain in the late 1940s with spectacular results. By using both pollens and fragmentary red deer antlers from the site, he showed that Star Carr was occupied during the spring and summer months (J. D. G. Clark, 1954). The preservation conditions at the swamp site were so good that he was able to recover other evidence of prehistoric lifeways, too, including a canoe paddle, rolls of birch bark, and the remains of a brush platform built out toward the water's edge. At about the same time, University of Chicago archaeologist Robert Braidwood led a multidisciplinary research team to the Near East on a broad-based study of the origins of agriculture. He excavated the 8,000-year-old farming village of Jarmo in the Zagros foothills of

Iraq, while zoologists studied domestic animal bones and geologists studied the evidence for recent climatic change in the area (Braidwood and Braidwood, 1983). These studies were the forerunners of the much more sophisticated multidisciplinary researches done today.

Currently, there are many avenues of research that provide information on hunting and gathering practices, and on agriculture, pastoralism, and even long-distance trade. Here are some major lines of evidence:

1. *Artifacts* such as axes, plow shares, and digging sticks, to say nothing of stone spear points, provide evidence for subsistence activities. The discovery of a plow share, for example, implies a more complex set of tools for cultivation, which penetrate deeper into the ground and can be used on a much wider range of soils, as happened in prehistoric Europe after 4200 years ago. But the evidence for hunting, gathering, and food production that comes from tools is necessarily limited. Very often, the food remains themselves provide more precise insights.

2. *Settlement data,* in the form of house foundations, temple ruins, and the surviving traces of complete camps, villages, towns, or cities, tell us much about the changing ways in which people have exploited their ever-changing environment (Wilk and Ashmore, 1987). Archaeologists working in the Valley of Mexico have shown how the prehistoric population distributions changed in response to the growth of the Aztec Empire and later as a result of the Spanish Conquest (Sanders, Parsons, and Santley, 1979).

3. *Rock paintings* and other art objects can sometimes provide information on ancient subsistence. Witness Figure 8.2 (p. 240), which shows a San hunter from southern Africa with his toolkit. Sometimes such evidence can also be used to interpret the function of incomplete artifacts found in archaeological deposits nearby (J. D. Clark, 1959).

4. *Indirect evidence* of subsistence activities comes in several ways, not only from geological studies but also from surprisingly esoteric sources. For example, we can learn much of the subsistence ecology of the early hominids at Olduvai Gorge by examining the cut marks on the broken animal bones associated with their tools (Bunn and Kroll, 1986; Potts, 1984a). These marks show that the hominids concentrated on meat and marrow-rich bones. It seems possible that our earliest ancestors competed with predators for much of their game meat, scavenging it from carnivore kills in hasty forays. If so, they were opportunistic foragers rather than true hunters, such as were found among later humans.

Fossil pollens from prehistoric swamps, and organic remains from wet sites like Ozette in Washington State and Monte Verde in Chile tell us much not only about ancient natural vegetation but also about more perishable artifacts made of wood, netting, or fiber (Fagan, 1988b). Pollens can reveal abrupt changes in tree cover resulting from forest clearance by early farming communities. Prehistoric farmers in Denmark and northern Germany, for example, burnt off and cleared forests for their fields 6000 years ago. As the forests were destroyed, characteristic cultivation weeds that infest newly planted wheat fields appear in the pollen diagrams for the first time. Both pollen analysis (palynology) and zooarchaeology (the study of ancient animal bones) enable one to look at the constantly changing relationship between a human cultural system and its environment, as well as at the ways in which people made their living. And, as time went on, both archaeologists and anthropologists began to look more closely at this very subject, called cultural ecology, which we discuss on the following pages. They found, for example, that there was a quantum jump in the number of archaeological sites in the Valley of Mexico once the Aztecs developed a distinctive form of swamp agriculture that doubled maize productivity over thousands of acres of hitherto unexploited land. By the time of the Spanish Conquest, the Indians were occupying every acre of potentially cultivable land in the area. This was in sharp contrast to earlier times, when far more selective, usually nonirrigation, agriculture was practiced (Fagan, 1984a).

5. *Food remains*, such as animal bones or seeds, offer direct evidence for types of food eaten and, by sophisticated analyses, can provide insights into overall dietary pattern as well. The remains of domestic animals or game can be identified by such parts as teeth, jaws, horns, and sometimes the articular ends of limb bones. One can not only establish the proportion of the diet which each type of animal supplied but also, in some cases, obtain invaluable data on butchery practices, the ages at which animals were killed (determinable by study of the teeth), and even the seasons at which the site was occupied. When Joe Ben Wheat excavated the 8000-year-old Olsen-Chubbock bison kill in Colorado, he found the bones of sixteen calves only a few days old. He concluded from known data about bison breeding seasons that the kill took place in late May or early June (Wheat, 1972; see also Speth, 1983).

Seeds are much harder to come by than animal bones and are often recovered using a flotation method: the soil is passed through water so that the fine seeds float on the surface (Ford, 1985; Hole, Flannery, and Neely, 1969). Dry caves in the United States and Mexico have yielded tens of thousands of once-edible seeds. Those from caves in the Tehuacán Valley in Mexico have shown how the inhabitants scheduled their gathering of wild plants with great care. The seeds yield an excellent chronicle of their early experiments with maize and other crops (Ford, 1985; MacNeish, 1978; J. Renfrew, 1973).

Food remains can come in many other forms, too. Fish and bird bones are highly informative and often provide evidence of specialist hunter-gatherer activities. Human feces can be subjected to detailed analysis and provide a fascinating insight into the diet of a site's inhabitants (Bryant, 1974). The ultimate objective of studying food remains is to understand the minutest details of a prehistoric society's adaptation to its environment.

CULTURE AS ADAPTATION — CULTURAL ECOLOGY

Since the 1950s, new views of human culture and its relationship to the natural environment have transformed ways in which archaeologists study world prehistory. Today, the notion that humans adapt to their natural environments seems obvious. But ecological interpretations of prehistoric times are a surprisingly new concept, partly because it is only recently that researchers have developed methods for studying ancient environments. At first they used isolated techniques, studying animal bones or employing pollen analysis. Then, in the 1950s and 1960s, a new body of ecological theory emerged, which owed much to the basic concepts of systems theory in the natural and physical sciences. The assumptions and statements of intent in this research led to new notions of culture — culture as adaptation.

Steward on environment

The American anthropologist Julian Steward was one of those who developed the idea that human cultures were adaptations to the subsistence and ecological requirements of a locality. Steward saw this adaptation as constantly changing. "No culture," he wrote, "has ever achieved an adaptation to its environment which has remained unchanged over any length of time" (Steward, 1970). This viewpoint contrasted sharply with that of many archaeologists of the time, who felt that human cultures were built by accumulation of cultural traits through diffusion and not as responses to ecological factors.

White on equilibrium

Another famous anthropologist, Leslie White, agrued that human culture is made up of many structurally different parts that interact; they react to one another within an overall cultural system (L. White, 1949). He pointed out that cultures could change in response to changes in the environment, but that one part of a cultural system could not change without triggering change in other segments — a prelude to the adoption of systems theory in archaeology. There is a relationship between a human cultural system and its natural environment, and the system is constantly adjusting to environmental changes. Steward and White assumed that successful adaptive patterns continue in use and act as an important stabilizing influence over a long period of time. From their work has developed a new recognition of the importance of cultural evolution in prehistory, not the cultural evolution of Tylor and Morgan, which implied that some human races are superior to others, but evolution based on many and increasingly complex adaptations to the natural environment. The study of the total way in which human populations adapt to and transform their environments is called *cultural ecology*.

Cultural ecology

Archaeologists who study cultural ecology are primarily interested in human cultures as systems interacting with other systems: other human cultures, the biotic community (other living things around them), and the physical environment. They are concerned not only with cultural evolution but also with reconstructing ancient environments and ways in which past cultures made their living (Fagan, 1988b; Sharer and Ashmore, 1987).

At this point, we should look more closely at environment and archaeology.

ENVIRONMENTAL ARCHAEOLOGY

The ultimate goal of environmental archaeology is to understand the relationships between human cultures and their environments, which involves, among other things, defining the characteristics and processes of the biophysical environment. This environment is the matrix for studying the human ecosystem, the interaction between human cultures and their natural surroundings. Archaeological sites, or distributions of them, are part of the human ecosystem (Butzer, 1982).

Biosphere

Human societies are a segment of the *biosphere*, which encompasses all the earth's living organisms interacting with the physical environment. The biosphere model is organized both vertically and horizontally. Vertically, genes and cells are found at the base; organisms, populations, and communities occur above them. Horizontally, the community, all the biological populations in a given area, functions together with the nonliving environment, in a biome.

Biomes are the largest terrestrial communities, major biotic landscapes on earth in which distinctive plant and animal groups live in harmony together. *Habitats* are the areas within a biome where different populations and communities flourish, each with hundreds of individual *sites,* specific locales with their own immediate settings. There are often transition zones between different habitats, and frequently there are areas of considerable importance to human communities exploiting specific resources, such as certain game or vegetable foods. These are known as *ecotones.*

Ecology is a study of functional relationships rather than genetic or phylogenetic ones. This purview is reflected in the concept of the ecological *niche,* the tertiary space occupied by an organism, its functional role in the community, and how it is constrained by other species and external factors.

Every ecosystem is maintained by the regulation of trophic levels (vertical food chains) and by patterns of energy flow (Figure 2.1). The complexities of

Biomes

Habitats
Sites

Ecotones
Ecology
Niche

FIGURE 2.1 A simplified energy cycle for an environmental system. (After Butzer, 1982)

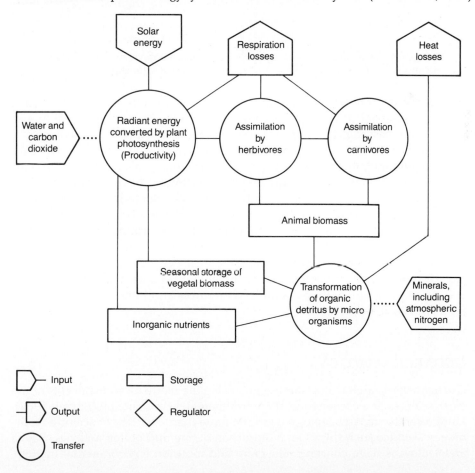

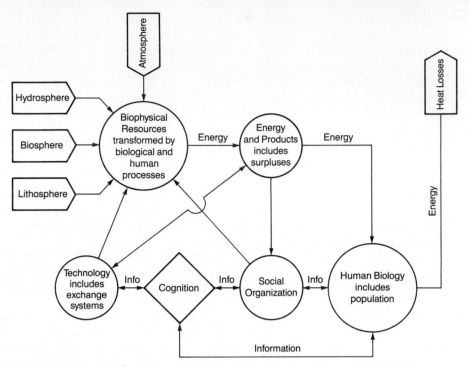

FIGURE 2.2 A much simplified energy cycle for a human ecosystem. This does not include provisions for storage of food and other resources. (After Butzer, 1982)

even modern ecosystems make them difficult to study empirically; prehistoric ones are impossible to reconstruct completely. Yet the broad conceptual framework of the ecosystem serves as a very useful research tool for archaeologists.

Human ecosystems differ from biological ecosystems in many ways (Figure 2.2). Information, technology, and social organization all play much greater roles. Human beings, both as individuals and as groups, have unique capacities for matching resources with specific objectives. They not only think objectively about such matching but also transform the natural environment to meet their objectives. Value systems and goal orientation are important to human ecosystems, as are group attitudes and decision-making institutions, especially in more complex societies. Any attempts to reconstruct prehistoric environments must take into account not only environmental resources and constraints but also the ways in which humans utilized resources and intervened in the environment and changed it.

GEOARCHAEOLOGY

Geoarchaeology

Geoarchaeology, archaeological research using the methods and concepts of the earth sciences, is a cornerstone of environmental reconstruction (Butzer, 1982). Until recently, geoarchaeology was little more than a battery of scientific techniques used for such things as radiocarbon dating and pollen analysis. But as archaeologists have concentrated more and more on environmental matters, and on changing human settlement distributions over long periods of time, they have come to appreciate the great importance of an integrated approach to environmental reconstruction. The new geoarchaeology fills this role (Butzer, 1982).

Ideally, and whatever their expertise, geoarchaeologists should be members of a multidisciplinary research team. They should work alongside the excavators in the field, collecting pollen and soil, and dating samples; recording stratigraphic profiles; relating the site to its landscape by topographic survey; and so on. Working closely with survey archaeologists, geoarchaeologists can locate sites on the natural landscape with the aid of air photographs, satellite images, and other remote-sensing devices. They can examine geological exposures and study the stratigraphic and sedimentary history of the entire region in a wider context vis-à-vis the sites found within it. Back in the laboratory, they can analyze maps and soil samples. Studying the sediments, they can work out the microstratigraphy of the site down to the centimeter relative to that of the surrounding area (Figure 2.3). They can also analyze site deposits for such properties as pH, organic content, and so on, to establish the effects of human activity on the sedimentary sequence. The ultimate objective is to establish the ecological and spatial frameworks for the prehistoric data that emerge from archaeological excavations and surveys.

This approach has been tried with success in many places, including the Nile Valley, where Karl Butzer (1981) has argued that the Ancient Egyptians constantly modified their state and economic structure to overcome external and internal crises, while maintaining the same basic adaptation to a floodplain environment for millennia.

Geoarchaeology is definitely not geology, since it deals not only with sediments but with human activity as well. People are geomorphic agents, just as the wind is. Accidentally or deliberately, they carry inorganic and organic materials to their homes. They remove rubbish, make tools, build houses, abandon tools. All these mineral and organic materials are subjected to all manner of mechanical and biochemical processes during and after the time the site is occupied. The controlling geomorphic system at a site, whatever its size, is made up of both natural elements and a vital cultural component. So the geoarchaeologist is involved with archaeological investigations from the very beginning, and is concerned not only with the formation of sites, and with the changes they underwent during occupation, but also with what happened to them after abandonment.

Thus, geoarchaeologists are deeply involved in the study of what are called *site formation processes* (Schiffer, 1983). These are the processes by which an abandoned prehistoric site is transformed into the archaeological record, the pattern of artifacts, food remains, and so on, that archaeologists investigate today. Site formation processes are still imperfectly understood, because archaeologists have only just begun to look at this type of environmental archaeology, the environment in which a site decayed after abandonment. Wind, earthworms, cattle trampling, even human feet can shift the position of artifacts, erode and deposit soil, and cause artifacts and food remains to disappear or even change shape. Geoarchaeologists use sedimentation studies, soil samples, and chemical analyses to study site formation processes.

Site formation processes

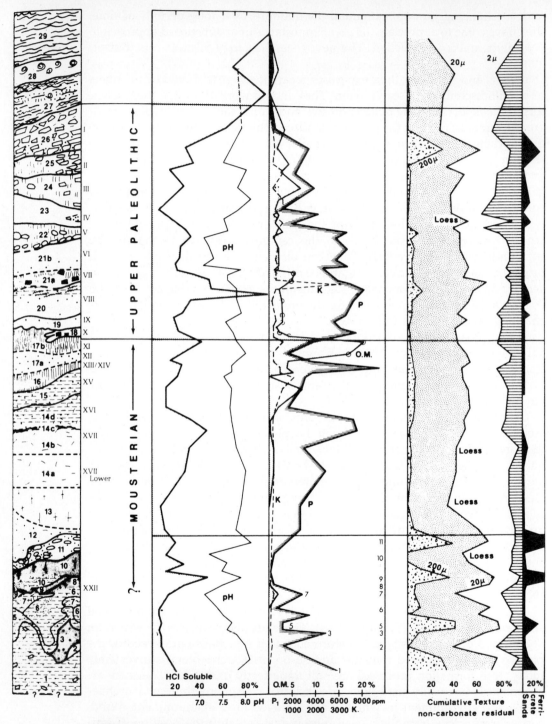

FIGURE 2.3 The complexities of microstratigraphy. A composite archaeosedimentary profile for Cueva Morin, a Paleolithic cave in northern Spain. The different sedimentary classes form the vertical columns; the actual stratigraphic layers appear at the left. (After Butzer, 1982)

Environmental archaeology involves, then, not only the study of ancient environments but also an examination of the highly localized environmental context in which the archaeological record of a site or area is created.

We return to geoarchaeology in Chapter 3, when we consider the environmental background to world prehistory.

PARTICIPATING IN CULTURE

Culture as adaptation — this statement is behind most contemporary interpretations of world prehistory. Leslie White (1949) called culture "man's extra-somatic means of adaptation." Culture is the result of human beings' unique ability to create and infuse events and objects with meaning that can be appreciated, decoded, and understood (Gamble, 1986b). To espouse this definition of culture as adaptation means that culture is *participated in* rather than *shared by* human beings (for extended discussion, see Binford, 1965). However, this participation differs greatly from place to place, and from time to time, resulting in variations in prehistoric material culture — the data for studying prehistory. This viewpoint contrasts sharply with that of culture historians. They tend to argue that all variability can be accounted for by a view of culture which explains patterning in the archaeological record as the result of shared ideas and cultural norms. In other words, assemblages of artifacts that are different represent different cultures, as Childe believed.

The debate between culture historians and those who believe that we do not know all the causes of variability in the archaeological record has gone on for more than a decade (Gamble, 1986b). As Clive Gamble points out, it is really a debate about how the archaeological record is formed. Are artifact assemblages generated by a shared set of experiences and deposited as a result of that phenomenon? Or does a cultural system leave behind a highly complex record of an adaptive strategy that defies easy interpretation?

The new school of thought uses a much more complex, *multidimensional* model to investigate the significance of patterning and variation in archaeological finds (Binford, 1983; Gamble, 1986b). This model is based on two fundamental assumptions:

Multidimensional model

- Since resources are not uniformly distributed within an environment, humans must expend energy in collecting and gathering them. They have to employ some form of adaptive strategy to minimize risk and make optimal use of seasonal phenomena, such as availability of vegetable foods and game migrations. These seasonal strategies rely on the potential of available technology, food storage capacity, and so on. Among hunter-gatherers, for example, these strategies utilize the mobility of individual groups and their flexible social organization to divide them into bands of different sizes, membership, duration, and purpose (Jochim, 1976).
- Under this approach, human activities and their cultural residues are distributed over the landscape through time and space. This scattering results from variations in the distribution and organization of energy. In other words, the archaeological record of world prehistory varies *over the landscape* as a result

of past behavior related to adaptive strategies (Foley, 1981; Gamble, 1986b). Thus, no one site can be taken to represent an entire adaptation; the focus for studying world prehistory must be regional.

This multidimensional approach means thinking of the formation of the archaeological record as reflecting the dimensions of time and space, and their variable impact on human adaptive strategies (Gamble, 1986b). Thinking of world prehistory in terms of culture as adaptation means explaining change and variation in the archaeological record by examining the behavioral content of the material remains of the past. This approach means examining such phenomena as the consequences of band mobility, site location, demography, storage, and the organization of technology. The concern is with long-term changes in adaptive strategies. Thus, the archaeological record of world prehistory consists of a record of observations of what Gamble calls "items of spent energy" — artifacts, features, food remains, sites, as well as environmental data. "The archaeological record is a structure of relationships between the distribution and form of matter as caused by energy sources acting on matter in the past" (Binford, 1981).

It follows that students of world prehistory have a major concern with how the archaeological record was formed, and how we interpret the static data of past human behavior — stone artifacts, broken bones, and so on — in terms of what was once dynamic human behavior in prehistoric times. There is information in the structure and organization of the archaeological record. To acquire this information, archaeologists have made use of several innovative approaches to the past, including ethnographic analogy, controlled experimentation, and middle range theory, a body of theory that seeks to bridge the gap between past and present.

ANALOGY AND EXPERIMENT

There is nothing obvious in the archaeological record. We cannot just pick up stones, bones, or potsherds and ask them what they can tell us about human behavior. The material remains of the past have to be decoded with the aid of a precise methodology if we are to understand their significance in terms of ancient behavior. Archaeological data are the results of behavior and not the behavior itself. This behavior can only be observed in a living cultural system. So, in a sense, this approach to world prehistory can be called a form of behavioral code cracking.

Archaeology, like history, is based on the principle of *uniformitarianism,* the assumption that the present provides observational data that enable us to unlock the information in written and unwritten records of the past. The use of analogy and experiment in archaeology is based on this principle — working from the present into the past.

Ethnographic analogy

Ethnographic analogy, comparing prehistoric societies with living peoples, has been a backbone of prehistoric archaeology for more than a century. Early analogies were simplistic, sweeping comparisons that assumed, for example, that the Inuit of the Arctic were living examples of Stone Age hunter-gatherers who had flourished in southwest France near the end of the Ice Age (Sollas, 1910). As we have seen, such arguments were closely tied to ideas of universal human progress.

Another form of analogy became popular in North America, where prehistory was, and still is, regarded as a form of anthropology in the past. This was the so-called *direct historical approach,* in which the archaeologist starts with a historical baseline, then excavates stratified sites that link the known, historical present with much earlier prehistoric cultures. A. V. Kidder (1927) used this approach with great success at Pecos pueblo in the Southwest in the 1920s, developing an outline chronology of pueblo occupation that extended back more than 2000 years. Given the long continuity of Indian culture in this area, the approach was fundamentally sound. Unfortunately, however, this direct and comprehensive way of comparing ancient and modern society is simply too elementary. There are far too many uncontrollable variables and too great a time depth between remote past and the present (for a discussion of analogy, see Wylie, 1985).

Direct historical approach

The modern attitude toward analogy is far more rigorous. During the past quarter century, archaeologists have refocused analogy in much more specific terms. They approach it in the context of a carefully defined problem, such as the function of an artifact, ways in which garbage was discarded, and so on. Here again, though, there are serious problems, because the earlier the site the more likely it is that site formation processes and other variables have affected the patterning of artifacts, food remains, and other phenomena in the ground.

Many archaeologists have turned to highly specific *artifact analogies* and have made exact replicas of prehistoric tools and weapons that they then tested under controlled conditions. Nicholas Toth (1985) has replicated hominid artifact assemblages from East Turkana and Olduvai Gorge in East Africa, artifacts more than 1.75 million years old. His experiments have demonstrated that our earliest toolmaking ancestors were adept stoneworkers, who were primarily interested in sharp flakes for cutting, sawing, and butchery (Chapter 4). Toth has even been able to show that some of the earliest toolmakers were left-handed by studying the flake scars on discarded cores and flakes. Jeffrey Flenniken (1988), an archaeologist of the American Northwest, learned how to make Paleo-Indian projectile points, which he tested against live animals. Combining studies of edge wear on ancient artifacts and modern replicas with careful "retrofitting" of flakes to discarded cores has proved a fruitful approach to the study of prehistoric stone technology.

Artifact analogies

Experimental archaeology has taken many other forms, too, and can be regarded as a form of analogy using controlled experimentation as a means of comparison. British archaeologist John Coles (1973) fabricated exact copies of European Bronze Age shields and swords, which were tested one against the other, showing that such weaponry was highly effective. Another fashionable form of experimental archaeology has been to build prehistoric settlements, then find volunteers to live in them for months, acting out the ancient lifeway as closely as possible. Such experiments are informative, and, when conducted under carefully controlled and specific circumstances, they are of great value. Artifact by artifact, even dwelling by dwelling, it is sometimes possible to make illuminating analogies about the ancient use of specific artifacts.

Modern archaeology still grapples with the problem of deciding the role of an artifact in prehistoric society. Since this "functionalist" approach considers an artifact as an integral part of the larger society in which it occurs, it should be possible to establish its role in the society. An analogy is set up between the modern society that most closely resembles the archaeological culture — and those least removed from it in time — in subsistence, technology, and environment. But even this apparently reasonable approach has serious objections. For example, we might want to know about the role of sandal making among the Great Basin Indians of 6000 years ago. Were sandals produced by men, women, individuals, or groups? If we consider sandal making an aspect of technology, we might turn to the ethnographic literature on San hunter-gatherers from southern Africa, in whose society sandals were sometimes features. Since women normally carry out domestic tasks among the San, one might argue that sandal making was a domestic task in the Great Basin and was done by women. However, even closer to home, the Pueblo Indians of the Southwest consider weaving a man's work, a task carried out in special ceremonial rooms, as it has been for centuries. Did the Great Basin people have a similar tradition of men performing domestic tasks? We do not know. No matter which analogical choice we make, we probably would not have much confidence in it.

Artifact analogies are now realized to have somewhat limited value. Controlled experiments with prehistoric artifacts, ancient agricultural methods, and early technology are more precise forms of analogy that lead logically into broader attempts to use modern hunter-gatherer or farming societies as a way of interpreting the past. This form of ethnographic analogy is based on ethnoarchaeology, sometimes called "living archaeology."

ETHNOARCHAEOLOGY

Ethnoarchaeology

Ethnoarchaeology is a form of ethnography with a strongly materialist bias (Gould, 1978). It is not just a mass of observed data on human behavior, the sort of simple, isolated analogy that Sollas made. It is the study of dynamic processes in the modern world. For example, the South African anatomist Raymond Dart claimed that the australopithecines, who lived in southern Africa more than a million years ago, made bone tools by twisting, fracturing, and hammering animal bone fragments. This, he claimed, was the first human culture, evolved long before people used stone artifacts. Biologist C. K. Brain tested Dart's hypothesis against a set of controlled observations on modern hyena dens. He was able to show that the bone accumulations in australopithecine caves had been created by predators, not hominids (Brain, 1981; Dart, 1957).

The most famous ethnoarchaeological studies have been carried out among hunter-gatherers: the San of the Kalahari Desert in southern Africa and the Nunamiut Eskimo caribou hunters of Alaska. The San research began when anthropologist Richard Lee undertook a long-term study of !Kung hunter gatherers. He collected a mass of data on hunting and gathering, including residence patterns, that were of potentially vital use to archaeologists working on prehistoric hunter-gatherer bands. Then an archaeologist accompanied the research team and made detailed studies of butchery techniques as well as plans of abandoned settlements of known, historical age. John Yellen's research (1977) yielded a treasure trove of data on house and camp arrangements, hearth locations, population densities, and bone refuse. For example, he points out that a San camp develops through conscious acts, such as the construction of windbreaks and hearths, as well as through such incidental deeds as the discarding of refuse and manufacturing debris (Figure 2.4). Yellen recognized communal areas, open spaces where dancing and distribution of food took place. Then there were family hearths for food processing and cooking. These and other activity areas leave different tracks in the archaeological record.

Lewis Binford's Nunamiut research (1978) concentrated on the food procurement systems of a group of caribou hunters. In a carefully designed piece of research, he wanted to find out as much as he could about their hunting and

FIGURE 2.4 A San camp in the ≠ Tum = / toa grove, Botswana, Africa, as plotted by John Yellen to show the layout of activity areas and artifacts. (After Lee and DeVore, 1976)

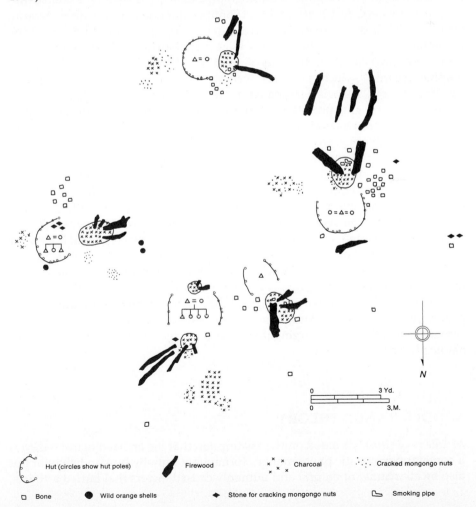

food-processing systems by studying the animal bones that resulted from the chase. He studied not only seasonal hunting but also the storage systems that carried the group from one year to the next — fresh meat is available only two months a year. By close study of the Nunamiuts' annual round, as well as their butchery and storage strategies, Binford was able to develop indices that measured the way the Eskimo used different caribou body parts and utilized their primary food resource. The Nunamiut research provided a mass of empirical data on human exploitation of animals and also showed just how local many cultural adaptations are. Thus, argues Binford (1983), many of the artifact differences recognized in the archaeological record are, in fact, reflections of highly localized adaptations to the environment.

The archaeological record contains evidence for the study of long-term processes. The problem for archaeologists is to gain access to this information. It is hardly surprising that prehistorians have used living societies as analogies for interpreting ancient ones. After all, they are the living cultural systems that are most relevant for understanding the patterning in prehistoric cultural materials. Nevertheless, anyone who uses ethnographic analogy is steering a course into dangerous waters. As Clive Gamble (1986b) eloquently says: "With increasing frequency it is possible to spot, in current archaeological studies, glimpses of the Nunamiut, !Kung, and other groups faintly camouflaged in palaeolithic costume." Martin Wobst (1978) warns of what he calls the "tyranny of the ethnographic record," which provides well-focused glimpses of living human cultural systems. There is a strong temptation to freeze these glimpses and use them as wide-ranging prototypes that are perceived as "fitting" observed patterns of prehistoric materials (for an admirable and sophisticated discussion, see Gamble, 1986b).

The fact remains, however, that we can only understand the past through the present (Spaulding, 1968), since there are no direct ways of observing prehistoric behavior. Ethnographic analogy does not consist of making isolated observations and fitting them to prehistoric examples. Rather, ethnoarchaeology provides a means of exploring the relationship between behavior (dynamics) and its material remains (statics). Living societies, especially varied hunter-gatherer adaptations, allow us to examine this critical relationship, to think about ways of investigating causes of variation in the archaeological record. Understanding the causes of variation in modern hunter-gatherer adaptations gives us a potentially powerful foundation for predicting and investigating just as varied adaptations in the remote past. A new body of archaeological theory is emerging that seeks to bridge the static past and the dynamic present.

MIDDLE RANGE THEORY

Middle range
theory

Middle range theory is based on the assumption that the archaeological record is a contemporary, static phenomenon, formed not only by human behavior but also by all manner of natural and humanly caused factors that buried artifacts, destroyed sites, rebuilt other settlements on them, covered them with wind-blown sand, and so on. These processes create the archaeological record — the phenomena that the archaeologist finds in the ground today. They provide the critical link between long-extinct, dynamic human behavior in the past and the static material properties common in both past and present — the artifacts we examine, pots that were used in the past, and similar types of vessels still used today. What middle range theory tries to do is treat the relationship between statics and dynamics, between human behavior and its material derivatives (Binford, 1978, 1981; Raab and Goodyear, 1984).

Middle range theory is still a new concept in archaeology and one that has raised considerably controversy. For instance, Lewis Binford considers that the archaeological record is static and material and contains no direct information on the relationship between human behavior and material culture. Others disagree and argue that it does (Schiffer, 1976). Just how much genuine middle range theory has yet been generated is still arguable, but the concept is certainly of value when studying the wear on the working edges of prehistoric stone tools and examining site formation processes. This narrow focus is likely to change in future years, since ethnoarchaeology and experimental archaeology provide unique opportunities to gather data for interpreting artifact patternings in the archaeological record and to integrate both statics and dynamics (for a critique, see Raab and Goodyear, 1984).

Using the living world as a means of interpreting prehistoric times will never be easy. Ethnography and ethnoarchaeology deal with living societies at a moment in time. In contrast, archaeology studies *long-term processes* of adaptation and change, using a data base of material culture that provides the observer with access to every aspect of highly variable prehistoric behavior over large areas simultaneously. Successful application of analogy, experimentation, and data from the ethnographic present depends on carefully formulated middle range theory and intricate, formal research designs that stress entire regions rather than specific archaeological sites (Gamble, 1986b).

The fundamental point is that human behavior both today and in the prehistoric past was an adaptation not to a single site but to environmental regions. Thus, to understand individual sites and artifact patternings, the archaeologist has to study regions. Robert Foley calls this *off-site archaeology*, the notion that the archaeological record, certainly of hunter-gatherers, should be perceived not as a system of structured sites but as a continuous pattern of artifact distribution and density over the landscape. As individuals and groups hunt and forage their way across this landscape, they leave behind material remains of their presence, a record that reflects their continual behavior within the region.

The off-site approach uses an ecological concept — a home range — as a way of establishing a link between the principles of ecological organization and the variable artifact densities that reflect mobile adaptations by people using the landscape (Foley, 1981). This approach allows the archaeologist to investigate variable artifact densities over a landscape "as signatures of long term adaptive strategies that have withstood many environmental changes and taken place within wider contexts of social and political change" (Gamble, 1986b, where a lengthy discussion appears).

MULTILINEAR CULTURAL EVOLUTION AND WORLD PREHISTORY

The approaches to world prehistory embodied in analogy, experiment, and middle range theory are concerned with understanding long-term processes through millennia of prehistoric times. They seek to interpret cultural variation and adaptation on a regional basis, especially among highly mobile hunter-gatherer populations. As we have seen, the relationship between ecological and social systems is a critical part of this approach.

These same social systems have evolved through the long millennia of prehistory, not in the simple linear way espoused by Victorian scholars but in increasingly complex ways. Each human society pursues its own evolutionary course, determined by the long-term success of its adaptation, via technology and social institutions, to its natural environment (Sahlins and Service, 1960). This concept of *multilinear evolution* (multiple-lined evolution) now is widely accepted as a general framework by students of world prehistory.

Some societies achieve a broad measure of equilibrium with their environment, in which adaptive changes consist of little more than some refinements in technology and the fine tuning of organizational structures. Other societies be-

Growth cycles   come involved in cycles of growth that are triggered by environmental change or from within society. If these changes involve either greater food supplies or population growth, there can be accelerated growth resulting from the need to feed more people or the deployment of an enlarged food surplus. Continued growth can place additional strains on the society, triggering technological changes, adjustments to social organization, or alterations in the belief system that provides the integrative force for the society.

Every society has its growth limits imposed by the environment and available technology, and some environments have more potential for growth than others. Certain types of sociopolitical organization, such as centralized control of specialized labor, are more efficient than others. The emergence of food production in Mesoamerica (Central America) and the beginnings of urban civilization there are both cases of societies having entered on a major growth cycle after centuries of relatively slow cultural evolution in the same regions. Adaptive changes have triggered technological innovation that has led to increased food supplies and higher population densities. Our own society is embarking on such a cycle today — with open-ended and dangerous consequences.

This sophisticated concept of multilinear cultural evolution led Elman Service, Morton Fried, and others to develop four broad stages of societal complex-

Stages of society   ity that were of great importance in prehistory, stages that are implicit throughout this book (Service, 1962):

1. *Bands* are associations of families that may not exceed twenty-five to sixty people. These bands are knit together by close social ties; they were the dominant form of social organization for most hunter-gatherers from the earliest times up to the origins of food production.

2. *Tribes* are clusters of bands that are linked by clans. A clan is a group of people linked by common ancestral ties, which serve as connections between widely scattered communities. Clans are important because they are a form of

social linkage that gives people a sense of common identity with a wider world than their own immediate family and relatives. They are much more of a kin than a political unit, and, as such, are not used as one of the major stages of social evolution in themselves.

3. *Chiefdoms* develop among some tribes, societies in which clan groups assume a ranking. One clan may achieve dominance because its members have extraordinary religious or organizational powers. The leaders of this clan may become chieftains, who act as social instruments for the control and redistribution of goods and services within the tribe as a whole. Chiefdoms, such as those found among the Hopewell people of the Midwest some 1500 years ago, are a transitional stage between the tribe and the state societies of the earliest civilizations.

4. *State-organized societies* develop from chiefdoms and are governed by a full-fledged ruling class and a hierarchy of social classes below them that includes such diverse groups as specialist craftspeople, merchants, peasants, and even slaves. State-organized societies of the past were first ruled by priest-bureaucrats, then gradually came under the rule of secular kings, who sometimes became despotic monarchs, often with alleged divine powers. This type of social organization was typical of the early literate civilizations and was the forerunner of the Classical civilizations of Greece and Rome.

There has been some criticism of this model (Dunnell, 1980; Plog and Upham, 1983). Most of the criticism is directed not at the stages themselves but at uncritical use of them. All too often, archaeologists have tended to use the stages as a way of fleshing out an incomplete record of the past (Creamer and Haas, 1985). To assume, for example, that a prehistoric society that displays some of the features of a tribal society actually had all of them is very naive, an interpretation far out of touch with reality. What is the point of studying ancient societies, if they are carbon copies of modern ones in their social organization? As we shall see, today's researches concentrate on using the archaeological record to expand and revise our understanding of different stages of human social organization. Archaeology is a unique and highly effective way of studying human cultural change in the past, and, as such, it adds a time dimension to studies of cultural evolution, as well as helps explain how cultural change takes place.

CULTURAL PROCESS, SYSTEMS, AND EVOLUTION

In recent decades not only has a mass of new information become available to archaeologists but also new and much more complex methods of studying cultural process have been developed. At the heart of the new methodology is an insistence that archaeological investigations be based on deductive research. This type of inquiry begins with formal research designs and testable hypotheses, which are then compared against data collected in the field.

Multilinear cultural evolution is the vital force that combines systems theory and cultural ecology into a closely knit, highly flexible way of studying and explaining cultural process (Sanders and Webster, 1978). When systems theory first come into fashion in archaeology during the 1960s, it was regarded as the

Systems theory

solution to all theoretical problems. Kent Flannery (1968a) studied early agriculture in Mexico's southern highlands. He discovered that between 10,000 and 4,000 years ago the highland peoples relied on five basic food sources — deer, rabbits, maguey, tree legumes, and prickly pears — for their sustenance. By careful predicting of the seasons of each food, they could schedule their hunting and gathering at periods of abundance and before animals gained access to the ripe plants. Flannery assumed that the southern highlands and their inhabitants were part of a large, open environmental system consisting of many subsystems — economic, botanic, social, and so on — that interacted with one another. Then something happened to jolt the food procurement system toward the deliberate growing of wild grasses. Flannery's excavations at dry sites dating to between 7,000 and 4,000 years ago showed wild maize cobs slowly increasing in size and other signs of genetic change. He suggested that the people began to experiment with the deliberate planting of maize and other grasses, intentionally expanding the areas where they would grow. After a long period of time, these intentional deviations in the food procurement system caused the importance of wild grass collecting to increase at the expense of other collecting activities until it became the dominant one. Eventually, the Indians created a self-perpetuating food procurement system, with its own vital scheduling demands of planting and harvesting that competed with earlier systems and won out because it was more durable. By 4000 years ago, the highly nutritious bean and corn staple diet of the highland peoples was well established.

Flannery's Mexican research dramatizes the importance of looking at cultural change in the context of the interrelationships between many variables. There is no one prime agent of cultural evolution but rather a series of important variables, all with complex interrelationships. When we seek to explain the major and minor events of prehistory, we consider the ways in which change took place, the processes and mechanisms of change, (cultural evolution, experimentation), and the socioeconomic stresses (population pressure, game scarcity, and so on) that trigger these mechanisms (Flannery, 1972).

The problem is that testing such multicausal models is a difficult task, involving rigorous methodologies for identification of the variables in the archaeological record as well as comparative studies of these variables in regions where a particular development (say, the emergence of civilization) occurred and where it did not, and also in societies that flourished immediately before its development (Redman, 1978). Flannery's systems approach has been criticized by some scholars for its heavy reliance on cultural evolution (Sanders and Webster, 1978). They point out that environmental stimuli are probably far more important then the universal evolutionary processes of multilinear evolutionists.

CURRENT DIRECTIONS

Evolutionary theory has yet to be explored systematically in archaeology. Flannery's methods are still fundamentally based on the anthropologists' notions of cultural evolution, a view that tends to emphasize variability in human culture as a whole at the expense of individual human actions and decisions. Just how important was the individual in prehistory, as opposed to biological, cultural, and environmental forces? Much current archaeological research is trying to move us closer to understanding the frameworks within which cultural process took place. Some of the exciting new directions of this research include the following:

Structural Archaeology and the Individual

Some archaeologists believe that there is much more to human culture than functions and activities. Behind all activities of any society, ancient or modern, are the logic and coherence that have to be understood in their own terms (Hodder, 1982). This "structure" of prehistoric society is defined as "the codes and rules according to which observed sets of interrelations are produced," the set of rules, as it were, that can be likened to those in chess or Pictionary. They are followed as people go about the business of surviving, adapting, and making a living. Structural archaeology is an attempt to get at objects as they were perceived by their original owners, at the symbolism of burial rites,and ultimately at the reasons why societies remain static, change, collapse, and so on. Structural archaeology is in its infancy, since few areas provide the enormous quantities of archaeological data that are needed to trace and observe the subtle changes in artifact patterning over time.

Evolution and World Prehistory

Without question, the greatest theoretical advances in world prehistory currently involve neoevolutionary theory. They have special relevance for the study of early prehistory. The principle of natural selection has long been the central dogma of evolutionary thought, accepted as a basic mechanism for evolution but little analyzed. All this has changed in recent years. A whole new body of evolutionary theory has equipped biologists with methods of investigating the processes as well as the patterns of evolution (Foley, 1984b). This wealth of new theory is finally having an impact on world prehistory (Dunnell, 1980), for natural selection may prove to be a means of explaining patterns of variation in human morphology and behavior. There are several approaches:

Sociobiology attempts to account for patterns of behavior among living populations in terms of increasing fitness (Chagnon and Irons, 1979; E. O. Wilson, 1978). Sociobiologists believe that cultural expression is a flimsy blanket for genetic imperatives. In other words, human behavior is partly explained by a form of genetic determinism — our actions are much more genetically directed than we might think. In contrast, most anthropologists believe that the greater part of human behavior is produced by our unique culture. *Sociobiology*

In another of the growing links between anthropology and biology, *behavioral ecologists* are using a comparative approach to biological evolution to place human characteristics within a general framework of animal variability. This and other emerging evolutionary approaches are concerned with the analysis of *Behavioral ecology* human adaptation from a biological perspective. All assume that patterns of adaptation in prehistoric times were the products of natural selection and can be interpreted in these terms. These new approaches assume that human biological evolution and human prehistory cannot be isolated one from the other. Human biological and cultural evolution must be placed in two contexts: the evolution of the animal community as a whole and that of local ecology. Human adaptation in prehistory is the result of ecological and evolutionary adaptations between humans and other species that make up the biological community (Foley, 1984b).

Community ecology

This new and powerful approach to early world prehistory would appear to make the study of human prehistory a branch of evolutionary biology. But it would be wrong to consider it so, simply because the data base for prehistory is quite different. Blind application of theoretical principles developed for studying living populations is dangerous, because they cannot be tested adequately against fossil and archaeological data. It is here the ethnoarchaeology, analogy, and experimentation, as well as middle range theory, have important roles to play.

Evolutionary theory will have its greatest impact on the study of early prehistory, on our understanding of the processes by which humans first peopled the diverse environments of the Old and New worlds. The new approaches analyze human adaptation and evolution as products of interactions between members of a much wider biological community. They approach early prehistory in two ways. One examines the geographic communities of which humans were a part. For example, the earlier periods of human evolution occurred in tropical Africa, when hominids were part of the tropical African community. Later on, humans settled in more temperate and arctic latitudes, where they were members of quite different biological communities. The second approach looks closely at the types of organisms that share ecological problems faced by our ancestors. As we shall see (Chapter 4), these are the large mammals.

Community evolution and ecology provide a perspective on early prehistory that allows one to identify, formulate, and analyze problems in prehistoric adaptation. Above all, they allow one to examine our remote ancestors in the context of the rest of the biological world instead of considering them as something unique and isolated, which they were not.

Our knowledge of world prehistory grows ever more complex, but our understanding of it is still grossly inadequate. Although we can discern some regularities, the general relationships and processes that have led to them remain little understood. This is where the new approaches typified by ethnoarchaeology and community evolution come in, approaches that will undoubtedly assume greater importance in the remainder of this century.

Cultural Complexity and Marine Resources

Earlier, we mentioned how archaeologists use the archaeological record to expand our understanding of emerging social complexity in the past. Everyone agrees that prehistoric farmers and early civilizations enjoyed progressively more complex social organization and cultural complexity. But what about hunter-gatherers? Were there Stone Age hunters and foragers who lived in more complex societies than the simple bands associated with such peoples as the San of southern Africa or most Australian aborigines? Many experts have pointed to the American Indians of the Pacific Northwest coast as an example of a more complex hunting and gathering society, one governed by powerful chieftains and enjoying rich ceremonial traditions and elaborate art traditions, as well as sedentary settlements.

Relatively few Stone Age hunter-gatherer societies are candidates for any degree of cultural complexity. Some possibilities include the Magdalenians, who lived in southwest France some 15,000 years ago; some fishing societies of southern Scandinavia some 7,000 years ago; and late "Archaic" peoples living in midwestern river valleys in North America about 4,000 years ago. Almost invariably, social complexity among prehistoric hunter-gatherers is associated with exploitation of freshwater or marine fish, shellfish, or sea mammals. Aquatic resources have the advantage of being both relatively plentiful and predictable, so much so that there are strong incentives for people to adopt sedentary lifeways along rivers, and at lake and ocean shores. Common sense would dictate that aquatic resources were exploited by human beings very early in prehistory. In fact, the full potential of marine and freshwater resources was only realized in a relatively few areas of the world, and then mostly within the past 10,000 years.

The debates about emerging social complexity in the Stone Age revolve around two opposing viewpoints. The first envisages the oceans as a kind of "Garden of Eden" (Binford, 1983). Proponents of this theory point to the enormous abundance of shellfish in many tidal areas, to seasonal fish runs up large rivers in many parts of the world, and to the great productivity of many estuaries and coastal waters easily exploited by shore-dwelling fisherfolk. This abundance allowed societies to become sedentary and to maintain population densities (Fladmark, 1978; Holmes, 1987; Moseley, 1975a).

In contrast, another group of archaeologists, many of them studying post–Ice Age hunter-gatherers in Europe, argue that aquatic resources were a strategy of last resort, a response to population pressure and shortages of terrestrial resources such as game and wild vegetable foods (Bailey, 1978; Gamble, 1986b). These authorities assume that marine and freshwater resources, no matter how productive, are much more labor intensive to harvest and are less nutritionally valuable than food sources on land.

David Yesner (1987) has recently taken a somewhat different viewpoint. He argues that the shift to the exploitation of aquatic resources was the result of decisions made by people living in periods of rapid environmental change, where population pressure was causing food shortages. The "optimal" strategy for people under these circumstances would be to turn to a resource that does involve more work, and is, perhaps, not as productive as big game.

All of these viewpoints assume, however, that maritime resources played a key role in the emergence of social complexity among Stone Age hunter-gatherers. The issue of social complexity comes into full play at the end of the Ice Age, when sea levels were rising and the climate warming up rapidly, forcing human populations all over the world to adapt to radically new circumstances, in temperate latitudes and more forested environments. The debates about social complexity and aquatic resources still continue, for no one knows exactly how decisive marine or riverine resources were in allowing high population densities and sedentary living, both essential prerequisities for social complexity. Nor do we know whether one can make analogies between prehistoric societies thousands of years old and complex Northwest coast Indian societies that flourished only a few centuries ago. There is an enormous chronological gap to be bridged.

Nevertheless, the debate about social complexity is of great importance to world prehistory, for many of the cultural phenomena associated with it, for example, tribal social organization and sedentary settlement, played a vital role in later prehistory, when farmers and later preindustrial civilizations flourished in many parts of the world.

Examining a satellite photograph of the earth or flying from Los Angeles to New York makes you realize one fundamental truth about world prehistory, which serves as a good starting point for the next chapters. Of all the millions of animals on earth, we are the only ones who have so relentlessly and universally transformed the face of the globe. We have done both bad and good, and we have at times caused lasting damage to the earth, damage that prompts some people to predict that the end of human existence is near. But we are also the only ones of a myriad of living creatures who have evolved the intellectual powers to guide our own destiny. It is this capacity that enables us to ask the question, Why are we here? This book cannot do much to answer that question, but it can give you an understanding of some of the complex processes in human prehistory that have led us to master and transform the earth.

GUIDE TO FURTHER READING

Binford, Lewis R. *In Pursuit of the Past*. New York: Thames and Hudson, 1983.
A basic account of processual archaeology, with lengthy discussions of ethnoarchaeology and middle range theory.

Butzer, Karl. *Archaeology as Human Ecology*. Cambridge: Cambridge University Press, 1982.
A basic account of cultural ecology and environmental archaeology from a geological perspective.

Fagan, Brian M. *In the Beginning* (6th ed.). Boston: Scott, Foresman/Little, Brown, 1988.
The early chapters of this textbook cover major theoretical developments.

Gamble, Clive. *The Palaeolithic Settlement of Europe*. Cambridge: Cambridge University Press, 1986.
Probably the most important synthesis of new approaches to prehistoric archaeology in a generation. Definitely a book for advanced readers.

Harris, Marvin. *The Rise of Anthropological Theory*. New York: Crowell, 1968.
A magnificent, if occasionally polemical, survey of theory in anthropology that covers many personalities mentioned in this chapter.

Meltzer, David, Fowler, Don D., and Sabloff, Jeremy A. (eds.) *American Archaeology Past and Future*. Washington, D.C.: Smithsonian Institution Press, 1986.
A series of essays that analyze the history and future of American archaeology. Essential reading for any serious student of world prehistory.

Salmon, M. *The Philosophy of Archaeology.* New York: Academic Press,1982.
A thoughtful book on the basic philosophies behind archaeology and its relationships to other intellectual disciplines.

Watson, Patty Jo, LeBlanc, Steven, and Redman, Charles L. *Archaeological Explanation: The Scientific Method in Archaeology.* New York: Columbia University Press, 1984.
A description of the basic principles of processual archaeology, widely used by serious students.

CHAPTER 3

The Great Ice Age

Preview

■ The later part of the Cenozoic, the age of mammals, was a period of rapidly changing and often intensely cold climate. These changes reached a peak during the Quaternary, the most recent period of earth history, which began about 1.6 million years ago. The Pleistocene or great Ice Age forms most of the Quaternary until about 10,000 years ago.

■ The Pleistocene is important because it is the only geological epoch contemporary with human activity. Its deposits offer unique opportunities for studying ancient environments and dating prehistoric human cultures.

■ The Pleistocene was once studied by means of glacial deposits and other land formations, as well as high levels. But deep sea cores provide the most accurate and comprehensive chronicle of climatic change during the Ice Age. These changes are mirrored by sequences of vegetation changes obtained from fossil pollens in waterlogged deposits on land.

■ The Pliocene/Pleistocene boundary is set arbitrarily at 1.6 million years ago, a date that coincides with a reverse in the earth's polarity at the end of the Olduvai Event.

■ About 730,000 years ago, the earth's polarity reverted to normal at the Matuyama/Brunhes boundary, a worldwide event identified in deep sea cores and loess deposits ashore. There have been at least eight cycles of glacial and interglacial climate since then.

■ Geologists divide the Pleistocene into Lower, Middle, and Upper subdivisions on the basis of paleomagnetic, climatic, and fossil changes. The Lower Pleistocene saw gradual cooling. Its fauna still included Pliocene animals. It ended with the Matuyama/Brunhes boundary 730,000 years ago. The Middle and Upper Pleistocene witnessed at least eight cycles of glacial and interglacial climate, including two major glaciations identified in northern Europe — Elster and Saale — separated by short interglacials.

■ The Upper Pleistocene began with the Eemian interglacial about 128,000 years ago. The climate cooled rapidly after about 118,000 and reached a cold climax about 18,000 years ago.

■ Postglacial times (the Holocene) began about 10,000 years ago. The climate reached a warm climax about 7,000 years ago. The global climate is now cooling.

■ Pleistocene climatic change radically affected the human settlement of the Old and New worlds, in terms of both broader ecological processes and *Homo sapiens's* successful ability to adapt to cyclical, and often drastic, environmental changes after 700,000 years ago.

The later part of the Cenozoic — the age of mammals — was, and still is, a period of rapidly changing and often intensely cold climate. These changes culminated during the Quaternary, the most recent period of earth history, which began about 1.6 million years ago (Haq et al., 1977). This period is sometimes called the *Age of Humanity*, for it was during that time that human beings first populated most of the globe. This chapter describes some of the major climatic and environmental changes that have taken place during the Quaternary, changes that were the climatic backdrop for some of the most important stages in human evolution (Goudie, 1983).

For most of geological time, the world's climate was warmer and more homogeneous than it is today. As long ago as the Miocene epoch (Table 3.1), land began to uplift in many places and mountains began to form, continuing through the Pliocene into recent time (Butzer, 1974; Flint, 1971). During the Oligocene, some 35 million years ago, the first signs of glacial cooling appeared, with the formation of a belt of pack ice around Antarctica. This was followed by a major drop in world temperatures between 14 and 11 million years ago. As temperatures lowered, glaciers formed on high ground in high latitudes. About 3.2 million years ago, large ice sheets formed on the northern continents, locking up enough water to lower world sea levels by about 130 feet (40m). Then, about 2.5 million years ago, glaciation intensified still more and the earth entered its present period of constantly fluctuating climate.

THE GREAT ICE AGE

The Quaternary (or Pleistocene) era had constant fluctuations between warm and intensely cold global climates. Climates as warm as or warmer than that of today were rare during the Quaternary. Called *interglacials,* they lasted only about 10,000 years each. The cold, *glacial* periods between them were not uniformly cold but fluctuated constantly between milder phases, called *interstadials,* and millennia of intense cold. Not that the interstadials were warm, far from it. They were merely slightly less frigid.

During Pleistocene times, climatic change repeatedly displaced plants and animals from their original habitats (Kurtén, 1968; Kurtén and Anderson, 1980; Martin and Klein, 1984). When a glacial period began, plants and animals usually fared better in lower altitudes and warmer latitudes. Populations of ani-

TABLE 3.1 Geological epochs from more than 60 million years ago. The curve demonstrates lasting temperature changes on earth since the late Miocene; the dotted line indicates lack of data. Notice that the general trend is toward cooler temperatures with fluctuations (Pleistocene temperatures are shown in Table 3.2).

Millions of years B.P.	Geological period	Geological epoch	Millions of years B.P.	Geological epoch	Temperature ← lower higher →
3 –	QUATERNARY	PLEISTOCENE	I ?		
10 –		PLIOCENE	I	PLEISTOCENE	
15 –					
20 –		MIOCENE	3 – ?		
25 –					
30 –		OLIGOCENE		PLIOCENE	
35 –	TERTIARY		10 –		
40 –					
45 –		EOCENE			
50 –					
55 –			15 –		
60 –				MIOCENE	
65 –		PALEOCENE			
70 –	CRETACEOUS	CRETACEOUS			
75 –			20 –		

mals spread slowly toward more hospitable areas, mixing with populations that already lived in those areas and creating new communities with new combinations of organisms. This repeated mixing surely affected the directions of evolution in many forms. No one knows exactly how many species of mammals emerged during the Pleistocene, although Björn Kurtén has estimated that no fewer than 113 of the mammal species now living in Europe and adjacent Asia appeared during the last 3 million years.

The Pleistocene is important because it is the only geological epoch contemporary with human activity. People lived and hunted over much of the terrain covered by its ice sheets and dwelt in arctic steppe zones during the more temperate interglacials. Stone Age humans killed many types of animals for food, animals whose butchered bones often are found in river gravels and other Pleistocene deposits in the Old World. Early hunters preyed on animals now extinct, whose carcasses sometimes sank into lake mud or washed into river backwaters, burying the skeletons for archaeologists to find thousands of years later.

With these fossils and careful study of geological deposits, a complex chronological record of the Pleistocene has been assembled, much of it based on temperature fluctuations recorded in deep sea cores (Goudie, 1983). Numerous branches of science — botany, zoology, geomorphology (the study of landforms), nuclear physics, and oceanography — have helped build up the story of the Pleistocene epoch we shall outline here.

STUDYING THE PLEISTOCENE

In the late nineteenth century, two Austrian geologists, A. Penck and E. Brückner, studied the glacial deposits in four northern Alpine valleys (Penck and Brückner, 1909). They identified at least four major Pleistocene glacial periods — Günz, Mindel, Riss, and Würm — which were named after Alpine valleys. These, they said, designated times when the ice sheets of the mountains extended into much lower altitudes than today. At the same time, vast ice sheets flowed southward from Scandinavia and arctic Canada, covering much of northern Europe and much of the northeastern and midwestern United States. Penck and Brückner argued that these glaciations were separated from each other by prolonged interglacials, when sea levels rose and the world enjoyed warmer and often drier climates (Table 3.2). When the longest interglacial was at its height, such animals as the hippopotamus were living in the Somme, Thames, and other European rivers.

For years, Pleistocene geologists accepted the Austrian scheme. They relied on river gravels, glacial deposits, and other crude geological indicators. They thought of the Pleistocene as being divided into three, perhaps four, major glaciations. But the inevitable advance of science and technology has changed all this and shown that the Pleistocene was far more complicated than was once suspected (a valuable historical summary can be found in Imbrie and Imbrie, 1979). There are indications from deep sea cores that there were at least seventeen glacial cycles during the 1.6 million years of the Pleistocene.

Deep Sea Cores

The science of oceanography relies heavily on deep sea core borers that bring up columns of sediment from the ocean floor. Sediments from these cores provide something that has never been discovered on land — a *continuous* stratigraphic record of Pleistocene events. These events can be fixed at key points by absolute dates such as radiocarbon dating, which is used on the uppermost sections of the cores. Paleomagnetic research (the study of ancient magnetism) on the full length of the columns provides another important perspective, for these studies have shown that the earth's magnetic field changed from reversed to normal 730,000 years ago.

TABLE 3.2 Geological events, climatic changes, and chronology during the Pleistocene (highly simplified), with approximate dates.

Temperature ← lower higher →	Dates (B.P.)	Periods	Epochs	Subdivisions	European glacials/ interglacials	North American glacials/interglacials	Human evolution	Prehistory	Three Age System
		Holocene	Holocene	HOLOCENE	Holocene	Holocene	*Homo sapiens sapiens* ←	Cities, agriculture Settlement of New World	IRON AGE BRONZE AGE NEOLITHIC MESOLITHIC
	10,000—								UPPER PALEOLITHIC
	118,000—	Quaternary	B r u n h e s	UPPER PLEISTOCENE	Weichsel (Würm)	Wisconsin			
	128,000—				Eemian	Sangamon			
				MIDDLE PLEISTOCENE	Saale (Riss)	Illinoian	*Homo sapiens* ←	Hunter-gatherers	LOWER AND MIDDLE PALEOLITHIC
			M a t u y a m a		Holstein	Yarmouth			
				LOWER PLEISTOCENE	Elster (Mindel)	Kansan	*Homo erectus*		
	730,000—		Pleistocene						
	1,600,000—	Tertiary	Olduvai Event / Pliocene				Early hominids and *Australopithecus*		

Note for the advanced reader and the instructor: Throughout this book I have used the glacial terminology applied to northern Europe in discussing the successive glaciations and interglacial periods in the Old World. This system follows Karl Butzer's definitive synthesis, *Environment and Archaeology*, 3rd ed. (Chicago: Aldine, 1974). Many still use the Alpine names preferred in earlier literature, but I have chosen to reduce confusion and recognize that not everyone will agree. For the newcomers, here are the equivalent names:

Alpine terms: Würm Riss Mindel *Northern European terms:* Weichsel Saale Elster

Uncertain climatic detail before 130,000 years ago

Matuyama and Brunhes

The earth's magnetic polarity was reversed during the so-called Matuyama epoch, changing to normal with the onset of the Brunhes epoch at 730,000 years ago. This important boundary is a stratigraphic marker of worldwide significance, because it can be identified both in deep sea cores and in volcanic rocks on land, where the boundary can be dated with potassium argon methods. The Matuyama/Brunhes boundary marks the arbitrary division between the Lower and Middle Pleistocene (see later) (Butzer and Isaac, 1975).

Deep sea cores produce long columns of ocean floor sediments that include the skeletons of small marine organisms that once lived close to the ocean's surface. These planktonic foraminifera consist largely of calcium carbonate. When alive their minute skeletons absorb oxygen isotopes. The ratio of two of these isotopes — ^{16}O and ^{18}O — varies as a result of evaporation. When evaporation is high, more of the lighter ^{16}O is extracted from the ocean, leaving the plankton to be enriched by more, heavier ^{18}O. When great ice sheets formed on land during glacial episodes, sea levels fell as moisture was drawn off for continental ice caps. During such periods, the world's ocean contained more ^{18}O in proportion to ^{16}O, a ratio reflected on millions of foraminifera. A mass spectrometer is used to measure the ratio, which does not reflect ancient temperature changes but is really a statement about the size of the oceans — and about contemporary events on land.

One advantage of sea cores is that with them you can confirm the climatic fluctuations by using several different lines of evidence. For example, you can analyze the changing frequencies of foraminifera and other groups of marine microfossils in the cores. By using statistical techniques, and assuming that relationships between different species and sea conditions have not changed, climatologists have been able to turn these frequencies into numerical estimates of sea-surface temperature and ocean salinity over the past few hundred thousand years (CLIMAP, 1976).

The core that serves as the standard reference for events during the past 700,000 years comes from the Solomon Plateau in the Pacific Ocean (core number V28–238; Figure 3.1; Shackleton and Opdyke, 1973). This core is a long way from the great European and North American ice sheets, but it, and many other such samples, records events of local climatic significance like glacial advances on a global scale. The Matuyama/Brunhes boundary occurs at a depth of 39.3 feet (1200 cm) in core V28 238. Above it, a saw-toothlike curve identifies eight complete glacial and interglacial cycles, a far more complicated picture of the Middle and Upper Pleistocene than comes from land sediments (Gamble, 1986b; Goudie, 1983).

Sea cores have produced a highly complex picture of Pleistocene climate. Lower Pleistocene cores show that the climatic fluctuations between warm and cold were relatively minor until about 800,000 years ago. Since then, periods of intense cold have recurred about every 90,000 years, with minor oscillations about 20,000 and 40,000 years apart. Many scientists believe that these changes are triggered by long-term astronomical changes, especially in the earth's orbit around the sun (Covey, 1984), which affect the seasonal and north-south variations of solar radiation received by the earth. Of course there are other factors, too, such as the amount of volcanic dust in the atmosphere (Gribben, 1978).

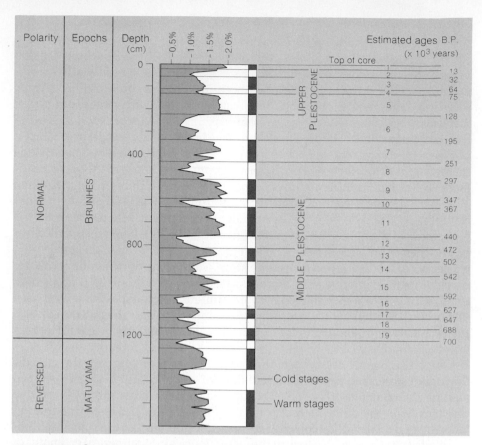

FIGURE 3.1 Stratigraphic record of the Pleistocene from deep sea core V28–238. The Matuyama/Brunhes boundary occurs at about 730,000 years ago. The saw-toothlike profile chronicles the relative size of the world's oceans and ice caps. (After Shackleton and Opdyke, 1973)

Land Observations

The major problem confronting Pleistocene geologists — and one of fundamental importance to archaeologists — is to correlate the continuous deep sea core record with the fragmentary data from land (Bowen, 1978; Gamble, 1986b). The geological record on land is much less complete than that from the ocean floor, partly because the forces of erosion, deposition, and earthquake movement are constantly changing the earth's surface (Bowen, 1978). The fragmentary deposits that do survive are extremely difficult to date either stratigraphically or in years, except in volcanic areas, where potassium argon dating can be used. Geologists rely heavily on deep layers of glacial, windblown dust and pollen-rich lakes and swamps for correlations between land and ocean.

Loess deposits

Loess deposits are deep layers of windblown dust that were laid down under dry, arctic steppe conditions during glacial periods. Strong winds blowing out from the ice caps carried loess over enormous distances, dropping it in thick belts that mantle much of China, central Europe, and parts of North America.

When the climate warmed up, these loess layers carried woodland or grassland, which formed rich soils that show up clearly in geological exposures, and they were often covered by later deposits of glacial dust. The loesses can be dated by paleomagnetic techniques and confirm what we already know from oxygen isotope sea core analyses: that the climate has fluctuated constantly between warm and cold for at least 1.8 million years. River terraces at Červený Kopec (red hill) near Brno in Czechoslovakia and elsewhere in central Europe have accumulated up to 328 feet (100 m) of Middle and Upper Pleistocene loess deposits. Here, the Matuyama/Brunhes boundary as well as eight cycles of glacial and interglacial climatic change that coincide well with those from core V28-238 can be identified (Kulka, 1977). It should be stressed, however, that these are the most general of correlations.

Pollen analysis (palynology) has long been used to study vegetational changes over lengthy periods of time, using sample cores taken from lake deposits and peat bogs. One lake core in northern Greece provides a vegetational sequence that goes back more than 600,000 years (Turekian, 1971). This finding can be correlated with deep sea cores. Pollen analysis can be used most profitably to study the last 130,000 years, when many more core sequences survived.

Pollen analysis

Animal remains have also long been used to make crude correlations of Pleistocene climatic changes. For example, the fossilized teeth of elephants provide an interesting chronicle of dramatic changes in elephant populations during the Ice Age, although these changes are of a very general nature. Since many mammals are relatively insensitive to rapid climatic change and can flourish in a wide range of climatic regimens, only the most general impression of a Pleistocene climate can come from such data. Studies of tiny mammals like rats and mice, however, can often provide a relatively sensitive picture of Pleistocene environments such as those at the famous early hominid sites at Olduvai Gorge, Tanzania, in East Africa.

Animal remains

In general terms, there appear to have been repeated climatic fluctuations on a cyclical basis every 90,000 years or so during the Middle and Upper Pleistocene, with a long-term trend toward drier and colder glacial episodes. The deep sea cores tell us that the transition from full glacial to interglacial conditions was a very rapid one in geological terms. This is dramatized by the celebrated Bering Land Bridge, a critical element in the first human settlement of the Americas (Chapter 7). The land bridge was at its full extent 15,000 years ago. Only 5,000 years later, the Siberian coastline of the Bering Strait had assumed its modern configuration (Hopkins et al., 1982).

LOWER PLEISTOCENE

The beginning of the Pleistocene is a purely arbitrary boundary defined by geologists for the sake of convenience (Table 3.2). The boundary between the Pliocene and Pleistocene is generally placed at about 1.6 million years ago, a point that coincides with a major geomagnetic reversal (the top of the so-called Olduvai Event), which can be recognized on a global basis (Haq et al., 1977.) By this time great mountain chains had formed in the Alps, Himalayas, and elsewhere. Landmasses had been uplifted; there was reduced connection between those latitudes and southern areas, lessening their heat exchange and causing greater temperature differences between them. Marine temperatures cooled gradually during the Pliocene. By 3 million years or so ago, northern latitudes, still warmer than today, were much cooler than they had been 70 million years before. A cooling of the northern seas 3 million years ago can be detected from finds of marine deposits in northern Europe and North America that show temperate, northern mollusks replacing warmer species.

The terms *Lower, Middle,* and *Upper Pleistocene* break the epoch into large subdivisions according to their fossils and climatic changes. The Lower Pleistocene normally includes surviving Pliocene animal fossils, as well as wild horses, cattle, elephants, and camels, all of which appear for the first time in the Pleistocene.

The Lower Pleistocene is still very imperfectly known. However, it is known from sea cores that climatic fluctuations between warmer and colder regimens were still relatively minor (Kurtén, 1968). It lasted about a million years, up to about 730,000 years ago, when the present phase of the earth's magnetic polarity began. Many Lower Pleistocene fossil beds come from Africa, where early hominids hunted both large mammals and smaller animals. This was the critically important time when *Homo erectus* evolved and human populations moved out of Africa into Asia and Europe.

MIDDLE PLEISTOCENE

The boundary between the Lower and Middle Pleistocene coincides with the Matuyama/Brunhes changeover some 730,000 years ago. Deep sea cores tell us that there have been at least eight glacial and interglacial cycles during the Middle and Upper Pleistocene (Figure 3.1; Table 3.2). The seesaw pattern of sea core changes suggests that although ice sheets formed gradually, deglaciation took place with great rapidity, during phases that geologists call *terminations,* which correspond with major sea level rises that flooded low-lying coastal areas. Lesser rises took place during interstadials. Street (1980) estimates that glaciers covered a full one-third of the earth's land surface during glacial maxima, while they were about as extensive as they are today during interglacials. Thus, during interglacials sea levels were within 18 to 30 feet (5 to 10 m) of present shorelines.

The fluctuations in ice sheets were mirrored by major vegetational changes away from the ice sheets. Treeless arctic steppe and tundra covered much of Europe and North America during cold periods but gave way to temperate forests during interglacials. Much less is known about changes in tropical latitudes, although it is thought that the southern fringes of the Sahara Desert expanded dramatically during cold periods: high percentages of windblown desert sand have been found in sea cores taken off West Africa.

In earlier editions of this book, I used a long-established sequence of glacial episodes and interglacials to subdivide both the Middle and Upper Pleistocene. Although many details of these periods have been modified by sea core research, it is still worth summarizing the major episodes, identified in Europe (Table 3.2).

The best glacial deposits in Europe come from northern Germany and are named after two rivers: the Elster and the Saale.

The *Elster* glaciation reached its height about 525,000 years ago. Ice covered much of central Britain, the Low Countries, and central Europe as far east as the Ural Mountains. The Alpine ice extended northward and local glaciers sat on the Pyrenees and the Caucasus, so that much of Europe between latitudes 40 and 50° N was arctic plains country, with severe winters in the Mediterranean. The North American equivalent was the Kansan ice sheet, which extended southward from three ice caps near the sixtieth parallel in Canada. Its southern limits were Seattle, St. Louis, and New York. At that time as much as 33 percent of the earth's surface was covered with ice, and sea levels were about 650 feet (197 m) below their present heights.

Elster **525,000 B.P.**

The succeeding interglacials brought much more temperate conditions, at times milder than today's in northern latitudes (Figure 3.2). It was during this period that human settlement of temperate latitudes really took hold, as small bands of hunters exploited the rich game populations of European river valleys (Chapter 5). The oscillations between warmer and colder weather, which are chronicled in Table 3.2, show a surprising regularity, with peaks of more tem-

Holstein **515,000 to 315,000 B.P.**

FIGURE 3.2 Generalized distribution of vegetation in Europe during the height of the Holstein interglacial. (After Butzer, 1971)

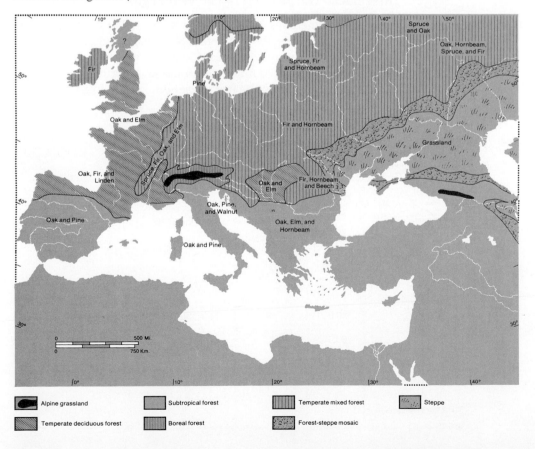

perate conditions between about 515,000 and 315,000 years ago but colder incidents breaking up the warmer climate.

The *Saale* glaciation coincided with the Illinoian in North America. In places, the Saale was fully as intense as the Elster, with an arctic climate persisting over much of the neighboring parts of Europe, which were marked by extensive loess deposits. But it was relatively short-lived, from about 180,000 to 128,000 B.P.

UPPER PLEISTOCENE

The Upper Pleistocene coincided with the last interglacial and glacial cycle, which began about 128,000 years ago. The detailed picture we have of this cycle gives us important clues as to the general nature of Ice Age climate — gradual glaciation, rapid deglaciation — in cycles that saw cold, dry weather prevailing over northern latitudes for some 60 percent of the past 730,000 years. Full interglacial conditions, when the climate was warmer than today, prevailed for very little time indeed.

The Upper Pleistocene is now divided into five stages, summarized in Table 3.3 (Gamble, 1986b).

Stage 1: Interglacial (128,000 to 118,000 years ago)

The last interglacial, sometimes called the *Eemian*, lasted only some 10,000 years. It saw global temperatures between 1 and 3° C warmer than today. The sea rose at least 20 feet (6 m) above its present level, ice sheets were much reduced, and temperate forest covered much of Eurasia and North America.

This interglacial was followed by the last glaciation, known to geologists by

TABLE 3.3   The Upper Pleistocene in Europe (much simplified).

Temperature ← lower higher →	Date (B.P.)	Stage	Subdivision		Human cultures
		5	POSTGLACIAL		MESOLITHIC
	8000—	4	LATE GLACIAL		
	20,000—	3	FULL GLACIAL	W	UPPER PALEOLITHIC
	30,000—			E I	
	40,000—		EARLY	C H	
	50,000—	2	LAST GLACIAL	S E	
	60,000—			L	MOUSTERIAN
	70,000—				
	118,000—	1	EEMIAN INTERGLACIAL		
Present climate					

many different names, the most common of which are *Weichsel* or *Würm* (used by European scholars), and *Wisconsin,* the term used for the North American manifestation. This glaciation lasted from about 118,000 to some 10,000 years ago and formed the backdrop for some of the most important developments in human prehistory: the final emergence of *Homo sapiens,* the Neanderthals, and the first human settlements in the Americas.

Weichsel **118,000 to 10,000 B.P.**

Stage 2: Early Last Glacial (118,000 to 32,000 years ago)

This stage is divided into two phases, an early one before 75,000 years ago, when there was temperate woodland in Europe and occasional periods of intense cold, and a glacial phase, with dry, arctic conditions. By 115,000 years ago, the North American ice sheets were expanding again and sea levels had already fallen an estimated 230 feet (70 m). Forests gave way to open grassland and scrub or steppe. Only two brief warmer episodes, about 105,000 and 82,000 years ago, interrupted the cooling, but from 75,000 years ago, glacial conditions persisted (Figure 3.3; Table 3.3).

Stage 2 **118,000 to 32,000 B.P.**

FIGURE 3.3 General distribution of vegetation in Europe at the height of the Weichsel glaciation. Land areas were larger than today's. Notice, too, the extent of the ice sheet. (After Butzer, 1971)

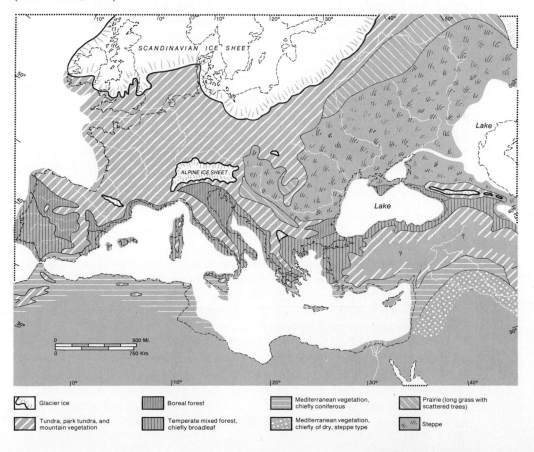

The Great Ice Age **75**

Stage 3: Full Glacial (32,000 to 14,000 years ago)

There was a brief warming up between 32,000 and 29,000 years ago, but glacial conditions intensified after 29,000, reaching their height about 18,000 years ago. The Scandinavian and North American ice sheets reached their maximum extent about 18,000 years ago, when the sea levels fell to at least 425 feet (130 m) below present shorelines. This drop led to the exposure of huge continental shelves, especially in southeast Asia. The Bering Strait between Siberia and Alaska became dry land and a refuge for humans and large mammals during the height of the last glaciation (Hopkins et al., 1982).

At this point the bitterly cold climate effectively blocked off huge areas of the world for human settlement. The North American ice sheet extended as far south as 39° N, the Scandinavian to 52° N. Snow lines on most mountains were lowered by as much as 3300 feet (over 1000 m). Barren polar deserts covered the dry northern latitudes of Siberia and Alaska on both shores of the Bering Strait. The European and North American climate was harsh, dry, and windy. World temperatures fell by as much as 60° F (15.5° C) near the ice sheets, between 37 and 48° F (2.7 and 8.8° C) in the tropics. Lower sea levels and cooler ocean temperatures resulted in less rainfall and atmospheric moisture transport.

The world's vegetation was very different during Stage 3. Treeless tundra vegetation extended south of the ice sheets, giving way to a wide belt of continental, cold steppe that extended from the Low Countries into China and from Siberia to the Mediterranean. The steppe was much narrower in North America, soon giving way to coniferous forest farther south. Huge zones of desert occupied more than half the earth's surface between latitudes 30°N and S, but some of today's desert areas — like the American Southwest, the northern Sahara, and the southern African deserts — were more hospitable, supporting scrub, grassland, and shallow lakes. The rain forests of tropical Africa and Asia gave way to open woodland and grassland; coral reefs and mangrove swamps contracted drastically as a result of cooler temperatures. However, despite the harsh world climate, humankind managed to survive and flourish in this very different world.

Stages 4 and 5: Late Glacial and Postglacial (14,000 years ago to the present)

The world climate remained extremely cold for about 4000 to 8000 years after the Stage 3 maximum. Then the ice sheets began to retreat, at times very rapidly — the Bering Strait, which was dry land as late as 15,000 years ago, was ocean again by 10,000. The onset of postglacial warming (sometimes called the Holocene) was prompted by many factors, among them proximity to the ice sheets that surrounded the North Atlantic, and fluctuated widely in different areas. But the decisive warming took place shortly before 9300 years ago. By that time sea levels were rising rapidly, especially in areas like Scandinavia, where the earth's crust was depressed by the massive weight of retreating ice sheets. The North Sea was flooded, and Britain was separated from the continent by approximately 8000 B.P. Pollen cores from Scandinavian and North

American swamps have chronicled the dramatic changes in vegetation that accompanied the warming trend, with steppe and tundra giving way in rapid succession to birch forests and then dense temperate oak woodland.

Perhaps the climatic changes in warmer latitudes were even more important for humanity. Some scientists believe that wild cereals and legumes migrated into the Near East about 11,000 years ago, as the present-day Mediterranean-type climate became reestablished at the end of the Stage 3 glaciation. Periods of increased rainfall between 12,500 and 5,000 years ago led to the expansion of equatorial forests far beyond their present limits, and to much wetter conditions in the Sahara and Arabia, which supported grassland and scrub, and, eventually, cattle herders. But by 5000 years ago, desiccation had set in, areas like the American Southwest and Sahara were much less hospitable, and, perhaps, changing climatic conditions accelerated the extinction of Pleistocene big game in North America and other areas.

Paleoclimatologists believe that our present interglacial peaked several thousand years ago, in North America some 7000 years ago, when deciduous forest reached its northern limits. It has been retreating since, as have the woodlands that once covered most of England, Scotland, and Wales. The world's climate appears to be getting colder again, as evidenced by the mountain glaciers and snowfields that have grown in many areas. More important, tropical deserts have expanded in the past 5000 years. But, especially in tropical and humid areas, human activity has played a more important role in changing the world's climate and vegetation than have natural processes. We can only guess at what climatic regimens will confront our descendants.

This broad framework of Pleistocene climate forms the general backdrop for human prehistory and is a key element in understanding the settlement of the globe by human beings over more than 2 million years. As we shall see, the earlier millennia of this colonization were part of a broader set of ecological processes that saw the simultaneous radiation of modern ungulate grazing animals into temperate latitudes as far north as Europe and northern China (Gamble, 1986b). But the long-term success of *Homo sapiens* was in the ability to adapt to the cyclical environmental changes that characterized the Pleistocene after 700,000 years ago. It should be stressed, however, that the archaeologist, working with individual sites, is more concerned with local environmental conditions, with the specifics of the ecological adaptations made by our ancestors. In the pages that follow, we examine human populations within the context of their own environments, using pollen analysis and other sophisticated scientific technologies to reconstruct not only human cultures but also the microenvironments in which they flourished.

GUIDE TO FURTHER READING

Bowen, David Q. *Quaternary Geology.* Oxford: Oxford University Press, 1978.
 An admirable general account of the study of the Quaternary in easily intelligible language.

Butzer, Karl. *Environment and Archaeology* (3d ed.). Chicago: Aldine, 1974.
A highly technical account of the geological and environmental complexities of the Pleistocene.

Flint, R. F. *Glacial and Quaternary Geology.* New York: Wiley, 1971.
The classic college textbook on the Ice Age. Although much outdated, it is still a primary source on basic glacial geology.

Gamble, Clive. *The Palaeolithic Settlement of Europe.* Cambridge: Cambridge University Press, 1986.
This sophisticated analysis of early European prehistory contains a succinct critical analysis of Pleistocene climate change.

Goudie, Andrew. *Environmental Change* (2d ed.). Oxford: Clarendon Press, 1983.
An admirable basic primer on the Pleistocene designed for undergraduates.

PART II

The First Humans

(c. 4 Million to 40,000 Years Ago)

The art of fabricating arms, of preparing aliments, of procuring the utensils requisite for this preparation, of preserving these aliments as provision against the seasons in which it was impossible to procure a fresh supply of them — these arts, confined to the most simple wants, were the first fruits of a continued union, and the first features that distinguished human society from the society observable in many species of beasts.

— Marquis de Condorcet

We describe the origins of humankind, and the early evolution of human culture from the first toolmakers up to the emergence of modern humanity.

CHRONOLOGICAL TABLE A

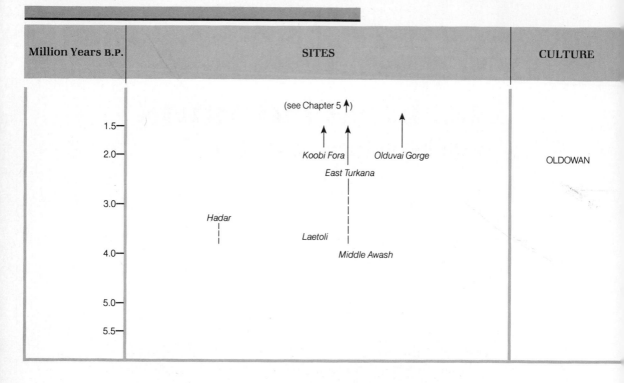

Million Years B.P.	SITES	CULTURE
	(see Chapter 5 ↑)	
1.5—		
2.0—	Koobi Fora ↑ ↑ Olduvai Gorge ↑	OLDOWAN
	East Turkana	
3.0—	Hadar	
	Laetoli	
4.0—	Middle Awash	
5.0—		
5.5—		

NOTE ON CHRONOLOGICAL TABLES

A chronological table appears at the beginning of most subsequent chapters; it covers the sites and cultures mentioned in the narrative. These sites and cultures, and their dates, are also listed in the chapter headings or in the margins opposite the place where they are mentioned. *Only sites and cultures in the headings or margins are listed.*

In addition to being keyed to the text, the chronological tables are labeled A, B, C, and so on and are cross-referenced at the beginning of each chapter. They form an interlocking sequence; the beginning and end of each chart are keyed to earlier and later chapters. The following key is used throughout the tables:

———————	A continuous line means the chronology is firmly established.
————————→	A line terminating in an arrow means the time span continues beyond the arrow.
———————	A line terminating with a horizontal bar means the limit of chronology is firmly established.
– – – – – – –	A broken line means the chronology is doubtful.
Hadar	A name in italics is an archaeological site, normally named after the locality at which it occurs.
?Hadar	A question mark beside a site name means its date is not firmly established.
ACHEULIAN	A name in capital letters is an archaeological culture, usually named after a type site, which in turn is labeled after a geographic location.

CHAPTER 4

Human Origins: The Emergence of "Handy Person"

(4.0 million to 1.6 million years ago)

Preview

◼ An evolutionary radiation of hominoids began in the Late Miocene, between 8 and 5 million years ago. It produced four lineages, at least one of which, human beings, is known to have been considerably modified.

◼ The apelike animals that formed the hominoid segment were probably tree living, with long arms and legs, and broad chests. They were knuckle walkers, eventually becoming bipedal, walking on two limbs.

◼ Molecular biology suggests that the chimpanzee, gorilla, and human shared a common ancestor some 5 to 4 million years ago.

◼ Early hominids faced three major adaptive problems: they were large mammals, they were terrestrial primates, and they lived in an open tropical savanna environment. They solved these problems by widening territorial ranges, scheduling food gathering, broadening their diet, and achieving great mobility and behavioral flexibility. Life on the savanna was adaptive for bipedal posture and a highly mobile lifeway.

◼ There were at least three, perhaps four, different hominid forms in East Africa by 2 million years ago, among them *Australopithecus africanus*, the more robust *Australopithecus robustus*, and a hominid with a larger brain but apelike limbs — *Homo habilis*. It is possible that a small, bipedal hominid identified as *Australopithecus afarensis*, living about 4 million years ago, was ancestral to later hominids. There is general agreement that *Homo habilis* is the probable ancestor of later human species — *Homo erectus* and *Homo sapiens*.

- The first toolmaking hominids were both hunters and scavengers, who relied heavily on wild vegetable foods. They returned habitually to places where they cached stone implements and processed parts of animal carcasses. It is thought these were not home bases but the prototypes of what were to become hunter-gatherer camps.

- Oldowan technology, the technology of *Homo habilis,* was based on the opportunistic production of sharp flakes, and perhaps choppers. It was in use from perhaps as early as 2.5 million years ago, up to about 1.5 million years ago. This type of flaking required the stoneworkers to be able to think in three dimensions, but it did not result in the kind of relatively standardized artifacts found in later prehistory. Increasing use of bifacial flaking techniques is thought to have developed over the million years or so that Oldowan technology was in use.

- *Homo habilis* was probably incapable of articulate speech, a characteristic of human beings that developed later in prehistory.

TABLE 4.1 Human development: 10 million to 10,000 years ago.

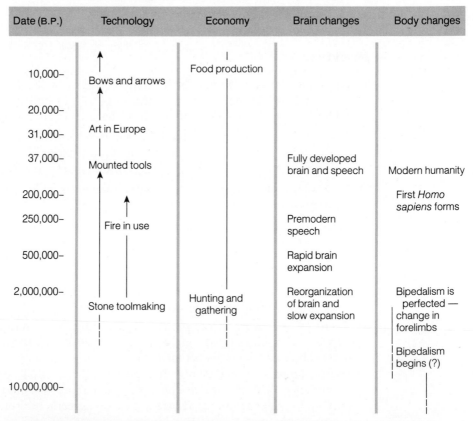

Date (B.P.)	Technology	Economy	Brain changes	Body changes
10,000–	Bows and arrows	Food production		
20,000–				
31,000–	Art in Europe			
37,000–	Mounted tools		Fully developed brain and speech	Modern humanity
200,000–				First *Homo sapiens* forms
250,000–	Fire in use		Premodern speech	
500,000–			Rapid brain expansion	
2,000,000–	Stone toolmaking	Hunting and gathering	Reorganization of brain and slow expansion	Bipedalism is perfected — change in forelimbs
				Bipedalism begins (?)
10,000,000–				

Note: The developments on this table appeared at the period indicated by the placement. They are assumed to continue until being either replaced or refined.

Nineteenth-century scientists pointed out that our closest living relatives were apes, such as the chimpanzee and the gorilla. All of us are members of the order of primates, which are placental mammals, most tree living, with two suborders: anthropods (apes, humans, and monkeys) and prosimians (lemurs, tarsiers, and other "pre-monkeys") (Huxley, 1863). The research of more than a century has shown that the many similarities in behavior and physical characteristics between the hominids (primates of the family *Hominidae*, which includes modern humans, earlier human subspecies, and their direct ancestors) and these closest living primate relatives can be explained by identical characteristics that each group inherited millions of years ago from a common ancestor. (For an overview of human development covered in Part II, see Table 4.1.)

THEORIES ON THE ORIGINS OF THE HUMAN LINE

The great Victorian zoologist Thomas Huxley spelled out his own opinion about the divergences between humans and apes in his classic *Man's Place in Nature* (1863): "The structural differences which separate man from the gorilla and chimpanzee are not so great as those which separate the gorilla from the lower apes." Huxley realized, though, that humans are separated from the higher apes by a gap between parallel lines, not a gap between locations along a single line. The gap measures divergent evolution from a common ancestor.

The question is, When did humankind separate from the nonhuman primates? Experts disagree violently about the answer.

Aegyptopithecus and *Sivapithecus*

Some 35 to 30 million years ago, large bands of small, fruit-eating primates known to paleontologists as *Aegyptopithecus* trooped through the lush, wet forests of the Nile Valley. These creatures were no larger than a fox and weighed no more than 9 to 10 pounds. Elwyn Simons (1984) has found their jaws and skulls near the Fayum Depression west of the Nile. The bones bear some resemblance to those of later primates in East Africa dating to the Miocene epoch, which lasted from 23.5 to 5.2 million years ago. It was in Africa that apes and humans diverged from the monkeys, but no one knows when this divergence took place. Was *Aegyptopithecus* the basic primate stock from which the great apes and humans radiated, or did the separation take place during the Miocene?

Seventeen million years ago the world looked very different from what it is today. Continental drift linked Africa and Arabia with Europe and Asia. Hitherto they had been separated by sea. New mountain ranges like the Alps formed, and the climate became cooler as atmospheric and ocean circulation patterns changed. As a result, previously separated animal species came into contact via the new land bridges, which led them into new habitats.

Several species of apes, some of which are now extinct, were already flourishing in Africa at the beginning of the Miocene, including a tree-dwelling, baboon-sized hominoidlike primate named *Proconsul africanus* (Rose, 1984;

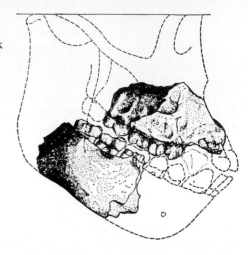

FIGURE 4.1 Composite reconstruction of the face of *Sivapithecus* from the Siwalik Hills, India. Partly based on teeth from Kenya, this reconstruction is highly tentative.

Ward and Kimbel, 1983). *Proconsul* fossils may date to as early as 22 million to around 18 million years ago (Pilbeam, 1985, 1986). *Proconsul* was an unspecialized primate. Its successors in Africa are unknown, but other Miocene hominoids occur in Europe and Asia, including *Ouranopithecus* from Greece and a better known, quite different form from Turkey, India, and Pakistan known as *Sivapithecus*, ranging in age from about 12 to 7 million years ago. *Sivapithecus* resembles the modern orang-utan in facial anatomy (see Figure 4.1) but otherwise is quite different. Its teeth and other features vary greatly from those of later hominoids, such as *Australopithecus* (see later). *Sivapithecus* is thought to have been an active climber and spent most of its time in the trees.

What do these fossils tell us about the evolution of our first ancestors? Let it be said at once that there is so little fossil evidence that any hypotheses are little more than intelligent guesswork. The basic anatomical pattern of the large hominoids appears in the Middle Miocene, 18 to 12 million years ago. One lineage of that first evolutionary radiation survives in modified form as the modern orang (Pilbeam, 1986). A second radiation begins in the Late Miocene, between 8 and 5 million years ago. This radiation eventually produces four lineages, at least one of which, human beings, is known to have been considerably modified. It is interesting to note that a similar evolutionary pattern occurs among other herbivores, like elephants. Early Miocene archaic elephant forms are replaced by a more modern radiation at the Early/Middle Miocene boundary. Late Miocene extinctions wipe out much of this radiation, but it also gives rise to a second Late Miocene radiation that produces most Pleistocene elephant lineages. In both cases, the patterns are monitoring changing climates and habitats — from warmer, less seasonal, more forested regimens to colder, more seasonal, and less forested conditions. Such changes occurred throughout the past 25 million years, but there were major, pulselike shifts between 17 and 14 million years ago, and again between 8 and 5 million years ago. These reflected changes in the configuration of continents, mountain systems, and antarctic ice (Figure 4.2) (Barry et al., 1985). Everyone agrees that the critical evolutionary radiation that produced the hominid line occurred in Africa.

Unfortunately, a vast chronological gap lies between *Ouranopithecus, Siva-pithecus*, and the earliest hominidae, the australopithecines, which date to approximately 4 million years ago. Donald Johanson and Maitland Edey (1981) refer to this gap rather picturesquely as a "black hole" in our knowledge of early human evolution. The critical period was between 10 and 5 million years ago, when the segment of the African hominoid lineage radiated to produce gorillas, chimpanzees, and hominids. In the absence of key fossils, we can only speculate as to the nature of the apelike animals that formed the hominoid segment during these millennia.

David Pilbeam (1986) has used existing fossils and evolutionary theory, as well as molecular biology, to guess — he can do no more — that these animals were mostly tree living, like *Sivapithecus*, with long arms and legs, and a broad chest. They would have used all fours in the trees, occasionally scrambling on the ground, using their knuckles, and even standing on their rear limbs at times. There was a marked difference in size between males and females, females perhaps weighing around 44 pounds (30 kg), males about double that. At least one

FIGURE 4.2 A much simplified version of how Old World monkeys, apes, and humans evolved. For later human evolution, see Figure 4.11.

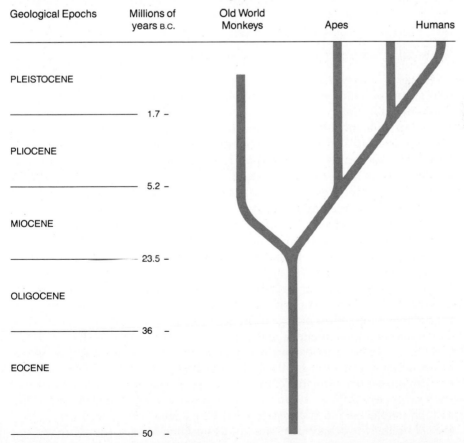

Geological Epochs	Millions of years B.C.	Old World Monkeys	Apes	Humans
PLEISTOCENE				
	1.7 –			
PLIOCENE				
	5.2 –			
MIOCENE				
	23.5 –			
OLIGOCENE				
	36 –			
EOCENE				
	50 –			

of the Late Miocene hominoid lineages led to the gorilla, a much larger, more terrestrial form.

Pilbeam goes on to speculate that a later hominoid lineage divided into western and eastern parts at least 5 million years ago. The western segment, the "proto-chimpanzee," remained dependent on fruit and other tree foods, scattered resources that required a flexible social organization. Both terrestrial and tree-living behaviors remained essential. Knuckle walking (see Figure 4.3) was important, because long arms and hands as well as grasping feet were still vital for climbing. They may also have adapted through smaller male body size, since smaller knuckle walkers were more efficient than larger ones. Early hominids became bipedal, walking on two feet, over a long period of time, perhaps as a result of spending more and more time feeding on plant foods on the ground. Bipedalism may have required less energy than moving around on four limbs. It might have had social advantages, too, allowing males to monitor females more efficiently when they were dispersed over larger areas (for full discussion, see Pilbeam, 1985, 1986).

Pilbeam's scenario is purely speculative; it reconstructs a "proto-hominid" that is quite different from anything known from the fossil record or living today. But the basic elements of his theoretical reconstruction are based on a diversity of clues from many lines of research.

Molecular Biology and Human Evolution

Some years ago, two biochemists, Vincent Sarich and Alan Wilson, developed a means of dating primate evolution. They believe that the albumin protein substances found in primate blood have evolved at a constant rate (Sarich, 1971; 1983). Thus the difference between the albumins of any pair of primates can be used to calculate the time that has elapsed since they separated.

Sarich and Wilson have shown that the albumins of apes and humans are more similar than those of monkeys and humans. Thus, they argue, apes and humans have a more recent common ancestry. They estimate that apes and Old World monkeys diverged approximately 23 million years ago, the gibbon and humankind only 8 million or so years ago, and that the chimpanzee, gorilla, and human last shared a common ancestor 5 to 4 million years ago. The apparent separation of apes and humans is so recent that statistically reliable numbers of differences have not yet accumulated.

Newer ways of comparing proteins and DNA are now refining the original "time clock" of evolutionary change and strongly imply some regular pattern of change along independent lineages. The new studies confirm that African apes and humans are similar, orangs roughly twice as distant, gibbons a bit more dissimilar than orangs. Intense controversy surrounds the relationships between humans, chimpanzees, and gorillas (Pilbeam, 1986), but many biologists agree that chimpanzees are humans' closest relatives. The precise relationships between any genetic differences and the geological time scale are still uncertain and are the subject of much discussion (see Gingerich, 1985).

We are unlikely to achieve a greater understanding of very early human evo-

FIGURE 4.3 Bipedalism and quadrupedalism. (a) Human bipedal posture. The center of gravity of the body lies just behind the midpoint of the hip joint and in front of the knee joint, so that both hip and knee are extended when standing, conserving energy. (b) A knuckle-walking chimpanzee. The body's center of gravity lies in the middle of the area bounded by legs and arms. When the ape walks bipedally, its center of gravity moves from side to side and up and down. The human center of gravity is displaced much less, making walking much more efficient. (After Zihlman) (c) A baboon. Baboons are quadrupedal and adapted to living on the ground.

lution unless we discover hominoid fossils dating to between 10 and 5 million years ago. Even when we do, the fossil record will probably be inconclusive, simply because the hominoid populations of Africa were probably very heterogeneous. A major focus of research will also be the environments to which such (still hypothetical) hominoids adapted. These 5 million years were periods of major environmental change. As recently as 5.5 million years ago, the Mediterranean basin dried up when it became separated from the Atlantic. This development must have had major effects on the climate and ecology of Africa, as well as influencing the evolution of many species. That such evolution took place seems certain. During this critical period the African savanna, with its residual forests and extensive grassland plains, was densely populated by many mammal species as well as specialized tree dwellers and other primates. Both the chimpanzee and the gorilla evolved in the forests, surviving from earlier times. On savanna plains other primates were flourishing in small bands, probably walking upright, and, conceivably, making tools. No fossil remains of these creatures have been found, so we do not know when primates first achieved the bipedal posture that is the outstanding human physical feature. Only future fossil discoveries will resolve the question. We can, however, model some of the ecological problems our earliest ancestors encountered.

THE ECOLOGICAL PROBLEMS FACED BY EARLY HOMINIDS

Selection

The evolutionary process is based on selection, which can be viewed in several ways (Foley, 1984b). For example, one can consider the emergence of the first humans in terms of adaptive, evolutionary change. Organisms are mostly in balance with their environment. An occasional mutation occurs that places an individual at a selective advantage within a population. Thanks to its reproductive advantage, the mutant form now spreads through the population, resulting in an improvement. As far as the behavioral evolution of the hominids is concerned, this process gives a model of terrestrial primates living in the increasingly dry environments of tropical Africa. Among one hominid group mutations led to adaptive shifts — bipedalism, toolmaking, meat eating, and so on. These shifts put the group at an advantage over other terrestrial primates.

Problem solving

Another approach sees evolutionary changes arising as solutions to problems faced by the organism in its environment. New adaptations are selected if they solve problems effectively. The selective agent is the organism's environmental problems. Under this scenario, the characteristics of a hunter-gatherer adaptation would appear among hominids if they were solutions to problems faced in the environment. Where do these environmental problems come from? One viewpoint sees a species' problems as the other species it eats, those with which it competes, and those which eat it. In other words, an evolutionary advance made by one species in an ecosystem can be seen as a deterioration of the environment for another. Thus, environmental problems are not inanimate forces but dynamic, evolving creatures. An organism has to evolve as rapidly as possible just to maintain its current ecological adaptation. L. van Valen, the biologist who developed this approach, calls it the "Red Queen" model: "Now *here*," the queen remarks in *Alice Through the Looking-Glass*, "you see, it takes all the running *you* can do, to keep in the same place."

Red Queen model

The Red Queen model is one appropriate theoretical framework for studying the behavioral evolution of the earliest hominids (Foley, 1984c). These populations underwent adaptive changes through natural selection to solve environmental problems caused by the broader ecological community. To analyze these changes requires identification of the ecological problems faced by the early hominids, and understanding of the relationship between these problems and the evolution of the tropical savanna community as a whole.

Adaptive Problems

Early hominids faced three major adaptive problems. They were large mammals, they were terrestrial primates, and they lived in an open tropical savanna environment.

Large mammals

Human beings are large relative to the majority of warm-blooded animals. Hominids have become larger through their evolutionary history, a change that has led to additional food requirements because of higher metabolic rates. This means that every individual has to range over a larger area to obtain food. Population densities must fall, because the carrying capacity of any territory is finite. There will be an increase in dietary breadth, for metabolic requirements will decrease relative to body size. It is interesting to observe that hunter-gatherers use a wider range of foods, many of lower quality, than do nonhuman primates. Larger mammals are more mobile than their smaller relatives. They cover more ground, which enables them to subsist off resources that are unevenly distributed not only in space but at different seasons. Mobility allows larger bodied animals to incorporate unpredictable, often seasonal resources in their diets. Larger mammals can also tolerate extremes of heat and cold, a capacity that may have contributed to the expansion of humans out of tropical latitudes later in prehistory. By the same token, increased body size has caused problems with regulating body heat. Thus, humans have sweat glands and are heavily dependent on water supplies.

Range and mobility

These and several other factors — such as increased longevity and brain enlargement — created adaptive problems for emerging humans. These problems resulted in a variety of solutions: wider territorial ranges, the need to schedule food gathering, broadening of diet, a high degree of mobility, and much greater behavioral flexibility. This flexibility included enhanced intelligence and learning capacity, parental care, and new levels of social interaction.

Being a Terrestrial Primate

An upright posture and bipedal gait are the most characteristic human physical features. Upright posture is vital, because it frees the hands for other actions, like toolmaking. Knuckle walking is a specialized way of walking in which the backs of the fingers are placed on the ground and act as main weight-bearing surfaces. Human arms are too short for us to be comfortable with this posture, used by football linemen and runners at the starting block. *Homo habilis* and other early hominids with their longer arms may have used knuckle walking more frequently. Knuckle walking may have been an intermediate stage between the ape's arboreal adaptation and the human bipedal posture. Bipedalism was a critical antecedent of both hunting and gathering and toolmaking (Tuttle, 1972; Washburn, 1967; Washburn and Moore, 1987).

The fall in temperatures during the Late Miocene resulted in increasingly open environments in tropical latitudes. With this reduction in forested environments there probably came a trend toward terrestrially adapted species. The main constraint on arboreal primates is body size. Thus, to be part of the general trend toward larger body size among mammals, such primates would have to be at least partially terrestrial in their habits. Some forty or more extinct and living primates, including the hominids, have adapted to a terrestrial existence. This secondary adaptation among tree-living forms may have occurred some time after 10 million years ago — expressed in the simplest terms, primates "came down from the trees" (Foley, 1984a). Coming down from the trees created three immediate problems for primates:

Open environments

Coming down from the trees

- Locomotion difficulties arise for animals with limbs adapted to moving through forests that are less efficient for moving on the ground. All terrestrial primates underwent some modification of their way of getting about, in the case of hominids a shift to bipedalism. We know that this selection was a powerful one. It was in existence at least 4 million years ago.

- Shelter becomes an acute problem in open country, where predators abound. Arboreal primates have special sleeping areas and are safe in the trees. Those adapted to living in open country return to trees at night, or use cliff faces or caves, even if they have to disperse. Large hominids that are safer from predators make ground nests, where they sleep and also seek shade on hot days — "home bases." Exactly what forms these home bases take is a matter of constant scientific debate.

- Competition for food is another pressing problem for primates who require high-quality plant food, abundant in the forests. Such foods are dispersed widely in open country. There are two possible solutions — either specialize in a small spectrum of plant foods and become an effective competitor or maintain a broad dietary niche and expand the range of foods consumed. It is striking that such a broad-based niche is characteristic of later hunter-gatherers in tropical environments. And, as part of human evolution, hominids expanded their food range to include meat.

The Red Queen model shows that the problems of being a terrestrial primate have major adaptive consequences that, in the long term, are directly relevant to the development of the behavioral characteristics of later hunter-gatherers.

Living in a Savanna Environment

Water supplies

Terrestrial primate populations can live in drier grasslands and woodlands, environments that present another set of challenging problems. Water supplies are certain to be restricted in distribution and by season, a critical environmental reality for hominids that need regular access to liquids. The distribution of water and hominid populations are closely connected. Further, plant foods in a savanna are of lower quality. Hominids had to compete with other animals for them. Most species were seasonal and of low productivity, so a great deal of time would have been expended in searching for and processing them. A whole range of species would have been needed to ensure year-round food supplies.

Plant foods

Most plant species that do occur in the savanna are grasses, which are largely unsuitable for primates — but not for a diverse population of herbivores. This secondary biomass of animals could have been a valuable walking food source if the hominids found a way of tapping it. But there were competitors — a great diversity of predators, who would also have eaten an occasional hominid if the opportunity arose.

The long-term solutions to living in the savanna centered around an adaptation that involved exploiting a broad but patchy subsistence base. The lifeway was highly mobile, the range dependent on restricted water supplies. Meat became part of the diet as a way of coping with long periods of plant scarcity. Among mammal species, these characteristics are associated with a trend toward larger brain size (Eisenberg, 1981).

The Adaptive Behavior of Later Hunter-Gatherers

Hunting and gathering have been the primary subsistence base of all human societies for more than 99 percent of human prehistory, in some areas, like the Arctic and parts of Africa and South America, until modern times (Foley, 1984c;

Lee and DeVore, 1976). Hunters and gatherers are human beings who survive by exploiting resources as they occur in the wild. It follows that they exert little control over their natural environment or its resources. This universal way of life shares certain general characteristics, which appear to relate directly to the problems faced by the earliest hominids (Binford, 1979, 1980):

Characteristic behavior

- Hunter-gatherers live at relatively low population densities.
- Their home ranges are larger than those of equivalent-sized mammals and primates.
- They live in small social units, often called bands, based on kin ties that regulate reproductive activity.
- They usually enjoy a mobile lifeway, focused on home bases that are used for many activities.
- They tend to be omnivorous; the proportion of meat, plant foods, or other resources they consume varies greatly from environment to environment.
- They employ some division of labor. The men hunt; the women collect plant foods (for female roles see Fedigan, 1986).
- In general, hunter-gatherer adaptations are highly flexible, and this flexibility has a direct relationship to the available resource base, territory, and band size.

This is a very general description that subsumes a great variety of hunter-gatherer adaptations, even within apparently uniform environments. But it describes, in general terms, human subsistence throughout most of prehistory. If the ecological model is on track in assuming that this lifeway evolved in response to selective pressures in the open savanna more than 2 million years ago, then we must examine the archaeological and fossil evidence to see at what point hunting and gathering appeared. Were the hominids of 2 million years ago true hunters and gatherers? Or were they far more apelike in behavior than their successors?

THE FOSSIL EVIDENCE FOR HUMAN EVOLUTION

Between 9 and 4 million years ago, the last common ancestral hominoid stock split into two main lineages that evolved into apes and humans. The details of this split are still a complete mystery, largely because fossil beds dating to this critical period are very rare in Africa (Figure 4.4). The fossil record proliferates after about 5 million years ago but is still fragmentary. The later record of human evolution has become a veritable battlefield between paleoanthropological titans (Lewin, 1987). The controversies are aired within the arid pages of scientific journals, in popular magazines, even on television talk shows. We can but navigate cautiously between the various schools of thought.

Australopithecus and *Homo*

In 1924, an anatomist named Raymond Dart identified a fossil primate in South Africa that displayed both human and apelike features. He named his find *Australopithecus africanus* (Latin for southern ape of Africa) (Figure 4.5). *A. africanus* was a gracile, small creature, in contrast to a second, more robust form

A. africanus

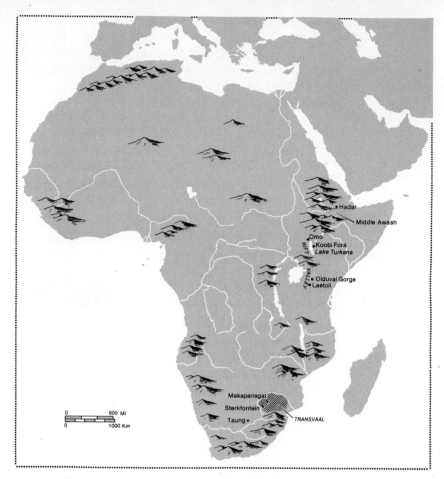

FIGURE 4.4 Archaeological sites in Africa mentioned in this chapter.

A. robustus

that turned up among the dozens of australopithecine fragments found in later years. This Dart named *Australopithecus robustus*, a squat, massively built primate with crested skull (Figure 4.6). None of the South African australopithecines could be dated by potassium argon methods, but they are estimated to be between 3 million and 800,000 years old (Dart, 1925; Pfeiffer, 1985; Rak, 1983).

For years, paleoanthropologists thought that *Australopithecus africanus* was the direct ancestor of humankind, that human evolution had proceeded in a relatively linear way through time. Then hominid fossils began turning up in East Africa, finds that showed human evolution to be much more complicated. The many fossil finds are confusing, so we describe them in chronological order (see Table 4.2).

Awash and Hadar

Middle Awash
4.1 to 3.9 million years ago

The earliest australopithecines from East Africa are very fragmentary. The Middle Awash area of Ethiopia has yielded some skull fragments and a solitary thigh bone piece, found in deposits potassium argon dated to between 4.1 and

FIGURE 4.5 *Australopithecus africanus* from Sterkfontein, South Africa. *A. africanus* was probably 42 to 50 in. (107 to 127 cm) tall; the females, weighing 40 to 60 lbs. (18 to 27 kg), were somewhat lighter than the males. The posture was fully upright, with the spinal curvature that places the trunk over the pelvis for balanced walking. (Apes do not have this curvature, nor are their legs proportionately as long as those of *Australopithecus*.) The foot was small, with a well-developed big toe. *Australopithecus* looked remarkably human, but with an apelike snout that was, however, less prominent than the ape's. The canines were small, and the incisors were vertical in the jaw, whereas the ape's slope outward. A flat nose was combined with a well-developed forehead, and the brow ridges were much less prominent than those of modern tree-living relatives. The brain had an average size of about 450 cc, much smaller than that of a modern human male (1450cc) and slightly larger than that of the chimpanzee (400 cc).

3.9 million years ago. The skull fragments come from an australopithecine with almost no forehead and brow ridges intermediate between those of apes and humans.

By far the most complete australopithecine finds earlier than 3 million years ago come from Hadar in northern Ethiopia (Johanson and Edey, 1981; Johanson and White, 1979; Kalb et al., 1984). When Maurice Taieb and Donald Johanson discovered a remarkably complete skeleton of a small primate at Hadar on the Awash River, they named it Lucy (Figure 4.7). Lucy was only 3.5 to 4.0 feet (1.0–1.2 m) tall and nineteen to twenty-one years old. Nearby, they found the remains of at least thirteen males, females, and children. Potassium argon dates for Hadar range between 3.00 and 3.75 million years ago. The Hadar hominid fossils are all from a single species of hominid, despite great variations in size. Some individuals stood 5 feet (1.5 m) tall and probably weighed approximately 150 pounds (68 kg), a far cry from the small, slender Lucy. These small creatures, however, were powerful, heavily muscled individuals, thought to be as strong as chimpanzees. All were fully bipedal, with arms slightly longer for their size than the arms of humans. They had humanlike hands, except that

Hadar
3.00 to 3.75 million years ago

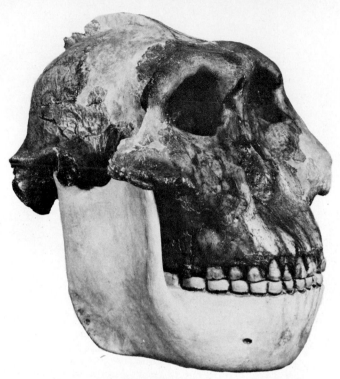

FIGURE 4.6 A robust australopithecine from Olduvai Gorge, Tanzania. The robust australopithecine was both larger and heavier than the *africanus* forms, with a more barrel-like trunk. The biggest contrasts were in the facial appearance and the teeth. *Australopithecus robustus* had a low forehead and a prominent bony ridge on the crest of the skull, which supported massive chewing muscles. Its brain was slightly larger than that of *A. africanus,* and *A. robustus* had relatively well-developed cheek teeth as well as larger molars.

their fingers were slightly more curved. The Hadar hominids had brains approximating the size of chimpanzee brains, ape-shaped heads, and forward-thrusting jaws. There is no evidence that they made tools.

The Hadar finds are of great importance, for they demonstrate that the fundamental human adaptation of bipedalism *predates* the first evidence of toolmaking and the expansion of the brain beyond the level found in our nearest living relatives, the African apes. But bipedalism also implies that later hominids were preadapted to utilize their hands for toolmaking.

Donald Johanson and Tim White believe that Lucy and the other Hadar hominids are a species of primitive australopithecine, the common ancestor of all later hominids, including Dart's *Australopithecus africanus.* They named this species *Australopithecus afarensis,* a designation that has caused intense controversy. Are the Hadar hominids a primitive form of the later *A. africanus,* or do they represent more than one hominid species? There are just too few specimens to tell. However, there seem to be greater resemblances to Miocene hominoids and living apes than to *A. africanus* (Stringer, 1984).

TABLE 4.2 Highly schematic chronology of Olduvai Gorge, Tanzania, with positions of fossils and tools.

10 cm
0

Date (B.P.)	Bed	Finds
Not less than 700,000	Bed IV	Acheulin hand axes
Not less than 1,000,000	Bed III	Acheulian hand axes
	Bed II[a]	Acheulian hand axes *Homo erectus*
		Homo habilis finds
	Bed I	Oldowan chopper tools
1,750,000		*Australopithecus boisei*
1,800,000		*Homo habilis* Stone structure
c. 2,200,000		Volcanic lava

[a]Broken line shows a possible break in the sequence.

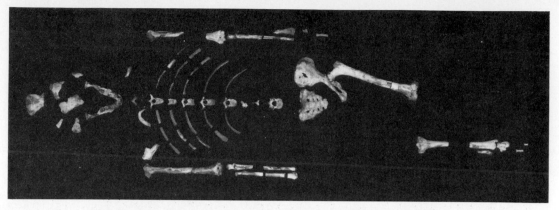

FIGURE 4.7 "Lucy," a fragmentary australopithecine from Hadar, Ethiopia.

Whatever the classification of the Hadar finds, they demonstrate that bipedalism was a hominid characteristic by 3.75 million years ago.

Bipedalism at Laetoli

Laetoli
**3.6 million years
ago**

Dramatic confirmation of hominid bipedalism by 3.75 million years ago comes from fossil-bearing beds at Laetoli in northern Tanzania, excavated by Mary Leakey and potassium argon dated to 3.75 to 3.59 million years ago. They have yielded not only the bones of extinct animals but also the incomplete jaws and teeth of at least thirteen hominids (M. D. Leakey et al., 1976; M. D. Leakey, 1978). The Laetoli hominids share many characteristics with those from Hadar, to the extent that Johanson believes they are the same species. But the most remarkable finds came from the buried bed of a seasonal river, where thin layers of fine volcanic ash once formed a pathway for animals traveling to water holes. The hardened surface of the ash, dated to more than 3.59 million years ago, bore the footprints of elephants, rhinoceroses, giraffes, a saber-toothed tiger, and many species of antelope. Leakey also identified a trail of prints of a fairly large bipedal primate, which, she estimated, stood nearly 4 feet (102 m) tall (Figure 4.8). "The tracks," she wrote, "indicate a rolling and probably slow-moving gait, with the hips swiveling at each step, as opposed to the free-striding gait of modern man." Unfortunately, no traces of bones of this primate have come from the excavations so far.

Turkana and Olduvai

The modern era of paleoanthropology dawned in 1959, when Mary and Louis Leakey found the skull of a robust australopithecine at Olduvai Gorge, a find potassium argon dated to 1.75 million years ago and named *zinjanthropus boisei* (Figure 4.6) (L. S. B. Leakey, 1951; M. D. Leakey, 1971). The gorge is a spectacular rift in the great Serengeti Plain of northern Tanzania, a place where earth movements have exposed hundreds of yards of lake beds belonging to a long-dried-up Pleistocene lake (Table 4.2). Later, a more gracile hominid came from a level slightly lower than that of the original robust skull, a fossil Louis

Leakey promptly named *Homo habilis* (handy person), on the grounds it was something quite different from the robust australopithecine nearby.

By the mid-1960s, there were hints that some form of more advanced hominid had lived in East Africa at the same time as *Australopithecus*. The evolutionary picture was further complicated by discoveries of fossil-bearing beds on either shore of remote Lake Turkana in northern Kenya. Richard Leakey and an international team of experts have located hundreds of square miles of Pliocene and Lower Pleistocene fossil-bearing sediments. The hominids include both australopithecines and individuals with unmistakably enlarged brains, including the famous Skull 1470 (Figure 4.9), which has a brain capacity of 775 cc, far larger than that of *Australopithecus*. This specimen, with a jutting face, like an *Australopithecus*, but a larger brain size, is thought to date to approximately 1.8 million years ago. The East Turkana finds include another skull, almost complete, of a hominid that is clearly from the genus *Homo*, dated to approximately 1.5 million years ago, and contemporary with australopithecines (Leakey and Lewin, 1977; Lewin, 1987).

East Turkana 1.8 to 1.5 million years ago

FIGURE 4.8 Pliocene hominid footprints from Laetoli, Tanzania.

FIGURE 4.9 A tentative reconstruction of Skull 1470 from East Turkana. Provisionally identified as *Homo*, this cranium is remarkable for its large brain capacity and rounded back.

Homo habilis

Koobi Fora
**2.5 million
years ago**

Olduvai Gorge
**1.75 million
years ago**

Even specialists are confused by the proliferation of hominids in East Africa by 2 million years ago, not only gracile and robust australopithecines but also other hominids with much larger brains. These hominids come from Koobi Fora and from Olduvai in Kenya and have cranial capacities between 650 and 800 cc. These larger brained individuals are generally assumed to represent the appearance of the genus *Homo*. Louis Leakey was the first to identify one of these hominids at Olduvai, so his label *Homo habilis* has stood the test of time.

If you had encountered *Homo habilis* 2 million years ago, you would have seen little to distinguish the new hominid from *Australopithecus*. Both were of similar height and weight, about 4 feet, 3 inches (1.3 m) tall and about 88 pounds (40 kg). Both were bipedal, but *Homo habilis* would have looked less apelike around the face and skull. The head was higher and rounder, the face less protruding. Some of the most significant anatomical differences involve the teeth. The molars were narrower, the premolars smaller, while the incisors were larger and more spadelike, as if they were used for slicing. However, microscopic teeth wear studies have shown that both *Australopithecus* and *Homo habilis* were predominantly fruit eaters, so there does not seem to have been a major shift in diet between the two forms.

The first *Homo habilis* fragments, which came from Bed I at Olduvai Gorge in the early 1960s (Figure 4.10), consisted of some skull and postcranial fragments of a larger brained hominid. Then Richard Leakey found the famous Skull 1470, a large-brained, round-headed cranium that confirmed the existence of *Homo habilis* in no uncertain terms. Thigh and limb bones from Koobi Fora and from Olduvai confirm that *Homo habilis* walked upright. The hand bones are somewhat more curved and robust than those of modern humans. This was a powerful grasping hand, more like that of chimpanzees and gorillas than humans, a hand ideal for climbing trees. An opposable thumb allowed both powerful gripping and precise manipulation of fine objects. With the later capacity, *Homo habilis* could have made complex tools.

A recent discovery of 1.8-million-year-old *Homo habilis* skull and limb bones at Olduvai Gorge has shown that this was a tiny hominid, standing about 3 feet (1 m) tall, about the same size as Lucy from Hadar. There was probably considerable difference in size between males and females (the new Olduvai specimen, labeled OH 62, is thought to be a female) (Johanson et al., 1987). This find throws important new light on hominid evolution between 4.0 and 1.5 million years ago, for it shows that the small size of *Australopithecus afarensis* persisted for much longer than had hitherto been suspected.

Three major anatomical changes took place during the 2.5 million years between *A. afarensis* and the emergence of much larger and more advanced *Homo erectus* some 1.6 million years ago (see Chapter 5). Brain size increased from about 450 cc in *A. afarensis* to 1000 cc in *Homo erectus*. There were further modifications to hip and limbs for bipedal locomotion, and a reduction in sexual dimorphism (size difference due to sex) between males and females. The latest

FIGURE 4.10   Olduvai Gorge, Tanzania.

Olduvai *Homo habilis* shows that the primitive body form and sexual dimorphism characteristic of earlier hominids vanished only with the emergence of much more advanced *Homo erectus*. These observations have important implications for deciding just how "human" *Homo habilis* was.

The specimen OH 62 suggests that *Homo habilis* was distinctly less human than had been thought. Skeletal anatomy from many finds gives a mosaic picture of both primitive and more advanced features, of a hominid that both walked bipedally and retained the generalized hominoid ability to climb trees. A telling clue comes from OH 62's upper arm bones, which, like Lucy's, are within 95 percent of the length of the thigh bone. The chimpanzee has upper arm and leg bones of almost equal length, while human upper arms are only 70 percent of the length of the leg bones. Almost certainly *Homo habilis* spent a great deal of time climbing trees, an adaptation that would make them much less human in their behavior, and presumably social structure, than had been assumed even a few years ago.

From Hominids to *Homo*

There is general consensus among the experts that *Homo habilis* is the probable ancestor of the later human species *Homo erectus* and *Homo sapiens*. The sharp disagreement begins when one examines the evolutionary relationships between *Australopithecus afarensis* and later hominids, and between *Homo habilis* and the australopithecines. As British physical anthropologist Chris Stringer (1984) puts it: "The field is littered with abandoned ancestors and the theories that went with them."

Earlier models argued that evolution had proceeded through unidirectional, gradual change, as if evolutionary mechanisms were simple. One such model designated *Australopithecus africanus* as the direct ancestor for subsequent members of the genus *Homo*, with *Homo habilis* an evolutionary intermediate between *Australopithecus* and *Homo erectus*.

Figure 4.11 and Table 4.3 summarize the fossil evidence and several major hypotheses for early human evolution. Donald Johanson and Tim White (1979) believe that *Australopithecus afarensis* from Hadar is ancestral to all later hominids. The australopithecines split off about 2.5 million years ago to form a specialized side branch, becoming more and more robust and eventually extinct. The *Homo* line led to *Homo habilis* and *Homo erectus* (Scheme A).

Scheme A

The Leakey family disagrees, and holds that a common ancestor of *Homo* and *Australopithecus* diverged fairly early, well before *Australopithecus afarensis* appeared (Scheme B).

Scheme B

A new *Australopithecus robustus* find from Lake Turkana, dating to 2.6 to 2.5 million years ago (Walker et al., 1986) has caused major modifications to the Johanson and White scheme, raising the possibility that the later australopithecines and *Homo* radiated rapidly and separately from a common ancestor (Scheme C). If such a rapid radiation took place, it was a unique event. Did hominids achieve some unique breakthrough in physiology or behavior? Was there a dramatic climate change? There are several variants on this new hypothesis (see Shipman, 1984).

Scheme C

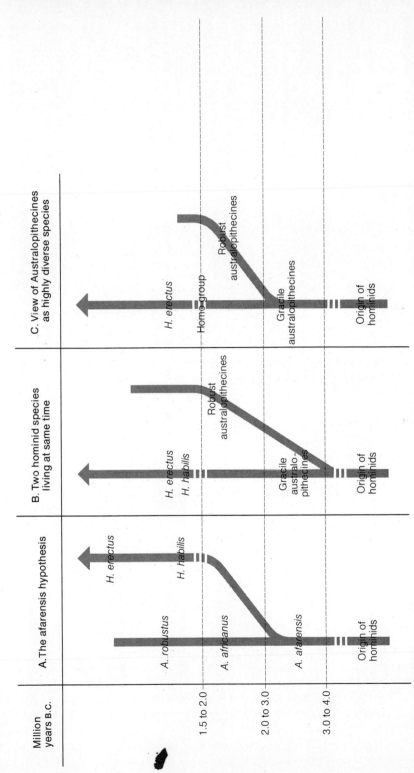

FIGURE 4.11 Three widely discussed, somewhat linear theories of early human evolution referred to in the text. Compare these with the "clado-gram" in Figure 4.12, which reflects much current evolutionary thinking.

TABLE 4.3 Four tentative groups of East and South African hominids, much simplified for this book.

Variables	Robust group	Gracile group	Homo group	Hadar/Laetoli group
Brain size	500–550 cc	450–550 cc	650–775 cc	Comparable to a chimpanzee
Teeth	Very large back teeth; relatively small front teeth	Large front and back teeth	Variable; generally smaller than robust and gracile forms	Small back teeth; large front teeth
Limbs	Some elements of limb bones differ from those of modern humans		Bipedal, but lower limbs still partially adopted to arboread life	Bipedal; arms slightly longer than *Homo sapiens*'s
Species and sites	*Australopithecus robustus* South Africa: Swarkrans, Kromdraal *Australopithecus boisei* East Africa: Olduvai, East Turkana, Omo	*Australopithecus africanus* South Africa: Taung, Sterkfontein, Makapansgat East Africa: Omo?, East Turkana	*Homo* East Africa: Olduvai and East Turkana South Africa: Sterkfontein	*Australopithecus afarensis* East Africa: Hadar and Laetoli
Dates	East Africa: c. 2,600,000 to c. 1,000,000 B.P. South Africa: no reliable dates	East Africa: c. 3,000,000 to c. 1,500,000 B.P. South Africa: no reliable dates	East Africa: c. 2,000,000 to c. 1,500,000 B.P.	East Africa: c. 4,000,000 to c. 3,000,000 B.P.

A CLADISTIC THEORY OF HUMAN EVOLUTION

In reality, the fossil hominid record compares poorly with that of many other mammalian groups, to the point that any theorizing about the relationships between the hominids of 4.0 to 1.5 million years ago is invalidated by the limitations of the field evidence.

However, there have been great changes in the interpretation of human evolution in the past decade, resulting from both many new discoveries and new theoretical advances. The most important development is a realization that hominid evolution involved a far greater level of species diversity than was previously thought (Foley, 1987). As Stephen J. Gould puts it (1977), human evolution is like a bush, rather than the ladder that has been used as an analogy for so long.

Human evolution can be seen as one or more adaptive radiations rather than a simple, one-way evolution of successive species. This view stems from *cladistics,* an analytic system for reconstructing evolutionary relationships. Classical evolutionary analysis is based on morphological similarities between organisms. So is cladistics, but with a difference — cladistic analysis concentrates not on features that identify common ancestry but on those that are derived independently and are unique to specific lineages. Inevitably, cladistics tends to emphasize diversity over homogeneity.

The current view of human evolution begins with a widely accepted assumption that the sequence of hominid evolution began with the australopithecines, followed by the emergence of *Homo habilis* through *Homo erectus* to *Homo sapiens.* But cladistics emphasizes considerable diversity at each stage, so much so that one cannot think of human evolution as simply a trend toward anatomically modern forms (Figure 4.12). As we have seen, the australopithecines were remarkably diverse, with the primitive *afarensis* form, the lightly built and later *A. africanus,* and the much more massive *A. robustus.* Between five and one million years ago, there was considerable adaptive radiation of australopithecines. The earliest members of the genus *Homo* were probably part of that radiation, *Australopithecus*-like forms with larger brains relative to body size. These forms are all classified as *Homo habilis,* but it seems certain that there was considerable variability and that several subspecies will be identified in the future. *Homo erectus* appeared about 1.6 million years ago and may also have been part of this adaptive radiation.

Homo erectus has long been considered the single human form to have lived on earth during much of the Lower and Middle Pleistocene (Foley, 1987). However, cladistic theorists argue that this all-embracing classification is based on primitive features that link the various fossils from Africa, Asia, and Europe. Derived features, such as some of the massive features found on Asian *Homo erectus* skulls, may in fact be evidence for several geographically defined forms, only one of which evolved into *Homo sapiens.* This view sees *Homo erectus* as an adaptive radiation of hominids in the Lower and Middle Pleistocene, with only a small part of this evolution resulting in the emergence of *Homo sapiens.* Under this theory, the archaic forms of *Homo sapiens* in Europe and Asia were merely local continuations of primeval local populations. It was only in Africa that *Homo erectus* gave rise to modern *Homo sapiens* (Brauwer, 1984). In other

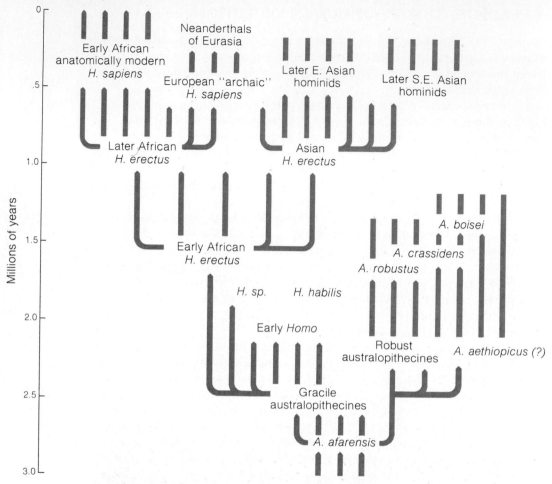

FIGURE 4.12 A diagram that sees the process of human evolution as a series of adaptive radiations. The basis for each radiation was a mixture of adaptations to local conditions and geographic isolation, isolation being especially important in later prehistory. The result was the evolution of diverse behavioral and ecological strategies and different species and subspecies. This model bears a much greater resemblance to models for other mammalian families, for it is a mistake to think of human evolution as different from that of other animals. (After Foley, 1987)

words, the pattern of human evolution based on the adaptive radiation seen with the australopithecines persisted into much later times.

ARCHAEOLOGICAL EVIDENCE FOR EARLY HUMAN BEHAVIOR

We must now examine the archaeological evidence for the emergence of distinctive human behavior, especially for the hunting and gathering lifeway that provided human subsistence for most of prehistory. Studying early human behavior is complicated by both poor preservation conditions and the vast time chasm that separates us from our remotest ancestors. In general terms, there are three lines of evidence that offer opportunities for testing hypotheses about early human behavior. One is scatters of artifacts and food remains that form the archaeological record for hominid activities, perhaps at predator kills, home bases, or meat caches. A second is manufactured artifacts; because of preservation conditions these are mainly objects made in stone. The transport of raw materials used to make these tools is also an important consideration. Last, surviving food remains, almost entirely fragmentary animal bones, can reveal valuable information about our remote forebears.

Evidence for Home Bases?

Later hunter-gatherers made habitual use of home bases, places where they returned to sleep, fabricate tools, cook food, and engage in a wide variety of social activities. Did the earliest humans have similar home bases?

The only archaeological evidence comes from East Turkana and Olduvai Gorge, where a number of concentrations of bones and stone tools dating to around 2 million years ago and later have been excavated and studied with meticulous care. It is important to note that no such concentrations have been found with the earlier Laetoli or Hadar hominids.

For years, Louis Leakey and other pioneer paleoanthropologists believed that these scatters were "living floors," places where our ancestors slept, made tools, and butchered game. These were home bases, they argued, on the assumption that the hominids who created the artifact concentrations were hunters and gatherers behaving like primitive versions of living bands. Recent thinking on the subject regards such assumptions as dangerous. In the first place, the archaeological record is very ancient, so much so that the only way one can hope to interpret it is with a thorough knowledge of the geological and other processes that have affected the bone and tool scatter since it was abandoned by its makers. Second, we now know much more about living hunters and nonhuman primates, enough to undermine confidence that direct analogies from such populations have any validity when dealing with 2-million-year-old hominid behavior. Third, a whole new generation of research involving controlled experimentation, edge wear studies, and other sophisticated approaches has thrown doubt on the notion that *Homo habilis* was a hunter at all (see Chapter 2).

If the Koobi Fora and Olduvai scatters are not home bases, what behavior do they represent? Some of the earliest manufactured tools in the world, some in association with animal bones, come from the Koobi Fora area of East Turkana (Isaac, 1981a; Isaac and Harris, 1978). Several localities have been excavated, among them a dry streambed where a group of hominids found the carcass of a hippopotamus about 1.8 million years ago. They gathered around and removed bones and meat from the dead animal with small stone flakes. The deposits in which the stones and flaked debris are found are so fine grained that they contain natural pebbles no larger than a pea. Thus, every lump of rock there was carried in by the hominids to make tools at the carcass. Some of the cores came from nearly 9 miles (14 km) away, presumably so the people could strike off

Living floors

Bone and stone accumulations

sharp flakes to butcher the carcass. This site provides clear evidence of tool-making, raw material transport, and butchering. But we simply do not know whether the hominids killed the hippopotamus. The site may represent a place where they paused briefly to scavenge meat from a predator kill or an animal that had died of natural causes. It was certainly not a home base.

Site FxJj50, also at Koobi Fora, is in an ancient watercourse, a place where the hominids could find shade from the blazing sun, located close to water and abundant supplies of stone for toolmaking (Figure 4.13) (Bunn et al., 1980). The site consists of a cluster of stone artifacts: choppers, crude scrapers, battered cobbles, and sharp-edged flakes. Approximately 2100 bones representing at least twenty vertebrates, mainly antelope, are associated with the tools, some of them bearing carnivore chewing marks. But there are clear signs that the bones were smashed and cut by hominids, for reconstructed fragments show signs of hammer blows and fine linear grooves that can have resulted only from cutting bone with stoneworking edges. The excavators noted the lack of articular ends of bones, a characteristic of bone accumulations resulting from carnivore kills. Could the hominids simply have chased away lions and other predators, then moved in on the fresh kill? We do not know, but there is a strong possibility that successful hunting played a relatively limited part in hominid life at this early date. Again, we cannot be sure this was a home base.

Another site also consists of a scatter of stone tools and broken animal bones, these from several antelope and larger mammals. The scatter lay on the surface of a dry streambed where water could still be easily obtained by digging in the sand. The banks of the watercourse were probably shaded by dense stands of

FIGURE 4.13 Excavation at site FxJj50 Koobi Fora, Kenya.

trees that provided both shelter and plant foods. Perhaps the people who left the tools and bones climbed into these trees at night. The site was so sheltered that even minuscule stone chips were still in place, unaffected by the strong winds that sweep over the area; the leaves, too, left impressions in the deposits. The nearest source of toolmaking stone is 2 miles (3.2 km) from the site, so the inhabitants must have carried in their tools, and, in all probability, portions of the several animals whose bones accumulated at the site. This type of behavior — the carrying in of food to a fixed location — is fundamentally different from that of the nonhuman primates.

Much of our present knowledge about the lifeways of the earliest hominids comes from Olduvai Gorge, where Mary Leakey plotted and recorded sites in Bed I at the base of the gorge (M. D. Leakey, 1971). The *Zinjanthropus* at Olduvai was found to be 1239 feet square (115 m²), consisting of more than 4000 artifacts and bones. Many artifacts and bones were concentrated in an area some 15 feet (4.5 m) across. A pile of shattered bones and rocks lay a short distance away, the bones perhaps piled in heaps as the marrow was extracted from them. A barer, arc-shaped area between these bone heaps and the pile of more complete fragments remains unexplained. Leakey wonders whether it was the site of a crude windbreak of branches, since the area lies in the path of today's prevailing winds.

Recent researches have approached the Olduvai locations from several angles (Bunn and Kroll, 1986; Potts, 1984a). Careful examination of the bones revealed that many of them had lain on the surface for considerable periods of time, perhaps as long as four to six, even ten, years, to judge from weathering patterns on modern East African bones. The bones of many different animals are found in the assemblages, and the remains of carcasses are from a very ecologically diverse set of animals. Limb bones predominate on the "floors," as if these isolated bones were repeatedly carried to the site. Furthermore, the stone tools found on the Olduvai surfaces were all imported from raw material sources some distance away.

What is one to make of this pattern of meat- and marrow-rich bones concentrated in a small area with stone tools? The percentage of carnivore bones is somewhat higher than the natural environment would suggest, about 3 percent in the Olduvai assemblages, as opposed to 1 percent for the local environment today (in one case the figure was as high as 21 percent). Was there then intense ecological competition for game meat between hominids and other carnivores? It seems possible that the presence of carnivores restricted the activities of hominids at Olduvai. They may have grabbed meat-rich bones from carnivore kills, then taken them to a place where they had a collection of stone tools. There they could have hastily cut off meat and extracted marrow before abandoning the fresh bones to the carnivores hovering nearby. The Olduvai sites may not have been safe from carnivores, and without fire or domesticated dogs, *Homo habilis* probably had to rely on opportunistic foraging. As we have already noted, many of the Olduvai bones bear both carnivore teeth marks and stone tool cuts, perhaps a reflection of competition for game meat. It is also worth noting that one hominid bone found at Olduvai had been gnawed by carnivores.

Were the Olduvai bone and artifact accumulations actual home bases, places to which the hominids returned to sleep, to feed their dependents, and to carry out other activities? We can be sure that the hominids transported toolmaking stone and portions of animal carcasses from one place to another. But we cannot be certain that they actually lived at the places where these objects were abandoned, in the way that hunter-gatherers do. Several experts believe that the accumulations were useful caches of stone artifacts to which bones and other food resources were taken for processing (Potts, 1984b). These caches may have lain near water supplies or predictable food supplies, or have been maintained throughout a group's range, so that they did not have to carry meat or stone very far. But the caches could have been dangerous places, locations to which carnivores came, attracted by the smell of fresh meat. It may have been adaptive for the hominids to minimize their time at the caches for this reason, because they had no means of defending their home bases.

All archaeology currently tells us is that the early Olduvai sites were places to which stone and food resources were carried. As such, the caches may be the predecessors to hunter-gatherer home bases, which were to come into being later in prehistory, conceivably with the regular use of fire for heat and protection.

Hunting and Scavenging

Taphonomy, edge wear studies, and other highly sophisticated approaches to the archaeological record of 2 million years ago have shown again and again the sheer folly of basing theories about early hominid behavior on crude analogies with contemporary hunting societies. Just for a start, the hominids belonged to a quite different species. Furthermore, their behaviors are not displayed by any living ape, nor indeed by all early hominids, some of whom never accumulated bones. At this stage, just about all we can do is pose fundamental questions about early lifeways:

- Did *Homo habilis* hunt game or merely scavenge meat? There seems to be some agreement that such humans were scavengers at least part of the time (Bunn and Kroll, 1986).
- But what kind of scavenging was the rule? Was it casual scavenging when the opportunity arose? Or did the hominids deliberately chase away predators from their kills while they seized pieces of the carcass?
- How much of the diet was meat? Do the bones at the Olduvai scatters represent many meals or one major meat-eating event?
- How important was foraging for plant foods? Did the hominids make a practice of sharing food, with both hunters and foragers returning to a home base to distribute their spoils among other members of their group?

For some time, paleoanthropologists have assumed that the meat and foraging diet was associated with home bases where food was shared, with momentous consequences for the evolution of human behavior (Isaac, 1978, 1984). Proponents of this school argue that meat is easily carried back to base and is a rich source of necessary amino acids. However, such explanations must be sup-

Caches

plemented by information on the ecological conditions under which early hominid meat eating occurred (for a detailed discussion, see Potts, 1984b).

As we have seen, diverse carnivore and ungulate communities developed in eastern and southern Africa by 4 million years ago, with a wide diversity of hominids as part of the mammalian community. Some scientists believe that new ways of adapting to a heterogeneous environment like that of the East African savanna developed opportunistically. Under some ecological conditions, they argue, an opportunistic shift in use of a food source such as meat could have led to a breakthrough in human behavior that had long-term significance.

In contrast, the Red Queen model (see The Ecological Problems Faced by Early Hominids earlier) argues somewhat differently — that species within communities are highly interdependent and competitive. With a wide diversity of predators in the savanna, hominids consuming meat would have to have competed successfully with carnivores to obtain it. This competitive ability was selected because meat eating became vital to survival and reproductive success, and the dangers of competing with carnivores were more than outweighed by the advantages of more available food supplies and increased reproductive success because of better nutrition and easily transportable meat for social feeding.

At present, it is difficult to choose between these general ecological models.

Modern studies of carnivorous animals provide some clues to the ecological conditions that correspond to behaviors often found in early hominids (Potts, 1984b). These researches have shown conclusively that no large mammal can live just by scavenging. Among lions and hyenas, for example, hunting and scavenging are complementary ways of obtaining meat; while live animals are always available, scavenged meat from carcasses killed by others is often favored. The great animal behaviorist George Schaller (1972) records that 60 to 70 percent of carcasses scavenged by Serengeti Plain lions in Tanzania were taken from other carnivores. Or sometimes the predators simply waited their turn at the meat. Lions are especially successful at this strategy because their social organization in prides allows them to protect their foraged meat from others.

Unlike carnivorous birds such as vultures, large carnivores such as lions have relatively fixed territories related to stationary breeding areas. They position themselves close to regular ungulate migration routes, where, for a few months, they prey off the thousands of animals that pass through. There is plenty of game for all and minimal competition. The rest of the year, the predators fall back on the resident ungulates, a much more diverse population in small numbers. With limited foraging ranges, scavenging these animals involves intense competition with other carnivores. Perhaps one can argue that under ecological conditions closely similar to those of the modern East African savanna, terrestrial and nomadic hominids could have fed off large numbers of scavenged dead mammals from a few migratory species with minimal competition for several months each year. It may be that the early hominids took advantage of the annual migration circuits of herbivores.

Some microscopic evidence from very early archaeological sites at Olduvai Gorge suggests that scavenging may have been much more important. Pat Shipman (1984) and others have examined dozens of broken animal bones

Scavenging

from Olduvai, peering at minute but distinctive cut marks resulting from such activities as butchery, disarticulation of carcasses, and skin removal. They made high-fidelity replicas of bone marks, then examined them under a scanning electron microscope, comparing the results with those obtained from a 2300-year-old agricultural settlement in Kenya, where the inhabitants were actively engaged in disarticulation, butchery, and other activities. They found that 90 percent of the 2300-year-old bones showed cut marks resulting from the disjointing of carcasses, but only 45 percent of those from Olduvai showed the same phenomenon. This was likewise true with butchery marks, those made when removing meat from bones. In contrast, about 75 percent of both the Olduvai and the 2300-year-old bones show the characteristic marks left by skin and tendon removal, which are especially visible on the lower limb bones since they had little meat on them.

Both disarticulation and butchery were surprisingly uncommon at Olduvai, so it seems doubtful the hominids were butchering and disjointing large animals and carrying them back to base. They seem to have obtained meat without cutting up too many carcasses. It is possible that they scavenged it from predator kills. A tantalizing clue came from thirteen Olduvai bones on which both carnivore and humanly made markings were present. In eight instances, the human marks *overlay* carnivore marks, as if the humans had scavenged the bones from carcasses that had already been killed by lions or other predators (see Potts, 1984a).

The diversity of animals, including nonmigratory species, represented in the Olduvai bone accumulations is striking. Richard Potts (1984b) believes that this represents the variety of animals found in a resident rather than a migratory ungulate population, where only a few species are represented. He argues that the hominids depended at least partially on resident animals in a situation where the generalization about large carnivores being hunters *and* scavengers might apply. Thus, the Olduvai hominids were hunting resident mammals as well as competing with other carnivores in scavenging activity.

By studying body part frequencies in Olduvai accumulations, Potts has shown that carnivore bone assemblages contain a high proportion of forelimbs, the body part usually removed first from a carcass by a scavenger. In accumulations where hominid activity had taken place, higher forelimbs are also common but hindlimbs are relatively abundant as well, as if the hominids were obtaining meat both early and later in the sequence of carcass disarticulation.

A variety of ecological and zoological approaches argue for the Olduvai hominids not being just scavengers; their bone collection activities were generally similar to those of some modern mammal carnivores. They probably hunted and scavenged. Judging from the mix of fore- and hindlimbs, some of the scavenging was opportunistic.

Plant Foraging and the Early Hominids

Beyond some microscopic wear traces from plant tissues on early stone artifacts, there is as yet no archaeological evidence for plant foods being consumed by early hominids. Yet a scanning electron microscope focused on tooth microwear has shown that some Lower Pleistocene hominids had diets very similar to those of modern nonhuman primates (Walker, 1981). Again, the arguments are theoretical. Clifford Jolly (1970) has written of a lengthy period when "basal" hominids — immediate ancestors to humans — were predominantly, if not exclusively, seed eaters. The recent discovery of *Homo habilis* limb bones revealed a far more arboreal anatomy than that previously assumed for a terrestrial, bipedal primate of 2 million years ago. Such adept tree climbers are certain to have relied on fruit and other plant foods, perhaps enjoying a diet closer to that of modern apes than to that of hunter-gatherers. We can be sure that plant foods were a major element in a broadly based early hominid diet.

Seed eating

TOOLMAKING

Other animals like chimpanzees make tools (Figure 4.14), but human beings manufacture tools regularly and habitually as well as in a much more complex fashion. In other words, we have gone much further in the toolmaking direction than other primates (Gowlett, 1984). One reason is that our brains allow us to plan our actions much more in advance. Prehistoric tools in all their simplic-

FIGURE 4.14 Chimpanzee using a stick as a tool to fish for insects. Chimpanzees also use objects for play and display, and carry them in their hands. Sometimes, they improve their sticks slightly with their teeth. They take leaves for cleaning the body and sipping water. Chimpanzees have inherited behavior patterns far closer to our own than to those of any monkey. (Goodall, 1986)

ity and sometimes extraordinary complexity provide a record of ancient decision-making processes. By analyzing the ways in which prehistoric stone artifacts — the most enduring of all technologies — were made, we can gain insights into the mind processes of the people who created them.

All studies of stone artifacts are based on the assumption that a sequence of removing flakes ultimately produced a finished artifact, whether simple or complex, to be used for a specific purpose (Figure 4.15). Many details of the world's earliest stone technology are debated, but there is no doubt that it was the work of individuals with an impressive knowledge of the properties of stone. They knew how to select the right rock, could visualize in three dimensions how to put it to use and flake it, had mastered the routine steps needed to create a tool, and were capable of passing this knowledge on to others.

The Oldowan Industry

Everyone has always assumed that the earliest stone technology would be very simple. When the Leakeys found crudely chipped stones in the long-buried lake beds at Olduvai Gorge, they were indeed nothing much to look at (Figure 4.15). (The Leakeys called their early tool assemblages Oldowan, after the gorge where they were first identified.) Most were broken pebbles and flakes, with flakes in the majority. Some Oldowan tools were so crude that only an expert can tell them from a naturally fractured rock, and the experts often disagree. All the Oldowan choppers and flakes strike one as extremely practical implements; many are so individual in design that they seem haphazard artifacts, not standardized in the way later Stone Age tools were. Classifying them is very difficult, for they do not fall into distinct types. The tools cannot be described as primitive, since many display a sophisticated understanding of stone's potential uses in toolmaking. We now know that the Olduvai hominids were adept stone toolmakers, using angular flakes and lumps of lava to make weapons, scrapers, and cutting tools. The tools themselves probably were used on skin too tough for teeth to cut. In all probability, the hominids made extensive use of simple and untrimmed flakes for many purposes.

Oldowan industries have been found on several sites in East Africa dating to between about 2.5 and 1.5 million years ago. There appears to be relatively little variability between different toolkits, and the artifacts show certain common technological features:

- Use of pebbles as raw material
- Cores with edges flaked from both sides (Figure 4.16)
- Some of the cores possibly fashioned into deliberate core tools (were these choppers?)
- Both heavy- and light-duty tool forms, some modified into crude scrapers

There is a tendency to describe the Oldowan as a very simple technology. It is true that there are few formal Oldowan tool types, but the artifacts show a skilled appreciation of basic stone-flaking techniques and flaking sequences that were envisaged in the mind's eye.

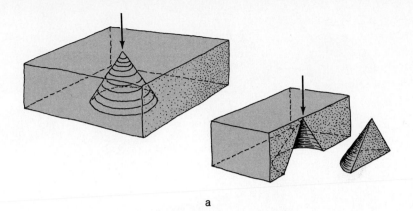

a

When a blow is struck on flinty rock, a cone of percussion is formed by shock waves rippling through the stone (left). A flake is formed (right) when the block (or core) is hit at the edge, and the stone fractures along the edge of the ripple.

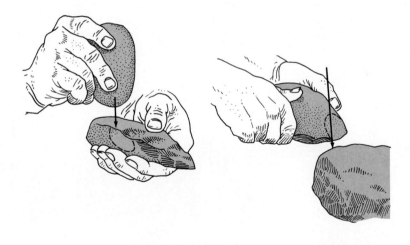

b

Using a hammerstone (left) and anvil (right).

FIGURE 4.15   Early stone technology. The principles of fracturing stone were fully understood by early stoneworkers, who used them to make simple but very effective artifacts. Certain types of flinty rock fracture in a distinctive way, as illustrated in (a). Early stoneworkers used a heavy hammerstone to remove edge flakes or struck lumps of rock against anvils to produce the same effect as shown in (b). Oldowan choppers were frequently made by removing a few flakes from lava lumps to form jagged working edges. Such artifacts have been shown by modern experiments to be remarkably effective for dismembering and butchering game. Perhaps it is small wonder that this simple stone technology was so long lasting.

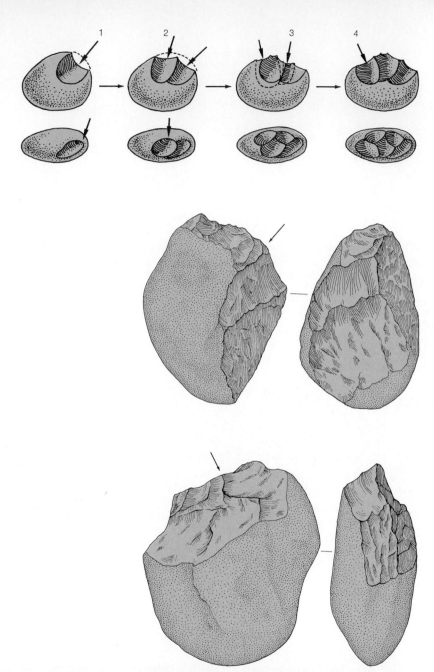

FIGURE 4.16 Oldowan technology. Many cobbles at Koobi Fora and Olduvai Gorge were used as cores to produce sharp-edged flakes. The technology was simple in the extreme. First, sharp blows were struck near the natural edge of a pebble to remove flakes. The pebble was then turned over and more blows struck on the ridges formed by the scars of the earlier flakes. A core with a jagged edge, perhaps sometimes used as a chopper, resulted. Many cores were "mined" for as many flakes as possible before being discarded. The figure shows two Oldowan cores from Olduvai Gorge. Arrows show flake edges. Front and side views (three-fifths actual size).

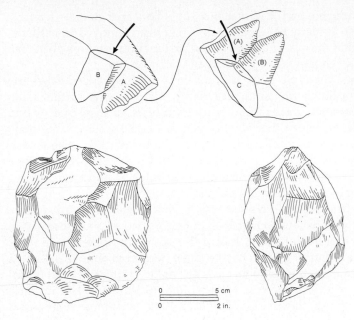

FIGURE 4.17 Making Oldowan bifaces. Above, a simplified picture of the process required for bifacial flaking. Below, a large Oldowan diskoidlike artifact from Chesowanja, East Africa, in plan and side views. The stoneworker used this bifacial technique but did not fashion the biface along a long axis, as later humans did (see Chapter 5). (After Gowlett, 1984)

For years, archaeologists have thought of the Oldowan as a static technological stage without any perceptible change. As more sites come to light and analytic techniques are refined, though, the Oldowan appears in a different light, as a simple, highly effective technology that grew more complex over time, with the appearance of crude bifacial working, in which cores were flaked on both sides (Figure 4.17) (Gowlett, 1986).

Mary Leakey (1971) studied the Oldowan choppers and flakes from the early hominid levels at Olduvai and divided the artifacts into different morphological forms. Her classification remained unchallenged until Nicholas Toth and a new generation of scholars approached early stone technology from a more holistic perspective (Toth, 1985). The objective of their studies is to learn as much as possible about early hominid behavior from the stone artifacts these people left behind. Such research is based firmly in experimental archaeology and middle range theory. It is founded on every aspect of technology, from raw material acquisition through artifact manufacture and use to discarding and incorporation of the tools into the geological record. As part of his work, Toth became an expert stone toolmaker and carried out edge wear and taphonomic studies on sites in East Turkana.

Toth emerged from his work with a very different view of the Oldowan. He points out that conventional approaches to the stone artifacts are based on the idea that the makers had premeditated artifact forms in mind. His experiments replicated thousands of Oldowan cores and flakes, and led him to argue that much of the variety in Oldowan artifacts was, in fact, the result of flake production. Many of the choppers from Olduvai and Koobi Fora are actually "waste," cores discarded when as many flakes as possible had been removed from them. Toth also observes that the size of available raw material can profoundly affect the size and variety of choppers and flakes at an Oldowan site.

Toth's experiments with replicated tools revealed that sharp-edged flakes are far more effective for butchering animal carcasses, especially for slitting skin. Flakes, then, were of much greater importance than hitherto suspected — but this does not necessarily mean that all choppers were just waste. Some may have served as wood-chopping and adzing tools, or for breaking open bones for their marrow. Edge wear studies of the few Oldowan flakes made of fine-grained materials have hinted at three possible uses: butchery and meat cutting, sawing and scraping wood, and cutting soft plant matter.

What are the implications of Toth's studies for our knowledge of early hominid cognitive skills? Toth believes our earliest ancestors had a good sense of the mechanics of stone tool manufacture, and of the geometry of core manipulation. They were able to find the correct acute angle needed to remove flakes by percussion. Not even modern beginners have this ability; it takes several hours of intensive practice to acquire the skill. While chimpanzees use sticks and crack nuts with unflaked stones, they rarely carry their "artifacts" more than a few yards. In contrast, the Koobi Fora and Olduvai hominids carried flakes and cores over considerable distances. This represents a simple form of *curation*, retaining tools for future use rather than just utilizing convenient stones. Toth hypothesizes that the hominids tested materials in streambeds and other locations, transported the best pieces to activity areas, and sometimes dropped them there, carrying the rest off with them. He also points out that they must have relied heavily on other raw materials, like wood and bone, and that stone artifacts do not necessarily give an accurate picture of early hominid cognitive abilities.

Curation

Without question, our ancestors became more and more dependent on technology. But the opportunistic nature of primeval stone technology is in sharp contrast to the better designed, much more standardized stone artifacts of later times.

THE DEVELOPMENT OF LANGUAGE

Cooperation, the ability to get together to solve problems of both subsistence and potential conflict, is a vital quality in human beings. We are unique in having a spoken, symbolic language that enables us to communicate our most intimate feelings to one another. One fundamental question about early prehistory surrounds this development: At what point did hominids acquire the ability to speak?

Our closest living relatives, the chimpanzees, communicate with no more than gestures and many voice sounds in the wild, while other apes use sounds only to convey territorial information. However, chimpanzees seem to have a natural talent for learning symbolic language under controlled conditions. A famous chimpanzee named Washoe was trained to communicate with humans, using no fewer than 175 sign language gestures similar to those of American

Washoe the chimp

Sign Language (Gardner and Gardner, 1969). After more than a year, Washoe could associate particular signs with specific activities, such as eating and drinking. Another chimpanzee, named Sarah, was taught to read and write with plastic symbols and acquired a vocabulary of 130 words, to the extent that she obeyed sequences of written instructions given with the symbols (Premack and Premack, 1972). The research continues, but there is no evidence that chimpanzees can combine visual symbols to create new meanings or use syntax. Sequences of signs produced by trained chimpanzees may have a superficial resemblance to the first multiword sentences produced by children, but beyond the stage of learning isolated symbols, an ape's language learning is severely restricted (Terrace, Sanders, and Bever, 1979).

Clearly, articulate speech was an important threshold in human evolution, because it opened up whole new vistas of cooperative behavior and unlimited potential for the enrichment of life. When did hominids abandon grunts for speech? There are only two potential lines of research. One uses *endocasts*, natural casts of the interior of the brain case. Dean Falk (1984) has studied the convolutions of early hominid endocasts and found that those of the early australopithecines are apelike. But the brain cell of Skull 1470 (Figure 4.10) is about 300 cc larger, and the frontal lobe of its endocast is more humanlike, especially in the Broca's area, the left hemisphere, where speech control is located.

Endocasts

Endocast research is much more generalized than detailed anatomical studies of the position of the voice box, the larynx, using both comparative anatomy and actual fossils to study differences between apes and humans. Jeffrey Laitman (1984) poses the two fundamental questions:

- What was the anatomy of our ancestors' vocal cords?
- How does it compare to that of modern humans?

The second line of research has been done by Laitman and others who studied the *position* of the larynx in a wide variety of mammals including humans. They found that all mammals except adult humans have a larynx high in the neck, a position that enables the larynx to lock into the air space at the back of the nasal cavity. Although this allows animals like monkeys and cats to breathe and swallow at the same time, it limits the sounds they can produce. The pharynx — the air cavity part of the food pathway — can produce sounds, but animals use their mouths to modify sounds, since they are anatomically incapable of producing the range of sounds needed for articulate speech.

Until they are about eighteen months to two years old, human children's larynxes are also situated high in the neck. Then the larynx begins to descend, ending up between the fourth and seventh neck vertebrae. How and why are still a mystery, but the change completely alters the way the infant breathes, speaks, and swallows. Adult humans cannot separate breathing and swallowing, so they can suffocate when food lodges in an airway. However, an enlarged pharyngeal chamber above the vocal cords enables them to modify the sounds they emit in an infinite variety of ways, which is the key to human speech.

Can one tell the position of the larynx from fossil skeletons? Fortunately, the shape of the base of the skull is highly informative. Most mammals have flat-based skulls and high larynxes, but humans have an arched skull base associated with their low larynx. Using sophisticated statistical analyses, Laitman and his colleagues ran tests on as many complete fossil skulls as possible. They found that the australopithecines of 4.0 to 1.0 million years ago had flat skull bases and high larynxes, while those of *Homo erectus,* dating to about 1.5 million years and later, show somewhat more curvature, suggesting that the larynx was beginning to descend to its modern position. It was only about 300,000 years ago that the skull base finally assumed a modern curvature, which would allow for fully articulate speech to evolve.

So it seems that language was a relatively late development, albeit one of vital importance. The real value of language, apart from the stimulation it gives brain development, is that with it we can convey feelings and nuances far beyond the power of grunts or gestures to communicate. We may assume that the first humans had more to communicate with than nonhuman primates, but it appears that articulate speech was a more recent stimulus to biological and cultural evolution.

THE EARLY ADAPTIVE PATTERN

The few early sites that have been excavated show that the first phase of human evolution involved shifts in the basic patterns of subsistence and locomotion, as well as new ingredients — food sharing and toolmaking. These led to enhanced communication, information exchange, and economic and social insight, as well as cunning and restraint. Human anatomy was augmented with tools. Culture became an inseparable part of humanity.

Opportunism

Archaeologist Glynn Isaac (1978) believes that opportunism is a hallmark of humankind — a restless process, like mutation and natural selection. The normal pressures of ecological competition were able to transform the versatile behavior of ancestral primates into the new and distinctive early hominid pattern. The change required feedback between cultural subsystems, such as hunting and sharing food. Weapons and tools made it possible to scavenge and butcher larger and larger animals. Vegetable foods were a staple in the diet, protection against food shortages. Foraging provided stability, and it may also have led to division of labor between men and women. Skin bags, bark trays, and perhaps baskets were useful in collecting food; sharing and manufacturing them encouraged the division of labor. The savanna was an ideal and vacant ecological niche for hominids who lived on scavenging, hunting, and foraging combined.

By a million years ago, the hominid lines had been pruned to the extent that one lineage, *Homo,* remained. Judging from the abundance of finds from East Turkana, the hominids of 2 million years ago appear to have been about as common as baboons are in the savanna today (Lewin, 1988a). The microwear patterns on the tooth surfaces of *Australopithecus* and *Homo habilis* show that both creatures flourished on a diet very similar to that of chimpanzees. But this pattern can be produced by all kinds of combinations of vegetable and meat foods, to the extent that the two species may have been ecologically separated by their different dietary preferences. Otherwise it would not have been possible for them to share the same area for very long. But this is purely intelligent speculation. The archaeological deposits in which both fossils and artifacts are found are simply too coarse grained to allow detection of even fairly major climatic and ecological changes.

The only clue to this separation may lie in *Homo habilis* appearing at about the same time as the first stone tools. These artifacts must have been connected with new ways of getting and processing foods, even with entirely new forms of diet. *Homo habilis* had a much larger brain, a development that was probably associated with an increase in economic and social complexity, and perhaps food sharing as well.

What sort of social organization did *Homo habilis* enjoy? However much we look at contemporary nonhuman primates, we cannot be sure. Most primates are intensely social and live in groups where the mother-infant relationship forms a central bond. The period of infants' dependency on mothers found in, say, chimpanzees, was probably lengthened considerably with *Homo habilis*. The larger brain size would mean that infants were born with much smaller heads than adults, at an earlier stage of mental maturity. This biological reality would have had a major impact on social organization and daily habits.

Baboons and chimpanzees live in groups that range from about a dozen individuals up to troops of a hundred or so. They occupy a relatively small territory, one with sufficient vegetable resources to support a considerable population density; this pattern contrasts sharply with the average hunter-gatherer band, typically a closely knit group of about twenty-five people of several families. The kind of systematic hunting such people engage in requires much larger territories and permits much lower densities per square mile. The few sites that have been excavated suggest that *Homo habilis* tended to live in bands that were much closer to those of modern hunter-gatherers. However, it would be a mistake to assume that they lived in actual hunter-gatherer bands. In all probability their social organization resembled more closely that of chimpanzees and baboons.

Chimpanzees and baboons live in a world created in their brains by the integration of sight, sound, smell, and touch. The more complex the inputs and their neural processing, the more complex the inner world built by the brain. It may well be that this increase in complexity is what underlies the cumulative growth in brain size that is such a distinctive feature of mammalian evolution, from amphibians to reptiles, then through mammals to humans. The world of *Homo habilis* was much less predictable and more demanding than that of even *Australopithecus*. What was it that was more complex? Why do we have to be so intelligent? Not for hunting animals or gathering food but for our interactions with other people. The increased complexity of our social interactions is likely to have been a powerful force in the evolution of the human brain. For *Homo habilis*, the adoption of a wider based diet with a food-sharing social group would have placed much more acute demands on the ability to cope with the complex and unpredictable. And the brilliant technological, artistic, and expressive skills of humankind may well be a consequence of the fact that our early ancestors had to be more and more socially adept.

GUIDE TO FURTHER READING

Foley, Robert (ed.) *Hominid Evolution and Community Ecology: Prehistoric Human Adaptation in Biological Perspective.* London: Academic Press, 1984.

A provocative set of essays on the ecological background to the evolution of humankind. Crammed with thoughtful commentary and imaginative theorizing on the emergence of humanity. Essential for the serious student.

Johanson, Donald C., and Edey, Maitland A. *Lucy: The Beginnings of Humankind.* New York: Simon and Schuster, 1981.

A well-written, racy account of the Hadar hominids that ranges widely over the major controversies of paleoanthropology. Superb descriptions of the research process and dating methods.

Lewin, Roger. *Bones of Contention.* New York: Simon and Schuster, 1987.

An entertaining account of the major personalities and controversies surrounding paleoanthropology. Admirable for the general reader.

Lewin, Roger. *Human Evolution* (2d ed.). Oxford: Blackwell Scientific Publications, 1988.

A lucid, multidisciplinary account of human origins full of stimulating ideas.

Tanner, Nancy M. *On Becoming Human.* London: Cambridge University Press, 1981.

A brilliant essay on human origins and male/female roles.

Weiss, Mark L., and Mann, Alan E. *Human Biology and Behavior* (5th ed.). Boston: Little, Brown, 1988.

A standard undergraduate text that presents the biological background to human evolution. Excellent graphics.

CHRONOLOGICAL TABLE B

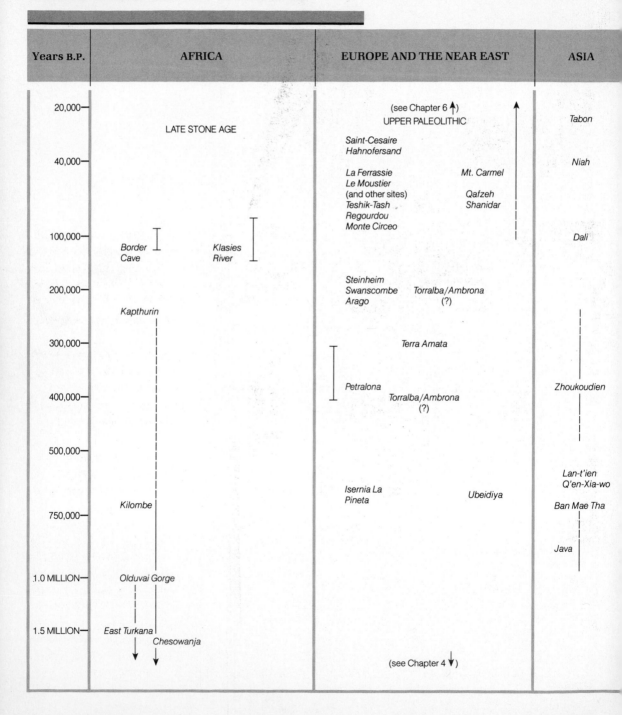

Years B.P.	AFRICA	EUROPE AND THE NEAR EAST	ASIA
20,000—		(see Chapter 6 ↑) UPPER PALEOLITHIC	Tabon
	LATE STONE AGE	Saint-Cesaire Hahnofersand	
40,000—		La Ferrassie Mt. Carmel Le Moustier (and other sites) Qafzeh Teshik-Tash Shanidar Regourdou Monte Circeo	Niah
100,000—	Border ⊥	Klasies	Dali
	Cave River		
200,000—		Steinheim Swanscombe Torralba/Ambrona Arago (?)	
	Kapthurin		
300,000—		Terra Amata	
400,000—		Petralona Torralba/Ambrona (?)	Zhoukoudien
500,000—			
			Lan-t'ien Q'en-Xia-wo
	Kilombe	Isernia La Ubeidiya Pineta	Ban Mae Tha
750,000—			
			Java
1.0 MILLION—	Olduvai Gorge		
1.5 MILLION—	East Turkana		
	Chesowanja	(see Chapter 4 ↓)	

CHAPTER 5

Toward Modern Humanity

(1.5 million to 40,000 B.P.)

Preview

■ *Homo erectus* first evolved in tropical Africa about 1.6 million years ago and was apparently the first hominid to adapt to climates as diverse as tropical forest, temperate, and near-arctic. Anatomically, *Homo erectus* was fully adapted to bipedal posture, had much more humanlike limbs than *Homo habilis*, and had a brain capacity that ranged between 775 and 1300 cc.

■ *Homo erectus* may have been the first hominid to tame fire, to use it for protection, warmth, and cooling.

■ About 700,000 years ago, *Homo erectus* moved from Africa into Asia and Europe. This spread coincided with a radiation of tropical carnivores and ungulates into temperate latitudes. The earliest known European human settlement is at Isernia La Pineta, Italy, dating to this time. The Zhoukoudien Caves of China were visited by *Homo erectus* bands from about 460,000 to some 230,000 years ago.

■ The successful colonists of northern latitudes were those who could exploit game animals distributed unevenly over a landscape with a climate of sharp seasonal contrasts. The key to this new adaptation was mobility, an opportunistic adaptation based on knowledge of resource distribution.

■ *Homo erectus*'s stone technology was oriented toward the making of stone axes, a wide range of flake tools, and choppers. Acheulian hand axes were shaped symmetrically around a long axis, multipurpose tools like the flake artifacts favored at many locations. Human technology between 1.5 million and 150,000 years ago shows considerable diversity, probably associated with different local adaptations and the availability of toolmaking stone.

■ *Homo erectus* hunted and foraged for food, perhaps developing effective social mechanisms to foster collaboration and enhanced communication in pursuit of large game. Torralba/Ambrona in Spain, and Terra Amata, France, provide examples of European settlements occupied by such early hunter-gatherers.

■ Anatomically modern humans *(Homo sapiens)* are thought to have evolved in tropical Africa some time before 100,000 years ago and to have spread into the Mediterranean Basin and the Near East about 45,000 years ago.

■ The Neanderthals first appeared in Europe, the Near East, and Asia well before 100,000 years ago, and flourished until replaced by modern humans about 35,000 years ago. Their more robust postcranial skeleton and skeletal anatomy set them apart from *Homo sapiens sapiens*.

■ Middle Paleolithic technology used techniques developed by Acheulian stoneworkers but yielded a wider variety of finished artifacts, some of them composite tools. Prepared and disk core technologies came into use and were important after 150,000 years ago. However, the Neanderthals employed a fundamentally simple stone technology with techniques that varied considerably from one location to the next for many reasons, among them raw material availability, climate, different activities, and subsistence needs.

■ The Neanderthals were the first human beings to bury their dead, suggesting at least rudimentary spiritual beliefs.

It would be a mistake to think of human evolution in terms of neat ladders of progression from one form to the next improved form. With only a handful of fossils to work with, and those fragmentary at best, there has been a tendency even for experts to think in linear terms. However, since human evolution has probably followed the pattern of that of other animal groups, we are likely to find more rather than fewer species in our ancestry. Instead of a ladder, one should think of a bush, with different branches representing new species that all became extinct, except for the one surviving form — *Homo sapiens*. We are a rarity in nature in that we are all from one species (Lewin, 1988a).

In Chapter 4, we noted how opportunism and adaptability were hallmarks of the first hominids, in terms of both diet and ecological exploitation. The australopithecines were not as adaptable as some of their hominid contemporaries. They lived at a time when baboons and other competitive primates were evolving rapidly, and they probably became extinct as a result of competitive exclusion. We must now examine their successors and those of *Homo*, humans who were capable of a far more complex and varied lifeway. These were hominids who used fire, made systematically manufactured rather than opportunistic tools, developed seasonal home bases, and were the first to settle outside Africa.

HOMO ERECTUS

Homo erectus
1.5 million to
?200,000 B.P.

The earliest unquestioned specimen of *Homo erectus* comes from East Turkana in Kenya, a skull dated to between 1.6 and 1.5 million years ago (Figure 5.1) (Leakey and Lewin, 1977). This fossil, with its massive brow ridges, enlarged brain size, and high forehead, is morphologically very close to examples of *Homo erectus* dating to a million years ago and earlier.

Richard Leakey and anatomist Alan Walker have recently discovered the virtually complete skeleton of a twelve-year-old *Homo erectus* boy on the western shores of the same lake, dating to about the same time period. The footprints of hippopotamuses and other animals nearby suggest that the decomposing corpse was trampled to pieces. From the neck down, the boy's bones are remarkably modern looking. But the skull and jawbone are more primitive looking, with brow ridges and a brain capacity perhaps as high as 700 to 800 cc, about half the modern size. The skeleton shows that the boy stood about 5 foot 6 inches (1.8 m) tall, taller than many modern twelve-year-olds. This new Turkana find tends to confirm many scientists' view that different parts of the body evolved at different rates, the body achieving fully modern form long before the head.

These finds date to much earlier points than the classic finds of *Homo erectus*, which were made as early as 1891. A Dutch doctor named Eugene Dubois found the skullcap of an apelike human in the gravels of the Solo River near Trinil in central Java (Pfeiffer, 1985). When, a year later at the same site, he found an upper limb bone that displayed many human features, he named his discovery *Pithecanthropus erectus* ("apeman who walks upright"). A vicious outcry greeted his announcement; Dubois was accused of heresy and his find-

FIGURE 5.1   Skull KNM-ER3733, East Turkana, Kenya.

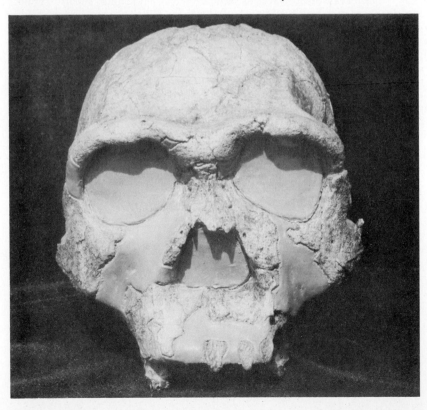

ings dismissed with contempt. Then, in 1928, a Canadian anatomist named Davidson Black announced the discovery of human teeth at Zhoukoudien Cave near Beijing (Weidenreich, 1946). A year later, Chinese archaeologist W. C. P'ei recovered a complete skullcap from the same cave; it closely resembled Dubois's Java finds. The human remains were associated with stone tools, crude bone artifacts, and the bones of hundreds of animals. A Dutch physical anthropologist, G. H. R. von Koenigswald, discovered more fossils in Java, examined the Chinese and Japanese remains, and described a new human form: *Homo erectus* (Figure 5.2) (Symon and Cybulski, 1981).

Homo erectus is known to have lived over a wide area of the Old World. Louis Leakey found a skullcap of *Homo erectus* in the upper levels of Bed II at Olduvai Gorge (Lewin, 1988a). This specimen came from levels dating to approximately a million years ago. In contrast, the Chinese finds are now estimated to date to between 500,000 and 350,000 years ago, while new *Homo erectus* finds from the Trinil area of Java have been potassium argon dated to between 900,000 and 600,000 years ago (Weiss and Mann, 1988). *Homo erectus* fossils have come to light in Morocco and Algeria and in Hungary and West Germany. None of the European finds can be dated, but they probably belong to approximately 500,000 years ago. Further, although fossil remains of *Homo erectus* are rarely encountered, their distinctive toolkit of stone axes and other artifacts is relatively commonplace and tells us much about their distribution and adaptations.

FIGURE 5.2   A plaster cast of *Homo erectus* from Zhoukoudien, China. The skull bones of *Homo erectus* show that these hominids had a brain capacity between 775 and 1300 cc, showing much variation. It is probable that their vision was excellent and that they were capable of extensive thought. The *H. erectus* skull is more rounded than that of earlier hominids; it also has conspicuous brow ridges and a sloping forehead. With a massive jaw, much thicker skull bones, and teeth with cusp patterns somewhat similar to those of *Australopithecus africanus* and modern humans, *H. erectus* had limbs and hips fully adapted to an upright posture. It stood over 5 ft., 6 in. (1.8 m) and had hands fully capable of precision gripping and many kinds of toolmaking.

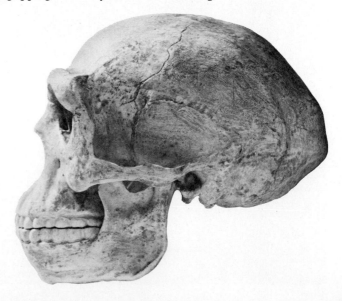

During *Homo erectus*'s long history, humanity adapted to a far wider range of environments, ranging from tropical savannas in East Africa to forested Javanese valleys, temperate climates in North Africa and Europe, and the harsh winters of China and northern Europe. *Homo erectus* was certainly capable of a far more complex and varied lifeway than previous hominids, and with such a wide distribution, it is hardly surprising that some variations in *Homo erectus* populations appear. For example, some had more robust skulls than others, while it is said that the Zhoukoudien skulls display a gradual increase in brain capacity from about 900 cc in 600,000-year-old specimens to about 1100 cc in 200,000-year-old individuals. In any case, *Homo erectus* was far more "human" than *Homo habilis*, a habitual biped, who had probably lost the thick hair covering that is characteristic of nonhuman primates. Unfortunately, we are unlikely to know when we lost our dense facial hair, because soft parts are never preserved. But it seems possible that this occurred when the dramatic enlargement of hominid brains recycled the developmental "clock" — perhaps with *Homo habilis* (Lewin, 1988a). In any case, *Homo erectus* certainly had abundant sweat glands and, presumably, in common with most tropical primates, relatively dark skin.

FIRE

Fire caused by natural conflagrations was certainly part of the savanna environment in which our earlier ancestors lived. Great grass and brush fires swept across open and wooded country during the dry months, especially, perhaps, when markedly drier conditions were widespread in East Africa about 1.7 million years ago (Clark and Harris, 1985). This was a time when the faunal communities of East Africa adapted to drier, more open grassland conditions. It was also about the time that *Homo erectus* first emerged. From this point on, there are signs that human behavior changed. The first archaeological sites appear at higher East African elevations, while less densely vegetated areas are more intensively occupied. Butchery sites containing the remains of large animals are more common. Stone technology becomes more complex, evidenced by the appearance of more elaborate hand ax–like artifacts and flake tools.

For years, archaeologists have argued that *Homo habilis* did not possess fire. There are no signs of hearths at Koobi Fora or Olduvai. Perhaps, went the argument, the East African environment was too warm for fire to be necessary. Thus, it was an innovation that allowed *Homo erectus* to settle cooler latitudes, perhaps 500,000 years ago. Recent excavations have turned up evidence of "hearthlike" arrangements of stone artifacts, fragmentary bones, and baked clay, clay that had been hardened by fire in antiquity at Chesowanja in the Kenya Rift Valley, a site dating to about 1.6 million years ago. Unfortunately, it has not proved possible to demonstrate that the inhabitants controlled the fire that hardened the clay. It is not until between one million and 700,000 years ago that fire is well documented in the archaeological record — significantly, in temperate China.

Chesowanja 1.6 million B.P.

It is not unreasonable to assume that the early hominids had learned to live with natural fires and were not afraid of them (Clark and Harris, 1985). Fire offers protection against predators and an easy way of hunting game, even insects and rodents, fleeing from a line of flames. The toxins from many common vegetable foods can be roasted or parched out in hot ashes, allowing people to use a wider range of plants in their diet (Stahl, 1984). The prevalence of such toxins may be the reason chimpanzees eat so many insects — still an important protein source for many African peoples, and perhaps for early hominids, too. Perhaps *Homo habilis* made the habit of conserving fire, taking advantage of long-smoldering tree stumps ignited by lightning strikes and other natural causes to kindle flames to light dry brush or simply scare off predators.

Hominid body size had increased dramatically with the appearance of *Homo erectus*. An ecological consequence of enlarged body size is extension of the home range, a fact well documented from animal behavior studies (Foley, 1984b). Larger quantities of food are needed because of higher metabolic rates. This may have been the time when hominids not only relied on smoldering tree stumps but also began to carry simple firebrands with them as protection against large predators. The new weapon would also allow them to move into more open country, where trees were much rarer, and to increase their home ranges into unfamiliar habitats.

Clark and Harris (1985) think it not unlikely that the conservation and taming of fire — as much as food sharing, meat eating, and new forms of sexual behavior — helped to forge close-knit family groups among hominid bands. The distribution of archaeological and hominid sites approximately 1.5 million years ago may reflect greatly increased home ranges, and, perhaps, the time when humans domesticated fire. It may be no coincidence that the earliest human settlement of Europe and Asia, of more temperate latitudes, occurred after *Homo erectus* appeared in East Africa and, perhaps, mastered fire.

THE RADIATION OF *HOMO ERECTUS*

Homo habilis and other contemporary African hominids were large mammals adapted to the tropical savanna (Roberts, 1984). They emerged in various forms before 2 million years ago, at a time when grasslands covered much of what is now rain forest in central Africa. *Homo habilis* depended on localized water supplies from lakes and streams to survive, but a major advantage of the savanna was its high diversity of herbivores. Between 5 and 1 million years ago, there were major, if little understood, fluctuations in world climate, which increased after about 900,000 years ago. After the Matuyama/Brunhes event of some 700,000 years ago (see Chapter 3), an intensification of glacial and interglacial cycles had profound effects on the ecological stability of Africa's tropical latitudes. During glacial maxima, savanna was distributed over much of what is now rain forest in central Africa. During interglacials, the savanna moved somewhat northward. The African savanna was periodically split into regions that were isolated, then reunited.

African hominids had to adapt to cyclical alterations between savanna, forest, and desert after 900,000 years ago. They could do so by migrating with the changing vegetational zones, as many other mammals did, or they could adapt to new environments, changing their dietary emphasis from meat to plant foods. Finally, they could move outside tropical latitudes altogether, into habitats that human beings had never occupied before.

Paleoanthropologists now believe that *Homo erectus* adapted to changed circumstances in all these ways, with hominids radiating out of Africa by way of the Sahara, when the desert was capable of supporting human life. Neil Roberts (1984) has likened the Sahara to a pump, sucking in population during wetter savanna phases and forcing hunter-gatherers out toward the Mediterranean during drier cycles. In radiating out of Africa, *Homo erectus* behaved just like other mammals in its ecological community.

Hominids were carnivores, and thus linked ecologically with other predators. There was widespread interchange of mammals between Africa and more temperate latitudes during the Pliocene and Lower Pleistocene. A major change in the mammalian populations of Europe took place about 700,000 years ago. Hippopotamuses, forest elephants, and other herbivores and carnivores like the lion, leopard, and spotted hyena seem to have migrated northward from Africa at this time. Migrations by the lion, leopard, and hyena — the animals with which hominids shared many ecological characteristics — were in the same direction as that taken by *Homo erectus*. Many paleontologists have noticed that the first European lions, leopards, and spotted hyenas reached enormous sizes, as if they enjoyed a successful adaptation in areas that were subject to far greater seasonal temperature fluctuations than the tropics. That the first successful human settlement of Europe and temperate Asia coincided with a radiation of a tropical mammal community from Africa seems plausible.

Earliest Human Settlement in the Near East and Europe

The earliest recorded human settlement in the Near East comes from the Ubeidiya site, near the confluence of the Jordan and Yarmuk rivers in Israel. Some human and animal bones are associated with simple choppers and some crude hand axes at this lakeside site. Unfortunately, Ubeidiya's dating is somewhat controversial, but an estimate of about 700,000 years ago, close to the Matuyama/Brunhes boundary, seems likely (Bar-Yosef, 1975).

Ubeidiya
700,000 B.P.

The earliest securely dated human artifacts yet found in Europe come from lake beds at Isernia La Pineta, southeast of Rome, Italy, stratified under volcanic deposits that have been potassium argon dated to some 730,000 years ago. The artifacts include flakes, scrapers, and choppers associated with bison, elephants, and other animals (Gamble, 1986b; Segre and Asconzi, 1984). None of the claims for even earlier European settlement have yet withstood close scrutiny, but by at least 350,000 years ago, human groups were living throughout western and central Europe, and perhaps even farther east.

Isernia La Pineta
c.730,000 B.P.

Homo erectus in Asia

In the present state of research, there is general agreement that Africa was probably the cradle of humankind. Despite several claims to the contrary, no australopithecine or *Homo habilis* fossils have come from tropical southeast Asia. Nor is there evidence of tropical radiation of hominids during the Lower

Pleistocene. *Homo erectus* is the earliest human being documented either in southeast Asia or in the Far East.

Southeast Asia

No australopithecine fossils have yet been identified from southeast Asia (G. G. Pope, 1984). The earliest traces of human settlement consist of three artifacts found in gravel deposits at Ban Mae Tha in northern Thailand. These split and flaked cobbles are dated through paleomagnetic and potassium argon studies to about 700,000 years ago (Pope et al., 1986). (There are also reports of 2-million-year-old stone choppers from India [Dennell et al., 1988]). Given what we know about the earliest prehistory of southeast Asia, it seems almost certain that these tools were made by *Homo erectus.* Dubois's *Homo erectus* finds and other more recent discoveries from Indonesia are thought to date to no earlier than about 700,000 years ago (G. G. Pope, 1984), a point in time that appears to coincide with the appearance of similar hominids in Europe and perhaps in China as well.

Homo erectus may have reached east Asia in the very late Lower Pleistocene, perhaps via the so-called Sunda shelf, low-lying ground that joined many of the southeast Asian islands during cooler cycles. This shelf appears to have acted as a faunal filter, preventing many tropical ungulate species from reaching the east. Southeast Asia was a tropical forest environment, with extensive patches of dense forest even during the driest periods of the Pleistocene. Geoffrey Pope (1984) believes that bamboo and other wood resources from these forests were of vital importance for the highly portable toolkit used by *Homo erectus* in this environment. They also point out that fire, perhaps tamed by these people, is an important component in forest technology. Thus, the crude stone choppers and flakes that may have formed the simple stone technology of Asia for tens of thousands of years were only a limited part of forest material culture. But such implements are all that remains of a Stone Age lifeway that was based not on the pursuit of large savanna animals but on smaller game and forest resources, many concentrated around natural springs, sinkholes, and caves.

China

There are two or three artifact assemblages from China that are claimed to date to the Lower Pleistocene, but the dates of all of them are uncertain (Chang, 1986). The earliest widely accepted traces of human activity date to after 700,000 years ago, during the Middle Pleistocene. The Lan-t'ien and Q'en-Xia-wo sites in central China have yielded specimens of *Homo erectus* that probably date to the early Middle Pleistocene, before 600,000 years ago.

The most famous and largest Middle Pleistocene site in China is the Zhoukoudien Caves, 28.5 miles (46 km) west of Beijing. Zhoukoudien consists of many caverns and fissures, the most famous of which is Locality I, where both stone implements and human fossils have been found. These caverns were visited by *Homo erectus* over an immensely long period of time, from about 460,000 to 230,000 years ago (Chang, 1986; Institute of Vertebrate Paleontology, 1981; Rukang and Shenglong, 1983). At least forty *Homo erectus* individuals have been found at Zhoukoudien, most of whom died before they were

Ban Mae Tha
c.700,000 B.P.

Lan-t'ien
Q'en-Xia-wo
600,000 B.P.

Zhoukoudien
460,000 to 230,000
B.P.

fourteen years old. Many of them appear to have perished from injuries; according to some physical anthropologists, some skulls were smashed open at the base to extract the brain, perhaps evidence for the earliest cannibalism in the world (Hooton, 1948).

The Zhoukoudien people visited the caves when the climate was perhaps a trifle warmer and moister than today. They hunted deer and other animals; more than sixty species are represented in the deposits. Lewis Binford, who examined some of the bones very hastily, claims that they were brought into the cave by scavenging predators, but the sample he studied was extremely small, and his conclusions are disputed (Binford and Ho, 1986; Binford and Stone, 1986). Charcoal, burned bone fragments, and ash accumulations that formed hearths show that *Homo erectus* used fire (Binford and Stone, 1986, claim that the people were not using fire).

About 100,000 stone implements come from Zhoukoudien, most of them made on flakes of rough-vein quartz. The people made choppers and scrapers, awls, crude points, and many multipurpose artifacts (Figure 5.3). The toolkit evolved through the 200,000 years of occupation, with the earliest artifacts tending to be larger, and made with simple percussion techniques. As time went on, the toolmakers turned to the bipolar technique and produced smaller implements, many of them made of finer raw materials.

Back in 1944, the Harvard archaeologist Hallam Movius studied the major Paleolithic sites of China and southeast Asia. He claimed that similar simple forms of choppers and chopping tools were used over enormous areas of south and southeast Asia, and the Far East during the Lower and Middle Pleistocene. He called this a "chopper-chopping tool complex," something quite different from the hand axes and flake tools so widely used by *Homo erectus* in Africa, Europe, and the Near East. The notion of this complex lingers on today, but most Asian archaeologists believe that Movius probably exaggerated the differences between east and west, despite the extreme rarity of hand axes in Asia. In fact, there may have been a broad continuum of stone technology and basic material culture throughout the world of *Homo erectus*. But within this contin-

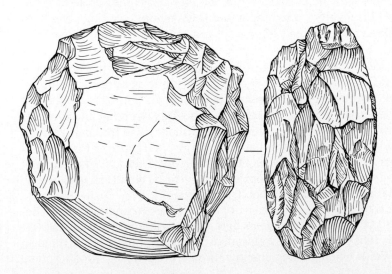

FIGURE 5.3 A crude chopping tool from Zhoukoudien, China. Front and side views (one-half actual size).

uum, there were innumerable local variations in both adaptation and culture, reflected only partially by the stone tools that have come down to us. It is probable that different *Homo erectus* bands throughout the Old World had ecological adaptations and social and cultural specializations that varied far more than their surviving artifacts suggest (Gowlett, 1986; Isaac, 1978). Furthermore, there was considerable but often inconspicuous cultural evolution during the long period when *Homo erectus* flourished in Africa, Europe, and Asia.

We still know little of the world of *Homo erectus*, beyond a certainty that humans had radiated far from their tropical homeland in Africa. By 700,000 years ago, *Homo erectus* had settled in temperate Europe and the Near East, was probably living in India, and was certainly present in southeast Asia and China. Human beings had now adapted to a far wider range of environments than ever before, where fire and efficient shelter were essential to survive dramatic contrasts in summer and winter climates. As far as is known, however, *Homo erectus* did not settle in extreme arctic latitudes, in what is now the USSR and Siberia. Nor did they develop the watercraft needed to cross from island southeast Asia to Australia, a landmass that remained isolated by the ocean throughout the Ice Age.

The Settlement of Temperate Latitudes

We must think of the first human settlement of temperate latitudes as part of a broader set of ecological processes, one of them the simultaneous radiation of modern grazing animals and new vegetational communities into Europe and other northern latitudes of the Old World. Humans were part of this vast animal community. Their long-term success resulted from their ability to adapt to the cyclical changes in the Ice Age environment, from temperate to much colder, then to full glacial conditions and an abrupt deglaciation as the climate warmed up again rapidly. The geologist Karl Butzer (1982) believes that these early human populations flourished in regions where dense, abundant, and predictable resources were to be found, isolated from other regions where similar conditions existed. The climatic changes of the Ice Age sometimes brought these isolated populations together, then separated them again, ensuring gene flow and genetic drift, and continued biological and cultural evolution, over the millennia.

The British prehistorian Clive Gamble (1986b) argues that the first settlement of temperate latitudes was not simply a case of an opportunistic species seizing a set of favorable environmental circumstances. He believes that by 730,000 years ago hominids had mastered the necessary hunting and foraging strategies to survive in much more diverse environments than tropical savanna. Most regions of the temperate world had the energy and resources for hominid settlement even when *Homo habilis* flourished. But *Homo habilis* had not evolved the long-term solutions for coping with cyclical climatic change and all the resource changes that resulted from it.

Gamble points out that most evidence for Middle Pleistocene settlement, between about 730,000 and 130,000 years ago, falls in periods when the climate was colder than today but not fully glacial, as it has been for most of the past 700,000 years, times when grazing animals formed the principal food resource in cooler latitudes. Plant and marine foods were much more costly to exploit and often sparse. The successful colonists of northern latitudes were those hominids who could exploit game animals distributed unevenly, at times very densely, over the landscape.

That is not to say, of course, that the hominids lived by hunting alone. They had to cope with long, sparse winter months, when their prey dispersed so widely that it was beyond human capacity to hunt them effectively. Gamble hypothesizes that the people searched for frozen animal carcasses, a winter strategy that was adaptive for highly mobile predators like humans. They had one advantage over other predators — their technology of sticks and wooden probes that could be used to unearth food buried in ice fissures or snowdrifts. This would have been a lower risk strategy if a large group worked together, searching for the predictable refrigerated carcasses of large animals that died during the winter months.

During the spring and summer the people would concentrate on hunting migratory game, eating their kills quickly, and stripping them of meat before other predators moved in. Both winter and summer lifeways of this type required compact territories, where the people remained highly mobile year-round. We can thus expect to find Middle Pleistocene sites clustered in regions with large areas of uninhabited country between them. Gamble points out that many known sites are near lakes and streams, perhaps the places where the bands most commonly hunted or scavenged meat, also where wood might have been found for tools and for the fires used to thaw frozen meat. The key to this entire adaptation was mobility; the bands could respond quickly to changes in resource distribution by moving into new areas. Gamble believes this was a primarily opportunistic adaptation based on knowledge of resource distribution rather than the result of deliberate planning. "Survival," he writes, using the Butzer model, "took place during the long acts in the regional theatres rather than among the attractions of the crush bars in the intervals" (1986b).

THE TECHNOLOGY OF *HOMO ERECTUS*

Oldowan technology was simple and opportunistic, and developed slowly over more than a million years ago. There is good reason to believe that the same primeval toolmaking survived long after *Homo habilis* had vanished, as an integral part of later toolmaking traditions. We can be fairly certain, too, that Oldowan stoneworking methods formed part of the legacy of the first hominids to later prehistory.

Neither *Homo habilis* nor *Homo erectus* relied exclusively on stone, for we can say with confidence that our remote ancestors also made use of wood, one of the most versatile raw materials known to humanity. Unfortunately, timber rarely survives in the archaeological record. The earliest known wooden artifacts consist of a wooden spear tip (or possible snow probe) from Clacton in eastern England, dating to about 200,000 years ago (Figure 5.4), and a 150,000-year-old wooden spear from Lehringen in Germany. Most insights into the technology of *Homo erectus* come from stone tools and the by-products associated with them.

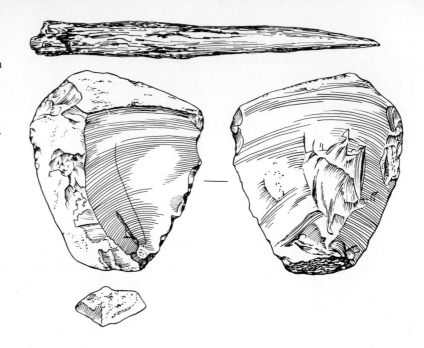

FIGURE 5.4 European wood and stone tools. At top, a wooden spear tip (perhaps a snow probe) from Clacton, England, dating to about 200,000 years ago (approximately one-eighth full size). Below, views of a flake from the same location. The upper surface is shown at left, the flake (lower) surface on the right. The striking platform is at the base (one-third actual size).

Both Oldowan technology and the artifacts fashioned by *Homo erectus* remained in use in various forms for immensely long periods of time. Oldowan stoneworking lasted for as much as a million years, its more diverse successor for nearly half as long again. There is a tendency to think of both technologies as monolithic, unchanging chronicles of human prehistory, fixed stages in human cultural evolution, partly because of the time scales involved and also because stone tools appear to have changed so little over hundreds of thousands of years. In fact, the technology of *Homo erectus*, like that of *Homo habilis*, displays considerable variability and development.

HOMINID SPECIES AND STONE TOOLS

The cladistic theory of human evolution highlights a basic phenomenon of early prehistory: the human artifacts of the Pleistocene are patterned in space and time in a general way that mirrors the pattern for early hominids. The earliest Oldowan stone artifacts appear at the same time as the genus *Homo*, while bifacially worked hand axes become commonplace as *Homo erectus* emerges in Africa. Later, the world divides into two broad technological provinces, a western with hand axes and an Asian without (wooden artifacts appear to have been in use in Asia for hundreds of thousands of years). The end of the Middle Pleistocene brought local changes throughout the Old World, technological changes like the Levallois and disk core techniques of stone tool manufacture that are found in Europe and Africa. Everywhere except tropical Africa, the technological continuity is striking, with hand axes being used by Mousterians in Europe and chopping tools lasting until late in prehistory in Asia. In Africa, however, the hand ax tradition gave way to the so-called Middle Stone Age over 150,000 years ago. This characteristic technology, with its scrapers and crude projectile points, was made for the most part on simple flakes. But in some places, people were making parallel-sided blades, which they fashioned into simple tools as early as 70,000 years ago. Everywhere else in the Old World, in Europe and Asia, blade technology appeared suddenly and abruptly between 40,000 and 25,000 years ago. The new technology was far more varied and specialized than anything ever used before.

What do these technological developments mean in evolutionary terms? Robert Foley believes they tell us something useful about the patterns and processes of human evolution. He has developed a cladogram that combines stages of hominid evolution and stone tool technologies associated with them (Figure 5.5). He argues that toolmaking was an ancestral trait of African hominoids,

FIGURE 5.5 A cladogram of human evolution that emphasizes the divergence of human taxa and associates stone tool technology with each taxon. Robert Foley uses this diagram to infer the origin of each at the branching points of the different lines. (Foley, 1987)

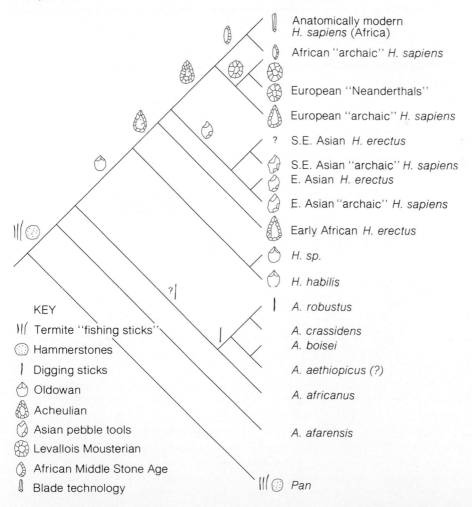

witness the penchant of chimpanzees for using sticks to fish for termites (Figure 4.14). Stone tool manufacture, a trait unique to *Homo*, appeared about 2.3 million years ago. (That is not to say that bone and wooden artifacts were not in use earlier, but they are not preserved in the archaeological record.) We have already mentioned that hand axes are associated with the emergence of *Homo erectus* in Africa, but the developments that occurred later are far more significant — local divergence of both human and artifact forms. What may have happened, Foley believes, was an ever greater anatomical and technological divergence, as outlying populations became more isolated from their remote African ancestors (Figure 5.6). In other words, stone tools developed in the same way as the morphological traits of human fossils. In the Lower and Middle Pleistocene they changed very slowly. The "archaic world," as Foley calls it, ended with the emergence of modern humans in Africa. From there *Homo sapiens* and a radically new technology dispersed throughout the Old World and eventually into the Americas (Figure 5.7). As Foley puts it, "One species, one technology."

This model is only provisional, formed from very basic data. But, at a general level, it fits well with what we know about early human fossils, technology, and molecular biology. Foley also believes that his model shows that earlier humans

FIGURE 5.6 The expansion of *Homo erectus* from sub-Saharan Africa. As *Homo erectus* colonized Asia and Europe, they diverged biologically (Foley, 1987). In Europe, the tradition of making hand axes persisted, while it was lost in Asia.

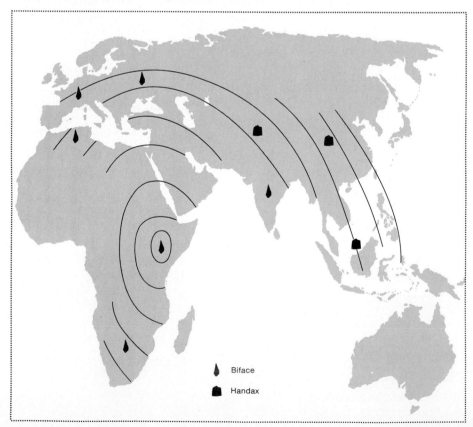

Biface

Handax

The First Humans

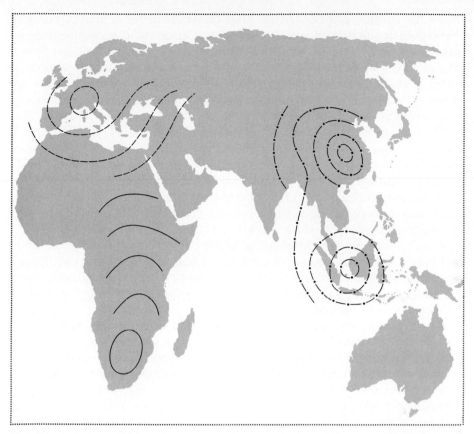

FIGURE 5.7 Robert Foley's view of the end of the archaic world about 130,000 years ago, when the descendants of African *Homo erectus* had diverged to form local centers for later human evolution. Foley identifies three populations: (1) Sub-Saharan Africa, the ancestors of modern humans; (2) Europe, the Mediterranean Basin, and central Asia, the Neanderthals, Mousterian, and related cultures; and (3) East Asia, archaic hominids with chopper or chopping tool cultures. This is probably a gross simplification of a very complex situation. (Foley, 1987)

behaved in very different ways from anatomically modern *Homo sapiens*. They may have used technology in far more limited ways, so the resulting artifacts show only the most constrained variability. Their technology may only have changed in response to geographic isolation, local raw material availability, and ecological needs. Perhaps the behavior of these earlier hominids was much more fixed and stereotyped than that of their descendants. The future direction of research into Foley's archaic world will involve theoretical models that take into account cladistic and other approaches to human evolution.

HAND AXES AND OTHER TOOLS

In Africa, Europe, and some parts of Asia, *Homo erectus* is associated with a distinctive toolkit that includes not only a variety of flake tools and sometimes choppers but bifacially flaked hand axes. These hand ax industries are grouped under the cultural label *Acheulian,* after the town of St. Acheul in northern France, where many such artifacts have been found. Hand axes come in many sizes and shapes; they are sometimes artifacts of great refinement and beauty (Figure 5.8), so much so that people ignore all the other tools *Homo erectus* made. In fact, human technology between 1.5 million and 150,000 years ago shows considerable diversity, probably associated with local adaptations and the availability of suitable raw materials.

The hand ax is one of the most common exhibits in the world's museums. It has been found over a vast area of the Old World, in all shapes and sizes, from crude tear-shaped forms, to ovals, tongue-shaped axes, and occasional finely pointed specimens that were evidently made with considerable care. Unlike the crude scrapers and choppers of the Oldowan, the Acheulian hand ax was an artifact with converging edges, which met at a point. The maker had to envisage the shape of the artifact, which was to be produced from a mere lump of stone, then fashion it not with opportunistic blows but with carefully directed hammer blows. Acheulian hand axes come in every size, from elegant oval types a few inches long to heavy axes more than a foot (0.3 m) long and weighing 5 pounds (2.3 k) or more. They must have been a versatile, thoroughly practical artifact to have continued in use so long.

What exactly were hand axes used for? Almost certainly they were held in the hand rather than being hafted on the end of a wooden shaft. They were simply too cumbersome, and, in any case, hafted tools probably did not come into use until much later. Conventional wisdom has it that they were multipurpose artifacts, used for grubbing up roots, working wood, scraping skins, and especially skinning and butchering large and small game. There is no question that they were highly effective butchery tools. Many archaeologists have tried not only cutting up antelope carcasses but also slicing through hippopotamus and elephant hide — with great success. In some ways, the hand ax was ideal for this purpose, because it could be sharpened again and again, and when it became a useless lump of stone, it could be recycled into flake tools. But you can achieve effective butchery with simple flakes as well, and a number of researchers have wondered whether the hand ax, which took longer to make, was not used for other purposes.

FIGURE 5.8 Acheulian technology. Hand axes were multipurpose artifacts that were shaped symmetrically around a long axis. As the hand ax from Kilombe, Kenya, of 700,000 years ago (top) shows, the stoneworker would sometimes use a minimum of blows to achieve the desired shape. Simple hammerstones were used to make many early hand axes and blanks for far more finished productions. Sometimes a bone hammer served to strike off the shallow flakes that adorn the margins of these tools (middle).

Later hand axes assume many forms, among them the finely pointed shape (bottom). Cleavers are thought to have been butchering tools, artifacts with a single, unfinished edge that has proved effective in modern experiments for skinning and dismembering game. As time went on, the stoneworkers used carefully prepared cores to fashion large flakes that served as blanks for axes and other artifacts. They also produced flakes that were used as opportunistic artifacts, for woodworking, and for many other purposes (see Figure 5.4).

Hand ax from Kilombe, Kenya, showing minimal flaking used to produce ax shape.

Using an animal bone to make a hand ax.

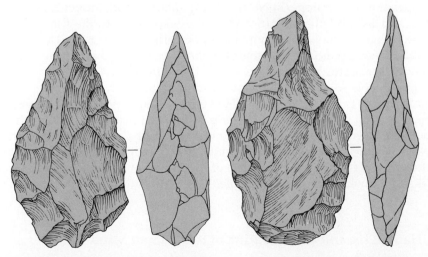

Two early hand axes from Bed II, Olduvai Gorge, Tanzania. Front and side views (three-quarters actual size).

Eileen O'Brien (1984) has argued that the hand ax was in fact a form of primitive discus. She points out that hand axes are most common on sites near watercourses and other places where big game customarily gathered, whereas they are much less common on sites away from such areas. Could they have been projectiles? O'Brien obtained a weighted fiberglass cast of a Kenyan hand ax that was nearly a foot (0.3 m) long and weighed 4 pounds, 3 ounces (2.6 kg). An expert discus thrower picked up the hand ax, held it by the butt, and put the point along his forearm. Then he hurled it again and again in an overarm, sidearm action. The hand ax spun horizontally, then suddenly changed its orientation in midair and early always fell to the ground on its edge or point. The average throw carried almost 100 feet (30.5 m), with an accuracy of about 2 yards (1.8 m) left or right of the throw line. Could the hand ax, with its streamlined shape, have been a far more effective projectile than the cores and stones that were the only weapons the first hominids had to protect themselves against predators and other enemies? Their only other — suicidal — alternative was hand-to-hand combat with the adversary. But with the discuslike hand ax, one could hunt big game from a relatively safe distance with lethal accuracy and defend oneself with drastically enhanced efficiency. Is it a coincidence that big-game hunting became a significant human activity just as *Homo erectus* developed a new tool that perhaps could be thrown? The thought is a tantalizing but highly controversial one.

In contrast to the earlier Oldowan, the Lower Paleolithic technology of *Homo erectus* varied greatly throughout its duration, reaching considerable heights of delicate artistry (Figure 5.9). In addition to hand axes, the new technology resulted in scrapers and other artifacts for woodworking, skinning, and other purposes. But hand axes remain the most characteristic artifact of many *Homo erectus* populations.

Acheulian culture 1,000,000 to 60,000 B.P.

Hand axes have been found over an enormous area of the Old World (Figure 5.10). Fine specimens are scattered in the gravels of the Somme and Thames rivers in northern Europe, in North African quarries and ancient Saharan lake beds, and in sub-Saharan Africa from the Nile Valley to the Cape of Good Hope. Acheulian tools are common in some parts of India, as well as in Arabia and the Near East as far as the southern shores of the Caspian Sea and perhaps even farther north. They are rare east of the Rhine and in the Far East, where chopping tools were commonly used until comparatively recent times (Butzer and Isaac, 1975; J. D. Clark, 1970; Howell and Clark, 1963). No one has been able to explain why hand axes have this restricted distribution. Were such multipurpose tools used only in big-game hunting camps? Was their use restricted by the availability of flint and other suitable raw materials? Did environmental conditions affect the hunters' choice of toolkits? Or were they used as projectiles in areas where big game abounded? We do not know.

Hand Axes and the Evolution of the Human Mind

While we recognize that *Homo erectus* made a wide variety of artifacts, the fact remains that the Acheulian hand ax is the most characteristic, and one of the most widely distributed tools made between 1.5 million and 150,000 years

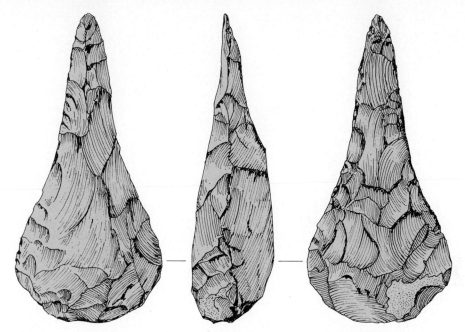

Acheulian hand ax from Swanscombe, England (one-third actual size).

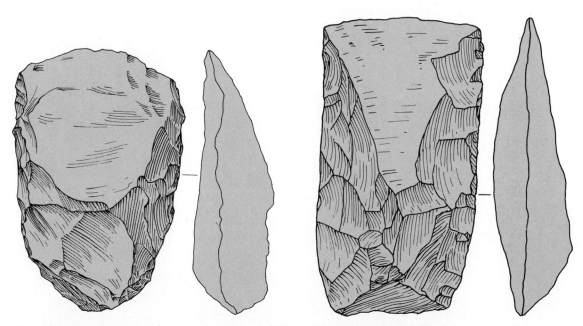

Two Acheulian cleavers, from Baia Farta, Angola (left) and Kalambo Falls, Zambia (right) (both one-half actual size).

FIGURE 5.9 Hand ax technology.

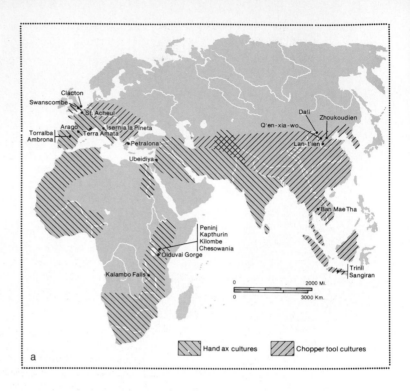

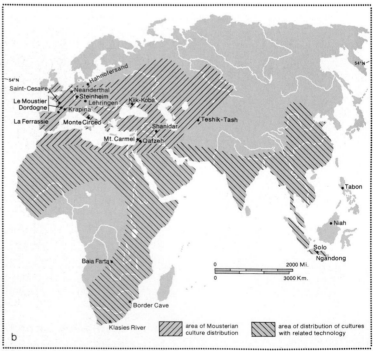

FIGURE 5.10 (a) Distribution of Lower Paleolithic hand axes and other stone tools, also showing location of sites mentioned in the first half of this chapter. (b) Distribution of Middle Paleolithic cultures, with locations of sites mentioned in text.

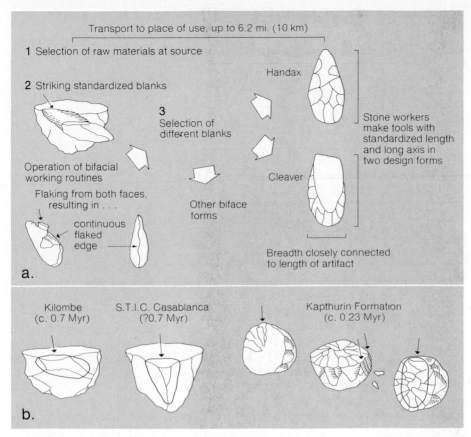

FIGURE 5.11 Making Acheulian bifaces. (a) The complex process used about a million years ago. (b) Early and late methods. The simple flaking process of 700,000 years ago (top) used in East and North Africa, compares with the expertise of the stoneworkers at Kapthurin, Kenya, 230,000 years ago (bottom). They prepared elaborately shaped cores to create flakes about 6 inches (16 cm) long as hand ax blanks. (After Foley, 1984b)

ago. It also provides us with an opportunity to consider the relationship between an artifact and the evolution of the mind.

John Gowlett (1984, 1986), who has thought profoundly about the relationship between early human technology and the evolution of the mind, believes that manufacture of the hand ax and the remainder of *Homo erectus's* toolkit, was the combination of a series of ideas, some derived from previous stoneworking experience, others from elsewhere, perhaps from observation of the environment or from woodworking. We do not know where hand axes first evolved. It is reasonable to assume that the technology began in Africa, where *Homo erectus* developed and where the earliest sites with such artifacts are found. Gowlett believes that a discoidlike artifact, a cobble flaked bifacially on all sides, was the general prototype for the hand ax. Discoids occur in Olduvai Beds I and II and at other early sites, like Peninj in Kenya and perhaps in East Turkana. Elongate these discoids and make them on large flakes, and you are approaching the shape of the hand ax, an artifact based on a design that stressed symmetry around the long axis.

Hand axes have a well-defined long axis, are bifacially flaked from the edge, usually all around, and tend to be symmetrical. They were the logical end result of long-used stone technology, made to a degree of standardization unimaginable in earlier times. Gowlett (1978) has studied the hand axes from Kilombe, Kenya, a site that dates to over 700,000 years ago. He found a very high statistical correlation between length, breadth, and thickness, standardization within a length of 3.14 to 9.40 inches (8–24 cm), which implies a well-defined mental image of the ideal end product shared by more than one person (Figure 5.11). "The artifacts which we see, and can measure, were present in the mind," he writes. *Homo erectus* had a geometrically accurate sense of proportion, which they imposed accurately on stone. Gowlett (1984) believes that this technology formed part of the fundamental preconditions for the much later development of art and mathematics.

Kilombe
700,000 B.P.

Acheulian technology was far from static. Another East African site, Kapthurin, near Kenya's Lake Baringo, contains hundreds of late Acheulian hand axes dating to about 230,000 years ago. The stoneworkers there used elaborately prepared cores, fashioned with perhaps forty or more strokes, as the blanks for a single large flake, a dramatic contrast to the three or four flakes removed in earlier millennia (Figure 5.11). The large flake that resulted was then bifacially flaked into an elegant, versatile hand ax in a wide variety of useful shapes.

Kapthurin
230,000 B.P.

Gowlett and others believe that the problem-solving abilities needed to fashion Acheulian artifacts of all types were much more complex than has sometimes been assumed. One suspects that *Homo erectus* was capable of implementing elaborate hunting and foraging strategies and engaging in social interactions that were a quantum jump beyond those of much more apelike *Homo habilis*.

TORRALBA AND TERRA AMATA

Without question, *Homo erectus* hunted and foraged for food, probably in far more effective ways than *Homo habilis*. Time and time again, hand axes and other butchering artifacts have been found in association with the bones of large game animals, which they were used to butcher. No one doubts that *Homo erectus* butchered such animals. But did the hunters actually kill such formidable herbivores as the elephant and rhinoceros? To do so would require social mechanisms to foster cooperation and communication abilities far beyond those of *Homo habilis*.

Evidence for butchery, and perhaps big-game hunting, comes from two remarkable Acheulian sites, at Torralba and Ambrona, northeast of Madrid in Spain (Gamble, 1986b; Howell, 1966). The Acheulians probably lived in this deep, swampy valley either 200,000 or 400,000 years ago (the date is disputed). Torralba yielded most of the left side of a large elephant that had been cut into small pieces, while Ambrona contained the remains of thirty to thirty-five dismembered elephants. Concentrations of broken food bones were found all over the site, and the skulls of the elephants had been broken open to get at the brains. In one place, the elephant bones had been laid in a line, perhaps to form

Torralba 400,000 or
200,000 B.P.

stepping stones in the swamp where the elephants had been dispatched (Figure 5.12). Both kill sites were littered with crude hand axes, cleavers, scrapers, and cutting tools.

The elephant bones at both sites were buried in clays that were once treacherous marsh. The original scenario for the sites had hunters watching the valley floors where the elephants roamed. At a strategic moment several bands would gather quietly, set brushfires, and drive the unsuspecting beasts into the swamps, where they could be killed and butchered at leisure. Karl Butzer (1982) argues that Torralba and Ambrona were on important game trails between summer and winter grazing areas. The hunters thus preyed on migrating elephants each spring and fall (Figure 5.13), dispersing into smaller groups during the other seasons. Other archaeologists believe that the elephant bone clusters are the result of natural phenomena, such as water action (Gamble, 1986b; Shipman and Rose, 1983), or that the hunters were actually scavenging meat from animals that perished when enmired.

Gathering wild vegetable foods such as nuts, berries, and seeds was undoubtedly important, although next to no evidence of this activity survives in

FIGURE 5.12 From Torralba, Spain, a remarkable linear arrangement of elephant tusks and leg bones that were probably laid out by those who butchered the animals.

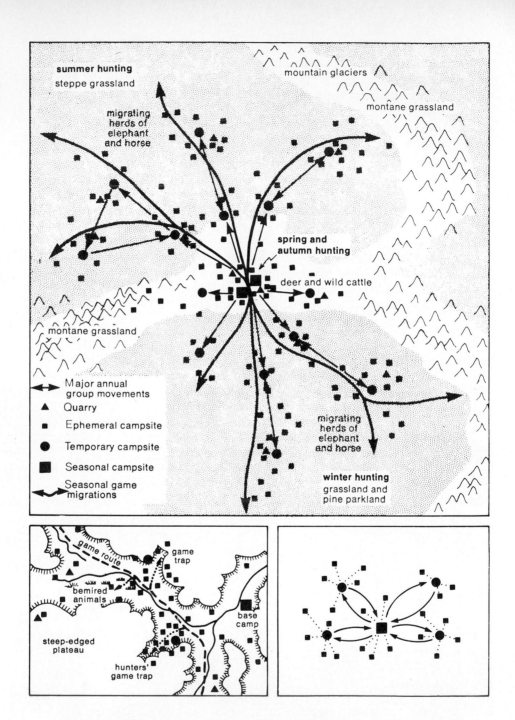

FIGURE 5.13 Reconstructed model for seasonal movement by Acheulian hunters at Torralba-Ambrona, Spain. (a) Interception of migrating animals in spring and fall. (b) Use of topography to secure game. (c) Schematic model of how the populations moved. The reconstructions were made using information recovered from excavations. (Butzer, 1982)

archaeological sites. Within their territory the hunters knew the habits of every animal and the characteristics of many edible vegetable foods and medicinal plants; they were familiar with the inconspicuous landmarks and strategic features. From sites like Terra Amata near Nice in France, we knew that they returned to the same locality year after year at favored seasons in search of specific foods.

Terra Amata was excavated by Henry de Lumley; it was occupied some 300,000 years ago (de Lumley, 1969). De Lumley excavated what he thought were a series of oval huts that consisted of shallow hollows 26 to 50 feet (8 to 15 m) long and 13 to 20 feet (4 to 6 m) wide, with an entrance at one end (Figure 5.14). When he cleared the hollows, he uncovered a series of posts approximately 3 inches (7 cm) in diameter that had once formed the walls. The bases of the posts were reinforced with lines of stones. The roofs were supported by center posts, and some huts had a hearth in the center. The excavators recovered the bones of wild oxen, stags, and elephants, as well as those of small rodents. There were even imprints of skins once laid on the floors. De Lumley records that the inhabitants never cleaned out their huts. They lived among butchered bones, discarded stone tools, even their own feces. The feces yielded numerous fragments of nuts and seeds that had flourished in the late spring and early summer. De Lumley concluded that Terra Amata was a seasonal camp, occupied by a band of hunter-gatherers who returned to the same locale year after year in search of vegetable foods and shellfish, another common find at the site.

Paola Villa (1983) threw serious doubt on this original interpretation when she tried refitting flakes from the site to one another, in order to reconstruct

Terra Amata
300,000 B.P.

FIGURE 5.14 Henry de Lumley's controversial reconstruction of a hut at Terra Amata, France.

stoneworking activity there. Over 40 percent of the refitted flakes came from different levels, implying that many specimens had been displaced vertically some 8 inches (21 cm). She believes that undetected natural phenomena such as soil creep, ice action, animal burrowing, even earthworm tunneling, transformed Terra Amata after its abandonment — to the point that de Lumley's houses of reeds and brush may not actually have existed. Terra Amata and many other sites of this age may have been disturbed so extensively since they were occupied that our interpretations of them will always be somewhat suspect.

Improvements in language and modes of communication are thought to have been a distinctive feature of *Homo erectus*'s style of life. With enhanced language skills and more advanced technology, it became possible for people to achieve better cooperation in gathering activities, in storage of food supplies, and in the chase. Unlike the nonhuman primates, who strongly emphasize individual economic success, Middle Pleistocene hunter-gatherers depended on cooperative activity by every individual in the band. The economic unit was the group; the secret of individual success was group success.Perhaps individual ownership of property was unimportant, since neither individuals nor groups as a whole had tangible possessions of significance. People got along well as individuals, as families, and as entire groups. The hunter-gatherers who followed *Homo erectus* did not necessarily inherit this advantage.

THE ORIGIN OF *HOMO SAPIENS*

When and where did *Homo sapiens sapiens,* modern humans, originate? This question remains one of the great controversies of world prehistory. Most people now believe that *Homo erectus* evolved into *Homo sapiens,* but there are few fossil remains from anywhere to document this vital transition. Except for a small overall increase in brain size, *Homo erectus* remained remarkably stable in evolutionary terms for more than a million years, until less than 500,000 years ago. We do not even know when the gradual transition began, or how it took place. Some researchers believe it began as early as 400,000 years ago, others much later, some time around or after 200,000 years ago.

Continuity or Replacement?

Over generations of debate, two major hypotheses have developed to explain the emergence of modern humans:

- The so-called candelabra model hypothesizes that *Homo erectus* populations throughout the Old World evolved independently, first to archaic *Homo sapiens,* then to fully modern humans. This continuity model, sometimes also called the Neanderthal phase hypothesis, argues for multiple origins of *Homo sapiens* and no migrations. Thus, according to it, modern geographic populations have been separated from one another for a long time, perhaps as long as a million years.

- The Noah's ark model takes the diametrically opposite view. According to it, *Homo sapiens* evolved in one place, then spread to all other parts of the Old World. This replacement model implies that modern geographic populations have shallow roots and were derived from a single source of relatively recent times.

These two models represent extremes, which pit advocates of anatomical continuity against those who favor rapid replacement of primeval populations. Until fairly recently, most anthropologists strongly favored the candelabra model. They did so because finds from western Europe and the Near East dominated academic discussion, largely because the largest numbers of fossils came from these areas. Furthermore, many deep, well-excavated caves and rock shelters appeared to document technological change from simple, relatively unsophisticated toolkits to the much more elaborate artifacts characteristic of *Homo sapiens.*

A torrent of new discoveries has turned our conception of Europe from one of the cradles of modern humans into somewhat of a backwater. The candelabra hypothesis was based in part on two famous 200,000- to 300,000-year-old European fossil skulls, from Swanscombe in England and Steinheim in Germany, thought to represent "Pre-sapiens" humans with larger brains and other modern features (Figure 5.15) (Ovey, 1964; Roe, 1981). Today more sophisticated cranial analysis has shown that both skulls display many archaic features, which are shared by newer European finds, among them the Petralona skull from Greece (400,000 to 300,000 years ago) and the Arago skull and jaws from the French Pyrenees (about 200,000 years ago). These finds appear to represent not Pre-sapiens populations but a very heterogeneous group of humans whose descendants were the Neanderthals of the last interglacial and Weichsel glaciation.

Petralona **400,000 to 300,000 B.P.**

Arago **200,000 B.P.**

Apart from the fossil evidence, basic principles of evolutionary biology make it appear unlikely that populations of *Homo sapiens* were living in central and western Europe for 200,000 years so isolated from one another that two different lineages could form.

Another important group of finds lent support to the candelabra model. These were the highly variable fossil populations found in the Mt. Carmel Caves in what is now Israel just before World War II (Garrod and Bate, 1937) — Neanderthals displaying startling anatomical variation compared with their European contemporaries.

Mt. Carmel **50,000 B.P. and earlier**

Was the Near East a cradle of *Homo sapiens*? Many new discoveries from southwest Asia and from sites like Qafzeh in Israel have confirmed that Near Eastern populations were very heterogeneous between 100,000 and 40,000 years ago. However, there is a considerable morphological gap between more archaic, and only slightly older, fossils and those displaying more modern features, such as reduced brow ridges, more rounded crania, and larger limbs. Eric Trinkhaus (1987) and other experts believe that the differences between these individuals make local evolution of *Homo sapiens* from Neanderthals unlikely.

Qafzeh **50,000 B.P. and earlier**

Such an evolution would require an adequate amount of time for anatomical change to take place. This time frame does not appear to exist in Europe, for re-

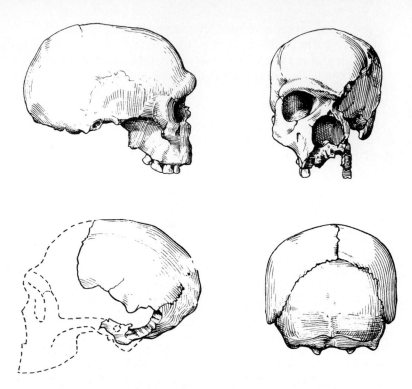

FIGURE 5.15 Steinheim (top) and Swanscombe (bottom) skulls (one-fourth actual size). The Swanscombe skull is shown with a tentative reconstruction of the missing parts.

Considerable controversy surrounds the classification of these and other European human fossils dating from about 300,000 to 120,000 years ago. Are they *Homo erectus* or archaic *Homo sapiens*? Chris Stringer and other paleoanthropologists have suggested that specimens like these, and other well-known finds, such as the Petralona skull from Greece and the Arago specimens from France, be placed in "grades" of *Homo sapiens*. Under this scheme, Steinheim and Swanscombe would be in *Homo sapiens* Grade 1, modern *Homo sapiens* being in Grade 3 or 4, depending on the scheme. This system is coming into widespread use as a convenient way of classifying Middle Pleistocene human fossils. It does not necessarily imply any evolutionary relationship between different grades (for full discussion, see Stringer et al., 1979).

Hahnofersand
Saint-Cesaire
**36,000 to
31,000 B.P.**

cent finds of Neanderthallike individuals from Hahnofersand near Hamburg, Germany, and Saint-Cesaire in the Charente (France) date to as late as 36,000 to 31,000 years ago. Anatomically modern humans were living in western Europe by this time. Very likely there was a period of coexistence and probably hybridization between the Neanderthals and the modern populations at about this time, when the latter had already replaced Neanderthals in the Near East.

Everything points not to anatomical continuity in Europe and the Near East but to replacement of primeval populations by *Homo sapiens*. Furthermore, Near Eastern excavations make it certain that *Homo sapiens* populations were living there as early as 45,000 years ago, earlier than they were in Europe. This may indeed have been the area from which modern people — perhaps we can call them *proto-Cro-Magnons* — spread into the north and replaced the Neanderthals some time later. The Noah's ark model, then, seems to fit the available evidence better. But the central question remains unanswered. Where did the proto-Cro-Magnons come from? We know from distributions of Neanderthal finds that there were contacts and gene flow with North Africa. Might tropical Africa have been the ancestral homeland of modern human beings?

Homo sapiens in Africa

Africa may have been the cradle of humankind, but for years it was regarded as a backwater in later prehistory, a place where modern humans arose very much later than they did in Europe. This long-held view coincided with what was known of late Stone Age archaeology in tropical Africa, where cultural innovations such as blade technology and art were thought to have appeared very late (J. D. Clark, 1970), arriving with *Homo sapiens* from the north. These ideas were formulated before radiocarbon chronologies and were based on a mere handful of fossil finds, among them the famous robust Broken Hill skull from Zambia, an archaic-looking cranium that seemed to epitomize a backward continent.

A new generation of research based on radiocarbon dates and sophisticated cave excavation has painted a radically different picture of African life after 200,000 years ago. We now know that Acheulian hand ax technology gave way to "Middle Stone Age" culture, with its more sophisticated flake tools and much more versatile toolkit, between 200,000 and 130,000 years ago in both east and southern Africa. The excavators of the Klasies River Mouth Caves in southeast Africa were able to correlate Middle Stone Age occupation with deep sea cores and date it to between 120,000 and 70,000 years ago. Numerous fragmentary human remains dating to between 125,000 and 95,000 years ago came from the Middle Stone Age levels, remains that displayed astoundingly modern features at a date far earlier than anything from the Near East or Europe (Singer and Wymer, 1982).

Klasies River
**120,000 to
70,000 B.P.**

Nor are the Klasies River finds unique. Border Cave, also in southern Africa, has yielded anatomically modern human remains dating to between 115,000 and 90,000 years ago (Beaumont, 1980). There are also scattered finds from East Africa (for a review, see Brauwer, 1984).

Border Cave
**115,000 to
90,000 B.P.**

Günter Brauwer (1984) believes he can identify at least three "grades" of *Homo sapiens* in sub-Saharan Africa. An "early archaic *Homo sapiens*" form was widely distributed from southern to northeast Africa some 200,000 years ago. These archaic populations had evolved from earlier *Homo erectus* populations and had larger cranial vaults and many other anatomical features akin to those of anatomically modern humans. The Broken Hill skull from Zambia belongs in this group. Brauwer's second group — "late archaic *Homo sapiens*" — includes fossils with mosaics of both archaic and modern features, with the latter tending to predominate. These specimens date to 100,000 years ago and earlier. His last group are anatomically modern individuals, with only a very few archaic features.

Brauwer believes that very early anatomically modern *Homo sapiens* was widely distributed in east and southern Africa as far back as the early Upper

Pleistocene, some 115,000 years ago, perhaps even earlier (see also Rightmire, 1984). He also believes that the developments that led to the emergence of *Homo sapiens* in east and southern Africa had run their course as early as between 100,000 and 70,000 years ago, far earlier than any equivalent developments in Europe or the Near East. At this time, the evolution of the classic and late Neanderthals had run its course in those areas.

In evolutionary terms, the transition from *Homo erectus* to archaic *Homo sapiens* seems to have occurred not quickly but relatively slowly and continuously. It is difficult to draw a line between the two species. In contrast, the "modernization" of the human skull into its present configuration took place considerably faster, some time at the very end of the Middle Pleistocene or the beginning of the Upper Pleistocene, by 100,000 years ago.

Molecular Biology and *Homo sapiens*

Molecular biology has played a significant role in dating earlier human evolution and is now yielding important clues as to the origins of *Homo sapiens* (Cann et al., 1987). Researchers have zeroed in on mitochondrial DNA (mtDNA), a useful tool for calibrating mutation rates because it accumulates mutations much faster than nuclear DNA. Mitochondrial DNA is inherited only through the maternal line; it does not mix and become diluted with paternal DNA. Thus, it provides a potentially reliable link with ancestral populations. When genetic researchers analyzed the mtDNA of 147 women from Africa, Asia, Europe, Australia, and New Guinea, they found that the differences among them were very small. Thus, they argued, the five populations were all of comparatively recent origin. But there were some differences, sufficient to separate out two groups within the sample — a set of African individuals and another comprising individuals from all groups. The biologists concluded that all modern humans derive from a 200,000-year-old African population, from which populations migrated to the rest of the Old World with little or no interbreeding with existing, more archaic human groups. While the mtDNA research tends to confirm what we know from archaeological evidence, it should be stressed that the results are highly provisional and the methodology still in its infancy. If one does accept the molecular chronology, how can the 200,000 year date be reconciled with that of about 100,000 derived from fossil evidence? The relationship between the genetic origin of the species and its manifestation in new anatomy remains a conundrum.

Ecology and *Homo sapiens*

For generations, anthropologists have tended to treat the origin of *Homo sapiens* as a unique event that took place outside the processes of evolutionary biology. The molecular research reminds us that this was not so. As Robert Foley (1984c) argues, one can only understand this event within a comparative ecological framework. Foley points out that modern humans were most likely to have originated within a single location. The savanna woodland of Africa around 100,000 years ago was an ideal environment for promoting the speciation of modern humans, he believes. Foley has studied monkey evolution in Africa and found that the widely dispersed populations had diverged; they did not continue on a single evolutionary course. Africa experienced considerable habitat fragmentation and re-formation during the alternating cold and warmth of the Pleistocene, fluctuations that enhanced the prospects of speciation among the continent's animals and plants. For example, Foley found that one monkey genus alone radiated into sixteen species at about the same time that modern humans may have evolved on the continent. These environmental shifts cannot have been too rapid or too severe, or the indigenous populations would have moved away or become extinct. The tropical environments of Africa consisted of a constant mosaic of changing environmental patterns, a mosaic which tended to foster local evolution. This contrasted with higher latitudes, where environmental changes were more marked and animal distributions changed significantly and rapidly over short periods of time.

Foley's monkey studies have convinced him that modern humans evolved in such a mosaic of tropical environments, developing distinctive characteristics that separated them from their archaic predecessors. Within tropical Africa's patchy environments were areas where food supplies were both predictable and of high quality. In response to such regions, some humans may have developed wide ranging behavior, lived in larger social groups with considerable kin-based substructure, and been highly selective in their diet. As part of these responses, some groups may have developed exceptional hunting skills, a technology so effective that they could prey on animals from a distance with projectiles. And with more efficient technology, more advance planning, and better organization of both hunting and foraging, our ancestors could have reduced the unpredictability of the environment in dramatic ways.

This ecological approach to modern human origins is still untested against archaeological evidence. But even at this stage in research there are unexplained anomalies between biology and archaeology. Once modern human beings had evolved, they manufactured a sophisticated tool technology, based on antler, bone, wood, and stone blade manufacture. This technology was far more advanced than anything made by their predecessors. But in Africa, at sites like Klasies River, the first modern humans were still making archaic toolkits, and their hunting skills were less developed than those of later millennia. Conversely, in Europe, there are instances of the new technologies being associated with Neanderthal fossils. The link between technology and anatomy is very loose, as if ideas and genes moved at different rates. But a number of lines of evidence strongly suggest that *Homo sapiens* originated in Africa and spread from there into other parts of the Old World.

The Spread of *Homo sapiens*

If tropical Africa was the cradle of modern humans, how and why did *Homo sapiens* spread into Europe and Asia (Brauwer, 1984)? The critical period was between 100,000 and 45,000 years ago, the date by which *Homo sapiens* is known to have been living in the Near East. The only major barrier to population movement between tropical Africa and the Mediterranean Basin is the Sahara, today some of the driest territory on earth. During the early Weichsel, the Sahara went through phases of relative aridity and greater rainfall. A cooler and wetter climate prevailed in the desert from before 100,000 until about 40,000 years ago, and again between 32,000 and 24,000 years ago. For long periods, the country between East Africa and the Mediterranean was passable, supporting scattered game herds and open grassland. The Nile Valley was always habitable, even during periods of great aridity in the desert. Thus, anatomically modern *Homo sapiens* may have hunted and foraged across the Sahara into the Nile Valley and the Near East in the early Weichsel. Then, as the Near East became increasingly dry and less productive, the newcomers may have responded to population pressure and food shortages by moving across the wide land bridge that joined Turkey to southeast Europe 34,000 years ago, spreading into the more productive steppe and tundra regions of Europe and western Asia.

How did *Homo sapiens* appear in eastern Asia?

Homo sapiens in Asia

Ideas about the origins of *Homo sapiens* in Asia pit those who believe in replacement theories against those who argue for modern human populations having evolved in different geographic regions (Wolpoff et al., 1984). Proponents of the latter viewpoint argue that there has been evolutionary continuity between Middle and Upper Pleistocene human populations in the region. They cite a number of fossil finds from China to support their view. These include an early *Homo sapiens* skull from Dali in Shanxi province, estimated to be some 100,000 years old, younger than the upper levels of Zhoukoudien. The cranium shares many features with earlier Chinese specimens, so Wolpoff and his colleagues argue that there are simply too many anatomical features in common between Middle and Upper Pleistocene Asians for *Homo erectus* to have been replaced abruptly by *Homo sapiens.*

Dali
100,000 B.P.

The same applies in southeast Asia, they argue, where about the only early *Homo sapiens* finds come from the extreme south, from Australia. The poorly dated *Homo sapiens* skull from the great cave at Niah in Borneo is believed to be about 40,000 years old, while an anatomically modern skull from Tabon Cave in the Philippines may date to about 23,000 B.P. Both these specimens are said to display features that link them to gene flow from farther north in Asia. By the same token, early Australian fossils from Lake Mungo, Kow Swamp, and elsewhere (Chapter 8) are said to display some anatomical continuity with late *Homo erectus* finds on the Asian mainland, notably from Ngandong in Indonesia (Wolpoff et al., 1984).

Niah
c.400,000 B.P.
Tabon
c.23,000 B.P.

The Wolpoff theory, if valid, has important implications. It means that east Asia was a major source for population movements to peripheral areas to the northeast (Siberia and the Americas), and the southeast and south (Australia). However, it should be stressed that there are almost no fossils to document this provocative and controversial theory. Many paleoanthropologists believe that the replacement theory is a better explanation for the evolution of *Homo sapiens* in Asia. (For a full discussion, see Wolpoff et al., 1984.)

THE NEANDERTHALS

Some people use the word *Neanderthal* to describe dim-witted, ugly people who are like apes, an insult aimed at those they consider dumb. This stereotype, and that of the shambling cave people so beloved of cartoonists, comes from mistaken studies of Neanderthal skeletons in the early years of this century. In fact, the Neanderthals were strong, robustly built humans with some archaic features like bun-shaped skulls and sometimes eyebrow ridges when compared with modern people. But there is every reason to believe they were expert hunters, nimble runners, and beings capable of considerable intellectual reasoning.

There are, of course, striking anatomical differences between Neanderthals and modern humans, both in the robust postcranial skeleton and in the more bun-shaped skull, sometimes with heavy brow ridges and a forward projecting face (Figure 5.16). These features are the reason this extinct hominid form is classified as *Homo sapiens neanderthalensis,* a subspecies of *Homo sapiens,* and not as *Homo sapiens sapiens,* a fully modern human.

In the century since the first Neanderthal skull from the German village of that name was unearthed, substantial numbers of Neanderthal individuals, most in western Europe, as well as contemporary human fossils from the Near East, Africa, and Asia, have been unearthed. They first appeared during the Eem interglacial, well before 100,000 years ago, but they were apparently few in number. Large Neanderthal sites occur in the Dordogne area of southwest France, where deep river valleys and vast limestone cliffs offered abundant shelter during the Weichsel glaciation (Bordes, 1968; Gamble, 1986b). The Neanderthal skeletons found in French caves look like anatomical anachronisms, with massive brow ridges and squat bodies. They walked upright and as nimbly as modern humans. They stood just over 5 feet tall (153 cm) and their forearms were relatively short compared with those of modern people. This "classic" variety of Neanderthal is confined to western Europe and is more noticeably different from *Homo sapiens* than its contemporary populations found elsewhere, especially around the shores of the Mediterranean and in Asia (Figure 5.7, p. 137). We find much variability among Neanderthals, who most often display less extreme features, particularly brow ridges and other cranial features, than the classic variety of western France. It is well demonstrated at the Mt. Carmel sites of et-Tabūn and es-Skhūl in Israel as well as at Krapina in central Europe (Stringer, 1988; Trinkhaus and Howells, 1979).

The morphological differences apparent between many Neanderthals and modern *Homo sapiens* are startling. How do these heavily built, beetle-browed people fit into the picture of human evolution? The great French physical anthropologist Marcellin Boule believed, in the 1930s, that the classic Neanderthals were clumsy, shambling people, so specialized that they became extinct while other populations provided the evolutionary basis for modern humans (Boule and Vallois, 1957). Erik Trinkhaus and William Howells (1979) reviewed Neanderthal populations from all over Europe and the Near East and point out that their anatomical pattern took approximately fifty millennia from 100,000 years ago to evolve, then stabilized for another fifty before changing rapidly to

Morphological differences

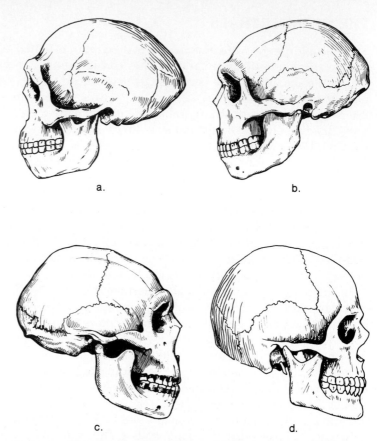

FIGURE 5.16 Comparisons of four fossil skulls and jaws. (a) The reconstructed *Homo erectus* skull has prominent brow ridges, a bun-shaped rear to the cranium, and a retreating chin. (b) A "classic" Neanderthal skull found at Monte Circeo, Italy, still has well-marked brow ridges and bun-shaped cranium, but an increased brain capacity. The skull is lower and flatter than those of modern humans, and the jaw is chinless. (c) The Shanidar Neanderthal from Iraq is a less extreme example, with a higher forehead, somewhat reduced brow ridges, and a much more rounded skull. (d) Modern skull with well-rounded contours, no brow ridges, high forehead, and a well-marked chin.

essentially modern human anatomy within a brief period of 5,000 years approximately 40,000 years ago. They point out that Boule was mistaken, partly because his definitive studies were made on an elderly individual suffering from arthritis and partly because much more skeletal material is now available. The Neanderthals had the same posture, manual abilities, and range and characteristics of movement as modern people. They differed from us in having massive limb bones, often somewhat bowed in the thigh and forearm, features that reflect the Neanderthals' greater muscular power. For their height, the Neanderthals were bulky and heavily muscled, and their brain capacity was slightly larger than that of modern humans, not because of greater intelligence but because of heavier musculature. Their antecedents are in the *Homo erectus* group, from which they inherited their heavy build, an adaptation so successful that it lasted for more than 100,000 years (Stringer, 1988).

EARLY *HOMO SAPIENS* ADAPTS

Although many details of the biological evolution of early *Homo sapiens* remain unresolved, we know a great deal about the many and diverse adaptations of these people. Their distinctive hunter-gatherer culture, which continued in the basic hominid tradition, is known from hundreds of sites in Africa, Asia, and Europe. The Neanderthals' *Mousterian* technology (named after the Le Moustier rock shelter in southwest France) was far more complex and sophisticated than its Acheulian predecessor, with many regional variations (Trinkhaus, 1983a). Many of the Neanderthals' artifacts were made for specific purposes. Like their *erectus* predecessors, the early *Homo sapiens* bands occupied large territories, which they probably exploited on a seasonal round, returning to the same locations year after year when game migrated or vegetables came into season. The Neanderthals were skilled hunters who were not afraid to pursue large game animals like the mammoth as well as reindeer and wild horses. They also caught birds and fish. It appears that many western European bands lived in caves and rock shelters during much of the year as a protection against arctic cold. During the summer months they may have fanned out over the tundra plains, living in temporary tented encampments (for details, see Gamble, 1986b). African hunter-gatherers developed woodworking toolkits for use in dense rain forests as well as on open savanna.

Mousterian culture
?100,000 to
40,000 B.P.
(Chapter 6)

Clive Gamble (1986b) believes that the Neanderthal adaptation in Europe was significantly different from that of earlier human populations. He points to significant changes in human settlement patterns, to a greater use of rock shelters and caves as well as repeated use of open sites as temporary stopping places by people away from the larger main group. This may have been a time when technology was more organized, when planning assumed greater importance — to reduce the risk of starvation. People were now developing hunting and foraging strategies based on four main herd species — bison, horse, red deer, and reindeer. Storage assumed much greater importance for surviving winter shortages, maximizing the meat culled from seasonally migrating animals. There may have been higher population densities, greater population stability, and more adaptive stability, with less risk of local populations dying out in times of stress.

For the new adaptive strategies, environmental knowledge was the key to effective planning. Factors like herd size, migration seasons, and predictability of animal movements assumed vital importance. Information was a highly valued commodity, and, Gamble believes, marriage patterns kept people tied to well-known territories without much interaction with their neighbors. This pattern of adaptation resulted in considerable interregional differences within the Neanderthal world. The southwestern areas of Europe, with their deep river valleys and large rock shelters, were occupied constantly, while more open areas to the north and east were more extensively exploited during periods of warmer climate and largely abandoned during glacial times. It is interesting to note that no Neanderthal sites have yet come to light north of 54°N (see Figure 5.10b).

STONE TOOL TECHNOLOGY

Middle Paleolithic technology

The stone technology used by the Neanderthals and other early *Homo sapiens* forms has often been subsumed under the label *Middle Paleolithic,* on the ground that the techniques used were distinct from those of *Homo erectus.* In fact, the basic differences are much less radical than has often been assumed, for well-established stoneworking methods from earlier times were simply adapted to produce a far more variable and diverse inventory of flake tools, including carefully shaped spear points and scrapers. The great debates about the technology of early *Homo sapiens* revolve around not the basic techniques but the meaning of different varieties of Mousterian and other cultures. For working purposes, it is best to assume that "Lower" and "Middle" Paleolithic technology form one broad continuum. The major changes in stone tool manufacture occur after 35,000 years ago, with the spread of *Homo sapiens sapiens* and "Upper Paleolithic" technology (Chapter 6).

Levallois and Disk Core Reduction Strategies

At Kapthurin and other East African sites, Acheulian stoneworkers demonstrated a remarkable skill at preshaping cores to produce large flakes for making axes and other artifacts. With such prepared core techniques, which were to assume great importance after 100,000 years ago, the core is shaped to predetermine the flake or blade that is to be removed. The *Levallois technique,* named after the Paris suburb where it was first found, produces broad, flat flakes, large blades, and triangular points (Figure 5.17). The *disk core technique* is designed to produce as many flakes of varying size as possible and results in residual cores with an approximate round shape. The size of the raw material lumps available to the stoneworker probably had a major effect on the flakes produced, for both techniques as well as simpler flaking were widely used in Europe, Africa, and Asia.

Tool Forms and Variability

Mousterian and other Middle Paleolithic tools were made for the most part on flakes, the most characteristic artifacts being points and scrapers (Figure 5.17). Some of these were *composite tools,* artifacts made of more than one component — for example, a point, a shaft, and the binding that secured the head to the shaft, making a spear. The edges of both points and scrapers were sharpened by fine trimming, the removal of small, steplike chips from the edge of the implement (Figure 5.18). These artifacts, almost universally distributed in Middle Paleolithic sites, were used in the chase, in woodworking, and in preparing skins. However, recent edge wear researches have revealed that many un-

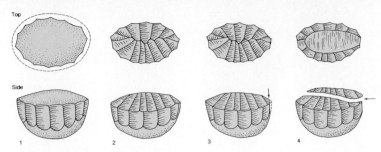

Making a Levallois core: (1) the edges of a suitable stone are trimmed; (2) the top surface is trimmed; (3) a striking platform is made, the point where the flake will originate, by trimming to form a straight edge on the side; and (4) a flake is struck from the core and removed.

A Levallois core from the Thames Valley, England (left), with the top of the core (left bottom), shown from above and the end view (left top). A typical Levallois flake is shown at the right: upper surface (center), lower (flake) surface (right), and cross section (left). Both artifacts are one-third actual size.

FIGURE 5.17 Prepared core techniques. Prepared cores were carefully flaked to enable the toolmaker to strike off large flakes of predetermined size.

The Levallois technique meant that the stoneworker would shape a lump of flint into an inverted bun-shaped core (often compared to an inverted tortoise shell). The flat upper surface would be struck at one end, the resulting flake forming the only product from the core. Another form was the disk core, a prepared core from which several flakes of predetermined size and shape were removed. The core gradually became smaller, until it resembled a flat disk. Disk cores were often used to produce points and scrapers.

trimmed flakes were used for cutting, scraping, and other tasks; they were convenient working edges when needed at a moment's notice (Gamble, 1986b).

The complexity of Mousterian technology is striking. The French sites have yielded a great diversity of Mousterian artifacts and toolkits. Some levels include hand axes; others, notched flakes, perhaps used for stripping meat for drying or pressing fibrous plants. Subdivisions of Mousterian technology have

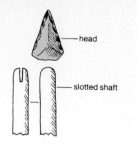 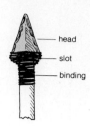

Stone-tipped Mousterian spear (a hypothetical example). The spear was made by attaching a pointed stone head to a wooden handle to form the projectile. The head probably fitted into a slot in the wooden shaft and was fixed to it with resin or beeswax; a binding was added to the end of the shaft.

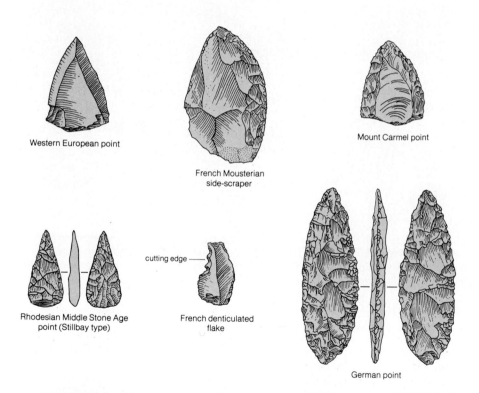

Western European point

French Mousterian side-scraper

Mount Carmel point

Rhodesian Middle Stone Age point (Stillbay type)

cutting edge —

French denticulated flake

German point

Mousterian artifacts.

FIGURE 5.18 Middle Paleolithic tools and technology. This technology was based on simple stone techniques that were used for tens of thousands of years before the emergence of early *Homo sapiens*. By 100,000 years ago, artifacts of many types were of *composite* form — made from several different parts. A wooden spear might have a stone tip, a flint scraper, a bone handle. Unfortunately, we know almost nothing about the bone and wood tools used.

been identified by the prevalence of specific tool types. The French archaeologist François Bordes has identified five traditions which he says represent the work of five distinct bands living in one territory at the same time (Bordes, 1968).

Not everyone agrees with Bordes. British archaeologist Paul Mellars hypothesizes that Mousterian technology evolved slowly through time and that the variations in toolkits were the result of slow cultural change, with various tools (such as the side scraper or hand ax) in fashion at different times. This, he feels, is a more likely explanation than ethnic differences or different activities (Mellars, 1973). In contrast, Sally Binford and Lewis Binford argue that Bordes's traditions reflect various distinct activities carried out within the same cultural system at different times of the year (Binford, 1983; Binford and Binford, 1966). Harold Dibble (1987) has studied Mousterian scraper technology, on the assumption that the various shapes of these artifacts represent a "reduction continuum," that is to say, a continuous process of flaking the edge of flake blanks. Thus, collections with more large side scrapers represent *less* intensive utilization of scrapers than those with greater variability in scraper forms. He argues that neither style nor function was the overriding factor in stone tool variability. Rather, the Neanderthals were using a fundamentally very simple stone technology, with both flaking techniques and reduction processes varying considerably in response to all kinds of external factors — raw material availability and size, climate, differing activities, and subsistence needs among them.

The Neanderthals and their contemporaries were developing tools for different activities far more quickly than ever before, perhaps at a time of growing human populations and slightly enhanced social complexity. But fundamentally Middle Paleolithic technology was simple, highly variable, and a logical development of technologies refined over many millennia.

THE ORIGINS OF BURIAL AND RELIGIOUS BELIEF

Although the Neanderthals were still hunter-gatherers and the world's population still small, life was gradually becoming more complex. Among them we find the first signs of religious ideology, of a preoccupation with the life hereafter. Many Neanderthals were buried by their companions. Neanderthal burials have been recovered from the deposits of rock shelters and caves as well as from open campsites. Single burials are the most common, normally accompanied by flint implements, food offerings, or even cooked game meat (evidenced by charred bones). One band of Siberian mountain goat hunters lived at Teshik-Tash in the western foothills of the Himalayas. They buried one of their children in a shallow pit, surrounding the body with six pairs of wild goat horns (Klein, 1969).

Burials at
Teshik-Tash

Another remarkable single burial came from Shanidar Cave in the Zagros Mountains of Iraq (Trinkhaus, 1983b). There a thirty-year-old man (born, incidentally, with a useless right arm) was crushed by a rockfall from the roof of the cave. He was buried in a shallow pit. Other single graves from France and central Europe were covered with red ocher powder.

Shanidar

One rock shelter, La Ferrassie near Les Eyzies in France, yielded the remains of two adult Neanderthals and four children buried close together in a campsite (Peyrony, 1934). Group sepulchers occur at other sites, too, more signs that the Neanderthals, like most living hunter-gatherers, believed in life after death. They may also have had beliefs that coincided with deliberate burial, but details will always remain hypothetical.

Some glimmers of insight into Neanderthal beliefs may come from their remarkable bear cults. The Neanderthals were skillful hunters who were not afraid to go after cave bears, which were about the size of Alaskan brown bears and weighed perhaps up to three-quarters of a ton. Like some modern northern hunters, the Neanderthals had a bear cult, known to us from bear skulls that were deliberately buried with ceremony. The most remarkable find was at

Regourdou in southern France, where a rectangular pit lined with stones held the skulls of at least twenty cave bears (Howell, 1974). The burial pit was covered with a huge stone slab. Nearby lay the entire skeleton of one of the bears. It seems likely that the cave bear became an integral part of these hunters' mythology, an object of reverence and an animal with a special place in the world.

Evidence of an even more remarkable ritual appeared in the depths of the Guattari Cave at Monte Circeo, 60 miles (96.5 km) south of Rome. A Neanderthal skull was found in an isolated inner chamber surrounded by a circle of stones (Blanc, 1961). The base of the skull lay upward, mutilated in such a way that the brain could be reached. The right side of the skull was smashed in by violent blows. Near the circle of stones lay three piles of bones, from red deer, cattle, and pigs (Figure 5.19). Although ingenious explanations for this curious ritual have been proposed, we shall never know why this sacrificial victim was

FIGURE 5.19 In the Guattari Cave of Monte Circeo, a human skull was found lying base upward in the center of a ring of stones. The condition of the skull, as well as other artifacts in the cave, gives evidence of a sacrificial murder.

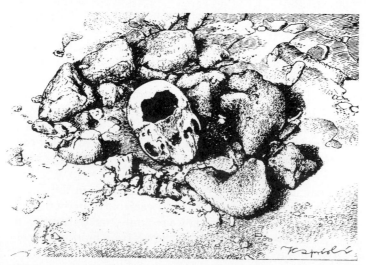

killed and beheaded outside the cave, his head then laid out as the centerpiece of an important ritual. Like the bear cult, cannibalism and other hunting rituals appear to have been part of human life and subsistence. We find in Neanderthals and their culture the first roots of our own complicated beliefs, societies, and religious sense.

GUIDE TO FURTHER READING

Bordes, François. *The Old Stone Age*. New York: McGraw-Hill, 1968.
A simple manual on the Paleolithic period that covers basic tool types and technologies. Invaluable for the beginning student.

Gamble, Clive. *The Paleolithic Settlement of Europe*. Cambridge: Cambridge University Press, 1986.
A full discussion of the fundamental issues surrounding the Middle Paleolithic adaption in Europe. For advanced readers.

Pfeiffer, John E. *The Emergence of Man* (4th ed.). New York: Harper and Row, 1985.
An articulate and complete account of early human evolution that focuses on behavior and culture as well as fossils.

Stringer, Chris. *The Neanderthals*. London: Thames and Hudson, 1988.
A sophisticated and up-to-date general account of the Neanderthals aimed at the serious general reader. Comprehensive summary.

PART III

Homo Sapiens and Hunter-Gatherers
(40,000 B.P. to Modern Times)

There is a passion for hunting something deeply implanted in the human breast.
— Charles Dickens, *Pickwick Papers*, 1836–37, Chapter 10

In this part we describe numerous cultural adaptations by *Homo sapiens sapiens* and the first settlement of Australia and the New World.

CHRONOLOGICAL TABLE C

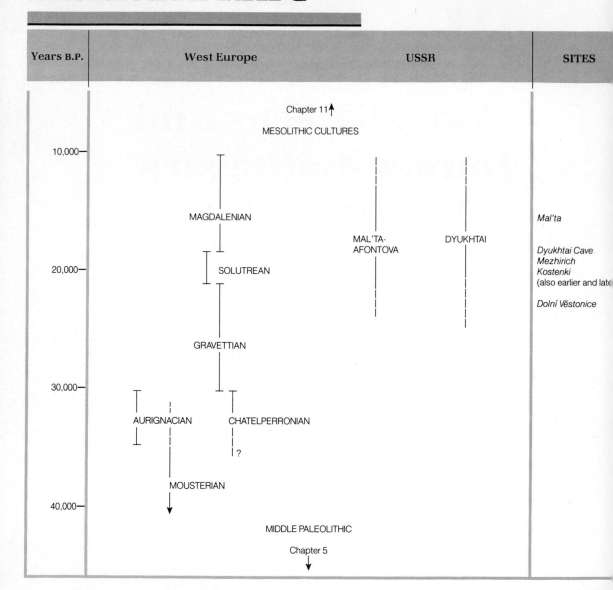

Years B.P.	West Europe	USSR	SITES

Chapter 11 ↑

MESOLITHIC CULTURES

10,000—

MAGDALENIAN

MAL'TA-AFONTOVA   DYUKHTAI

SOLUTREAN

20,000—

GRAVETTIAN

30,000—

AURIGNACIAN   CHATELPERRONIAN

?

MOUSTERIAN

40,000—

MIDDLE PALEOLITHIC

Chapter 5

Mal'ta

Dyukhtai Cave
Mezhirich
Kostenki
(also earlier and late

Dolní Věstonice

Note: There is probably considerable overlap between Western European Upper Paleolithic cultures.

CHAPTER 6

Europeans and Northern Asians

(c. 40,000 to 8,000 years ago)

Preview

- ▨ *Homo sapiens sapiens* spread rapidly through the Old World after 40,000 years ago, a marked biological and cultural break reflected by the sudden appearance of anatomically modern humans and of more refined and efficient tool technologies.

- ▨ Over the millennia after 40,000 B.P. there was an increasing trend toward greater specialization and flexibility in the hunter-gatherer lifeway.

- ▨ It seems most likely that *Homo sapiens sapiens* populations replaced *Homo neanderthalis* in most places rather than evolving from them.

- ▨ The technological changes of the Upper Paleolithic were foreshadowed tens of thousands of years earlier in tropical Africa, and in the Near East. Complex adaptive forces including the need for more economic methods of using fine-grained rock led to the new technologies.

- ▨ Upper Paleolithic technology was based on both blades and flakes, producing a wide range of scraping and graving tools as well as backed knives. In time, antler and bone technologies assumed great importance in colder latitudes, perhaps as substitutes for, and to supplement, wooden artifacts.

- ▨ The transition between Middle and Upper Paleolithic in Europe was a rapid one, occurring around 32,000 years ago. The new cultures were characterized by frequent readaptations to changing climatic conditions, as people exploited a rich mammalian biomass. The sheer diversity of the Ice Age environment gave hunter-gatherer bands great flexibility, and resulted in a considerable diversity and complexity among Upper Paleolithic cultures, especially the Magdalenian with its intricate artistic traditions. The Magdalenian flourished after about 16,000 years ago until the end of the Ice Age about 5,000 years later.

- Upper Paleolithic settlement in Europe coincided with long-term trends toward a restructuring of social relations after 32,000 years ago, together with a great proliferation of tool forms. There may have been more structured relationships between different bands. These people may have subsisted off migratory game animals as well as other foods, and many may have lived in southwest France in smaller territories.

- The Upper Paleolithic cultures of southwestern France lived in relatively close juxtaposition. At certain times of the year, they may have come together for communal hunts and a variety of social functions. It is thought that Magdalenian society may have become organized around social hierarchies, ranked kin groups such as are found on the Pacific Northwest coast.

- Upper Paleolithic art flourished for more than 20,000 years, and involved a complex symbolism revolving around the relationships between animals, humans, and the natural environment. It died out after 13,000 years ago, when Postglacial forest, river, and coastal adaptations replaced the big-game hunting traditions of the late Ice Age.

- In Russia and Siberia, big-game hunting traditions flourished during the last climax of the Weichsel glaciation. Siberia saw two distinctive Upper Paleolithic traditions — Mal'ta-Afontova and Dyukhtai — in existence about 18,000 years ago.

- The Dyukhtai tradition may have connections with Upper Paleolithic cultures to the south, in northern China, and has direct links to Paleoarctic cultural traditions in Alaska.

Chronological Table C

In the final analysis, the long millennia of prehistory have seen humankind become ever more efficient at extracting energy from its environment. The first hominids branched out into unfamiliar environments that took them away from an almost total dependence on forest fruits. *Homo habilis* was a scavenger as well as a collector, perhaps even an occasional hunter, a lifeway that further deepened the scope of our predecessors' lives. *Homo erectus* radiated into temperate latitudes, into the Near East, Europe, and Asia. These more advanced hominids were probably hunters as well as scavengers, who relied on enhanced cooperation for success in the chase. Once they became serious hunters, people could tap rich supplies of energy-rich meat, as well as vegetable foods. But hunters were, at first, yet another carnivore in a world well populated by successful carnivores. The transition to the new lifeway must have been slow, at times painful, and may have occurred in several stages. There can be little doubt that increased efficiency as a carnivore played an important role in the emergence of both archaic *Homo sapiens* and anatomically modern *Homo sapiens sapiens*. In Chapter 5, we explored current thinking about the emergence of *Homo sapiens sapiens* in tropical Africa and hypothesized that anatomically modern humans spread from the tropics into North Africa and the Near East about 45,000 years ago. From there, *Homo sapiens* may have entered Europe at a time of low sea level, crossing the land bridge that connected the Balkans with

Radiation of *Homo sapiens* **45,000 B.P. and later**

Homo Sapiens and Hunter-Gatherers

Turkey across the Dardanelles (for full discussion, see Brauwer, 1984; Stringer et al., 1984). This chapter chronicles the cultural changes that result from this (still hypothetical) replacement of European Neanderthals by anatomically modern humans and looks at the vigorous hunter-gatherer cultures that flourished in the northern parts of the Old World between 40,000 years ago and Postglacial times (Figure 6.1 shows sites in Chapters 6 and 8).

INCREASED EFFICIENCY

Is there any evidence for humanity becoming a more efficient carnivore after 40,000 years ago, when *Homo sapiens sapiens* first emerged? Some fascinating indications come from coastal caves in South Africa, among them Klasies River Mouth and Nelson's Bay (Binford, 1984; R. Klein, 1979). Richard Klein found that the people who inhabited these caves lived not only off vegetable foods but off game and marine resources as well. Klasies River was occupied between about 120,000 and 70,000 years ago, then abandoned until about 5,000 years ago. The early inhabitants collected limpets and also pursued seals and penguins. But they took few fish; they preferred game on the hoof, especially such

Klasies River
Nelson's Bay
**100,000 to 70,000
B.P.**

FIGURE 6.1   Map showing archaeological sites mentioned in this chapter and Chapter 8.

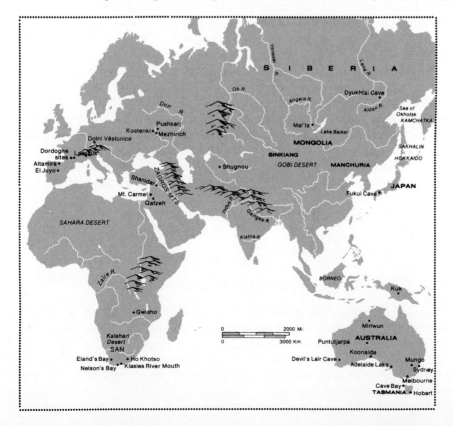

docile animals as the eland and bastard hartebeest. They did kill some more formidable beasts like the buffalo, black wildebeest, and roan antelope but in much smaller numbers, and some of the meat was perhaps scavenged. Interestingly, the bones of these individual species came from either very old or young individuals, which is the sort of age pattern found with predator kills. Only the eland and bastard hartebeest were taken at all ages. Klein believes that they may have been driven into traps or over cliffs.

The Nelson's Bay Cave was occupied by modern *Homo sapiens* populations after 15,000 years ago. Again, eland and bastard hartebeest were common, taken at all ages, perhaps using game drives. But the Nelson's Bay folk took bush pigs and warthogs, much fiercer and more formidable prey. Not only that, they used nets and fish hooks to catch a wide range of ocean fish. They also lived off flying sea birds like cormorants. One could argue, of course, that the Klasies River people simply preferred game on the hoof, but the relative abundance of wild pigs strongly suggests that the Nelson's Bay hunters were much more expert and capable of exploiting a far wider range of game. They may have used the bow and arrow, although there is as yet no evidence of this from Nelson's Bay. While the eland lives in widely dispersed herds, other antelope do not and would have been much more vulnerable to efficient hunting. Klein notes that several large mammal species became extinct 12,000 to 10,000 years ago, an event that cannot be accounted for by environmental changes alone. It seems possible that *Homo sapiens* was the destroyer, altering for the first time the delicate ecological balance between humans and their natural environment. We should note that there were large-scale big-game extinctions in North America, too, only a few millennia after hunter-gatherer populations expanded rapidly.

In some parts of the world, the changeover from archaic to modern *Homo sapiens* was a rapid, even dramatic one. The transformation was both biological and cultural, but these two aspects did not necessarily coincide. The biological break was the appearance of anatomically modern human beings, the cultural in part a refinement of long-established toolmaking practices and the introduction of numerous specialized artifacts for the chase, bone and wood working, and many other activities. These toolkits played an important role in hunter-gatherers' increased ability to influence their environment, and in the sharp rise in the efficiency of their lifeway. It is only in the past 15,000 years that specialized hunting and gathering developed in many parts of the world (Bailey, 1983.)

SPECIALIZED HUNTING AND GATHERING

"Specialized" hunting and gathering implies concentration on a limited number of natural resources to the exclusion of many others. Examples of specialized hunter-gatherers are the Plains Indians of North America, who concentrated on the buffalo, and the Pacific Northwest coast peoples, expert fisherfolk, who were able to acquire large food surpluses by exploiting seasonal salmon runs and other fish species.

Many specialized hunter-gatherers concentrated heavily on wild vegetable foods. In fact, gathering has always been of major importance to hunter-gatherers. Kay Martin and Barbara Voorhies (1975), who studied ninety hunting and gathering societies, found that 75% of them relied more heavily on collecting than on hunting. Only a quarter were predominantly hunters. The Foraging importance of gathering (foraging) has been dramatized by Richard Lee's researches among the present-day !Kung San of the Kalahari Desert in South Africa (Lee, 1979). He found that the !Kung live in an inhospitable, dry woodland environment where game is now rare. They gather the nutritious mangetti nut as a primary food all year round. The remaining vegetable foods are selected from at least eighty-five edible species known to the !Kung, of which only eight are major foods (Figure 6.2). All of them are seasonal favorites, one is a root that provides water at times of the year when people have to venture far afield in search of food, away from water supplies. So plentiful are edible vegetable foods that the !Kung San have two choices when favorite species become exhausted: eat less desirable foods near home, or walk farther, perhaps shifting

FIGURE 6.2 !Kung women gathering food.

their camp. Long before the least desirable foods are eaten, the people have moved to a new site.

Few hunters and gatherers are left, and it is difficult to know whether the !Kung life of relative security and leisure is typical of most prehistoric hunter-gatherers. We can be sure that some groups, such as the reindeer hunters of southwestern France 15,000 years ago, were far better off in terms of potential food sources than other groups living in less favorable environments. What is revealing, however, is the efficient way in which the !Kung relate to their environment, for this is surely typical of all *Homo sapiens sapiens* hunter-gatherer societies, probably to an even greater extent than in earlier millennia. The !Kung know their environment intimately, and they know what to expect from it.

Flexibility

They can gather their food when they need it and do not have to store it for days. This subsistence strategy is a conservative adaptation, based on plants and animals that come back naturally year after year. Hunter-gatherers tend to put in a constant amount of work, unlike the agriculturalists' sharply seasonal activity of planting and harvest. One of the most striking features of the hunter-gatherer lifeway wherever it can still be observed is its flexibility, both in food gathering and in a social organization normally based on the small band and the nuclear family. Perhaps it was this flexibility and resulting built-in insurance against lean years that made hunting and gathering the most lasting of all human lifeways. (For a recent assessment of !Kung research, see Schrire, 1984.)

NEANDERTHALS AND *HOMO SAPIENS SAPIENS*

If anatomically modern *Homo sapiens* spread from Africa into the Near East and Europe, the question immediately arises, What happened to the Neanderthals? Their sudden disappearance and replacement by modern humans has sparked some of the most vigorous controversies in archaeology and some scintillating, if speculative popular novels. How did the Neanderthals become extinct? Were they attacked and killed by anatomically more advanced newcomers? Or did they interbreed with anatomically modern humans and adopt new cultural adaptations? It is hardly surprising that the fossil record give us no clues, for it is far too incomplete. While some of the more pronounced facial features of the classic Neanderthals, like their brow ridges, did begin to recede in some later populations, this is far from a conclusive sign that the one population gave way to the other. And the first *Homo sapiens* populations, like the famous Cro-Magnon people of southwest France, while robustly built, show no anatomical signs that can be called transitional from the Neanderthals (Figure 6.3). Their robustness still lies within the range of variation of modern populations, albeit at the robust end. It seems most likely the *Homo sapiens sapiens* replaced *Homo neanderthalis* rather than evolving from them (Ronen, 1982).

Current thinking has it that *Homo sapiens sapiens* evolved from early *Homo sapiens* in tropical Africa, and ultimately from *Homo erectus*, by phyletic (evolution of different biological lines) change and by hybridization from earlier populations that displayed considerable variation (see Chapter 5). If this evolution took place in sub-Saharan Africa, did modern people evolve from the Neander-

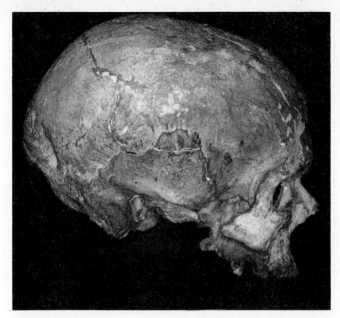

FIGURE 6.3 *Homo sapiens sapiens* from Cro-Magnon rock shelter, Les Eyzies, France, dating to between 40,000 and 35,000 years ago. (Courtesy of Milford Wolpoff)

thals elsewhere? The Near Eastern hunter-gatherer populations of 50,000 to 45,000 years ago displayed considerable anatomical variation that has been exhaustively studied. The older Neanderthal-like individuals buried in caves like et-Tabūn in Israel and Shanidar in Iraq were anatomically quite similar to European Neanderthals (Stringer, 1988; Trinkhaus, 1981). In contrast, the people buried at Skhul Cave and Qafzeh in Israel date to around 40,000 years ago, perhaps much earlier, and were anatomically closer to modern humans. There is a striking morphological gap between the two groups, which were separated by several millennia. The chronology for Qafzeh may be much earlier (Stringer, 1988). Despite the morphologically heterogeneous populations, almost certainly modern humans evolved elsewhere.

Near Eastern
Neanderthals

THE UPPER PALEOLITHIC TRANSITION

The biological transition from Neanderthals to *Homo sapiens sapiens* is still the subject of much debate; however, the replacement theory is most strongly favored. Can we, then, document the transition in technological and cultural terms?

The final chapter of human biological evolution was accompanied by considerable technological changes, but these changes were far less dramatic than has sometimes been claimed. For generations, experts on the Stone Age assumed that the appearance of *Homo sapiens sapiens* was associated with the invention of radically new, much more advanced technologies that involved, among other things, the use of punches to produce fine, parallel-sided blades and a proliferation of specialized tools, not only in stone but in antler and bone

FIGURE 6.4 Upper Paleolithic technology. The classic stoneworking technology used for Upper Paleolithic tools was based not only on percussion and the use of bone hammers but on punch-struck blades. Various methods were used to strike off the blades, using a hand-held or chest-impelled punch to produce parallel-sided blades (below). The punch allows intense pressure to be applied to a single point on the top of the core and channels the direction of the shock waves. Parallel-sided blades were made into a variety of tools, among them burins and scrapers, which were typical of all stages of the Upper Paleolithic. Burins (below, opposite) were used for grooving wood, bone, and particularly antlers, which were made into spears and harpoon points. The chisel ends of burins were formed by taking an oblique or longitudinal flake off the end of a blade. Burins also were used to engrave figures. End scrapers were used on wood and bone as well as skins. A strong trend toward the production of smaller blades developed in Europe and Asia after 20,000 years ago. Heat treatment enabled stone-workers to use pressure and other new retouch methods to remove fine, flat flakes from artifact surfaces (Price et al., 1982).

Upper Paleolithic technology was based on efficient use of toolmaking stone, an important point in environments where such materials may have been harder to find. It also relied heavily on composite tools, of which stone elements were only a part. Many small blades and bladelets were mounted in handles or sockets, as barbs or knives. A diverse bone and antler projectile point technology came into use after 35,000 years ago, greatly enhancing hunting effectiveness. After 20,000 years ago, Upper Paleolithic people began to use another deadly, and highly effective, device, the spear-thrower. This leverlike artifact with a weight on the outer end extended the throwing arc and the range and accuracy of the weapon, an important consideration with large animals. After about 15,000 years ago, the Magdalenian people decorated many of their spear-throwers with finely crafted animals, often headless.

Many Upper Paleolithic stone tools were employed in woodworking, for the people made use of many perishable materials that do not survive in the archaeological record. A small imprint of three-braided plant fibers from the famous Lascaux Cave in southwest France shows that cordage may have been important for making nets and snares, both for use on land and for catching fish.

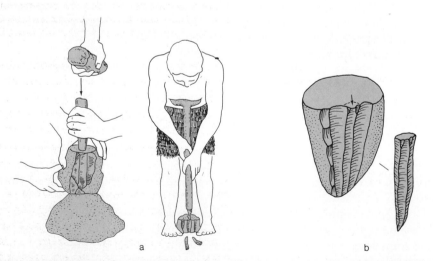

(a) Two punch techniques and (b) a typical product, a core and a blade struck from it. The dotted line and arrow show the point where the next blade will be struck off from the core.

as well. While there is no doubt that such innovations did appear in the Upper Paleolithic, careful examination of earlier technological traditions shows that they were foreshadowed tens of thousands of years earlier.

Africa and the Near East

Rock shelters and caves in east and southern Africa have yielded large tools made on blades fabricated by skilled percussion from carefully prepared cores. The same peoples of 100,000 years ago were using composite tools and a wider range of artifacts than many of their predecessors. In the Near East, great caves and rock shelters like et-Tabūn and Mugharet el-Wad at Mt. Carmel, Israel, and Shanidar, Iraq, document thousands of years of Neanderthal toolmaking. These sites were visited again and again by hunter-gatherer bands from more than 70,000 years ago right into modern times.

Near Eastern Mousterian technology

The Mousterian levels in these caves contain tens of thousands of carefully retouched flakes and side scrapers, as well as the bones of large deer and wild cattle (Marks, 1983). As Arthur Jelenik (1981), has pointed out, this technology was a very simple and conservative one that displayed considerable variability within fairly restricted limits. This variability included some horizons where large bladelike blanks were made with sophisticated percussion flaking. The Mousterian levels are covered by further occupation levels containing different toolkits that gradually replaced earlier artifact forms and technologies. In these, the long, parallel-sided blades that were the first stage in making stone tools were removed from cylindrical flint cores with a punch and a hammerstone (Figure 6.4). Some blades were up to 6 inches (15.2 cm) long. The tools made from them varied greatly; many were designed for specific tasks and, in later millennia, mounted in handles. The great British prehistorian Dorothy Garrod (1951) believed that the occupation levels of the Mt. Carmel Caves and neighboring sites documented a technological transition from Middle to Upper Paleolithic toolmaking. But subsequent research (summarized by Marks, 1983)

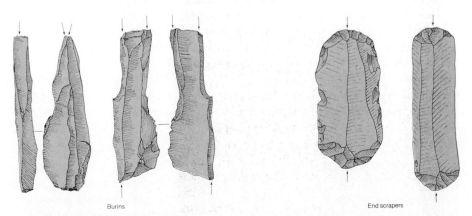

Burins   End scrapers

Burins and end scrapers. Arrows indicate the chisel ends of burins and the scraping edges of end scrapers.

has proved that Near Eastern technology was changing much earlier and that Upper Paleolithic toolkits and stoneworking may have resulted from new adaptive strategies resulting from climate change and other factors.

Anthony Marks believes that Upper Paleolithic technology resulted from far more than dramatic inventions and the rapid adoption of new ideas. Complex adaptive forces, still only dimly understood, were at work. Marks himself (1983) studied the transition between the Middle and Upper Paleolithic in Israel's Negev Desert. He describes Mousterian settlement there as "radiating," that is to say, the people lived at well-defined base camps near water and fine-

grained rock, exploiting a small area intensively. To do so, they used smaller sites, situated in different parts of their territory, for various activities. Around 45,000 years ago, the climate was wetter; there was considerable vegetation and abundant game resources in the Negev, sufficient to allow hunter-gatherer populations to concentrate in relatively small areas.

This settlement system changed radically with *Homo sapiens* and the Upper Paleolithic. The people now used a much larger territory for carefully scheduled exploitation of seasonal resources. The key to survival was mobility, for the climate was much drier. This mobility meant a lifeway that involved a different way of using fine-grained rocks. Previously the stoneworkers had made much use of the Levallois technique, a relatively uneconomical approach to stone flaking, ideal when flint was abundant. But the Upper Paleolithic bands could not always camp near sources of good stone, so they experimented with more economical flaking methods, often carefully selecting the raw material to pro-

duce elongated blanks, and eventually punch-struck blades. Marks believes that these new techniques did not develop suddenly with *Homo sapiens* but that they were the logical result of millennia of gradual adjustment to a more mobile lifeway, in which careful curation of raw materials was essential. There were, he points out, many different evolutionary paths to Upper Paleolithic technology before the distinctive punch-struck blade became commonplace.

Europe

Western Europe is the most thoroughly studied cultural province in the Stone Age world (Gamble, 1986b), but the transition there between Middle and Upper Paleolithic still remains a cultural enigma (Mellars, 1973; R. White, 1982). Was there a gradual changeover between the Neanderthal world and that of anatomically modern humans in this area about 35,000 years ago, or was the change abrupt? Randall White (1982) lists a series of long-term trends that characterize the Upper Paleolithic:

- A tendency toward high population densities after 35,000 years ago.
- More regular social gatherings.
- Much more stylistic variation in stone artifacts that were patterned in time and space. Perhaps these represent different territorial or social boundaries, perhaps a higher level of information exchange between isolated groups.
- Much greater emphasis on the working of bone and antler. Again, these tools display formal stylistic variation, perhaps with social significance.

- Some shift toward the hunting of herd animals that carry antlers for much of the year, especially in cold latitudes.
- Growing importance of personal ornamentation as a way of communicating corporate and personal identity.
- Obtaining of materials from distant sources, probably through structured exchange involving cooperation with other groups.

White believes there was a total restructuring of social relations during the critical transition period. It was then that corporate and individual identities became important and were enhanced by the skilled working of antler, bone, and stone, and by the use of ornaments. The Upper Paleolithic may have seen more structured relationships between the inhabitants of different geographic areas, expressed not only in trade but in better defined hunting territories and other social relationships. White believes that we should examine this transition on a very broad canvas. One of the most important questions is establishing whether *Homo sapiens sapiens* had to adapt to the close presence of other human groups as a matter of survival. In later prehistoric times, relationships with neighbors were to assume ever-increasing importance in adaptive strategies for long-term survival.

We cannot possibly describe the full diversity of hunter-gatherer peoples who flourished in all parts of the globe after 35,000 years ago, so our narrative concentrates on the following major developments:

- The hunter-gatherer cultures that flourished in southwest France and northern Spain between 35,000 and 8,000 years ago. These cultures are of particular importance because of their adaptation to the last cold snap of the Weichsel glaciation and their remarkable artistic traditions.
- The big-game hunting cultures that developed on the west Russian plains and Siberia.
- The early settlement of the arctic latitudes of northeast Asia, from which the first settlement of the New World may have developed.
- The first human settlement of the Americas and the cultural traditions that stemmed from it.
- The early history of surviving hunter-gatherers in tropical latitudes, especially the Australians and the San peoples of southern Africa.

EUROPEAN HUNTER-GATHERERS: 35,000 TO 8,000 YEARS AGO

The transition between Middle and Upper Paleolithic in western Europe is often thought to have been swift, with the Neanderthals vanishing rapidly after the anatomically modern Cro-Magnons arrived. Scientists had always assumed that the new technology in this area was the work of *Homo sapiens sapiens*, until two 32,000-year-old Neanderthal skeletons were discovered in a level containing Upper Paleolithic artifacts (Leveque and Vandermeersch, 1982). However, all known human skeletons after that date are those of *Homo sapiens sapiens*.

Central and western Europe was cold and dry during much of Upper Paleo-

Upper Paleolithic transition in Europe

lithic times, with great ice sheets covering large expanses of northern latitudes. South of the ice sheets, thousands of square miles of steppe-grassland with occasional stands of trees covered much of the unglaciated land. There were many local variations, with extensive tree growth in deep river valleys and other sheltered areas. A rich mammalian community flourished in these diverse environments. It included bison, horses, reindeer, and mountain goats in more rugged areas; large herbivores like the mammoth, woolly rhinoceros, and wild ox were common on the open steppe. The human inhabitants could exploit not only a rich animal biomass but a wide variety of plant foods, including blueberries, raspberries, acorns, and hazelnuts. The climate was changing constantly, so the people had to readapt by altering their diet, hunting and gathering strategies, and technology. Much of the great variability in Upper Paleolithic culture results from such readaptations.

The Upper Paleolithic of Europe began about 35,000 years ago and witnessed constant changes in human behavior over the next 25,000 years. These millennia have been subdivided into a series of cultural periods, each with its own technology and technological innovations (Table 6.1; Figure 6.4) (Movius, 1973). At first French archaeologists, who developed this cultural sequence from excavations in caves and rock shelters, thought of each period as a rigid "epoch," like a geological layer. But today the cultural phases are seen as changes stimulated by a variety of complex and little understood factors. Some of them may have been responses to practical needs, others purely dictates of fashion or small technological innovations.

As time went on, major regional differences emerged throughout central and western Europe (Gamble, 1986a). These can be identified from stone and antler tool types, by contrasting stone technologies. As Randall White (1986) remarks, it is almost as if barriers to communication were arising, as if there were regional dialects in Europe for the first time.

Settlement Strategies and Lifeways

The Upper Paleolithic peoples of southwest France have long been thought of as one of the prehistoric models for the cave people so beloved of twentieth-century cartoonists. While it is true that much of our knowledge of their cultures comes from French caves and rock shelters, these were by no means the only settlements occupied after 35,000 years ago. Southwest France is remarkable for its high density of Upper Paleolithic sites within a restricted area, sites that were sometimes intensively occupied over long periods of time.

Diverse food
resources

Between 35,000 and 12,000 years ago, the climate of this region was strongly oceanic, with cool summers and mild winters by Ice Age standards. Summer temperatures may have been in the 53.6 to 59° F range, with winter readings around 32° F (Mellars, 1985). The vegetation growing season was longer than on the open plains to the north and east, and snow cover was considerably less. Thus, food resources for large herbivores were more readily available, perhaps resulting in a much higher density of game animals as well as more plentiful edible foods. This was a region of diverse food resources (Jochim, 1983), reflected not only in tree pollens in sheltered archaeological sites but in the range of animals recovered from them. The people were mainly subsisting off reindeer, but they also took wild ox, red deer, bison, ibex, chamois, woolly rhinoceros, and mammoth. The sheer diversity of the environment gave the human inhabitants economic security. In years when reindeer migrations were unpredictable, there were other sources of animal protein close at hand, to say nothing of plant foods.

Many of these resources were relatively predictable. There were seasonal reindeer migrations, from the higher ground to the east in summer to the deep river valleys of the west in winter, where food resources could be found even in the coldest months. Paul Mellars (1985) believes that the hunters could intercept animals from a broad range of species, many of them migratory, from an ecological range extending perhaps some 62 miles (100 km) on either side of their home bases. Michael Jochim (1983) argues that large-scale salmon fishing during seasonal runs was a major factor in the evolution of complex hunter-gatherer societies in this region. The concentration of settlement along riverbanks, at places where the salmon runs were most predictable, was a logical response to predictable food resources. Effective exploitation of salmon runs requires not only efficient fishing technology but the services of considerable numbers of people to dry and store the thousands of fresh fish before they spoil.

Food resources

Unfortunately, Jochim's argument has a serious weakness, for very few salmon bones have been found in the region's Upper Paleolithic sites (Mellars, 1985). Although fish hooks and harpoons, as well as fine engravings of salmon and seals, are known from many later Upper Paleolithic sites, it appears likely that hunting of large mammals was the predominant subsistence activity between 35,000 and about 10,000 years ago. Fishing does seem to have assumed much greater importance at the very end of the Ice Age, perhaps as forests encroached on open grazing grounds and rising sea levels brought more fish to French rivers (Mellars, 1985; Pfeiffer, 1985).

Whatever the precise makeup of Upper Paleolithic diet in southwest France, there were direct adaptive responses to these highly favorable ecological conditions. Population densities were locally much higher than in other parts of Europe, with groups living in the same locations for much of the year, close to seasonal concentrations of food resources. They exploited these resources with high efficiency, Mellars believes, and some part of the population almost permanently lived in certain key locations. Smaller groups then exploited more distant resources in summer and according to need.

The people tended to choose many of their settlement sites with reference to plentiful water supplies and good views of the surrounding landscape, so they could observe game and perhaps their neighbors. More than 90 percent of all known sites are close to springs or riverbanks. The bands could live wherever they wanted, for they had the technology to survive hard winters in the open. Some of the largest cave and rock shelter sites lay close to river fords, places, perhaps, where migrating reindeer would cross each year. One such site is Laugerie Haute near Les Eyzies, were the skeletons of several reindeer lay between the great rock shelter and the river ford. When the people occupied a rock shelter or cave, it invariably faced south, so they could benefit from the sun's rays on cool days. They appear to have erected tents and hide curtains in the shelters for additional protection. Some overhangs lay near places where it was

Settlement preferences

TABLE 6.1 Much simplified outline of the Upper Paleolithic cultural traditions of western Europe from 40,000 to 8,000 years ago.

The most commonly accepted scheme has two parallel cultural traditions flourishing from about 34,000 until 30,000 years ago, the Chatelperronian characterized by backed knife blades, and the Aurignacian favoring scrapers and sharpened blades (opposite, bottom). The Gravettian with its fine-backed blades became dominant after 30,000 years ago. Thereafter, there were considerable regional variations.

The Solutrean, a culture that relied on sophisticated "cooking" of large pieces of flint so that it became porcelainlike in texture, flourished in France and Spain. The stoneworker could exert pressure on the flake edges to produce magnificent leaf-shaped spear points (opposite, right). Pressure flaking never took hold in Europe, where many variations of Gravettian culture are found. In the west, the Magdalenian tradition, which relied heavily on antler and bone (opposite, top). emerged about 18,000 years ago.

It should be noted that all Upper Paleolithic cultures in this area relied heavily on blade technology and on scrapers, burins, and other simple blade artifacts.

With the retreat of the ice sheets after 12,000 years ago, Stone Age peoples adapted their cultures to more forested environments, where exploitation of woodlands and coasts was important to survival. These Mesolithic cultures, with their distinctive microlithic technology, lasted until farming spread into Europe about 8000 years ago, reaching the northwest about 7500 years ago.

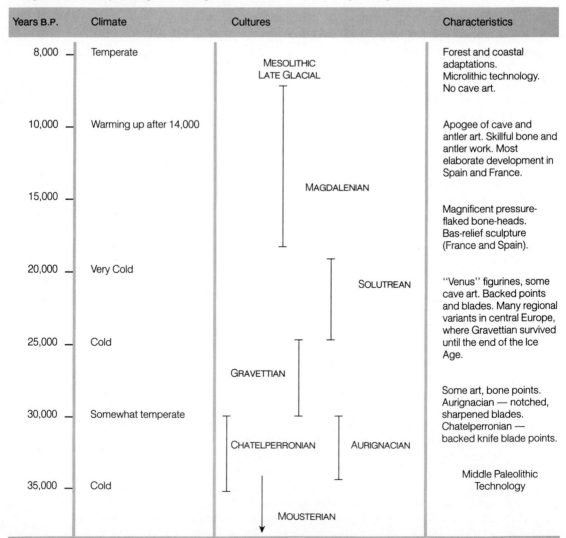

Years B.P.	Climate	Cultures	Characteristics
8,000	Temperate	MESOLITHIC LATE GLACIAL	Forest and coastal adaptations. Microlithic technology. No cave art.
10,000	Warming up after 14,000		Apogee of cave and antler art. Skillful bone and antler work. Most elaborate development in Spain and France.
15,000		MAGDALENIAN	Magnificent pressure-flaked bone-heads. Bas-relief sculpture (France and Spain).
20,000	Very Cold	SOLUTREAN	"Venus" figurines, some cave art. Backed points and blades. Many regional variants in central Europe, where Gravettian survived until the end of the Ice Age.
25,000	Cold	GRAVETTIAN	
30,000	Somewhat temperate	CHATELPERRONIAN AURIGNACIAN	Some art, bone points. Aurignacian — notched, sharpened blades. Chatelperronian — backed knife blade points.
35,000	Cold		Middle Paleolithic Technology
		MOUSTERIAN	

Magdalenian

Harpoons

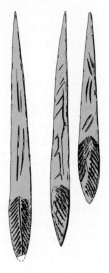

Bone points with
beveled bases for mounting

"Parrot beak" burin with inclined chisel edge

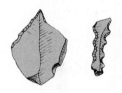

Stone tools

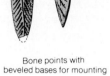

Spear thrower (a hypothetical
drawing of one in use)

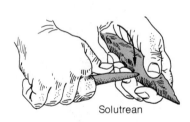

Solutrean

Aurignacian

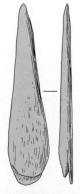

Split-base bone point
(split used for mounting)

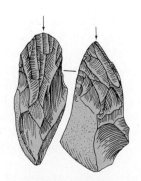

Steep scraper
(scraping edge indicated)

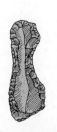

Blade with sharpened
notches

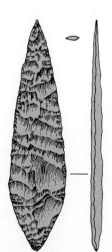

possible to stampede reindeer, horses, and other herd animals over precipitous cliffs. In the open, some groups laid out pavements of river cobbles as foundations for wood, skin, or sod structures. Sometimes they heated the pebbles first, perhaps so they could lay them over frozen ground to form a secure platform.

Social Life and Group Size

Many of the largest French Upper Paleolithic sites are close to places where seasonally abundant resources like reindeer could be exploited by large numbers of people. Other settlements were much smaller, little more than temporary camps occupied by a few families. Perhaps it is significant that the larger sites — like Laugerie Haute and Laugerie Basse or La Madeleine, the type site of the Magdalenian — contain many more art objects. The bands may have come together into larger social units at locations where abundant resources were available for a few months or weeks to cooperate in the food quest. Such aggregations could not have lasted year-round, partly because the environment would not support so many people in one place for long. If modern hunter-gatherers are any guide, the bands probably had no mechanisms for resolving disputes, except that practiced by modern San — walking away. This is what anthropologist Richard Lee (1979) calls "voting with your feet."

The days, weeks, even months of aggregation are the high point of the year in living hunter-gatherer societies, as they must have been in Upper Paleolithic times. This was the time of marriage and initiation ceremonies, of highly intense rituals, in which the fine art objects of the people may have played important roles. This was when shamans told tales and wove spells, when the forces of the ancestors and the spirit world were invoked to ensure the continuity of life and the success of the hunt. It was also a time when men and women exchanged artifacts, ornaments, and exotic raw materials from near and far. Seashells from the English Channel and the Mediterranean, Baltic amber, and other exotica — items that were sometimes imbued with special magical, social, or prestige value — were apparently exchanged from hand to hand. Many of these may have been given and received as gestures of social obligation between individuals and groups.

Social Organization and Complexity

The Upper Paleolithic societies of southwest France lived in relatively close juxtaposition, in a diverse environment with rich, predictable food resources. For at least part of the year, these societies may have lived a relatively sedentary existence and come together in much larger aggregations. Under these circumstances, it is reasonable to expect that their social organization would become more complex than was normal among egalitarian band societies. The evolution of social complexity among prehistoric hunter-gatherer societies is a much-debated topic (for a set of essays, see Price and Brown, 1985), but in the case of the Magdalenian of southwest France, we can predict some social complexity with confidence.

Magdalenian culture was elaborate and sophisticated, to the point that we can predict that more sedentary living and larger group size might have re-

Social structure

Social complexity

sulted in social change (Mellars, 1985). Certain individuals may have acquired greater social prestige or authority that enabled them to organize and coordinate the activities of other members of the society. They might have organized communal hunts and the distribution of food, and have mediated in domestic conflicts. In time, Magdalenian society might have become organized around social hierarchies, ranking systems such as are found among modern hunter-gatherer societies like the Northwest Coast Indians of North America. There may have been other trends toward greater social complexity — a new, and strong, sense of attachment on the part of different social groups to the lands they occupied and exploited, with neighbors or other groups being excluded from them. Extended family networks and kin groups would have become more elaborate, enlarged to encompass relationships with people living at some distance, outside the extended family. As part of this elaboration, we can envisage more structured marriage rules that restricted patterns of interaction between different regional populations (Wobst, 1976).

These changes are largely hypothetical, simply because archaeology rarely preserves evidence for rank differentiation or marriage rules. But Mellars and others have argued that changes of this nature were inevitable when hunter-gatherers lived in larger groups, within relatively small territories, and at the same spot for much of the year. Certainly, the sometimes elaborate decorations of seashells, bracelets, even sewn clothing associated with the dead argue for complex spiritual beliefs, many involving abstract symbolic images of the Ice Age world that we will never be able to recover.

Upper Paleolithic Art

Nearly 200 caves bearing wall paintings and engravings are known from southwest Europe, mainly France and Spain. Some 10,000 sculpted and engraved art objects have come from Upper Paleolithic sites across Europe, far into Siberia, and in Africa. Upper Paleolithic people were brilliant artists in stone, antler, bone, clay, ivory, and wood. They used paint on rock walls, sculpted in bas-relief and the round, and made musical instruments (R. White, 1986). The artists created thousands of naturalistic images of animals, sometimes human and humanlike forms, and dozens of enigmatic signs. All of this art conveys complex, long-forgotten ideas, a symbolic world of spirit animals and spirit humans, of forces benevolent and evil. Generations of archaeologists have grappled with the meaning of the art (Pfeiffer, 1982), so far with little success.

The earliest artworks appear to come from the Aurignacian, dating to perhaps as early as 32,000 years ago. (There are some scratched Mousterian and Chatelperronian bones, but these hardly constitute art.) The Aurignacians carved some animals in the round in ivory and made simple paintings and engravings of animals and human sexual organs. British archaeologist Mark Newcomer has made an exact copy of a 32,000-year-old Aurignacian bone flute and played it, evidence that musical sounds were made early in the Upper Paleolithic (R. White, 1986).

Gravettian artists executed incised engravings on walls and blew or brushed pigment against their hands to make imprints on cave walls. They also fash-

Aurignacian art 32,000 B.P.

Gravettian art c. 25,000 B.P.

ioned "Venus" figurines, sculptures and bas-reliefs of females, often with pendulous breasts, sometimes pregnant, and with exaggerated sexual characteristics (Figure 6.5). Many scholars believe these were female fertility figurines. They have been found from Russia in the east to the Dordogne of France in the west, most in deposits dating to about 25,000 years ago. We have no means of knowing whether, in fact, these were fertility figures, but they seem to have been associated with a relatively short-lived set of beliefs that were in use over a wide area of Europe.

Bas-reliefs, friezes of animals like wild horses that adorn places where the people lived, came into fashion during the Solutrean. The Solutreans also painted animals on cave walls, but 80 percent of all known Upper Paleolithic art comes from the Magdalenian, beginning around 18,000 years ago. The earlier Magdalenian saw some remarkable cave painting, from places like Lascaux, painted some 17,000 years ago. Lascaux's walls were covered again and again with depictions of wild horses, bulls, reindeer, and many other animals. Many of the animals were painted with long, distorted necks and thick bodies, as if the artists were unaware of perspective (Figure 6.6). The paintings also include squiggles, spaghettilike patterns, and tentlike symbols (Windels, 1965). A Great Hall of the Bulls features four immense wild bulls, drawn in thick, black lines, with some of the body details filled in. Horses, deer, a small bear, and a strange unicornlike beast prance with the great bulls in a fantastic display of blacks,

Cave art
32,000 B.P.

FIGURE 6.5 Paleolithic art. Venus figurines from Brassempouy, France (left) and Dolní Věstonice, Czechoslovakia (right).

FIGURE 6.6 A giant stag painting from Lascaux, France.

browns, reds, and yellows that truly brings the animals to life in a flickering light. It is hard to believe that the paintings are at least 17,000 years old.

The earliest tradition reached its height with an explosion of antler- and bonework after 18,000. The hunters decorated their harpoons, spear points, spear-throwers, and other artifacts with naturalistic engravings, fine carvings of wild animals, and elaborate schematic patterns. Even fine eye details and hair texture were shown by delicate graving strokes. But the Magdalenians are most famous for their beautiful rock art, paintings and engravings deep in the caves of northern Spain and southwest France. At Altamira, in northern Spain, Altamira you walk deep into the hillside to enter a low-ceilinged chamber where the painters left fine renderings of bison in red and black (Figure 6.7) (Breuil, 1908). By painting and engraving the animals around natural bulges in the rock, the artists conveyed a sense of relief and life. In cave after cave, the hunters left jumbled frenzies of large and small game and animals, hand impressions, dots, and signs, many of which must have had symbolic significance.

An enormous and highly speculative literature concerns the motives behind this remarkable art (Conkey, 1981; Mellars, 1985; Pfeiffer, 1982). Originally, Henri Breuil and other experts (Breuil, 1952) argued that the caves were sacred places where the hunters gathered to perform rituals and sympathetic magic that would ensure the fertility of game and the success of the hunt. Even the signs on the cave walls were interpreted as snares and traps (Grasiosi, 1960). Today we know a great deal more about symbolic behavior and the art that goes with it, and much more about how hunter-gatherer societies function. The latest cave art research has concentrated not only on the art itself but on the con-

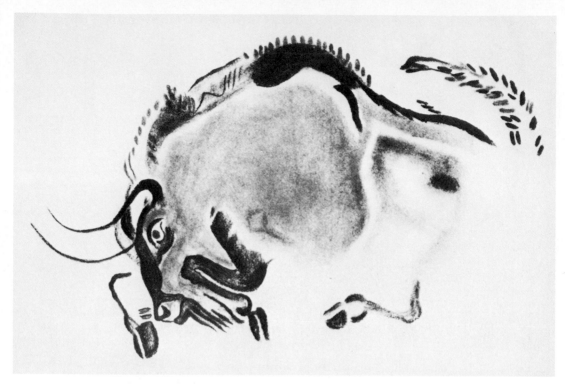

FIGURE 6.7 A bison in a polychrome cave painting in Altamira, Spain.

texts in which it appears. French prehistorian Andre Leroi-Gourhan argued in 1965 that the art was not random but part of a system of meanings, an expression of worldview that organized Upper Paleolithic life. By counting the associations of subjects and clusters of motifs, Leroi-Gourhan found that certain themes, among them female figures, appeared in rock shelters and better lit locales, while others frequented dark caverns. There are differences in the distribution of art, too. Bison, for instance, dominate northern Spanish cave walls, but they rarely occur on portable objects. Perhaps the social contexts of wall and portable art were different (see N. Hammond, 1974; Ucko and Rosenfeld, 1967).

Alexander Marshack (1972, 1975) has carried out detailed microphotographic studies of Paleolithic art and shown that many of the visual forms are ecologically and seasonally related. Rather than concentrating on the naturalistic pictures of animals, he has studied the hundreds of nonnaturalistic pieces, with their patterns of lines, notches, dots, and groupings of marks (Figure 6.8). On some pieces, the marks were made with different tools at different times. These pieces, which Marshack named "time-factorial" objects, were used, he believes, as sequential notations of events and phenomena, predecessors of calendars. Marshack has examined hundreds of specimens stretching back as far as the Lower Paleolithic. He found duplicated designs, systematic groups of dots and notches that were either counting tallies or the beginnings, he feels, of a writing system; but, he suggests, they differ from later, more formal writing

Nonnaturalistic pieces

systems that could be read by everyone: the Magdalenian and earlier notations were for the engraver alone to read, even if he explained them to others on occasion. To formulate such a system required thought and theoretical abstractions far more advanced than those hitherto attributed to hunter-gatherers of this age. Of course, Marshack's ideas are controversial, but they come out of the type of ground-breaking research that produces exciting new interpretations and insights into Stone Age life.

Today, we know that many hunter-gatherer groups use ritual and art, creating and manipulating visual forms to structure and give meaning to their existence. Many ethnographic studies have shown how symmetry and other artistic principles may underlie the designs of many art traditions and characterize every aspect of daily life, from social relationships to village planning. The people may use relatively few symbols to communicate meanings. Very often it is the context of the symbols that reveals the meaning. For the Upper Paleolithic artists, there were clearly continuities between animal and human life and with their social world. Thus, their art was a symbolic depiction of these continuities. The artists did not choose just any wall or piece of antler or bone for their drawings, nor just any animal or geometric form to depict. Their selections were deliberate, symbolic acts that provide clues to the significance of the world's earliest artistic tradition.

Some archaeologists believe that the underground art, with its accurate depictions of reindeer and other animals at different times of the year, may have been a kind of storehouse of knowledge about the environment, passed from generation to generation. One such 14,000-year-old sanctuary comes from El

FIGURE 6.8 Engraved bone, 8.2 in (21 cm) long, from La Marche, France, which was intensively studied by Marshack. The close-up shot shows tiny marks in two groups, each engraved by a different point, with a different type of stroke. (©Alexander Marshack, 1972)

Juyo Cave in northern Spain. Alternating layers of animal bones and rosettelike features made by filling cylindrical containers with earth and turning them upside down (like sand castle molds) form a mound about 29.5 inches (75 cm) high. Twenty-five bone points and a stone carved into a half human–half feline face lay close by. The excavators believe this was a shrine (Freeman and Echegaray, 1981). (For a full discussion of different possible interpretations, see Conkey, 1981, 1983; N. Hammond, 1974; Pfeiffer, 1982).

About 13,000 years ago, the Magdalenians seem to have stopped painting and engraving deep caves. Most art after that appears at cave entrances and in rock shelters, always exposed to the light of day. The paintings and engravings were no longer naturalistic, and they vanished altogether about 11,000 years ago. By this time, much warmer climatic conditions had brought forest to the open plains, and the large arctic animals depicted in the earlier art were largely extinct. The brilliant efflorescence of Magdalenian culture had been replaced by new adaptations — to forests, rivers, and coasts. By this time, cave and antler art had given way to a complex symbol system, much of it painted on flat pebbles (Courand, 1985).

RUSSIA AND SIBERIA

The vast, undulating plains of western Russia and central Europe as far east as the Ural Mountains were a much less hospitable environment for Stone Age hunter-gatherers than the deep, well-watered valleys of the West. There were no convenient caves or rock shelters. For warmth and shelter the inhabitants of this area had to create artificial dwellings with their own tools and locally available raw materials. It may be no coincidence that few archaeological sites are found on these frigid plains, with their nine-month winters and short summers, until Upper Paleolithic times. The Neanderthals and early Upper Paleolithic populations may have ventured onto the steppe during the warmer summer months. But it took some significant technological innovations, providing better cultural adaptations to bitter cold, to allow people to live there year-round. One important invention may have been the perforated bone needle, which enabled people to fabricate tailored layers of clothing, for layered garments provide the best protection against subzero temperatures. Advances in bone and antler technology may also have played a decisive role in arctic adaptation, for they allowed not only more efficient hunting but the development of such important artifacts as the spear-thrower, a highly effective weapon against large, gregarious animals.

Only a few rivers dissect the west Russian plains, among them the Don and the Dnieper. It is no coincidence that ancient river terraces were the most common locations for Stone Age hunting settlements. These were often promontories overlooking the river, where the hunters could spy on the movements of the herds of arctic elephant (mammoth), woolly rhinoceros, and wild horse that flourished in the valleys (Dolukhanov, 1982). At the height of the last glaciation, this area was a treeless periglacial landscape, a meadow steppe in warmer interstadials. It was a very inhospitable environment but one where hunter-gatherer societies flourished for thousands of years. Winter temperatures may have averaged −30 to −40° F, summer maxima rarely reaching 64°.

Soviet archaeologists have found traces of human settlements on these plains going back into Mousterian times. But most Upper Paleolithic finds date to the period between 18,000 and 14,000 years ago, when scattered hunter-gatherer bands lived in what were often spectacular mammoth bone structures (Soffer, 1985). The Mezhirich site overlooks the Dnieper River southeast of Kiev; it is a 15,000-year-old settlement of five houses, covering an area of some 110,000 square feet (10,219 m²) (Kornietz and Soffer, 1984). Each house was about 13 to 22 feet (4 to 7 m) across and up to 850 square feet (78.9 m²) in area (Figure 6.9). Foundation walls of massive mammoth bones supported an intricate framework of smaller limb bones, vertebrae, and other parts, sometimes arranged in fine herringbone patterns. The roof was supported by uprights that were stuck into holes broken through large mammoth bones, and the entire structure was almost certainly covered with elephant hide. Hearths and work areas lay inside the houses, which seem to have been occupied over long periods of time. More hearths and deep storage pits that kept meat refrigerated in the permafrost soil lay between the houses.

Mezhirich
15,000 B.P.

The Mezhirich dwellings are thought to have housed about fifty people, each dwelling taking ten men about five or six days to complete, a considerable investment of effort. Since mammoth bone dwellings found at other locations are less elaborate, it may be that this settlement was of unusual importance. The inhabitants hunted not only mammoth but also other large mammals, as well as taking river fish and birds. Judging by the evidence from several sites, they pursued mammoth in autumn and winter, reindeer in spring and early summer, fur-bearing animals in winter, and waterfowl in summer (Dolukhanov, 1982). So many mammoth bones were used in house construction that the people may have scavenged them from carcasses on the plains in addition to using their own kills. Soviet archaeologists report that seashells from between 400 to 500 miles (643 and 804 km) away came from the Mezhirich houses, while amber, a stone thought by many prehistoric peoples to have magic qualities, was traded in from 100 miles (160 km) away.

Mezhirich is far from unique. The famous Kostenki sites on the Don River have yielded large, irregular dwellings partially scooped out of the earth (R. Klein, 1969; McBurney, 1976). The floor plans are so irregular that it is difficult to be sure what the house plan was. In some cases, several circular structures up to 15 feet (4.6 m) in diameter were built together in a huge depression with a row of hearths down the middle. Bands of considerable size must have congregated in these tented areas (Figure 6.10).

To the east of the western plains stretches Soviet central Asia, a vast area of continental territory that covers not only northern Afghanistan but the arid Turan depression and the central Asian highlands. The archaeology of this area is still little known, although research has made rapid strides in recent years (Davis, 1987; Ranov and Davis, 1979). There are numerous Mousterian sites dating to the early part of the Weichsel glaciation, as they do in the West, displaying different toolkit variations that probably reflect different seasonal activities. It is not yet known when the transition to the Upper Paleolithic took

Soviet central Asia

FIGURE 6.9 Excavation of Dwelling 4 at Mezhirich, USSR.

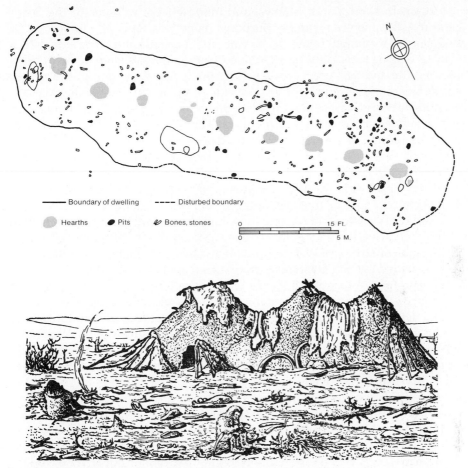

FIGURE 6.10 The plan of a long house (top) from Kostenki IV, USSR, and a reconstruction based on the finds at Push Kari. The latter was nearly 40 ft long by 12 ft wide (12.0 by 3.7 m) and stood in a shallow depression.

place, but there is a possibility that it occurred somewhat later than in the West, for early Upper Paleolithic sites are few and far between.

The Upper Paleolithic of Soviet central Asia is known from a late Weichsel culture that was widespread in caves, rock shelters, and open sites, but is still not well known. The Shugnou site southwest of the city of Samarkand lies at an altitude of 6700 feet (2000 m), one of the highest Upper Paleolithic sites in the world. Soviet archaeologists found five occupation layers in a site above a mountain river, yielding evidence of big-game hunting, of horses, wild oxen, wild sheep, and goats, dating to at least 20,000 to 15,000 years ago. Pollen grains suggest that weather conditions were somewhat cooler and wetter than today. The hunter-gatherer population of central Asia may have been sparse for thousands of years, perhaps owing to unfavorable climate conditions, but this is pure conjecture. Population densities rose at the end of the Pleistocene, and human settlement expanded into higher elevations.

Mammoth skins, bones, sinews, and marrow were valuable to the Soviet central Asian peoples for many purposes. Bone was especially important for fuel; burned mammoth bones have come from Kostenki and other sites. House frames, digging tools, pins, needles, and many small tools were made from the bones of the hunters' prey. Wood was naturally less important in the treeless environment of the steppe. In this difficult environment, we would expect an economy based at least in part on lumbering beasts, whose carcasses could support many hungry mouths and fuel fires. The technology of the plains made much use of fire for warmth and for hardening the tips of spears. Indeed, fire was vital in the human armory as people moved outward to the arctic frontiers of the Paleolithic world.

Soviet central Asia was subjected to cultural influences from both the flake and blade traditions of the West and the chopper-chopping tool traditions of the Far East. Consequently, stone tools here frequently were based on stone cobbles and were simple, highly effective artifacts that rarely achieved the sophistication or artistry of Western traditions. The same amalgam of cultural traditions filtered into Siberia in far eastern Asia (Larichev et al., 1987).

Siberia

Remote from Atlantic and Pacific weather patterns, Siberia is dry country with harsh, dry winters and short, hot summers. Treeless plains predominate in the far north and extend to the shores of the Arctic Ocean. Rainfall was so sparse during the Weichsel glaciation that the great ice sheets of the West never formed here. Herds of gregarious mammoths grazed on the tundra and on the edges of the river valleys, where small bands of hunter-gatherers weathered the long winters. The archaeology of this enormous area and of northeast Asia is still little known, despite long-term excavation campaigns by Soviet archaeologists in recent years (Bryan, 1978; Chard, 1974; R. Klein, 1971; Muller-Beck, 1982). Nonetheless, Siberia and northeast Asia are of vital importance, for they were the staging areas from which the first settlement of the Americas took place, across the Bering Strait. A number of key issues confront anyone working in this area:

- What was the date of the first human settlement of the far northeast?
- Was there a pre-*sapiens* population in Siberia before 35,000 years ago?
- What technological and cultural traits are found in the Far East that can be identified in the New World?

Soviet archaeologists have identified two different Upper Paleolithic cultural traditions in Siberia and northeast Asia. These are known as the Mal'ta-Afontova, a tradition associated with simple, edge-trimmed tools; and the Dyukhtai, associated with stone knives and spear points which are flaked on both sides.

The Dyukhtai tradition is found mostly east of the Yenesei Basin. The Soviet archaeologist Yuri Mochanov believes he has found Dyukhtai sites on the Aldan River that are 35,000 years old, but the dating is suspect (Mochanov, 1978). Dyukhtai Cave itself and nearby open sites make it certain that small populations of hunter-gatherers were in this region by at least 18,000 years ago. This was a long-lived tradition, of sparse arctic populations surviving on large and small mammals. The people made spear points that were carefully flaked on both sides, as well as used large pebbles that may have served as butchery tools (Figure 6.11). The effective exploitation of this area depended on a suc-

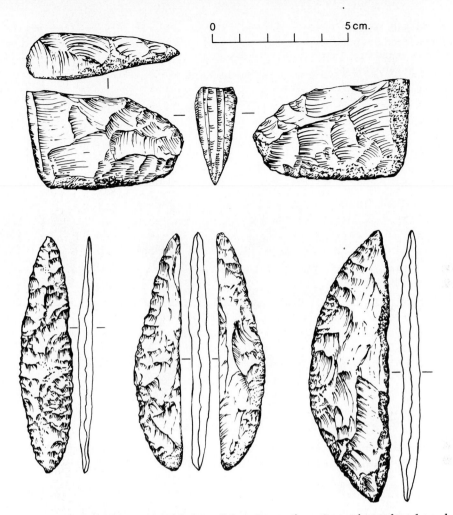

FIGURE 6.11 Artifacts of the Dyukhtai tradition. At top, four views of a wedge-shaped core, used to make tiny blades. At bottom, three bifacially flaked projectile heads. The wedge-shaped core is a characteristic artifact found on both sides of the Bering Strait in contexts of approximately 10,000 B.P. It is, of course, a by-product of the production of fine microblades.

cessful adaptation to the open tundra and on the special skills of big-game hunting. As in the West, the plains people would have had to range widely over a huge territory in search of their prey, camping near the kills for a few days and returning to favored spots year after year when the prey were plentiful.

The Mal'ta-Afontova tradition is best known from the Yenesei Valley and the Lake Baikal region. The Mal'ta site itself was occupied by people who lived in long houses and hunted both arctic and plains game (Gerasimov, 1958). Their tools included Upper Paleolithic scrapers and burins, as well as edge-trimmed points and scraping tools that are obvious survivals from Middle Paleolithic traditions. The Mal'ta people were expert boneworkers who carved female and bird figurines (Figure 6.12). The Mal'ta-Afontova tradition has been radiocar-

Mal'ta-Afontova tradition
earlier than 22,000 B.P. to 10,000 B.P. and later

FIGURE 6.12 Figurines from Mal'ta, Siberia. A bone figurine (actual size), two views; and an ivory bird (two-thirds actual size).

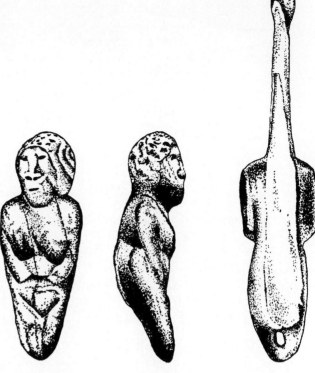

bon dated to as early as 20,900 ± 300 years ago in the Yenesei Valley, and Mal'ta itself has been carbon dated to approximately 14,500 years ago.

MAL'TA-AFONTOVA, DYUKHTAI, AND THE FIRST AMERICANS

As we shall see in Chapter 7, the Americas were first settled from Siberia, probably across a low-lying land bridge that connected Siberia to Alaska until some 14,000 years ago. Thus, in archaeological terms, we must look for the origins of the first Americans in Siberian cultural traditions, which themselves originated in Siberia or farther afield. The Mal'ta-Afontova tradition is thought to have strong links with Upper Paleolithic cultures to the west, but fewer ties to the east. It appears, therefore, to have little relevance to the first settlement of the New World. The Dyukhtai tradition was well established over much of northeast Asia at about the time the first human settlement of the Americas took place, but the origins of this microblade complex are still a complete mystery (Larichev et al., 1987). The only clues come from northern China, where microblades were being used at least 22,000 years ago, and probably earlier (Chung and Pei, 1986; Olsen, 1987). These possible connections are of some interest, since Christy Turner (1984) believes that the closest dental connections be-

Dyukhtai tradition ?18,000 to 12,000 B.P.

Chinese and Japanese microblade cultures ?22,000 to ? B.P.

tween the Old and New worlds 15,000 years ago lie in northern China and northeast Asia.

Microblade traditions are also found in Japan, where human beings may have settled about 150,000 years ago (the exact date is highly controversial) (Anderson, 1987; Ikawa-Smith, 1980; Reynolds and Barnes, 1984). Traces of human settlement before 30,000 years ago are rare, except for the lowermost levels of Fukui Cave in northern Kyushu, which yielded two bifacial tools and several flakes, radiocarbon dated to older than 31,000 years ago (Aikens and Higuchi, 1981; Anderson, 1987).

Throughout east Asia, later Stone Age cultures were characterized by a wider variety of adaptations and a great diversity of blade tools, including projectile heads and scrapers. This diversity is well documented in Japan, where, by 12,000 years ago, sea levels were rising and the landmass area available to hunter-gatherers shrank considerably. In Postglacial times, many Asian groups settled by coastlines and lakeshores, just as they did in Europe. They began exploiting a wide range of land and maritime resources in many different climatic zones. And in some areas where resources were concentrated, people began to adopt more sedentary settlement patterns and live in well-defined territories. In Japan, for example, shellfish collecting provided a relatively stable subsistence base for the Jomon people. As early as 12,500 years ago, they made clay vessels, which they used for steaming mollusks and making vegetable foods palatable. These are some of the earliest clay pots ever made, but the same cultural development may have taken hold elsewhere, as Stone Age people adapted to radically new environmental conditions and exploited an even wider resource base. And, as Postglacial times continued, the people turned to another logical adaptive strategy, deliberate growing of crops and taming of animals to ensure more reliable food supplies.

Jomon **12,500** B.P. to **2,300** B.P.

By the time the Dyukhtai tradition of northeast Asia gave way to new Postglacial cultural traditions and pottery was being used in Japan, human populations were well established in the Americas. Whatever their ultimate ancestry, we know they were direct descendants of the Stone Age populations who had flourished in Ice Age Siberia thousands of years earlier. And the primeval human populations of both northeast Asia and the New World were distant descendants of the *Homo sapiens sapiens* populations that had originated in more temperate and tropical latitudes millennia before.

GUIDE TO FURTHER READING

Bordes, François. *The Old Stone Age*. New York: McGraw-Hill, 1968.
    A basic manual on Stone Age artifacts with a strong emphasis on western Europe. Excellent illustrations of tool forms.

Clark, J. G. D. *The Earlier Stone Age Settlement of Scandinavia*. Cambridge: Cambridge University Press, 1975.
    A fundamental source on Mesolithic Europe. Well illustrated and multidisciplinary.

Clark, J. G. D. *Mesolithic Prelude*. Edinburgh: Edinburgh University Press, 1979.
    A brief essay on the Mesolithic for the general reader.

Gamble, Clive. *The Palaeolithic Settlement of Europe.* Cambridge: Cambridge University Press, 1986.
Provocative essay on the European Stone Age. Essential for all serious students of the subject.

Grasiosi, Paolo. *Palaeolithic Art.* New York: Abrams, 1960.
A superb compendium of Paleolithic cave and mobile art with a clear text that is a joy to read. More descriptive than analytic.

Leroi-Gourhan, A. *The Dawn of European Art: An Introduction to Palaeolithic Cave Painting.* Cambridge: Cambridge University Press, 1984.
An introduction that gives a useful summary of major sites and fresh theories on the art.

Pfeiffer, John. *The Creative Explosion.* New York: Harper and Row, 1982.
A wide-ranging, popular treatment of early cave art for the general reader.

Soffer, Olga. *The Upper Palaeolithic of the Central Russian Plains.* New York: Academic Press, 1985.
An account of Mezhirich and other Upper Paleolithic sites. An exemplary essay on the Stone Age in the Ukraine.

CHRONOLOGICAL TABLE D

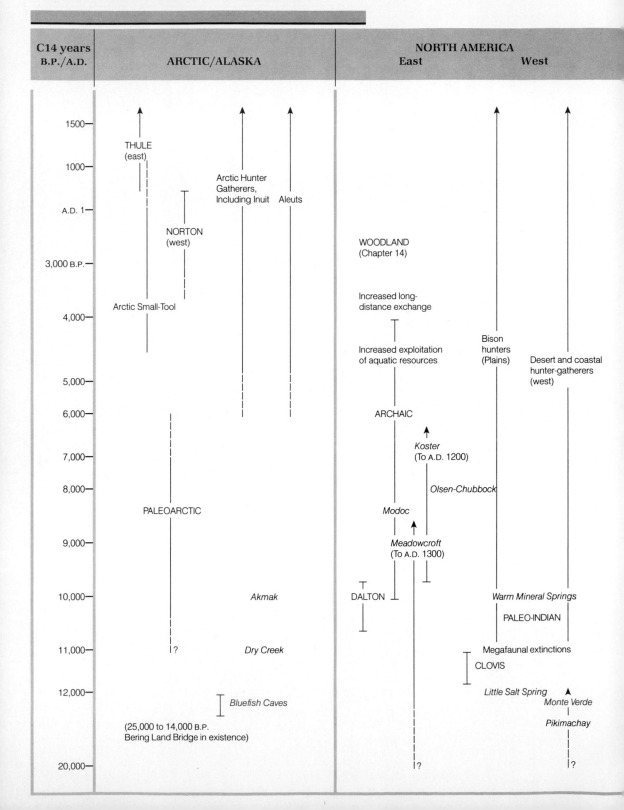

C14 years B.P./A.D.	ARCTIC/ALASKA	NORTH AMERICA East	West

- THULE (east)
- Arctic Hunter Gatherers, Including Inuit
- Aleuts
- NORTON (west)
- Arctic Small-Tool
- WOODLAND (Chapter 14)
- Increased long-distance exchange
- Increased exploitation of aquatic resources
- Bison hunters (Plains)
- Desert and coastal hunter-gatherers (west)
- ARCHAIC
- Koster (To A.D. 1200)
- Olsen-Chubbock
- PALEOARCTIC
- Modoc
- Meadowcroft (To A.D. 1300)
- Akmak
- DALTON
- Warm Mineral Springs
- PALEO-INDIAN
- Dry Creek
- Megafaunal extinctions
- CLOVIS
- Bluefish Caves
- Little Salt Spring
- Monte Verde
- Pikimachay
- (25,000 to 14,000 B.P. Bering Land Bridge in existence)

1500—
1000—
A.D. 1—
3,000 B.P.—
4,000—
5,000—
6,000—
7,000—
8,000—
9,000—
10,000—
11,000—
12,000—
20,000—

The First Americans

Preview

■ The earliest human settlement of the Americas is now generally agreed to have come across the Bering Strait during the last glaciation. During the coldest millennia of that glaciation, a land bridge, part of a landmass named Beringia, connected Siberia and Alaska. It is known to have existed from about 25,000 to 14,000 years ago.

■ The precise date of first settlement is much disputed. Some scholars believe that it was before 15,000 years ago, others that it occurred at the very end of the last glaciation, when big-game hunters crossed into Alaska. However, the earliest dated human settlement of arctic North America occurred around 12,000 years ago, at Bluefish Caves in the Yukon Territory.

■ Farther south in the Americas, there is indisputable evidence for human occupation about 12,000 years ago from Meadowcroft Rock Shelter in North America and Pikimachay Cave in Peru, as well as at a few other scattered locations. Meadowcroft and Pikimachay are believed by some archaeologists to have been occupied as early as 20,000 years ago, but the evidence is disputed.

■ The Clovis tradition of North America dates to between 11,500 and 11,000 years ago and was the first widespread big game hunting culture as far south as Mexico. About 11,000 years ago, the Ice Age big game became extinct, and the human inhabitants of the Americas adapted by turning to more diverse hunting and foraging activities.

■ Many varieties of hunting and gathering culture developed in the Americas after 10,000 years ago. The Desert traditions of the Far West made efficient use of favored locations by lakes, rivers, and swamps, as well as coastal resources, while Archaic societies in the Eastern Woodlands developed highly effective ways of exploiting vegetable foods and aquatic resources. Many varieties of hunter-gatherer adaptation, often involving precise scheduling of gathering activities, developed in Central and South America during the same period. It was among some of these specialized foraging groups that early American agriculture began.

■ The hunter-gatherer cultures of the Aleutian Islands and the Arctic developed from earlier Paleoarctic traditions based on fishing and sea mammal hunting. Aleut and Inuit cultures can be recognized in the archaeological record at least 3000, perhaps 4000 years ago.

Ever since the Americas were first colonized, people have speculated about where the pre-Columbian populations of the Western Hemisphere came from (Wauchope, 1962). Canaanites, Celts, Chinese, Egyptians, Phoenicians, and even the Ten Lost Tribes of Israel have been proposed as ancestors of the native Americans (Willey and Sabloff, 1980). By the early nineteenth century, field research and museum work had begun to replace the wild speculations of earlier scholars. People began to dig in Indian mounds. Spanish and American explorers rescued the temples of Mesoamerica from the rain forest.

A wise and sober scholar named Samuel Haven summarized myths and legends about pre-Columbian Indian beginnings in 1856. He concluded that the New World was initially settled from across the Bering Strait, designating the earliest Americans as northeastern Asiatics who migrated into North America at an unknown date. (See Figure 7.1 for sites mentioned in this chapter.) Most archaeologists now agree with Haven that the first Americans set foot in the New World by way of the Bering Strait. The Bering route is accepted because at times the strait formed a land bridge between Asia and Alaska during the Wisconsin (equivalent to Weichsel) glaciation (Figure 7.2).

Chronological
Table D

CONTROVERSIES OVER FIRST SETTLEMENT

For all the agreement about the Siberian route, intense controversies surround the beginnings of human settlement in the Americas (Bryan, 1978; Fagan, 1987; Shutler, 1983). These controversies revolve around three fundamental questions:

■ How long ago did humans settle in the Americas?
■ What toolkit did they bring with them, and what was their lifeway?
■ What was the ultimate ancestry of the first American Indians?

Although a few scholars still believe that people were living in the Americas as early as 250,000 years ago, or before the emergence of modern *Homo sapiens* about 35,000 years ago, there are absolutely no valid archaeological grounds for such hypotheses. No generally accepted 200,000-, or even 50,000-year-old sites have come from the Americas, nor have any human fossils other than those of anatomically modern individuals been discovered. Furthermore, the archaeological record in the Old World strongly suggests that no one occupied the northern latitudes of northeast Asia or the Siberian coasts of the Bering Sea this early (Fagan, 1987). On logical grounds, we are left with two competing hypotheses, each with passionate advocates:

Homo Sapiens and Hunter-Gatherers

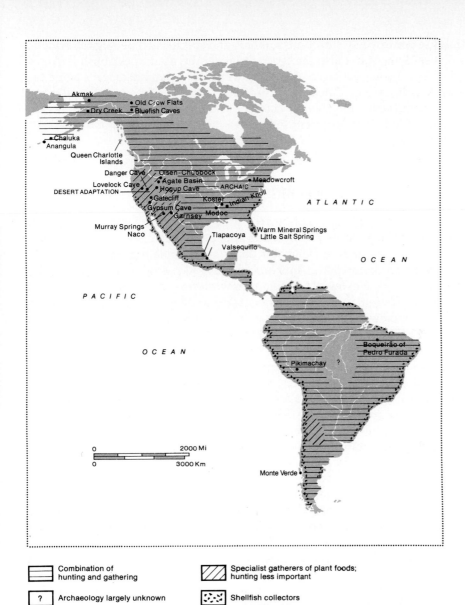

FIGURE 7.1   Prehistoric hunter-gatherers in the New World. Sites mentioned in the text are indicated. (For the Bering Land Bridge, see Figure 7.2.) The diagonally hatched areas show the distribution of specialized hunter-gatherers after 7000 years ago.

The *Pre-Clovis* hypothesis holds that the Americas were colonized by *Homo sapiens* some time during the Wisconsin glaciation, perhaps as early as 30,000 years ago, or even earlier.

The *Clovis* hypothesis argues that the first Americans crossed into the New World at the very end of the Wisconsin glaciation, perhaps as recently as about 15,000 years ago, and penetrated south of the Upper Pleistocene ice sheets as they retreated.

Intense controversy surrounds not only the specific archaeological evidence for first settlement but also the criteria that can be used to establish it (for extended discussion, see Fagan, 1987). However, most archaeologists agree that securely radiocarbon dated, well-stratified cultural remains of undoubted human manufacture are the only acceptable evidence. So far, data of this quality have eluded even persistent search, leaving one of the major mysteries of world prehistory still unsolved.

ICE SHEETS AND LAND BRIDGES

As we have seen in Chapter 6, human settlement in Siberia and northeast Asia is documented as early as 18,000 years ago, perhaps somewhat earlier. These Dyukhtai people remain somewhat of an enigma, for dating Siberian sites situated in subarctic landscapes requires sophisticated geological and geomorphological field work. However, judging from western and central Europe, human settlement of extreme arctic environments expanded about 18,000 years ago, a date that coincides well with the apparent first appearance of hunter-gatherer culture in the far northeast. If we accept the notion that *Homo sapiens* was living near the shores of the Bering Strait about 18,000 years ago, how did people cross into Alaska, only a short distance away?

At the time we are considering, world sea levels were as much as 330 feet (100 m) lower than today — so low that a land bridge stood where the Bering Strait now separates Asia and Alaska. (Sea levels drop when quantities of ocean water are frozen into continental ice sheets.) The strait formed part of a now almost submerged landmass known to geologists as Beringia. Only parts of west and east Beringia are dry land today — in Siberia and Alaska.

Bering Land Bridge
50,000 to 40,000 B.P.

25,000 to 14,000 B.P.

Since modern *Homo sapiens* emerged, the Bering Land Bridge has been dry land for two periods, potential "windows" when human beings could have hunted their way from Asia to Alaska. The first was about 50,000 to 40,000 years ago and the second about 25,000 to 14,000 years ago. The low-lying land bridge was a continuation of the Siberian steppe-tundra, a landscape that extended like a peninsula from Asia eastward to the vast Wisconsin ice sheets that covered North America (see Figure 7.2). We know from deep sea cores that Beringia was a dry plain, with brief, warm summers; long, extremely cold winters; and continual winds. At first glance, the land bridge would seem like a most inhospitable place for human settlement, especially at the height of a glaciation. But its plains gave way to many marshy areas, where lush meadows provided ample summer fodder for large grass-eating mammals like the mammoth, as well as for wild horses, musk oxen, and other arctic species. The Upper Pleistocene fauna of this general area included many species that are intolerant of deep snow, although they may have flourished in the dry environment, moving from one grazing ground to another as the snow thawed during the summer. Judging from modern arctic environments, the density of game may never have been high, but it may have been up to three and a half times that of today, partly because of a much greater abundance of willow shrub, which is thought to have provided as much as 50 percent of mammoth diet. This was no land teeming in milk and honey but a very savage climate indeed. Nevertheless, it

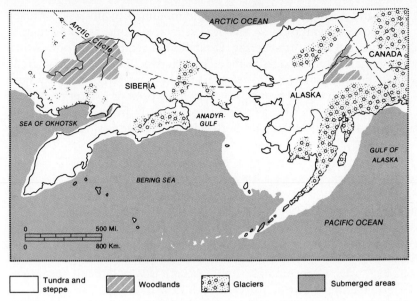

| | Tundra and steppe | | Woodlands | | Glaciers | | Submerged areas |

FIGURE 7.2 The Bering Land Bridge as reconstructed by the latest research.

may have been capable of supporting a human population of between fifteen and twenty-five people per 386 square miles (1000 sq km), a figure roughly equivalent to that for modern Eskimos living off the land and sea alone (for a fascinating set of essays on Beringia, see Hopkins et al., 1982).

The Bering Land Bridge may have been an inhospitable environment, but it was, apparently, capable of supporting human life during two periods when modern *Homo sapiens* was on earth. Of these two windows, the first appears to immediately predate the appearance of our direct ancestors. This was also a time when, apparently, there was no human settlement in northeast Asia (our archaeological knowledge is, of course, very incomplete). The most likely period when human beings could have used the land bridge would have been during the second window, at the height of the late Wisconsin glaciation. Under these circumstances, we should look for traces of human settlement in Alaska, then east Beringia, sometime between 25,000 and 14,000 years ago.

Could the first Americans have made their way across the strait by boat? We know that people colonized the remote landmass of Australia before 30,000 years ago, and that they could only have done so by crossing over some 55 miles (88 km) of open water even at the height of the glaciation, when sea levels were much lower than today. But these were more benign tropical waters, where such hazards as floating ice, strong arctic winds, and the ever-present danger of hyperthermia were unknown. The risks in the far north were much greater. Even in summer fogs and rough seas make the strait a chancy place, while to cross winter pack ice is to invite disaster.

Unfortunately, we have no means of knowing whether the coastal Dyukhtai people or their predecessors may have had skin boats, even kayaks, for their long-abandoned settlements lie under modern sea levels. But we do know that the predominant dietary source for arctic Stone Age hunters over an enormous area of Europe and Asia was big-game and land mammals of all sizes, with apparently much less concentration on seasonal vegetable foods, fish, and marine mammals. To venture onto the Bering Land Bridge required no new skills, merely the big-game hunting skills that characterized generations of arctic hunters. That the first crossing into Alaska was by land rather than by boat seems likely, simply on logical grounds. It may have been only later that arctic peoples adapted to Postglacial coasts and crossed freely from Asia to Alaska, maintaining social and cultural ties on both sides of the Bering Strait.

FIRST SETTLEMENT — ALASKA

Dyukhtai people were well established in Siberia during the last glacial maximum, for their characteristic small blade tools and distinctive wedge-shaped cores have been found over wide areas of northeast Asia, in contexts that date to 18,000 years ago. If they were the first settlers, it would be logical to find similar artifacts in Alaska. Unfortunately, field research is very difficult because of the remote terrain and severe climate (Dumond, 1987a; Morlan, 1983). As Richard Morlan says, it is rather "like looking for a needle in a haystack (and a frozen one at that)."

**Old Crow Flats
?30,000 B.P.**

For years, traces of human settlement as early as 30,000 years ago were thought to occur in eroding deposits at Old Crow Flats in the Yukon Territory, near the border between Alaska and Canada (Morlan, 1983). The area has yielded a number of fossil mammoth bones, of which a hundred or so are claimed to have been made into artifacts and many more altered for casual use. Several of these bones have been radiocarbon dated to between 29,000 and 25,000 years ago. Unfortunately, none of these specimens has been found in its original geological context. All come from redeposited levels, layers shifted by water, erosion, or some other natural force. Thus, their date is suspect. Nor do many experts accept the modified specimens as artifacts, arguing that they were split and polished by nature. Old Crow remains a controversial location, one that at present cannot be taken to establish human settlement in Alaska.

**Bluefish Caves
?15,000 to
12,000 B.P.**

The first Alaskans are still a very shadowy entity, known only from confusing scatters of stone artifacts and a few stratified locations. The earliest of these is the remote Bluefish Caves in the Yukon, about 40 miles (64.4 km) southwest of Old Crow. Some 15,000 years ago, the caves lay within sight of windswept glacial lakes. Jacques Cinq-Mars (1979) found a layer of tightly packed, undisturbed loess in the caves, with mammoth and other bones, microblades, a wedge-shaped core, and some trimming flakes. Cinq-Mars obtained bone collagen dates from several animal fragments and believes that this stratified site contains evidence of human occupation between 15,000 and 12,000 years ago, perhaps earlier. If this site is accepted as valid, it is one of the earliest in the Americas.

Bluefish may have been occupied while the land bridge was still dry land, but soon afterward the low-lying plain was submerged, although parts of the Alaskan coastline were up to 60 miles (96 km) offshore as late as 10,000 years ago. A handful of sites document human settlement in the millennia coinciding with, and following, submergence. Most of these contain microblades and small cores, bladelets that are far smaller than the normal Upper Paleolithic blade so well known from the Old World. So far, there are few signs of distinctive Upper Paleolithic blades in Alaska. A few sites, like Dry Creek in the northern foothills of the Alaska Range, offer tantalizing clues. The lower levels of this location have yielded cobbles, flakes, and thin bifacial knives but no microblades; they are radiocarbon dated to about 11,100 years ago (Powers and Hamilton, 1978). A later occupation, dated to about 10,700 years ago, does contain microblades and other small artifacts. Roger Powers believes the earlier Dry Creek level contains "Upper Paleolithic" tools similar to those from a Siberian site said by Soviet archaeologists to belong within the Dyukhtai tradition.

Dry Creek
11,100 B.P.

Elsewhere, isolated artifact scatters and dates lie between 12,000 and 11,000 years ago, but later sites almost invariably contain microblades and wedge-shaped cores, belonging to an ill-defined "Paleoarctic" tradition dating to later than 11,000 years ago, by which time there was well-documented human settlement far to the south. This description in general terms probably masks considerable cultural diversity. The most famous locality is the 10,000-year-old site at Akmak, on the Onion Portage. Akmak lies in a river valley that has been a migration route for caribou since the earliest human settlement in the region (D. Anderson, 1970). This site consists of little more than a scatter of characteristic tools that once lay by a shelter long since eroded away.

Akmak
10,000 B.P.

Some archaeologists believe that there are some connections between the Dyukhtai artifacts of northeast Asia (Chapter 6) and those of the Paleoarctic tradition, but it would be unwise to pursue these analogies too far until many more sites have been dug on both sides of the Bering Strait. Some of the stone-working techniques practiced by Paleoarctic groups are broadly similar to those used by Stone Age people in northern China as early as 15,000 years ago (Chung and Pei, 1986) and in Japan between approximately 14,000 and 10,000 years ago (Ikawa-Smith, 1978). Again, it would be easy to read a great deal into these parallels, but in fact their very existence has been barely established, from only a few widely separated sites.

The date of first settlement in the far north remains an enigma, for there are so few sites that even vaguely precise chronologies are out of the question. However, by broad process of elimination, we can suggest that

- It is unlikely that there was human settlement in the Americas before about 25,000 years ago, when the Bering Strait became dry land for about 10,000 years.
- The Bering Land Bridge was capable of supporting big-game hunters, as was the steppe-tundra to the west during the height of the last glaciation.

First settlement of Alaska most likely took place between 25,000 and about 14,000 years ago, perhaps toward the end of that period, when hunters followed mammoth and other game to higher ground. However, the earliest archaeological evidence for such settlement is at the most 15,000 years old, perhaps less.

The toolkits used by the first settlers may have been generally Upper Paleolithic. However, the earliest documented toolkits from either side of the Bering Strait are based on wedge-shaped cores and microblades, artifacts associated with the Dyukhtai tradition of Siberia, and perhaps with caribou hunting.

As far as can be established, the predominant lifeway in extreme arctic latitudes of Europe and Asia during the last glacial climax was based on big-game hunting (Gamble, 1986b). That this lifeway also predominated on the Bering Land Bridge and in Alaska during the same period seems unquestionable. Once the ice sheets retreated, however, many Ice Age big-game species became extinct, and big-game hunting bands had to adapt to a far more diverse tundra and birch forest environment. This environmental diversity is reflected in considerable toolkit variation within Alaska's Paleoarctic tradition.

A possible scenario for first settlement, then, has tiny groups of big-game hunters crossing into Alaska at a time when Ice Age mammals were still to be found, perhaps between 25,000 and 15,000 years ago. Some of these people, perhaps numbering only in the dozens, were the first to move southward into the temperate latitudes that lay beyond the great ice sheets covering much of Canada and the Rocky Mountains.

There remains one fundamental question: Why did humans settle in the New World at all? Was it an inner urge that caused the first Americans to endure the harsh climate of the Bering Land Bridge? Or was there some more prosaic reason?

Two great population dispersals occurred during prehistory, the first when *Homo erectus* emerged from the tropics about a million years ago. The second took place after the emergence of *Homo sapiens sapiens* between 40,000 and 35,000 years ago (Lewin, 1988), when the first human populations crossed from the Old World into the New and Australia was inhabited for the first time. The exact dates of this later dispersal are still highly uncertain, but it seems to have occurred soon after modern people appeared. The explanation for these sudden dispersals seems to lie mostly in the fact that humans tended to behave as other animals did. Rather than responding to an inborn restlessness, the first Americans were probably behaving in the same way as other animal predators. They spent their days tracking the game herds that formed an important part of their subsistence, and when Siberian game herds moved onto the Bering Land Bridge during the coldest millennia of the last glaciation, their human predators followed. And the higher ground to the east — Alaska — formed part of the same hunting grounds.

BIOLOGICAL EVIDENCE FOR THE FIRST AMERICANS

For more than a century, anthropologists have pointed to biological similarities between Siberians and North American Indians. Christy Turner (1984) of Arizona State University has studied the changing physical characteristics of native American teeth, especially their crowns and roots, and compared them with those of Old World populations. These dental features are more stable than most evolutionary traits, with a high genetic component that minimizes the effects of environmental differences, sexual dimorphism, and age variations. After examining more than 4000 individuals, ancient and modern, Turner has developed a series of hypotheses about the first settlement of the Americas based on dental morphology (Figure 7.3).

Turner points out that prehistoric Americans display many fewer variations

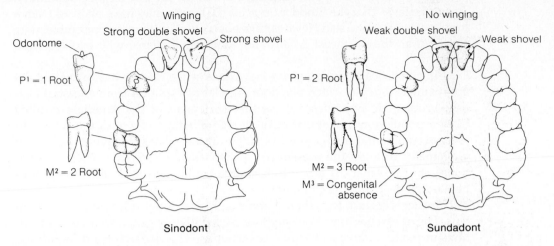

UPPER JAW

Sinodont

Sundadont

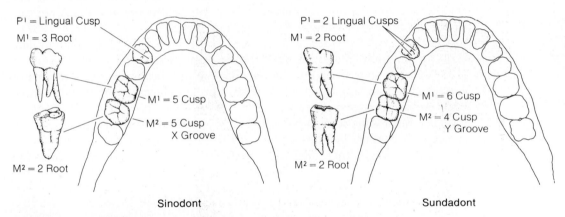

LOWER JAW

Sinodont

Sundadont

FIGURE 7.3 Dental morphology and the first Americans. Some of Christy Turner's theories about the peopling of America are based on differences between the teeth of so-called Sinodonts (northern Asians and all native Americans) and Sundadonts (eastern Asians). Sinodonts display, among other features, strong incisor shoveling (scooping out on one or both surfaces of the tooth), single-rooted upper first premolars, and triple-rooted lower first molars.

in their dental morphology than do eastern Asians. He calls these characteristics "Sinodonty," a pattern of dental features that includes incisor shoveling, single-rooted upper first premolars, triple-rooted lower first molars, and other attributes. Sinodonty only occurs in northern Asia and the Americas. Turner's earliest evidence for Sinodonty comes from northern China about 20,000 years ago, but he believes that it emerged much earlier, perhaps as early as 40,000

Sinodonty

years ago. European Upper Paleolithic skeletons do not display Sinodonty. Turner believes that the Sinodont northern Chinese may have evolved from a primeval southeast Asian *Homo sapiens* population, whom they resemble more closely than the northeast Asians and American Indians, who evolved from them.

Using statistics to study evolutionary divergence, Turner has calculated the approximate dates at which Sinodont populations split off from ancestral Chinese groups. He hypothesizes that first settlement of the Americas resulted from a population movement through east Siberia and across the now-submerged continental shelf around 14,000 years ago. Two subsequent population movements brought the present-day Athabaskan and Eskimo-Aleut populations into the Americas a few thousand years later. Neither of these groups penetrated deep into the continent.

If Turner is correct, then there is some biological support for a late settlement date. His researches have been supported by studies of genetic marker distributions in modern American Indian populations. The research team found that more than 14,000 Central and South American Indians in their samples share the same Gm Allotypes (variants in a protein found in the blood). Since interbreeding populations share sets of such variants, the genetic experts believe there was a single primeval migration of hunter-gatherers into the Americas, who evolved later by cultural differentiation (for discussion, see Fagan, 1987).

Dental morphology and genetic research hint strongly at a relatively late date for first settlement. So does the linguistic work of Joseph Greenberg (1987). He has compiled a massive data base on the vocabulary and grammar of American Indian languages, which leads him to believe that there were three basic Indian linguistic groups: Amerind, Aleut-Eskimo, and Na-Dene (Athabaskan). Most American Indian languages are in the Amerind group, whose speakers Greenberg believes arrived before 11,000 years ago. It is only fair to point out, however, that some linguists consider Greenberg's classifications too broad.

THE CASE FOR LATE WISCONSIN SETTLEMENT

Exactly the same problem — lack of sites — arises when we look for archaeological evidence of Late Wisconsin settlement south of the great ice sheets. Until fairly recently, most archaeologists believed that first settlement took place about 13,000 years ago, after the retreat of the Laurentide ice sheet. Those who argue for earlier settlement point to the toolkits used by the human inhabitants of the Americas at that time, suggesting that their projectile points and hunting artifacts are quite unlike the Dyukhtai tools of Siberia. They developed, then, from an earlier technological tradition that still awaits discovery.

Everyone agrees that the connections between 13,000-year-old toolkits south of the ice sheets and the few of this age known from the far north and Asia are tenuous at best. Proponents of late settlement argue that this situation is hardly surprising given the long distances, the great isolation of the first Americans, and the diversity of environments. Those who support earlier colonization believe that we have yet to find the primeval American toolkit. Decades of ardent search have produced only a handful of sites that *may* date to earlier than 15,000 years ago (Bryan, 1978; Fagan, 1987; Shutler, 1983).

The lack of evidence is depressing, to the point that many claims are based on emotionalism and specious argument from minimal data. There are numerous claims for early North American settlement based on poorly dated scatters of projectile heads and flaked tools from deep caves and open sites in many parts of the United States. Many of these have been disproved by later investigation, through use of improved dating methods, or by application of more sophisticated artifact analysis techniques (Fagan, 1987).

Before examining the possible evidence for Late Wisconsin settlement, we should consider the possible routes by which human beings spread from the north into the Americas.

ICE-FREE CORRIDORS AND SEA COASTS

If tiny bands of hunter-gatherers penetrated the fastnesses of Beringia during the Late Wisconsin glaciation, how, then, did they reach the heart of the Americas? Again, the route of first settlement is fraught with controversies about hypothetical routes and the boundaries of ice sheets.

North America was very different during the Wisconsin glaciation. We know from deep sea core studies that the Wisconsin began some 117,000 years ago, with an inexorable cooling of world temperatures. Great ice sheets covered much of northern North America during the Early Wisconsin, until about 60,000 years ago. Between 60,000 and about 25,000 years ago, there was a prolonged period of glacial retreat and sea levels rose, severing Asia and Alaska. With the possible exception of a much reduced ice sheet around Hudson Bay, most of North America was freed of glacial barriers. For these 35,000 years, any (hypothetical) human settlers would have encountered environments not very different from modern tundra and boreal forest.

The Late Wisconsin, the earliest time period when human settlement seems possible, began about 25,000 years ago. The so-called Laurentide glaciers, centered on Labrador and the Keewatin areas of Canada, expanded south, west, and east, eventually fusing into a huge frozen wilderness. At its maximum about 18,000 years ago, the Laurentide ice sheet extended from the Atlantic seaboard across the Great Lakes region into southeast Alberta. The mountain ranges of southern Alaska and British Columbia were heavily glaciated at the time, forming the Cordilleran glacier complex in the west. The Cordilleran extended about 30 miles (48 km) south of Seattle as recently as 14,500 years ago, apparently reaching its maximum extent after the Laurentide.

Late Wisconsin
25,000 B.P.

Clearly, these great Late Wisconsin ice barriers would have inhibited travel between Beringia and the southern latitudes of the New World. But did they stop human settlement altogether? In the 1950s, Canadian geologists reported that the Cordilleran ice flowed down the eastern flanks of the Rockies but apparently did not join the Laurentide ice sheet. Despite a lack of reliable maps, the idea of an "ice-free corridor" soon took hold of archaeologists' imaginations. "Doubtless it was a formidable place," wrote Thomas Canby of the National Geographic Society (1979), "an ice-walled valley of frigid winds, fierce snows, and clinging fogs . . . yet grazing animals would have entered, and behind them would have come a rivulet of human hunters." The picture is a compelling one — but was it reality?

The ice-free corridor has been mapped more thoroughly in recent years, to the point that we can be sure it was no superhighway for Stone Age hunters. In some places the ice sheets did merge. In others, especially in the far north and south, there was a corridor, but it twisted and turned through the roughest of terrain, country restricted by chill meltwater lakes, often with biologically sterile shores. At best the Late Wisconsin ice-free corridor was a barren and impoverished landscape. Even if it was passable, there is a good chance that there was no incentive to cross it between about 25,000 and 15,000 years ago, for much better food resources lay in Beringia. And, in any case, we lack evidence that human settlers had made Beringia their homeland earlier than 15,000 years ago.

If an interior route was used, chances are that it was traversed during a time of glacial retreat, sometime after 15,000 years ago, when the Laurentide glaciers shrank rapidly. But, if the ice-free corridor was a barrier to human settlement, could people have passed down ice-free coastal areas along the Alaskan and British Columbian coasts into temperate regions? Knud Fladmark (1978) believes that the Late Wisconsin northwest coasts were relatively warmer and more productive than other areas, to the extent that they might have sustained human life. Unfortunately, however, we do not know whether these areas were accessible from mainland Beringia, or, indeed, whether there were Late Wisconsin populations on the land bridge at all. If such people did exist, their sites are buried deep beneath modern sea levels. The earliest documented settlement occurs on the Queen Charlotte Islands of British Columbia, between 12,000 and 10,000 years ago (Fladmark, 1978). Many archaeologists believe that much earlier coastal settlement is unlikely, on the (perhaps dangerous) assumption that everything we know about the earliest settlers suggests they were terrestrial hunters and gatherers, with a lifeway adapted in part to the pursuit of large Ice Age mammals.

Queen Charlotte Islands 12,000 to 10,000 B.P.

ARCHAEOLOGICAL EVIDENCE FOR LATE WISCONSIN SETTLEMENT

A number of sites throughout the Americas have been claimed as evidence for Late Wisconsin settlement, mainly caves and rock shelters (Fagan, 1987). The most important are worth individual review.

Meadowcroft Rock Shelter

Meadowcroft 12,000 B.P. (perhaps as early as 19,000 B.P.) to 700 B.P.

Meadowcroft Rock Shelter lies 30 miles (48.2 km) southwest of Pittsburgh, Pennsylvania, a sheltered location close to permanent water supplies. James Adovasio excavated and dated the eleven levels of the shelter with more than seventy radiocarbon dates. They show that it was occupied from nearly 700 years ago back to at least 12,000, and perhaps to 19,000 years ago (Adovasio et al., 1984, 1986).

Adovasio's meticulous excavations establish human occupation at 12,000 years ago beyond any doubt. The controversy begins in a layer he calls Stratum IIa, a level divided into three subunits, the upper two of which date to between about 12,950 and 7,950 years ago. The lowermost subunit of IIa is sealed from its successors by rock fragments and has yielded seven radiocarbon dates, ranging from 19,600 to 13,240 years ago. Adovasio claims that the 19,600 B.P. date is associated with materials of indisputable human manufacture, overlying a sterile Stratum I.

This claim is questioned by geologist-archaeologist C. Vance Haynes (1980) and others, who argue that the Stratum IIa charcoal samples contain dead carbon, in the form of coal particles from much older layers that have permeated the soil through groundwater. After exhaustive retesting, Adovasio sticks to his claim, and the controversy is, in many people's view, still unresolved.

There are also some other problems with Meadowcroft. The very early levels contain coniferous and hardwood vegetable remains, ground cover that were typical of the area after the Late Wisconsin but not during the glaciation itself, when tundra was nearby. Adovasio argues that Meadowcroft may have enjoyed a sheltered location despite its proximity to ice sheets, making it a favorable place for big-game hunters.

Meadowcroft remains a tantalizing question mark, a conundrum that will only be unraveled with the discovery of comparable sites nearby.

At the time of writing, there is no archaeological evidence for human settlement of North America in Late Wisconsin times.

Mesoamerica and Latin America

The evidence for Late Wisconsin human occupation is also sparse south of the Rio Grande. Richard MacNeish believes there is evidence for a "chopper-chopping tool" stage of human occupation in Mesoamerica dating to more than 30,000 years ago (MacNeish, 1986; MacNeish and Nelken-Terner, 1983). This probably mythical formulation consists mostly of undated surface finds and artifacts from river terraces.

MacNeish's second stage, marked by "bone tools and a unifacial industry," is dated to between 30,000 and 15,000 years ago. One of his key sites is Valsequillo, near Pueblo in central Mexico, where thirteen apparent unifacial stone tools lay with the bones of extinct animals at five locations. The finds came from stratified gravels, the upper levels of which contained bifacial tools. A date of 21,850 ± 850 years is claimed for a freshwater shell near one of the stone flakes (Irwin-Williams, 1978). Unfortunately, Valsequillo is questionable because the geology is suspect. The gravels containing the early artifacts may be 200,000 years old. Some scholars have questioned both the associations of animals and artifacts, and the humanness of the earliest "tools." MacNeish places the famous Tlapacoya mammoth bones from near Mexico City in the same stage; they are claimed to have been found with simple flakes and other artifacts in contexts dating to between about 24,000 and 22,000 years ago. Unfortunately, there are again serious doubts about the validity of this association.

Valsequillo
?21,850 B.P.

Tlapacoya 24,000 to 22,000 B.P.

MacNeish is a fervent believer in early human settlement in Mesoamerica. It is only fair to point out that most scholars favor a later date, for the earliest indisputable finds date to about 11,000 years ago, roughly contemporary with early human occupation to the north (Figure 7.4).

Supporters of Late Wisconsin and even earlier settlement reserve their greatest enthusiasm for a series of finds from South America, scattered between Venezuela and northern Chile (Bryan, 1978, 1986). Alan Bryan has gone so far as to hypothesize that human settlers fanned out over South America long before 20,000 years ago.

Pikimachay Cave

Pikimachay 14,200 B.P. (perhaps earlier)

Richard MacNeish excavated the deep Pikimachay Cave high in the Andes foothills of southern Peru (MacNeish et al., 1980, 1981). He identified three major occupation groups in the cave, a relatively recent one and a second occupation with large crude bifaces, some projectile points, and choppers as well as sloth, horse, camel, and puma bones radiocarbon dated to 14,200 ± 180 years. This single radiocarbon date identified one of the earliest Postglacial occupations in the Americas.

The earliest Pikimachay level consists of jumbled earth and cemented soil containing deer and sloth bones as well as crude tools, radiocarbon dated to between 20,250 and 19,650 years ago. Quite apart from the large statistical errors for the dates, the crude artifacts have been called into question, despite MacNeish's claims. The evidence for 20,000-year-old occupation at Pikimachay is questionable.

Boqueirão of Pedro Furada

Boqueirão of Pedro Furada ?30,000 B.P.

The Boqueirão of Pedro Furada rock shelter in northeast Brazil contains deep, sandy layers with pebbles and gravel beds in them (Guidon and Delibrias, 1986). Niede Guidon excavated 9.8 feet (3 m) into the cave and unearthed "traces of human occupation [that] succeed one another throughout the stratigraphic sequence." She believes the shelter was occupied again and again by a small human band, the earliest of whom left large circular hearths, as well as stone pebble tools, mainly "pieces with blunt points obtained by . . . convergent flakings," along with a variety of other tools. Guidon claims occupation as early as some 32,000 years ago, with continuing occupation between 30,000 and 12,000 years ago. She believes she has found a piece of rock with two painted lines — the first American rock art — in a hearth dated to 17,000 ± 400 years ago.

FIGURE 7.4 Points found with mammoths in Mexico. The length of the middle point is approximately 3 in (8.1 cm).

What are we to make of this discovery, few details of which have yet been published? The Pedro Furada deposits are claimed to contain the remains of camps alongside a stream, and the layers may well be part of a streambed themselves. Are the "hearths" actually of human origin? Were the proposed artifacts, which look unconvincing to the dispassionate eye, actually humanly manufactured? Have chemical analyses of the red pigment from the 17,000-year-old "painting" been completed? Until definitive answers to these questions are forthcoming, Guidon's claims lack scientific authority, and the site must remain doubtful.

Monte Verde

Located in a small river valley in southern Chile, this 13,000- to 12,500-year-old streamside settlement is covered by a peat bog, so that not only stone and bone but wooden artifacts as well survive (Dillehey, 1984). Thus far only a portion of the site has been excavated, revealing two parallel rows of rectangular houses, joined by connecting walls. The skin-covered houses were 9 to 13 feet (3 to 4 m) square, with log and crude plank foundations and a wooden framework. Clay-lined hearths, wooden mortars, and large quantities of vegetable foods were found in the houses. A short distance away lay a wishbone-shaped structure associated with chewed bolo plant leaves (used today to make a form of medicinal tea), mastodon bones, and other work debris. This may have been a work area. The Monte Verde people exploited a very wide range of vegetable foods, including wild potatoes; they also hunted small game and perhaps mammals like extinct camels and mastodons (it is possible that they scavenged such meat, however). Monte Verde was in a forest, with abundant vegetable foods all year round. The site was almost certainly a long-term campsite. What is fascinating is that 90 percent of the stone artifacts are crude river pebbles. It is clear that wood was the most important raw material. It was certainly used for spears and digging sticks, and for hafting stone scrapers, three of which have survived in their wooden handles. Sites yielding simple flaked stone artifacts like those from Monte Verde have been found elsewhere in South America, as far south as Patagonia, but this is the first place that anyone has been able to make more complete discoveries.

The Monte Verde investigations are still in progress, although they hint that early American society may have been much more sophisticated than had been realized. Other locations like Pikimachay and Meadowcroft are located in more open country. The Monte Verde site shows just how scanty the archaeological record of the first Americans is, and just how little we are likely to find out about them until more waterlogged sites come to light.

Archaeological evidence for human settlement of Mesoamerica and South America before Postglacial times is still lacking.

After more than a century of searching, the earliest archaeological sites in the Americas date to around 14,000 to 13,000 years ago, and even these occupations are poorly documented. As the years go on, and the intensity of archaeological research throughout the New World picks up, the chances of finding indisputable evidence for Late Wisconsin, or even earlier, human settlement seem ever remoter. Add to this the realities of full glacial environments in the far north, the evidence from genetics and dental morphology, and the distribution of archaeological sites in northeast Asia as we know it, and a compelling case can be made for late settlement.

In all probability, the first Americans crossed into east Beringia (Alaska) from the Bering Land Bridge, perhaps at the very end of the last glaciation. Then, as the ice sheets retreated 14,000 years ago, a mere handful of people hunted their way southward into the heart of a virgin continent. In the millennia that followed, human predators underwent a population explosion in the new lands, adapting to a great diversity of Late Glacial and Postglacial climates everywhere between the ice sheets and Tierra del Fuego.

THE PALEO-INDIANS

About 11,500 years ago, the highly distinctive Clovis culture appeared on the Great Plains of North America and much farther afield. These *Paleo-Indian* people are the first well-documented inhabitants of the New World, but many questions still remain about their ancestry and lifeway. What is certain, however, is that the Clovis culture was relatively short-lived. Judging from dated sites in the west, most sites were occupied during the five centuries after 11,500 years ago. We now move onto solid prehistoric ground, for the archaeological record suddenly mushrooms from nothing to a well-documented scatter of locations from coast to coast in North America, with well-established Paleo-Indian occupation in Mesoamerica and Latin America as well.

Clovis

Clovis 11,500 to 11,000 B.P.

Although Paleo-Indian occupation is known from both eastern and western North America, the Clovis culture is best known from the Great Plains. At the end of the Wisconsin glaciation, the areas in the rain shadow of the western mountains of North America were dominated throughout the year by the dry mid-Pacific air mass. Most rain fell, and still falls, in spring and early summer, supporting short grasses that keep much of their biomass beneath the soil. This structure helps retain moisture in the roots, providing mammoths, bison, and other ruminants with high-quality nutrients in the dry fall and into the winter. These grasslands expanded at the end of the Wisconsin and were colonized by herds of ruminants who were selective feeders. They were also the home of scattered bands of Clovis people. Within a few centuries, tiny hunter-gatherer bands had spread to both North American coasts and as far south as Guadalajara, Mexico.

The western plains of North America offer a highly diverse range of environments with a variety of protein-rich grasses and shrubs that once supported a browsing and grazing mammalian fauna, which in turn provided subsistence for a small number of hunter-gatherers (Frison, 1978). However, life was not easy for the bands, as they had to respond to different distributions of animals and plants each year, conditions which depended on rainfall, snowfall, runoff from the mountain peaks, and so on. The realities of the climate meant that the people had to collect dried meat and vegetable foods in the summer months and store them against the bitter winter. Each family group probably moved at least fifty to one hundred times a year, tending to visit the same campsites year after year, taking all their belongings with them. Archaeologically, they left very little behind, so the evidence for prehistoric occupation of the Plains normally is limited to remains of large bison kills and scatters of broken flakes and projectile points.

The Clovis culture is known mainly from kill sites in the west, places where the hunters dispatched and butchered such animals as the mammoth and bison. At Murray Springs, Arizona, for example, the people killed mammoth and bison, butchering them at separate locations, with a campsite nearby. Eleven bison died at Murray Springs, yielding enough meat to support up to fifty to one hundred people, perhaps many fewer. Distinctive Clovis projectile points and other tools were found among the bones. At Naco, Arizona, no fewer than eight points lay in one mammoth carcass. Perhaps between four and eight hunters, a fifth of a band of about twenty to forty people, killed the great beast. The hunters partially dismembered their quarry, sometimes making piles of the disarticulated bones.

Everyone agrees that the Clovis people hunted both big game and smaller animals, besides foraging for wild vegetable foods during spring, summer, and fall. But big-game hunting was probably the most important part of their subsistence. Large animals like the mammoth and bison could provide meat for weeks on end, as well as valuable by-products for household possessions, tents, even clothing. George Frison (1978) and others believe that Clovis hunters tended to concentrate on solitary mammoths, for their spear technology could not stop an elephant in its tracks, just wound it severely. They would stalk herds, concentrating on straying animals, sometimes perhaps driving them into swamps (for extended discussion, see Haynes, 1982). The hunters would wound an animal, then take their time to kill it with thrusting spears.

Clovis people, and other Paleo-Indian groups, used a portable toolkit that included bone, stone, and wood artifacts. Preservation conditions allow us to know most about their stone technology, often based on precious, fine-grained rock from widely separated outcrops. The hunters traveled great distances for their stone, trading it in core form for hundreds of miles. These cores were like a savings account, carried around so that flakes could be used to make finely pressure-flaked projectile points. The finished heads were mounted in wood or bone foreshafts set on the end of spear shafts. Once the spear penetrated an animal, the foreshaft would break off. The hunter could then rearm his spear with a new foreshaft in a few moments. Damaged points were resharpened and used again.

Besides projectile points, the Clovis toolkit included butchering tools, scrapers, and dozens of untrimmed stone flakes used as convenient knives. The people used bone, and presumably wood, for foreshafts and spears, as well as other artifacts. These artifacts bear little resemblance to the microblades and fine cores of the Dyukhtai tradition from Siberia. Haynes (1982) and others believe that they have roots in Upper Paleolithic big-game hunting traditions in the Old World. Under this scenario for first settlement, the fluted projectile point was an indigenous development in temperate North America. But, goes the argument, big game and mammoths were to the Upper Paleolithic hunter what the reindeer is to the Laplander or the caribou to the inland Inuit. These authorities also believe that *general* similarities exist between Clovis stone and bone tools and those from classic mammoth-hunting sites in east Europe and the Ukraine. Thus, they speculate that the first settlement of North America was part of a primeval big-game hunting tradition that spread from northeast Asia into the New World. The descendants of these people wandered farther south, pursuing their favorite game, the mammoth. Eventually they reached the Canadian prairie, where they encountered new mammoth species and a greater bounty of other big game.

This scenario for first settlement is almost as inadequately documented as those espousing earlier dates. But the cumulative sum of the limited data tends to support rather than undermine it (Fagan, 1987).

BIG-GAME EXTINCTIONS

The Clovis people flourished for about 500 years, and then, about 11,000 years ago, they vanished abruptly, to be replaced by a multitude of hunting and gathering cultures. This sudden disappearance coincides with one of the great mysteries of modern science — the catastrophic extinction of Ice Age big-game animals in the Americas. Many large animals became extinct throughout the world at this time but nowhere as drastically as in the Americas. Three-quarters of the large mammalian genera there vanished abruptly at the end of the Pleistocene (Martin and Klein, 1984; Martin and Wright, 1967).

Overkill

Why did the American fauna die off so suddenly? Speculations have been long and lively. One theory that has long held on is that the large mammals were killed off by the Paleo-Indian bands' intensive hunting, as they preyed on large herds of animals that had formerly had relatively few predators to control their populations. This overkill hypothesis is weakened by the fact that many Pleistocene animals disappeared before the heyday of the Paleo-Indians. Besides, the Indians existed in very small numbers, and they had other subsistence activities as well. Surely the animals would have adapted to changed conditions and new dangers. Instead, the extinctions accelerated after the hunters had been around for a while; the modern bison, for example, never adapted to mounted hunters.

Climate change

Change in climate gives a second hypothesis for the cause of extinction. Changing environments, spreading aridity, and shrinking habitats for big game may have reduced the mammalian population drastically. Strong objections face this hypothesis too. The very animals that became extinct had already survived enormous fluctuations in Pleistocene climate without harm. If they had once migrated into more hospitable habitats, they could have done so again. Furthermore, the animals that became extinct were not just the browsers; they were selected from all types of habitat. This too-simple climate change hypothesis is supported by the notion that desiccation leads to mass starvation in game populations, an idea refuted by ecological research in Africa. What actually happens is that the smaller species and those with lower growth rates adapt to the less favorable conditions, leaving the population changed but not defunct (Olivier, 1982).

A third hypothesis cites the great variation in mean temperatures at the end of the Pleistocene as a primary cause of extinction. In both New and Old worlds, the more pronounced seasonal contrasts in temperature climates would Seasonal contrasts have been harder on the young of species that are born in small litters, after long gestation periods, and at fixed times of the year. These traits are characteristic of larger mammals, precisely those which became extinct. The less equable climate at the end of the Pleistocene, then, would have been a major cause of late Pleistocene extinctions in North America.

All three hypotheses have truth in them. Complex variables must have affected the steps that led to extinction, with intricate feedback among the effects of intensive big-game hunting, changing ecology, and the intolerance of some mammalian species to seasonal contrasts in weather. It may be that the hunters, being there as persistent predators, were the final variable, causing more drastic mammalian extinctions than might otherwise have occurred.

LATER HUNTERS AND GATHERERS

As the world climate warmed up rapidly at the end of the last glaciation, New World environments changed drastically. The great ice sheets of the north shrank, mountain snow lines and sea levels rose, and forest vegetation established itself in hitherto glaciated regions. If one word can be used to describe these momentous changes it is *diversity*, a great diversity of local environments — lush river floodplains, great deserts, grassy plains, miles upon miles of boreal and deciduous woodland. And the late Paleo-Indians and their successors adapted to this great diversity with brilliant success and ingenuity. In general, the west and southwest United States became drier, but the East Coast and much of the Midwest grew densely forested. The large Pleistocene mammals became extinct, but the bison remained a major source of food. In the Southeast, the more favorable climate brought drier conditions, which meant less standing water, markedly seasonal rainfalls, and specialization among humans for fishing or intensive gathering instead of big-game hunting. Many areas had much economic diversity, as we see among the desert gatherer peoples of the Tehuacán Valley in Mexico. They flourished between 12,000 and 9,000 years ago, at the same time hunter-gatherers in the Pacific Northwest were probably taking advantage of seasonal salmon runs in the fast-moving rivers.

North American climate and sea levels seem to have stabilized close to their modern configurations about 8000 years ago. Three thousand years later, human populations started to grow more rapidly. Almost everywhere in temperate North America the number of archaeological sites mushroomed within a millennium. The stage was set for rapid cultural, economic, and social change in many areas, change that was still climaxing as European explorers and colonists arrived in the New World.

Eight thousand years ago, the human population of North America was still sparse, scattered in a myriad of isolated hunter-gatherer bands. Judging from sites in many areas, people spent most of the year living in small family groups, exploiting large hunting territories. They might have come together with their neighbors for a few weeks during the summer months at favored locations near rivers or nut groves. The bands would have held ceremonies, exchanged wives, and traded fine-grained rocks and other commodities. Then they would have gone their separate ways, following migrating game, trapping small animals, and foraging for wild vegetable foods.

At first there was plenty of vacant territory to go around, continues this hypothetical scenario. But in time natural population growth and the low carrying capacity of the land combined to restrict mobility. Several long-term adaptive trends developed.

First, the extinction of the Ice Age megafauna meant that hunters focused on smaller mammals, especially the white-tailed deer. Inevitably, people turned to alternative food sources, including wild vegetable foods, birds, mollusks, and fish. Wild vegetable foods were a particularly favored dietary source, especially in areas like river valley bottoms and lakeshores, where they were seasonally abundant and diverse.

Second, there was a long-term trend toward less mobility, toward base camps that were occupied for many months of the year. These served as anchors for larger territories, which were exploited seasonally from outlying settlements. This settlement pattern was by no means universal, but it took hold in areas where there was an unusual diversity of food resources. Examples of base settlements are to be found in the desert west, in midwestern and southeastern river valleys, and in the Northeast.

Third, some areas witnessed a move toward sedentary settlement, occupation of the same settlement year-round, or for most of year. This type of settlement is different from a base camp used on a seasonal basis, even if the occupation lasts for many months. It implies a permanent settlement within a highly restricted territory, a settlement lying within easy reach of sufficient game, vegetable, and aquatic resources to enable the occupants to stay through every season of the year. Sedentary settlement is hard to identify in the archaeological record, except through the presence of substantial dwellings or cemeteries. Such occupation was well established in some midwestern river valley bottoms by 4000 years ago and perhaps in favored coastal areas, such as southern California and the Pacific Northwest, somewhat later.

These trends coincided with accelerating population growth in more favored areas after 4000 years ago.

Such was the diversity of North American environments in Holocene times that only a few relatively limited areas witnessed sedentary settlement and large-scale population growth. Perhaps it is no coincidence that it was in some of these areas, notably midwestern and southeastern river valleys and the Southwest, that people turned to the cultivation of domesticated plants.

Surviving Big-Game Hunters

In only one region — the arid grasslands from the frontiers of Alaska to the Gulf of Mexico — did big-game hunting survive. This was the "Great Bison Belt," which lay in the rain shadow of the western mountains (Fagan, 1987). The short grass range of the Plains was an ideal environment for the bison, one of the few Ice Age big-game species to adapt to Holocene conditions. The Postglacial descendants of the Ice Age steppe bison have increased digestive efficiency to cope with the high-fiber, low-nutrient dead grass of winter. They can feed in deep snow and are less selective eaters than many of the Ice Age species that died out. By 10,500 years ago, bison were the dominant species in all archaeological sites through the bison belt.

10,500 B.P.

At first glance, the Great Plains appear homogeneous, even monotonous. But close examination reveals many subtle differences — stream courses and water holes where game congregated, places where longer grass and seasonal water favored larger bison herds. The late Paleo-Indians and their successors, who preyed on the herds right into historic times, could only survive by a careful, planned utilization of the Plains' complex ecosystem (Frison, 1978).

After 10,000 years ago, numerous variations of bison-hunting cultures appeared on the Plains, all of them using portable toolkits that bear a strong resemblance to those of their Clovis ancestors. Stone-tipped projectile heads with carefully thinned and ground bases made spear-throwers and spears effective weapons for bison hunting. At least seven major forms are known, with names like Eden, Folsom, Plainview, and Scottsbluff — to mention only a few (Frison, 1978; Haynes, 1982; Irwin and Wormington, 1970). Whether all these forms actually represent distinct cultural entities is a matter of controversy. The entire Paleo-Indian toolkit was highly portable and capable of being used for a wide variety of purposes, everything from woodworking to bison butchery.

10,000 B.P.

Most Plains sites are kill locations, strategic places where mass game drives could be organized. Such drives were far from daily events, perhaps taking place every couple of years or so. To pursue bison on foot means days of patient stalking and an intimate knowledge of the animals' habits. Perhaps several bands would cooperate in a game drive. They would encircle a few beasts or, more often, stampede a herd into a swamp or a narrow defile. In some cases, they would drive the frightened animals over a cliff or into dune areas. The archaeological evidence for such activities comes from a series of sites, among them the Agate Basin site in eastern Wyoming, where, judging from the age of the animals, the hunters apparently maneuvered ten to twenty animals into an arroyo bottom in late February or early March (Frison, 1978). The hunters then drove them upstream until they reached a natural trap in the gully, where the confused bison could be killed with stone-tipped spears.

The Olsen-Chubbock site in Colorado is an example of a kill site where approximately 200 bison of all ages were stampeded into a deep, narrow arroyo, probably during the summer or fall (Frison, 1978; Wheat, 1972). Because the skeletons of the prehistoric bison faced north, the excavators concluded that the wind was blowing from the south on the day of the hunt. The stampeding herd was driven into a gully and could not catch the scent of the people waiting for them at the arroyo. The hunters' artifacts were scattered around the carcasses of their quarry (Figure 7.5): scraping tools, stone knives, and flakes used for dismembering the bison.

Olsen-Chubbock 8000 B.P.

Smaller communal hunts were probably much more commonplace. John Speth's excavations at Garnsey, New Mexico (1983), chronicle such a kill. About 400 years ago, a group of hunters visited a small gully where they knew bison would congregate in late March or early April. Instead of killing every animal on sight, they tended to concentrate on the males. Speth believes this preference was because male bison are in better condition in the spring, when

FIGURE 7.5 A layer of excavated bison bones from the Olsen-Chubbock site in Colorado, where a band of hunters stampeded a herd of bison into a narrow arroyo.

Homo Sapiens and Hunter-Gatherers

their bone marrow has a higher fat content. Fattier meat is an important source of energy and essential fatty acids and is difficult to come by after the lean winter months. So if Garnsey hunters killed a cow, they consumed only the choice, fatter parts.

Bison hunting was practiced on the Plains right up until the advent of the horse and the repeating rifle, but Paleo-Indian peoples flourished throughout North America. Clovislike projectile points are known from many locations in the East, including Meadowcroft Shelter in Pennsylvania. Herds of caribou may have provided sustenance in northern sites around the Great Lakes and in the Northeast (Dragoo, 1976). Paleo-Indian hunting and gathering economies may have varied a great deal from region to region, some bands specializing in big game, others in fishing or gathering, depending on the resources available in each territory. This variation is reflected in Paleo-Indian archaeological sites that can vary from kill locations to shell middens. That hunting was important in places where large game was abundant seems unquestionable, but this activity diminished rapidly in importance as the big game became extinct.

The Desert West

Economic emphasis shifted in the arid West and Southwest. As big game became scarce, many hunting bands relied more heavily on wild vegetable foods that required much more energy to collect and process than game meat. In the Great Basin, smaller animals such as rabbits, squirrels, and deer became more common prey. At the same time, gathering of vegetable foods grew to dominate economic life, combined with some fishing and, in maritime areas, exploitation of shellfish. We are fortunate that arid climates in Utah, Nevada, and elsewhere have preserved many plant and vegetable foods eaten by these early hunter-gatherers. By 9000 years ago, a distinctive desert form of Archaic culture had been developed over much of the western United States by small bands camping in caves, rock shelters, and temporary sites.

Desert tradition **9000 B.P. to modern times**

Excavations at later sites like Danger Cave in Utah and the Gypsum and Lovelock sites in Nevada reveal that the hunters were making nets, mats, and baskets, as well as rope (Figure 7.6) (Heizer and Berger, 1970; Irwin-Williams, 1968; Jennings, 1957, 1975). The Hogup Cave in Utah has yielded one of the world's most complete and longest archaeological culture sequences (Aikens, 1970). The site displays gradual adaptations at one settlement, changing it from a base camp to a short-stay camp that was associated with other base camps or with horticultural villages after people learned how to produce food. At all these sites the inhabitants used digging sticks to uproot edible tubers, and much of their toolkit consisted of grinding stones used in preparing vegetable foods. Most Great Basin peoples were obliged to be constantly on the move, searching for different vegetable foods as they came into season and camping near scanty water supplies. Only a few communities living near relatively permanent food sources or good fishing grounds could afford a more sedentary life.

Danger Cave
Gypsum Cave
Lovelock Cave

Hogup Cave

The deposits at Gatecliff Rock Shelter near Austin, Nevada, are 40 feet (12.1 m) deep and span more than 8000 years of human occupation. The inhabitants lived by valleyside streams in the winter, then moved up to the shelter in

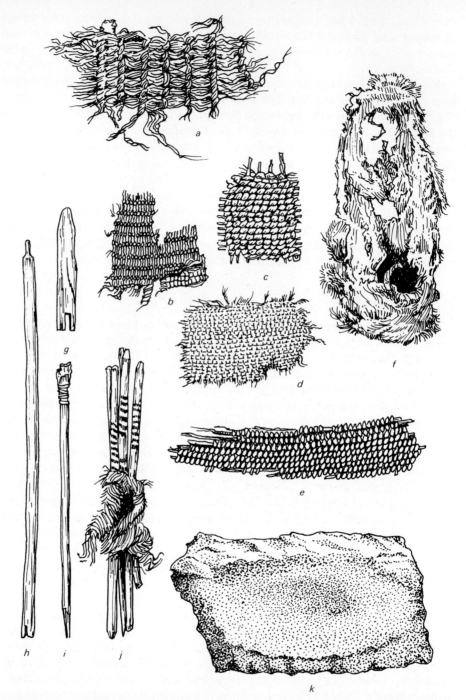

FIGURE 7.6 Artifacts from Danger Cave, Utah, preserved by the dry climate. (a and b) Twined matting; (c) twined basketry; (d) coarse cloth; (e) coiled basketry; (f) hide moccasin; (g) wooden knife handle, 4.5 in (7.4 cm) long; (h) dart shaft, 16 in (41 cm) long; (i) arrow shaft with broken projectile point in place, 33 in (84 cm) long; (j) bundle of gaming sticks, 11.5 in (29 cm) long; (k) milling stone.

the summer, gathering piñon nuts on the mountain slopes as well as hunting game, just as Shoshone Indians did in recent times (D. Thomas, 1973; Thomas and Bettinger, 1983).

Most western prehistoric societies continued to live by hunting and foraging right up to European contact. It was only in the most favored areas that people could stay in one place for months on end. One such location was Lovelock Cave in Nevada, where the base camp overlooked a lake rich in fish and waterfowl. The people hunted their prey with bows and arrows, using extremely lifelike reed duck decoys. Human feces show that over 90 percent of the Lovelock inhabitants' diet came from the lake area, including wetland grasses, fish such as chub, ducks, and mud hens. The plant remains testify to year-round occupation (Heizer and Berger, 1970).

The southern California coast was another hospitable area, first exploited by small bands blending fishing with marine mammal hunting as early as 8000 years ago. The coastal population remained sparse except in favored areas, where much more elaborate societies evolved. For example, the historic Chumash people of the Santa Barbara Channel area congregated in large, more or less permanent villages ruled by local chiefs, who maintained trading contacts over extensive areas of the West (Moratto, 1985). Such sedentism was possible because of exceptional resource diversity. From November to March, the Chumash subsisted on dried meat and stored vegetable foods. They also collected shellfish and caught fish in the dense kelp beds close inshore. Come spring, they ranged far afield, collecting plants and tubers. Summer brought tuna and other warm-water fish to local waters. The people caught enormous quantities of fish from their canoes. Pine nuts and acorns were gathered in the fall and stored for the leaner months ahead. The Chumash hunted marine mammals and scavenged stranded whales whenever the opportunity arose. This maritime bounty resulted from upwelling that replenishes the surface layers of the Santa Barbara Channel with nutrients and zooplankton. At least 125 fish species flourished in local waters, part of an incredibly diverse range of food resources that enabled not only relatively sedentary settlement but higher population densities — as many as 15,000 people living near the shores of the channel and on the offshore islands at European contact.

8000 B.P.

Eastern North America

While the Great Plains are dominated by grasslands, eastern North America, the region from the Mississippi Valley eastward, is covered by deciduous woodlands, and the Southeast by evergreen forest. Superficially, this could be considered a homogeneous natural environment with no sharp geographic barriers to interaction between different human groups, but in fact the area includes an almost bewildering array of microenvironments (Caldwell, 1958; Stoltman and Barreis, 1983). As a result, it is almost impossible to generalize about cultural developments after first settlement some 11,000 years ago (for general and regional summaries, see Barreis and Stoltman, 1983; Mason, 1981; Morse and Morse, 1983; Muller, 1986; B. Smith, 1986; Snow, 1980).

Archaic tradition
10,500 to 3,000 B.P.
and modern times

Paleo-Indian bands settled widely over the Eastern Woodlands from as far north as Nova Scotia to southern Florida. The most dramatic finds come from natural sinkholes in Florida. During the early Holocene, when sea levels were much lower than today, many rivers left large sinkholes that were favored game areas and places where vegetable foods were also to be found. Carl Clausen, Wilburn Cockrell, and others (Fagan, 1987) have investigated several such locations. At Warm Mineral Springs in Sarasota County, a male burial dating to about 10,000 years ago lay on a ledge 42.6 feet (13 m) below the modern water level. Ground sloth bones and other extinct animal remains occurred in the same horizons as human remains higher up in the hole. Parts of the Warm Mineral Springs site may be older than 11,000 years. (For discussion, see Fagan, 1987.)

Warm Mineral Springs 10,000 B.P.

Little Salt Spring, not far away, yielded the collapsed shell of a giant tortoise killed about 12,000 years ago. The hunter thrust a wooden stake between shell and plastron, then turned the tortoise over and cooked the meat in the shell (Figure 7.7). A wooden boomeranglike artifact remarkably like those of modern Australian aborigines came from the same site.

Little Salt Spring 12,000 B.P.

The Florida Paleo-Indians and their contemporaries farther north combined hunting with foraging, turning to the pursuit of the white-tailed deer and other smaller mammals as the Ice Age megafauna vanished. By 10,000 years ago, a widespread shift to more generalized hunting and gathering was under way, as the peoples of the Eastern Woodlands exploited a broad variety of foods — both

10,000 B.P.

FIGURE 7.7 Little Salt Spring, Florida. A Paleo-Indian had fallen into the spring and swum to a dry ledge, where he found a turtle that he cooked for food. When the meat ran out, he starved to death.

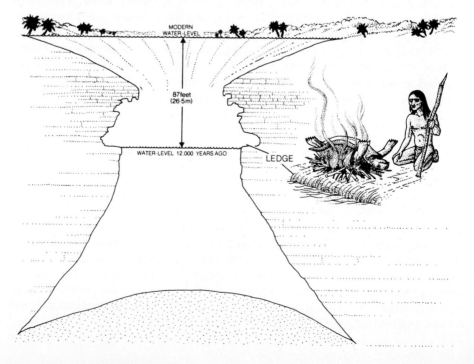

forest resources like gray squirrels and annual nut harvests, and pioneer seed-bearing grasses. It seems certain that small game, fish, mollusks, and vegetable foods assumed greater importance in the eastern diet after about 10,500 years ago. Inhabitants were part of the broad-spectrum hunting and gathering tradition known as the *Archaic*, which lasted until about 3000 years ago in many areas (for alternative terminology, see Stoltman, 1978).

During the many millennia of the Archaic, there was a long-term trend toward increased efficiency and success in exploiting forest and river valley resources, a shift called "Primary Forest Efficiency" by Joseph Caldwell in a landmark paper (1958). The Archaic has been subdivided into early, middle, and late stages on the basis of stylistic changes in projectile points and the introduction of slate tools, copper artifacts, and other technological innovations (see Griffin, 1967, for details), but the basic patterns of Archaic life were established early on and are known to us from excavations and surveys in northeast Arkansas and the Little Tennessee River Valley (Chapman et al., 1982; Morse and Morse, 1983; B. Smith, 1986).

The Dalton tradition flourished over a wide area of the Southeast and Midwest from about 10,500 to 9,500 years ago. Dan Morse and Phyllis Morse argue that in northeast Arkansas, Dalton band organization allowed a network of stable local family bands of twenty to thirty people who regularly used base camps centered on watershed territories (Morse and Morse, 1983). There they exploited easily accessible shallow-water fish, vegetable foods, seasonal nut harvests, and deer, with the women marrying into neighboring bands in nearby river valleys, thereby maintaining trading links between each drainage, contacts that ensured ample supplies of fine-grained chert over large areas. | **Dalton 10,500 to 9,500 B.P.**

By about 8000 years ago, warmer and drier climates were developing in the East, culminating in the so-called Hypsithermal episode of 6500 to 6000 years ago (Delcourt and Delcourt, 1981). The major rivers of the Midwest and Southeast stabilized their courses, while prehistoric population densities were still low. The highest concentrations of population were in areas like major river valley bottoms and lakeshores, which offered the greatest diversity of aquatic, game, and vegetable foods. In some favored areas, there was a slow trend toward living within more circumscribed territories and toward more sedentary settlement, made possible by an abundant constellation of seasonal foods. | **8000 B.P.**

The famous Koster site in the Illinois River Valley, with its fourteen stratified occupation levels, provides an extraordinary chronicle of human exploitation of a midwestern river valley from about 9500 years ago until A.D. 1200 (Struever and Holton, 1979). The first visitors to camp at Koster were Paleo-Indians, but about 8500 years ago, an early Archaic camp there covered about 3/4 acre (0.3 ha). An extended family group of about twenty-five people returned to the same location again and again, perhaps to exploit rich fall nut harvests in the area. Between 7600 and 7000 years ago, there were substantial settlements of rectangular, pole, brush, and clay houses that were occupied for most if not all the year, covering about 1 3/4 acres (0.7 ha). During spring and summer the inhabitants took thousands of fish, gathering freshwater mussels and hickory nuts in fall. Perhaps the people moved to the nearby uplands to hunt deer in winter. As long as this Middle Archaic population remained stable, they could find most of their food resources within 3 miles (4.8 km) of their settlement. It | **Koster 9500 B.P. to A.D. 1200** ... **7600 to 7000 B.P.**

was not until much later, after 4500 years ago, that the Koster people began exploiting a wider range of food resources.

A similar trend toward exploiting a relatively narrow range of wild foods is documented at other midwestern sites, among them the Modoc Rock Shelter near the Mississippi River (Brown and Phillips, 1983; Fowler, 1958). Modoc was occupied between about 10,000 and 4,000 years ago. As time went on, it became more and more of a base camp, where people lived for much of the year while they caught fish and exploited nut harvests. Both Koster and Modoc show that the Middle Archaic adaptation was a conservative one, requiring at least a degree of careful scheduling to maximize the potential of nut harvests and to capitalize on the game that fed on the rich forest mast (undergrowth) each fall. In this sense, Caldwell's Primary Forest Efficiency was achieved very early in the Archaic.

By about 4500 years ago, there had been a dramatic increase in the use of riverine resources over much of the Southeast and Midwest, perhaps coinciding with the onset of the Hypsithermal, when the stabilized river bottoms provided an abundance of oxbow lakes and swamps, where fish abounded and native grasses, shellfish, and other foods were to be found. Some of the river valleys lay on seasonal waterfowl migration routes, too, providing a bounty of food in spring and fall. This enhancement of aquatic habitats increased potential food supplies over long sections of river floodplains. As Bruce Smith (1986) puts it, there was an "opportunistic response to the advantageous emergence of a localized, seasonally abundant, dependable, and easily collected resource." This response led to the gradual adoption of sedentary lifeways in many parts of the Eastern Woodlands. Perhaps it is better described as a shift toward centrally based wandering, which involved a seasonally mobile lifeway and regular returning to the same base location for much of each year, especially during the summers.

Archaic populations in the East rose sharply after 6000 years ago, especially in favored areas. The Hypsithermal opened up vast areas of eastern Canada to caribou and human settlement. Rising sea levels and warming ocean temperatures allowed a steady northward expansion of fish and shellfish habitats. Flooded estuaries allowed more up-river fish runs in spring and fall. Nut-bearing forests spread farther north, into parts of the Great Lakes region, and river valley bottoms were exceptionally diverse and rich environments for Archaic hunter-gatherers.

In all probability, Archaic population growth was a response not only to environmental change but also to technological and subsistence advances, as well as new settlement patterns that took advantage of new riverine environments. The more sedentary living that accompanied the growth in many areas allowed people to store nuts and other winter foods on a much larger scale than if they were always on the move. This storage, in turn, created larger food surpluses, the ability to support higher population densities year-round, and opportunities for kin groups and individuals to play important roles in controlling labor and the redistribution of food and luxury goods. By the same token, people lived within more restricted territories, and there was far more local cultural variation.

There were also long-term changes in the ways people interacted with one

Modoc 10,000 to 4,000 B.P.

4500 B.P.

another and their neighbors. The smaller territories inhabited by more people contained a diversity of food resources and raw materials, but there was always something lacking. Such items had to be sought from elsewhere, by making a special journey or maintaining regular economic and social contacts with groups living nearer to the sources of what was needed. Over time, these trading connections assumed ever greater importance in the yearly round. They became a source not only of valued possessions and raw materials but of social connections and prestige — a way of maintaining "diplomatic" relations with the outside world. These interactions also affected population densities, especially when demand for prestige items, such as copper objects or seashells, soared. More and more hands would be needed to increase the output of food and trade goods. The intensification of hunting and foraging to meet these demands would lead to population increases — and to the emergence of social ranks based on prestige and social and economic power within previously egalitarian societies.

The Late Archaic witnessed much greater regional variety in hunter-gatherer culture in the East (B. Smith, 1986; Snow, 1980). The so-called Central Riverine Archaic was the most elaborate and well developed of all eastern Late Archaic traditions, for it was centered on midwestern and southeastern river valleys with a superabundance of aquatic, game, and vegetable foods. Between 5900 and 4800 years ago, a village covering 5 acres (2 ha) flourished at Koster (Struever and Holton, 1979), housing perhaps 100 to 150 people in substantial homes. The inhabitants did not concentrate on faster-water fish like their predecessors. Instead they speared and netted thousands of shallow-water species, like bass and catfish. One Illinois fish biologist has estimated that the people could have taken between 300 and 600 pounds (136 and 272 kg) of fish flesh per acre from backwater lakes that covered hundreds of acres. The people still collected shellfish and exploited the fall hickory and acorn harvests, but they now collected many more seed plants, including marsh elder, a swamp-side grass, grinding the seeds with pestles and mortars. In spring and fall, they would also shoot and trap thousands of migrating waterfowl. Everything from this Late Archaic settlement points to greater efficiency at food procurement, accompanied by exploitation of a broader spectrum of potential foods.

Similar broad-spectrum exploitation is found at other midwestern sites, among them the celebrated Indian Knoll site in Kentucky (C. H. Webb, 1968), which has yielded more than 1000 burials. Judging from these graves, the people still lived in fairly egalitarian societies, even if a few individuals were buried with prized possessions, such as turtle-shell ornaments or copper ornaments from Lake Superior (for other Late Archaic sites, see Jeffries, 1987; Winters, 1967).

By 6000 years ago, the diverse hunter-gatherer populations of the East were living under very different social conditions than their remote ancestors, in territories with restricted boundaries, cherishing tenuous social and economic links that connected individual to individual, kin to kin, through valleys and entire drainages, over hundreds, even thousands of miles of North America. The long-distance exchange of materials associated with these networks first appeared about 6000 years ago and escalated over the next 3000 years. Lake Superior native copper, hematite, Atlantic and Gulf Coast seashells, jasper

Central Riverine
Archaic 6000 B.P.

Koster 5900 to
4800 B.P.

from eastern Pennsylvania, chert and other fine-grained rocks — all these materials were exchanged between individuals and passed "down the line," just as obsidian was in the Neolithic Near East.

As studies of Lake Superior copper have shown, exotic artifacts and materials acquired greater prestige the farther they were traded (Figure 7.8). Within this context of regular social gatherings and exchanges, a greater degree of social differentiation based on reciprocity may have developed in Late Archaic society. This may have been nothing more than a ranking between younger and older members of society, or perhaps the emergence of one kin group as the "ranking" one. Judging from burial customs, both kin-based and individual social ranking took place within a context of increasingly elaborate ritual life. Perhaps some of the richly adorned burials from Late Archaic cemeteries are those of individuals who achieved social rank not by force or through virtue of birth but because of their personal qualities as traders and diplomats, as people who helped break down the social, economic, and political isolation that came with restricted mobility.

More intensive exploitation of food resources, even some cultivation of native plants, greater sedentism, regular social interaction and long-distance exchange, increased ceremonialism — these were the culminating elements in Late Archaic life that were to persist into the last few centuries before Christ, when new, much more elaborate burial customs appeared in the Eastern Woodlands (Chapter 14). In some areas of the Northeast and eastern Canada, much of the Archaic hunter-gatherer tradition survived until modern times, until people came into contact with European explorers (Morison, 1971).

FIGURE 7.8 Archaic copper artifacts (approximately one-half actual size).

Specialized Hunter-Gatherers in Mesoamerica and Latin America

The hunter-gatherers of the central and southern portions of the New World enjoyed a wide variety of specialized adaptations after 9500 years ago. Sites of these specialized hunter-gatherer groups have been excavated from Mexico to Tierra del Fuego. One characteristic adaptation has been identified in the Andes, and another flourished on the uplands of eastern Brazil (Lynch, 1978, 1980; Rick, 1980). As in North America, intensified hunting and gathering concentrated the human population in favored localities such as lakeshores and seacoasts, where resources were unusually abundant.

Sophisticated hunting and gathering strategies ensured food at all seasons. Kent Flannery has shown, for instance, that the hunter-gatherers of the Tehuacán Valley in Mexico had a regular, almost scheduled, annual round of hunting and gathering activities that caused the population to gather in large camps during the plentiful season and scatter into small groups during the lean months (Flannery, 1968a). The people obtained a balanced diet by using different food procurement systems that varied in importance with the time of year.

Tehuacán
1000 B.P.

Some of these specialized hunter-gatherers remained at the simple hunting and collecting level because of limitations in their environment and plentiful natural resources, making economic change unnecessary. However, in some areas of Mesoamerica and on the coast and highlands of Peru, hunter-gatherer bands began to experiment with the deliberate planting of vegetable foods, perhaps in attempts to expand the areas in which certain favored vegetable foods were found. These experiments became one of the vehicles of dynamic cultural change that resulted from the first development of agriculture in the New World (Chapter 14).

The southernmost extremities of Latin America were inhabited until recent times by scattered bands of hunters and fishermen. The Ona, Yaghan, and Alacaluf peoples are vividly described by early missionaries who settled among them. They lived in small bands, using only the crudest shelters of skins or grass and driftwood, with nothing but skin for body covering during the height of the antarctic winter. Shellfish, some game, fruits, berries, and fish provided a simple diet, and for tools they had none of the more sophisticated weapons made by more northern hunters. Tierra del Fuego, however, was occupied remarkably early, and it is thought that the Fuegian tradition began as early as 6000 B.P., if not earlier. Many roots of these most southerly prehistoric humans lie back in early hunting cultures that elsewhere were replaced thousands of years before by more advanced farming cultures.

Fuegian Indians
6000 B.P. to
modern times

ALEUTS AND INUIT

We started the story of the first Americans with Alaska, and now end with a brief return to arctic latitudes to trace the origins of the Aleuts and Inuit, whose remarkable hunter-gatherer cultures survived long beyond European contact into recent times. The origins of both the Aleut and the Inuit go back many thousands of years into prehistory, and their ultimate ancestry may lie both in Asian roots and in local cultural evolution. The differences between them are more cultural than physical and reflect varied adaptations to arctic maritime environments. It is logical for us to end this chapter with the Arctic, for the Inuit were the first native Americans to come into contact with Europeans, in Greenland and in the extreme continental Northeast (Dumond, 1987a,b).

Paleoarctic tradition 11,000 to 6,000 B.P.

As we have seen, the earliest cultural tradition which makes any archaeological sense at the moment is the Paleoarctic tradition, which was flourishing by about 11,000 B.P. and had some connections with contemporary cultures in Siberia. The Paleoarctic people were tundra-dwelling hunter-gatherers, whose culture and language *may* be the ancestor of both Inuit and Aleut culture and language. It should be noted that both peoples are the most Asian of all indigenous Americans. By 9000 years ago, these two peoples had moved south as far as the Alaskan peninsula. Only a millennium later they had settled in the Aleutian Islands.

9000 B.P.

6000 B.P.

By 6000 B.P., there was more cultural diversity in the Arctic, as specialized adaptations developed on the coast and in the interior, and some American Indian groups moved northward into formerly glaciated regions in the interior. On the Pacific Coast, and in the eastern Aleutians, the Aleutian tradition was among those which emerged.

Aleutian tradition 8700 B.P. to modern times

The Aleuts have been in their island homeland twice as long as the Inuit have been in Greenland (Laughlin, Marsh, and Harper, 1979). The ancestors entered the archipelago at a time when the sea level was lower than it is today. Their ancestry is perhaps in the Norton tradition (see later; Dumond 1987a). The earliest occupation dates to approximately 8700 B.P. at Anangula, about a third of the way along the chain, at the terminus of the Bering Land Bridge. An-

FIGURE 7.9 Aleuts returning from a sea otter hunt, probably in the 1890s. They are wearing eye visors made of wood. Photograph by an unknown government surveyor.

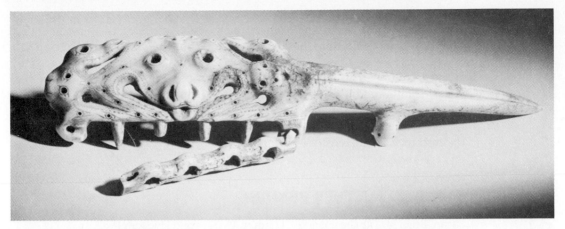

FIGURE 7.10 Ornamented ivory object, perhaps a comb, from the Seward Peninsula in Alaska (Northern tradition and style). Length: 10.2 in (26 cm).

angula lies on a cliff 65.5 feet (20 m) above sea level and probably was occupied for at least 500 years, by an estimated group of at least one hundred (Aigner, 1970; Laughlin, 1980). The inhabitants lived by fishing, sea mammal hunting (Figure 7.9), and fowling, an ideal strategy for an isolated, stable marine environment. The nearby and later site of Chaluka carries the story of Aleutian occupation up to recent times. Radiocarbon dates suggest that the eastern and western ends of the Aleutian archipelago were occupied approximately 3000 years ago, the people expanding outward from the Anangula area as the population density grew.

The origins of the Inuit (Eskimo) cultural tradition of modern times may lie in the Arctic Small-Tool tradition, a distinctive small-artifact technology that appeared in Alaska approximately 4300 years ago. The Arctic Small-Tool people may have had strong connections with Siberia and are thought to have been nomadic land mammal hunters who preyed on caribou and musk ox (Giddings, 1967). Some settled in Alaska; others wandered as far east as Greenland by 4000 B.P., becoming the first people to settle in the eastern Arctic. The eastern Small-Tool tradition eventually evolved into the long-lived Thule tradition, whose people were the first native Americans to come into contact with Europeans (Maxwell, 1985).

The Arctic Small-Tool tradition began to disappear in Alaska some 3500 years ago, to be replaced by cultures based on the intensive hunting of both sea mammals and land animals. This tradition, called the Norton tradition, in turn gave rise to the Thule tradition, which is thought to have originated among whale hunters in the Bering Strait. This tradition first emerged in the first millennium after Christ and developed into a highly distinctive sea mammal hunting culture with all the Inuit artifacts so well known from popular publications — among them, the kayak, the umiak (open skin boat), and toggled harpoons, as well as fine ivory work (Figure 7.10). Many of the Inuit, especially those who hunted whales, lived by then in larger settlements. In approximately A.D. 900 the Thule people started to expand to the south, and then to the east. Thule whale hunters appeared in the arctic islands of the east in approximately

Marginal notes:

Arctic Small-Tool tradition **4300 to 3500 B.P.**

Norton tradition (west) **3500 B.P. to A.D. 500**

Thule tradition **A.D. 500 to modern times**

A.D. 1000, where their open-water hunting techniques could be used with great effect. By the time the Thule reached northwest Greenland, the Norsemen had been living in the southern parts of the island for some time (Wahlgren, 1986).

Inuit cultural traditions, like those of the Fuegians and other hunter-gatherer groups, continued to flourish after European contact, but within a few centuries, traditional lifeways were modified beyond recognition and exotic diseases decimated hunter-gatherer populations. Today, few of America's hunter-gatherers still practice their millennia-old lifeways: there are no longer the resources or the territory for them to do so.

GUIDE TO FURTHER READING

Fagan, Brian M. *The Great Journey.* London: Thames and Hudson, 1987.
A general, analytic discussion of the evidence for first settlement.
Hopkins, David M., et al. (eds.) *Paleoecology of Beringia.* New York: Academic Press, 1982.
A fascinating and highly technical set of essays about the Bering Land Bridge that discusses everything from animal life to sea level changes.
Jennings, Jesse D. *Ancient Native Americans.* 2d ed. 2 vols. New York: Freeman, 1983.
A comprehensive volume of essays on the archaeology of North, Middle, and South America, each written by an established authority. Up-to-date, highly technical, and crammed with useful information.
Shulter, Richard, Jr. (ed.). *Early Man in the New World.* Beverly Hills: Sage Publications, 1983.
Authoritative, well-written essays on what we know in the 1980s about the first Americans. Strongly recommended.
Smith, Bruce D. "The Archaeology of the Southeastern United States: From Dalton to de Soto, 10,500–500 B.P.," *Advances in World Archaeology* 5 (1986): 1–92.
A superb analytic synthesis of southeastern archaeology that has broad application elsewhere in the Eastern Woodlands. This is an excellent example of contemporary approaches to North American prehistory.

CHRONOLOGICAL TABLE E

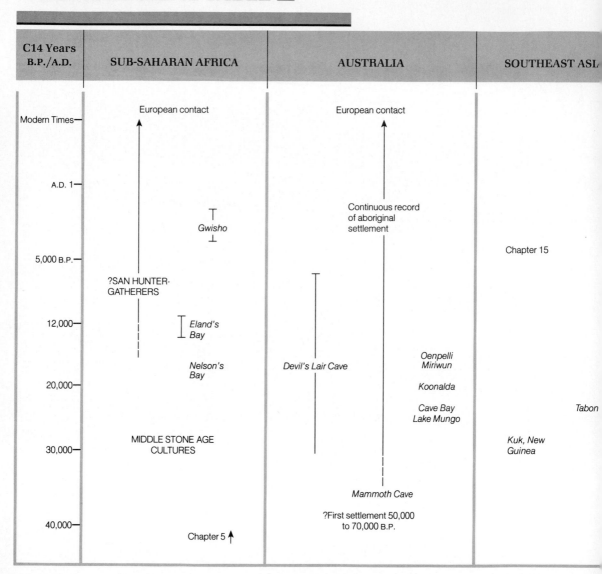

C14 Years B.P./A.D.	SUB-SAHARAN AFRICA	AUSTRALIA	SOUTHEAST ASL

CHAPTER 8

Africans and Australians

Preview

- Like hunter-gatherers in northern latitudes, the post-Pleistocene peoples of tropical regions adopted increasingly diverse economies after 10,000 years ago. They also made much use of the bow and arrow. Toolkits became smaller and more lightweight as a result.

- Judging from excavations in southern Africa, the Postglacial populations of Africa may have turned their attention to smaller browsing animals, food gathering, and aquatic resources, continuously adapting to changing environmental conditions. The densest human populations were probably concentrated in areas of abundant water and diverse animal and plant resources. The result was probably a much greater diversity of hunter-gatherer societies throughout much of Africa, a diversity from which living societies like the San arose.

- The San of southern Africa flourished in savanna woodland country that was rich in game and vegetable foods. Their lively rock art depicts their hunting and gathering activities. These paintings, and the waterlogged Gwisho sites in central Zambia, have shown that their portable toolkits changed little over the centuries. The San's highly flexible band organization of today doubtless ensured the continued viability of prehistoric hunter-gatherers as well. They also lived at small campsites, which were often reoccupied at certain seasons of the year for many generations.

- During much of the Weichsel glaciation, New Guinea and Australia formed a single landmass, called Sahul.

- It has been estimated that human settlement of Sahul goes back 70,000 to 50,000 years, although the earliest archaeological sites date to about 32,000 years ago.

- The archaeological record shows that the Australian lifeway changed little during its long history, but there were steady, slow changes in tool technology. The Tasmanians were isolated in their homeland as sea levels rose at the end of the Pleistocene and, as a result, did not acquire some of the later mainland tool types, such as the boomerang.

■ Living archaeology and ethnographic analogy play an important part in our interpretation of the prehistory of tropical hunter-gatherers.

Chronological
Table E

The end of the Weichsel glaciation had less profound effects on tropical latitudes than on northern latitudes. However, it did result in minor shifts in rainfall patterns, which may have had a significant effect on the distribution of critically important game populations and cereal grasses. The archaeological record for the many hunter-gatherer populations of southern latitudes consists for the most part of thousands of stone implements from dozens of isolated sites (Allchin, 1966). Instead of attempting a detailed chronicle of isolated local cultures, we concentrate on two adaptations of particular interest — those of the San peoples of southern Africa and those of the Australian aborigines. Both these peoples continue to display a wide range of relatively specialized adaptations that include not only hunting and gathering but fishing and exploitation of shellfish as well.

The modern hunter-gatherer populations of Africa and Asia are among the very few survivors of the longest-lived and perhaps most viable of all human lifeways. Only 15,000 years ago, probably everyone lived by hunting and gathering. Ethnographer George Peter Murdock (1968) has estimated that perhaps 15 percent of the world's population was still hunting and gathering at the time Columbus landed in the New World. We are fortunate that modern anthropological studies of the San and Australians have given us at least a few insights into the traditional lifeways of southern hunter-gatherers.

AFRICAN HUNTER-GATHERERS: PAST AND PRESENT

As we saw in Chapter 5, *Homo sapiens sapiens*, anatomically modern humans, probably evolved in Africa, perhaps as early as 100,000 years ago. The long millennia of the Weichsel glaciation saw the peoples of Africa evolving ever more efficient ways of hunting and foraging. These changes are still little

Nelson's Bay
15,000 B.P.

known, except in southern Africa. At Klasies River Mouth and Nelson's Bay Cave in South Africa, Richard Klein (1979) has documented the major changes in subsistence patterns that took place during the later Stone Age. After some 15,000 years ago, the inhabitants of Nelson's Bay were enjoying a far more varied diet than their predecessors. They took bush pigs and warthogs, as well as larger antelope like the eland and hartebeest. The people used nets and fish hooks to catch ocean fish, something their ancestors had never done. They also lived off flying birds like the cormorant. One reason for this more diverse lifeway may have been that many species of larger antelope became extinct at the end of the Ice Age, an event that is difficult to account for on environmental grounds alone. Perhaps human hunters played a role in accelerating the process of extinction, at the same time adapting to Postglacial conditions with a more diverse subsistence strategy.

We know very little about the climate of sub-Saharan Africa at the height of the last glaciation, but John Parkington (1987) and others believe that the human populations living at the southern tip of the continent were sparse. Parkington notes that larger animals appear to have been more common before about 9000 years ago and hypothesizes that small bands of hunter-gatherers may have roamed over large territories in search of large, gregarious animals. There is, however, almost no evidence to support this scenario, and much of the southern part of Africa may have been wet, cold, and windy during glacial times.

By about 9000 years ago, the world's southern oceans were warmer than today. It was not until 3000 years later, during the so-called Postglacial climatic optimum, that northern seas achieved higher temperatures. This is because of different land and water distributions in the two hemispheres, with Antarctica being much colder than the Arctic Ocean. Warmer, drier conditions in southern Africa led to more succulent vegetation at the expense of grassland and heath, with major changes in human subsistence. These changes are hard to document. John Parkington (1987) has chronicled one changing scenario at Eland's Bay Cave in the far south. Thirteen thousand years ago, the inhabitants hunted large and medium-sized antelope. But between 11,000 and 9,000 years ago, they turned their attention to smaller browsing animals, with estuarine and marine animals, as well as limpets, becoming ever more common. By 8000 years ago, the entire coastal plain was flooded, with only small browsing animals, mussels, and fish being taken. Then Eland's Bay Cave was abandoned suddenly, never to be reoccupied.

Eland's Bay **13,000 to 8,000 B.P.**

After 11,000 B.P. the quantity of food bones increases dramatically, as does the variety of ostrich eggshell beads, water containers, bone tools, decorated bonework, and other artifacts (Figure 8.1). Parkington believes that this intensification in domestic activity was due to environmental change, to the dramatic encroachments of the Postglacial ocean. Eland's Bay Cave was first visited, then lived in for long periods of time as the coastal plain shrank. Finally, the people moved into the interior or elsewhere along the shore when this stretch of coastline was no longer productive. It would be a mistake to describe the major changes in artifact inventories or subsistence as evolving culture change. Rather, they may reflect continuous adaptation to rapidly altering climatic conditions, changes that were reflected by other adaptive shifts elsewhere on the coast, as at Nelson's Bay, and also in the warm interior.

The long-term trend over the past 15,000 years may have been toward smaller "food parcels" (Parkington, 1987). Many late Stone Age caves and rock shelters in southern Africa were used much more regularly in Postglacial times, as if mountain and near-coastal locations were extremely favorable places to settle, places where smaller browsing animal herds would be concentrated. The warming trend in the earlier millennia of Postglacial times may have led to increased aridity in many parts of the interior, with the densest human populations concentrated in areas of abundant water and diverse animal and plant resources. The result was probably a great diversity of hunter-gatherer societies throughout much of Africa.

Hilary Deacon (1979) has excavated several late Stone Age rock shelters and caves with exceptional care. He believes that there was a trend toward hunting

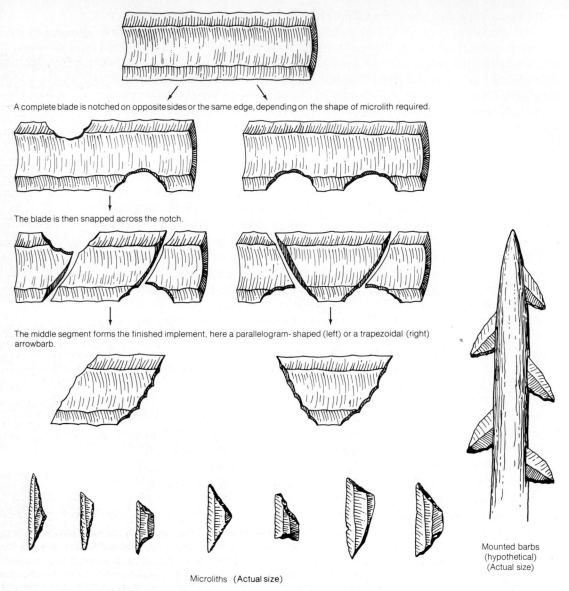

A complete blade is notched on opposite sides or the same edge, depending on the shape of microlith required.

The blade is then snapped across the notch.

The middle segment forms the finished implement, here a parallelogram-shaped (left) or a trapezoidal (right) arrowbarb.

Microliths (Actual size)

Mounted barbs
(hypothetical)
(Actual size)

FIGURE 8.1 Microliths. Stages in manufacturing a microlith, a small arrow barb, or similar implement made by notching a blade and snapping off its base after the implement is formed.

smaller game, and especially the exploitation of plant foods. Rabbits, tortoises, and both grasses and root plants became vital components in the hunter-gatherers' diet. Just when plant foods came to be of overwhelming importance is much debated, but they were especially significant after about 2000 years ago, when herding peoples were settled in extreme southern Africa (Chapter 12), perhaps when the newcomers squeezed hunter-gatherers into more limited territories, away from cattle grazing grounds (for full discussion, see Parkington, 1987).

The same general trend toward increasingly specialized subsistence strategies may also have developed in other parts of sub-Saharan Africa, just as in other parts of the world. The peoples of the open savanna lived off the abundant game populations and supplemented their diet with seasonal gathering of the rich vegetable resources of the woodland. Other bands settled on the shores of lakes and on riverbanks and lived by fishing. This valuable and reliable source of protein encouraged more lasting settlement and increased specialization. The rain forest peoples of the Zaire River Basin in central Africa were unable to hunt such a wide range of game as their savanna counterparts, so they relied heavily on vegetable foods and wild roots.

The later Stone Age hunter-gatherers of the eastern and southern African savanna are comparatively well documented not only from archaeological sites but also from their own rock paintings and engravings. Rock paintings are notoriously hard to date, but it is possible that Stone Age artists were at work in southern Africa as early as 20,000 years ago. They were certainly painting the walls of caves they visited 8000 years ago. Modern ethnographic and historical records connect the San peoples who live today in the Kalahari Desert with this ancient artistic tradition. Their Stone Age lifeway survived into the twentieth century and appears to have changed relatively little for thousands of years.

The Gwisho hot springs in central Zambia provide evidence for a basically **Gwisho 3500 B.P.** similar subsistence pattern at least 3500 years ago (Fagan and van Noten, 1971). Because the lower levels of the sites among the springs were waterlogged, many organic artifacts and food remains have survived, giving an exceptionally complete picture of Stone Age life in the region. The economy and material culture of the Gwisho people show a striking resemblance to those of modern San peoples in the Kalahari, although, of course, there are environmental differences (R. B. Lee, 1979; R. B. Lee and DeVore, 1976; Yellen, 1977). The Gwisho people hunted many species of antelope and caught fish in shallow pools of the nearby Kafue River. The waterlogged levels contained more than 10,000 plant remains, from only eight species, all of which were apparently collected to the exclusion of many other edible species. Nearby lay some fine arrowheads and some of the wooden artifacts made by the inhabitants, including some simple digging sticks used for uprooting tubers. These tools are identical to those used by Kalahari San today. There were traces of a grass and stick shelter, of hearths, and of layers of grass that may have served as bedding. Thirty-five burials were deposited in the soil of the campsites. The deposits were littered with hundreds of stone arrow barbs and tiny scraping tools that lay alongside pestles and grinding stones used to process the vegetable foods that were an important part of the Gwisho diet. So little have gathering habits changed in the past 3000 years that a San from the Kalahari was able to identify seeds from the excavations and tell archaeologists what they were used for.

The Gwisho hot springs are informative, for they confirm ethnographic observations made about the present-day San. Like that of their modern successors, the toolkit of the Gwisho people was highly portable, and much of it was disposable. Except for bows and arrows, the Kalahari San improvise many of their tools from the bush as they need them, making snares fom vegetable fibers and clubs from convenient branches. The women use digging sticks like the Gwisho artifacts for digging tubers and a softened antelope hide, or kaross, as a garment and carrying bag. Their only other artifacts are a pair of pounding stones for breaking up nuts. The Gwisho site contained both digging sticks and pounders. We know from cave paintings that the San used karosses for thousands of years, and we can assume they were used at Gwisho and elsewhere.

Like those of the San, the Gwisho home bases were little more than small clusters of brush shelters. The average present-day !Kung San camp holds approximately ten to thirty people. The small population of !Kung territory leads to a continuous turnover of the composition of camp populations. This constant change is a reality reflected in the !Kung's highly flexible kinship system. Every member of a band has not only close family ties but also kin connections with a much wider number of people living all over !Kung territory. The !Kung kinship system is based on an elaborate network of commonly possessed personal names, which are transmitted from grandparent to grandchild. People with similar names share kin ties even if they live some distance from one another. This network is such that individuals can move to a new camp and find a family with which they have kin ties to accept them. The resulting flexibility of movement prevents total social chaos. Presumably, the prehistoric San had a similar social organization to aid survival.

The vivid San paintings and engravings depict the game hunted, the chase, and life in camp (Lewis-Williams, 1981; Vinnecombe, 1976). The San drew running hunters, people fishing from boats, and scenes of gathering honey and vegetable foods (Figures 8.2 and 8.3). The hunters can be seen stalking game in disguise, hotly pursuing wounded quarry, even raiding the cattle herds of their agricultural neighbors of later centuries. David Lewis-Williams (1981), who has studied ethnographic records of San bands, has shown convincingly that many of the paintings depict complex metaphors that represent symbolic values in the San world. Each superimposition of paintings, each relationship between

FIGURE 8.2 A running San hunter from Ho Khotso, Lesotho, southern Africa. From a late Stone Age painting colored purple-red. The figure is approximately 8 in (21 cm) high.

human figures and animals had profound meaning to the artists and the people. For instance, many of the paintings depict eland with dancers cavorting around them (Figure 8.4). Lewis-Williams believes the dancers were acquiring the potency released by the death of the eland. The dancers go into trances so powerful that they become eland themselves (Figure 8.5). This symbolism survived into the nineteenth century. When Victorian anthropologist George Stow

FIGURE 8.4 A trance dance being executed by San shamans. Their elongated bodies convey the sense of being stretched out experienced by people in altered states of consciousness. Dots along the spine of the central figure depict what the San describe as a "boiling" sensation felt as supernatural power rises up the spine and "explodes" in the head. The power is derived from certain animals, like the eland depicted to the right.

FIGURE 8.5 A curing dance among the San from the Nyae Nyae area of Namibia. Dances like this may have formed part of the ritual behind prehistoric rock paintings.

(Lewis-Williams, 1981) showed some rock painting pictures to an elderly San couple, the woman began to sing and dance. The man begged her to desist because the old songs made him sad. But eventually he joined in, and Stow watched the couple reliving the symbolism of past days. Only now, more than a century later, are archaeologists trying to probe this forgotten world.

A.D. 1

Prehistoric hunter-gatherers enjoyed the savanna woodlands of eastern and southern Africa undisturbed until approximately 2000 years ago, when the first farming peoples (other African folk) settled by the banks of the Zambezi and Limpopo rivers (Phillipson, 1984). The San placed second in the resulting competition for land: the farmers wanted grazing grass and prime land for cultivating, so they drove off the bands of San hunter-gatherers, who had to retreat into less favored areas. Some took up the new economies and married into farming communities. White settlement in South Africa increased the isolation

A.D. 1800

of the San. As the pressure on their hunting grounds grew, the San moved into mountainous areas and desert regions. Even there they were harassed and hunted. Some of the white settlers went shooting them on Sunday afternoons.

The doomed San of South Africa calmly continued to paint scenes of cattle raids and of European ships and wagons. They even depicted red-coated English soldiers on their expeditions into the mountains. By the end of the nineteenth century, there were no San painting in South Africa, and the art of stone toolmaking had all but died out. The last stoneworkers used glass bottle fragments to make their sharp arrowheads. They found this unusually pure "stone" vastly preferable to their usual quartz pebbles (Peringuey, 1911; Schapera, 1930).

A.D. 1890

PREHISTORY OF THE AUSTRALIANS

The Australian aborigines encountered by Captain Cook and other early European explorers were still living in the Stone Age; they were all hunter-gatherers and used a technology that could have stepped right out of prehistory (Figure 8.6). Their ancestry has excited the interest of anthropological archaeologists ever since: Where did the Australians come from, and how long ago did people first settle on this remote continent? (Lourandos, 1987; Mulvaney, 1975; White and O'Connell, 1982).

The natural area in which to look for Australian origins is, of course, southeast Asia. When sea levels were at their lowest, during the height of the Weichsel glaciation, perhaps 50,000 years ago, only a relatively short open-water passage separated Australia from the islands that lie off southeast Asia (Figure 8.7) (Allen, Golson, and Jones, 1977). Everyone agrees that a broad gene pool of southeast Asian origin ultimately gave rise to the human populations of Pleistocene and later Australia. Whether there was just one primeval settlement or different populations arriving at various times is still uncertain. Unfortunately, the archaeological evidence in southeast Asia is too sparse for any close comparisons between Australian toolkits and those of their Asian contemporaries. Tropical New Guinea was connected to mainland Australia until about 8000 years ago. There were areas of highland glaciation as well as human occupation dating to at least 30,000 years ago, and perhaps much earlier. There are some very general resemblances between tanged flaked tools from New Guinea and surface finds in Australia (Lourandos, 1987).

The constant fluctuations of sea level during the Weichsel glaciation had profound effects on the geography of Australia. For at least 80 percent of the time humans have lived on the continent, New Guinea and Australia were joined by a continental shelf, now submerged by higher, post–Ice Age water. This single landmass is known as Sahul. For about the first 40,000 years of their history the peoples of Sahul shared a common history. Then at the end of the Weichsel, sea levels rose and separated the two countries (Figure 8.7). Sunda, another submerged landmass, joined the islands off mainland Southeast Asia.

Sahul

Throughout this period, the climate fluctuated constantly. About 20,000 to 15,000 years ago, Tasmania was part of the Australian mainland, present coastlines were far inland, and much of the region was considerably drier. The first traces of human settlement in Australia may date to as early as 50,000 years ago, but no evidence of such occupation has yet come to light. This is hardly

FIGURE 8.6 An Australian aborigine with his lightweight hunting kit. This somewhat romanticized portrait was drawn by François Peron, a naturalist attached to the Baudin Expedition of 1802.

surprising, since most archaeological sites are the remains of short-term out-door encampments that contain little more than hearths and stone tools.

Lake Mungo **33,000 to 22,000** B.P.

The earliest dated sites are from dry Lake Mungo in west New South Wales. A series of carbon patches appear to be hearths, associated with simple stone artifacts and some heavily encrusted human bones. The hearths contained fish bones, some birds, shellfish, and a few mammal fragments. A series of radio-carbon dates place this occupation in the range 33,000 to 22,000 B.P. (White and O'Connell, 1982). The skeletal remains are entirely of modern people, who may have reached Australia as early as 50,000 years ago (J. M. Bowdler, Jones, and Thorne, 1970).

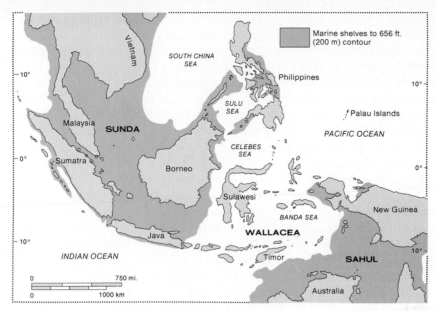

FIGURE 8.7 Ice Age, Southeast Asia. Low sea levels exposed dry land off Southeast Asia and between Australia and New Guinea during the last glaciation, creating Sahul and Sunda.

As in the Americas, there are precious few sites dating to earlier than 10,000 years ago. The Devil's Lair Cave in the southwest part of west Australia contains occupation levels that date from earlier than 27,000 B.P. — perhaps much earlier (Dortch and Merrilees, 1973). Nearby Mammoth Cave was excavated early in this century without good stratigraphic control, but many bones from extinct marsupials (pouched animals) were found. There is a possibility that this site may be as much as 40,000 years old, although the evidence is inconclusive (White and O'Connell, 1982).

The only other piece of archaeological evidence contemporary with Lake Mungo comes from Kuk in highland New Guinea, where firecracked and humanly transported rocks have been dated to about 30,000 years ago (White and O'Connell, 1982). It is probable that Sahul was settled between 70,000 and 50,000 years ago, during times of low sea level, but this is a mere guesstimate. New ax finds from New Guinea's Huon Peninsula may date to as early as 30,000 B.P. (Groube et al., 1986).

Kuk, New Guinea
c. 30,000 B.P.

How did the actual settlement occur? Almost certainly as a result of accidental voyages. At no time was the southeast Asian mainland joined to Sahul. But many of the islands off the mainland are less than 6 miles (10 km) apart. These islands could easily have been reached intentionally on simple rafts, or even floating logs. The more distant islands, though, were probably colonized by accident, when people drifted offshore. It is interesting to note that almost no Asian animals colonized the islands, so the settlement of Sahul was probably unintentional, and even if the shortest sea routes were used, the trip would have involved at least one open-water crossing of over 50 miles (80.4 km). Therefore, the human settlement of Sahul was probably a very slow process, with no return voyages, that may have started in the Ice Age, since human settlement on the mainland took place at least a million years ago.

At present, it is impossible to go far beyond speculation. Few archaeologists have worked in any part of Sahul, many of the early sites are on the ocean floor, and initial human settlement was very sparse indeed.

Once settlement was established, on a continent that was three times its present size, we can assume that humans spread slowly through the entire region. By 20,000 years ago, people were certainly living around the modern coasts and on the fringes of the desert. By 10,000 years ago, they had settled in all the major environmental zones. And by that time Tasmania was separated from the mainland by the rising waters of the Bass Strait. How did this colonization take place? Some argue that it was a relatively rapid process, a matter of pursuing big game, or of the population doubling every twenty years or so, a natural rate of increase that would give rise to the modern density of indigenous Australians in about 2000 years. But there are too many variables for this model to be truly convincing, among them birth spacing and physiology. Another hypothesis holds that the first settlers were coastal peoples, who later moved into the interior. While many of the first colonizers may have been coastal peoples, it seems more likely that the interior would have been settled at the same time as the coast, and, in any case, the notion that the earliest sites were coastal is as yet unproven (for detailed arguments, see White and O'Connell, 1982). White and O'Connell have compared the Australian situation to that in America, where some people (Martin, 1973) believe that colonization by big-game hunters led to a very rapid settlement as far south as Patagonia. They believe that it would take hunter-gatherers a considerable time to adapt to the many environments between the Plains and Tierra del Fuego, that this process took many millennia, and that the settlement of both America and Australia was a very slow process. The main barriers to rapid human settlement were not the environments but people's ability to learn how to exploit them. Generations of field work are needed to underpin any of these hypotheses.

Miriwun
18,000 B.P.

Between 25,000 and 10,000 years ago, the population of Australia may have reached approximately modern levels, an estimated 300,000 people. Sites in this time bracket have been found throughout Australia, at Miriwun in the north, a shelter dating to nearly 18,000 years ago (Dortch, 1977). Another famous location is Koonalda in southern Australia, a cave on a treeless plain where hearths and flint nodules were discovered at a mining site and date to between 24,000 and 15,000 years ago. Some wavy patterns made by human hands have been found on the soft limestone walls and may be very old (R. Wright, 1971).

The same traditions of stoneworking and bone technology found in these early sites survived almost unchanged for thousands of years (R. Wright, 1977). for instance, flakes showing wear patterns characteristic of adz blades made by modern aborigines date back as far as 20,000 years ago, and the same bone points used to fasten skin clothes in historic times have been found deep in the prehistoric levels of Devil's Lair. The Australian aborigines were famous for their artistic traditions and elaborate ceremonial life. Abundant traces of ritual belief have been found in Australian sites. The Devil's Lair site yielded stone plaques, a deep pit, and human incisor teeth that had been knocked out with a sharp blow: such evulsion of teeth was a long-lived Australian tradition. If the Koonalda engravings are as old as claimed, then some Australian art is as ancient as European Upper Paleolithic artistic traditions.

Despite the essential conservatism of Australian stoneworking practices, some regional variations did appear over the millennia. Steep-edged scrapers, which were probably used as woodworking tools, were made over a wide area of Australia during much of the Upper Pleistocene. These, and crude flake tools, remained in use until recent times; they were joined after 6000 B.P. in some areas by stone points set on shafts and other microliths. There is good reason to believe that aboriginal technology developed within Australia over a long period in response to local needs, and without the benefit of cultural innovation from outside (Figure 8.8).

Some idea of the simple level of early Australian life can be obtained from the saga of the Tasmanians (Plomley, 1969). When the first European voyagers visited Tasmania in 1642, they found bands of hunter-gatherers living on the island. The Tasmanians lasted precisely eighty years after European settlement in 1802. They had no shafted tools (that is, tools composed of stone heads or points with wooden shafts or handles) and relied instead on scrapers and chop-

FIGURE 8.8   Australian aborigines making stone tools.

pers somewhat like those used by early hunter-gatherers on the mainland; they lacked the boomerangs, spear-throwers, shields, axes, adzes, and lightweight stone tools the Australians of the mainland had when they first entered written history. Tasmania was settled when it was attached to the mainland during the Weichsel glaciation, but many of the earliest sites are probably buried under the sea.

Cave Bay
22,000 B.P.

The earliest archaeological record of occupation is from a cave at Cave Bay on Hunter Island, now isolated from Tasmania by the higher sea level that cut Tasmania away from Australia as well. The cave was used by occasional visitors, who left sparse occupation levels behind them dating from around 22,700 to 18,000 years ago. (S. Bowdler, 1984). The result of Tasmania's isolation was that its populations, although forming part of the Australian cultural group, never received the later cultural innovations that spread through Australia after sea levels rose. Harry Lourandos and others have suggested that Tasmanian adaptations preserved a rather specialized lifeway that was typical of much of Australia during the late Weichsel into modern times (for discussion, see Lourandos, 1987).

Fortunately for archaeology, at least some investigations of aboriginal culture have been made that have important bearing on the interpretation of the archaeological record. Richard Gould (1977) spent many months among the

FIGURE 8.9 Comparison of a prehistoric campsite at Puntutjarpa Rock Shelter, Australia, with a modern aboriginal campsite in the same area. Note that the modern encampment can be subdivided into living areas by using informants' data and anthropological observation, while the archaeological site is devoid of such information, consisting merely of artifact patterns.

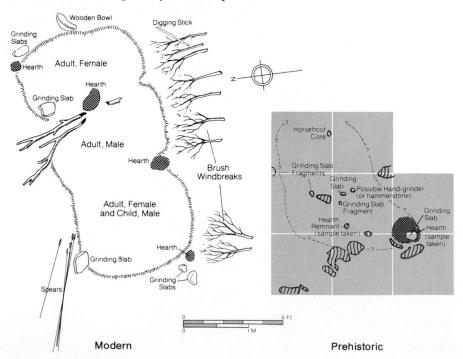

Ngatatjara people of the Western Desert, carrying out ethnographic investigations that had objectives somewhat similar to those of Richard Lee among the San in Africa: he was interested in their cultural ecology and in the ways ethnographic observations could be used to interpret the archaeological record. His aboriginal informants took him to Puntutjarpa Rock Shelter, a site that they still visited regularly. Gould excavated the occupation levels in the shelter and found that people had lived there for more than 6800 years. The later stone implements were almost indistinguishable from modern Ngatatjara tools, to the extent that Gould was able to compare the wear patterns on both ancient and modern artifacts and decide which 5000-year-old tools had been mounted on shafts and which had not. He also compared modern living surfaces with equivalent features found in the rock shelter (Figure 8.9).

The study of living aborigine bands shows just how conservative Australian lifeways have been. There were few major technological innovations during Australian prehistory. Indeed, it was possible for the prehistoric Australians to maintain a thoroughly viable lifeway with minimal technology and but the simplest of artifacts. The Tasmanians, for instance, used only two dozen or so tools to hunt and forage. The great elaboration of Australian and Tasmanian culture was in social and ritual life, neither of which can readily be recovered by archaeological investigation. That much of this activity was designed to maintain the delicate balance between the aborigines and the available resources in their environment was no coincidence (White and O'Connell, 1982). A belief in such balance lay at the very core of Australian life.

GUIDE TO FURTHER READING

Clark, J. Desmond. *The Prehistory of Africa*. London: Thames and Hudson, 1970.
A synthesis of African prehistory with emphasis on the Stone Age.

Gould, Richard A. *Living Archaeology*. Cambridge: Cambridge University Press, 1980.
A definitive primer on ethnoarchaeology that covers most major field research conducted thus far. Excellent on basic principles.

Lee, Richard B. *The !Kung San*. Cambridge: Cambridge University Press, 1979.
If there is one classic ethnographic study of hunter-gatherers, this account of the Kalahari San and their complex ecology is it. Strongly recommended to give the reader a clear understanding of hunter-gatherer lifeways.

Lewis-Williams, David. *Believing and Seeing: Symbolic Meanings in Southern San Rock Art*. New York: Academic Press, 1981.
A superb, well-argued study of the meaning of prehistoric rock art in southern Africa that should be read by anyone interested in this subject.

White, J. Peter, and O'Connell, James. *A Prehistory of Australia, New Guinea, and Sahul*. New York: Academic Press, 1982.
The definitive analytic synthesis of the prehistory of Australia. A superb, even masterly account.

Farmers
(c. 12,000 Years Ago to Modern Times)

Agriculture is not to be looked on as a difficult or out-of-the-way
invention, for the rudest savage, skilled as he is in the habits of the
food-plants he gathers, must know well enough that if seeds or roots
are put in a proper place in the ground they will grow.
— Sir Edward Tylor, 1883

The beginning of food production — of agriculture and animal domestication — was one of the catalytic events of human prehistory. Part IV not only
describes the sequence of farming cultures in all parts of the world but also ana-
lyzes some of the recent theories about the origins of farming. We will start with
the theoretical background and then study farming in geographic areas. With
the beginnings of food production we find the first signs of rapidly accelerating
cultural evolution, of processes that are still operating at a record pace. However, our understanding of the early millennia of farming is incomplete. The archaeological evidence outlined here is extremely sketchy and often stretched to
the limit to produce a coherent narrative. Future research is certain to modify
drastically the story set forth in the following chapters.

CHAPTER 9

Plenteous Harvest: The Origins

Preview

■ The domestication of plants and animals was one of the momentous developments in world prehistory because the new economic strategies resulted in increased and stabilized food supplies but generally at a higher energy cost.

■ Food production proved dramatically successful. Ten thousand years ago almost everyone in the world was hunting and gathering. By 2000 years ago hunter-gatherers were in a minority.

■ The advent of food production brought more sedentary settlements, improved storage facilities, and new toolkits designed for agriculture and food storage. Population increases appear to have preceded, and followed, the beginnings of food production.

■ The first theories for the origins of food production were formulated in terms of a single genius who invented agriculture. Others hypothesized that increased desiccation at the end of the Pleistocene concentrated plants, humans, and animals in a close symbiosis, which resulted in domestication. V. Gordon Childe refined this theory and postulated a Neolithic Revolution.

■ Modern theories have moved from a Neolithic Revolution toward ecological explanations, which suggest that a variety of factors interacted to cause humankind to experiment with the deliberate cultivation of cereal and root crops. According to this account, food production was developed in several areas of the world more or less at the same time.

■ Robert J. Braidwood with his nuclear zones, Lewis Binford with theories of demographic stress, and Kent Flannery with a systems approach to agricultural origins all argue that the development of food production was a gradual process, in which hunter-gatherers moved from scheduled gathering activities to experimentation with food crops at the edges of areas where potential domesticates were abundant.

■ Mark Cohen has suggested that population pressure was a major factor in the development of food production. He argues that the only significant puzzle is why people turned from hunting and gathering, a relatively low-risk activity, to agriculture, which, at least initially, was a high-risk and much more arduous venture. It could be that the changeover occurred when environmental imbalance caused people to fall back on less desirable foods and therefore to try to grow food for themselves. This would be a logical step for people familiar with the germination of plants.

■ Wherever food production took hold, it seems possible that a few underlying demographic, subsistence, and environmental variables favored a shift toward agriculture and animal domestication. These factors can only be identified in a general way. Future research will concentrate on pinpointing local selective pressures that led to a shift toward food production.

■ Studies of prehistoric diets tend to suggest a general decline in the quality, and perhaps the length, of human life with the advent of food production. People may have turned to agriculture only when no other alternatives were available.

■ Domesticated herds assured a regular meat supply, isolating species from a larger gene pool for selective breeding under human care. As a result of domestication, animals and humans increased their mutual interdependence. The process of domestication took a considerable time, but in time, penned, gregarious animals became a food "reserve," protected, stored, and maintained against hard times.

■ A long period of deliberate gathering and experimentation preceded the domestication of root and cereal crops throughout the world. With cereal grasses, this meant selecting for a tough rachis, the hinge that joined seed to stalk and allowed deliberate harvesting of the grain.

■ Food production resulted in more sedentary human settlement, more substantial housing, elaborate storage technologies, and special implements for clearing, cultivating, and harvesting crops. All these new technological developments led to greater interdependence and to long-distance exchange of raw materials and finished artifacts.

Some 12,000 years ago, as part of the process of adapting to radically different Postglacial environments, some hunter-gatherer groups took a momentous step. They began to experiment with the deliberate growing of wild cereal crops and to tame small mammals as means of expanding their food supply. It is difficult for us, buying our food from supermarkets, to appreciate how awesome were the consequences to human history of agriculture and the domestication of animals. For more than 99 percent of our existence as humans, we were hunter-gatherers, tied to the seasons of vegetable foods or movements of game. However, with economies based on the production of food, people could influence their environment and sometimes control its ecological balance, with drastic consequences for their descendants.

CONSEQUENCES OF FOOD PRODUCTION

The new food-producing economies proved dramatically successful. Ten thousand years ago virtually everybody in the world lived by hunting and gathering. By 2000 years ago most people were farmers or herders and only a minority were still hunter-gatherers. The spread of food production throughout the world took only about 8000 years. The problem for anthropologists is not only to account for why people took up agriculture but also to explain why so many populations adopted this new, and initially risky, economic transition in such a short time. Food production spread to all corners of the world except where an environment with extreme aridity or heat or cold rendered agriculture or herding impossible or where people chose to remain hunters and gatherers. In some places, food production was the economic base for urbanization and literate civilization; but most human societies did not go further than subsistence-level food production until the industrial power of nineteenth- and twentieth-century Europe led them into the Machine Age.

Food production resulted, ultimately, in much higher population densities in many locations, for the domestication of plants and animals can lead to an economic strategy that increases and stabilizes available food supplies, although more energy is used to produce them. Farmers use concentrated tracts of territory for agriculture, and for grazing cattle and small stock if they practice mixed farming. Their territory is much smaller than that of hunter-gatherers (although pastoralists need huge areas of grazing land for seasonal pasture). Within a smaller area of farming land, property lines are carefully delineated, as individual ownership and problems of inheritance arise. Shortages of land can lead to disputes and to the founding of new village settlements on previously uncultivated soil (Childe, 1936; Struever, 1971).

More enduring settlements brought other changes. The portable and lightweight material possessions of many hunter-gatherers were replaced by heavier toolkits and more lasting houses (Figure 9.1). Grindstones and ground-edged axes were even more essential to farming culture than they were to gathering societies. Hoes and other implements of tillage were vital for the planting and harvesting of crops. New social units came into being as more lasting home bases were developed; these social links reflected ownership and inheritance of land and led to much larger settlements that brought hitherto scattered populations into closer and more regular contact.

Food production led to changed attitudes toward the environment. Cereal crops were such that people could store their food for use in winter (Figure 9.1). The hunter-gatherers exploited game, fish, and vegetable foods, but the farmers did more; they *altered* the environment by the very nature of their exploitation. Expansion of agriculture meant felling trees and burning vegetation to clear the ground for planting. The same fields then were abandoned after a few years to lie fallow, and more woodland was cleared. The original vegetation began to regenerate, but it might have been cleared again before reaching

FIGURE 9.1 A pole-and-mud hut typical of the Middle Zambezi Valley, Africa (left). Such dwellings, often occupied fifteen years or longer, are more lasting than the windbreak or tent of the hunter-gatherer. At right is a grain bin from an African village, used for cereal crops. Storing food is a critical activity of many hunters and farmers.

its original state. This shifting pattern of farming is called *slash-and-burn agriculture*. Voracious domesticated animals stripped pastures of their grass cover, then heavy rainfalls denuded the hills of valuable soil, and the pastures were never the same again. However elementary the agricultural technology, the farmer changed the environment, if only with fires lit to clear scrub from gardens and to fertilize the soil with wood ashes. Hunter-gatherers had deliberately set fires to encourage the growth of new grass for their grazing prey. In a sense, shifting slash-and-burn agriculture is merely an extension of the age-old use of fire to encourage regeneration of vegetation.

Food production resulted in high population densities, but growth was controlled by disease, available food supplies, water supplies, and particularly famine. Many peoples who were constantly on the move controlled their populations by deliberately spacing births. Early agricultural methods depended heavily on careful selection of the soil. The technology of the first farmers was hardly potent enough for extensive clearing of the dense woodland under which many good soils lay, so potentially cultivable land could only be that which was accessible. Gardens probably were scattered over a much wider territory than is necessary today. One authority estimates that, even with advanced shifting agriculture, only 40 percent of moderately fertile soil in Africa is available for such cultivation (Allan, 1965). This figure must have been lower in the early days of agriculture, with their simpler stone tools and fewer crops.

In regions of seasonal rainfall, such as the Near East, sub-Saharan Africa, and parts of Asia, periods of prolonged drought are common. Famine probably was a real possibility as population densities rose. Many early agriculturalists must have worriedly watched the sky and had frequent crop failures in times of drought. Their small stores of grain from the previous season would not have carried them through another year, especially if they had been careless with their surplus. Farmers were forced to shift their economic strategy in such times. We know that the earliest farmers availed themselves of game and vegetable foods to supplement their agriculture, just as today some farmers are obliged to rely heavily on wild vegetable foods and hunting to survive in bad years (Scudder, 1962, 1971). Many hunter-gatherer bands collect intensively just a few species of edible plants in their large territories. Aware of many other edible vegetables, they fall back on those only in times of stress; the less favored foods can carry a comparatively small population through to the next rains. But a larger agricultural population is not so flexible and quickly exhausts wild vegetables and game in the much smaller territory used for farming and grazing. If the drought lasts for years, famine, death, and reduced population can follow.

THEORIES ABOUT THE ORIGINS OF FOOD PRODUCTION

Why did people choose to grow their own crops? What caused food production to be adopted in thousands of human societies and with such rapidity?

Early Hypotheses

Speculations about the origins of agriculture go back for more than a century. The first theories envisaged a solitary genius who suddenly had the brilliant idea of planting seed (Roth, 1887). Others argued for a severe drought at the end of the Pleistocene, which concentrated animals, plants, and humans in oases with permanent water supplies where people tamed the flora and fauna for their own purposes. No one still looks for a single genius or for the earliest maize cob. Rather, modern theory concentrates on the complex processes that caused gradual changes in human subsistence patterns (G. Wright, 1971).

Childe: Neolithic Revolution

One of the first scholars to work with excavated data was V. Gordon Childe, who proposed a major economic revolution in prehistory — the Neolithic Revolution (Childe, 1936, 1952). This transformation took place during a period of severe drought, a climatic crisis that caused a symbiotic relationship to be forged between the humans and animals in fertile oases. The new economies ensured a richer and more reliable food source for people on the edge of starvation.

Childe's hypothesis was a refinement of the oasis theory and was widely accepted, but no one has yet found convincing traces of drier climate at the end of the Pleistocene. Other early scholars began to examine the hilly regions above the lowlands of Mesopotamia to see if they might have been the cradle of early food production, for it was there that fossils of potentially domesticable animals and wild cereals were found (Peake and Fleure, 1927).

Braidwood: nuclear zones

Systematic field work into the origins of food production began only in the late 1940s. Robert J. Braidwood of the University of Chicago mounted an expedition to the Kurdish foothills of Iran to test Childe's theories. Geologists and zoologists on the expedition produced field evidence causing Braidwood to reject the notion of catastrophic climatic change at the end of the Pleistocene, despite minor shifts in rainfall distribution. Nothing in the environment, Braidwood argues, could have necessitated the radical shift in human adaptation proposed by Childe (Braidwood and Braidwood, 1983). Braidwood feels the economic change came from the "ever increasing cultural differentiation and specialization of human communities." Thus, he argues, people were culturally receptive to innovation and experimentation with cultivation of wild grasses. They had begun to understand and manipulate the plants and animals around them in "nuclear zones," that is to say, areas where potentially domesticable cereals and animals flourished in the wild. One of these zones was the hilly flanks of the Zagros Mountains in Iraq and the upland areas overlooking the Mesopotamian lowlands. Braidwood is convinced that the human capacity and enthusiasm for experimentation made it possible for people to domesticate animals and grow crops. However, his hypothesis does not explain *why* food production was adopted.

In 1952, Carl O. Sauer published a remarkable essay on agricultural origins, in which he analyzed the ecology of food production. He saw the origins of food production as a change in the way culture and environment interact. Sauer proposed southeast Asia as a major center of domestication, where root crops were grown by semisedentary fishing folk. Few scholars were prepared to accept Sauer's theory that the idea of domestication diffused from southeast Asia to the Near East. Yet Sauer has proved remarkably prophetic about the importance of root crops and the antiquity of food production in southeast Asia, for evidence of possible root cultivation may date to as early as 11,000 B.P. in Spirit Cave, Thailand (Solheim, 1971). He insisted on the importance of continuous adaptation to the origin of food production. Sauer's was a pioneer interpretation of how food production began.

Sauer: ecology

A Transition

Lewis Binford (1968) rejects Braidwood's contention that human nature brought about agriculture and argues that demographic stress favored food production. At the end of the Pleistocene, he hypothesizes, people flowed from some of the world's seacoasts into less populated areas because of rising sea levels as the world's glaciers retreated. These movements led to demographic stress where potentially domesticable plants and animals were to be found; consequently the development of agriculture was adaptively advantageous for the inhabitants of these regions. Like Braidwood's, Binford's theory has several weaknesses, not least among them being the repeated fluctuations of sea levels in earlier interglacials. Why did they not lead to similar demographic stress and culture change?

Binford: demographic stress

Kent Flannery has argued that the transition from hunting and gathering to food production was a gradual process (Flannery, 1968a). In a classic paper that examined the mechanisms by which Mesoamericans took up agriculture (Chapter 2), he maintains that the preagricultural peoples of Mesoamerica who later became agriculturalists adapted not to a given environment but to a few plant and animal genera whose range cut across several environments. Using pollen and animal bone analyses from preagricultural sites, Flannery listed the animals and plants upon which these people depended — among them were century plant leaves, cactus fruits, deer, rabbits, wild waterfowl, and wild

Flannery: systems approach

grasses, including corn. Foods such as the century plant were available all year. Others, such as mesquite pods and deer, were exploited during the dry season, but cacti were eaten only during the rains.

To obtain these foods people had to be in the right place at the right season, and the time depended on the plants, not the people: foragers had to plan around the seasons. In other words, their system for procuring food was scheduled. A minor change in any part of the system was reflected in the group's scheduling and might preclude their exploiting foods whose season conflicted with the new schedule.

Maize

Genetic changes in corn eventually made it increasingly important to the people who used it. Corn (maize) became slightly more productive and so tended to become more important in the diet. Gradually more and more time was spent cultivating it, and groups had to reschedule their activities to accommodate this change. Because a group could not be in two places at once, foods that were procured at times when corn had to be planted or harvested would necessarily be neglected.

In another paper (1965) Flannery considers the problems of Near Eastern food production. He stresses that it was not the planting of seeds or the herding of animals that was important but the fact that people moved out to niches to which they were not adapted and removed pressures of natural selection, which allowed more deviants to survive and eventually be selected for characteristics not beneficial under natural conditions. According to Flannery and his colleagues Frank Hole and J. A. Neely (Hole, Flannery, and Neely, 1969), approximately 20,000 years ago people began to shift from a hunting and gathering way of life to a more specialized economy, including the use of both storage pits and ground stone tools to crush pigments and tough grass seeds. Seasonal use of the environment was typical of many parts of the Near East and Mesoamerica, with different wild foods scheduled for separate seasons. What upset this equilibrium between culture and environment?

Flannery took Binford's demographic model, in which population growth in southwest Asia was greatest in the optimum habitats of the seasonal hunters and gatherers of the hilly flanks and the Palestine woodlands. The population increases caused new groups to split off into more marginal areas, where the inhabitants tried to produce artificially, around the *margins* of the optimum zone, stands of cereals as dense as those in the heart of the zone.

There are several implications of this hypothesis. First, the hunter-gatherer populations in the optimum areas increased before food producing began. This supposition can be tested in the archaeological record by searching for evidence of dense settlement in the optimum areas and large kill sites and other signs of a culture that hunted and collected food intensively to support its numbers. Second, the earliest evidence of food production will appear on the margins, in sites where the material culture is strikingly similar to that of the hunter-gatherers in the best areas. Finally, there will be more than one center of domestication for both plants and animals. The advantage of Flannery's hypothesis is that it can be tested in the field, although the testing is likely to be arduous and time-consuming. Measuring population increases before food production started will be particularly difficult, if such increases occurred.

Now that we can look at world prehistory on a far wider canvas than the pioneers could, we know that agriculture appeared in widely distributed parts of the world at approximately the same time — in the Near East, China, southeast Asia, and the Americas. An increasing preoccupation with population has caused those following up on Flannery's work to look more closely at prehistoric demography. Mark Cohen (1977) has argued that population pressure on a global scale caused many widely separated hunter-gatherer cultures to abandon gathering because their growing populations had reached the limit that their food resources could support. This point, argues Cohen, was reached at or near the same time on all the major landmasses except Australia. Cohen assumes that early agriculture was a logical development of existing gathering and plant conservation techniques and that agriculture was neither easier nor a more secure subsistence base than hunting and gathering. All that can be said for it is that it yields more calories, especially carbohydrates, per acre of land. He goes on to assume that hunter-gatherer populations had mechanisms for controlling excessive local population growth but that population densities rose steadily throughout early prehistory. Thus, he concludes, a single explanation for the appearance of agriculture can be invoked for the entire world — population pressure.

Cohen: population growth

Cohen's tantalizing hypothesis is difficult to support from archaeological evidence because some variables — such as population size, age-sex structures in society, and many demographic factors — are very hard to recover from archaeological research. The crux of his hypothesis is that early agriculture offered only one major advantage — increased food yield. In the short term, the per capita workload increased and the quality of diet probably declined. An agriculturalist's life is far more arduous than that of a hunter-gatherer. The only circumstances under which people would experiment with a new food procurement system would be those that held a serious ecological imbalance; such an imbalance can be accounted for only by population growth that upsets the efficiency of hunting and gathering for small populations. Once less palatable wild foods were being consumed, the only possible recourse for a growing population would be to start producing its own food. This, after all, is a logical step for people familiar with the germination of plants and used to manipulating vegetable foods for their use.

No one denies that food production led to higher population densities and indeed ignited a population explosion (Figure 9.2) (Lewin, 1988a). But there is no evidence for very high population densities in the Near East or Mesoamerica during the millennia when agriculture was taking hold, certainly not for the sorts of density that cause chronic food shortages. (For a discussion of this problem in Tehuacán, see Flannery, 1983; Stark, 1986.)

"PUSH," "PULL," AND "SOCIAL"

Barbara Stark (1986), divides modern theories about the origins of agriculture into three broad categories: "push," "pull," and "social." Each can be criticized on various grounds (for a detailed theoretical analysis, see Rindos, 1984).

The push theories are based on relationships between populations and resources. They are an extension of economist Ester Boserup's argument (1965), that food production systems of any type are highly flexible. Thus, hunter-gatherers responded to less favorable relationships between population densities and available resources by intensifying their hunting and foraging (Clark and Yi, 1983). Population growth is often cited as the villain when resource imbalances arise; sometimes this growth results from more sedentary settlement, when people are packed more tightly into a local area where diverse resources occur. There is less mobility and more intensive exploitation of resources because everyone has less territory to move around in, a situation that may have arisen in parts of the Near East and in Mesolithic northwest Europe.

Environmental changes are important because they can affect the balances between human populations and resources, and the costs or benefits of hunting and gathering as opposed to agriculture or animal domestication. There is also another dimension of environmental change — risk. All environments involve some element of risk for hunter-gatherer societies, risk that manifests itself in periodic food shortages. These can be caused by drought cycles, long, cold winters, or unpredictable floods, to mention only a few possibilities.

Risk casts the whole notion of population growth in a very different light, for we cannot think of rising population densities in a linear way. We can argue, for instance, that regular episodes of food shortages, whether annual or over many years, will tend to regulate population size. Of course the frequency and duration of risk are vital factors, for a human population will tend to respond to lengthy stress from risk by moving away. However, frequent, and often predictable, risks are often countered by technological innovations. People will develop ways of storing wild seeds in pits or special granaries, dry thousands of salmon caught in annual runs, carry powdered bison meat in leather bags as they move. Many of the early crops domesticated by prehistoric people were easily stored. Thus, a straightforward cultural solution to food shortages and the stress resulting from them may be to cultivate familiar wild plants and do-

FIGURE 9.2 World population changes since the beginnings of food production. There has been an explosion in population densities in the past 10,000 years.

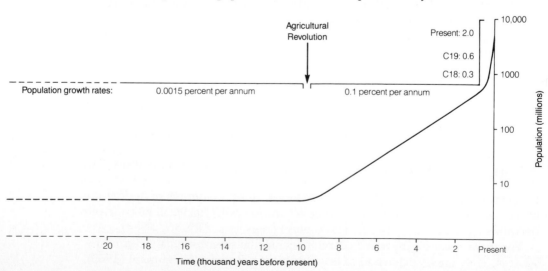

mesticate common prey, so people can draw on a predictable stored resource in scarce months. This is not to say that population densities were not a critical factor in prehistory. They were, but the risk and stress conditions associated with them were also important.

Push theories tend to concentrate on three interdependent factors: sedentism, population-resource imbalances, and factors of risk. Unfortunately, all three are difficult to identify from archaeological sites. For this reason, push theories have tried to identify population growth that occurred before and during the adoption of food production, or argued that climatic change induced the "risk" that pushed people to the new economies.

Pull models focus on ecological factors, such as local variability in food resources and the interactive effects of human exploitation on them. Proponents of these models talk of opportunities for the introduction of agriculture, of people turning to superior local resources when the moment came (see Minnis, 1985; Reidhead, 1980; Rindos, 1984). What happens is that some resources, say wild wheat or barley, or wild goats, or teosinte grasses, are perceived as attractive. People make more and more use of them, to the point that they eventually domesticate them. Flannery's research in Mesoamerica (1968a) already cited falls under this approach. In later field work, he and others (1985) claim they could simulate the origins of agriculture in the valley of Oaxaca, Mexico, without invoking either population growth or environmental change as a major factor. The research team argues that both variations in annual rainfall that affected wild plant yields and natural variability in plant populations led to a gradual shift in subsistence strategies from foraging to intentional cultivation.

The crux of pull models is trying to identify the processes that caused people to shift to deliberate cultivation. Did a set of cost-benefit equations make agriculture more attractive than foraging, the optimum food procurement strategy at the time? Or did cultivation enable the new farmers to widen their adaptive niche? Were species added to their diet in order of the energy cost required to use them? What about such factors as nutritive value, seasonal availability, storage potential, and nonfood use? Both genetic changes and changes in availability encouraged by human beings can alter the economic value of animal and plant species.

Push models give population growth a relatively minor role, mainly as a reality that prevented people from reverting to hunting and gathering. But one may ask why, then, food production did not take hold much earlier? Surely there were many previous occasions when conditions were favorable for people to start cultivating plants? Here population models for prehistory offer some clues. We know there was gradual overall population growth during the Stone Age. The constant cyclical changes of the last 700,000 years of the Ice Age must have led to periods of occasional environmental stress among hunter-gatherer populations. However, it was not until after the spread of *Homo sapiens* after 40,000 years ago that there was accelerating intensification of hunter-gatherer lifeways — and this intensification was even more pervasive in early Postglacial times. Thus, a relatively late date for the adoption of food production seems most likely (Stark, 1986).

Social models look to social factors that led to intensified hunting and gathering and eventually food production. Barbara Bender (1985) argues that hunter-gatherer societies were becoming more complex, with far more elaborate, hierarchical social organizations. She points to the increasing abundance of trade objects and the appearance of richly decorated burials before food production began. Perhaps, she hypothesizes, an expansion of trade, and of political alliances between neighboring groups, created new social and economic pressures to produce more and more surplus goods, not only foodstuffs but other objects as well. This in turn led to more sedentary lifeways. Evidence for this model is still weak, for it is very difficult to document social factors or demography from archaeology.

Whatever the general explanation for the beginnings of food production, we still have to account for local variations in the time it took to adopt the new economies. David Harris (1978, 1980) argues that hunter-gatherers in subtropical zones like the Near East and highland Mesoamerica were beginning to manipulate potential domesticates among wild grasses and root species at the end of the Ice Age. Dependence on such foods probably came earlier in these regions, where there were only a few forageable species. Such dependence was essential to long-term survival. In contrast, populations in more humid tropical regions, like the African and Amazonian rain forests, probably did little more than manipulate a few wild species to minimize risk in lean years — as a corollary, many African agricultural peoples turn to hunting and gathering in lean years to this day. The archaeological record shows that agriculture was established considerably earlier in the subtropical Near East, Middle and South America, southeast Asia, and India than it was in humid, tropical zones, undoubtedly because that environment was rich in game and wild vegetable foods. Furthermore, domesticated crops and animals were more susceptible to irregular rainfall, locusts and other insect attacks, and endemic stock diseases. A strong and sustained incentive to obtain food must have been a prerequisite for a lasting shift from foraging to agriculture.

Harris points out that many variables have to be understood before we can reconstruct the conditions under which agriculture was first regarded as profitable activity. We are searching for a set of conditions in which population pressure, distribution of plants, the rate at which the environment is changing, even techniques of harvesting wild grasses, all play their part in making agriculture work. Then there are variations among the potentially domesticable plants and animals, some of which resist domestication because of their long life span or because parts of their lives take place outside human control. The seasonal distribution of wild vegetable foods or game could also have prevented experiments in domestication, when the seasons during which these wild foods were exploited coincided with the times of year when it was important that experimenting farmers stay near their growing crops. Under these circumstances, people would tend to pursue their traditional food-getting strategies rather than risk their lives for an uncertain outcome.

Most theories about the origins of food production are far from easy to test. It is difficult to link complex models with actual field data, largely because the models do not lend themselves to quantification. The immediate future is unlikely to yield any new insights into the kinds of factor that led to food production. What future research will yield is more regional data, more local models that pin down easily identifiable environmental and other conditions. Even gathering this data may be difficult, for it is not easy to be precise about environmental conditions or to make sufficiently exact reconstructions of the way people acquired food. Until such reconstructions are made, we cannot identify with certainty the selective pressures that favored cultivation and animal domestication (Stark, 1986).

Wherever food production took hold, it seems possible that a few underlying demographic, subsistence, and environmental variables favored a shift toward the growing of crops and the taming of animals. So far, we have been unable to identify them except in the most general way. We know that both environmental and demographic push variables played an important role in the origins of food production and that they operated in conjunction with such factors as the changing relative costs and benefits of different food sources, as well as compelling social circumstances as yet little understood. The challenge for the future is to test various explanatory models against field data from many areas, to clarify the diverse reasons why people first started agriculture and animal domestication.

As we shall see in the chapters that follow, food production took hold in many parts of the world in Postglacial times, in response to a wide variety of conditions.

NUTRITION AND EARLY FOOD PRODUCTION

Was food production a real improvement in human lifeways? For generations archaeologists have argued that human health improved dramatically as a result of agriculture, as people worked less and lived on more reliable food supplies (Butzer, 1982; Childe, 1952). In recent years, Ester Boserup (1965) and others have argued that in fact agriculture brought diminishing returns in relation to labor expended in the new systems that were adopted to feed many more people. Richard Lee's studies of the !Kung San of the Kalahari Desert tend to support her views. They show that these hunter-gatherers, and presumably others, had abundant leisure and worked less than farmers. Some nutritionists point out that foragers may have had better balanced diets than many farmers, who relied heavily on root or cereal crops. Further, farmers, with their sedentary settlements and higher population densities, were much more vulnerable to famine than their hunter-gatherer predecessors. They would also have been more vulnerable to gastrointestinal infections and epidemics (Cohen and Armelagos, 1984).

While the theoretical controversies swirl, actual empirical data is still hard to come by. Some pioneer nutrition studies based on the skeletons of early farmers suggest some incidence of anemia and slow growth resulting from malnutrition. Signs of physical stress are even harder to come by. But ten regional studies of prehistoric populations have suggested a *decline* in mean age expectancy in agricultural populations, which contradicts the commonly held perception. Taken as a whole, such paleopathological studies as have been published suggest a general decline in the quality, and perhaps the length, of human life with the advent of food production. It should be pointed out, however, that there are many unknowns involved, among them changes in fertility and population growth rates, which caused the world's population to rise even if general health standards and life expectancy fell. (For details, consult Cohen and Armelagos, 1984. See also Buikstra et al., 1986.)

What impact these studies will have on population pressure theories about the origins of agriculture is still uncertain. Certainly, any shift to food production caused by increasing population pressure could be reflected in a decline in overall health and nutrition displayed by prehistoric skeletons. It is likely that the next generation of theories about early agriculture will be based on researches into the paleopathology of pioneer farming populations.

In the final analysis, people probably turned to food production only when other alternatives were no longer practicable. The classic example is the aborigines of extreme northern Australia, who were well aware that their neighbors in New Guinea were engaged in intensive agriculture. They, too, knew how to plant the top of the wild yam so that it regerminated, but they never adopted food production, simply because they had no need to become dependent on a lifeway that would reduce their leisure time and produce more food than they required.

HERDING: DOMESTICATION OF ANIMALS

Potentially tamable species like the wild ox, goat, sheep, and dog were widely distributed in the Old World during the Upper Pleistocene. New World farmers domesticated only such animals as the llama, the guinea pig, and the turkey, and then only under special conditions and within narrow geographic limits. It is possible that the domesticated dog crossed into the New World with the first Americans before 15,000 years ago or that it was domesticated elsewhere in the Americas, but the evidence is uncertain.

Having one's own herds of domesticated mammals ensured a regular meat supply. The advantages to having a major source of meat under one's control are obvious. Later, domesticated animals provided by-products, such as milk, cheese, and butter, as well as skins for clothes and tent coverings and materials for leather shields and armor. In later millennia, people learned how to breed animals for specialized tasks such as plowing, transportation, and traction (Clutton-Brock, 1981).

Domestication implies a genetic selection emphasizing special features of continuing use to the domesticator (Ucko and Dimbleby, 1969). Wild sheep have no wool, wild cows produce milk only for their offspring, and undomesticated chickens do not lay surplus eggs. Changes in wool bearing, lactation, or egg production could be achieved by isolating wild populations for selective breeding under human care. Isolating species from a larger gene pool produced domestic sheep with thick, woolly coats and domestic goats providing regular supplies of milk, which formed a staple in the diet of many human populations.

No one knows exactly how domestication of animals began. During the Upper Pleistocene, people already were beginning to concentrate heavily on some species of large mammals for their diet. The Magdalenians of southwest France directed much of their life toward pursuing reindeer. At the end of the

Pleistocene, hunters in the Near East were concentrating on gazelles and other steppe animals. Wild sheep and goats were intensively hunted on the southern shores of the Caspian Sea. Gregarious animals are those most easily domesticated; they follow the lead of a dominant herd member or all move together.

Hunters often fed off the same herd for a long time, sometimes deliberately sparing young females and immature beasts to keep the source of food alive. Young animals captured alive in the chase might be taken back to the camp and grow dependent on those who caged them, thus becoming partially tamed. A hunter could grasp the possibility of gaining control of the movements of a few key members of a herd, who would be followed by the others. Once the experience of keeping pets or of restricting game movements had suggested a new way of life, people might experiment with different species (Flannery, 1969; Higgs and Jarman, 1969). As part of domestication, animals and humans increased their mutual interdependence.

The archaeological evidence for early domestication is so fragile that nothing survives except the bones of the animals kept by the early farmers, and differences between wild and domestic animal bones are often so small initially that it is difficult to distinguish them unless very large collections are found. In the earliest centuries of domestication, corralled animals were nearly indistinguishable from wild species.

One way of differentiating between domestic and wild beasts is to age an animal find by its dentition — the number, kind, and arrangement of its teeth. Hunters normally kill animals of all ages but strongly prefer adolescent beasts, which have the best meat. However, herd owners slaughter younger sheep and goats, especially surplus males, for meat but keep females until they are no longer productive as breeding animals. In some early farming sites, such as Zawi Chemi in the Zagros Mountains in the Near East, the only way domestic sheep could be identified was by the early age at which they were slaughtered or by bone crystal analysis (Perkins, 1964).

The process of animal domestication undoubtedly was prolonged, developing in several areas of the Near East at approximately the same time. Although animal bones are scarce and often unsatisfactory as evidence of early domestication, most authorities now agree that the first species to be domesticated in the Near East was the sheep, 10,500 years ago or so. Sheep are small animals living in herds, whose carcasses yield much meat for their size. They can readily be penned and isolated to develop a symbiotic relationship with people.

Cattle are much more formidable to domesticate, for their prototype was *Bos primigenius,* the wild ox much hunted by Stone Age people (Figure 9.3). Perhaps cattle were first domesticated from wild animals that were penned for food, ritual, and sacrifice. They may have been captured from wild herds grazing in the gardens.

It should be noted that some animals, such as sea mammals, resist domestication because much of their lives is spent out of range of human influence. As mentioned, most early successes with domestication took place with gregarious animals. Kent Flannery (1969) has pointed out that penned gregarious animals can, in a sense, be regarded as a "reserve" of food, protected, stored, and maintained against hard times.

CULTIVATION: DOMESTICATION OF PLANTS

Many fewer wild vegetable foods were domesticated than foraged over the millennia (J. Renfrew, 1973). In the Old World, wheat, barley, and other cereals that grow wild over much of Asia and Europe became cultivated. In the New World, a different set of crops was tamed. These included Indian corn *(Zea mays)*, the only important wild grass to be domesticated. Root crops such as manioc and sweet potatoes, chili peppers, tobacco, and several types of bean were all grown. Common to both Old and New Worlds are gourds, cotton, and two or three other minor crops (Ford, 1985).

Carl Sauer (1952) pointed out that seed crops such as maize were first grown in Mesoamerica, and root crops such as manioc and potatoes were grown more commonly in South America. This fundamental distinction also applies in the Old World, where tropical regions had many potential domesticates such as the yam and gourds. In southeast Asia and tropical Africa, a long period of intensive gathering and experimenting with the deliberate planting of wild root crops probably preceded the beginnings of formal agriculture. Perhaps, however, the transition from gathering to cultivation of root crops was almost unconscious, for many tubers are easy to grow deliberately. The African yam, for example, can be germinated simply by cutting off its top and burying it in the ground. The hunter-gatherer bands who were familiar with this easy means of conserving their food supplies may simply have intensified their planting efforts to supplement shortages caused by changed circumstances. As with animals, however, certain heavily exploited species tended to resist domestication; among them were the long-lived trees like the oak and plants whose life spans were so long that they inhibited human selection. They also tended to cross-pollinate, a process that undoubtedly discouraged human efforts to trigger or control genetic variation.

In the Old World, the qualities of wild wheat, barley, and similar crops are quite different from those of their domestic equivalents. In the wild, these grains occur in dense stands (J. G. D. Clark, 1970). The grasses can be harvested easily by tapping the stem and gathering the seeds in a basket as they fall off. This technique is effective because the wild grain is attached to the stem by a

FIGURE 9.3 *Bos primigenius,* the aurochs or wild ox, as depicted by S. von Herbenstain in 1549. It became extinct in Europe in 1627, although recent breeding experiments have reconstructed this formidable beast.

brittle joint, or *rachis*. When the grass is tapped, the weak rachis breaks and the seed falls into the basket.

The conversion of wild grass to domestic strains must have involved some selection of desirable properties (Figure 9.4) (Harlan, Delvet, and Stemler, 1976). To cultivate cereal crops extensively, the yield of an acre of grass has to be increased significantly. If the yield remains low, it is easier to gather wild seeds and save the labor of cultivation. A tougher rachis must be developed to prevent the seed from falling on the ground and regerminating. By toughening the rachis, people could control propagation of the grass, sowing it when and where they liked and harvesting it with a knife blade or sickle (Harlan, 1967). Certain patterns of grass harvesting, such as the hand and sickle methods used in the Near East even today, tended to select for useful mutants like the tough rachis, thereby reinforcing the trend toward control of the grasses. The mutations that did take place helped already adaptable wild grasses to grow outside their normal wild habitats (Vavilov, 1951; Zohary, 1969). Early farmers seem to have grown cereals with remarkable success, but they probably succeeded only after long experimenting in different places.

TECHNOLOGY AND DOMESTICATION

The technological consequences of food production were, in their way, as important as the new economies. A more settled way of life and some decline in hunting and gathering slowly led to long-term residences, lasting agricultural

a   b

FIGURE 9.4 (a) The wild ancestor of a primitive wheat *(Triticum boeoticum)* contrasted with (b) its cultivated form *(T. monococcum)*. (Both two-thirds actual size.)

styles, and more substantial housing. As they had done for millennia, people built their permanent homes with the raw materials most abundant in their environment. The early farmers of the Near East worked and dried mud into small houses with flat roofs; these were cool in summer and warm in winter. At night during the hot season people may have slept on the flat roofs. Some less substantial houses had reed roofs. In the more temperate zones of Europe, with wetter climates, timber was used to build thatched-roof houses of various shapes and sizes. Early African farmers often built huts of grass, sticks, and anthill clay. Nomadic pastoralists of the northern steppes had no concern with a permanent and durable home, yet they, too, took advantage of the related benefits of having a domestic food supply: they used the skins to make clothing as well as tents to shelter them during the icy winters.

Agriculture is a seasonal activity, with long periods of the year when the fields are lying fallow or are supporting growing crops. Any farmer is confronted with the problem of keeping food in ways the hunter-gatherer never has to ponder. Thus, a new technology of storage came into being. Grain bins, jars, or clay-lined pits became an essential part of the agricultural economy for stockpiling food for the lean months and against periods of famine. The bins might have been made of wattle and daub, clay, or timber (see Figure 9.1). Basket-lined silos protected valuable grain against rodents.

Hunter-gatherers use skins, wood containers, gut pouches, and sometimes baskets for carrying vegetable foods back from the bush. Farmers face far more formidable transport problems: they must carry their harvest back to the village, keep ready-for-use supplies of foods in the house as opposed to in storage bins, and store water. Early farmers began to use gourds as water carriers and to make clay vessels that were both waterproof and capable of carrying and cooking food (Figure 9.5). They made pots by coiling rolls of clay or building up the walls of vessels from a lump and firing them in simple hearths. Clay vessels were much more durable than skin or leather receptacles. Some pots were used for several decades before being broken and abandoned. Pottery did not appear simultaneously with agriculture. It came into use at different times in many widely separated places. For example, the Jomon hunter-gatherers of Japan were making simple clay pots at least 10,500 years ago. They lived a more or less sedentary life by their shell middens, using clay vessels long before agriculture became part of their way of life (Aikens and Higuchi, 1981). In the Near East, however, pottery was first used by farmers approximately 8000 years ago (Mellaart, 1975).

For tens of thousands of years, people dug up wild edible roots with simple wooden sticks, sometimes made more effective with the aid of a stone weight. The first farmers continued to use the digging stick to plant crops a few inches below the surface, probably on readily cultivable soils. They also used wooden or stone-bladed hoes (and, much later, iron) to break up the soft soil. These they fitted with short or long handles, depending on cultural preference. European and Near Eastern farmers made use of the ox-drawn plow in later millennia, at first with a wooden-tipped blade, then bronze, and later iron (Chapter 16). The plow was an important innovation, for it enabled people to turn the soil over to a much greater depth than ever before. Every farmer has to clear wild vegeta-

FIGURE 9.5 Pottery manufacture. A common method of potmaking was to build up the walls from coils of clay (top). The pot was then smoothed and decorated (left), and fired, in either an open hearth (right) or a kiln. These pictures illustrate Pueblo Indian pottery-manufacturing techniques from the southwest United States and are, of course, not necessarily typical of all potters.

tion and weeds from the fields, and it is hardly surprising to find a new emphasis on the ax and the adz. The simple axes of pioneer farmers were replaced by more elaborate forms in metal by 4500 years ago in the Near East. Present-day experiments in Denmark and New Guinea have shown that the ground and polished edges of stone axes are remarkably effective in clearing woodland and felling trees (Figure 9.6) (Cranstone, 1972). In later millennia, the alloying of copper and bronze, and later, the development of iron cutting edges, made forest clearance even easier.

New tools meant new technologies to produce tougher working edges. At first the farmers used ground and polished stone, placing a high premium on suitable rocks, which were traded from quarry sites over enormous distances. Perhaps the most famous ax quarries are in west Europe, where ax blanks were traded the length of the British Isles, and Grand Pressigny flint from France was prized over thousands of square miles. In the Near East and Mexico, one valuable toolmaking material was obsidian, a volcanic rock prized for its easy work-

FIGURE 9.6 Using a stone adz to fell a tree. A Tefalmin farmer at work in 1966, in New Guinea.

ing properties and its ornamental appearance. Early obsidian trade routes carried tools and ornaments hundreds of miles from their places of origin. By using spectrographic techniques, scientists have been able to trace obsidian over long distances to such places of origin as Lipari Island off Italy and Lake Van in Turkey (Renfrew and Dixon, 1976).

All these developments in technology made people more and more dependent on exotic raw materials, many of which were unobtainable in their own territory. We see the beginnings of widespread long-distance trading networks, which were to burgeon even more rapidly with the emergence of the first urban civilizations.

We still know tantalizingly little about the ways humankind began to exercise control over food resources. We know that in the Near East there was a dramatic shift in human subsistence patterns 10,000 years ago, in northern China about 7,000 years ago, and in Mesoamerica some 5,000 years ago. But some fascinating clues suggest that people were exercising some sort of control over their food supplies very much earlier. Perhaps Upper Paleolithic people who specialized in hunting reindeer or mountain goats made some attempts to manage the prey herds. Conceivably, too, hunter-gatherers living on the fringes of tropical rain forests could have engaged in deliberate opportunistic horticulture, planting yams and other food plants that could be regenerated for future use. The beginnings of the agricultural revolution may have taken hold many thousands of years before the explosion came. After all, we should never forget that humans have always been opportunistic, and the planting of food crops and the first taming of animals may have simply resulted from such opportunism.

GUIDE TO FURTHER READING

Childe, V. Gordon. *Man Makes Himself.* London: Watts, 1936.
    Classic Childe arguments for a Neolithic Revolution that summarize all the evidence in favor of a revolutionary change in prehistory when food production began.
Cohen, Mark. *The Food Crisis in Prehistory.* New Haven: Yale University Press, 1977.
    An original and thought-provoking essay on the origins of agriculture that advocates population as a major factor.
Cohen, Mark, and Armelagos, George J. (eds.). *Paleopathology at the Origins of Agriculture.* New York: Academic Press, 1984.
    A volume of essays that test basic hypotheses about the origins of food production. Technical but fascinating.
Renfrew, Jane. *Palaeoethnobotany: The Prehistoric Food Plants of the Near East.* London: Methuen, 1973.
    An admirable synthesis of the archaeology of plant remains in the Old World. Much valuable material on basic methodology.
Rindos, David. *The Origins of Agriculture: An Evolutionary Perspective.* New York: Academic Press, 1984.
    A provocative discussion of the origins of agriculture that evaluates competing theories.

Sauer, Carl O. *Agricultural Origins and Dispersals.* New York: American Geographical Society, 1952.

A short essay full of original ideas about root as well as cereal crops, although the archaeological evidence is much outdated.

Struever, Stuart (ed.). *Prehistoric Agriculture.* Garden City, N.Y.: Natural History Press, 1971.

An anthology of articles that brings together the major theories about early agriculture.

CHRONOLOGICAL TABLE F

C14 Years B.P.	NEAR EAST			EGYPT	TROPICAL AFRICA	ANATOLIA	TEMPORATE EUROPE AND THE BALKANS
	Lowlands	Foothills					
				Chapter 17 ↑	Chapter 17 ↑	Chapter 19 ↑	Chapter 20 ↑
4,000—					?Agriculture in West Africa		
5,000—		Chapter 16 ↑		UNIFICATION			Stonehen
					Saharan cattle herders		Megaliths Cardial w
6,000—			BADARIAN				
				Fayum			Brzesc Kujawski · CHASSE BANDKERA
7,000—		Jarmo	Merimde				TRIPOLY
	Jericho		?Early agriculture				Starčevo
8,000—						Çatal Hüyük	
						Hacilar	
9,000—	A R C H A I C	Ali Kosh					KARANOVO Argissa-Maghula
		Mugharet el-Wad	QADAN			Çayönü	
10,000—		Abu Hureyra 'Ain Mallaha					
	N E O L I T H I C	Ganj Dareh					
11,000—		NATUFIAN	Zawi Chemi Shanidar				
12,000—							
	Chapter 8 ↑						Chapter 6

CHAPTER 10

The Origins of Food Production in the Near East

Preview

■ The Near East was cool and dry from about 20,000 to 15,000 years ago, with dry steppe over much of the interior. Human populations were sparse and highly mobile until conditions warmed up at the end of the Ice Age and forests spread. The development and spread of agriculture took place under unusually favorable environmental conditions.

■ Stone Age hunter-gatherers expanded south into the Negev and Sinai as conditions warmed. Occasional larger settlements situated on ecotones appeared, some apparently occupied for much of the year. One such culture was the Natufian, which flourished as early as 12,000 years ago. There was a trend toward more sedentary life, associated with intensification of hunting and gathering, also a shift toward deliberate planting and harvesting of cereal grasses.

■ The Neolithic of the Levant began about 10,500 years ago and lasted until about 5,750 years ago. Archaic Neolithic sites date to between 10,500 and 9,600 years ago in this area. Most were small settlements, but Jericho was protected with a stone wall and watchtowers and covered a much larger area.

■ The farmers of the Archaic Neolithic hunted gazelles, wild goats, and other species. They were efficient, selective hunters. Sheep and goats abruptly replaced gazelles at Abu Hureyra and other sites after 9000 years ago, as if herding was introduced to the Levant at this time.

■ In the Zagros Mountains, herding was well established by 10,000 years ago, by which time farmers were living on the Mesopotamian lowlands to the south.

- Anatolia was a diverse, favorable environment for hunter-gatherers in the Early Holocene. Agriculture and animal husbandry developed in this area at least 9500 years ago. Widespread trading in obsidian and other exotic materials connected Neolithic villages in Anatolia with others hundreds of miles away. Some settlements, like Çatal Hüyük, occupied 7500 years ago, achieved considerable complexity as a result of trading activity.

- Cultural development proceeded separately in each area of the Near East described in this chapter. In each, food production emerged independently, although there were trading links between regions. It was only later, after 7000 years ago, that broader cultural unity developed.

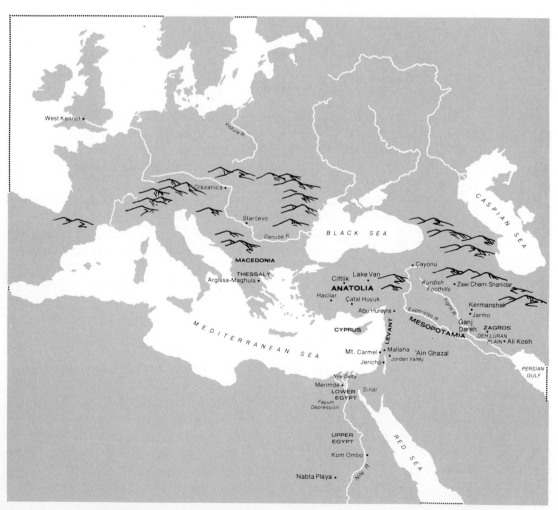

FIGURE 10.1 Early farming sites in the Near East, Europe, and the Nile Valley.

Much of the theorizing about early food production has stemmed from archaeological research in the Near East, where many early farming settlements are found (see Figure 10.1) (G. Wright, 1971). Agriculture and settled life developed in three regions of the Near East: Anatolia, the Zagros Mountains and Mesopotamia, and the Levant. The time when food production began is called the *Neolithic,* the "period in which a pattern of village settlement based on subsistence farming and stockbreeding became the basis of existence for communities throughout the Near East" (Moore, 1985). The Neolithic of the Near East began about 10,000 years ago nearly everywhere and lasted until the sixth millennium B.C. in Mesopotamia and until as late as 6000 years ago in the Levant.

Chronological Table F

THE NEOLITHIC ENVIRONMENT

Deep sea cores and pollen studies tell us that the Near Eastern climate was cool and dry from about 20,000 to 15,000 years ago, during the late Weichsel (Moore, 1985). Sea levels dropped more than 300 feet (100 m); much of the interior was covered by dry steppe, with forest restricted to the Levant and Turkish coasts. Between 15,000 and 10,000 years ago, climatic conditions warmed up considerably, reaching a maximum about 5000 years ago. Forests expanded rapidly at the end of the Ice Age, for the climate was still cooler than today and considerably wetter. Many areas of the Near East were richer in animal and plant species than they are now, making them highly favorable for human occupation. The development and spread of agriculture took place in unusually favorable environmental conditions.

HUNTING AND GATHERING

As Barbara Stark (1986) has emphasized, understanding the origins of agriculture means understanding the lifeway of the hunter-gatherers that preceded the first farmers. Unfortunately, we know almost nothing about the late Stone Age hunters of the Near East, except those in the Levant. Between 20,000 and about 12,000 years ago, sparse populations of highly mobile hunters and gatherers inhabited the Levant from northern Syria to the Negev Desert (Bar-Yosef, 1987). The interior plateau was probably too cold and dry for these people, who enjoyed a highly mobile lifeway and were widely dispersed in tiny settlements across the landscape. They concentrated on hunting gazelles and fallow deer, as well as gathering wild vegetable foods. Andrew Moore (1985) believes that environmental conditions on the open steppe of the time were probably quite severe, especially for people who subsisted for the most part on sparse game populations. Thus, he argues, this may have been the first time some groups collected wild cereal grasses to help tide them over food shortages.

20,000 to 12,000 B.P.

In time, the climate began to improve, with rising temperatures and rainfall that created a rich forest and steppe environment over much of the Levant. Stone Age hunters now expanded south into the Negev and the Sinai, and into favorable areas far to the east. Most campsites were still small, but occasional larger settlements, situated on ecotones (the boundaries of several ecological zones), occurred, some covering as much as 8,611 to 21,528 square feet (800 to 2000 sq m). These were small villagelike encampments, some apparently occupied for most, if not all the year. The inhabitants lived in circular huts or pit dwellings. This may be a sign that plant foods were assuming far greater importance in the local diet, a trend that encouraged the use of larger, more permanent settlements (Moore, 1985). One such culture was the Natufian, named after a valley in Israel, which flourished over much of the coastal strip from southern Turkey to the fringes of the Nile River (Bar-Yosef, 1987).

Natufian
**12,000 to
10,000 B.P.**

The Natufians hunted gazelles (perhaps even semidomesticated them) but obtained much of their food from stands of wild cereal grasses (Garrod, 1957; Mellaart, 1975). Their toolkits included flint sickle blades, of which the cutting edges bear a characteristic gloss that was achieved by friction against grass stalks; the kits also contained bone handles in which the blades were mounted (Figure 10.2).

'Ain Mallaha
10,000 B.P.

Natufians began to live in fairly permanent settlements. 'Ain Mallaha in northern Israel, for example, covers at least half an acre, with circular houses on stone foundations. Storage chambers were an integral part of the houses, a clear sign of increasing sedentariness. Stone bowls, mortars, and paved floors are also common, and many burials reflect greater social differentiation by their varying amounts of adornment. This increasing social complexity logically precedes the more elaborate class structure of later urban life, but other Natufians

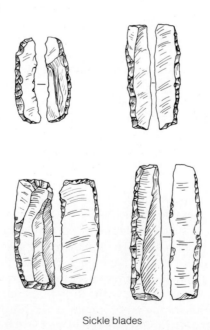

FIGURE 10.2 Natufian sickle blades and a bone handle for such blades. This handle (approximately one-half actual size) bears a deer's head.

Sickle blades

Sickle handle

were still living in rock shelters and caves like Mugharet el-Wad at Mt. Carmel. Mugharet el-Wad
A relative abundance of trade objects, such as seashells, seems to indicate expanded bartering in both house and rock-shelter communities. Trading was destined to spread greatly in future millennia.

There are signs, too, that the population rose sharply, perhaps reducing the size of foraging territories, even under the more favorable conditions of 10,000 years ago. This rise may have reinforced the trend toward more sedentary life, a move apparently associated with intensification of hunting and gathering as well as a shift toward deliberate planting and harvesting of cereal grasses. Moore (1985) believes these innovations first developed among people living on the better watered steppe landscape. In the forest, the people turned toward more intense gathering of acorns and other stable plant foods, for mortars and grinders are common on sites of the time in once-forested areas.

THE NEOLITHIC OF THE LEVANT

The Neolithic of the Levant began about 10,500 years ago and lasted until about 5,750 years ago, in various stages of development.

"Archaic Neolithic" sites dating from about 10,500 to 9,600 years ago are Archaic Neolithic 10,500 to 9,600 B.C. found from the Aleppo region of Syria as far south as the southern Sinai, but only as far east as the interior plateau, with just a few outliers in the Euphrates Valley. Most lie on low ground, near well-watered, easily cultivable land. Every settlement was considerably larger than earlier hunter-gatherer camps. The people lived for the most part in circular or oval one-room houses, often partially dug into the ground. These stone, mud, or mud-brick dwellings were between 13.0 and 19.6 feet (4 and 6 m) in diameter, densely clustered together in tightly knit communities.

Most Archaic Neolithic villages covered at most a couple of acres. In dra- Jericho 10,500 B.P matic contrast, the settlement at Jericho extended over at least 9.8 acres (4 ha). A temporary Natufian camp had flourished at the bubbling Jericho spring at least 10,500 years ago (Kenyon, 1981). But a more lasting farming settlement quickly followed. Soon these people, whose technology did not include clay vessels, were building massive walls around their town. A rock-cut ditch more than 9 feet (2.7 m) deep and 10 feet (3.2 m) wide was bordered by a finely built stone wall complete with towers (Figure 10.3). The beehive-shaped huts of Jericho were clustered within the defenses. The communal labor of wall-building required both political and economic resources on a scale unheard of a few thousand years earlier. Why walls were needed remains a mystery, but they must have been for defense, resulting from group competition for scarce resources. Some recent geomorphological researches hint that the walls may have been flood-control works (Bar-Yosef, 1986).

The earliest Archaic Neolithic populations were descended from Stone Age peoples, for many of their simple artifacts and their circular houses strongly recall those of earlier times.

The population of the Levant increased considerably between 9600 and 8000 years ago. More than 140 sites are known, scattered throughout the Le-

FIGURE 10.3 Excavated remains of the great tower in early Jericho.

vant and far east onto the Syrian plateau. Many of them are much larger than the first farming settlements. Abu Hureyra in northern Syria covers nearly 28 acres (11.5 ha), larger even than Jericho at this time.

Abu Hureyra
c. 11,500 to 10,000 B.P.
c. 9,500 to 7,000 B.P.

Abu Hureyra began life as a small village settlement of pit dwellings with simple reed roofs supported by wooden uprights (Moore, 1979) (Figure 10.4). Using fine screens and flotation equipment, the excavators recovered thousands of wild vegetable foods, including wild einkorn, rye, and barley. Abu Hureyra lies outside the present-day range of these wild cereals. However, between 11,500 and 10,000 B.P., when the site was first occupied, the climate was somewhat warmer and damper than it is today. As a result, the village lay in a well-wooded steppe area where animals and wild cereals were abundant. At

FIGURE 10.4 Abu Hureyra, Syria. *Top:* The mound of Abu Hureyra from the southwest. The site, which overlooks the Euphrates floodplain, consists of two superimposed settlements. The earliest dates to between c. 11,500 and 10,000 B.P. A later farming village was occupied c. 9,500 and 7,000 B.P. *Bottom:* The earlier settlement consisted of a series of interconnecting pits dug into the natural subsoil. These were roofed with poles, branches, and reeds to form huts. Part of a later rectilinear house can be seen near the top of the picture.

any rate, some hunter-gatherer groups such as the Hureyra people gathered in more permanent settlements and harvested wild cereals as a deliberate subsistence strategy. The inhabitants also had access to a reliable meat source, Persian gazelles that arrived from the south each spring. The arrivals were apparently killed en masse each year, the meat stored. With such a favorable location, Abu Hureyra slowly increased in size to 300 to 400 people, until deteriorating climatic conditions, and perhaps deforestation due to heavy firewood consumption, caused them to leave. In its heyday, its people may have enjoyed a higher degree of social organization than that found in nomadic hunter-gatherer societies (Lewin, 1988b).

A later farming settlement at Abu Hureyra was occupied about 9500 years ago and covered nearly 30 acres (12 ha). Visitors to the village would have found themselves wandering through a closely knit community of rectangular, one-story mud-brick houses, joined by narrow lanes and courtyards. The multiroom dwellings had black burnished plaster floors, sometimes decorated with red designs. Each was probably occupied by a single family.

FIGURE 10.5 Plastered Neolithic skull from Jericho, perhaps evidence for an early ancestor cult.

FIGURE 10.6 Plaster figurines from 'Ain Ghazal, Jordan.

Similar types of house occur at Jericho and other contemporary settlements, where the dead were buried within the settlement, sometimes under house floors. At Jericho, 'Ain Ghazal in Jordan, and elsewhere, the people would sever the head and deposit it alone or with a cache of skulls. At both sites, they sometimes modeled the features of the deceased in painted plaster, perhaps in some form of ancestor cult (Figures 10.5 and 10.6). But there are no signs of differences in individual status in society.

The farmers of the Archaic Neolithic 10,000 years ago hunted gazelles, wild cattle, pigs, goats, and other game species. None of the bones shows the characteristic morphological features of domesticated animals. Judging from the proportions of immature gazelles at some sites, the people were very efficient, selective hunters. This pattern of animal exploitation began millennia earlier, during the Upper Paleolithic. Sheep and goats very rapidly replaced gazelles as the principal meat supply at Abu Hureyra and elsewhere after about 9000 years ago. At the same time, there are signs that cattle and pigs were subject to increasing human control. By this time, the domestication of sheep and goats had proceeded to the point that their morphology is clearly that of domesticated animals (see Moore, 1985, for references). About 8500 years ago, it appears that the local gazelle herds were depleted: sheep and goats now composed 60 percent of all meat consumed (Legge and Rowley-Conwy, 1987).

Emmer wheat, barley, lentils, and peas were grown in the Archaic Neolithic from as early as 10,000 years ago. Even quite early on, agricultural methods were relatively sophisticated, cereals being rotated with pulses to ensure high crop yields and sustained soil fertility. An effective system of allowing fields to lie fallow also enabled larger sites. Abu Hureyra and Jericho were occupied continuously over many centuries as a result. Many settlements became trading centers, for the numbers of imported materials and exotic objects rise dramatically after 9000 years ago. The farmers were using obsidian from Anatolia, turquoise from Sinai, seashells from the Mediterranean and Red Sea. The volume of trade was such that many villagers used small clay spheres, cones, and disks to keep track of commodities traded. These tokens are thought to have been a simple recording system (Schmandt-Besserat, 1978).

By 8000 years ago there was considerable variation in farming culture throughout the Levant, caused by local cultural developments. But the farmers maintained fleeting contacts with communities many hundreds of miles away, even with peoples living in quite different culture areas in the Zagros and Anatolia.

THE ZAGROS AND MESOPOTAMIA

As in the Levant, the sequence of Neolithic cultures in the Zagros foothills and Mesopotamia can be divided into an earlier stage, from about 10,000 to 8,000 years ago, and a later Neolithic, lasting until about 7,000 years ago. There were sporadic contacts between these areas and the Levant, but cultural developments in this region were parallel to and independent of those at Abu Hureyra, Jericho, and other western locations.

Thanks to the pioneering work of Robert Braidwood (L. Braidwood, 1982), who looked for agricultural origins on the hilly flanks of Mesopotamia, we know more about the highlands, where agricultural conditions were less favorable, than we do about early food production on the lowlands, the undulating northern Mesopotamian steppe, where the Assyrian civilization flourished. To the south, the sandy Mesopotamian plain accumulated deep layers of silt through the Holocene. Early farming settlement there is probably buried under feet of alluvium. Only small farming villages preserved under great city mounds like those of Ur and Eridu tell us anything about early farming settlement in these regions, and they date to not much earlier than about 7000 years ago.

During the late Ice Age, human groups probably lived on the warmer lowlands. In the very early Holocene, the mountains were cool and dry, so agriculture probably began on the lowlands first, a natural habitat for wild cereals and pulses. As the climate warmed up, people moved into the mountain valleys of Zagros, open steppe country with seasonal resources spaced vertically up hill slopes. This was ideal country for herding sheep and goats, to the extent that herding may have developed earlier here than in other parts of the Near East (Moore, 1985).

Zawi Chemi Shanidar **11,000 B.P.**

Some 11,000 years ago, wild goats were a primary quarry for the hunters and gatherers exploiting the resources of the foothills. The people of a small encampment named Zawi Chemi Shanidar in the mountains of Kurdistan were hunting and gathering at this time, living in small, circular huts. Dexter Perkins (1964) studied the animal bones from the site and found that the inhabitants were killing large numbers of immature sheep, as if they had either fenced in their grazing grounds or so tamed the sheep that they could control the age at which they were killed. Zawi Chemi may have been a summer encampment on the steppe. Pollen studies show an increase in cereal grasses during the occupation, perhaps evidence of cultivation (Moore, 1985).

Ganj Dareh **10,500 B.P.**

High in a mountain valley near Kermanshah lies another early farming village named Ganj Dareh, first occupied about 10,500 years ago (P. E. L. Smith, 1978). The earliest settlement was probably a seasonal camp used by hunters and gatherers, but a later occupation, around 9000 years ago, consisted of a small village of rectangular mud-brick houses, some two stories high. The lower stories may have been used for storage, because clay bins have been found in them. Ganj Dareh represents the beginnings of permanent settlement in the Zagros, based on goat and cattle herding and possibly agriculture. Contemporary sites contain clear evidence for changes in goat bone morphology indicative of full domestication.

Jarmo **7000 B.P.**

One of the best-known Zagros farming villages is Jarmo, a permanent hill village southeast of Zawi Chemi occupied more than 7000 years ago (Braidwood and Braidwood, 1983). Jarmo was little more than a cluster of twenty-five houses built of baked mud, forming an irregular huddle separated by small alleyways and courtyards. Storage bins and clay ovens were an integral part of the structures. The Jarmo deposits yielded abundant traces of agriculture: seeds of barley, emmer wheat, and minor crops were found with the bones of sheep and goats. Hunting had declined in importance — only a few wild animal bones testify to such activity — but the toolkit still included Stone Age–type tools with sickle blades, grinding stones, and other implements of tillage. Jarmo contains exotic materials such as obsidian, seashells, and turquoise traded into the Zagros from afar. There are also numerous clay tokens, perhaps, again, evidence for a recording system connected with long-distance trade. Jarmo was a fully permanent, well-established village engaged in far more intensive agriculture than its predecessors. More than 80 percent of the villagers' food came from herds or crops.

Ali Kosh **10,000 to 8,000 B.P.**

Below, on the lowlands, farming began along the eastern edge of the flat Mesopotamian plain at least as early as in the Levant. The well-known Ali Kosh site on the plains of Khuzistan, north of where the Tigris and Euphrates join waters, chronicles human occupation from as early as 10,000 years ago. Ali Kosh began life as a small village of mud-brick rectangular houses with several rooms (Hole et al., 1969). As time went on, the houses became larger, separated from each other by lanes or courtyards. The people herded goats and sheep, which may have been driven to highland pastures in the mountains during the hot summer months. This transhumance pattern continues in the area to this day. Emmer, einkorn, barley, and lentils were cultivated from the earliest days of Ali Kosh. Hunting and gathering were important, as were fish and waterfowl from a nearby marsh. This well-excavated site documents more than 2000 years of farming and herding on the lowlands, a time span that saw the development of improved cereal strains and the first appearance of irrigation as a way of intensifying agricultural production.

Agriculture and herding were well established in the lowlands when Ali Kosh was founded some 10,000 years ago. As in the Levant, cereal cultivation and animal husbandry were probably developed by hunter-gatherer groups in the very early Holocene. (For details of the late Neolithic in the Levant and these areas, see Moore, 1985.)

ANATOLIA

Anatolia (Turkey) was a diverse, favorable highland and lowland environment for human settlement from early on in the Holocene. However, the earliest evidence for farming and animal herding there dates from about 9500 years ago. We can only assume that the new economies were developed in this region somewhat earlier, and that sites to document the transition await discovery. Certainly, there is no reason why food production could not have developed here as early as 10,000 years ago.

Çayönü **9400 to 8000 B.P.**

Neolithic Çayönü in southeast Turkey was occupied from about 9400 to 8000 years ago (L. S. Braidwood, 1982; R. J. Braidwood and Cambell, 1980). The first phase of occupation lasted about 650 years, when the inhabitants lived in separate rectangular houses of various designs. The people cultivated cereals and pulses, collected wild vegetable foods, and relied increasingly on domesticated sheep for meat after 8700 years ago. Çayönü represents a relatively developed form of Neolithic life, remarkable only for the sudden adoption of sheep herding, a phenomenon also found at Abu Hureyra in Syria. Perhaps the inhabitants of both sites started herding sheep as a result of contact with shepherd peoples from the highlands to the east, who had been herding small stock for a long time (Moore, 1985; Ryder, 1982).

Hacilar **8700 B.P.**

On the Anatolian plateau, James Mellaart (1975) excavated a remarkable early farming village at Hacilar, which was founded approximately 8700 years ago. Seven phases of occupation took place at Hacilar before its inhabitants moved. They lived in small rectangular houses with courtyards, hearths, ovens, and plastered walls.

No pottery was used at Hacilar, but basketry and leather containers probably were. Barley and emmer wheat were cultivated, and some wild grass seeds were also eaten. The bones of sheep or goats and cattle and deer were present, but there was no evidence for the domestication of any animal except the dog. Hacilar was a simple and unsophisticated settlement, probably typical of many communities in the Near East in the early millennia of farming.

Most Neolithic sites in central and east Anatolia were within easy reach of the rich obsidian sources near Lake Van and elsewhere. Villages close to the volcanic flows where the fine stone came from used it almost exclusively for artifacts, trading a great deal of obsidian to communities near and far in the form of prepared blade cores. Small quantities of Anatolian obsidian traveled hundreds of miles into the Levant and as far as the Persian Gulf (Renfrew and Dixon, 1976). Trace element analyses of artifacts from many sites show that the patterns of exchange were exceedingly complex, as different sources came into, and went out of, fashion (Moore, 1985).

The simplicity of many Anatolian farming villages contrasts dramatically with a more complex settlement engaged in widespread trading activity. The great mound of Çatal Hüyük covers 32 acres (13 ha); it was a town of numerous small houses built of sun-dried brick, which were designed to back onto one another, occasionally separated by small courtyards. Roofs were flat, and the outside walls of the houses provided a convenient defense wall (Figure 10.7). The town was rebuilt at least twelve times after approximately 8000 years ago, presumably when the houses began to crumble or the population swelled.

Çatal Hüyük
8000 to 7000 B.P.

A most remarkable feature of Çatal Hüyük is its artistic tradition, preserved in paintings on carefully plastered walls and in sculptures, some of them parts of shrines (Figure 10.8). Most depict women or bulls. Some paintings show women giving birth to bulls. Much art was about fertility and the regeneration of life, and figurines of women in childbirth have been found.

Much of Çatal Hüyük's prosperity resulted from its monopoly on the obsidian trade from quarries in nearby mountains. Obsidian was but one of many materials traded by Near Eastern farmers after 10,000 years ago. Marine shells, jadeite, serpentine, turquoise, and many other exotic commodities moved from

FIGURE 10.7 Schematic reconstruction of houses and shrines from Level VI at Çatal Hüyük, Anatolia, showing their flat-roof architecture and roof entrances.

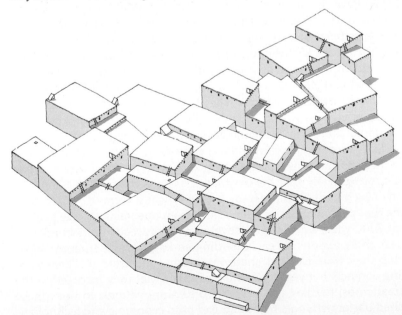

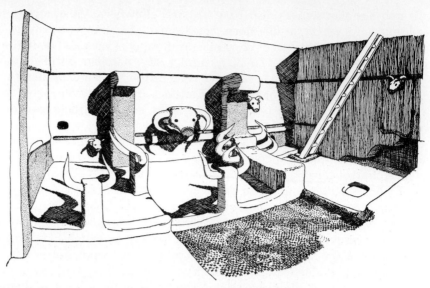

FIGURE 10.8 Reconstruction of the east and south walls of Shrine VI.14 at Çatal Hüyük, Anatolia, with sculptured ox heads, horns, benches, and relief models of bulls and rams. The shrine was entered by the ladder at right.

village to village through a myriad of barter transactions. Perhaps these regular exchanges were used not only to obtain exotic materials but also to cement social relationships. Andrew Moore (1985) believes that this widespread exchange of raw materials accelerated the diffusion of all manner of innovations far and wide, among them sheep herding, the introduction of pottery, and, eventually, copper and bronze metallurgy.

Just how important the obsidian trade was in the area has been shown by spectrographic analyses of fragments of the volcanic glass in hundreds of sites between Turkey and Mesopotamia. The trace elements in obsidian are so distinctive that it is possible to identify the natural source of the glass by this analysis and to reconstruct the distribution of obsidian from dozens of localities. Colin Renfrew and others were able to identify no fewer than twelve early farming villages that had obtained obsidian from the Ciftlik area of central Turkey (Renfrew, Dixon, and Cann, 1966). The study showed that 80 percent of the chipped stone in villages within 186 miles (300 km) of Ciftlik was obsidian. Outside this "supply zone," the percentages of obsidian dropped away sharply with distance, to 5 percent in a Syrian village, and one-tenth of a percent in the Jordan Valley. Renfrew and his colleagues argue that regularly spaced villages were passing approximately half the obsidian they received to their more distant neighbors. Much early farming trade probably was a form of "down-the-line" bartering that passed various commodities from one village to the next.

Until about 7000 years ago, cultural development proceeded independently in each of these three regions. In each, herding and agriculture emerged separately. Not that they were isolated one from another, far from it. There were regular trading contacts between each area, contacts that may have led to the spread of cereal crops, herding, pottery, and other innovations. In time, these well-established barter networks helped spread both economic and technological innovations throughout the ancient Near East. This is why similar developments, and intensifications of agricultural production, occur at about the same time in several places. The Near Eastern Neolithic itself was not the point at which cereal agriculture and herding first began. These developments occurred much earlier, among late Ice Age hunter-gatherers. But the Neolithic saw the culmination of them, saw the new economies become the foundations of human diet throughout the Near East. Major changes in settlement patterns ensued. Sustained population growth took hold some time after farming became commonplace and agriculture sufficiently productive to feed many more people.

The development of the new food-producing economies took place in two stages. The first saw some agriculture and control of animals, but most of the diet came from game and wild vegetable foods. Then, about 8000 years ago, more productive cereal grains and cattle, sheep, goats, and pigs were completely domesticated, creating the fully agricultural and stock-raising economy that was to persist into historic times, albeit in elaborated forms.

This was a time of profound social change, when human societies developed new mechanisms for social control, settlement of disputes, and regulation of the cultivation and inheritance of land. The new Near Eastern societies were still egalitarian, their economy based on the productive abilities of the nuclear family. But, judging from the plastered skulls from Jericho, 'Ain Ghazal, and other Neolithic sites (see Figure 10.5), complex rituals and ancestor cults were already defining the relationship between living people and the spiritual world, the world of soil fertility, bountiful crops, and the ancestors.

GUIDE TO FURTHER READING

Bar-Yosef, O. "Late Pleistocene Adaptations in the Levant," in Olga Soffer (ed.) *The Pleistocene Old World: Regional Perspectives.* New York: Plenum Press, 1987, pp. 219–236.
An authoritative synthesis of late Upper Paleolithic cultures in the Near East designed for the serious reader.

Hole, Frank, Flannery, Kent V., and Neely, J. A. *The Prehistory and Human Ecology of the Deh Luran Plain.* Ann Arbor: Museum of Anthropology, University of Michigan, 1969.
An exemplary monograph on a lowland Mesopotamian excavation. Excellent discussion of subsistence changes after 10,000 years ago.

Kenyon, Kathleen. *Excavations at Jericho,* vol. 3. Jerusalem: British School of Archaeology, 1981.
The monograph on the early levels at Jericho. A fascinating specialist publication.

Mellaart, James. *The Earlier Civilizations of the Near East.* London: Thames and Hudson, 1975.
A summary of early farming societies in the Levant and Turkey. Excellent for advanced students.

Moore, Andrew T. "The Development of Neolithic Societies in the Near East," *Advances in World Archaeology* 4 (1985):1–70.
An exemplary and thoroughly up-to-date synthesis of the subject matter covered by this chapter. Strongly recommended for its clarity and taut thinking.

CHAPTER 11

Early European Farmers

Preview

- We can only understand the emergence of food production in temperate Europe by analyzing Postglacial hunter-gatherer cultures in the region.

- The term *Mesolithic* is used to describe hunter-gatherer societies that flourished in Europe from about 10,000 years ago until the introduction of farming to northwest Europe about 5,500 years ago.

- The Mesolithic was once thought to be a cultural hiatus. However, it is now seen as a period when the hunter-gatherer quest intensified, with some groups adopting almost sedentary lifeways, to the point that they could be classified as "affluent hunter-gatherers."

- The Maglemose, Kongemose, and Ertebølle period adaptations, based on increasingly intense exploitation of terrestrial and land resources, span the Mesolithic of southern Scandinavia. Elsewhere in Europe, contemporary Mesolithic settlements were often situated on the boundaries of ecological zones.

- Agriculture and animal husbandry in southeast Europe probably developed partially as a result of indigenous adaptive shifts to more intensive exploitation of cereals and wild sheep, and also because of the "drift" of domestic animals and cereals from the Near East. Cereal cultivation and animal domestication are known from Greece as early as 8000 years ago.

- The Bandkeramik complex documents the first settlement of southeast European farmers in the Middle Danube and on the light loess soils of central Europe just after 6000 years ago.

- Food production began over most of Europe during the subsequent millennium, largely by indigenous Mesolithic people adopting sheep, pottery, and cereals, which they considered of immediate advantage to them.

- The megalithic tombs of the Mediterranean Basin and west Europe document a trend toward greater cultural diversity after 6000 years ago. They are thought by some observers to be symbols of the continuity of human life.

The origins of agriculture in Europe have always been thought of in terms of the Near East, the spread of cultivation techniques, crops, and animal domestication from the southeast into temperate latitudes of Europe and Asia. This viewpoint, which originated long before the days of V. Gordon Childe (Chapter 2), has regarded the temperate zones as the fringe of the ancient world, as a recipient rather than an innovator (Childe, 1925). Today, people no longer talk of farmers and metallurgists flooding into temperate regions from the innovative East. Like the inhabitants of the Near East, the Europeans of 10,000 years ago encountered major climate change and adapted to radically new conditions in many ways. One of these adaptive pathways was food production. As in the Near East, we can only understand the early history of farming in Europe by examining the changes in hunter-gatherer life that took hold as the Ice Age ended over 10,000 years ago (for discussion, see Zvelebil, 1986).

Chronological Table F

MESOLITHIC PRELUDE

In many parts of the world, the terrestrial climatic changes at the end of the Ice Age were far from dramatic. The Near East saw increasing aridity in some areas, but human adaptations remained much the same as they were during the late Ice Age. Southern Europe, for example, was home to deciduous oak forests and many land mammals like the red deer, roe deer, and wild pig, which spread into more northerly latitudes as the climate warmed up (Price, 1987). Farther south, climatic shifts were subtle, with accompanying minor changes in human adaptations until farming and animal domestication took hold a few thousand years later. The most dramatic changes in human societies were in northwest Europe, where forest and coastal hunter-gatherers replaced tundra reindeer hunters. It is to these societies that *Mesolithic* is often applied, a term used to refer to the period of Postglacial times in Europe that preceded the introduction of farming (J. G. D. Clark, 1975, 1979). The Mesolithic spans about 4,500 years, from about 10,000 years ago until the introduction of farming in northwest Europe about 5,500 years ago.

The Mesolithic is a temperate and boreal forest adaptation that is confined to the northern Old World. In the New World, Postglacial societies lived on a continent where geographic barriers run north to south and where people had colonized the landscape relatively recently. Thus, they faced a very different set of opportunities, described in Chapter 7.

Mesolithic 10,000 to 5,500 B.P.

For generations, archaeologists thought that European hunter-gatherers went into decline at the end of the Ice Age. The great artistic traditions vanished, the vast herds of Pleistocene arctic animals became extinct. According to this view, Europeans eked out an impoverished existence among forests and along lake- and seashores during the Mesolithic, a brief transitional period that ended with the arrival of farming peoples in temperate Europe some 8000 years ago. The great British prehistorian Grahame Clark has long disagreed, calling the Mesolithic a "prelude to fundamental advances in the development of culture" (1979). As Barbara Stark (1986) has pointed out in the Americas, much of our understanding of early farming has to come not from the farmers themselves but from cultural processes among earlier hunter-gatherer societies. This viewpoint has meant that the Mesolithic has assumed new importance in archaeological thinking, as a period when hunter-gatherers in the temperate zone developed a range of Postglacial adaptations. These adaptations differed from those contemporary in the Near East but still paralleled them in many ways. Any understanding of the origins of food production in Europe must start with a discussion of cultural developments among Postglacial Stone Age hunter-gatherers in temperate zones.

Cultural Hiatus and Affluent Alternatives

The traditional view of the Mesolithic had Europe populated by scattered bands of impoverished hunters and gatherers, who had lost much of their capacity for economic and social relations (for discussion, see Rowley-Conwy, 1986). This notion of a cultural hiatus has crumbled in the face of recent sophisticated ecological researches. Instead of impoverished environments, each change in Postglacial forest composition probably brought greater ecological productivity. A range of forest ungulates such as red and roe deer replaced the migratory reindeer that was so important in Ice Age times. Plant foods such as nuts assumed much greater importance in Mesolithic life. These favors may have contributed to an increase in Mesolithic populations. Coasts, estuaries, and lakes were highly productive, especially with such seasonal resources as salmon, water birds, and sea mammals, many of them relying on seasonal plankton production in the oceans. Many of these aquatic foods could be taken and stored, especially by people who occupied relatively permanent encampments near where several such resources were to be found. Thus, larger populations were possible in some areas, among people who relied on seasonal resources and used such nonseasonal foods as shellfish to "plug" the gaps (Rowley-Conwy, 1986). Some of these more sedentary groups enjoyed a bounty of food sources and a complexity of lifeway that has been called "affluent foraging" (see Chapter 2).

Were all Mesolithic peoples affluent foragers? The interplay of different resources varied dramatically throughout Europe, with its seasonal climates and productive environments. This was not a hostile environment peopled by only minimally complex hunter-gatherer bands but one where a great variety of adaptations was possible. At least two general models have been proposed for Mesolithic Europe:

- Lower latitudes supported somewhat generalized environments, where highly mobile bands exploited evenly dispersed animal and plant resources, shifting camp regularly as local resources were exhausted (Binford, 1980).
- Higher latitude environments were more uneven in productivity and resource reliability, having few species in larger numbers. These were specialized environments, where human groups moved less often and frequently directed their moves toward the exploitation of a single seasonal resource like caribou. Larger numbers of people sometimes congregated for seasonal hunts.

These are, of course, by no means the only models for Mesolithic life that could be put forward, but they serve to remind us that this was a period when

European populations enjoyed a wide range of adaptations, from peoples with highly mobile lifeways to permanently settled, "affluent" peoples who dwelt in large villages or base camps, such as are found in northwest Europe and by the Iron Gates area of the Danube River (Rowley-Conwy, 1986).

The Mesolithic, then, was a period of broad variation in economic and social life, with some intensification of the food quest where environmental conditions dictated it.

Clive Gamble (1986a) points out that the adaptive trends seen in the European Mesolithic are not particularly innovative; indeed most of them have their roots in a much earlier restructuring of the organization and use of resources with the arrival of modern humans in temperate latitudes some 35,000 years ago. The Upper Paleolithic saw much greater exploitation of regional resources and an enhanced ability to adapt to extremes of both glacial and fully interglacial climates. This restructuring gave Europeans the ability to solve the problems of exploiting not just a few resources but many different ones at once. This ability became vital at the end of the Ice Age, when food management strategies came into use that were able to cope with extremely varied combinations of food resources. These strategies included some elements that were of critical importance when people began to grow crops and tame animals: adaptations that were attuned to scheduling of seasonal activities connected with growing and harvesting seasons, and systems of information sharing. The Mesolithic hunters' schedule was comprehensive and flexible enough to cope with anything and could easily accommodate strategies that relied on deliberate cultivation of the soil or careful animal husbandry.

Complexity among hunter-gatherer societies is one of the "hot" topics in world prehistory today. By *complex*, we mean those hunter-gatherer groups who live sedentary or semisedentary lives, live in sizable settlements that could be called villages, and construct large, durable dwellings that are used over long periods of time. Complex hunter-gatherers often store food and manipulate the environment in ways that can alter the availability or abundance of food resources (Rowley-Conwy, 1986). Many of these activities were once thought to be characteristic of agricultural societies, but researches into living and recently extinct hunter-gatherer societies show that such signs of "complexity" not only occur in living cultures but also perhaps existed in much earlier prehistoric cultures.

The classic example of a living "complex" hunter-gatherer society is the Northwest Coast Indians, who lived in semipermanent villages of large planked houses and exploited food resources intensively. They enjoyed an elaborate social organization and ceremonial life controlled by important kin leaders. These leaders served as chieftains, with weighty economic, political, and spiritual powers. Examples of complex hunter-gatherers in remote prehistory are harder to find. Some authorities believe that the Magdalenians of southwest France enjoyed a degree of social complexity, with, perhaps, some social differentiation between individuals. The Mesolithic Ertebølle peoples of southern Scandinavia (see later) were often packed into relatively limited territories with such diverse resources that sedentary settlement was possible. They buried their dead in cemeteries. The grave goods from these burials provide some as yet inconclusive evidence for social differentiation. In both these prehistoric cases, however, there is evidence of considerable intensification of the food quest, with both game and vegetable foods, and sometimes aquatic resources, efficiently and heavily exploited. This intensification, and the sedentism that accompanies it, may have been a preliminary for the emergence of more complex social orders, even if they did not reach their full elaboration in earlier prehistory, as they did in recent times in the Pacific Northwest and other areas.

Cultural Innovations

Efficient food management strategies involved more effective technology, too — more diverse toolkits for hunting forest animals and exploiting coastal resources such as sea mammals and shallow-water fish. The Mesolithic peoples who lived along the shores of the newly emerging Baltic Sea developed an astonishing range of fish spears, nets, harpoons, and traps, many of them preserved in waterlogged sites. Spears and arrows were tipped with tiny stone barbs, while bone and antler served the same purpose. Ground-edged tools came into use for woodworking and processing forest plants. Large canoes, some of them dugouts hollowed from tree trunks, were in evidence. We know that Stone Age people were crossing open water as early as 12,000 years ago, for miners were visiting the island of Melos in the Mediterranean to collect obsidian that was traded far and wide (Torrence, 1986).

Many Mesolithic groups lived in larger, more permanent settlements, a number of them located on strategic bays or near lakes or rivers. Some locations were probably used year-round, or certainly for many months, anchored by abundant aquatic resources nearby. There were smaller camps and specialist activity areas, too. Everything points to greater internal differentiation in society and to more intensive subsistence activities. Nuts and shellfish became far more important, and hunters took a far wider range of game than their Ice Age predecessors. It was not the dietary staples but merely the diversity of food resources exploited that changed.

Perhaps the most profound changes were those in population densities and social organization, both notoriously difficult phenomena to identify in the archaeological record. At the end of the Upper Paleolithic, Grahame Clark (1979) has identified three major "social territories" between the Netherlands, Poland, and southern Sweden. Three distinct cultures (Ahrensburgian, Swiderian, and Bromme) each covered territories of about 38,610 square miles (100,000 sq km). But as the Postglacial wore on, these territories were rapidly reduced in size. By 8000 years ago, there were at least fifteen territories in this same area, identified by different artifact styles or distributions of raw materials. Each of these zones was about 5791 to 7722 square miles (15,000 to 20,000 sq km) in extent. This pattern may reflect major changes in the distribution, density, and social organization of Mesolithic populations. Douglas Price (1983) points out that as these changes were taking place, new artifact forms, and presumably other innovations, were spreading across wide areas of Europe. Among them was a characteristic trapeze-shaped microlith widely used as an arrow barb by later Mesolithic peoples that appeared all over the continent about 8000 years ago, perhaps somewhat earlier in southeast Europe (J. G. D. Clark, 1960). The Mesolithic ended with the rapid spread of agricultural economies into southeast

Europe about 8000 years ago. From there they spread sporadically into central Europe by 6500 years ago and to the northwest after 5500 years ago.

The European Mesolithic testifies to a continuity in human culture from Ice Age times, but this continuity was based on continuous adjustment to changing Postglacial environments. And, in time, the same Mesolithic societies readapted to the warmest millennia of Postglacial times not only by shifting their hunting and foraging methods but by taking up new subsistence practices, often within the context of their existing society (Price, 1983).

Regional Variants

The Mesolithic flowered most vigorously in northwest Europe and is well known from waterlogged coastal sites in Britain and southern Scandinavia. Three broad divisions of the northern Mesolithic are recognized (J. G. D. Clark, 1975; Price, 1985).

The Maglemose Period (9500 to 7700 years ago)

Maglemose
9500 to 7700 B.P.

The Maglemose was a time of seasonal exploitation of rivers and lakes, combined with terrestrial hunting and foraging. Inland late spring and early summer settlements are represented by the Ulkestrup site in Denmark, where the people lived in large huts with bark and wood floors on a peat island in a swamp by a lake. One hut lay close to poles where canoes were once moored. A large wooden paddle lay nearby. The Maglemose people used bone and antler barbed points for fishing, trapped birds, and hunted such animals as red deer, wild ox, and pig. In fall, the bands foraged for hazelnuts and other edible plant foods, killing elk and other game in winter, when, apparently, fishing was less important.

The Kongemose Period (7700 to 6600 years ago)

Kongemose
7700 to 6600 B.P.

Kongemose sites mainly come from Baltic Sea coasts, along bays and near lagoons, where the people exploited both marine and terrestrial resources. Many Kongemose sites are somewhat larger than Maglemose ones; among the better known is the now submerged Segebro settlement in brackish water near the southwest Swedish coast. This settlement covered 164 by 82 feet (50 by 25 m) and was occupied year-round, but mainly in spring and summer. Carbon isotype analyses of human bones from Segebro show that fish and sea mammals constituted most of the diet, with no fewer than sixty-six species of animals found in the site. Not only fresh- and saltwater fish, but red deer, elk, boars, and seals were commonplace. Like the Maglemose people, Kongemose hunter-gatherers used small stone microlithic arrow barbs as well as artifacts and weapons of bone, antler, and wood.

The Ertebølle Period (6600 to 5200 years ago)

Ertebølle
6600 to 5200 B.P.

Ertebølle was the culmination of Mesolithic culture in southern Scandinavia (Price, 1983, 1987). By this time, the Scandinavians were occupying many coastal settlements year-round, subsisting off a very wide range of food resources indeed. These included forest game and waterfowl, shellfish, sea mammals, and both shallow- and deep-water fish. There were smaller, seasonal coastal sites, too, many for specific activities, such as deep-water fishing, sealing, or the hunting of migratory birds. The Aggersund site in Denmark was occupied for a short period in the autumn, when the inhabitants collected oysters and hunted some game, especially migratory swans (Price, 1985).

Inland, the Ertebølle people occupied both large and small summer and winter settlements. The Ringkloster site, also in Denmark, was occupied some 5500 years ago. The inhabitants concentrated on hunting wild boars but also collected nuts and trapped pine martens. Skinned carcasses are almost intact, for the hunters were after pelts.

Ertebølle technology was far more elaborate than that of its Mesolithic predecessors — a wide variety of antler, bone, and wood tools for specialized purposes such as fowling and sea mammal hunting were developed, including dugout canoes up to 32.8 feet (10 m) long.

With sedentary settlement comes evidence of greater social complexity. Some Ertebølle communities buried their dead in cemeteries, with the bodies placed in various positions, and also with dog interments. The Vedbaek Bogebakken cemetery in Denmark dates to about 6000 years ago and contains the graves of at least twenty-two people of different ages. Everyone was buried in an extended position, at least three people after injury or a violent death. Men and women were deposited with different grave goods, older people with red deer antlers. Other Ertebølle cemeteries from Denmark contain evidence of violent death; some people had projectile points in their ribs. There are also traces of cannibalism (Price, 1985). One forty-year-old man buried at Skateholm was deposited in a wooden coffin, his body sprinkled with red ocher and associated with an antler harpoon, ground stone axes, and other tools.

The trend toward more sedentary settlement, the cemeteries, and occasional social differentiation revealed by elaborate burials are all reflections of an "intensification" among these relatively "affluent" hunter-gatherers of 5000 years ago. Mesolithic societies intensified the food quest by exploiting many more marine species, making productive use of migratory waterfowl and their breeding grounds, and collecting shellfish in enormous numbers. This intensification is also reflected in a much more elaborate and diverse technology, more exchange of goods and materials between neighbors, greater variety in settlement types, and a slowly rising population throughout southern Scandinavia. These phenomena may, in part, be a reflection of rising sea levels throughout the Mesolithic, inundations that flooded many cherished territories. There are signs, too, of regional variations in artifact forms and styles, of cultural differences between people living in carefully delineated territories and competing for resources (Price, 1985).

Mesolithic cultures are much less well defined elsewhere in Europe, partly because the climatic changes were less extreme than in southern Scandinavia, and because there were fewer opportunities for coastal adaptation. In many areas, settlement was confined to lake- and riverside locations, widely separated one from another by dense forests. Many Mesolithic sites were located on ecotones, transitional zones between different environments, so that the inhabitants could return to a central base location, where they lived for much of the year, close to predictable resources such as lake fish. But they would exploit both forest game and other seasonal resources from satellite camps. In central Europe, for example, Michael Jochim (1976) believes that some groups lived during the winter in camps along the Danube, moving to summer encampments on the shores of neighboring lakes. In many areas like Spain, there appears to have been intensified exploitation of marine and forest resources. There was a trend nearly everywhere to greater variety in the diet, with more attention being paid to less obvious foods and to those, like shellfish, that require more complex processing methods than game and other such resources.

These trends took hold in Mesolithic societies throughout Europe at a time when Near Eastern societies were already experimenting with the deliberate growing and domestication of crops and animals. After about 8000 years ago, farming was well established in parts of the Aegean and southeast Europe. During the 2500 years that followed, European Mesolithic societies gradually adjusted to these new subsistence practices, abandoning the hunter-gatherer lifeways that had sustained their immediate and remote ancestors for hundreds of thousands of years. (For detailed discussion and regional surveys of the European Mesolithic, see the essays in Zvelebil, 1986; also Price, 1987).

THE TRANSITION TO FARMING IN EUROPE

Did farming spread into Europe as a result of diffusion from the Near East, or did food production develop independently in the temperate zone? There are almost as many theories about this controversial subject as there are archaeologists; the theories pit diffusionists against those who argue that Europeans developed their own farming culture in southeast Europe more than 8000 years ago.

Radiocarbon Dates and Prehistoric Europe

The conventional wisdom that agriculture and metallurgy had spread into temperate Europe from the Near East was overturned by radiocarbon chronologies, which have radically altered our view of European prehistory. V. Gordon Childe and his diffusionist contemporaries worked before radiocarbon dates were available. All chronologies of epochs before approximately 5000 years ago, when civilization emerged in the Near East, were based on artifact typologies and inspired guesswork. The first radiocarbon dates showed that agriculture and metallurgy had begun in Europe much later than in the Near East, and there seemed nothing wrong with the traditional hypotheses.

When people started to calibrate radiocarbon dates against tree-ring chronologies, they found that European time scales between 3500 and 7000 years ago had to be corrected several centuries backward (Fagan, 1985; Klein et al., 1982; C. Renfrew, 1970; Suess, 1965). Egyptian historical (that is, from the written record) chronology from 5000 years ago now agrees more closely with calibrated C14 dates, rather than being several centuries too recent, as it was before.

British archaeologist Colin Renfrew has now moved the dates for temperate Europe back far enough to rupture the traditional diffusionist links between the

Near East and Europe (Figure 11.1) (C. Renfrew, 1973): that is, it is now apparent that events in Europe were contemporary with those in the Near East and not a later result of the spread of Near East culture. Using historical dates for the Mediterranean has thrown what Renfrew aptly calls a "fault line" across the Mediterranean and southern Europe. This line marks a chronological boundary, to the west of which radiocarbon (C14) dates after 5000 years ago have been pushed back by calibration, making them older than the accurate, historically attested dates for the eastern Mediterranean and the Balkans, which are east of the fault. Of course, this fault line is a methodological boundary, but it serves to show that prehistoric Europeans were much less affected by cultural developments in the Near East than Childe had suggested. They adopted metallurgy and other innovations on their own, just as early as many such inventions were brought into use in the Near East (C. Renfrew, 1973).

Greece and the Balkans

One reason that everyone assumed for so long that agriculture spread into Europe from the Near East was that they thought of Europe as one geographic entity and Turkey and the rest of the Near East just across the Dardanelles as another (Dennell, 1983). This artificial barrier combined with an assumption that rising population densities caused surplus farmers to spill over into Europe, bringing goats, sheep, and Near Eastern cereal crops with them. But there is no evidence of uncomfortably high population densities anywhere in Anatolia at this time (although our knowledge is incomplete). Furthermore, the earliest

FIGURE 11.1 Chronology of Europe and calibration of C14 chronology. With the uncalibrated chronology, the traditional view of European prehistory had agriculture and other innovations spreading northwestward from the Near East and eastern Mediterranean into continental Europe. The calibrated chronology has hardly affected the dates after 5000 B.P. for the eastern Mediterranean and sites to the southeast of the fault line. The calibrated dates after 5000 B.P. for sites to the west and northwest of the fault line, however, have been pushed back several centuries, so that the old notion of innovation from the east is replaced by new theories postulating less eastern influence. (C. Renfrew, 1973)

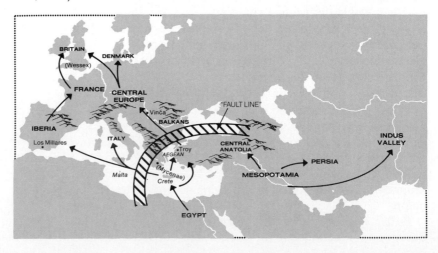

farming sites in southeast Europe are situated in very favorable places, which could only have been familiar to people who had lived in the region for many generations. However, it is undeniable that food production began in the Near East about 10,000 years ago, and some 2,000 years later in southeast Europe. How, then, are we to account for the chronological gradient?

The assumption that the natural distributions of wild cereals and of potential animal domesticates have remained unchanged since the Early Holocene is at best questionable (Dennell, 1983). As many authors have pointed out, human activity alone may have drastically reduced present-day ranges to the point that all we record are residual distributions. Late Glacial and Early Holocene pollen diagrams from northern Greece demonstrate that barley and perhaps other cereals were present in southeast Europe long before farmers appeared, about 8000 years ago. Cereal grasses may have moved into temperate Europe ahead of woodlands in Early Holocene times. Pulses may also have grown in Europe — the evidence is uncertain. As for potential animal domesticates, wild sheep are known to have flourished, albeit in scattered groups, in Upper Paleolithic Europe. At least one of these groups survived in southern France into Postglacial times.

Robin Dennell (1983) argues that the development of food production in southeast Europe went through three phases.

First, climatic conditions in the Early Holocene favored more plant growth. Grasses like einkorn and barley became more abundant, growing in dense stands that could be harvested in sufficient quantities to support a family for a year (for a modern experiment, see Harlan, 1967). However, in reality, most groups probably relied on shorter term supplies, as wild plant harvests were unpredictable. So they moved on and obtained much of their diet from hunting and other foraged foods.

A second stage began when trees colonized the areas previously occupied by grasses. This change would have scattered grass stands, decreasing the amount of grasses worth harvesting by human groups. But the grasses were worth maintaining as a seasonally important food. So the people may have ring-barked tree trunks or burned the forest to clear space for wild grasses to grow. The harvested plots would gradually revert to woodland, where young shoots would attract deer, wild sheep, and other animals. Dennell (1983) believes that a simple interdependence between plant harvesting and animal exploitation developed in areas where woodlands were expanding at the expense of cereals. In such areas, human beings lived in small, transitory settlements, many of them seasonal camps — just the kinds of site found in the southern European Mesolithic (see Zvelebil, 1986).

A third phase saw the establishment of permanent agricultural settlements. Through either local bartering or natural means, large-grained tough-rachis cereals were introduced into southeast Europe. These were Near Eastern cereals like emmer and bread wheat that were more predictable and productive than wild cereals. But they required much more work to cultivate and careful sowing in specially prepared and selected fields. The farmers had to weed and protect their growing crops. All this extra effort involved creating special fields and gardens for crops, a mosaic of cultivated land based on carefully chosen soils and a rotation system that allowed exhausted soils to rest. Both domestic emmer and bread wheat extract large quantities of nutrients from the soil, which could be replaced by underplanting nitrogen-fixing legumes and using animal manure. This new farming habitat involved the integration of cultivation and animal husbandry into a closely knit subsistence strategy based on individual households supplying their own food needs.

This model envisages food production in southeast Europe as a largely indigenous development, stimulated in part by the immigration of some domestic plants and animals from across the Dardanelles. It also accounts for the chronological gradient, a time lag that resulted from the gradual "drift" of new crops and domesticated animals from the Near East.

Argissa-Maghula
8000 B.P.

The earliest known evidence of food production in Europe comes from the Argissa-Maghula village mound in Greek Thessaly (Figure 11.2). The inhabitants cultivated emmer wheat and barley. Domestic cattle, sheep, and pig bones

Franchthi
8000 B.P.

in the lower levels of the site date to before 8000 years ago. The Franchthi Cave in southern Greece was occupied in Mesolithic times and continued in use for many thousands of years. Farming appeared there about 8000 years ago. These people had trading contacts with the Aegean islands (Dennell, 1983; Jacobsen, 1981). Since domesticated crops appeared abruptly at Franchthi, it is reasonable to suppose that cereal agriculture had been developed somewhat earlier.

In the Balkans to the north, the earliest farmers used their intimate knowledge of local conditions to settle on fertile agricultural soils on floodplains and elsewhere (Tringham, 1981; Whittle, 1985). Many of them lived in compact vil-

FIGURE 11.2 Archaeological sites in temperate Europe and the distribution of Bandkeramik (Danubian) pottery, Cardial ware, and western Neolithic.

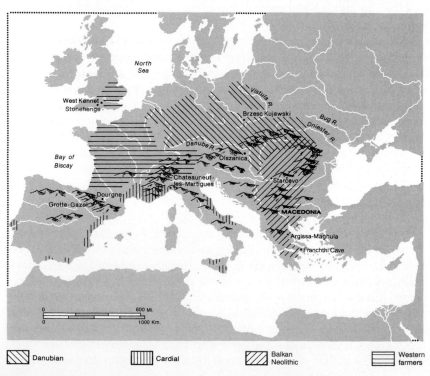

Farmers

lages of one-room dwellings built of baked mud plastered on poles and wicker (Tringham et al., 1980). These Karanovo culture settlements were occupied over long periods. Farming villages were built on brown forest soils and alluvial river plains, and the economy was based on cultivated wheat and barley and domesticated sheep and goats. A number of culture traits, including *Spondylus* shells (a characteristic Mediterranean mussel much valued because it could be used for ornamentation), clay seals and figurines, and reaping knives, show continuing connections with the Mediterranean world. The Starčevo site near Belgrade gives a vivid picture of the economic life and pottery styles of this widespread culture. This is an area with great environmental variability and ranges in temperature. For example, there are fertile plains and spring areas where the soils are permanently moist. It was here that many farming communities settled in the same locations for centuries, just as Near Eastern and Anatolian farmers had done. The largest mounds are found where good arable soils are most widespread. It was in this area that metallurgy developed approximately 5000 years ago (see Chapter 20).

Karanovo culture

THE SPREAD OF FARMING INTO TEMPERATE EUROPE

Between 7000 and about 5000 years ago, cereal cultivation and animal husbandry spread to most parts of temperate Europe through a very complex set of population movements and adaptive processes that are still little understood. These temperate zones are ones with year-round rainfall and marked contrasts between winter and summer seasons. Timber and thatch replaced the mud-brick architecture used so effectively for houses in Near Eastern villages (Melisauskas, 1978). Agricultural techniques had to reflect the heavier soils and perennial rainfall of European latitudes, but the first introduction of farming coincided with a warm, moist phase, when midsummer temperatures were at least 2° C higher than today (Butzer, 1974). The forest cover was mainly mixed oak, shadier tree cover that reduced the grazing resources of large game animals such as deer and wild cattle. Much of the indigenous Mesolithic population was settled by coasts, lakes, and rivers, on ecotones, where they could exploit several ecological zones from summer and winter camps. The first European farmers settled on the mostly loess soils of central Europe, which were lightly wooded, fertile, and easily tilled with simple digging sticks and hoes (Starling, 1985).

7000 to 5000 B.P.

Bandkeramik 7300 B.P.

These newcomers are known as the *Bandkeramik* complex (or sometimes as the Danubians), so named after their distinctive linear-decorated pottery (Figure 11.3). Their first colonization of the Middle Danube was a small-scale one about 7300 years ago. It appears that small groups of people migrated along river valleys, avoiding areas where Mesolithic folk lived. Their farming territories were widely spaced and apparently very small, perhaps on the order of about 500 acres (202 ha), of which about a third to a tenth was in cultivation at one time (Dennell, 1983; Howell, 1987). The people lived in hamlets made up of individual farmsteads, separated by about 100-yard (90-m) intervals. Individual houses were rectangular, from 18 to 46 feet (5.4 to 14.02 m) long, made

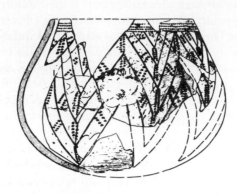
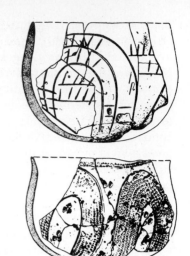

FIGURE 11.3 Danubian *Linearbandkeramik* (linear pottery) from Sittard, Holland, with characteristic line decoration (one-fourth actual size).

of timber and thatch, presumably sheltering families, their grain, and their animals (Champion et al., 1984; P. Phillips, 1980). Population estimates of between forty and sixty people per village seem not unreasonable, with a new settlement being founded as the population expanded (F. Hammond, 1981).

The Bandkeramik people cultivated barley, einkorn, emmer wheat, and minor crops including flax. These they grew using systems of crop rotation and fallowing that enabled the farmers to remain in the same place for long periods of time, sometimes even growing hedges to delineate their fields. Cattle were important in Bandkeramik life, as were sheep, goats, and dogs. Population growth after first settlement was slow. As each settlement grew, companion villages were founded nearby, gradually infilling the gaps between widely spaced neighboring communities. Within four or five centuries, population densities in parts of Germany rose from 1 per 386 square miles (1000 sq km) to 1 per 46 square miles (120 sq km).

By 6000 years ago, cereal crops and domesticated animals were widely used in southeast and central Europe, and perhaps also in southern France. These farming communities were surrounded by scattered hunter-gatherer societies. The Bandkeramik people had spread far west to southern Holland, where they had settled by 6800 years ago, and east to the Vistula River and the Upper Dniester. In the prime agricultural areas, the people relied heavily on their cattle, sheep, and pigs. They may have moved their herds onto the northern European plain for part of the year. The Brzesc Kujawski site in southern Poland was inhabited by summer cattle herders, who also gathered wild vegetable foods and caught perch in northern streams (Bogucki, 1988). Eventually farmers settled on heavier soils. We find regional variations of Danubian culture in many parts of central Europe. Some farmers had to rely more on hunting and gathering because the soils of their gardens did not yield enough food to support their families. Defensive earthworks appeared later, as if vigorous competition for land had caused intertribal stress.

SOCIAL CHANGES, LINEAGES, AND THE INDIVIDUAL: 5500 TO 4400 YEARS AGO

Bandkeramik settlement was limited to very specific parts of the landscape — to the edges of plateaus overlooking medium-sized streams in areas of loess soils (Howell, 1987). The people deliberately selected places where damp lowland pasture coincided with tracts of light, friable upland soils. They were cultivating fertile soils, land where hoe-using farmers could grow emmer wheat and other crops year after year, manuring their fields with cattle dung and domestic waste. Cattle were an important element in Bandkeramik economy, pointing to a "pioneer" economy introduced from southeast Europe rather than an indigenous farming culture that made full use of local plants and game animals.

The Bandkeramik people built large, permanent timber houses, investments in time and labor that would have been totally uneconomic if they were engaged in slash-and-burn agriculture and shifted their villages regularly (Figure 11.4). Bandkeramik sites formed clusters of settlements, separated from one another by distances of 12.4 or 18.6 miles (20 or 30 km). Up to a dozen or more houses stood in each settlement; the houses were, apparently, rebuilt in much the same place again and again. Bandkeramik settlements were occupied over long periods of time, so that a basic site, and the social structure within it, was maintained over many generations. There was continuity of residence location and inheritance from one generation to the next. In some areas, settlements were closely packed within small areas, each hamlet owning a territory of 37 acres (15 ha) or so. This was not because land was in short supply but because factors such as trade and local outcrops of flint and other materials may have played a role.

All of these characteristics point to farming societies that were producing food at the household level but with cooperation between different lineages at the settlement level — to build houses, erect enclosures, and herd cattle (for discussion, see J. Thomas, 1987). The first settlement in an area was, perhaps, the senior one, the place where the elder of the senior lineage lived, where the group's cemeteries and ritual enclosures were to be found. In the cemeteries, there were two general distinctions among grave goods: between graves of males and females, and those of young and old. Political power and social authority may have been in the hands of a group of older men, who controlled

FIGURE 11.4 Plan of a Bandkeramik long house from Olszanica, Poland, with wall trenches, postholes, pits, and other features.

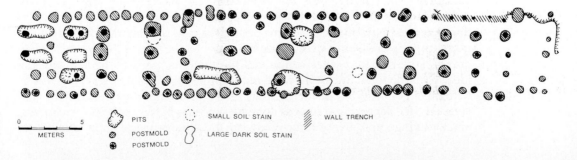

0	5		PITS		SMALL SOIL STAIN		WALL TRENCH
METERS			POSTMOLD		LARGE DARK SOIL STAIN		
			POSTMOLD				

cattle ownership and the exchange of cattle and other exotic commodities with other settlements. In Bandkeramik society, then, a complex network of social relations controlled productivity. Lineages within society formed the links between people and the lands of their ancestors.

About 5500 years ago, Bandkeramik settlements became more clustered and turned into villages. Many were protected by earthen enclosures, and divergent pottery styles hint that there were well-defined territories for different settlement clusters (J. Thomas, 1987). There were divergent developments in northwest Europe, with its communal megalithic tombs, and southeast Europe, where the dead were buried in cemeteries. This was a time when more elaborate burial traditions developed throughout Europe, as ancestor cults became more complex.

Megaliths and other corporate tombs may have originated as monuments designed to bring a sense of common identity to scattered farming communities. It may be that those buried in them were revered kin leaders, whose genealogical ties with the ancestors were of paramount, and collective, importance. Julian Thomas (1987) believes that as more and more effort was put into building large monumental tombs, their function changed. They became important power symbols among local populations, and the rituals that surrounded them became enmeshed in political relationships between different groups. Kinship still fashioned patterns of local production at a time when trade networks were intensifying throughout Europe. People, goods, and livestock were exchanged in ways that linked them to genealogical realities, to ceremonial life, marriage rules, and many other realities.

Between about 4800 and 4400 years ago, another change in burial customs took hold throughout Europe. For the first time, individual graves as well as communal sepulchers appeared. S. J. Shennan (1982) has argued that group-based ideologies were replaced by new beliefs that reinforced individual power and prestige. It would have been very hard for a single elder to preempt political and economic authority in Bandkeramik society. There were simply too many kin ties and reciprocal obligations to overcome, as well as the collective bond with the ancestors. But by being buried separately, in a burial adorned with elaborate grave furniture, a prominent elder could take on the role of sole male ancestor, the fountain of authority over land ownership, a role now assumed by his successor. Inheritance of land and wealth from one individual to another was now legitimized.

This is, of course, a speculative scenario but one supported by telling clues. There are many cases in which men and women were buried together in a single grave. This, argue some archaeologists, means monogamous marriages rather than the polygamous ones of lineage-based Bandkeramik society. The dominance of male burials from this period suggests that men were of great importance in establishing descent and rights of inheritance. Many individual graves were dug into older communal monuments, perhaps to reinforce the idea that individual ancestors were more important than collective ones. The rich grave goods found in such burials reveal new emphases in society: many weapons like daggers and swords appear, as well as battle axes, fine ornaments, and drinking cups. Everything points to the emergence of individuals who thought of themselves as warriors. Personal achievement and prestige were associated with males, who were involved in expanding exchange networks that handled luxury goods like amber, gold ornaments, and weapons. These were the symbols of prestige, the means of cementing individual relationships and political links, reciprocal obligations.

There are striking differences in the people buried, too. Bandkeramik farmers lavished their finest goods on older individuals. The later individual burials are those of men in their prime, indicating that personal achievement was the avenue to power and prestige.

Andrew Sherratt (1981) believes that the introduction of plow agriculture was a seminal development in Europe. Plows are known to have been used as early as 5600 years ago, but Sherratt says they came into far more widespread and intensive use about 4600 years ago, at a time when a number of other innovations or products reached Europe from the Near East. These included sheep shearing, milking, horse riding, and the use of oxen for traction. He goes so far as to argue for a "secondary products revolution," which transformed both settlement patterns and social organization throughout Europe. Julian Thomas (1987) disagrees and believes that social change was necessary for the plow and other innovations to succeed. The existing pattern of hoe agriculture and lineage-based production would have militated against new technologies.

Plow agriculture allows fewer people to work an acre of land, so more land would be cleared, making an individual's fields more widely scattered, sometimes close to the outer limits of daily walking. The result was a much more dispersed settlement pattern, with a rapid expansion onto heavier soils and hitherto uncultivated areas around 4600 years ago. With much more acreage to clear, and the technology to do it, the farmers of 4500 years ago were less tied to ancestral lands and the realities of household production and the kin ties these imply. Fewer people worked in the field, creating "unproductive" individuals in greater numbers, and there were compelling needs for social change. So, in place of the kin-based society arose a new social order in which individual success, prestige, and inheritance of land were the norm — with momentous consequences for the Europeans.

While the Bandkeramik complex was developing in central Europe, a mosaic of different subsistence patterns emerged on the Russian plains to the east between 8000 and 6500 years ago (Dolukhanov, 1986; Telegin, 1987). The areas best suited for farming, such as intermountain basins, were settled by agricultural peoples, while hunter-gatherers continued to exploit the river basins, like those of the Bug and Dniester rivers. The farmers and foragers interacted with one another, living in complementary environments, where one did not threaten the other. By 6500 years ago, Bandkeramik peoples had moved as far east as the Ukraine, bringing a mixed farming economy with them. They settled on the higher terraces of major rivers, still interacting with Mesolithic folk in the valley bottoms. Both Mesolithic and Neolithic peoples maintained their own identities. Farming reached its greatest extent in the forest-steppe regions of west Russia with the Tripolye culture some 6000 years ago (Figure 11.5). Soon after this, the farmers finally submerged the Mesolithic foragers of the valleys, perhaps because they relied extensively on cattle, whose grazing demands may

6500 B.P.

Tripolye
6000 B.P.

FIGURE 11.5 A Tripolye culture village.

have competed with hunter-gatherers' foraging needs. Some 4800 years ago, the climate deteriorated, making cultivation less viable. At this point balanced economies emerged, relying on stockbreeding on the steppe and farming in the forest-steppe, a balanced dynamic that survived into recent times, with important historical consequences.

FRONTIERS AND TRANSITIONS

The Bandkeramik expansion created a "frontier" in many parts of Europe between farming communities and Mesolithic groups. It would be a mistake to think of this as a rigid boundary between different peoples, for both hunter-gatherer and farming societies have a tendency to stay within their own territories and to continue the way of life with which they are familiar (Dennell, 1983). By the same token, however, the peoples who lived on either side of the frontier inhabited a far from closed world. They knew of one another's presence, traded with each other, and interacted through an intricate web of contacts that were beneficial to both sides. There can be no doubt that Mesolithic people were well aware of cereal crops and domesticated animals. But, in many cases, they saw no advantage in adopting a new way of life that involved a great deal more work with few significant changes in the diet.

More likely, as Robin Dennell (1983) has argued, they incorporated some aspects of Neolithic culture into their lives, those that gave them immediate advantage. These could have included clay vessels for storage and cooking, perhaps status items acquired by trade that were soon copied by local women. Cereal crops and sheep may have been valuable, simply because they solved problems of winter food supplies. Stored nuts, wild cereal grains, and dried deer meat or fish may have been Mesolithic winter staples. Sheep have lower feeding requirements than deer, have higher reproductive and growing rates, and can be used to keep woodland open for cereal growth. It would have been easy for Mesolithic people to graft sheep and domestic cereals onto their existing hunting and gathering practices. Dennell (1983) believes that these processes of assimilation caused farming to spread over much of temperate Europe after 8000 years ago and continued until as late as 5500 years ago, when many Scandinavian groups finally adopted food production.

Marek Zvelebil and Peter Rowley-Conwy (1984) take the argument a stage further, distinguishing three transition phases from hunting and gathering to farming:

- An "availability phase," when farming is known to Mesolithic peoples and there is some exchange of materials and information. Both farmers and hunter-gatherers are still independent units.
- A "substitution phase" that has two forms: (1) Farmers move into and settle hunter-gatherer territory in competition with the indigenous residents, and (2) hunter-gatherers add cultivation or animal husbandry to their range of subsistence activities. During this phase, there is competition for land, food, and raw materials, and perhaps social competition as well.
- A "consolidation phase," when food production becomes extensive and widespread, with hunting and gathering becoming subsistence strategies in emergencies. Farmers have now occupied the best soils and are using secondary areas with more intensive farming methods. By this time, the frontier has vanished.

The Zvelebil-Rowley-Conwy model serves as a descriptive device for analyzing the spread of food production into west and central Europe, but more data is needed to bolster it.

MEDITERRANEAN AND WEST EUROPE

New artifacts, such as pottery, and food sources, such as sheep, were added to hunter-gatherer adaptations as farming took hold in central Europe and farther afield. This transitional phase lasted for centuries throughout Europe. In many areas the new items added to existing practices, but they did little to change the fundamental structure of Mesolithic society or lifeway. The full-scale adoption of farming economies in areas like west Russia took a long time to achieve, whereas in other areas, like Britain, a full changeover occurred within five centuries or so.

In the Iron Gates region of the Danube Valley, coastal Yugoslavia, central Italy, and southern France, pottery, cereal crops, and sheep appeared, but there was little immediate change in daily life. Many sites where such artifacts occur are in the same type of setting as Mesolithic settlements, where hunting continued for centuries, even millennia. Sheep were in use in southern France in the Early Holocene, but the people were still hunter-gatherers. In the Mediterranean Basin, the long-term changes were an expansion in the use of obsidian and much wider ranging trade in this material after 7000 years ago. Obsidian is found on three Mediterranean islands, including Sardinia, and was now regularly traded to neighboring islands and the mainland. This trade was part of a widespread network of contacts, linked partly by sea, that carried seashells, exotic rocks, and later copper ore the length and breadth of the Mediterranean.

This trade also coincided in general terms with the manufacture of distinctive pottery styles decorated with impressions of seashells, among them the cockle shell, *Cardium* (Figure 11.6). This motif has given rise to the term *Cardial ware* to describe a range of indigenously developed pottery styles that mark the first use of clay vessels by Western peoples. Like sheep and goats, and perhaps cereal crops, pottery was adopted long before fully fledged farming economies emerged in the western Mediterranean and west Europe (Whittle, 1985).

The decisive shift from hunting and gathering in the West took place in the sixth millennium before Christ, with sheep and goats being acquired by trade, exchange, or theft considerably earlier, cereal crops arriving somewhat later. In southeast France, the Châteauneuf-les-Martigues Rock Shelter contains Mesolithic levels with small percentages of sheep dating to before 7000 years ago. Sheep became established later and eventually superseded wild cattle, pigs, deer, even rabbits, in the people's diet. Cereals also appear at this vast shelter, situated near a lagoon between the coastal plain and the hills (Whittle, 1985). The Grotte Gazel and Dourgne sites on the eastern side of the Pyrenees have also yielded sheep bones in Late Mesolithic levels, radiocarbon dated to between 7800 and 6800 years ago. These sheep were herded on the slopes of the Pyrenees long before impressed pottery was introduced into the region along with cultivated plants and other domesticated animals (Geddes, 1983, 1985).

Other French sites document scattered occurrences of sheep becoming more important in the centuries before 6000 B.P. There was no major change in the

Châteauneuf-les-Martigues **7000 B.P.**

Grotte Gazel

Dourgne **7800 to 6800 B.P.**

6000 B.P.

FIGURE 11.6 Cardium-shell-impressed pottery from southern France (one-fourth actual size).

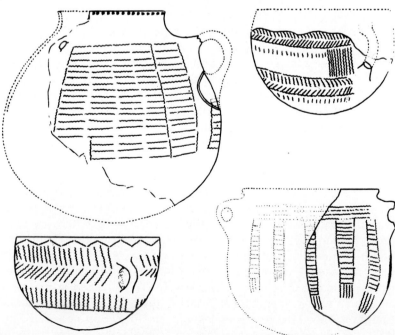

West until the emergence of the Chassean culture in the following millennium. The Chasseans were fully fledged mixed farmers who opened up thousands of acres of hitherto unexploited territory to agriculture (Whittle, 1985).

By this time, a series of fishing villages were thriving on the shores of the Swiss lakes, communities with close links to the Chassean (Lee, 1866; Muller-Beck, 1961). They were occupied by cattle and sheep farmers who cultivated barley and wheat as well as many minor crops, including cider apples and flax (used for textiles) (Figure 11.7). Their houses were built on the damp ground between the lake reed beds and the scrub brush of the valley behind. The first dwellings were small rectangular huts, but they eventually gave way to larger, two-room houses. Some villages grew to include between twenty-four and seventy-five houses clustered on the lakeshore, a density of population much the same as that of modern Swiss villages, which have approximately thirty households.

In the extreme northwest, food production was adopted comparatively late. From 8000 years ago through 6000 years ago, the newly isolated Mesolithic peoples of Britain developed with little or no significant contact with the continent. The earliest traces of pottery and forest clearance appeared soon after 6000 years ago, with well-documented cereal agriculture by 6300 years ago. The same processes may have operated here as in west Europe. Robin Dennell (1983) theorizes that European farmers did not cross the Channel and settle in Britain. Rather, Mesolithic peoples experienced population pressure about 6000 years ago, perhaps as a result of forest expansion due to warmer climate, and

FIGURE 11.7 Sample prehistoric stone axes mounted in deer antler handles from the Swiss lake dwellings, typical of those used by early farmers in Europe.

also because of population growth. Hunting became more difficult, so the people began clearing woodland to provide more animal forage and plant foods, and to make hunting more predictable. The people also increased their exploitation of marine resources, and seafaring techniques developed, leading to contacts with other coastal communities in Britain and on the continent. Eventually, Mesolithic populations in Britain became aware of new food resources like domestic cereals and sheep and acquired them. Ample open grassland was available for herding and cultivation in southern Britain. Within five centuries or so Mesolithic populations had transformed themselves into farmers with their own distinctive cultural traditions. Somewhat similar processes probably led to the adoption of agriculture and stock rearing among Mesolithic Scandinavians.

THE MEGALITHS

Early European farming societies were basically egalitarian, with the family, as the basic productive unit, at the center of a web of intricate kin ties and reciprocal social relationships that linked communities near and far, and tied people to the land of their ancestors. There was probably equal access to resources, with sufficient food being produced to feed individual families. In a real sense, the subsistence farming economy *was* society (Champion et al., 1984). In general, Early Neolithic burials in Europe do not reflect any social differentiation between individuals.

But there are signs of variation, notably in the intensity of trading activities through barter networks and in burial customs. A slow process of social change can be documented throughout Europe after 6000 years ago, moving toward greater emphasis on craft specialization and burial ritual, and the emergence of regional trading centers that controlled exchange networks, and perhaps ritual as well. The famous megalithic tombs of the Mediterranean and west Europe are one symbol of this trend toward social change.

As early as 6000 years ago, some French farmers were building large communal stone tombs, known to archaeologists as *megaliths* ("large stone" in Greek) (Figure 11.8). Megaliths are found as far north as Scandinavia, in Britain, Ireland, France, Spain, the western Mediterranean, Corsica, and Malta. For years, scholars thought that megaliths had originated in the eastern Mediterranean approximately 4500 years ago and spread westward into Spain with colonists from the Aegean, who had carried a custom of collective burial and their religion with them. Megalithic tombs were believed to have then been built in west Europe, witnesses to a lost faith perhaps spread by pilgrims, missionaries, or merchants. With their massive stones and large burial chambers, megaliths remained one of the mysteries of European prehistory (Daniel, 1973; C. Renfrew, 1967, 1973).

This popular and widely accepted hypothesis was badly weakened by C14 dates from France that turned out to be earlier than others from west Europe. Furthermore, new calibrated dates have placed Spanish megalithic sites and their associated culture as early as approximately 6000 years ago, much earlier than their alleged prototypes in the Aegean. Thus, megaliths were being built in

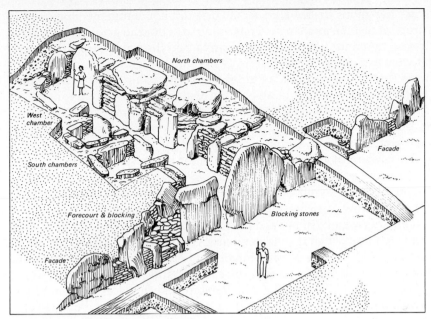

FIGURE 11.8 Interior of a megalithic chamber tomb in West Kennet, England, C14 dated to approximately 5500 years ago. (Piggott, 1965)

west Europe at least a millennium before massive funerary architecture became fashionable in the eastern Mediterranean. This remarkable freestanding architecture is a unique local European creation (P. Phillips, 1980).

What exactly were megaliths? Were they the surviving remains of a powerful religious cult that swept west Europe, or did they symbolize the emergence of new, more sophisticated political and social structures in the West? Colin Renfrew (1983) has argued that the tradition of communal burial developed in very early west European farming societies and that it is manifested by the famous long barrows of southern Britain (Figure 11.8), many of which had stone boulder, megalithic, interiors. The long barrows were fairly small structures, requiring not more than about 5,000 to 10,000 worker-hours to build (a figure equivalent to twenty men taking fifty days). Between 6000 and 5500 years ago, these barrows were associated with more elaborate monuments, among them enclosed earthworks (often called "causewayed camps"), which are known to have been protected by timber palisades. Recent excavations have shown that these camps were littered with human bones, many of them skeletons from which the flesh had weathered in the open. Perhaps these camps were places where the dead were exposed for months before their bones were deposited in nearby communal burials.

As time went on, the argument goes, burial ceremonies revolved around even larger monuments, the so-called henges, stone- and wood-built circles of which Stonehenge in southern Britain is the most famous (Figure 20.6, p. 480). In this sense, megaliths of all types formed a kind of settlement hierarchy on the prehistoric landscape, a hierarchy that may have reflected profound changes in European society.

Another ingenious theory argues that megalithic monuments appeared in west Europe at just the moment when farming took hold all across Europe. This final colonization must have had a major impact on the stable Mesolithic societies that were exploiting coastal resources along the Atlantic Ocean and North Sea shores from the Bay of Biscay in France to the Baltic. Indeed, Mesolithic stone tools have been found in association with some French megaliths. Ian Kinnes (1982) believes that megaliths first appeared in the margins of Neolithic society, along the Atlantic Coast, where competition with Mesolithic groups may have been most acute. Perhaps, he believes, the megaliths served as territorial markers, signs of ancestral ownership of the surrounding land.

Colin Renfrew and others have called megaliths the "tombs of the living," lasting humanly made symbols of the continuity of human life, as well as symbols of the continuity of ownership of land from one generation to the next. The annual round of religious rituals at places like Stonehenge reinforced this continuity, and, at a time when population densities were rising sharply, the megaliths associated with them became important symbols of political and social continuity. They also reinforced the political, economic, and spiritual power of those who supervised the building and worship at such places as Stonehenge. That such supervision was necessary is certain, for it has been estimated that Stonehenge required at least 30,000 worker-hours to complete. So the appearance of megaliths and the hierarchy of more elaborate stone and wooden monuments associated with them may have foreshadowed profound social changes in prehistoric Europe that came with the increasing use of bronze and other metals (Chippindale, 1983).

A complex set of processes governed the emergence of food production in temperate Europe, processes only rarely involving the movement of entire populations from one region to the next. Here, as in other parts of the world, one should think of agriculture not as a miracle invention, or in terms of conquest, but as yet another instance of how readily hunter-gatherers adapted to new opportunities and conditions. As is so often the case in prehistory, continuity was as important as change, but this continuity was born of inherent flexibility, an ability to adapt to new circumstances.

GUIDE TO FURTHER READING

Champion, T. G., et al. *Prehistoric Europe.* New York: Academic Press, 1984.
  An up-to-date summary of European prehistory, with a major emphasis on trade, subsistence, and social organization.

Clark, J. G. D. *Prehistoric Europe: The Economic Basis.* Palo Alto: Stanford University Press, 1952.
  The classic essay on prehistoric European economic life. Still of immense value to the general reader.

Dennell, Robin C. *European Economic Prehistory: A New Approach.* New York: Academic Press, 1983.
  An enjoyable essay on European prehistory that formed my ideas on this chapter. Strongly recommended for newcomers to the subject.

Phillips, Patricia. *The Prehistory of Europe.* Bloomington: Indiana University Press, 1980.
A synthesis of Old World prehistory that is a fundamental source on a key area of the world. A technical but clearly written account for the informed reader.

Renfrew, Colin. *Before Civilization.* New York: Knopf, 1973.
A well-written essay on recent advances in European prehistory that concentrates on the calibration of radiocarbon dating. Essential reading for any more-than-casual student of Old World archaeology.

Trump, David. *The Prehistory of the Mediterranean.* New Haven: Yale University Press, 1980.
Another synthesis of Old World prehistory that, like the Phillips text, is a fundamental source on a key area of the world. For the informed reader.

Whittle, Alastair. *Neolithic Europe: A Survey.* Cambridge: Cambridge University Press, 1985.
A summary of the European Neolithic for the more advanced reader.

Zvelebil, Marek (ed.). *Hunters in Transition.* Cambridge: Cambridge University Press, 1986.
A volume of articles that describe basic Mesolithic theory and analyze the Neolithic transition in various parts of Europe.

CHAPTER 12

Early Farmers of Africa

Preview

■ Some archaeologists believe that agriculture and animal domestication first took hold in the eastern Sahara about 10,000 years ago, among people who left the Nile Valley after catastrophic flooding some 12,000 years ago. Increasing aridity about 7000 years ago then caused some of these nomadic cattle herders and farmers to settle in the Nile Valley, where food production was well established by 7000 years ago.

■ The earliest Egyptian farmers probably had little need for irrigation agriculture, the introduction of which appears to have coincided with the political unification of Egypt approximately 5000 years ago.

■ The Sahara was sufficiently well watered to support cattle-herding peoples from approximately 7500 to 5000 years ago. With the desiccation of the desert, Saharan peoples moved southward into sub-Saharan Africa, where they domesticated summer rainfall crops like sorghum and millet.

■ Cattle-herding people were living in East Africa by 5000 years ago, and cattle may have been domesticated there much earlier. But agriculture and domesticated animals did not spread to tropical Africa as a whole until the advent of ironworking, approximately 2000 years ago.

FIGURE 12.1   The Nile, close to the First Cataract.

Chronological
Table F

Like the Tigris and Euphrates in Mesopotamia, the lower reaches of the Nile
River flow through wide areas of rich, easily cultivable floodplain soil. (See Figure 10.1, p. 276.) This context gave the Nile Valley the same potential of becoming a center of early agriculture and civilization as Iraq. But the Nile floodplain
is wider, with more predictable annual floodwaters, which were easier to control than those of the twin rivers. The Egyptians could water their highly productive fields very easily by modifying natural basins to retain floodwater
(Aldred, 1986; Fedden, 1977; Trigger, 1983). The Nile Valley was always an isolated oasis, a slash of green, fertile land flowing between desert bastions (Figure
12.1). There were intervals of higher rainfall, however, one of them between
11,000 and 8,000 years ago, when there was some runoff at the edges of the
valley. This would have made it possible for Neolithic farmers to cultivate the
margins of the gullies leading down from the desert. The Nile Valley floor itself
consisted for the most part of seasonally flooded natural basins that supported
grass and brushland. People lived on higher levees along the river, where trees
grew and settlements escaped the annual inundation.

HUNTER-GATHERERS ON THE NILE

During the last millennia of the Ice Age, the Nile Valley was a rich, diverse habitat, abounding in game of all sizes and in wild vegetable foods. Fish and waterfowl added to the bounty of resources. From about 15,000 years ago until perhaps as late as 6,500 years ago, a diverse population of hunter-gatherers exploited these resources. They are grouped under the name *Qadan culture* by archaeologists (J. D. Clark, 1971). The Qadan is best known from microlithic tools found on riverside campsites near the Nile. In the earlier stages of the Qadan, fishing and big-game hunting were important, but large numbers of grindstones and grinding equipment came from a few localities, which seems to show that gathering wild grains was significant to at least part of the economy. Some Qadan settlements were probably large and occupied for long periods. The dead were buried in cemeteries, in shallow pits covered with stone slabs. Some pits held two bodies. In six instances, small stone tools were embedded in the bones of these Qadan people, who must have met a violent end (Wendorf, 1968).

Other distinct cultural traditions are known to have prospered in the Nile Valley at this time. Around Kom Ombo, upstream of Qadan country, Stone Age hunter-gatherers lived on the banks of lagoons and flood channels of the Nile, seeking game in the riverside woodlands and on the plains overlooking the valley. They fished for catfish and perch in the swamps. Here, too, wild grasses were important in the economy from approximately 14,000 years ago (Wendorf and Schild, 1980).

AGRICULTURAL ORIGINS ON THE NILE

The Nile Valley is unusual in that its water supplies depend not on local rainfall but on annual floods from far upstream in Ethiopia. Thus, fluctuations in these inundations had a profound effect on the pattern of Holocene settlement along the Nile. A series of catastrophic floods about 12,000 years ago apparently brought an intensification of hunting, gathering, and fishing in the valley to a halt, delaying the development of food production along the Nile for as long as 2000 years.

For years, people assumed that cereal crops and domesticated animals were introduced into the Nile Valley from southwest Asia sometime after 10,000 years ago (Childe, 1952). In recent years, this viewpoint has been rejected. Fekri Hassan (1986) has spent many years studying climatic change in the Nile Valley and eastern Sahara. He believes that food production began very early in, of all places, the eastern Sahara Desert. During the Early Holocene, he argues, the Sahara was wetter than today, and the catastrophic Nile floods caused people living in the river valley to spill over onto the harsh, poorly watered desert plains. Those who remained alongside the Nile probably took advantage of the fish resources of the great river, while those who left the valley followed game animals onto the stunted grassland plains of the Sahara with no idea of the major climatic fluctuations that were to follow.

The areas that are now desert were, like all arid regions, very susceptible to cycles of higher and lower rainfall, resulting in major, sudden change in distributions of plants and animals. Hassan argues that these shifts in the Saharan environment led the people who preyed on the sparse desert fauna to manage the wild resources they hunted and gathered, especially wild oxen, which must have regular water supplies to survive. The human population was never large, and the people probably lived in small bands, subsisting off a wide variety of plant and game resources, at the same time engaging in some small-scale cattle herding. The very flexibility and mobility of hunter-gatherer life in these marginal lands probably made pastoralism adaptive. The people may have extended the distributions of stands of wild cereal grasses by deliberate cultivation as well. It is thought that some cattle bones found in the Egyptian part of the eastern Sahara are from domesticated beasts dating to between 10,000 and 8,000 years ago, a date for domesticated cattle far earlier than that from Greece (Chapter 10). Domesticated barley is known from the Nabta Playa site in the Western Desert and dates to about 8000 years ago (Wendorf et al., 1984).

Nabta Playa 8000 B.P.

While J. Desmond Clark (1971) originally argued that the valley was pre-adapted to agriculture, Hassan believes that agriculture was introduced into the Nile from neighboring desert regions as the climate grew progressively drier after 7000 years ago. The earliest dated Neolithic settlements from the Nile Valley, both from Egypt and the Sudan, date to between 6300 and 5300 years ago. Hassan believes that the nomadic peoples of the desert now included the fertile river valley in their wanderings, moving in and out of the desert as conditions warranted, as they do in the Sahel at the southern fringes of the Sahara today. These movements, he believes, were especially significant after 4500 years ago, when conditions became very arid indeed. This was also a time of exceptionally low Nile floods, so the sparse agricultural sites dating from early farming times are probably buried under many feet of later river alluvium. Hassan argues that irregular population movements involving small numbers of people continued for thousands of years and came into the valley from many desert regions. The result was considerable cultural diversity within the Nile Valley, resulting from both immigration and fusion with existing populations.

6300 B.P.

If Hassan's theory is correct, the Nile Valley supported a scatter of farming settlements as early as 7000 years ago, perhaps earlier. Many were probably little more than temporary camps of crude matting or reed shelters. Only a few have been excavated, among them one found on the shores of a former lake in the Fayum Depression to the west of the Nile Valley (Caton-Thompson and Gardner, 1934). The inhabitants lived at a simple subsistence level by fishing and hunting both crocodiles and hippopotamuses. They cultivated wheat and barley and kept both sheep and goats. The floodplain settlements were more like the village of Merimde near the Nile Delta. There a cluster of oval houses and shelters were built half underground and roofed with mud and sticks (Hoffman, 1979). An occupation mound 7 feet (2 m) high accumulated over 600 years from approximately 6130 B.P. Simple pottery, stone axes, flint arrowheads, and knives were in use. Agriculture and the cultivation of cereal crops are evidenced by grains stored in clay pots, baskets, and pits. Dogs, cattle, sheep or goats, and pigs were kept. Farming at a subsistence level was characteristic of large areas of the Nile floodplain for thousands of years (Hoffman, 1979).

Fayum 6000 to 4000 B.P.

Merimde 6900 to 6500 B.P.

Other farmers who flourished along the Upper Nile are known to us mainly from cemetery burials. Like their northern neighbors, they used bows and arrows in the chase, many tipped with finely flaked arrowheads. Emmer wheat and barley were cultivated, and cattle and small stock provided much of the meat. Settlements here were typified by mud-brick and transient architecture.

The dead, however, were buried with some ceremony — in linen shrouds and covered with skins. The women wore ivory combs and plaited their hair. This culture, named the *Badarian* after a village where the first settlements were found, is thought to have been broadly contemporary with Merimde (Butzer, 1976; Hays, 1984; Hoffman, 1979).

Badarian culture
5700 B.P.

The early farming communities of the Nile continued to use the forested riverbanks for settlement (Butzer, 1976; Trigger, 1968). Animals grazed in the flat grasslands of the plain for most of the year, and crops were planted on wet basin soils as the waters receded. Game was still abundant in the Nile Valley 6000 years ago; even so, the people ventured to the edge of the deserts in search of gazelles and other small animals. They buried their dead in huge cemeteries overlooking the Nile, where the graves would not take up valuable agricultural land.

The unification of Egypt into a single state took place approximately 5100 years ago. Agriculture was practiced for at least 2000 years before this event. The density of population was probably low enough that the people had no need of either government or government-regulated irrigation canals. They made use of natural floods and drainage basins to grow their crops. One authority has estimated that an average Nile flood would have allowed early Egyptian farmers to harvest grain over perhaps two-thirds of the floodplain of the Nile (Hamden, 1961). The first appearance of irrigation seems to have coincided with the unification of Egypt and is described in Chapter 17.

THE SAHARA

Many people think of the Sahara as a vast sand sea, one of the most desolate places on earth. But in fact the Sahara is a highly diverse, albeit dry, region that has undergone major climatic changes during the past 12,000 years. Before 8000 years ago, there were shallow lakes in the central and southern Sahara that supported hippopotamuses and many species of fish. Many prehistoric hunting camps have been found on these long-dry lakes (A. B. Smith, 1984). Similar hunter-gatherer groups flourished along the Nile in the Sudan.

After a short drying period around 7000 years ago, climatic conditions in the central and southern Sahara improved (Rognon, 1981). The lakes expanded and filled again. This time cattle herders camped by their shores. The earliest cattle bones come from a cave in southwest Libya dated to about 5000 B.P., but they may be as much as 7000 years old. Pastoralists were widespread in the central and southern Sahara during the fourth millennium B.C., and it seems certain that they were making use of wild cereal grasses and perhaps cultivating such tropical crops as sorghum. Opinions vary as to how domestic animals reached the Sahara. The most common hypothesis has goats and sheep being introduced to North Africa about 8000 years ago, with cattle domestication about a millennium later. It is thought that wild cattle in the Sahara were the source of local domestication.

The cattle herders had but the simplest of possessions, unsophisticated round-based pots and flaked and polished adzes. They also hunted with bow and arrow. The Saharan people left a remarkable record of their lives on the walls of caves deep in the desert. Wild animals, cattle, goats, humans, and scenes of daily life are preserved in a complicated jumble of artistic endeavor extending back perhaps to 7000 years ago (Lhote, 1959). The widespread distribution of pastoral sites of this period suggests that the Saharans were ranging their herds over widely separated summer and winter grazing grounds.

About 5500 years ago, climatic conditions deteriorated. The Sahara slowly became drier and lakes vanished. Rainfall rose in the interior of west Africa, and the northern limit of the tsetse fly belt moved south (this insect is endemic to much of tropical Africa and is fatal to cattle). So the herders shifted south, following the major river systems into savanna regions. By this time, the Saharan people were probably using domestic crops, experimenting with such summer rainfall crops as sorghum and millet as they moved out of areas where they could grow wheat, barley, and other Mediterranean crops (for a full discussion, see J. D. Clark, 1984).

SUB-SAHARAN AFRICA

At the end of Pleistocene times, the indigenous inhabitants of sub-Saharan Africa were already adapted to many kinds of specialized environment. Some lived by intensive fishing, others by gathering or hunting, depending on their environment. In a primitive way the techniques of food production may have already been employed on the fringes of the rain forests of west and central Africa, where the common use of such root plants as the African yam led people to recognize the advantages of growing their own food (J. D. Clark, 1984; M. Harris, 1968). Certainly the yam can easily be germinated by replanting its top. This primitive form of "vegeculture" may have been the economic tradition onto which the cultivation of summer rainfall cereal crops was grafted as it came into use south of the grassland areas on the Sahara's southern borders (Harlan, DeWet, and Stemler, 1976; McIntosh and McIntosh, 1981).

Vegeculture (plant manipulation)

The East African highlands are ideal cattle country and the home of such famous cattle-herding peoples as the Masai today. They were inhabited by scattered bands of hunter-gatherers living around mountains near the plains until about 5300 years ago, when the first cattle herders appeared. Their emergence may be connected with shifts in climatic zones that opened up the highlands to pastoral peoples for the first time (Ambrose, 1984). These cattle people may have moved between fixed settlements during the wet and dry seasons, living off hunting in the dry months and their own livestock and agriculture during the rains (Bower, 1984).

Stone Age cattle herds appeared in other parts of sub-Saharan Africa as well, in the grasslands south of the Sahara in west Africa and even at the extreme southern tip of Africa. These Khoikhoi people were still flourishing when Portuguese explorer Bartholomeu Dias rounded the Cape of Good Hope in A.D. 1488. The explorers who had dealings with them commented on their simple material culture and constantly nomadic lifeway, which was finely attuned to the seasonal Cape environment. They are known to have lived on the Cape for at least 2000 years (Elphick, 1977; R. Klein, 1984). It is not known how they reached their homeland. The Khoikhoi did not long survive European settlement in the seventeenth century, and their lifeway is extinct today.

Approximately 2000 years ago, with the arrival of ironworking, the practices of producing food and keeping domestic animals spread throughout the African continent (Phillipson, 1977). For thousands of years after the Near East had started to enjoy literate civilization, San hunter-gatherers continued to flourish on the rich savanna woodlands of east and southern Africa. Their environment was so rich that they had no incentive to take up the new economies, even if they were aware of them. Agriculture finally came to the savanna when widespread forest clearance was made easier by iron tools and tougher working edges, starting approximately 2000 years ago.

GUIDE TO FURTHER READING

Butzer, Karl. *Early Hydraulic Civilization in Egypt.* Chicago: University of Chicago Press, 1976.
    A fundamental source on Ancient Egyptian irrigation that has great relevance to this chapter.
Clark, J. Desmond, and Brandt, Steven A. (eds.). *From Hunters to Farmers.* Berkeley: University of California Press, 1984.
    A set of scholarly essays summarizing recent evidence for early agriculture in Africa. Excellent for specialists, but definitive.
Hoffman, Michael A. *Egypt Before the Pharaohs.* New York: Knopf, 1979.
    A fascinating study of prehistoric Egypt that not only recounts key discoveries but also recalls the archaeologists who made them. The first detailed account of this subject for many years, written for the general reader.
Oliver, Roland, and Fagan, Brian M. *Africa in the Iron Age.* Cambridge: Cambridge University Press, 1975.
    A general history of Africa from approximately 500 B.C. that covers much of the material in this chapter in a wider historical context.

CHRONOLOGICAL TABLE G

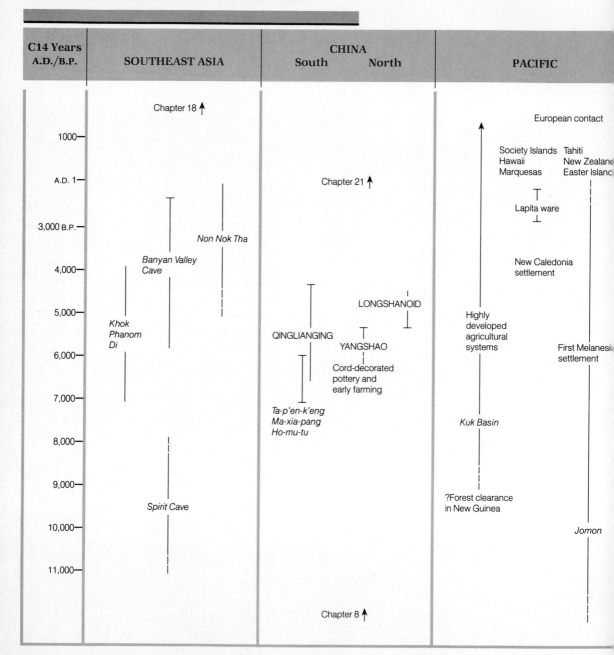

C14 Years A.D./B.P.	SOUTHEAST ASIA	CHINA South	North	PACIFIC

Chapter 18 ↑

European contact

1000—

Society Islands   Tahiti
Hawaii   New Zealand
Marquesas   Easter Island

A.D. 1—   Chapter 21 ↑

Lapita ware

3,000 B.P.—

Non Nok Tha

New Caledonia
settlement

4,000—   *Banyan Valley
Cave*

LONGSHANOID

5,000—

*Khok
Phanom
Di*   QINGLIANGING

Highly
developed
agricultural
systems

First Melanesian
settlement

6,000—   YANGSHAO

Cord-decorated
pottery and
early farming

7,000—

*Ta-p'en-k'eng
Ma-xia-pang
Ho-mu-tu*

8,000—   Kuk Basin

9,000—

?Forest clearance
in New Guinea

10,000—   *Spirit Cave*

Jomon

11,000—

Chapter 8 ↑

CHAPTER 13

Asia: Rice, Roots, and Ocean Voyagers

Preview

- Southeast Asia is widely believed to have been an early center of root crop domestication. The archaeological evidence from Spirit Cave, Thailand, and other sites is still insufficient to establish whether people were hunting and gathering a broad spectrum of animal and vegetable foods 11,000 years ago or were deliberately planting some individual species.

- Rice was, and still is, a key cereal crop in Asia. Its origins are still not certain. Rice cultivation appeared at Khok Phanom Di in Thailand approximately 7000 years ago. The date of the earliest rice cultivation in China is unknown but may be as early. The widespread dispersal of rice cultivation in China is thought to be associated with the Longshanoid cultures, after 5000 years ago.

- The human settlement of the Pacific was dependent on Asian root crops. The Kuk Basin in New Guinea has yielded traces of forest clearance and drainage as early as 9000 years ago, with the cultivation of taro and yams probably beginning as early as 6000 years ago.

- The first settlement of Melanesia is believed to have been associated with the development of trading networks. First settlement may have occurred as early as 6000 years ago, with the widespread Lapita pottery tradition flourishing about 2000 years ago and being used as far east as Samoa.

- Polynesia was settled within the last 2500 years: the Marquesas were colonized approximately A.D. 400, Hawaii some 1350 years ago, and Easter Island approximately A.D. 500. The Polynesians were technologically in the Stone Age, but they developed powerful chiefdoms that were at the height of their power when the first Europeans arrived in the eighteenth century.

■ New Zealand was first colonized by Polynesians in A.D. 900 or so, but the introduction of the sweet potato led to rapid population buildup that coincided with the emergence of Maori culture approximately 600 years ago. The Maori developed a warlike society with constant competition for prime agricultural land.

Chronological Table G

Fifteen thousand years ago much of southeast Asia was inhabited by hunter-gatherers whose stone toolkits reveal remarkable uniformity over large areas of the mainland and islands (Bellwood, 1985). These stone assemblages do not necessarily reflect a stagnation of cultural innovation or a simple lifeway. Rather, it seems certain that the people were exploiting a broad range of game and vegetable foods (Glover, 1977).

15,000 to 8,000 B.P.

Very few scientific excavations have been made on sites that cover the period 15,000 to 8,000 years ago, when food production may have begun in this region (Gorman, 1969, 1971). The controversies about early food production in southeast Asia surround two questions:

- When did people first start to cultivate root crops?
- What are the origins of rice cultivation (rice being the vital staple cereal crop in much of Asia throughout later prehistory)?

EARLY FOOD PRODUCTION IN THAILAND

As Carl Sauer has pointed out (1952), the domestication of root crops is difficult to identify in the archaeological record at the best of times. The only way that one can deduce cultivation is by examination of vegetable remains found in excavations, comparing these finds with the modern flora and extrapolating modern uses of the flora into the past, on the assumption that use patterns have not changed.

Spirit Cave
11,000 to 9,000 B.P.

Chester Gorman's excavations at Spirit Cave in northeast Thailand took him to a limestone cave overlooking a small stream (see Figure 13.1). He found that the lowest levels of the site were formed more than 11,000 years ago (for a summary, see Bellwood, 1985). What he called Hoabhinian tools, including small flakes and choppers, came from these horizons, and it was clear that such tools were used for a long time. Gorman was able to identify quantities of seeds from the Hoabhinian levels. When botanists examined these finds, they found that the people had eaten almonds, betel nuts, broad beans, gourds, water chestnuts, peppers, and cucumbers. Douglas Yen of the Bishop Museum in Honolulu visited the area and collected modern floral specimens for comparative purposes (Yen, 1977). He even ate some of the wild foods himself. He noted that there were at least eight wild species of yam in the area and that the seeds found in Spirit Cave were from plants that can be collected in the wild and have a variety of dietary, medicinal, and other uses. The botanists had great difficulty in establishing whether the Spirit Cave seeds were domesticated or wild and in fact have produced no definite grounds for calling them deliberately planted.

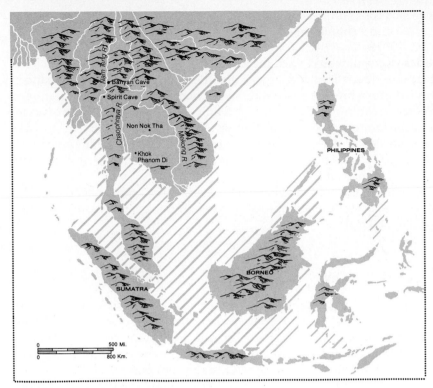

FIGURE 13.1 Southeast Asian sites mentioned in this chapter. Shaded areas show the extent of low sea levels during the Weichsel glaciation.

The Spirit Cave finds provide no firm evidence for domestication of plants as early as 11,000 years ago, but despite the uncertainty of the botanical evidence, Wilhelm Solheim (1971) and others have claimed that southeast Asia was a major center of early plant and animal domestication. There is certainly insufficient evidence from the few excavations in the area to make such a claim. However, there are indications of the following:

- There was a wide variety of yams and other potential domesticates in Thailand and elsewhere; these were exploited by hunter-gatherers at the end of the Pleistocene.
- In the case of yams, there were enough species present for people under demographic or other stress to experiment with hybridization if they wished.
- In view of these two factors, there is no reason to doubt that food production could have begun in this area quite independently from other regions.

As we have pointed out before, yam planting is very simple, and hunter-gatherers are well aware that deliberate cultivation is possible. The problem is to identify the factors that led people to deliberate experimentation with various plants. In the absence of firm archaeological evidence, we can speculate that primitive shifting agriculture, with a combination of diverse crops and some animal herding, may have had its origins in a broad spectrum of hunting and gathering, as it did in other regions of the world. In the final analysis, all that is needed for a culture to make the transition are some clearings at the edge of the forest and a simple digging stick, already used for gathering, to plant the crop (Yen, 1977).

Charles Higham, who studied the animal bones from Spirit Cave and other localities in northern Thailand, argues that the large range of species found in the sites indicate a broadly based hunting economy that focused on deer, pigs, and arboreal creatures such as monkeys (Higham, 1972). Perhaps the caves reflect only the hunting aspect of an otherwise agricultural economy; in any case, there was no sign of domestic animals in the collections. Chester Gorman believes that this broadly based hunting was a preadaptation to early animal domestication (Gorman, 1969, 1977).

The case for indigenous development of agriculture and animal domestication in southeast Asia is still unproven, although there is no reason to believe that it did not take place.

RICE CULTIVATION

Rice is one of the world's staple crops, yet surprisingly little is known about its origins (Bellwood, 1985). It was certainly one of the earliest plants to be domesticated in the northern parts of southeast Asia and southern China. Botanists believe that the rices and millets ancestral to the present domesticated species radiated from perennial ancestors around the eastern borders of the Himalaya Mountains at the end of the Ice Age (Whyte, 1983). There is fairly general agreement that the wild annual ancestor of modern cultivated rice was first domesticated somewhere between northeast India, northern southeast Asia, and southern China (Chang, 1986). The initial cultivation of rice is thought to have taken place in an alluvial swamp area where there was plenty of water to stimulate cereal growth. Perhaps this cultivation occurred under conditions where seasonal flooding made field preparation a far from burdensome task (Bellwood, 1985). Such conditions could have been found on the Ganges Plain in India, in northern Thailand, and in China's lower Yangtze Valley, where the earliest records of cultivated rices are found, outside the modern range of wild rice, as early as 7000 years ago.

Peter Bellwood (1985) hypothesizes that a sedentary lifeway based on the gathering of wild rice developed in areas like this at the beginning of the Holocene, with systematic cultivation resulting from a response to population growth, climatic change, or some other stress. Kwang-Chih Chang (1986) believes that truly domesticated rice first developed in southern China, where cooler weather and a shorter growing season exerted greater selection pressure on the early cultivated cereals and made them more dependent on human care. These ideas are based on the most inadequate of evidence, and we may learn that rice was domesticated in several different areas by 7000 years ago, perhaps considerably earlier.

Evidence for early rice cultivation in southeast Asia is still very sketchy. The material culture of the Spirit Cave people shows a distinct change after about 9000 years ago. From then until approximately 7600 years ago, the inhabitants began to use adzes, pottery, and slate knives. The knives strongly resemble later artifacts used for rice cultivation in parts of Indonesia and could be interpreted as a suggestion that cereals were cultivated near the site — but this is pure speculation.

By 8500 years ago, people were moving from the hills onto river plains and into lowland areas. River plains were the best places for the intensive cultivation and simple irrigation needed to grow rice. Crop yields, far superior to those from small highland root crop gardens, were ample and easily obtained. But whether this supposed population movement was associated with the beginnings of rice cultivation is a matter of conjecture.

Charles Higham (1984a; 1988) has excavated an early rice farming community at Khok Phanom Di in Thailand, a settlement that was close to coastal mangrove swamps between 7000 and 4000 years ago but is now over 12 miles (19.3 km) from the seashore. The site covers 12.3 acres (5 ha), is 39 feet (12 m) deep, and contains rice specimens and other evidence of agriculture. Higham hypothesizes that the inhabitants of the coastal plains took up wild rice cultivation as sea levels rose, inundating the game and woodland resources of the fertile shoreline. Other rice specimens come from Banyan Valley Cave in northern Thailand and Non Nok Tha, a low mound on a Mekong River tributary in the same general area (Bayard, 1970, 1972). Gorman found rice husks in Banyan levels dating to between 7500 B.P. and A.D. 800, none of which the botanical experts could positively identify as fully domesticated. Experiments with milling stones showed that the husks had been ground by a quite different method from that used by modern rice farmers in the area. Yen, whose studies of rice can surely be described as comprehensive, speculates that the Banyan finds are the result of a form of gathering plus selective cultivation of wild rice — a stage in the gradual domestication of the cereal. There are many wild species in the region, several of which could have been candidates for cultivation.

Non Nok Tha may have been occupied before 5000 to 4000 years ago, but it was abandoned at some time before 2000 years ago. (The chronology is controversial.) The excavators found traces of rice in the form of grain impressions on clay pots in the lowest levels. They point out that the site dates to the time when the lowlands were already settled and argue that this means that the rice was probably cultivated. Bones of domesticated cattle came from the same site. The inhabitants were sedentary farmers depending on rice and cattle for most of their diet. Hunting and gathering were less important than in earlier millennia, when highland sites were occupied all year.

Rice cultivation has become the major cereal crop agriculture of the world, but its origins are still uncertain. Southeast Asia did not suffer from the drastic climatic charges of northern latitudes. No prolonged droughts or major vegetational changes altered the pattern of human settlement in this region. Only dramatic rises in low sea levels altered the geography and environment of southeast Asia, creating islands from dry land and reducing the amount of coastal floodplain available to hunters and gatherers. Conceivably, these major changes in coastline and available land surface were among many factors that moved the inhabitants of southeast Asia to experiment with plants and domestic animals.

Khok Phanom Di
7,000 to 4,000 B.P.

Non Nok Tha
5000 B.P. to A.D. 1

EARLY FARMING IN CHINA

"In the wealth of its species and in the extent of the genus and species potential of its cultivated plants, China is conspicuous among other centers of origin of plant forms." Thus wrote the great Russian botanist N. I. Vavilov more than thirty years ago (Vavilov, 1951). Like the archaeology of early agriculture in southeast Asia, that of China is still in its infancy, but agriculture seems to have appeared separately in three major areas of China: the southern coastal, the eastern coastal, and the north (Keightley, 1983).

Southern and Eastern China

No one knows when agriculture first began in southern China, but Chang (1986) hypothesizes that it may have begun as early as 12,000 years ago with the cultivation of roots and tubers. It is possible that the broad spectrum of ways of exploiting wild vegetable foods in southeast Asia may have been practiced in southern China too.

For much of Postglacial times, the Chinese environment was warmer and wetter than today. These conditions meant that forests were widespread at lower elevations. Lakes were larger, and many waterside locations offered environments with plentiful animal and plant resources (for details, see Chang, 1986). These local areas of rich diversity were probably a key to early experiments with food production, just as they were elsewhere in the world.

10,000 B.P.

Some ill-defined Upper Paleolithic stone industries record the presence of hunter-gatherer societies throughout China immediately before 10,000 years ago; these peoples were probably the first to experiment with cultivation and animal domestication. Unfortunately, their lifeways are virtually unknown to us.

Early food production appears to have developed in many regions of China, regions that were to interact with one another throughout later prehistory. The Lake T'ai-hu region of the lower Yangtze Valley east of Shanghai is one such area, a lacustrine environment with a wealth of plant and aquatic resources, and abundant freshwater vegetation that could be not only exploited but deliberately cultivated as well. More than a hundred early farming sites are known from this region, of which at least twenty have been excavated. Wang Tsun-kuo divides the Lake T'ai-hu sites into three phases, the earliest two dating to be-

7000 to 5000 B.P.

tween about 7000 and 5000 years ago (for full discussion, see Chang, 1986).

The earliest Lake T'ai-hu "Ma-xia-pang" sites occur on slightly higher ground or artificial mounds near rivers and ponds. The people lived in rectangular houses built of timber with carefully fashioned mortise and tenon joints and sand, shell, or clay floors. The people grew rice and a plant named the water caltrop, as well as bottle gourds. They used domesticated dogs, water buffalo, and pigs, hunting a wide variety of mammals, birds, and fish. Wood, bamboo, antler, and bone served to manufacture arrowheads, trowels, needles, and many other artifacts. Stone-bladed adzes and axes were used for woodworking, while animal-shoulder-bladed hoes turned the soil. The people were skilled potters and expert farmers, whose economy depended heavily on raising annual crops of sun-loving aquatic plants that grow naturally in marshes and lakes. These crops, species like lotus seed and water chestnut, were raised in rotation with rice. Later phases of this distinctive and well-established farming culture witnessed much greater sophistication in pottery forms and considerable elaboration of material culture.

Parallel farming cultures are known from other parts of southern China, where rice cultivation was well established at least 7000 years ago. One such contemporary culture was the Ho-mu-tu, south of Shanghai, dating to about the same period as Ma-xia-pang. Ho-mu-tu itself lies in a marshy area and was once surrounded by forests and ponds and a great diversity of natural resources. Four cultural layers have been radiocarbon dated to between about 7000 and 6000 years ago, all of them from wooden pile dwellings on the damp shores of a lake. This remarkable site has yielded beautifully mortise-and-tenon-joined building planks, as well as bone hoes and coarse black pots decorated with cord impressions. This is ideal rice-growing country, and it was hardly surprising to find abundant rice in the site, as well as the remains of bottle gourds and numerous wild vegetable foods. The Ho-mu-tu people were skilled hunters who kept water buffalo, pigs, and dogs. Ho-mu-tu was roughly contemporary with Khok Phanom Di in Thailand, and the cord-decorated pottery made by the Ho-mu-tu people is widespread in southern China, as well as in Taiwan, southeast Asia, and Japan. Ho-mu-tu c. 7000 to 6000 B.P.

Many other early farming traditions are known to have emerged in southern China after 7000 years ago (for details, see Chang, 1986). Many scholars think of the monsoon areas of southeast Asia as a nuclear area for early food production, all the way from southeast India to mainland China and the offshore islands of southeast Asia. Much of the earliest agricultural development may be associated with the widely distributed cord-decorated pottery traditions found in Ho-mu-tu and other mainland sites. Offshore, the Ta-p'en-k'eng culture of Taiwan is one of the better known of early farming traditions, a culture of people who lived close to lakes and rivers. As early as 7000 years ago, the Ta-p'en-k'eng people were engaged in intensive fishing and shellfish collecting, as well as hunting and foraging. Chang (1986) believes they may have been gardening as well. It is likely that this is but one of many cord-decorated cultural traditions that flourished over this vast area in the millennia after the first development of agriculture. Ta-p'en-k'eng 7000 B.P.

By 5000 years ago, much more sophisticated agricultural societies were flourishing on the Yangtze River and farther afield (Chang, 1986). The archaeology of these traditions is known primarily from cemetery excavations that show slow changes in grave goods (Pearson, 1981). The earliest graves indicate few social differentiations, but later sepulchers show not only a much wider variety of artifacts — pottery, bone and stone tools, jade objects, and other ornaments — but an increase in the number of elaborately adorned burials. Richard Pearson, who has analyzed several cemeteries, argues that they demonstrate an increase in concentration of wealth, a trend toward ranked societies, and a shift in the relative importance of males at the expense of females; the latter trend may be associated with the development of more intensive agriculture, an activity in which males are valued for their major roles in cultivation and production of food and manual labor is carried out by women, when land is plentiful and shifting cultivation is the rule of the day.

Northern China

The earliest farming traditions of the south are represented by the widespread cord-decorated pottery cultures that date to before 7000 years ago. Another set of early farming traditions emerged in the north, either independently or as a result of interaction with the south (Chang, 1986).

Northern Chinese agriculture has one great contrast with that of the south: It is based heavily on cereals and seeded plants. The first northern agricultural communities were sited in the central regions of the Yellow River Valley (Figure 13.2). The area is a small basin, forming a border between the wooded western highlands and the swampy lowlands to the east. Pollen analysis has provided evidence for a prolonged period of warmer climate from approximately 8000 to 4000 years ago, when favorable rainfall patterns and greater warmth made this nuclear area a fine place for agriculture (Ho, 1969).

During the glaciations of the Pleistocene, loess soils were formed over a wide area of the north. The fine, soft-textured earth was both homogeneous and porous and could be tilled by simple digging sticks. Because of the concentrated summer rainfall, cereal crops, the key to agriculture in this region, could be grown successfully. The indigenous plants available for domestication included the wild ancestors of foxtail millet, broom-corn millet, sorghum, hemp, and the mulberry. Ancient Chinese farmers developed their own cultivation techniques, which persisted for thousands of years before irrigation was developed. Although irrigation gradually became the basis of the agricultural economies of

FIGURE 13.2 Early Chinese farming cultures, with names of three major local variants shown. Yangshao sites occur both within the northern shaded area and outside it. Southern sites of corded pottery are found in the Kwangtung, Fukien, and Taiwan areas.

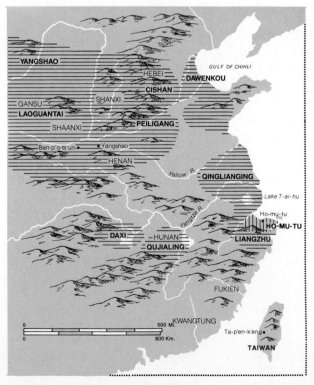

Egypt, the Indus Valley, and Mesopotamia, it was not important in northern China until much later (Ho, 1969).

The earliest millennia of northern Chinese agriculture are still a blank on the archaeological map. Two hypotheses are possible. We can assume that the inhabitants of the Yellow River region passed through a long phase of experimental cultivation and intensive exploitation of the indigenous flora before developing their own distinctive agricultural techniques, or we can assume that food production was developed farther south in China and adopted later in the north. Neither hypothesis can be tested with the available evidence. It is known that early farming villages were associated with coarse, cord-marked pottery found on the banks of the Yellow River in western Henan province. Perhaps these vessels are related to the cord-decorated pottery traditions of southern China, southeast Asia, and Taiwan.

Three early agricultural traditions have been identified in northern and central China, each of them dating to about 7000 years ago: the Cishan, Peiligang, and Laoguantai (Figure 13.2) (Chang, 1986). They share certain features: the keeping of dogs and pigs and the cultivation of foxtail millet. The villagers built semisubterranean houses, dug large storage pits, and relied on hunting and gathering as well as cultivation.

Early farming 7000 B.P. and earlier

The middle reaches of the Yellow River have yielded the Yangshao culture, which dates to before 7000 to about 5200 years ago (Chang, 1986). Similar villages have been found over much of the Yellow River Basin, an area as large as the early centers of agriculture in Egypt and Mesopotamia.

Yangshao 7000 to 5200 B.P.

Many Yangshao villages were undefended settlements built on ridges overlooking the floodplains, situated to avoid flooding or to allow maximal use of floodplain soils. The villagers lived in fairly substantial round or oblong houses partly sunk into the ground. Yangshao houses had mud-plastered walls, timber frames, and steep roofs (Figure 13.3). Usually there were cemeteries outside the villages. Sometimes the villages had a special area for pottery kilns, where the

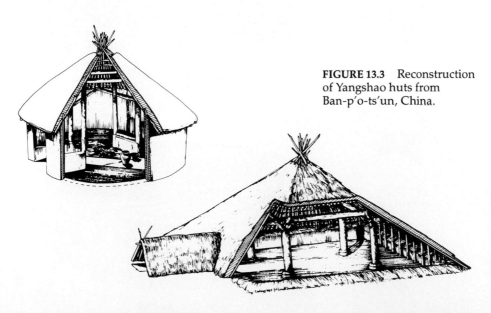

FIGURE 13.3 Reconstruction of Yangshao huts from Ban-p'o-ts'un, China.

characteristic Yangshao painted funerary vessels favored by the households were manufactured.

Some Yangshao people moved their settlements regularly but returned to the same sites again and again. Using hoes and digging sticks, they cultivated fox-tail millet as a staple crop. Simple dry-land slash-and-burn farming probably supplemented riverside gardens. Irrigation may have been practiced as early as 6000 years ago, however. Dogs and pigs were fully domesticated. Cattle, sheep, and goats were less common. Hunting and gathering were still significant, as was fishing, for which hooks and spears were employed.

Each Yangshao village was a self-contained community, of which thousands flourished in the river valleys of northern China. The Yangshao farmers were distributed over a comparatively limited part of northern China, from eastern Gansu in the west to the Yellow River and northwestern Henan in the east. There were other local variants such as Dawenkou and Qingliangang (Figure 13.2) (Chang, 1986). By 5000 years ago, the features of a characteristic, and thoroughly Chinese, culture was already clear. The earliest Chinese farmers had developed a distinctive naturalistic art style (Figure 13.4). The unique Chinese style of cooking with steam is attested by the discovery of cooking pots identical to later specialized cooking vessels. Jade was worked; hemp was used for making fabrics; skilled basketry was practiced; even the Chinese language may have roots in Yangshao. There can be little doubt of the indigenous origins of Chinese cereal agriculture, although, theoretically, long-established trade

FIGURE 13.4 Yangshao pottery from Ban-po, China (approximately one-fourth actual size). The fish motifs often used to decorate Yangshao pottery can be clearly seen (other motifs are drawn separately).

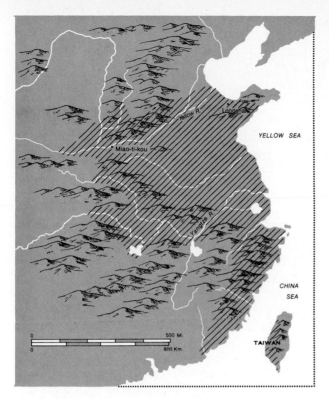

FIGURE 13.5 Approximate distribution of later farming cultures in China (shaded area).

routes to the West could have brought new ideas, including some crops, especially to the Far East, in later millennia.

The Yangshao culture itself had a relatively restricted distribution in northern China, centered on the Yellow River Valley. The expansion of the Yangshao was largely confined to gradual taking up of land by villages that split off from the larger settlements and needed new gardens. Still, the success of the agricultural adaptation led in part to population increases and greater elaboration of material culture, resulting in the evolution of more complex farming cultures, some concentration of wealth in privileged hands, and more intensive food production. Inevitably, too, farming peoples in both the north and the south spread into hitherto uncultivated areas, taking up new lands (Figure 13.5). Soon many regional variations of peasant farming culture were flourishing throughout China. The village settlements follow a pattern of river valleys and seacoasts, each regional variant connected to others by a network of waterways. The development of food production in China was a long process that occurred at much the same time throughout the land, with people adapting their crops and farming techniques to local conditions.

The typical later (Longshanoid) farming settlement — insofar as it is possible to generalize — was larger than that of the Yangshao. The settled, permanent villages were often protected by earthen walls. Millet seems to have been a staple crop in the north, while domestic cattle, sheep, and goats, and perhaps the horse were added to the economy. Hunting and gathering as well as fishing were locally important. The economy changed but little from earlier times, ex-

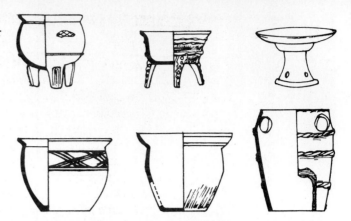

FIGURE 13.6 Some typical Longshanoid vessels used for cooking and other purposes, from Miao-ti-kou, China (scale not recorded).

cept for increased productivity, some evidence of better organization of village life (witness the communally built walls), and the addition of rice to the crops grown. Remains of rice grains have been found in later northern villages, giving reason to believe that rice cultivation spread into northern China from the south, where fertile floodplains with their lush water meadows provided an effective environment for rice growing. The introduction of rice to the north would have reduced dependence on dry agriculture and, presumably, led to the use of irrigation and modification of agricultural technology.

These farmers are thought to have been one of the groups responsible for the rapid spread of rice cultivation not only through the mainland but on the offshore islands of southeast Asia and far into the Pacific. Certainly, their more intensive agriculture, substantial settlements, and more elaborate material culture were among the roots of Chinese civilization (Figure 13.6).

JOMON AND EARLY AGRICULTURE IN JAPAN

Jomon tradition
12,500 to 2,300 B.P.

As we learned in Chapter 6, the Jomon people of Japan were using pottery as early as 12,500 years ago, living near coasts and lakeshores, and exploiting a wide range of game, vegetable foods, and shellfish (Ikawa-Smith, 1980). More than 10,000 Jomon sites are known, most of them from Honshu in central Japan. All are linked by a common cultural tradition that lasted for thousands of years, but there were probably different ethnic groups, who perhaps spoke different languages and adapted to diverse environments. The Jomon people hunted deer and other game with bows and arrows, collected thousands of shellfish, mainly in the spring, and fished much of the year. At first they caught all types of fish, but as time went on they concentrated on a few carefully selected species, inshore and lake fish as well as deepwater forms such as the bonito and tuna. Above all their diet depended heavily on wild vegetable foods such as acorns, nuts, and edible seeds. They lived in relatively sedentary settlements, perhaps because of carefully scheduled seasonal hunting, gathering, and fishing activities. Others believe that they supplemented these activities with cultivation of root crops, cereals, or simply by careful management of nut trees. The evidence for agriculture is still sketchy, but it seems possible that the

FIGURE 13.7 Jomon gray-bodied molded jar, of conical form with loop handles and decorated with combwork.

Jomon people flourished by developing an elaborate technology for processing and storing huge stocks of nuts, an activity they may have combined with cultivation of milletlike plants.

The Jomon tradition lasted from as early as 12,000 years ago until as late as 2,300 years ago. During this period, the focus of settlement shifted from the coasts to central Honshu and to the northern shores of Japan. By 7000 years ago, the inhabitants of Honshu were enjoying an elaborate material culture, including finely made ritual clay pots adorned with intricate decorations (Figure 13.7). The people often lived not in the caves and simple pit houses of earlier times but in large clusters of wooden houses with elaborate hearths. After 5000 years ago, the climate began to cool, overpopulation may have strained the carrying capacity of arable land, and clearance of natural vegetation affected hunting activities. Hence, the population declined and the major centers of Jomon occupation moved toward the coasts. In the south, the inhabitants of Kyushu took up rice and barley cultivation after 3000 years ago (for a lengthy discussion, see Akazawa, 1982).

The basis for what was to become traditional Japanese society was formed during the Yayoi period, which began after 2300 years ago, when new crops and technologies spread through the islands. Japan was unified into a single state in approximately A.D. 600, by which time complex, stratified societies were commonplace throughout the archipelago.

Yayoi **2300 B.P.**

Unification
A.D. 600

AGRICULTURE IN ISLAND SOUTHEAST ASIA

Peter Bellwood (1985) believes that the first stages of food production in island southeast Asia involved the swamp cultivation of rice at least 6500 years ago. As populations rose slowly, people began dry farming of rice, millet, and other

6500 B.P.

plants where the rains were relatively predictable. After about 4500 years ago, food production expanded into the equatorial regions of island southeast Asia, where people lived in damp, often densely forested environments. There they could not always clear land completely or burn it off. So they may have developed cultivation systems that required less forest clearance, with greater emphasis on fruit trees like bananas and root crops like taro and yams. Agricultural systems of this type are widespread in parts of Indonesia and on islands in Melanesia in the Pacific. These systems spread throughout island southeast Asia, and all over the Pacific islands, after 4500 years ago.

Agriculture based on fruit trees and root crops may have developed independently in New Guinea, where taro is grown in naturally rich soils or as a first crop in newly cleared forest gardens. The older New Guinea crops include both taro and yams, cultivated at higher elevations. Today, they are combined with the sweet potato, an American cultigen introduced relatively recently that allows agriculture at lower altitudes and far greater crop yield.

Startling evidence for early forest clearance is reported from raised coastlines on the Huon Peninsula in New Guinea, where large polished stone axes may date to more than 40,000 years ago, but unfortunately this discovery is still largely unpublished (Groube et al., 1986). Inland, Jack Golson, J. Peter White, and others have researched early agriculture in the New Guinea highlands using both pollen analysis and the study of old irrigation channels to amplify the archaeological record (Allen, 1969; Golson, 1977). There are traces, at approximately 9000 years ago, of deliberate diversion of river water in the Kuk Basin, which have been interpreted to mean that the people were cultivating taro or yams at a very early date. The evidence is still uncertain, although signs of increased erosion in the area may be the result of forest clearance for taro or yam gardens, or, possibly, for the deliberate growing of indigenous New Guinea plants (White and O'Connell, 1982).

By 6000 to 5500 years ago, much more organized agricultural works are found in the Kuk Basin. There is pollen evidence for quite extensive forest clearance in the general area. These works may have been created for yam and taro crops, while indigenous plants were grown on the better drained soils between the channel banks. After 4000 years ago, the first highly developed drainage systems occurred in the area, a sign that a much more intensive agriculture was expanding. After 2500 years ago, the people depended more and more heavily on dry and wet agriculture, for the forest resources they had relied on were replaced by an environment that had been altered permanently by human activity. A slow population growth would have resulted eventually in the taking up of uncleared land. After that was exhausted, the only option would have been to shorten the fallow periods on cleared gardens — something which, if taro was the crop, would have resulted in lower crop yields.

The archaeological and pollen analysis investigations of Golson and others have produced firm evidence for sedentism, forest clearance, stone agricultural tools, and water-control techniques in the New Guinea highlands by 6000 to 5000 years ago. What is uncertain, however, is the means by which food production began in New Guinea. Was it developed locally with introduced plants after the local hunter-gatherers had manipulated indigenous plants for centuries? Or did the people manipulate local plants as a result of adopting a few introduced crops first? Whatever the answer to these questions, it appears that the New Guinea highlands were an area where people created an artificial garden environment as a result of a long period of experimentation, in which they were raising plants *within* their natural environment. By exploiting a wide range of tropical animals and plants, the people may have become more sedentary and later might have started to plant small plots of root crops; ultimately, they would have intensified their food production until they modified their environment beyond recognition. This hypothetical model for early agriculture in New Guinea may serve as a possible model for other tropical areas in Asia as well.

AGRICULTURE IN THE PACIFIC ISLANDS

The origins of the peoples of the Pacific islands have fascinated scientists since the eighteenth century (Figure 13.8) (Moorehead, 1966), but most authorities now look to southeast Asia for the origins of the Melanesians and Polynesians. They point out that settlement of the offshore islands depended on the successful cultivation of root crops such as taro and the yam, as well as breadfruit, coconuts, and sugarcane. Chickens, dogs, and pigs were also valued as food and

FIGURE 13.8   Map of Pacific sites. Shading shows distribution of Lapita pottery.

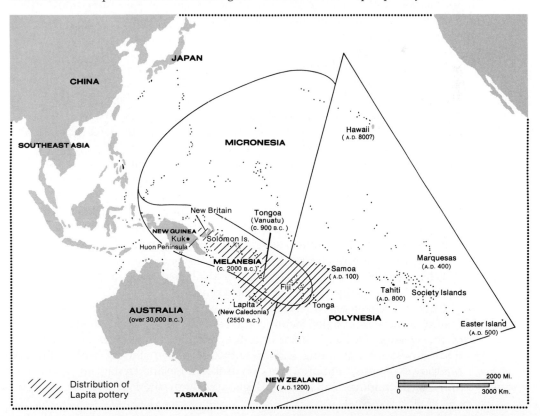

were domesticated in Asia before being introduced to the Pacific. Why did these foods have to be established in the diets and farming repertoires of the island settlers? Small animals such as pigs and chickens could readily have been carried from island to island in canoes, as could easily germinating root plants such as the yam. Both food sources allowed a sizable population to spread to many hundreds of small islands separated by miles of open water.

The Pacific islanders show no features attributable to American Indian stock. Their physical attributes had probably stabilized before any cultivators left the Asian mainland. Their languages are similar to Thai and other southeast Asian dialects and bear no resemblance to native American speech. Artifacts such as ground and polished axes and adzes, shell fish hooks, and canoes can be paralleled generally on the western shores of the Pacific.

The first settlement of the Pacific islands is closely connected with the early cultivation of yams, and especially of taro. As we pointed out earlier in this chapter, taro and yams were probably domesticated in southeast Asia before the development of rice cultivation, but exactly when and where they were first grown is unknown. In all probability, there were several centers of early domestication within southeast Asia.

HOW WAS THE PACIFIC SETTLED?

Today, the Pacific island groups are divided culturally into three major areas: Polynesia, Micronesia, and Melanesia (Figure 13.8). These cultural divisions are entirely valid in the twentieth century but gradually lose their validity as we move back into the more remote past (Bellwood, 1987a; Kirch, 1982). People have tended to think that the Pacific was settled in a series of fast-moving, dramatic migrations that took adventurous canoers into the farthest recesses of the ocean in a few short centuries. Thus, they argue, the cultural differences between the islands have been present since the earliest times. However, archaeological excavations have painted a very different picture, of a gradual and highly complex process of settlement from west to east. This process began soon after the end of the Ice Age and continued right into the present millennium. As immigrants moved ever farther out into the Pacific, they settled islands that were more and more isolated, and sometimes biotically more impoverished, so they had to adapt to new conditions, often quite different from those in their homelands. It would appear, then, that the diverse cultural patterns of the Pacific islanders developed over many centuries of adaptation to isolated environments (Terrell, 1986).

Why were the Pacific islands settled at all? Here archaeologists and anthropologists have indulged in an orgy of speculation.

Current archaeological research in lowland and island Melanesia points to maritime trade as a major factor in the settlement of the hundreds of islands of the western Pacific. The social and economic complexities of Melanesian trading systems have long excited anthropologists, starting with Bronislaw Malinowski, whose immortal work on Trobriand island trading still forms part of the basic training of all anthropologists (Malinowski, 1922). It is now known that related trading systems link all parts of coastal New Guinea and much of Melanesia. Although Malinowski concentrated on the ceremonial aspects of the trade, these networks carried an enormous diversity of everyday and exotic goods and commodities ranging from foodstuffs to manufactured items. Anthropologists have shown that these trade networks circulated commodities in huge rings that were reciprocal and self-perpetuating. Concerned as they are with material culture and technology, archaeologists have begun to look closely at this trade and the objects carried by it as a means for interpreting the archaeological record of early settlement (Allen, 1977).

Most long-distance trade was conducted by intermediaries or specialist merchants who traveled in sea-going canoes. They made their living by trading food surpluses for manufactured goods. The navigational abilities of the Pacific islanders have long been the subject of vigorous academic controversy, much of which, however, has now been dispelled by some compelling studies of indigenous navigational techniques; these studies were done by anthropologists and practical small-boat seafarers. One school of thought argued that long-distance voyages by early islanders were one-way accidental trips, when canoes were blown out to sea (Sharp, 1957). Early navigators were helpless, this school argued, to counteract ocean currents. Their views have been sharply challenged by those who have studied the well-developed maritime technology of the Polynesians (Vadya, 1959). They point out that nearly all the long trips attributed to the Polynesians were from north to south, which involved simple dead-reckoning calculations and an elementary way of measuring latitude from the stars. Anthropologist Ben Finney (1967) made detailed studies of Polynesian canoes and navigational techniques; his findings support a notion of deliberate one-way voyages, sparked as much by necessity — drought or warfare — as by restless adventure. Evidence for the carrying of women, animals of both sexes, and plants for propagation, however, shows that colonization was the deliberate aim.

Amateur seaman David Lewis (1972) completed a remarkable study of Polynesian navigation, voyaging under prehistoric conditions and accumulating navigators' lore from surviving practitioners of the art. He found that navigators were a respected and close-knit group. Young apprentices learned their skills over many years of making passages and from orally transmitted knowledge about the stars and the oceans accumulated by generations of navigators. The navigational techniques used the angles of rising and setting stars, the trend of ocean swells, and the myriad inconspicuous phenomena that indicate the general direction and distance of small islands. The navigators were perfectly capable of voyaging over long stretches of open water, and their geographic knowledge was astonishing. They had no need for the compass or other modern aids, and their landfalls were accurate. Lewis's findings confirm those of Finney and others who believe that deliberate voyages colonized even remote islands.

By looking at oral traditions, archaeological excavations, and some linguistic data, A. Pawley and R. C. Green have dated the expansion of farming peoples into island Melanesia to approximately 6000 years ago and as far as New Caledonia to at least 4000 years ago (Bellwood, 1987a; Green, 1979; Jennings,

Melanesia
6000 to 4000 B.P.

FIGURE 13.9 Lapita pottery from Melanesia.

Lapita ware
1600 B.C. to A.D. 1

1979). These settlers are thought to have introduced agriculture, domesticated animals, and pottery to Melanesia. A later manifestation of this expansion is associated with a characteristic pottery style known as Lapita (Groube, 1971; Jennings, 1979). This is seen as a specialized invention that spread widely through the islands when the double-hulled canoe came into use. This canoe was part of the evolution, we are told, of efficient trading networks that were maintained by regular two-way voyages over distances up to 372 miles (600 km). Obsidian trade was conducted through these networks and has been identified by using trace elements in the raw material to track rocks from the eastern Solomon Islands to a source in New Britain (Bellwood, 1978, 1979). Some people believe that the makers of Lapita pottery were traders and seafarers, but so little is known about them that this is probably a premature hypothesis. Certainly, trade played an important role in the colonization of Melanesia.

Lapita pottery itself was decorated with impressed designs and made of clay tempered with shell (Figure 13.9). It is found from the Santa Cruz islands as far east as Vanuatu, Fiji, Tonga, and Samoa. It is generally dated to the last thousand years before Christ, but seems to have gone out of fashion approximately 1800 years ago (Kirch, 1982).

Polynesia
150 B.C. to A.D. 800

From Melanesia canoes voyaged to Polynesia, taking the plants and domestic animals of their home islands with them. The antiquity of human settlement in Polynesia is approximately 2000 years (Jennings, 1979; Kirch, 1982). It is thought that the Polynesians originated in the Fiji area before the great elabora-

FIGURE 13.10 Bone fish hooks from Polynesia.

tion of Melanesian culture after A.D. 1. After a lengthy period of adaptation in western Polynesia, small groups began to settle the more remote islands. The Marquesas were settled by A.D. 400, and the Society Islands and Tahiti by A.D. 800 (Oliver, 1977). The first canoes arrived in Hawaii some 1350 years ago, and on Easter Island by A.D. 500 (Emory, 1972; Kirch, 1985). The human settlement of Polynesia seems to have taken approximately 2500 years from its beginnings, in the hands of people who were still, technologically speaking, in the Stone Age. They relied heavily on stone axes and adzes, and an elaborate array of bone and shell fish hooks (Figure 13.10). The crops the people planted varied from island to island, but breadfruit, taro, coconut, yams, and bananas were the staples. The food surpluses generated on the larger islands were used as a form of wealth. (For a valuable discussion of the colonization process, see Kirch, 1982, 1984, 1986.)

When the French and British visited Tahiti in the eighteenth century, they chanced upon the center of a vigorous eastern Polynesian society (Oliver, 1977). The islands were ruled by a powerful hierarchy of chiefs and nobles, many of them descendants of the canoe crews who had settled the archipelago. The chiefs acquired prestige by controlling and redistributing wealth and food supplies. Their formidable religious and social powers led them to warfare and to the undertaking of elaborate agricultural projects and the erection of monu-

FIGURE 13.11   A *marae* on Tahiti.

mental shrines and temples of stone: the famous *maraes* of Tahiti are typical examples (Figure 13.11). On remote Easter Island the people erected vast statues, as much as 32 feet (9.8 m) high. They are thought to be images of deified ancestors associated with different kin groups.

The full diversity of Polynesian culture is still imperfectly understood, for archaeological research has hardly begun in the South Seas, but it is certain that the Polynesians were making ocean voyages on a large scale at a time when the Greeks and Romans were little more than coastal navigators.

Settlement of New Zealand

New Zealand is the largest and among the most remote of all the Pacific islands; it is actually two large islands. It has a temperate climate, not the tropical warmth enjoyed by most Polynesians. Despite this ecological difference, New Zealand was first settled by Polynesians who voyaged southward in comparatively recent times and settled on the North Island. Maori legends tell of a migration from Polynesia in the mid-fourteenth century A.D. Settlers including Toi Ete'hutai, who came to New Zealand in search of two grandsons blown away from Tahiti during a canoe race, may have arrived 400 years before. The earliest

C14 dates for New Zealand archaeological sites are a matter of controversy but they are within the present millennium (Bellwood, 1978; Davidson, 1985).

First settlement
? A.D. 900

The temperate climate of the North Island formed a southern frontier for most of the basic food plants of Polynesia. The yam and gourd can be grown only there, but the sweet potato can be cultivated in the northern part of the South Island if adequate winter storage pits are used. The Polynesian coconut never grew in New Zealand. The earliest settlers relied heavily on hunting, fishing, and gathering. Even later, though some peoples specialized in food production, others did not, especially on the South Island, where many settlements were close to abundant ocean resources (Prickett, 1983).

The first settlers found great flocks of flightless Moa birds, cumbersome and helpless in the face of systematic hunting. They hunted the Moa into extinction within a few centuries. Fish, fern roots, and shellfish were important throughout New Zealand's short prehistory. The introduction of the sweet potato made a dramatic difference to the New Zealanders, for the tubers, if carefully protected from cold, could be eaten in the winter months, and some could be kept for the next year's planting. Sweet potatoes have a large crop yield and are thought to have contributed to a rapid population buildup, especially on the North Island. This, in turn, led to competition among groups for suitable agricultural land to grow the new staple (Davidson, 1985).

Maori
A.D. 1400

When the Moa became extinct, the Maori had few meat supplies except birds, dogs, and rats. Their only other meat source was human flesh. The archaeological record of Maori culture from approximately A.D. 1400 onward shows not only population growth but an increasing emphasis on warfare, evidenced by the appearance of numerous fortified encampments, or *pa's*, protected with earthen banks. The distribution of *pa's* coincides to a large extent with the best sweet potato lands (Bellwood, 1970; Groube, 1970). In the course of a few centuries, warfare became a key element in Maori culture, to the extent that it was institutionalized and an important factor in maintaining cohesion and leadership in Maori society. The booty of war was not only *kumara* (sweet potato) but the flesh of captives, which became a limited part of the Maori diet.

Maori warfare, mainly confined to the North Island, where more than 5000 *pa's* have been found, was seasonal and closely connected with the planting and harvest of sweet potatoes, when everyone was busy in the gardens. Military campaigns were short and intense, very often launched from the sea in war canoes up to 78.7 feet (24 m) or more in length (Figure 13.12). These elaborately carved vessels could hold as many as 150 men on a short expedition. So formidable was the reputation of the Maori that European ships avoided New Zealand ports for years before permanent white settlement was achieved. The last Maori war ended in 1872, by which time the indigenous population had been decimated by disease, warfare, and European contact.

GUIDE TO FURTHER READING

Bellwood, Peter. *Man's Conquest of the Pacific.* Oxford: Oxford University Press, 1978.
  A summary of the prehistory of the Pacific that covers every corner of this vast ocean. For the advanced reader, but crammed with useful information.

FIGURE 13.12 Maori war canoe recorded by Captain Cook in the eighteenth century.

Bellwood, Peter. *The Prehistory of the Indo-Malaysian Archipelago.* Sydney: Academic Press, 1986.

A valuable summary of southeast Asian mainland prehistory.

Chang Kwang-Chih. *The Archaeology of Ancient China* (4th ed.). New Haven: Yale University Press, 1986.

The definitive account of Chinese prehistory in the English language. A highly technical work truly designed for the advanced student or professional archaeologist.

Davidson, Janet. "New Zealand Prehistory," *Advances in World Archaeology* 4 (1985):239–292.

An exemplary article on general trends in New Zealand prehistory with a very complete bibliography.

Jennings, Jesse D. (ed.). *The Prehistory of Polynesia.* Cambridge, Mass.: Harvard University Press, 1979.

A series of essays that provide a state-of-the-art summary of Pacific prehistory.

Lewis, David. *We the Navigators.* Honolulu: University of Hawaii Press, 1972.

An account of traditional Polynesian navigational methods based on both local lore and experiments navigating a yacht without a compass and sextant. What makes this book fascinating is that the author is a practical seaman himself.

CHRONOLOGICAL TABLE **H**

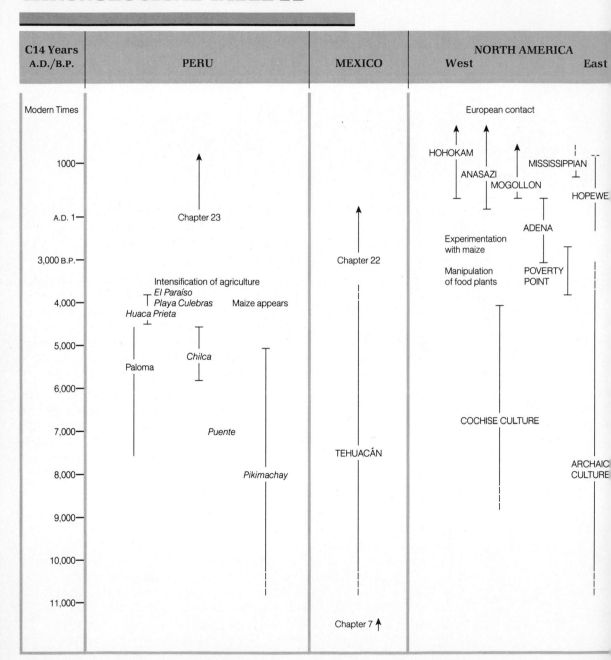

C14 Years A.D./B.P.	PERU	MEXICO	NORTH AMERICA West	East
Modern Times			European contact	
1000—			HOHOKAM	MISSISSIPPIAN
			ANASAZI	
			MOGOLLON	HOPEWE
A.D. 1—	Chapter 23		ADENA	
			Experimentation with maize	
3,000 B.P.—		Chapter 22	Manipulation of food plants	POVERTY POINT
	Intensification of agriculture			
	El Paraíso			
4,000—	Playa Culebras Maize appears			
	Huaca Prieta			
5,000—	Chilca			
	Paloma			
6,000—				
7,000—	Puente		COCHISE CULTURE	
		TEHUACÁN		
8,000—	Pikimachay			ARCHAIC CULTURE
9,000—				
10,000—				
11,000—				
		Chapter 7		

...sed on crops quite different from those grown ...ps included manioc and sweet potato, while ...staple cereal. Domesticated animals included ...pig.

...evolved from a native grass named teosinte ...Tehuacán Valley of southern Mexico as early ...lture spread from southern Mexico and Gua- ...e north and south. A long tradition of fishing ...ave way to food production in some areas by ...The Ayacucho area of the Andes provides ...n the highlands of Peru by 5500 years ago.

...North American Southwest by approximately ...ago, sedentary villages and a much greater ...haracteristic of the Southwest, leading to the ...llon, and Anasazi cultural traditions. Hoho- ...o be ancestral to American Indian groups still

...nidwestern parts of North America by 7000 ...groups domesticated native plants like sun- ...e and bean agriculture were late develop- ...0. After 3000 years ago, a series of powerful ...and Midwest, peoples among whom elabo- ...ding of burial mounds and earthworks were commonplace. The Adena tradition emerged about 2700 years ago and was replaced by the Hopewell in approximately A.D. 200. Both traditions depended on long-distance trade in essential commodities and cult objects for much of their prosperity. A preoccupation with death and status was at the focus of Hopewell life, for their burials show extraordinary lavishness. Twelve hundred years ago the center of economic, religious, and political power shifted to the Mississippi Valley with the emergence of the Mississippian tradition, which is thought to owe much to Mexican cosmology. The Mississippian had powerful religious and secular leaders; it survived in a modified form until European contact in the sixteenth century.

Chronological
Table H

The American Indians domesticated an impressive range of native New World plants, some of which — like maize, potatoes, and tobacco — were rapidly adopted by European farmers after contact.

The most important staple crop was Indian corn, properly called maize, the only significant wild grass in the New World to be fully domesticated. It remains the most important food crop in the Americas, being used in more than 150 varieties as both food and cattle fodder. Root crops formed another substantial food source, especially in South America, and included manioc, sweet potatoes, and white potatoes. Chili peppers were grown as hot seasoning; amaranth, sunflowers, cacao, peanuts, and several types of bean were also significant crops. Some crops, such as cotton and gourds, are common to both Old and New worlds but were probably domesticated separately (see Pickersgill, 1972).

In contrast to Old World farmers, the Indians had few domesticated animals, including the llama of the Andes, and alpacas, which provided wool. Dogs appeared in the Americas, and the raucous and unruly turkey and the muscovy duck were domesticated.

Most archaeologists now agree that there were two major centers of plant domestication in the Americas: Mesoamerica for maize, beans, squash, and sweet potatoes, and the highlands of the central Andes for root crops. There were also four major areas of later cultivation activity: tropical (northern) South America, Peru, Mesoamerica, and eastern North America.

MESOAMERICA: TEHUACÁN AND THE ORIGINS OF MAIZE AGRICULTURE

Maize was the staff of life for many native Americans when Christopher Columbus landed in the New World. It was cultivated over an enormous area of the Americas, from Argentina and Chile northward to Canada, from sea level to high in the Andes, in low-lying swampy environments and in arid lands. Hundreds of races of domesticated maize evolved over the millennia, each a special adaptation to local environmental conditions.

The origins of domesticated maize are still the subject of great controversy, which centers on the relationship between a wild grass named teosinte (*Zea mexicana*) that grows over much of Mesoamerica and early strains of domesticated maize (for a comprehensive review, see Galinat, 1985). The botanist George Beadle (1981) concludes that "it now seems quite likely that a teosinte of some 8,000 to 15,000 years ago was the direct ancestor of modern corn and was transformed into a primitive corn through human selection." According to Beadle, there was a mutation in the tunicate gene in an ancestral form of teosinte that converted the hard fruit cases of the grass into shallow, softer cupules that carried elongated glumes, which enclosed and protected the kernels. This change made wild teosinte much easier to thresh (Galinat, 1985). The transformation to a domesticated form of early maize may have taken place simultaneously in many areas and may have occurred within a very short time, perhaps only a century.

There are impressive grounds for considering teosinte the wild ancestor of maize. A perennial teosinte found in Mexico in recent years has been crossbred with maize. Experiments have shown that teosinte can be "popped" by being placed in a fire, on a hot rock, or on heated sand, just like the popcorn we consume at the movies. Dry teosinte seeds can be cracked with even a simple grindstone, too, or softened before eating by soaking in water.

The hypothetical scenario for maize domestication goes as follows (Figure 14.1) (Galinat, 1985). The process may have started as an unintentional by-product of gathering wild teosinte, for gathering would lead to selective pressure for harvestable types of the grass, with their spikes condensed into fascicles. Such condensation made it harder for the seeds to scatter. In time, this form of teosinte would become established by campsites and in abandoned middens. These colonies would automatically diverge toward greater domestic kinds of variation, from which human beings could select the most useful types. In time, too, humans would remove weeds from these teosinte stands, then start deliberately planting the more useful types. So the female teosinte spike became canalized down a pathway leading toward maize. Cultivation and fertilization of semiwild grass populations were followed by attempts to sow selected seed from the most desirable types. At first the planted teosinte was no more productive than wild forms, but it was easier to harvest, a critical stage in the process of domestication. When people began selective harvesting and planting of transitional forms of teosinte, the grass's reproductive strategy changed to dependency on human intervention. A genetic revolution followed, in which attributes that made harvesting easier and favored teosinte's use as a human food had a selective advantage.

The archaeological record for transitional forms of teosinte is sadly lacking, perhaps because the domestication process was very rapid. Some of the oldest maize cobs discovered in archaeological sites, as well as ancient teosinte grasses, do bear marks of earlier transformations. One maize cob from Tehuacán Valley in Mexico dating to about 7000 years ago appears to show some intermediate features between teosinte and maize, but it may be a degenerate form. The earliest known archaeological occurrence of condensed teosinte comes from Tlapacoya in the Valley of Mexico and dates to about the same time (Galinat, 1985).

Traces of early experimentation with the deliberate cultivation of crops such as maize and squash have come from regions in Mexico, notably from Sierra Madre, Sierra de Tamaulipas, and the Tehuacán Valley (Figure 14.2). The dry, highland Tehuacán Valley in southern Mexico has many caves and open sites and is sufficiently arid to preserve seeds and organic finds in archaeological deposits. This was the valley that Richard MacNeish (1970, 1978) chose as a promising area in which to seek the origins of domesticated maize. MacNeish soon found domestic maize cobs dating back to approximately 5000 years ago,

FIGURE 14.1 The various stages in an apparent transformation from teosinte to maize. The earliest teosinte form is (a), the stabilized maize phenotype (e). The harvesting process increased condensation of teosinte branches and led to the husks becoming the enclosures for corn ears. (After Galinat, 1985)

but not until he began digging in the small Coxcatlán rock shelter did he find maize that even vaguely resembled what at that time was considered the hypothetical ancestor of maize. Coxcatlán contains twenty-eight occupation levels, the earliest of which dates to approximately 12,000 years ago. MacNeish eventually excavated twelve sites in Tehuacán, which revealed a wealth of information about the inhabitants of the valley through nearly 12,000 years of prehistory.

MacNeish found that the earliest Tehuacán people lived mainly by hunting horses, deer, and other mammals and also by collecting wild vegetable foods (MacNeish, 1978). These hunters used stone-tipped lances in the chase. They also hunted large numbers of jackrabbits, probably in organized drives. MacNeish estimates that 50 to 60 percent of the people's food came from game 12,000 years ago, and only 30 to 40 percent 9,000 years ago. Hunting seems to have been the major activity all year round (Table 14.1).

12,000 to 9,000 B.P.

TABLE 14.1 MacNeish's sequence for Tehuacán summarized.

Years	Phase	Characteristics
A.D. 750 to 1531 100 B.C. to A.D. 750 800 to 100 B.C.	VENTA SALADA PALO BLANCO SANTA MARIA	Spanish contact: A.D. 1531 Village life Village life
3,450 to 2,800	AJALPAN	Establishment of village life. Single-season economy with spring and summer agriculture.
4,250 to 3,450	PURRON	Hamlet villages and appearance of pottery. Agriculture important, but few details known.
5,350 to 4,250	ABEJAS	Seasonal economy, with hunting important in the winter, collecting in spring, simple agriculture in summer and fall. Some year-round settlements, small food surpluses.
6,950 to 5,350	COXCATLÁN	Seasonal scheduling of hunting and gathering. Planting of domesticates in spring and summer. Very limited food surpluses. Maize cultivated.
8,950 to 6,950	EL RIEGO	Seasonal scheduling of gathering and hunting. Seed planting appeared late in phase during summers. Food storage more important.
11,950 to 8,950	AJUEREADO	Lance ambushing of game important. Rabbit drives and small game significant. Less gathering than in later phases? Seasonal camps, no food storage.
Before 12,000	Hunter-gatherers	

Note: For full details, see Richard MacNeish, *The Science of Archaeology.* North Scituate, Mass.: Duxbury Press, 1978.

After 10,000 years ago, the game population declined slowly, and the people turned more and more to wild vegetable foods. Instead of hunting all year round, the Tehuacán bands scheduled their food gathering on a seasonal basis and were able to exploit the vegetable and other foods in their environment very effectively without overtaxing the available resources. Approximately 7000 years ago, the first deliberate planting took place, stemming from a desire to improve the location and abundance of favorite foods. This cultivation resulted in genetic changes, and soon the planted seeds were being laid out in special gardens.

7000 B.P.

The inhabitants of Coxcatlán seem to have continued this trend after 7000 years ago, planting potential domesticates, including some form of maize, in spring or summer. They grew foods that when stored would tide them over lean months: beans, amaranth, and gourds. The people lived in larger and more permanent settlements, grinding their maize with quite well-made grindstones (metates). The maize itself was smaller than modern strains and probably much

Coxcatlán

Legend:
- Nuclear areas for agriculture
- Mogollon
- Hohokam
- Anasazi
- Woodland (Adena and Hopewell)
- Mississippian

FIGURE 14.2 Archaeological sites and culture areas mentioned in this chapter. (After Meggers, 1973)

5400 B.P.

like teosinte (Figure 14.1). Still, only a tiny proportion of Tehuacán's diet came from domestic sources, compared with the period after 5400 years ago, when up to 30 percent of the diet came from agriculture; much of the produce was maize cobs that were larger than those of earlier centuries, clearly the descendants of earlier wild forms. (Recent research suggests earlier heavy dependence on maize [Farnsworth et al., 1985].)

By this time, the scheduled gathering and nomadic settlement patterns of earlier times had been replaced by more sedentary villages; these were small hamlets that moved very rarely and depended on agricultural systems that planted crops in fields. The villages were located near fertile flatlands and consisted of pit houses with brush roofs. Their ample storage facilities helped the people live through the lean months (Flannery, 1976).

The sequence of events at Tehuacán is by no means unique, for other peoples were also experimenting with cultivation. Different hybrid forms of maize are found in Tehuacán sites; these were not developed locally and can only have been introduced from outside. Dry caves elsewhere in northern Mesoamerica show that other cultures paralleled the cultural events in Tehuacán. On the other hand, the highland lakes of the Valley of Mexico and elsewhere may well have supported sedentary communities subsisting on fish and wild vegetable foods as well as experimenting with amaranth, corn, and other crops as early as the sixth millennium B.C. (Niederberger, 1979).

Plant domestication in Mesoamerica was not so much an invention in one small area as a shift in ecological adaptation deliberately chosen by peoples living where economic strategies necessitated intensive exploitation of vegetable foods. Kent Flannery has hypothesized as to how this shift in adaptation might have occurred. In a classic paper on the southern highlands of Mesoamerica, he tried to understand how the human population of this area took up agriculture (Flannery, 1968a). He assumed that the people and their homeland were part of a single, complex system composed of many subsystems — economic, botanical, social, and so on — that interacted with one another. Flannery pointed out that these people had no fewer than five carefully scheduled food-gathering systems that were in use at different seasons of the year. By being able to predict what vegetable foods came into season at different times of the year, the people were able to schedule their harvesting activities. Scheduling and use of seasonal food permitted these and many other Mesoamerican peoples to exploit their environment highly effectively without overtaxing any of the available food sources. Between 10,000 and 4,000 years ago, the people lived by using these basic procurement systems, but something caused the Mesoamericans to concentrate more heavily on wild grasses: both teosinte and foxtail millet. Between 7000 and 4000 years ago, the cob size of maize increased, and maize was crossed with related forms to produce a hybrid species that was the ancestor of modern maize. Some species of beans became more permeable in water and developed softer pods. Flannery argued that the highland people began experimenting with the planting of maize and other grasses, deliberately increasing the areas where they would grow. After a long time, these deviations in the food procurement system caused the importance of grass collection to increase at the expense of gathering other seasonal foods until the new activity, with its vital planting and harvesting schedules, became the dominant activity, one that was self-perpetuating from year to year.

Earlier theories of the origins of maize assumed that it was domesticated in many areas of the Americas from six or more presumed wild races. But modern pollen studies have shown convincingly that there was never a wild *Zea* with a wide range that extended outside southern Mexico and Guatemala. Recent hypotheses are based on theories of genetic drift and the founder principle. They argue that the first maizelike cultivars of teosinte from southern Mexico and Guatemala appear to have spread rapidly. A primitive form of eight-rowed maize *(Maiz de ocho)* with soft glumes represented at Tehuacán was the common ancestral corn that spread thousands of miles from its original homeland after 7000 years ago. Subsequent derivatives of this basic maize developed in many different North and South American environments, as well as in Mesoamerica (Galinat, 1985).

EARLY FOOD PRODUCTION IN PERU

Peruvian coast

The Peruvian coast forms a narrow shelf at the foot of the Andes, crossed by small river valleys descending from the mountains to the sea. These valleys are oases in the desert plain, with deep, rich soils and blooming vegetation where water is plentiful. For thousands of years Peruvians have cultivated these valley floors, building their settlements, pyramids, and palaces at the edges of their agricultural land. Because conditions for preservation in this arid country are exceptional, the archaeological record often is quite complete. The coast itself forms a series of related microenvironments, such as rocky bays where shellfish are abundant, places where seasonal vegetable foods nourished by damp fogs are common, and the floors or sides of river valleys flowing into the Pacific. One would assume that a combination of these microenvironments would provide a rich and uniform constellation of food resources that could normally be exploited with ease from relatively sedentary base camps (Moseley, 1975b). However, the bountiful maritime environment occasionally is disrupted by a warm countercurrent known as El Niño, which can flow for as long as twelve months. El Niño occurs at highly irregular intervals, perhaps every six years and sometimes much longer. It reduces marine upwelling so much that the fish migrate elsewhere, and thus one of the coastal peoples' staple diet sources is greatly reduced. This phenomenon is so unpredictable that the people could not store food against its arrival; they also could not move from the coast, and they did not have the offshore vessels needed for deepwater fishing. Their only strategy was to limit their population densities to the lowest levels of available natural resources until such time as they developed alternative food sources, such as maize grown by intensive irrigation agriculture (Raymond, 1981; Yesner, 1980).

The archaeological evidence for the Peruvian coast is incomplete for the period immediately preceding early food production. During the dry winter months the inhabitants collected shellfish and other marine resources, and hunting and vegetable foods were more important in the summers. After 7000 years ago, however, more efficient collecting strategies came into use, with greater attention to maximally exploiting natural food sources. Fishing, in particular, became more important. Between approximately 6200 and 4500 years ago, Peruvian coastal peoples depended on marine resources — fish, sea birds, and mollusks — for much of their diet. During the warmest and driest period after the Pleistocene, the coastal people moved closer to the shore, dwelling in larger and more stable settlements. Along with the shift to more lasting coastal dwelling came the development of sophisticated equipment for deep-sea fishing. As early as 7500 years ago, the coastal peoples were manipulating plants for their own purposes. The Paloma site on the central coast was occupied more than 7500 years ago, a settled community with numerous simple huts and grass-lined pits where the inhabitants stored food against the occasional lean year. The people relied heavily on fishing and gathering but also manipulated some plant species, including tuberous begonias, gourds, squashes, peppers, and possibly peanuts. They may also have kept llamas, the same species used by the Incas for load carrying in the Andes (Benfer, 1982).

A later coastal settlement that perpetuated the same subsistence pattern

7000 B.P.

6200 TO 4500 B.P.

Paloma 7500 to 4500 B.P.

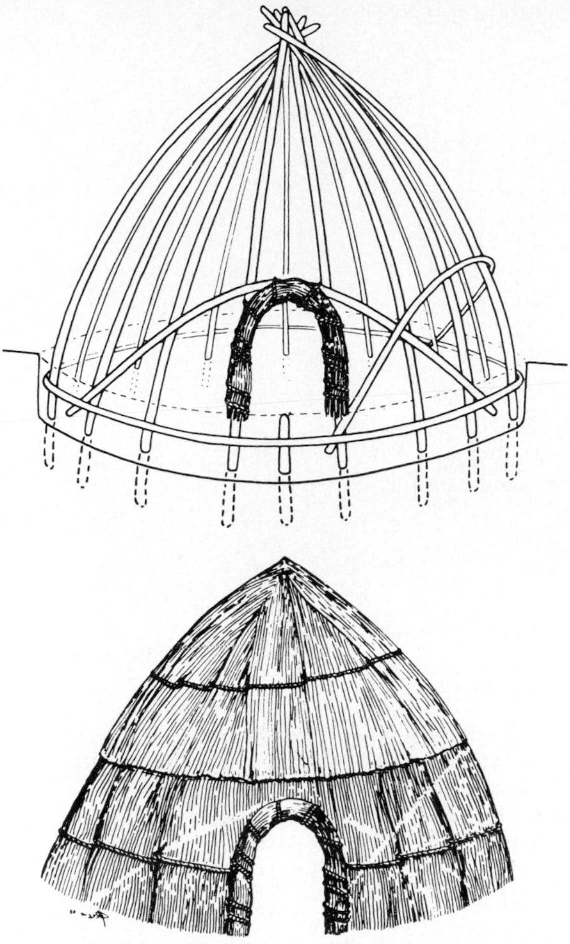

FIGURE 14.3 Reconstruction of a Chilca house. (After Willey, 1971)

flourished at Chilca, 45 miles (72 km) south of present-day Lima. Frederic Engel (1966) excavated refuse heaps there and C14 dated the earlier Chilca occupation to between 5800 and 4650 years ago. When the site was in use, it probably lay near a reedy marsh, which provided both matting and building materials as well as sites for small gardens. The Chilca people lived on sea mollusks, fish, and sea lions; they apparently hunted few land mammals. They cultivated jack and lima beans, gourds, and squashes, probably relying on river floods as well as rainfall for their simple agriculture.

Chilca **5800 to 4650 B.P.**

One remarkable Chilca house was uncovered: a circular structure, it had a domelike frame of canes bound with rope and covered with bundles of grass (Figure 14.3); the interior was braced with bones from stranded whales. Seven burials had been deposited in the house before it was intentionally collapsed on top of them. The skeletons were wrapped in mats and all buried at the same time, perhaps because of an epidemic.

The new emphasis on fish, increased use of flour ground from wild grass seed, and availability of cultivated squashes provided new sources of nutrition for some coastal groups. This supply may ultimately have set off a sustained pe-

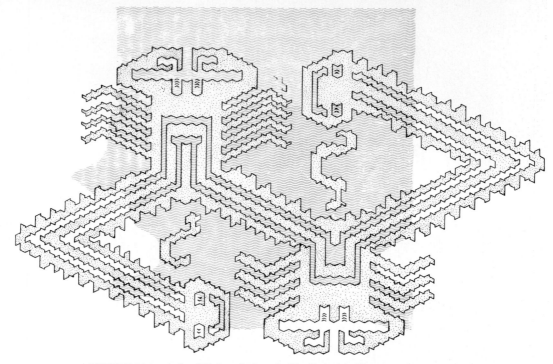

FIGURE 14.4 A double-headed snakelike figure with appended rock crabs revealed by plotting the warp movements in a preceramic twined cotton fabric from Huaca Prieta, Peru. The original length was approximately 16 inches (14 cm). The shaded area indicates the surviving textile. Double-headed motifs have persisted through more than 3000 years of Peruvian art. (Courtesy of Junius Bird)

riod of population growth. Certainly the succeeding millennia saw many permanent settlements established near the ocean; the people combined agriculture with fishing and mollusk gathering. Domesticated cotton first appeared around 4500 years ago. Squashes, peppers, lima beans, and other crops remained staple foods until recent times. Maize and other basic foods were still unknown. Agriculture remained a secondary activity much later than it did in Mesoamerica.

One later site is Huaca Prieta, a sedentary village that housed several hundred people on the north coast of Peru between 4500 and 3800 years ago (Bankes, 1977; Hyslop et al., 1987). The vast refuse mound there contains small one- or two-room houses built partially into the ground and roofed with timber or whalebone beams. The inhabitants were remarkably skillful cotton weavers who devised a sophisticated art style with animal, human, and geometric designs.

Maize made its first appearance on the coast at Playa Culebras, another important and contemporary settlement south of Huaca Prieta (Engel, 1957; Willey, 1953). This and other settlements show greater emphasis on permanent architecture not only in domestic buildings but also as large ceremonial struc-

4500 B.P.

Huaca Prieta **4500 to 3800 B.P.**

Playa Culebras

tures. A complex of stone and mud mortar platforms lies at El Paraíso on the floodplain of the Chillón Valley, some distance from the sea. At least one mound had complexes of connected rooms built in successive stages. Settlements such as El Paraíso obviously depended more on agriculture than earlier sites had. By the time the temple complexes were built there, after 3800 years ago, loom-woven textiles and pottery had come into widespread use (Figure 14.4). All the major food plants that formed the basis of later Peruvian civilization were employed.

4300 to 3800 B.P.

Most of our knowledge about the early history of food production in the highlands is from discoveries by MacNeish and others in the Ayacucho region of central Peru (MacNeish, 1978; Moseley, 1978). Food resources in the highland valleys are separated in vertically spaced microenvironments, like layers of a cake. Rarely was it possible for the inhabitants of a valley to exploit all these microenvironments from one locality, nor are they uniformly distributed in all highland valleys. Economic variability between mountain valleys was great, and no one food provided a staple diet. The carrying capacity of the highland valleys depended on the ways in which their populations exploited the resources. On the coast, intensified exploitation of the marine and vegetable resources led to population growth, but the reverse ultimately occurred in the highland valleys. There, deforestation, soil erosion, and temporary desiccation partly generated by agriculture reduced carrying capacities after A.D. 500.

Peruvian highlands

The early hunter-gatherers of the highland valleys are thought to have exploited only a small portion of the potential resources. According to MacNeish, finds at Pikimachay Cave and elsewhere indicate several subsistence options — hunting various sizes of mammal including the great sloth and varied small creatures, and collecting many species of plant food. These options were exercised by priority rather than by season, the notion being that one acquired food with the minimum effort. Approximately 11,000 years ago, however, the subsistence strategies changed. There is reason to believe that seasonal exploitation had replaced other options, with hunting, trapping, and plant collecting at high altitudes important in the dry season. During the wetter months, collecting and possibly penning small game, as well as seed collecting, were dominant activities.

Before 11,000 B.P.

11,000 B.P.

Guitarrero Cave (Figure 14.5) lies 1.5 miles (2.5 km) above sea level in the Andes (Lynch, 1980). The site was first occupied about 12,000 years ago. Common beans date from deposits about 10,600 years old, while lima beans occurred around 9000 years ago. Wild ancestors of the lima are found in rain forests east of the Andes. It is possible that people living in the forests to the east first domesticated the lima bean and that the domesticated strains later spread to drier areas to the west of the mountains.

After 7000 to 6500 years ago, the archaeological evidence becomes more abundant. In the Ayacucho-Huanta region twenty-five dry- and wet-season camps have been found that provide signs of continued exploitation of wild vegetables as well as game during the dry season. The Pikimachay Cave levels of this period yielded wet-season living floors. There, wild seeds are abundant along with remains of gourds and seeds of domesticated quinoa and squash. Game remains are very rare, as if a vegetable diet, whether wild or domesti-

7000 to 6500 B.P.

Pikimachay

FIGURE 14.5 Guitarrero Cave, looking toward the Andes.

cated, was of prime importance during the wet months. Another wet-season locality, Puente Cave, yielded a few bones of tame guinea pigs as well as the remains of many small wild mammals. Grinding stones and other artifacts used for plant collecting, or perhaps incipient agriculture, are also common at Puente. Throughout this period, many wet-season camps became larger and more stable, their use extending over longer periods of the year.

After 6000 years ago, the Ayacucho peoples relied more on food production. The potato was cultivated. Hoes appeared, as well as domesticated corn, squashes, common beans, and other crops. Guinea pigs were certainly tamed,

and llama were domesticated in central Peru by at least 5500 years ago. By this time, too, there was more interaction between coast and interior, trade in raw materials, and some interchange of domesticates. MacNeish believes corn spread from the north, ultimately from Mesoamerica, into Ayacucho. Root crop agriculture may have diffused from highland Peru into the lowlands, too.

The Ayacucho sequence is illustrative of the complex adaptive shifts that took place in many parts of South America after 7000 years ago. In both highlands and lowlands, the beginnings of agriculture were a gradual adjustment, with food production gradually supplanting gathering as the major subsistence activity. On the Peruvian coast, gathering of vegetable foods and fishing were supplemented by irrigation farming as early as 5000 years ago, while the highland peoples were cultivating a variety of crops by the same time, crops that amplified the horizontally stacked natural resources of their mountain homeland.

EARLY FARMERS IN SOUTHWESTERN NORTH AMERICA

Eleven thousand years ago the southwest United States was populated by hunter-gatherers whose culture was adapted to desert living (Cordell, 1984a, b; Lipe, 1978). A distinctive foraging culture, the Cochise, flourished in southeast Arizona and southwest New Mexico from about this time. The Cochise people gathered many plant foods, including yucca seeds, cacti, and sunflower seeds. They used small milling stones, basketry, cordage, nets, and spear-throwers. Many features of their material culture survived into later times, when cultivated plants were introduced into the Southwest.

Cochise **11,000 to 3,000 B.P.**

We do not know exactly when maize was introduced into the Southwest, but a reasonable estimate seems to be about 2500 years ago, give or take a couple of centuries (Berry, 1985). For decades, southwestern archaeologists have assumed that indigenous Archaic hunter-gatherer peoples adopted maize. Under this theory, based on some erroneous early dates for southwestern corn, the new agriculture had little impact on age-old hunter-gatherer economies. There was the slowest of shifts from hunting and gathering to a primary dependence on agriculture. For instance, Cynthia Irwin-Williams and C. Vance Haynes (1970) have suggested that an elementary southwestern culture emerged approximately 5000 years ago, at a time when there was slightly higher rainfall and increased food resources for growing hunter-gatherer populations to feed on. The various bands of the Southwest maintained widespread communication networks, which enabled them to share information about new plant foods and other innovations. It seems likely not only that the Archaic peoples were familiar with the germination of seeds but also that they occasionally manipulated wild plants by careful irrigation and weeding, as Great Basin peoples did in historic times. However, there is a considerable difference between occasionally helping wild foods grow, while not disturbing the annual gathering round, and taking up deliberate cultivation as a priority that competes with one's basic foraging schedule.

Early maize farming

With a much more recent date for maize cultivation, the earliest maize cobs are only a few centuries earlier than the emergence of a series of highly distinctive southwestern cultures. Thus, argues Michael Berry (1985), the transition was far from gradual; it was abrupt and dramatic. He believes that changes in the Cochise culture about 2500 years ago were sufficiently major to suggest that agricultural peoples dispersed into the Southwest at the time. He believes the primary reason for this dispersal was a drought throughout the Southwest between about 2950 and 2650 years ago. The early maize sites are confined to the Mexican Highland section of the Southern Basin and Range. But after 2200 years ago, when the climate was wetter and cooler, the highlands were much less densely populated. Perhaps the new conditions made the maize growing season in the highlands too short, while the agricultural potential of areas like the Colorado Plateau was enhanced. Then, after A.D. 300, there are the first signs of agricultural settlement in the Sonoran Desert, as conditions on the plateau deteriorated and the Hohokam and Mogollon traditions emerged in the Southwest. To cultivate maize, a plant that is not self-propagating for any length of time, requires a total commitment to its planting, maintenance, and harvesting from one year to the next. This process demands at least a semi-sedentary existence and a conscious shift away from wild vegetable food gathering during much of the year, the growing months. Berry points out that there are no signs of such a transition in the Southwest, by peoples who had hunted and foraged for thousands of years. Rather, he argues, agriculture was introduced by small groups of farmers whose cultural ties, even if indirect, were ultimately with Mesoamerica.

2300 B.P.

By 2300 years ago, experimentation and new hybrid varieties of maize introduced from the south had led to sedentary villages and much greater dependence on farming. The cultural changes of the period culminated in the great southwestern archaeological traditions: Hohokam, Mogollon, and Anasazi (Cordell, 1984b).

Hohokam ?2300 B.P. to A.D. 1500

The Hohokam tradition has long been thought to have originated in the Cochise. No one knows exactly when the tradition emerged, but it was probably in the first five centuries of the Christian era. However, Emil Haury, who dug the important Snaketown site in the Gila River Valley, believes that the Hohokam people were immigrants from northern Mexico, who brought their pottery and extensive irrigation agriculture with them (Haury, 1976). Under this scenario, the newcomers soon influenced the lifeway of the local people, and a desert ad-

FIGURE 14.6 A scheduled agricultural round. Diagram showing how the Pima Indians of the Southwest, descendants of the Hohokam, schedule their plantings and harvests around rainfall seasons. The Hohokam probably relied on a similar annual round. The thickness of the shaded area reflects relative plenty of food resources. (From Jesse D. Jennings, *Ancient Native Americans*, New York: Freeman, 1978, p. 349)

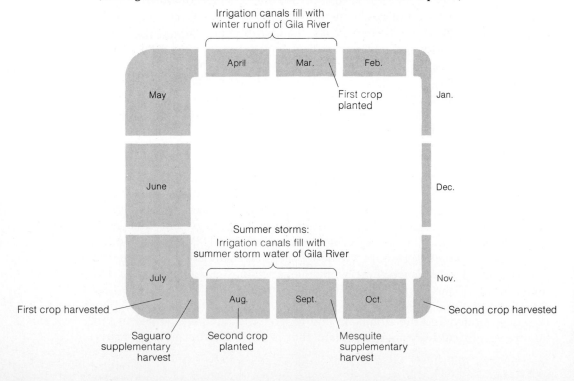

aptation of Hohokam resulted. But recent research tends to discount the migration theory. Reexamination of the Snaketown data and further field work suggest that the Hohokam enjoyed complex trading and ceremonial relationships with peoples living all over the Southwest and northern Mexico. As time went on, this trade expanded, perhaps within the context of a common ceremonial system centered on the ball courts and other ceremonial structures at Snaketown and other focal points. In all probability, the Hohokam was an indigenous culture, one that acquired much greater social complexity through time (for a discussion, see Fish and Fish, 1977; Wilcox, 1980, 1985).

Hohokam subsistence was based on maize, beans, cucurbits, cotton, and other crops, as well as on gathering. The people planted their crops to coincide with the biannual rainfall and flooding patterns. Where they could, they practiced irrigation from flowing streams; otherwise they cultivated floodplains and caught runoff from local storms with dams, terraces, and other devices. Hohokam people occupied much of what is now Arizona. Their cultural heirs are the Pima and Papago Indians of today (Figure 14.6).

Hohokam culture evolved slowly over as long as 2000 years. There are at least five stages of the culture, culminating in a Classic period from approximately 850 to 500 years ago, when large pueblos (communal villages) were built and canal irrigation was especially important. At this time and somewhat earlier Mexican influences can be detected. These include new varieties of maize, the appearance of platform mounds and ball or dance courts at Snaketown and elsewhere, and imports such as copper bells. Does this mean that Mexican immigrants transformed Hohokam culture, or were there internal factors that caused greater elaboration of local society at the same time as some ideas arrived from Mexico? Archaeologists remain divided on this point.

Originally, anthropologists believed the Mexican influence was transitory and weak, but excavations at a prehistoric town named Casas Grande in northern Chihuahua, Mexico, have changed their minds (Di Peso et al., 1974). (This site should not be confused with Casa Grande, Arizona.) At the height of its prosperity in the thirteenth century A.D., Casas Grande boasted approximately 1600 rooms and housed more than 2200 people. The dig showed that its inhabitants exchanged turquoise and painted pottery from the Southwest for marine shells and exotic bird feathers from Mexico. Local traditions connect Casas Grande with a settlement named Paquimé that was more of a Mexican town than an Indian pueblo. The archaeologists argue that Paquimé was founded by Mexican traders from the south, possibly itinerant merchants known to the Aztec as *pochteca*, who often served as spies. Perhaps they used their powerful religious beliefs to strengthen their control of the trade with the north. Perhaps, too, contacts between the Hohokam and Mexican civilization were far more regular than once was suspected.

The Mogollon tradition emerged from Archaic roots between 2300 and 1700 years ago and disappeared as a separate entity between 1100 and 500 years ago, when it became part of Anasazi (Haury, 1936; Lipe, 1978). The Mogollon is well known from dry caves in New Mexico as an agricultural tradition in which hunting and gathering in the highlands were always important. Mogollon agriculture depended on direct rainfall, with only very limited use of irrigation. The people lived in small villages of pit dwellings with timber frames and mat or

Mogollon
2300 to 1700 B.P.

brush roofs. Their material culture was utilitarian and included milling stones, digging sticks, bows and arrows, fine baskets, and characteristic brown-and-red pottery.

At least six regional variants of Mogollon are known, and there were five chronological stages, the fifth ending approximately 500 years ago. Early Mogollon villages often were located on high promontories close to more fertile lands. The settlement pattern varied from area to area but had a tendency toward larger sites and increased populations throughout the life of the tradition. By A.D. 1500 pueblos of several hundred rooms had developed in some areas, but by this time Mogollon had become part of the western pueblo Anasazi tradition.

Anasazi
Last 2000 years

The Anasazi tradition is, in general terms, ancestral to the cultures of the modern Pueblo Indians — the Hopi, Zuni, and others (Judd, 1954, 1964; Zubrow, 1971). Its emergence is conventionally dated to 2000 years ago, but this is a purely arbitrary date, for Anasazi's roots lie in Archaic cultures that flourished for a long time before. The Anasazi people made heavy use of wild vegetable foods, even after they took up maize agriculture seriously, after A.D. 400. Most of their farming depended on dry agriculture and seasonal rainfall, although they, like the Hohokam, used irrigation techniques when practicable. They made use of flood areas, where the soil would remain damp for weeks after sudden storms. Moisture in the flooded soil could be used to germinate seed in the spring and to bring ripening crops to fruition after later rains. However, this is a very high-risk type of agriculture, and the Anasazi relied on wild resources to carry them through lean years.

Anasazi chronology is well established thanks to the use of dendrochronology on beams from abandoned pueblos. The tradition is centered in the "Four Corners" area, where Utah, Arizona, Colorado, and New Mexico meet. There are at least six Basketmaker and Pueblo subdivisions of Anasazi; each marked a gradual increase in the importance of agriculture and the emergence of some larger sites with *kivas*, ceremonial sweathouses. Pueblos, which are complexes of adjoining rooms, occurred more frequently after A.D. 900; the population congregated in fewer but larger pueblos after A.D. 1180. These were located in densely populated areas, some of them moved from the open to under cliff overhangs, the so-called cliff dwellings. Some of the features of these sites, such as turrets and loopholed walls, appear to be defensive.

At the same time people concentrated in larger sites, there was depopulation of many areas of the northern Southwest. The reasons for these changes are imperfectly understood. In some areas, such as Chaco Canyon, New Mexico, the concentrated populations may have enjoyed roads, extensive irrigation systems, and more elaborate social and political organizations as well as trading connections with widespread areas of the Southwest, but most pueblos seem to have been more egalitarian in their organization and relatively self-sufficient. It may be that the changes generated by the developments in Chaco and elsewhere caused people to congregate more closely. Alternatively, it has been argued that some climatic and environmental changes, as yet little understood, may have caused major shifts in the settlement pattern. More likely, a combination of environmental, societal, and adaptive changes set in motion a period of turbulence and culture change.

FIGURE 14.7   Pueblo Bonito, New Mexico, dated by dendrochronology to A.D. 919–1130. The round structures are kivas.

By approximately A.D. 500, the basic Anasazi settlement pattern had evolved and above-the-ground houses were being substituted for the pit dwellings of earlier centuries. The pit dwellings developed into kivas, subterranean ceremonial structures that existed in every large village. Large settlements of contiguous dwellings became the rule after A.D. 800, with clusters of "rooms" serving as homes for separate families or lineages. Large settlements like Pueblo Bonito developed around A.D. 1100; this was a huge D-shaped complex of 800 rooms rising several stories around the rim of the arc (Figure 14.7). The room complexes surrounded courts, with the highest stories at the back. They formed a blank wall; a line of one-story rooms cut off the fourth side. Within the court lay the kivas, always one great kiva and usually several smaller ones. The great kivas were up to 60 feet (18.2 m) in diameter, with wide masonry benches encircling the interior. The roof was supported by four large pillars near the center, where a raised hearth lay. Two subterranean, masonry-lined rooms were situated on either side of the fireplace. A staircase leading from the floor of the kiva to the large room above it gave access to the sacred precinct.

The period between A.D. 1000 and 1300 was one of consolidation of population into a few more congested settlements, where more elaborate social organizations may have developed. The pueblos were probably communities run for the collective good, with at least some ranking of society under a chieftain. In modern Hopi society, clan superiority and kinship lineages played an important role in the election of chieftains. Thrust into close intimacy by the nature of pueblo architecture, the people developed well-integrated religious and ceremonial structures to counteract the tensions of close living.

The Anasazi enjoyed a relatively elaborate material culture at the height of their prosperity; at this time they were making distinctive black-and-white pottery, well-formed baskets, and fine sandals. However, their architecture was neither very sophisticated nor particularly innovative. Baked mud and rocks were formed into boxlike rooms; a roof of mud rested on horizontal timbers. Room after room was added as the need arose, using local materials and a simple architectural style entirely appropriate for its environment.

The southwestern farmer won success by skillfully using scarce water resources and bringing together soil and water by means of dams, floodwater irrigation, and other systems for distributing runoff. Planting techniques were carefully adapted to desert conditions, and myriad tiny gardens supplied food for each family or lineage. This successful adaptation is also reflected in the architecture.

AGRICULTURAL SOCIETIES IN EASTERN NORTH AMERICA

The Archaic hunter-gatherer traditions of eastern North America enjoyed many regional variations in material culture; these occurred because the people concentrated on different, locally abundant food sources (Jennings, 1983; Muller, 1978; B. D. Smith, 1986). In general, however, the lifeway was similar among them: a seasonal one, based on a very broad spectrum of game and vegetable foods (Brose, 1980). As long as the population density was low, every band could react relatively easily to changes in local conditions. Since many of their favorite vegetable foods were subject to cycles of lean and abundant years, a flexibility in choice and movement was essential. However, as population grew slowly throughout the Archaic, this flexibility was increasingly restricted and the people tended to specialize in local resources that were available most of the year. They developed better storage techniques and fostered closer contacts with their neighbors through exchange networks that handled foodstuffs and other commodities. The development of these types of response may have required more complex social organization than the simple band structure of earlier times, and it is no coincidence that burial patterns during the Late Archaic, approximately 3700 years ago, reflect greater differentiation in social status.

3700 B.P.

Under these circumstances, perhaps it was inevitable that Late Archaic peoples in the Eastern Woodlands turned to the deliberate cultivation of food plants to supplement wild plant yields. The first domesticated plants to reach eastern North America were gourds that originated in eastern Mexico and diffused across Texas into the Southeast and major midwestern river valleys (Ford, 1985). The earliest identifiable plant is a small squash, *Cucurbita pepo*, dated to about 7000 years ago in Illinois. Large and small varieties of hard-shelled pepo gourd were bred over the centuries, both for containers and for their edible seeds. The bottle gourd, *Lagenaria siceraria*, arrived several thousand years later (Asch and Asch, 1985).

Mexican gourd cultigens preceded the domestication of several native plants. By 4000 years ago, these included sunflower, sumpweed *(Helianthus annuus)*, and goosefoot. Most of these species flourished in river valleys where there were many and diverse wild vegetable foods, and they may have first been cultivated to supplement natural stands. Sumpweed was widely cultivated in the Midwest in the first millennium B.C., while sunflowers were prized for their edible seeds and oil by the same period. Several species were grown outside their natural ranges, but it seems likely that domestication of these native plants first took hold in the lower Mississippi River Delta, where wild ancestors of these species grow in abundance (Ford, 1985). It is significant that none of the domesticates required the kind of wholesale adaptive shift in year-round routine that maize cultivation demanded of its practitioners. Maize and bean agriculture did not flourish in the Eastern Woodlands until much later in prehistory (Stoltman, 1978).

After 4000 years ago, we find increasing signs of preoccupation with burial and with life after death, a new ideological foundation for local society in the East. These burial cults shared many practices, among them cremation, the deposition of exotic objects with the dead, and the custom of building burial mounds.

More intensive exploitation of food resources, greater sedentism, regular social interaction and exchange, a degree of social ranking, increased ceremonialism — these were the culminating elements in Late Archaic life in eastern North America. While most groups still lived in temporary encampments, or even sizable base camps used for most, if not all, the year, the Poverty Point culture of the lower Mississippi Valley and adjacent Gulf Coast offers a dramatic contrast. More than one hundred Poverty Point sites form ten regionally discrete clusters within natural geographic boundaries, each apparently grouped around a regional center.

Poverty Point
3600 to 2600 B.P.

The earliest Poverty Point sites date to about 3600 years ago, forming the oldest component in a cultural sequence that lasted for 1000 years. Poverty Point itself is the nexus of the culture and stands on Macon Ridge overlooking the Mississippi floodplain, near the confluence of six rivers (Figure 14.8). This was a strategic point from which to trade up and downstream, to receive and exchange raw materials and finished products. Some of the exotic materials at Poverty Point came from as far as 621 miles (1000 km) away. And the leaders of Poverty Point not only exchanged materials with peoples far away but redistributed them to regional centers in their own culture area.

Poverty Point with its great earthworks is a remarkable contrast to the humble base camps elsewhere in the East. Six concentric semicircular earthen ridges are divided into segments. They average about 82.0 feet (25 m) wide and 9.8 feet (3 m) high and are set about 131 feet (40 m) apart. Their significance is a complete mystery, beyond a suspicion that they were connected with astronomical

FIGURE 14.8 Poverty Point, Louisiana. *Top:* Aerial view of the site taken about forty years ago, showing the six concentric earth ridges. The ridges and intervening hollows (swales) show up as light and dark stripes in the fields. Mound A, covered with trees, is at center left. The white, straight line running diagonally across the picture is a modern road. *Bottom:* The south side of Mound A. The steps lead to the summit, which is now 70 ft (21.3 m) above the surrounding terrain.

observations. To the west lies an artificial mound more than 66 feet (20 m) high and more than 660 feet (200 m) long. A person standing on this mound can sight the vernal and autumnal equinoxes directly across the center of the earthworks to the east. These are the points where the sun rises on the first days of spring and fall. Built between 3000 and 2600 years ago, Poverty Point took more than 1,236,007 cubic feet (35,000 cu m) of basket-loaded soil to complete, a task that would have taken 1350 adults laboring 70 days a year 3 years to complete. Estimates of Poverty Point's population are hard to come by, but even a population of 1000 people makes the site unique for the period. At present, the significance of this extraordinary site and associated culture is little understood (Webb, 1968).

The Poverty Point culture went into decline approximately 2700 years ago, just as mound building reached new heights in the Ohio Valley, to the northeast (Otto, 1980).

Adena

By 2700 years ago, the people of eastern North America enjoyed a tradition of long-distance trading that had flourished for centuries. The trade carried not only prosaic commodities such as stone ax blades but also large quantities of prestigious imports such as conch shells and copper artifacts, most of which were deposited in the graves of their owners. Perhaps the trade reflects the emergence of new chiefdoms in which exotic goods were status symbols, but the evidence is uncertain (Gibson, 1964).

Adena **2700 B.P. to A.D. 200**

Between 2700 B.P. and approximately A.D. 200, the Adena culture flourished in the Ohio Valley. It relied not only on hunting and gathering but also on the cultivation of squash and local weedy plants (Muller, 1986). Maize agriculture may or may not have been practiced. The focus of Adena was the central Ohio Valley, with outliers as far northeast as New Brunswick in Canada and deep into the Southeast. There is a temptation to think of Adena as nothing more than burial mounds, when in fact these conspicuous monuments are merely one aspect of a flourishing village culture ruled, it is thought, by chieftains who were powerful kin leaders. The loyalties people felt to their lineages were so strong that the villages commemorated the dead not only with imposing burial mounds but with extensive earthworks as well.

Adena earthworks follow the contours of flat-topped hills and form circles, squares, and pentagons, enclosing areas perhaps as much as 350 feet (105 m) in diameter. The earth used to make the enclosures came from just inside the walls, giving a false impression of an interior moat. These were probably cere-monial compounds rather than defensive earthworks. The Adena people built large burial mounds, some placed inside enclosures, others standing indepen-dently outside. Most are communal rather than individual graves. The most im-portant people lie in log-lined tombs. Their corpses are smeared with red ocher or graphite. Nearby lie ceremonial soapstone pipes and tablets engraved with curving designs or birds of prey. Some prestigious individuals were buried in-side round houses, which were burned down as part of the funeral rites. Occa-sionally, the burial chamber was left open so that bodies could be added later. Dozens of people from miles around piled basketfuls of earth to form an impos-ing burial mound for a single ruler. More often, the mounds were piled up grad-ually over the years, as layers of bodies were added. However, the vast majority of less important Adena people were cremated: only their ashes were placed in-side the burial mound.

Despite the Adena concern with the afterlife, the basic life of the people re-mained unchanged from earlier times. They lived in groups of villages and

FIGURE 14.9 Reconstruction of an Adena house from the posthole pattern shown at left.

0   8 Ft.

0   2.5 M.

larger settlements that shared communal earthworks and burial mounds. Sometimes they occupied single-family dwellings (Figure 14.9), occasionally much bigger communal houses capable of holding as many as forty people. We know from the Koster excavations that the Indians probably turned to agriculture when the population grew to a point at which wild food sources were no longer sufficient. The highest densities of game and vegetable were concentrated on very narrow strips of land, mostly in river valleys. The intervening woodlands offered much less to hunters and gatherers. When population densities increased, the people could either have moved to marginal areas or taken up farming, with all the social and economic adjustments that such change implied.

Hopewell

Hopewell c. 2200 B.P. to c. 1400 B.P.

The Hopewell tradition first appeared in Illinois approximately 2200 years ago. Its religious cults were such a success that they spread rapidly from their heartland as far as upper Wisconsin and Louisiana and deep into Ohio and New York State. For nearly 1000 years, the Midwest experienced a dramatic flowering of artistic traditions and of long-distance trade that brought copper from the upper Great Lakes region, obsidian from Yellowstone, and mica from the southern Appalachians. Some archaeologists call this the Hopewell Interaction Sphere (Caldwell, 1958). The Hopewell people themselves lived in relatively small settlements and used only the simplest of artifacts to plant, hunt game, and fish. They wore leather and woven clothes of pliable fibers. Much wealth and creative skill were lavished on a few individuals and on their life after death. At first glance, the exotic artifacts and ritual traditions of the Hopewell seem completely alien to the indigenous culture of the area, but a closer look reveals the links between the underlying traditions and the magnificent art

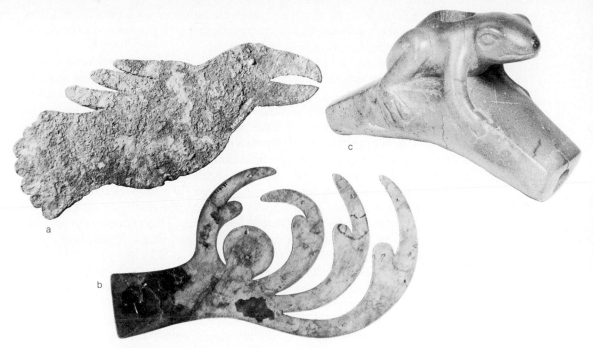

FIGURE 14.10 Hopewell artifacts: (a) raven or crow in beaten copper; (b) bird claw in mica; (c) soapstone frog.

created by Hopewell artisans. Their manufactures were traded from hand to hand throughout Hopewell territory in a vast network of gift-giving transactions that linked kin leaders with lasting, important obligations to one another (Brose and Greber, 1980).

The cult objects associated with this trade are found in dozens of Hopewell burial mounds and tell us something of the rank and social role of the people with whom they are buried. Some of the exotic grave goods, such as pipe bowls or axes, were buried as gifts from living clan members to a dead leader. Others were personal possessions, cherished weapons, or sometimes symbols of status or wealth. Hopewell graves contain soapstone pipe bowls in the form of beavers, frogs, birds, bears, and even humans. Skilled smiths fashioned thin copper sheets into head and breast ornaments that bear elaborate repoussé animal motifs (Figure 14.10). There were copper axes and arrowheads, trinkets as well as beads. A few specialists cut mica sheets into striking lustrous silhouettes of human figures, bird talons, and abstract designs. Most of these artifacts were manufactured by a few craftspeople working near major outcrops or sources of raw materials. They were distributed via the same trade networks that carried foodstuffs and tools throughout Hopewell territory. Most of them show surprisingly little wear, as if they were soon buried with their owners.

Hopewell burial mounds are much more elaborate than their Adena predecessors. For example, Cook's Mound in Louisiana rises 40 feet (12 m) and is more than 100 feet (30 m) across. Its builders followed the established custom when they buried 168 bodies within an extensive earthen platform. Then they placed a further 214 corpses on the platform before covering the entire sepulcher with a large mound. Another Hopewell burial mound complex in Ohio, appropriately named Mound City, contains no fewer than twenty-four mounds inside an enclosure covering 13 acres (5.2 ha).

The decline of the Hopewell culture after A.D. 400 is still imperfectly understood, but it is possible that a rapid and dramatic population increase strained the limits of the economic system, causing competition between trading networks and rupturing long-established economic and political relationships. It is possible, too, that as agriculture became more efficient and spread to other groups, there was an increase in population and in the number of settlements, so much so that there was greater competition for land. This in turn would have led to the development of local rule by chieftains that could have challenged the overbearing powers of those who controlled the centuries-old burial cults (Dragoo, 1976). We do not know why the center of religious and political power had spread southward from the Ohio Valley into the lower Mississippi bottomlands by A.D. 800, but the shift may be connected with the realization that maize offered great potential as a food staple.

Eight-rowed maize (*Maiz de ocho*) originated as a Southwestern strain pre-adapted to higher altitudes and northern latitudes. From there, it gradually spread along riverine areas toward the Northeast, ultimately reaching New England in about A.D. 1400. Corn was known and present in eastern North America for some time before its dietary staple potential was realized in the Late Woodland and Mississippian cultures of the Midwest. The lush floodplain of the lower Mississippi was ideal for cultivating high-yielding maize strains and also for growing beans. Beans arrived after the full potential of maize agriculture was realized. They had not only the advantage of a high protein value but also the asset of compensating for the amino-acid deficiencies of corn. The new agricultural adaptations were a considerable success. Soon the "Mississippian" people were expanding into the tributary valleys of the great river, until they flourished over a large area of the Mississippi drainage between Iowa and northern Louisiana.

Many archaeologists link the Adena and Hopewell cultures into a single "Scioto" tradition, while the term *Woodland* often is used to describe eastern cultures after the introduction of pottery in approximately 2600 B.P.

Mississippian

Mississippian
c. A.D. 800 to
European contact

The Mississippian culture first appeared along the lower Mississippi, then spread along the major floodplain corridors formed by the river's tributaries. The Mississippian is basically restricted to the fertile plains formed by meanders of the great river and its tributaries; this distribution has always been assumed to be because of the availability of easily tilled soils. In fact, we know now that this restricted distribution was owing to the complex adaptation that the people developed in an area with well-defined bands of arable soils that were fertilized by spring floods just before planting season. They lived in valleys with many lakes and swamps, where fish trapped by receding floods were plentiful and migrating waterfowl paused to rest in spring and fall. The Mississippian people not only grew maize, squashes, and beans but they also relied heavily on seasonal crops of nuts, fruits, berries, and seed-bearing plants. They hunted deer,

FIGURE 14.11 The central portion of Cahokia Mounds as it may have appeared around A.D. 1150, at its peak.

raccoon, and turkey, and shot thousands of migratory waterfowl in spring and fall. Fish and waterfowl may have composed up to 50 percent of the diet of the villagers living within the meander zones of the floodplain (B. D. Smith, 1975, 1978).

Most of the Mississippian population lived in small, dispersed homesteads or sometimes in compact villages. The larger communities and ceremonial centers that have been the focus of archaeological attention for a century constitute a small minority. In all probability, the villagers visited their local center only for scheduled seasonal ceremonies, major funerals of kin or high-status individuals, mutual defense in times of war, and fulfillment of their labor obligations for building fortifications or mounds. There may have been seasonal changes in settlement patterns. Judging from historical accounts of Indian warfare, isolated families may well have come together in larger defended communities during the summer warfare season, dispersing to their homes in the fall.

By A.D. 900, the larger Mississippian communities housed between 100 and 150 people and were fortified with defensive palisades. The largest Mississippian center was Cahokia, on the east bank of the river at St. Louis (Figure 14.11) (M. D. Fowler, 1969, 1978). Cahokia once contained more than one hundred earthen mounds and catered to a population of at least 30,000 to 35,000 people. It was a great ceremonial center; its mounds and plazas dominated the countryside for miles. Monk's Mound at the center of Cahokia rises 102 feet (32 m) above the floodplain and covers 16 acres (6.4 ha) (Figure 14.12). This gigantic mound is as tall as a ten-story building and was erected in at least four stages between the ninth and eleventh centuries A.D. Millions of basketloads of soil deposited by thousands of people went into this monumental earthwork. On the summit stood a thatched temple at the east end of an enormous central plaza. Around the plaza rose other mounds, temples, warehouses, administrative buildings, and the homes of nobles. The entire "downtown" area covered

FIGURE 14.12 Aerial view of Monk's Mound, Cahokia, Illinois, taken in 1983. (Courtesy Cahokia Mounds State Historic Site)

more than 200 acres (80.1 ha) and was fortified by a log fence with gates and watchtowers. Numerous mounds and lesser communities lay outside the walled interior core of Cahokia, each with its own plazas and burial mounds. The pole-and-thatch houses of the residential areas extended over 2000 acres (809 ha), the clusters of houses being separated by several acres of land. There is every reason to believe that Cahokia was planned and controlled by a powerful central authority.

Cahokia was by no means unique. It lay in the north of Mississippian territory, while its southern rival was Moundville in Alabama. Dozens of small centers and towns sprang up between the two. More than just sacred places for annual ceremonies of planting and harvest, the centers were markets and focal points of powerful chiefdoms. Cahokia owed some of its importance to the manufacture and trading of local salt and chert, a fine-grained rock used to make hoes and other tools. Above all, Cahokia and its neighbors were the places where the Mississippian leaders displayed their political and religious power.

We know little about how Mississippian society functioned, but it seems likely that the floodplain was ruled as a series of powerful chiefdoms, by an elite group of priests and rulers who lived somewhat separated from the rest of the population. The chieftains probably monopolized most long-distance trade and were the living intermediaries with the ancestors and the gods. As in the Hopewell culture, high-ranking individuals went to the next world in richly decorated graves, with clusters of ritual objects of different styles that betokened various clans and tribes. One small Cahokia burial mound yielded the skeleton of an important man wearing a robe into which had been woven 12,000 shell beads. Six servants lay by his side, together with a copper roll, polished game stones, and some mica slabs. No fewer than fifty-three women, perhaps slaves, had been buried in a mass grave nearby.

Was the Mississippian an indigenous cultural development? The debate has raged for more than half a century. It seems likely that the basic cultural traditions evolved in the Mississippi Valley in the late first millennium A.D., for the entire culture depended on a complex adaptation to a highly specialized environment. However, there are signs of Mexican influence in the layout of plazas and imposing mounds and in the emphasis on public ceremony and display that seems characteristic of the largest ceremonial centers.

Unfortunately, we know almost nothing of the elaborate rituals and beliefs of Mississippian society. The few clues come from surviving examples of Mississippian art, many of them from the Moundville sites. So pervasive are the design motifs — human hands with an eye in the palm, sunbursts, or weeping eyes — that the experts believe that a distinctive "Southern cult" flourished throughout Mississippian country. Southern cult motifs appear on pottery, were embossed on Lake Superior copper, and were incised on imported Gulf conch shells. Perhaps the most famous Mississippian cult objects are the so-called effigy jars, which bear human faces, some with signs of face painting and tattoos. Others are representations of the heads of sacrificial victims, their eyes closed and mouths sewn tightly shut. Often, the effigies are weeping, perhaps denoting a connection between tears, rain, and water in Mississippian cosmology.

The Southern cult appears to have been an amalgam of indigenous Indian and Mexican themes. Wind, fire, sun, and human sacrifice are common motifs. One persistent artifact is a small copper mask depicting a long-nosed god who bears a close resemblance to the god of the merchants found at many Mexican sites. Perhaps it was these *pochteca*, or traders, who introduced Mexican religious beliefs to the Mississippi Valley, but no Mexican artifacts have yet come from Mississippian settlements.

This remarkable society flourished until the sixteenth century. Then, in 1540 to 1542, Spanish conquistador Hernando de Soto encountered Creek Indian chiefs in the South who still lived in fortified towns with temple mounds and plazas. The smallpox he brought with him decimated center after center, weakening Mississippian culture beyond recovery. Nevertheless, when Europeans began to colonize the South in the seventeenth century, they came up against a powerful alliance of fifty large Creek Indian settlements in what is now Alabama and Georgia. To the west lived the Chickasaw and Choctaw, while the

Cherokee to the north numbered more than 60,000, distributed in at least one hundred settlements. The first missionaries who worked among the Cherokee recorded dimly remembered folktales of mound building in earlier centuries.

GUIDE TO FURTHER READING

Jennings, Jesse D. *The Prehistory of North America* (2d ed.). New York: McGraw-Hill, 1975.

———(ed.). *Ancient Native Americans.* 2 vols. New York: Freeman, 1983.
Two volumes by a leading Americanist that summarize the culture history of the Americas. *Ancient Native Americans* contains essays by various authorities, some with a stronger theoretical background than others.

MacNeish, Richard. *The Science of Archaeology.* North Scituate, Mass.: Duxbury Press, 1978.
An account of MacNeish's research in Mexico and Peru that summarizes the work and contains much commonsense advice about contemporary archaeology.

Moseley, Michael E. *The Maritime Foundations of Andean Civilization.* Menlo Park, Calif.: Cummings, 1975.
A clearly written, informative essay on the origins of food production and civilization in Peru that was an important basis for this chapter.

Muller, Jon D. *Archaeology of the Lower Ohio River Valley.* New York: Academic Press, 1986.
An excellent summary of this important region, with fine discussions of different adaptations to local environments.

Willey, Gordon R. *An Introduction to American Archaeology, North and Middle America,* vol. 1, and *South America,* vol 2. Englewood Cliffs, N.J.: Prentice-Hall, 1966, 1971.
The definitive accounts of the culture history of the Americas as of the late 1960s. Strongly recommended for the advanced reader. Somewhat outdated but still one of the ultimate authorities.

Old World Civilizations

(5000 Years Ago to Modern Times)

The great tide of civilization has long since ebbed, leaving these scattered wrecks on the solitary shore. Are those waters to flow again, bringing back the seeds of knowledge and of wealth that they have wafted to the West? We wanderers were seeking what they had left behind, as children gather up the coloured shells on the deserted sands.

— Austen Henry Layard

As in Part IV, a discussion of the theoretical background and the major controversies precedes the narrative prehistory. Part V deals with the beginnings of complex states and urban civilization. These chapters present an unconventional account of early civilization in that they deal with lesser known parts of the world, such as Africa and southeast Asia, as well as the Near East. Research in Africa and Asia has hardly begun; future excavations in these regions are likely to throw significant new light on such much-debated issues as the importance of ceremonial centers and long-distance trade in the emergence of complex societies. Once again, the reader is urged to start with the theoretical background before embarking on the narrative culture history.

CHAPTER 15

The Development of Civilization

Preview

■ V. Gordon Childe's pioneer definition of the Urban Revolution was widely accepted; it centered on the development of the city, metallurgy, food surpluses, writing, and a unifying religious force. Unfortunately, his criteria are not universal enough to be generally applicable.

■ Evolutionary models of the development of sociopolitical units give us a framework for looking at the mechanisms that led to the emergence of urban societies.

■ We summarize various commonly held theories about how complex societies began, describing the major potential causes for civilization. These include ecological stress, population stress, technological change, irrigation agriculture, and the notion of the hydraulic civilization. Exchange networks, religion, ceremony, warfare, have all been espoused as potential factors.

■ Kent Flannery has used an ecologically based systems approach to early civilization, arguing that the emergence of complex societies was a gradual process caused by many interacting factors. One must look at the processes and mechanisms by which the necessary changes took place. The ultimate objective is to establish the set of rules by which a complex state could have come into being. Religious and informational factors seem to have been key elements in the regulation of environmental and economic variables in early civilization.

■ Elizabeth Brumfiel argues for a social or "structural" approach to the origins of states. She believes that the social structure of a society ultimately determines its transformation over time. Pressures for state formation are triggered in some social and cultural systems but not in others. The search for causes therefore involves identifying the structures that lead to state formation and the conditions that determine their distribution in time and space. This process means focusing on ecological variables and the obstacles and opportunities they present to individuals pursuing political goals in different societies. In other words, how is ecological opportunity or necessity translated into political change?

CIVILIZATION

Everyone who has studied the prehistory of human society agrees that the emergence of civilization in different parts of the world was a major event in human adaptation. The word *civilization* has a ready, everyday meaning. It implies "civility," a measure of decency in the behavior of the individual in a civilization. Such definitions inevitably reflect ethnocentrism or value judgments, because what is "civilized" behavior in one civilization might be antisocial or baffling in another. These simplistic understandings are of no use to students of prehistoric civilizations seeking basic definitions and cultural processes.

Civilization

The generally agreed upon, special attributes that separate civilizations from other societies can be listed as follows:

- Urbanized societies, based on cities, with large, very complex social organizations. The early civilization was invariably based on a specific territory like, say, the Nile Valley, as opposed to smaller areas owned by individual kin groups.
- Symbiotic economies based on the centralized accumulation of capital and social status through tribute and taxation. This type of economy allows the support of hundreds, often thousands, of non–food producers such as smiths and priests. Long-distance trade and the division of labor, as well as craft specialization, are often characteristic of early civilizations.
- Advances toward record keeping, science and mathematics, and some form of written script.
- Impressive public buildings and monumental architecture.

These attributes are by no means common to all early civilizations, for they take different forms in each.

CITIES

Archaeological research into early civilization concentrates on the origin and development of the city. Today the city is the primary human settlement type throughout the world, and it has become so since the industrial revolution altered the economic face of the globe. The earliest cities assumed many forms, from the compact, walled settlement of Mesopotamia to the Mesoamerican ceremonial center with a core population in its precincts and a scattered rural population in villages arranged over the surrounding landscape. The cities of the Harappan civilization of the Indus were carefully planned communities with regular streets and assigned quarters for different living groups. The palaces of the Minoans and Mycenaeans functioned as secular economic and trading centers that served as a focus for scattered village populations nearby.

A *city* is best defined by its population, which is generally larger and denser than that of a town or village. A good and generally used rule of thumb is a lower limit of 5000 people for a city. However, numbers are not a sufficient determinant: many people can congregate in a limited area and still not possess the compact diversity of population which enables the economic and organizational complexity of a city to develop. It is this complexity that distinguishes the

City

city from other settlement types. Most cities have a complexity in both organization and nonagricultural activities which is supported by large food surpluses. Further, the city is a functioning part of a complex system of different settlements that rely on its many services and facilities.

AN URBAN REVOLUTION?

Since archaeological research into early civilization has concentrated on excavations of ancient cities and ceremonial centers, it was perhaps inevitable that the first attempts to explain the origins of civilization focused on the city and its implications.

Early scholars who debated the origins of civilization were concerned with the cultural evolution of humankind from a state of savagery toward the full realization of human potential. This, in their Victorian eyes, was civilization. They considered that their civilization had originated in Ancient Egypt and that bold mariners had spread its ideas all over the globe. These simplistic hypotheses collapsed in the face of new archaeological discoveries in Mesopotamia and the Nile Valley in the early decades of this century. With the discovery of Sumerian sites and early Egyptian farming villages, scholars came to realize that early civilization had developed over a wide area and a considerable span of time.

The first relatively sophisticated theories about the origins of urban civilization were formulated by V. Gordon Childe, of Neolithic Revolution fame (Chapter 2). Childe claimed that his Neolithic Revolution was followed by an Urban Revolution, when the development of metallurgy created a new class of full-time specialists and changed the rules of human social organization (Childe, 1936, 1956). He argued that the new specialists were fed by food surpluses raised by the peasant farmers. The products of the craftsworkers had to be distributed, and raw materials had to be obtained from outside sources. Both needs reduced the self-reliance of peasant societies. Agricultural techniques became more sophisticated as a higher yield of food per capita was needed to support the nonagricultural population. Irrigation increased productivity, leading to centralized control of food supplies, production, and distribution. Taxation and tribute led to the accumulation of capital. A new class-stratified society came into being. Writing was essential for keeping records and for developing exact and predictive sciences. Transportation by water and land was part of the new order. A unifying religious force dominated urban life as priest-kings and despots rose to power. Monumental architecture testified to their activities.

The notion of an Urban Revolution dominated archaeological and historical literature for years, but this hypothesis has flaws as an all-embracing definition of civilization and a description of its development. Childe's criteria are far from universal. Some highly effective and lasting civilizations, such as those of the Minoans and the Mycenaeans, never had cities (Redman, 1978; C. Renfrew, 1973). The Maya built elaborate ceremonial and religious centers with semiurban populations concentrated around them, surrounded by a more scattered rural population clustered for the most part in small villages. Writing was absent from the Inca civilization of Peru. The Maya and Aztec scripts were used in

Urban Revolution

part for administering an elaborate calendar. Some craft specialization and religious structure are typical of most civilizations, but it cannot be said that these form the basis for an overall definition of civilization.

American archaeologist Robert Adams (1966) stresses the development of social organization and craft specialization during the Urban Revolution. He raises objections to the Childe hypothesis, arguing that the name implies undue emphasis on the city at the expense of social change, the development of social classes and political institutions. Many of Childe's criteria, like the evolution of the exact sciences, have the disadvantage of not being readily preserved in the archaeological record. Furthermore, Childe's Urban Revolution was identified by lists of traits, although the name implies emphasis on the *processes* of culture change. Childe believed technological innovations and subsistence patterns were at the core of the Urban Revolution. Adams directed his work toward changes in social organization; he describes early Mesopotamia and central Mexico as following "a fundamental course of development in which corporate kin groups, originally preponderating in the control of land, were gradually supplemented by the growth of private estates in the hands of urban elites" (R. M. Adams, 1966). The eventual result was a stratified form of social organization rigidly divided along class lines (Service, 1962, 1975).

Adams: social organization

LATER THEORIES ABOUT THE ORIGINS OF CIVILIZATION

By the time Adams was criticizing Childe's Urban Revolution, people were beginning to investigate the many interacting factors that led to the emergence of complex states. Everyone agreed that complex societies appeared during a period of major economic and social change, but different scholars gave emphasis to various possible factors that contributed to the rise of civilization. These factors include ecology, population growth, technology, irrigation, trade, religious beliefs, and even warfare. In the pages that follow, we examine some of these factors, realizing that no one development led, on its own, to the emergence of cities and civilization.

Ecology

Many have said that the exceptional fertility of the Mesopotamian floodplain and the Nile Valley was a primary reason for the emergence of the cities and states in these regions. The fertility and benign climate led to the food surpluses that were capable of supporting the craftsworkers and other specialists who formed the complex fabric of civilization (Wheatley, 1971). This notion was the foundation of what was known in the 1920s and 1930s as the Fertile Crescent theory.

Reality, of course, is much more complicated. The true surplus was probably one of capacities, a *social surplus*, which is one that consciously reallocates goods or services. A social surplus is created by a society's deliberate action, through some form of governmental force. In a sense this is a taxation authority, a person or organization that wrests surplus grain or other products from

Social surplus

those who grow or produce them. Another problem with the Fertile Crescent theory is that the environments of all the major centers of early civilizations are far too diverse, in altitude above sea level, for example, for any assemblage of environmental conditions to be set forth as the requisites for civilization's start.

Even on the Mesopotamian floodplain, which superficially appears to be a uniform environment, specialized zones of subsistence vary greatly. Wheat was grown on the Assyrian uplands; barley did better on the margins of swamps and near levees on the plain. Both these winter cereals were staples. Near the permanent watercourses, low-lying orchards ripened in the summers, together with garden crops such as dates. The date crop was a beautiful supplement to the spring cereal harvests, ripening in the fall. Mesopotamian agriculture was combined with cattle herding on cereal stubble and fallow land in the permanently settled areas; many herds were grazed by nomads on the semiarid steppes beyond the limits of settled areas. Fish, too, taken from the rivers and swamps that also had reeds for building material, provided vital protein. Adams (1966) argues that these ecological niches, effectively exploited, forged an interdependence that was reflected in increased specialization in subsistence activities, as each segment of Mesopotamian society provided a part of the food supply and, ultimately, social surplus.

Complex subsistence patterns like these were almost certainly active in Mesoamerica and southeast Asia, to say nothing of Egypt, although the evidence is very incomplete. Even in the best documented areas, evidence comes from later, well-documented periods, and we can only surmise that complexities were similar in earlier times. The integration of several ecological zones, each producing a different food as a main product, into one sociopolitical unit probably took place as the first ceremonial centers came into being. A localized center of power could control different ecological zones and the products from them, a more deliberate hedge against famine that was indispensable for planning food surpluses. This is not at all the same as saying that favorable ecological conditions caused trade and redistributive mechanisms, and therefore some form of centralized authority, to develop. Rather, ecology was only one component in a close network of the many changes that led to civilization, a subsystem of interactive forces among a great many subsystems in equilibrium.

Population Growth

Thomas Henry Malthus argued as long ago as 1798 that human reproductive capacity far exceeds the available food supply. Many people have argued that new and more intensive agricultural methods created food surpluses. These in turn led to population growth, more leisure time, and new social, political, and religious institutions, as well as the arts.

Ester Boserup, among others, has criticized this point of view. She feels that population growth provided the incentive for irrigation and intensive agriculture (Spooner, 1972). Her theories have convinced others that social evolution was caused by population growth. No one has explained, though, why the original populations should have started to grow. By no means all farming populations, especially those using slash-and-burn cultivation, live at the maximum density that can be supported by the available agricultural land, and population often is artificially regulated. Claiming that population growth explains how states were formed necessitates finding out why such decisions would have been made.

Slash-and-burn, or *swidden,* agriculture with its shifting cultivation is very delicately balanced with the rest of its ecosystem. Populations are dispersed and have relatively little flexibility in movement or growth because the land has low carrying capacity and relatively few ecological niches to carry edible crops (Allan, 1965). More lasting field agriculture is far more intensive and exploits much more of the environment in an ordered and systematic way. The Mesopotamian example shows how effectively a sedentary population can manipulate its diverse food sources. The more specialized ecosystem created by these efforts supports more concentrated populations. It creates conditions in which more settlements per square mile can exist on foods whose annual yields are at least roughly predictable.

Most significant concentrations of settlement that might be called prototypes for urban complexes developed in regions where permanent field agriculture flourished. However, unlike the period immediately after food production began, there is no evidence for a major jump in population immediately before civilization appeared. Also, a dense population does not seem to have been a precondition for a complex society or redistribution centers for trade. We have no reason to believe that a critical population density was a prerequisite for urban life.

Technology

In Mesopotamia, again our best documented area, agricultural technology did not advance until long after civilization began. The technological innovations that did appear (the wheel, for example) were of more benefit to transportation than to production. Copper and other exotic materials were at first used for small-scale production of cult objects and jewelry. Not until several centuries after civilization started were copper and bronze more abundant, with demand for transportation and military needs burgeoning. Then we see an advance in technology or an increase in craftspeople. Technology did evolve but only in response to developing markets, new demands, and the expanded needs of the elite.

Irrigation

Most scholars now agree that three elements on Childe's list seem to have been of great importance in the growth of all the world's civilizations. The first was the creation of food surpluses, used to support new economic classes whose members were not directly engaged in food production. Agriculture as a way of life immediately necessitates storing crops to support the community during the lean times of the year. A surplus above this level of production was created by both increased agricultural efficiency and social and cultural changes. Specialist craftsworkers, priests, and traders were among the new classes of society that came into being as a result.

Second, agricultural economies may have tended to concentrate on fewer, more productive crops, but they remained diversified so that the ultimate subsistence base still was relatively wide. The Ancient Egyptians relied on husbandry, especially in the Nile Delta. The diversity of food resources not only protected the people against the dangers of famine but also stimulated the development of trade and exchange mechanisms for food and other products and the growth of distributive organizations that encouraged centralized authority.

The third significant development was intensive land use, which probably increased agricultural output. Intensive agriculture usually implies irrigation, often hailed as one fundamental reason for a civilization's inception. Archaeologists have long debated how significant irrigation was in getting urban life started. Julian Steward and Karl Wittfogel argue that irrigation was connected with development of stratified societies (Steward et al., 1955; Wittfogel, 1957). The state bureaucracy had a monopoly on hydraulic facilities and created the

Irrigation and the
Hydraulic State

Hydraulic State; in other words, the social requirements of irrigation led to the development of states and urban societies. Robert Adams (1966) takes a contrary view. He feels that the introduction of great irrigation works was more a consequence of dynastic state organizations, however much the requirement of large-scale irrigation subsequently may have influenced the development of bureaucracies.

Adams's view is based on studies of prehistoric irrigation in Mesopotamia, as well as observations of irrigation in smaller societies. Large-scale irrigation had its roots in simpler beginnings, perhaps in cooperation between neighboring communities to dam streams and divert water into fields where precious seeds were sown. The floodplain of the Tigris and Euphrates rivers, with its long, harsh summers, could be cultivated only by irrigation with canals, which had to be dug deep enough to carry water even when the rivers were at their lowest. No means of lifting water was found until Assyrian times, and the earliest inhabitants of the delta were obliged to dig their canals very deep and to keep them that way. Silting, blockage, and flooding were constant dangers, requiring endless worker-hours to keep the canals flowing. It paid the earliest delta farmers to live within a limited geographic area where canal digging was kept to a minimum, but even then organizing the digging would have required some centralized authority and certainly more restructuring of social life than the intercommunity cooperation typical of many smaller agricultural societies that used irrigation.

Building and maintaining small canals requires neither elaborate social organization nor population resources larger than those of one or several communities. Large-scale irrigation requires technical and social resources of a quite different order. Huge labor forces have to be mobilized, organized, and fed. Maintenance and supervision require constant attention, as do water distribution and resolution of disputes over water rights. Because those living downstream are at the mercy of those upstream, large irrigation works are viable only as long as all who enjoy them remain within the same political unit. A formal state structure with an administrative elite is essential.

Early irrigation in Mesopotamia was conducted on a small scale (R. M. Adams, 1966, 1981; Adams and Nissen, 1972). Natural channels were periodically cleaned and straightened; only small artificial feeder canals were built. Maximum use was made of the natural hydrology of the rivers. Most settlement was confined to the immediate vicinity of major watercourses. Irrigation was organized by individual small communities. Large-scale artificial canalization did not take place until long after urban life appeared. The same is true of Ancient Egypt, where construction of large artificial canals seems to have been the culmination of long evolution of intensive agriculture.

Growth of Trade

The origins and evolution of complex societies in human prehistory have long been linked to burgeoning trade in essential raw materials such as copper and iron ore, or in luxuries of all types. However, claiming that a dramatic increase in trading was a primary cause of civilization grossly oversimplifies a complicated proceeding. Trade is two things: a helpful indicator of new social developments and a factor in the rise of civilization. Many commodities and goods are preserved in the archaeological record, including gold and glass beads, seashells, and obsidian mirrors. These finds have enabled archaeologists to trace trade routes through the Near East, Europe, and other regions. With the many analytic methods for looking at the sources of obsidian, stone ax blanks, and metals, people now realize that prehistoric trade was much more than a few itinerant tradespeople passing objects from village to village (Sabloff and Lamberg-Karlovsky, 1975).

Prehistoric trade frequently is thought of as a variable that developed at the same time that sociopolitical organization was becoming more complex. This notion goes back to the long-established hierarchy of bands, tribes, chiefdoms, and states and to a linear, evolutionary way of looking at civilization's origins. It has been assumed that trade proceeded from simple reciprocal exchange to the more complex redistribution of goods.

Trade as an institution could have begun when people sought to acquire goods from a distance for prestige and individual profit. The decision to acquire any commodity from afar depends both on how urgent the need for it is and on the difficulties in acquiring and transporting it. Much early trade was based on obtaining specific commodities, such as copper ore or salt, that had peculiar and characteristic problems of acquisition and transport. There was no such thing as trading in general. Trade in any one commodity was almost a special branch on its own. Clearly such items as cattle or slaves are more easily transported than tons of iron ore or cakes of salt; the former move on their own, but metals require human or animal carriers or wheeled carts. To ignore these differences is to oversimplify the study of prehistoric trade.

In more complex societies, the ruler and his immediate followers were generally entitled to trade and to initiate the steps leading to acquisition of goods from a distance. The king might employ merchants or traders to do the work for him, but the trade was in his name. The lower-class traders of Mesopotamian society were more menial and were often bound by guilds or castes. These were carriers, loan administrators, dealers — people who kept the machinery of

Trade and exchange networks

trade going. Both the royal merchant and the lower-class trader were distinct from peoples such as the Phoenicians, who relied on trade as a continuous activity and a major form of livelihood.

Trade before markets were developed can never be looked at as the one cause of civilization or even as a unifying factor. It was far more than just a demand for obsidian or copper, for the causes of trading were infinitely varied and the policing of trade routes was a complex and unending task. It is significant that most early Mesopotamian and Egyptian trade was based on rivers, where policing was easier. When the great caravan routes opened, the political and military issues — tribute, control of trade routes, and tolls — became paramount. The caravan predates the great empires, a form of organized trading that kept to carefully defined routes set up and armed by state authorities for their specific tasks. The travelers were bent only on delivering and exchanging imports and exports. These caravans were a far cry from the huge economic complex that accompanied Alexander the Great's army across Asia, or the Grand Mogul's annual summer progress from the heat of Delhi in India to the mountains, moving half a million people including the entire Delhi bazaar.

Trade itself has been analyzed intensively by both economists and anthropologists (Polyani, 1975). They distinguish between internal trade, between neighboring communities in the same tribal area or state, and external trade, with other peoples, states, or areas. They examine trade in the form of gifts, such as that probably conducted by the Hopewell people of the North American Midwest (Chapter 14), which is really barter; and they consider trade by treaty, which results from political agreement. Formally administered trade is another important category, normally conducted from a port of trade, a place that can offer military security, commercial and loading facilities, and a safe haven for foreign traders.

There has been much debate about the origins of the market — both a place and a style of trading administration and organization. The market encourages people to develop one place for trading the relatively stable, almost fixed, prices for staple commodities. This does not, however, mean regulated prices. The trade market is a network of market sites (marketplaces) at which the exchange of commodities, especially the *mechanisms* of the exchange relationship, from an area where supplies are abundant to one where demand for the same materials is high is regulated to some degree.

This emphasis on mechanisms led C. C. Lamberg-Karlovsky, William Rathje (Sabloff and Lamberg-Karlovsky, 1975), and others to study market networks and the mechanisms by which supplies are channeled along well-defined routes, profits are regulated and fed back to the source, providing further incentive for more supplies, and so on. There may or may not be a marketplace; it is the state of affairs surrounding the trade that forms the focus of the trading system and the mechanisms by which trade interacts with other parts of the culture. Taking a systems approach to trading activity means regarding archaeological finds as the material expressions of interdependent factors. These include the need for goods, which prompts a search for supplies, themselves the product of production above local needs, created to satisfy external demands. Other variables are the logistics of transportation and the extent of the trading network, as well as the social and political environments. With all these vari-

Systems approach

ables, no one aspect of trade is an overriding cause of culture change or of evolution in trading practices. Hitherto, archaeologists have concentrated on trade in the context of objects or as an abstraction — trade as a cause of civilization — but have had no profound knowledge about even one trading network from which to build more theoretical abstractions.

The reality is that long-distance trade was carefully melded with fluctuating demands and availabilities of supplies. It is not enough to think of trade in terms of distribution of exports and imports (Kohl, 1978). Any study of prehistoric trade has to consider also the production and consumption of the goods involved. Were they essential raw materials or exotic luxuries, finished manufactures or ax blanks that were completed at their destination? Was the trade continuous or seasonal, carried on by specialist traders, only by the wealthy, or by everyone? Changes in the volume and nature of trade can influence and modify not only production in a society but its social and economic structures as well. For example, we know that the Aztec merchant could purchase the title *Lord*, presumably as a measure of his status as a successful trader. There was room for private dealing, specialist merchants, commodities markets, perhaps even smuggling and tax evasion. Archaeologists cannot understand a trading network without analyzing the social and economic structures of each society participating in the exchange, for, in many cases, they became interdependent, often without realizing that they were. Until there is much more systematic study of the data for early trade, no one will fully understand trade's influence on nascent civilization anywhere.

Warfare

Robert Carneiro (1972) has suggested a "coercive theory" of state origins. Based on the archaeology of Peruvian coastal valleys, it argues that areas like these valleys, where the amount of agricultural land is very limited and circumscribed by desert, are the ones where states may well form through a predictable series of events. Carneiro's scenario begins with autonomous farming villages scattered over the valley landscape. As the population grows and more land is taken up, the communities start fighting and raiding one another's fields as they compete for limited acreage. Soon some village leaders emerge as successful warlords, become chieftains, and preside over larger tribal politics. But the valley population continues to grow and warfare continues to intensify until the entire region falls under the sway of one warrior-ruler, who presides over a single state centered within the valley. Then, this ambitious ruler and his successors start raiding neighboring valleys. Eventually a powerful state emerges and rules over several valleys, which creates much larger civilizations.

The Carneiro hypothesis is difficult to test, but an attempt to do so in the Santa Valley, Peru, has produced an interesting picture of changing settlement patterns. Suffice it to say here that there are no signs of the kinds of dispersed, autonomous village that Carneiro's scenario begins with. The processes that shaped the emergence of state societies in the Santa Valley appear to have been much more complex and multifaceted than just tribal warfare. David Wilson (1983) points out that the only "coercive" processes came in about A.D. 400, when the Moche people carved out a multivalley state by military conquest of neighboring valleys. Their conquest took place long after complex, irrigation-based societies flourished in the Santa Valley. As with irrigation hypotheses, reality is much more complex than the straightforward scenario Carneiro developed.

There is an attractive simplicity in the idea that the early city was a mighty fortress to which the surrounding tribes would run in times of stress. Thus, goes the argument, they came to depend on one another and their city as a fundamental part of society. However, warfare can be rejected as a primary cause of civilization without much discussion, since large military conflicts appear to have been a result of civilization not a direct cause of it. For one thing, the earliest ceremonial centers apparently were not fortified. For another, in earlier times, the diffuse social organization of village communities had not yet led to the institutional warfare that resulted from the concentration of wealth and power in monopolistic hands. Only when absolute and secular monarchs came to power did warfare become endemic, with raiding and military campaigns designed to gain control of important resources or to solve political questions. This type of warfare is a far cry from the tribal conflict common to many peasant societies. It presupposes authority.

Religion

Religion has been ignored by many writers who favor trade and production as major forces in civilization's beginnings. Yet shrines and sacred places are common in agricultural settlements of great antiquity, such as Jericho, Çatal Hüyük, and Las Haldas (Peru) (Wheatley, 1971). These religious shrines were predecessors of the great ceremonial centers of Mesopotamia and Egypt, Mesoamerica, and Peru. In each part of the world where civilization appeared, ceremonial centers were preceded by inconspicuous prototypes tended by priests or cult leaders. These people must have been among the first to be freed of the burden of having to produce food, supported by the communities they served. In every region the ceremonial center was the initial focus of power, exchange, and authority, an authority vested in religious symbolism and organized priesthoods.

Priesthoods

Priesthoods may have become powerful authorities as people worried more about the cycles of planting and harvest and the soil's continuing fertility. It is no coincidence that the Mesopotamians' earliest recorded gods were those of harvest and fertility, or that in Mexico Tlaloc was the god of rain and life itself. These preoccupations may have become the focus of new and communal belief systems. Those who served the deities of fertility thus became people of authority, the individuals who controlled economic surpluses, offerings, and the redistribution of goods. The temple became a new instrument for organizing fresh political, social, and religious structures.

As society grew more complex, more sophisticated ethics and beliefs provided a means for sanctioning the society's new goals. The temple was an instrument for disseminating these new beliefs, a means for the new leaders to justify their acts and develop coherent policies. Symbolic statements describing society served as models not only for behavior and belief but also for the ceremonial centers that perpetuated and formulated them.

The Ceremonial Center

The nucleus of the first cities was some form of temple or ceremonial center, the edifice around which the business of the state, whether secular or religious, went on (Eliade, 1954, 1959). These centers were either very compact, like the Mesopotamian *ziggurat*, or dispersed, like Mayan examples. Those of the Mesopotamians and Chinese were relatively compact, with a reasonably dense population around them. Many Maya centers, such as Tikal in Guatemala, were huge urban complexes, with dense city and rural populations (N. Hammond, 1982). The priestly elite and rulers who lived at the center were surrounded by retainers and craftsworkers. The rural population in the environs was probably bound to the ceremonial center both economically and by kinship. As a ceremonial center became a focus for a group of independent settlements, it supplied reassurance or what Chinese historian Paul Wheatley calls "cosmic certainty." It was "the sanctified terrain where [the common people were] guaranteed the seasonal renewal of cyclic time, and where the splendor, potency, and wealth of their rulers symbolized the well-being of the whole community" (Wheatley, 1971). The rural population felt no alienation from those who lived at the center; the distinction was between the ruler and the ruled.

This classic interpretation of the ceremonial center is long established, notably in writings by Mircea Eliade (1959). To this school of thought, the ceremonial center was not a prime mover of civilization but an instrument of "orthogenetic transformation." The religious and moral models of society provided a sacred canon circumscribing economic institutions and laying out the social order. It ensured the continuity of cultural traditions and was recited in temples, where the Word of the Gods rang out in reassuring chants passed from generation to generation. The ceremonial center was a tangible expression of this continuity.

Eliade and the ceremonial center

Eventually the ceremonial center was transformed by the rising secular kings, who were sometimes installed by force. As the kingship's power grew, the ceremonial center's political power declined, although its religious functions were faithfully retained. In Mesopotamia, church and state separated when the power of the temple ruler, or *en*, was restricted to religious matters after 5000 years ago. The *lugal*, or king, assumed the secular and often militaristic leadership of the state (Kramer, 1963).

We can detect secularization of the ceremonial center in the appearance of the palace, where the secular king resided. The king himself might have enthusiastically believed in the state faith, but his functions were almost entirely secular, even if he used religion to justify his actions. He might have assumed a divine role himself. When the palace appears, we find the royal tombs standing as garish and splendid monuments to the awesome political and social power behind them.

SYSTEMS AND CIVILIZATIONS

Everyone seems to agree that urban life and civilization came into existence gradually, during a period of major social and economic change. The earlier linear explanations invoking irrigation, trade, or religion as a major integrative force are inadequate for our purposes.

Adams: multiple
causes

Robert Adams has been a pioneer in looking at multiple causes of state formation. Back in 1966 he argued that irrigation agriculture, increased warfare, and "local resource variability" were three factors vital in newly appearing civilization. Each affected society and one another with positive feedback, helping them reinforce each other. The creation of food surpluses and the emergence of a stratified society were critical developments. Irrigation agriculture and more intensive horticulture could feed a bigger population. Larger populations and increased sedentariness, as well as trade with regular centers for redistributing goods, were all pressures for greater production and increased surpluses, actively fostered by dominant groups in society. The greatly enlarged surpluses enabled those who controlled them to employ large numbers of craftsworkers and other specialists who did not themselves grow crops.

Adams develops his thesis further by arguing that some societies were better able to transform themselves into states because of the favorable variety of resources on which they could draw. Higher production and increased populations led to monopolies over strategic resources. These communities eventually were more powerful than their neighbors, expanding their territories by military campaigns and efficiently exploiting their advantages over other peoples. Such cities became the early centers of religious activities, technological and artistic innovations, and the development of writing (Figure 15.1).

FIGURE 15.1 Hypothetical model of the state's beginnings. (Compiled from R. M. Adams, 1966) Compare with Figure 15.2.

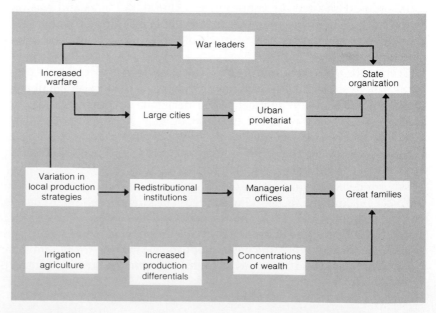

Kent V. Flannery (1972) has a more complex and somewhat abstract scheme further explaining the state's origins. He and others see the state as a very complicated living system, the complexity of which can theoretically be measured by the internal differentiation and specialization of its subsystems, such as those for agriculture, technology, religious beliefs, and so on. The ways these subsystems are linked, as well as the controls that society imposes on the system as a whole, are vital. Archaeologists who think this way make a fundamental distinction between

- The *processes* of culture change, the succession of changes by which the early states developed their new complexity.
- The *mechanisms*, the actual ways in which the processes of increasing complexity occurred.
- The socioenvironmental *stresses* that select for these mechanisms. Socioenvironmental stresses can include food shortages, warfare, and population growth, and are by no means common to all states.

"An explanation of the rise of the state then centers on the ways in which the processes . . . took place," writes Flannery.

A series of subsystems operate in human cultural systems, subsystems that interact with one another, just as the cultural system as a whole interacts with the natural environment. Each subsystem is regulated by a control apparatus that keeps all the variables in a system within bounds so that the survival of the system as a whole is not threatened. This apparatus of social control is vital, for it balances subsistence needs with religious, political, social, and other ideological values. There is a well-defined hierarchy of regulation and policy, ranging from those decisions under the control of individuals to institutions within society with specialized functions (such as acquiring the information necessary to regulate the system), on up to the basic, highest order propositions, those of societal policy. These abstract standards or values lie at the heart of any society's regulation of its cultural system. Not only crops and domesticated animals but all sorts of subtle relationships and regulatory measures make up the basis of a civilization (see Figure 15.2 for an example from Mesopotamia).

The management and regulation of a state is a far more elaborate and centralized undertaking than that of a hunter-gatherer band or a small chiefdom. Indeed, the most striking difference between states and less complicated societies is the degree of complexity in their ways of reaching decisions and their hierarchic organizations, not in their subsistence activities. Any living system is subjected to stress when one of its many variables exceeds the range of deviation that the system allows it. The stress may make the system evolve new institutions or policies. Such coping mechanisms may be triggered by warfare, population pressure, trade, environmental change, or other variables. These variables create what Flannery calls an "adaptive milieu" for evolutionary change. His specific mechanisms include "promotion" and "linearization," when an institution in a society may assume new powers or some aspect of life may become too complex for a few people to administer. Both mechanisms lead to greater centralization, caused by selective pressures on the variables that produced the coping mechanisms.

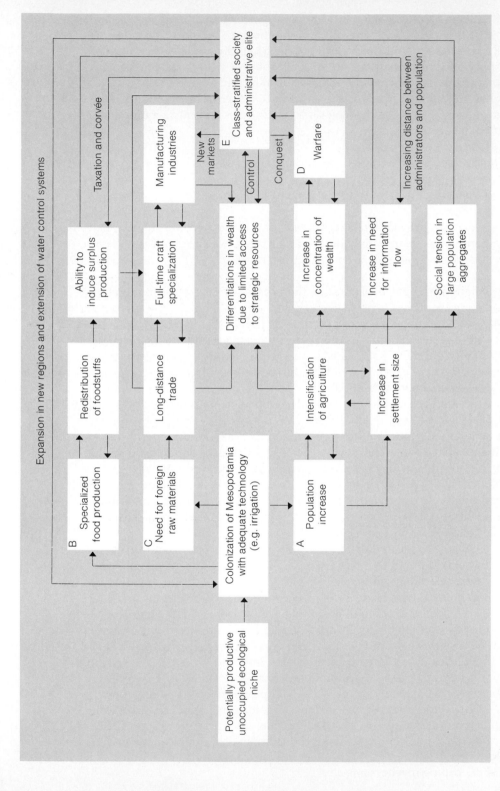

FIGURE 15.2 A systems diagram showing the interrelationships between cultural and environmental variables that led to increased stratification of class structure in early Mesopotamian urban society. (Developed by Charles Redman, 1978)

The ultimate objective of a systems analysis of how a civilization began could be the establishing of rules by which the origins could be simulated, but such rules are a goal for the future. Flannery lists fifteen beginning rules that could affect the cultural evolution of a simple human population forming part of a regional ecosystem. These rules can lead to new models for understanding the cultural evolution of civilization. Such models are certain to be most complex. We now have to be specific about the links between subsystems — distinguishing between the mechanisms and processes and the socioenvironmental pressures which are peculiar to each civilization and have, until now, been the means by which we have sought to explain the origins of civilization (Redman, 1978). Religious and informational factors now appear to be key elements in the regulation of environmental and economic variables in early civilizations and, indeed, in any human society.

Flannery's ecologically based theories have enjoyed a relatively long life compared with some other hypotheses, but they face the objection that testing multicausal models is very difficult indeed. William Sanders and David Webster (1978) point out that Flannery's approach relies heavily on cultural evolution and invokes a number of universal processes that affected the formation of complex societies (see also Binford, 1983), when in fact the environment in Mexico and other centers of early state formation was much more complex and variable. In his classic study of the Basin of Mexico (1979), Sanders shows how the Aztec created and organized huge agricultural systems that spread over the shallow waters of the basin's lakes. The variability of the basin environment meant that the Aztec had to exploit every environmental opportunity afforded them. Thus, he argues, the state organized large-scale agriculture to support a population of up to 250,000 just in and close around the Aztec capital, Tenochtitlán.

ECOLOGICAL AND STRUCTURAL APPROACHES

Two theoretical approaches to the emergence of states have dominated archaeological thinking in recent years (Brumfiel, 1983). The first originates in the pioneer work of Julian Steward in the 1950s, relating state formation to the challenges offered by the local environment. Population growth and pressure are thought to be the dynamics that fuel the process of state formation. The initial stages of state formation are claimed to be accelerated by the ecological benefits the people accrue from more centralized (state) organization. The second approach argues that states came into being as a result of certain social and cultural conditions. This "structural" approach, which owes much to Karl Marx and Friedrich Engels, argues that even societies with stable populations and balanced relationships with their environments possess an internal dynamic that fuels their progress toward greater social complexity. In other words, social components of society are more important than general conditions within a human population as a whole.

The ecological approach to state formation has focused attention on the effectiveness of centralized organization as a way of solving social and environmental problems. A powerful leader has the information at his or her disposal

Ecological approach

to make decisions along with the ability to command people's labor and to collect and redistribute the results of that labor. Thus, goes the argument, states arise in social and environmental contexts where centralized management solves problems effectively.

Centralized organization was at the core of Wittfogel's arguments for hydraulic civilizations, but, as we have seen, his theories proved invalid when it was shown that large-scale irrigation developed in Egypt and Mesopotamia long after urban civilizations had emerged. Management has been the focus of many other theories, too — theories that invoke the need to distribute food within a region; to organize the procurement of metals, salt, or other essentials from outside; to maintain defense or conduct wars of conquest (Carneiro, 1972); or to perform a multitude of interlocking functions (Flannery, 1972). Kent Flannery's systems approach to state formation (1972) epitomizes the management view, for it argues that effective leadership endowed emerging states in many parts of the world with the ability to deal with a great diversity of ecological and population problems.

Flannery's hypotheses have been elaborated even further, because we have to account for one unquestionable fact. Complex states only arose in a few locations at certain moments; state formation is not a universal phenomenon. Those who espouse the ecological approach have focused on the complex interactions between population growth and the local environment. In the Valley of Mexico, for example, William Sanders and Barbara Price (1968) argue that rapid population growth caused serious problems for small-scale societies after centuries of relatively egalitarian political organization. States emerged because they were beneficial as a way of organizing both increased food supplies through intensified agriculture, and trade and external relations with neighbors. Thus, states would only emerge in certain environmental settings, those with especially severe population problems or shortages of agricultural land. Effective, centralized management of food production, through state-organized irrigation systems and other means, and of trade, could bring ecological imbalance under control within a short time.

But the ecological approach has problems. How, for example, does one tell which environments would foster state formation? Fertile floodplains like Mesopotamia? Coastal river valleys like those in Peru? Or areas where land is in short supply, also coastal Peru? States have arisen in regions where there are few geographic constraints, like the Maya lowlands of Mesoamerica, and in the Nile Valley, where the distribution of resources is uniform. Further, civilizations have arisen without any sign of rapid population growth in Iran and other parts of the Near East. And while agricultural intensification often accompanied state formation, it occurred in many forms — in the adoption of swamp garden agriculture (Maya lowlands), in the diversion of river water into flood basins (Egypt), and by exploitation of different ecological zones (Aegean). The classic models, like Flannery's, of the origins of state-organized societies rely on positive feedback between population growth and recurring population pressure to maintain the cultural system in a state of evolutionary change, or on some other device. These models result invariably in complex feedback diagrams, which are fine in general theory but very difficult to document with archaeological data (for a full critique, see Brumfiel, 1983).

Elizabeth Brumfiel (1983) names the "social" approach to the origins of the state the "structural approach." Under this rubric, the social structure of a society ultimately determines its transformation over time. Perhaps the most commonly invoked structure is that of social conflict, first espoused by Marx and Engels more than a century ago. They believed that new technological innovations like metallurgy led to new economic institutions like slavery that divided society into ranked classes. The state, with its special mechanisms for maintaining law and order, came into being as a way of reducing social conflict. Although Engels was obviously wrong in invoking technological innovation as a catalyst for civilization, some anthropologists believe that the state did develop as a means of suppressing conflict between social classes. However, Elman Service (1975) among others argues that Engels was entirely wrong. Social inequality, or social ranking, evolved as a result of the intensification of social institutions like tribute and taxation in goods and labor that were commonplace in chiefdoms, societies less developed than states. In other words, social inequality was already in existence.

Brumfiel: structural approach

Service (1975) also points out that there is no evidence for class conflict wars in early civilizations, as Engels would have had us believe. Service believes that there were political reasons for state formation. Many early chieftains were in insecure positions. Thus, he argues, they secured permanent dominance by developing new political structures to bolster their authority. Brumfiel (1983) notes that "if, in certain types of political systems, threats to the leader's status are regularly generated," then one might be able to formulate an alternative to the Marxist social conflict theories, a theory "that explains the state as a consequence of conflicts resulting from political, rather than economic, structures."

We know that many historic chiefdoms were politically insecure, faced with constant rebellions and threats to their authority. Tahitian chiefs faced competition for power and prestige (Oliver, 1977), as did Hawaiian rulers. They achieved power by a combination of aggressive warfare, trading, and control of irrigated lands (Earle, 1978). Thus, argues Brumfiel, the structure of societies where political systems involve weak, permanent leadership can lead to social conflict that has both a political and an economic basis. "The process of state formation might be nothing more (or less) than a series of effective strategies designed and implemented by beleaguered rulers to survive . . . challenges to power," she writes. At first, the strategies used to maintain power might vary greatly, everything from politically motivated marriage alliances with neighbors to regional trade or outright wars of conquest. But as time goes on, the rulers' options would widen, since they would be less constrained by the realities of their own insecurity and local conditions. However, in many cases the limited potential of the underlying agricultural system, or the realities of the environment which might limit communication or trade (as happened in Hawaii) may profoundly affect the prospects for state formation. Environmental factors play an important role in structural models of state formation, just as they do in ecological ones.

The crux of the Brumfiel argument is simple: that pressures for state formation are triggered in some social and cultural systems but not in others, hence the historical distribution of early states in the world. Thus, a search for the causes of state formation involves identifying the structures that lead to state formation and the conditions that determine their distribution in time and space. In particular, we need to focus on population ecology, on how "ecological variables present obstacles and opportunities to individuals pursuing their political goals in various structural contexts" (Brumfiel, 1983).

Brumfiel supports her structural model with an analysis of Aztec state formation in the Valley of Mexico (Brumfiel, 1983; for a description of Aztec civilization, see Fagan, 1984a). She hypothesizes that the Aztec state came into being in four "logically discrete" steps:

First, competition intensified between petty kingdoms in the valley. This intensification crystallized in the famous Triple Alliance, formed in A.D. 1434 by the rulers of Aztec Tenochtitlán, Texcoco, and Tlacopán. Second, the emerging rulers centralized their power by organizational reforms that reduced the power of subordinate rulers and the nobility, thereby eliminating much of the competition for political leadership. Next, the Triple Alliance further consolidated its power by undertaking ambitious public works in the Valley of Mexico, not only wars of conquest but temple building, causeway and canal construction, and massive swamp agriculture. Each of these stages was made possible by the structural changes that preceded it, as was the final development. This was the emergence of a complex bureaucracy that oversaw the affairs of state, with specialized administrative personnel and several levels of decision making.

By the time of the Spanish conquest, in 1519–1521, the population of the Valley of Mexico was about four times that of earlier periods; the state was performing many of the ecological functions that one might expect of powerful bureaucratic and political systems (Brumfiel, 1983; Sanders, Parsons, and Santley, 1979). This structural model directs attention away from purely ecological factors to the specific problem of what implications ecological variables have for prestate political orders. In other words, the question that faces students of state formation is how ecological opportunity or necessity is translated into political change. What were the goals of the political actors, who were pursuing their individual goals while states were coming into being? Which ecological variables were obstacles? Which were opportunities? Until we have the answers to these questions, it will be difficult to develop any general theories of state formation.

GUIDE TO FURTHER READING

Adams, Robert M. *The Evolution of Urban Society*. Chicago: Aldine, 1966.
> An essay on the origins of civilization that stresses social and economic change, based on the author's field work in Mesopotamia and comparative data from the New World.

Brumfiel, Elizabeth. "Aztec State Making: Ecology, Structure, and the Origin of the State," *American Anthropologist* 85, no. 2 (1983): 261–284.
> A lucid and provocative analysis of the origins of states that uses the Aztec as a model. Represents much current thinking on the subject.

Childe, V. Gordon. *Man Makes Himself*. London: Watts, 1936.
> Perhaps the classic exposition of the revolution theory of civilization by a master at eloquent writing. Outdated but seminal.

Flannery, Kent V. "The Cultural Evolution of Civilizations." Palo Alto, Calif.: *Annual Review of Ecology and Systematics*, 1972. Pp. 399–426.

A masterly summary of the systems approach to early civilization that demonstrates the complexities of explaining the past.

Redman, Charles L. *The Rise of Civilization: From Early Farmers to Urban Society in the Ancient Near East.* San Francisco: Freeman, 1978.

A book that covers all the theories about the origins of civilization of the 1960s and 1970s and the key sites and concepts for the advanced student. Strongly recommended as a follow-up to this volume.

Sanders, William T., Parsons, Jeffrey R., and Santley, Robert S. *The Basin of Mexico: Ecological Processes in the Evolution of a Civilization.* New York: Academic Press, 1979.

An exemplary area study of highland Mesoamerican civilization that is crammed with wisdom about the study of complex societies. Also an unusually thorough archaeological study. Technical, but strongly recommended.

CHRONOLOGICAL TABLE I

C14 Years A.D./B.P.	MESOPOTAMIA/IRAN	EGYPT	TROPICAL AFRICA	INDUS	SOUTHEAST ASIA
1500—			European contact / *Zimbabwe* / Emergence of West African states		Historic times / *Angkor*
1000—					
500—	Historic times	Historic times		Historic times	Mekong Delta city-states
A.D. 1—		Roman occupation Ptolemies	Bantu origins Ironworking / MEROE		
	Cyrus BABYLONIAN EMPIRE / *Assur*	LATE PERIOD		King Darius's invasion of India	Indigenous state
3,000 B.P.—	ASSYRIAN EMPIRE			Ironworking Painted gray wares	
		NEW KINGDOM	Early food production in West Africa		
4,000—	Hammurabi of Babylon / Sargon of Agade / *Lugalzagesi*	MIDDLE KINGDOM / OLD KINGDOM		HARAPPAN CIVILIZATION	
	ELAMITES / SUMERIAN CIVILIZATION		Hunter-gatherers		*Ban Chiang*
5,000—	Jemdet Nasr / PROTO- ELAMITES / Uruk	ARCHAIC PERIOD / UNIFICATION			
	Tepe Yahya / *Susa*	Amratian			?
6,000—				Early food production	
	Ubaid / *Eridu*				
7,000—		Chapter 12 ⬆	Chapter 12 ⬆	*Mehrgarh*	
	Samarra / HALAFIAN				
8,000—	*Hassuna* / Chapter 10 ⬆				Chapter 13 ⬆

CHAPTER 16

Mesopotamia and the First Cities

Preview

▓ Approximately 8000 years ago highland peoples began to settle in northern Mesopotamia in areas where agriculture was possible using seasonal rainfall. These Hassuna people lived in close contact with other societies downstream that developed irrigation agriculture.

▓ Approximately 7500 years ago Halafian painted wares appeared over a wide area of northern Mesopotamia and Anatolia; they are thought to have coincided with the emergence of chiefdoms in this area. Two hundred years later the first farmers settled in the Mesopotamian delta.

▓ The first inhabitants of the delta practiced small-scale irrigation and lived in groups of communities linked by trade networks. In time, some, like Eridu, became ceremonial centers and towns. By 6500 years ago, the population of Eridu may have been as large as 5000 people.

▓ A rapid evolution to urban life ensued — marked by rapid population growth, congregation of people in small cities, and development of long-distance trade. The emerging city of Uruk and its satellite villages epitomize the period between 5600 and 5000 years ago, when its temple (*ziggurat*) was the center of ritual and economic life. This new urban society was organized in distinctive, stratified social classes.

▓ Writing developed around 5400 years ago, as a recording system for long-distance business transactions. It is thought to have evolved from a system of clay tokens that had been in use for several thousand years. Copper metallurgy developed at about the same time on the highlands and soon came into widespread use.

▓ By 4900 years ago, Sumerian civilization was in full swing in the southern Mesopotamian delta. Irrigation agriculture and long-distance trading were vital elements in this literate, urban society. Unlike Egypt, Mesopotamia never achieved political unification under the Sumerians. Rather, dozens of city-states vied for political and economic supremacy. The Sumerians depended heavily on trading with areas outside Mesopotamia. Their relationships with Proto-Elamites living in Khuzistan to the east were of critical importance. Approximately 5000 years ago the Proto-Elamites gained some degree of control over major trading centers on the Iranian plateau, centers that supplied obsidian, chlorite vessels, and other commodities and luxuries to Sumer.

▇ Sumerian civilization flourished until approximately 4000 years ago, when it was eclipsed by Babylonian power. In the late second millennium B.C. the city of Assur in the north nurtured the Assyrian Empire, which was extended by vigorous and despotic kings during the first half of the succeeding millennium. The Assyrian Empire at one time stretched from the Mediterranean to the Persian Gulf.

▇ The Assyrian Empire fell in 612 B.C., and the power vacuum was filled by the Babylonians under the rule of Nebuchadnezzar. Babylon fell to Cyrus of Persia in 534 B.C., and Mesopotamia became part of the Persian Empire.

Chronological Table I

The delta regions and floodplain between the Tigris and Euphrates rivers form a hot, low-lying environment, much of it inhospitable sand, swamp, and dry mud flats. Yet this region, Mesopotamia (Greek for "land between the rivers"), was the cradle of the world's earliest urban civilization (Fagan, 1979; Lloyd, 1980). From north to south, Mesopotamia is approximately 600 miles (965 km) long and 250 miles (402 km) wide. (Figure 16.1 shows its location.) The plains are subject to long, intensely hot summers and harsh, cold winters. Before 7500 years ago, the floodplain may have been uninhabited except for a few nomadic groups. Dry agriculture, which relies on seasonal rainfall, was totally impracticable, and the plants and animals of the highlands around Mesopotamia were unable to tolerate the climatic extremes of the delta.

There are few permanent water supplies away from the great rivers and their tributaries. However, once watered, the soils of Mesopotamia proved both fertile and potentially highly productive. The agricultural potential of the areas close to rivers and streams could be realized for the first time. By 7000 years ago and perhaps earlier, village farmers were diverting the waters of the rivers. Within 2000 years the urban civilization of the Sumerians was flourishing in Mesopotamia.

THE FIRST CITIES

With continued improvement in the effectiveness of agriculture and development of such technological innovations as pottery, the village communities of the Zagros foothills, east of Mesopotamia, achieved a more efficient subsistence base, which fed a gradually increasing farming population. These technological and economic changes were far from spectacular: by at least 8000 years ago, farmers were living on the Assyrian plains, at first in areas where they could

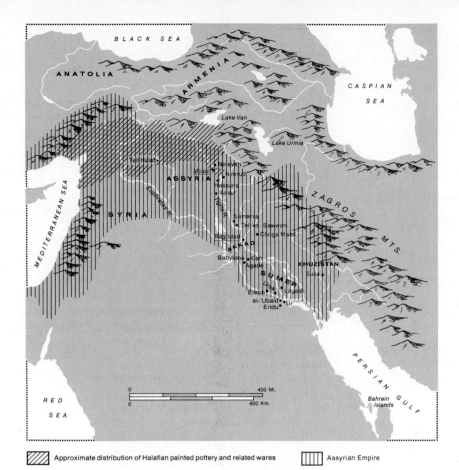

▨▨ Approximate distribution of Halafian painted pottery and related wares   ‖‖‖ Assyrian Empire

FIGURE 16.1 Sites and culture distributions mentioned in this chapter. (Tepe Yahya and Shar-i-Shokhta lie to the east of the map.)

rely on seasonal rainfall to water their crops; later they settled by the rivers, with animals and crops that could tolerate the climate of the lowlands. There they developed simple irrigation methods to bring water to their fields.

The first farmers to settle in Assyria were scattered over the undulating plains in small village settlements like Umm Dabaghiyah (Kirkbride, 1975; Lloyd, 1983; Oates and Oates, 1976; Redman, 1978) that contained a few huts and storage bins made of packed mud. Commonly the houses, which were probably entered from the roof, consisted of two or three rooms with small doors. Ovens and chimneys were integral parts of the houses. The successive occupation layers of these sites are filled with pottery handmade of coarse clay and painted or incised with dots, circles, and other designs (Figure 16.2). Such wares — named Hassunan pottery, after Hassuna, the first village of this type excavated — are found over a wide area of the north, from the upper Tigris Valley to the plains west of the modern city of Mosul.

Hassuna **8000 B.P.**

The regions between Mosul in the north and Baghdad in the south were inhabited by irrigation farmers by at least 7500 years ago. We know this from

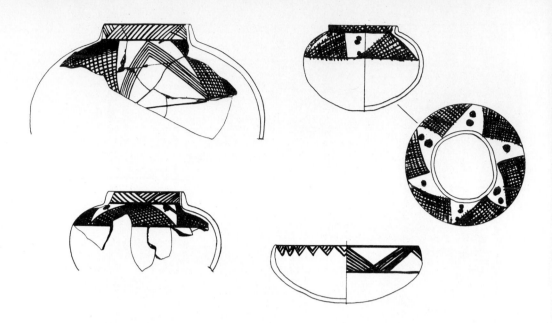

FIGURE 16.2 Early Mesopotamian painted pottery: above, vessels from Hassuna; below, Samarra-type vessels from Hassuna.

discoveries of villages in the region of Samarra, on the fringes of the Mesopotamian delta. Samarran culture painted pottery (Figure 16.2), which comes from such sites as Tell es-Sawwan and Choga Mami, reveals early farming villages situated in areas where irrigation agriculture was the only viable means of food production (Oates, 1973). The Samarran sites near Choga Mami are situated along low ridges parallel to nearby hills, where irrigation could be practiced with the least effort. Traces of canals are found at Choga Mami, as are wheat, barley, and linseed, a crop that can be grown in this area only when irrigation is used. Choga Mami itself lies between two rivers where floodwaters could be diverted across the fields and then drained away to prevent salt buildup. This is a relatively easy form of irrigation to adopt. Presumably, later refinements in technology enabled other farming settlements to move away from naturally flooded areas into regions where more extensive irrigation was necessary. There is every indication that the Samarrans were advanced farmers who lived in substantial villages which, in the case of Choga Mami, may have covered up to 14.8 acres (6 ha) and housed more than 1000 souls. The other excavated Samarran village, Tell es-Sawwan, was surrounded by a ditch and a wall, as if defense was a major consideration.

The Samarrans occupied relatively low-lying territory between the arid delta of the south and the dry-agriculture areas of the Hassunans to the north. Their newly developed irrigation techniques and heat-tolerant strains of wheat and barley enabled them to settle in areas that were hitherto inaccessible. Their sedentary and permanent settlements and great reliance on agriculture allowed them to forge community and external social and economic bonds that provided a catalyst for more complex societies to develop in future millennia.

Approximately 7500 years ago, many village farmers in the Near East began to make a characteristic style of painted pottery, abandoning the monochrome wares they had made before. The new fashion spread from southwest Turkey around the shores of Lake Van, famous for its obsidian, and as far east as the Zagros Mountains. The most brilliantly painted pottery was made in northern Iraq by the inhabitants of Tell Halaf, whose enormous kilns produced bowls, dishes, and flasks adorned with elaborate, stylized patterns and representations of people and animals (Figure 16.3). The Halafian cultural tradition flourished in what had once been Hassunan territory, and the people maintained regular contact with the Samarrans to the south.

The Halafians still lived in much the same way as their predecessors and made no startling agricultural or technological innovations, but they developed new contacts between villages hundreds of miles apart, trading such commodities as obsidian, semiprecious stones, and other luxury items. Their pottery is remarkably similar from one end of Halafian territory to the other; continuous and effective interaction over wide areas must have taken place. It has been suggested that this was the result of a major change in social organization, whereby tribal villages of earlier times were linked under chiefdoms. As with the Hopewell in North America, these new elite groups required greater communication and the sharing of status goods such as painted pottery to reinforce their authority (Redman, 1978).

Approximately 7300 years ago, the first farmers to live on the delta of the

FIGURE 16.3 Halafian vessel from Iraq.

south moved onto the floodplains. They settled on riverbanks, where they could obtain water without digging huge ditches or carrying it long distances. At first the farmers do not seem to have done much more than clear out natural, clogged channels, occasionally digging small feeder canals for gardens already sited to take advantage of natural drainage. These simple irrigation works made it possible to grow vegetables in addition to cereal crops. Cattle probably were penned in lush pastures, conceivably on a communal basis. The abundant fish and waterfowl were important dietary supplements. Fruit of the date palm may have been a vital staple.

We do not know anything about how the first inhabitants of the Mesopotamian delta acquired or developed the skills needed to survive in their harsh environment. Interdependence among members of the community was essential, because raw materials suitable for building houses had to be improvised from the plentiful sand, clay, palm trees, and reeds between the rivers. Digging even the smallest canal required at least a little political and social leadership. The annual backbreaking task of clearing silt from clogged river courses and canals can have been achieved only by communal effort. As both Robert Adams (1966) and Kent Flannery (1972) point out, the relationship between developing a stratified society and creating food surpluses is close. Distinctive social changes came from the more efficient systems for producing food that were essential in the delta. As food surpluses grew and the specialized agricultural economies of these 'Ubaid villages became successful, the trend toward sedentary settlement and higher population densities increased. Expanded trade networks and the redistribution of surpluses and trade goods also affected society, with dominant groups of 'Ubaid people becoming more active in producing surpluses, which eventually supported more and more people who were not farmers. The village of al-'Ubaid itself was built on a low mound and consisted of huts of mud brick and reeds, sometimes with roofs formed from bent sticks

'Ubaid period
7300 to 5600 B.P.

al-'Ubaid

(R. M. Adams, 1981; Adams and Nissen, 1972; Redman, 1978). The al-'Ubaid people relied on hunting and fishing as well as cereal crops, reaping their grain with sickles of clay, sometimes fitted with flint blades. Goats, sheep, and some cattle were herded on the floodplain.

Al-'Ubaid and similar small hamlets were clustered in groups, many with their own small ceremonial center. The villages were linked by kinship and clan, with one clan authority overseeing the villagers' affairs and, probably, the irrigation schemes that connected them. In time the small village ceremonial centers grew, as did the one at Eridu (first settled around 6750 years ago, when **Eridu 6750 B.P.** the Tell Halaf people were still making their painted pottery in the north).

Eridu consisted of a mud-brick temple with fairly substantial mud-brick houses around it, often with a rectangular floor plan. The craftsworkers lived a short distance from the elite clustered around the temple, and still farther away were the dwellings of the farmers, who grew the crops that supported everyone. By 6500 years ago, the Eridu temple had grown large, containing altars and offering places and a central room bounded by rows of smaller compartments. It has been estimated that the population of Eridu was as high as 5000 at this time, but exact computations are impossible.

'Ubaid society was fully developed by 6350 B.P.; its institutions and material **6350 B.P.** culture are found all over Mesopotamia. At every sizable 'Ubaid settlement the temple dominated the inhabitants' houses.

As Mesopotamian society grew in complexity, so did the need for social, political, and religious institutions that would provide an integrative function for everyone. The settlement of Uruk epitomizes cultural developments just before Sumerian civilization began. Anyone approaching Uruk could see the great zig- **Uruk period** gurat, the stepped temple pyramid, for miles (Figure 16.4). Built with enormous **5600 to 5000 B.P.** expenditure of work as a community project, the ziggurat and its satellite temples were the center of Uruk life. The temples were not only storehouses and places of worship, they were also redistribution centers for surplus food. Hundreds of craftsworkers labored for the temple as stonemasons, copperworkers, weavers, and at dozens of other specialized tasks. None of these people tilled the ground or worked on irrigation; they formed a distinctive class in a well-stratified society (Lloyd, 1978).

The entire life of Uruk and its connections with cities, towns, merchants, and mines hundreds of miles away revolved around the temple. The ruler of Uruk and the keeper of the temple was the *en*, both secular and religious leader. His wishes and policies were carried out by his priests and by a complex hierarchy of bureaucrats, wealthy landowners, and merchants. Tradespeople and craftsworkers were a more lowly segment of society, and under them were the thousands of fishers, peasants, sailors, and slaves that formed the bulk of Uruk's burgeoning population.

In its heyday, approximately 4800 years ago, Uruk was far more than a city. **4800 B.P.** Satellite villages extended out for at least 6 miles (10 km), each with its own irrigation system. All provided food for those in the city, whether grain, fish, or meat. Each settlement depended on the others for survival, at first because each provided things essential for a well-balanced existence; later they needed protection from outsiders who would have plundered their goods. The Mesopota-

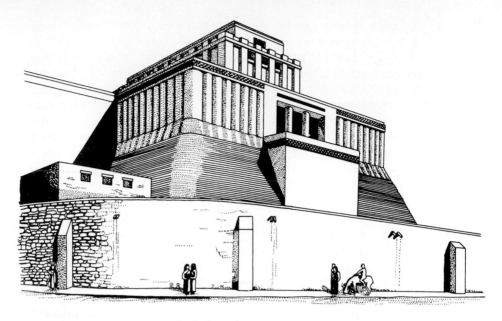

FIGURE 16.4   Reconstruction of an Uruk temple at Eridu. Notice the great platform supporting the temple and the drainage pipes in the walls. Below is a photograph of the great ziggurat (temple mound) of Ur, built approximately 4000 years ago.

mian city had developed an elaborate system of management with a well-defined hierarchy of rulers and priests, landowners and bureaucrats, traders and peasants. This system organized and regulated society, meted out reward and punishment, and made policy decisions for the thousands of people who lived under it.

By 5400 years ago, the Sumerians' commercial transactions were so complex that the possibilities for thievery and accounting mistakes were endless. It was not possible to keep all the details in one's head. Many people used marked clay tokens, which they carried around on strings. Eventually some clever officials made small clay tablets and scratched them with incised signs that depicted familiar objects such as pots or animals (Schmandt-Besserat, 1978). From there it was a short step to more simplified, conventionalized, wedge-shaped (cuneiform) signs that were modeled closer and closer to phonetic syllables and spoken language (Figure 16.5). Now trade could expand, unfettered by the limitations of the human memory. At first, specially trained scribes used cuneiform to record inventories and commercial transactions. Soon they began to explore the limitless opportunities afforded by the ability to express oneself in writing. Kings used tablets to trumpet their victories and political triumphs. Fathers chided errant sons, and lawyers recorded complicated land transactions. Sumerian poetry includes love stories, great epics, hymns to the gods, and tragic laments bemoaning the destruction of city after city (Kramer, 1963). Temple records and accounts tell us much not only of economic and social organization but also of Mesopotamian folklore and religion.

On the plateau to the north, copper tools and ornaments had been in use for centuries, first appearing as early as the fifth or sixth millennium B.C. (for chronology, see Hassan, 1987). Copper was intensively used in Iran during the fourth millennium and was imported into the delta areas of Mesopotamia as early as 5500 years ago, probably earlier. It came into widespread use in the Jemdet Nasr period. Although many peasant societies were aware of the properties of native copper, and both the early Egyptians and the American Indians made hammered ornaments from it, the softness of the metal limits the uses to which it can be put. Eventually, though, people familiar with kiln firing of pottery developed techniques for smelting copper ore. Copper is fine and lustrous and makes admirable ornaments. Its economic advantages (in terms of sharp cutting edges) were less obvious until metalsmiths learned to alloy copper with tin or arsenic to produce bronze and other forms of tougher metal. Once alloying was understood, copper assumed a more important place in agriculture and warfare.

By 5000 years ago, copper specialists had begun to work in most Mesopotamian cities, smelting and casting weapons and ornaments of high quality. Some cities attempted to maintain a monopoly on copper weapons and tools by training specialist craftsworkers and controlling trade in ingots and artifacts. The later development of bronze weapons can be linked to the rise of warfare as a method of attaining political ends, for cities such as Eridu and Uruk were not isolated from other centers. Indeed, they were only too aware of them. Ur of the Chaldees, a city much smaller than Uruk, was only 75 miles (120 km) away. The two were rivals for centuries, constantly bickering, competing in trading,

**Jemdet Nasr period
5350 to 4900 B.P.**

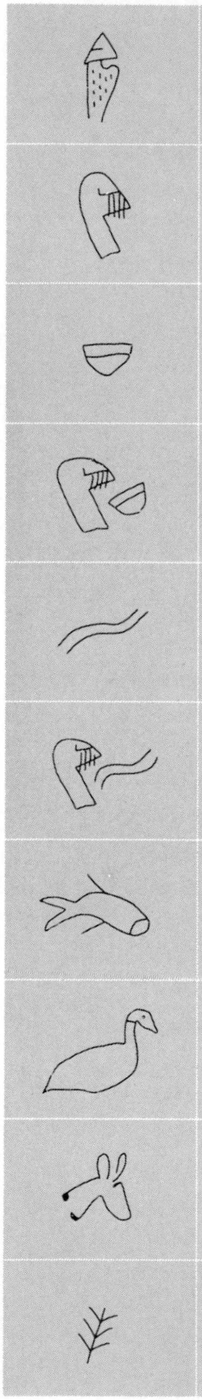

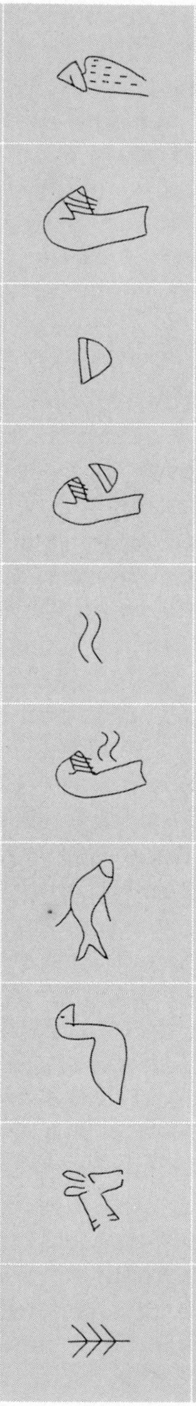

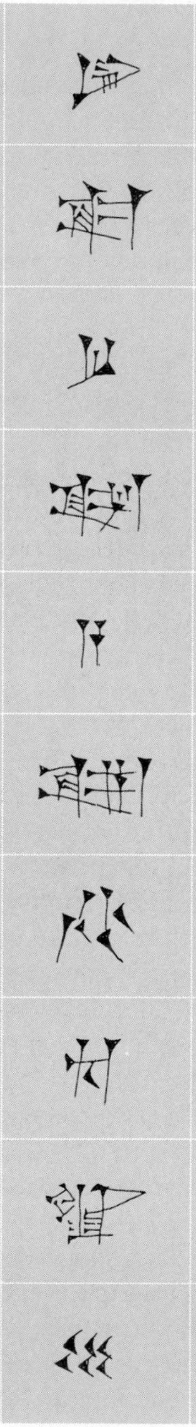

Earliest pictographs (3000 B.C.)	Denotation of pictographs	Pictographs in rotated position	Cuneiform signs c. 1900 B.C.	Basic logographic values Reading	Meaning
	Head and body of man			lu	Man
	Head with mouth indicated			ka	Mouth
	Bowl of food			ninda	Food, bread
	Mouth + food			kú	To eat
	Stream of water			a	Water
	Mouth + water			nag	To drink
	Fish			kua	Fish
	Bird			mušen	Bird
	Head of an ass			anše	Ass
	Ear of barley			še	Barley

FIGURE 16.5 Development of Sumerian writing, from a pictographic script to a cuneiform script, and then to a phonetic system. The word *cuneiform* is derived from the Latin word *cuneus*, meaning "a wedge," after the characteristic impression of the script.

and fighting with each other. Cities soon had walls, a sure sign that they needed protection against marauders. All the elements that made up Sumerian civilization were now in place.

SUMERIAN CIVILIZATION AND TRADE

By 4900 years ago, Sumerian civilization was in full swing in the southern delta. Archaeologically this status is reflected in increased wealth (Kramer, 1963). Metal tools became much more common, and domestic tools as well as weapons proliferated. Technologically, they were far in advance of earlier tools. Smiths began to alloy copper with tin to produce bronze. Armies and farmers were equipped with wheeled chariots and wagons. With a shift in political power from priests to kings, Mesopotamian rulers became more despotic, concentrating the wealth of the state and controlling subjects by military strength, religious acumen, and taxation, as well as economic incentive.

The cities' power depended in part on intensive agriculture, which irrigation and fertile Mesopotamian soils had so encouraged that rural populations rose sharply. The plow, which depended on draft oxen trained to pull it through the soil for a deeper furrow, was invented and increased agricultural yield. Plows were not used in the New World, where there were no potentially domesticable draft animals except the llama, and the rice farmers of Asia did not have much use for such a tool either, but it did permit higher yields of cereal crops and supported larger urban and rural populations in the Old World.

Trading was an integral part of Sumerian life, a multifaceted operation absorbing the energies of many people. The redistribution systems of the cities combined many activities, all controlled by the centralized authority that ruled the settlements. Food surpluses were redistributed, and raw materials were obtained from far away for the manufacture of ornaments, weapons, and prestigious luxuries. We have every reason to believe that specialist merchants handled commodities such as copper. If later historical records are any guide, there was wholesaling and contracting, loans were floated, and individual profit may have been a prime motivation.

Demands for raw materials appear to have risen steadily, spreading market networks into territories remote from the home state. For these long-distance routes to succeed, political stability at both ends was essential. An intricate system of political, financial, and logistical checks and balances had to be maintained, requiring an efficient and alert administrative organization.

The raw materials traded by the Sumerians included metals, timber, skins, ivory, and precious stones such as malachite. Many could be found only in the remote highlands to the north and east of Mesopotamia and were traded in bulk from the late third millennium B.C. onward. Wheeled vehicles and boats became vital in trade and warfare. Horses, asses, and oxen were put to drawing heavy loads.

Flourishing trade routes expanded along the delta waterways, especially up the placid Euphrates, which was easily navigable for long distances. This great river, whose ancient name *Uruttu* means "copper," transmitted raw materials from the north and trade goods from the Persian Gulf to the Mediterranean.

Well before 5000 years ago, the Euphrates joined many scattered towns, transmitting to all the products of Sumerian craftsworkers and a modicum of cultural unity.

Mesopotamia lacked the mineral and stone resources that were plentiful on the Iranian plateau to the east and in Anatolia. The Sumerians and their successors obtained them by trading their food surpluses in the form of grain, dried fish, and other perishable goods as well as textiles for basic raw materials. This capacity to produce surpluses was vital to Mesopotamian trading activities. This dependence on long-distance trading made the Mesopotamians vulnerable to the activities of their neighbors and even peoples living at a considerable distance from their homeland (Kohl, 1978).

THE PROTO-ELAMITES

While early farmers were settling the inhospitable Mesopotamian delta, other peoples were beginning to cultivate the area between the Zagros foothills and the Tigris and Euphrates (Lamberg-Karlovsky, 1978; Wright and Johnson, 1978). During the sixth and early fifth millennia B.C., small farming villages flourished in the heart of Khuzistan. The people were irrigation farmers who herded goats, sheep, and cattle as well. So many of their sites are known that it seems certain that areas such as the Deh Luran Plain were intensively settled by this time. During the next thousand years or so, Khuzistan was still densely populated, and village settlements grew larger and larger. It was about this time that the famous archaeological site of Susa began to achieve special prominence.

The earliest occupation levels at Susa are broadly contemporary with the late 'Ubaid occupation of Mesopotamia. The first village on the site was approximately 61.7 to 74 acres (25 to 30 ha) in area and was inhabited by metal-using farmers. Strong Mesopotamian influence can be detected in slightly later levels at Susa, as if there was at least some colonization of Khuzistan by Uruk people from the delta toward the end of the fourth millennium B.C.

Approximately 5200 years ago, a distinctive cultural tradition known as the *Proto-Elamite* (Elamite is a language) appeared at Susa and elsewhere in Khuzistan. The Proto-Elamite state seems to have evolved in what is now southwest Iran, but within a short time its distinctive tablets, seals, and ceramic types came to be found in widely scattered sites on the Iranian highlands. Their clay tablets have turned up in settlements in every corner of the Iranian plateau, in central Iran, and on the borders of Afghanistan.

The Proto-Elamite expansion took place over a very short time and appears to have been connected with a desire to control both key trade routes on the Iranian plateau and access to sources of important raw materials.

The most thoroughly excavated site on the plateau is Tepe Yahya, which was a prosperous rural community between 5400 and 5200 years ago (Lamberg-Karlovsky, 1973, 1978). The inhabitants were already importing such raw materials as obsidian and chlorite (steatite). After 5200 B.P., Tepe Yahya grew and was engaged in much more intensive trading activities. It is at this period that

8000 B.P.

Susa

Proto-Elamites
5200 B.P.

Tepe Yahya
5400 B.P.

Proto-Elamite artifacts are found in the site, which seems to have served as a political center that coordinated trade by surrounding settlements. The Tepe Yahya area was a center of chlorite bowl production, for abundant deposits of this raw material are found nearby. The bowls produced at Tepe Yahya and elsewhere were definitely luxury items, so highly prized in Mesopotamia that they may have caused keen competition among those rich enough to afford them (Kohl, 1975). Chlorite tools and ornaments were so popular that they occur over a very wide area of the Iranian plateau as well as on islands in the Persian Gulf, and at Moenjo-daro, one of the major cities of the Harappan civilization of the Indus Valley (Chapter 18).

The plateau trading networks also extended onto the Susiana Plain, south of the Hindu Kush, where a multitude of river valleys lead south to the Indus floodplain. The village of Shar-i-Shokhta, a small community of mud-brick houses, stood by the banks of Lake Helmand in east Iran. Traders brought fragments of lapis lazuli embedded in limestone from the distant Hindu Kush to Shar-i-Shokhta. There artisans chipped away the limestone and turned the semiprecious stone into beads. The beads, and lumps of raw lapis, were then traded across the desert to Mesopotamia and also north into southern Turkmenia, probably in exchange for grain, a valued commodity in this dry area (N. Hammond, 1973).

The chlorite vessels produced near Tepe Yahya were made by local artisans, perhaps working part-time or at certain seasons of the year, but the trade itself seems to have been managed by the Proto-Elamites, people who acted as middle agents in the long-distance trade between Mesopotamia and the distant plateau. In a sense the Sumerians controlled this trade through the laws of supply and demand. Their needs resulted in a degree of economic control of foreign areas without actual political control. The Proto-Elamites, however, seem to have recognized a political and economic opportunity which stemmed from their strategic position between Mesopotamia and Iran, so they expanded their sphere of interest onto the plateau. Their efforts at controlling trade and raw materials do not seem to have lasted very long. Perhaps their administrative and political system became overtaxed by the new demands on it. Conceivably the benefits of political control did not justify the effort in terms of trade generated. In any event, Proto-Elamite artifacts vanish from the archaeological record within a few centuries.

Even if the Proto-Elamites failed in their bid to control trade on the plateau, they certainly continued to flourish in Khuzistan. Susa itself grew into a great city, where the trade routes between Mesopotamia and the East converged. The Elamite state emerged in all its complexity after 5000 years ago and came under **Elamites 5000 B.P.** the domination of Akkadian kings from central Mesopotamia for a while, but by 4000 years ago the Elamites were strong enough to attack and destroy Ur of the Chaldees in Sumer. The Elamites' power and importance depended on their geographic position at the center of a network of trade routes that led to the Iranian plateau, to the Persian Gulf, and to most city-states in the lowlands. Elamite history shows us how no great civilization can be considered in isolation, for no complex society flourishes without depending on political and economic factors outside its boundaries. In the case of the Sumerians and Elamites, as well as the many communities on the Iranian plateau, interdependencies developed that linked lowlands and highlands in lasting ways (Kohl, 1978).

THE WIDENING OF POLITICAL AUTHORITY

By 4800 years ago, Mesopotamia held several important city-states, each headed by rulers who vied with the others for status and prestige. Political authority was most effective at the city level, with the temple priests as the primary controllers of trade, economic life, and political matters. Inevitably, as society became more complex, the priests were increasingly concerned with secular matters, such as the organization of irrigation systems that expanded as population densities rose and more and more prime agricultural land was put under cultivation. As the Mesopotamian delta became an environment increasingly controlled by human activities, the people began to concentrate in larger cities under secular leaders, abandoning many smaller towns. The motive for this shift was as much defense as population increase, for both Sumerian inscriptions and the archaeological record tell of warfare and constant quarreling between neighbors. Competition over natural resources intensified as each state raised an army to defend its water rights, trade routes, and city walls. The onerous tasks of defense and military organization passed to despotic secular kings supposedly appointed by the gods. As the wealth and power of the cities increased, so did internecine strife. Such states as Erech, Kish, and Ur of the Chaldees had periods of political strength and prosperity when they dominated their neighbors. Then, just as swiftly, the tide of their fortunes would change and they would sink into obscurity. Then there were the nomadic peoples of the surrounding mountains and deserts, who encroached constantly on settled Sumerian lands. At times, peoples such as the Gutians disrupted city life so completely that any form of travel became an impossibility.

Some Sumerian cities nurtured powerful and wealthy leaders. When Sir Leonard Woolley (1934) excavated a royal cemetery in Ur of the Chaldees (Figure 16.6), he found a series of kings and queens who had been buried in huge graves with their entire retinue of followers. One tomb contained the remains of fifty-nine people who were poisoned to accompany the king, even courtiers and soldiers, as well as serving women. Each wore his or her official dress and insignia and had lain down to die in the correct order of precedence, having taken poison. Some archaeologists believe that these are not royal graves but the result of a macabre fertility ceremony (Lloyd, 1983).

The first Sumerian ruler to have ambitions wider than merely controlling a few city-states was Lugalzagesi (approximately 4360–4335 years ago). Not content with control of Uruk, Ur, Lagash, and several other cities, he boasted of overseeing the entire area from the Persian Gulf to the Mediterranean. The god Enlil, king of the lands, "made the people lie down in peaceful pastures like cattle and supplied Sumer with water bringing joyful abundance" (Kramer, 1963). Sumerian contacts with the outside world should not be judged in terms of conquering armies but in the context of their constant trading, which was an integral part of their civilization. The people of Sumer traveled far and wide in search of raw materials and luxury imports. Life without trade was impossible.

Lugalzagesi
4360 B.P.

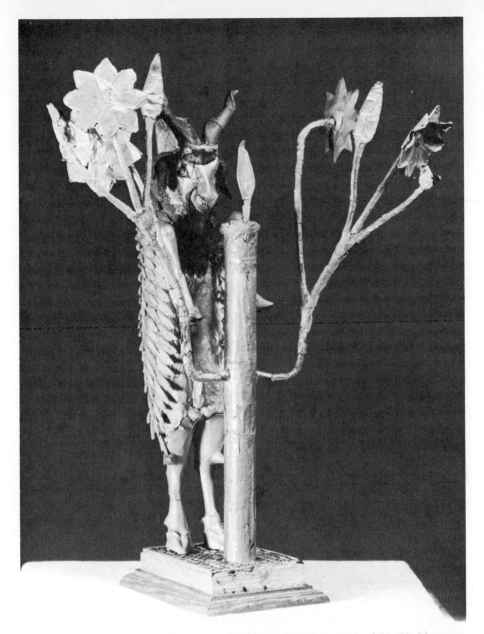

FIGURE 16.6   A famous ornament from the Royal Cemetery at Ur of the Chaldees, entitled "Ram in the Thicket." The wood figure was covered with gold leaf and lapis lazuli, the belly in silver leaf, and the fleece in shell.

They carried their political and religious ideas as far as the shores of the Mediterranean and maintained at least tenuous contacts with dozens of city-states in the Near East. The Sumerians not only developed a civilization but also were the first people to record their literature and beliefs in writing. They set down age-old legends of great floods and of warring gods that were to survive through the millennia to become part of the Old Testament and the cultural heritage of Western civilization.

THE ASSYRIANS

As Sumerian civilization prospered, urban centers also sprang up in northern Mesopotamia. Soon Assyrian cities began to compete with the delta city-states for trade and prestige. Approximately 4370 years ago, a Semitic-speaking leader, Sargon, founded a ruling dynasty at the town of Agade, south of Babylon. This northern house soon established its rule over Sumer and Assyria by military campaigns and skillful commercial ventures. After a short period of economic prosperity, the new kings were toppled by highland tribes from the north. Mesopotamia entered a time of political instability, but by 3990 years ago the ancient city of Babylon was achieving prominence under Semitic rulers, culminating in the reign of the great king Hammurabi 3790 years ago.

Hammurabi set up a powerful commercial empire reaching out from Mesopotamia as far as Assyria and the Zagros. The unity of his empire depended on a common official language and a cuneiform writing system. Small city-states for the first time influenced world culture far more than their geographic territory appears to justify, an influence based on economic and political power maintained by despotic rule and harsh power politics. By this time, Mesopotamian influence was so great that weapon types used by Babylonian armies had spread to Russia, Europe, and the western Mediterranean.

One of the cities of the north that flourished for a long time was Assur on the Tigris, the mounds of which contain the remains of Sumerian temples (Postgate, 1977). The merchants of Assur traded far to the east and west, as well as controlling the trade down the Tigris. Assur came into great prominence during the reign of King Assur-uballit I (1365 to 1330 B.C.), who incorporated the prime cereal-growing lands of northern Assyria into a new empire that his successors extended over a vast territory from the Mediterranean to Egypt, and as far as the Persian Gulf. Great military kings such as Shalmaneser, Assurnasirpal, Sargon, and Tiglath-Pileser were absolute despots, to whom warfare and prestige became veritable obsessions. When Assurnasirpal completed his palace at Nimrud he threw a party for the 16,000 inhabitants of the city, 1,500 royal officials, "47,074 men and women from the length of my country," and 5,000 foreign envoys (Postgate, 1977). The king fed this throng of more than 69,000 people for ten days, during which time his guests ate 14,000 sheep and consumed more than 10,000 skins of wine.

The last of the great Assyrian kings was Assurbanipal, who died in approximately 630 B.C. When he died, the Assyrian Empire entered a period of political chaos. The Babylonians achieved independence, and Assyrian power finally was broken in 612 B.C. when Nineveh was sacked by the Persians and Babylonians. For forty-three years, the mighty Babylonian king Nebuchadnezzar ruled over Mesopotamia and turned his capital into one of the showpieces of the ancient world. His double-walled city was adorned by magnificent mud-brick palaces with elaborate hanging gardens, a great processional way, and a huge ziggurat. It was to Babylon that a large contingent of Jews were taken as cap-

Sargon 4370 B.P.

Babylon 3990 B.P.

Hammurabi 3790 B.P.

Assur

Assyrians c. 1350 to 612 B.C.

tives after Nebuchadnezzar's armies sacked Jerusalem, an exile immortalized by the lament "By the waters of Babylon we sat down and wept" (Psalm 137:1).

The Babylonian Empire did not long survive the death of Nebuchadnezzar in 556 B.C. His successors were weak men who were unable to resist the external forces that now pressed on Mesopotamia. The armies of Cyrus the Great of Persia took Babylon virtually without resistance in 534 B.C., and Mesopotamia became part of an empire even larger than that of the Assyrians. By this time, the effects of constant political instability and bad agricultural management were beginning to make themselves felt. The Mesopotamian delta was a totally artificial environment by 4000 years ago, and poor drainage and badly maintained irrigation works in later centuries led to inexorable rises in the salt content of the soil and to drastic falls in crop yields. Nothing could be done to reverse this trend until modern soil science technology and irrigation techniques could be imported to the delta at vast expense.

Cyrus **534 B.C.**

GUIDE TO FURTHER READING

Fagan, Brian M. *Return to Babylon*. Boston: Little, Brown, 1979.
　　A history of archaeological research in Mesopotamia that starts with the first Arab geographers and ends with modern excavations.

Kramer, Samuel. *The Sumerians*. Chicago: University of Chicago Press, 1963.
　　The classic account of Sumerian civilization, written by one of the foremost experts on Sumerian cuneiform tablets and literature. A model of what such books should be.

Lloyd, Seton. *The Archaeology of Mesopotamia* (2d ed.). London: Thames and Hudson, 1983.
　　A synthesis of Iraqi archaeology that concentrates mainly on the early civilizations. Strong on archaeological data, well illustrated, and informative on architecture.

Oates, David, and Oates, Joan. *The Rise of Civilization*. Oxford: Elsevier Phaidon, 1976.

Postgate, Nicholas. *The First Empires*. Oxford: Elsevier Phaidon, 1977.
　　Two volumes in the Making of the Past series that describe for the lay reader the cultures and civilizations discussed in this chapter in more detail than is possible here. Recommended for paper writers.

CHAPTER 17

Pharaohs and African Chiefs

Preview

■ By 5600 years ago, the average Egyptian probably lived much as people do today in some Upper Nile villages.

■ These pre-Dynastic people lived at a time of gradual population growth and enrichment of the native culture, probably as a result of expanded trading contacts. The number of luxury goods increased, metallurgy was introduced from Mesopotamia, and social structure seems to have become more elaborate.

■ The acquisition of writing by the Egyptians probably was one of the catalytic events that led to the unification of Egypt and the emergence of civilization there. The process of unification culminated under the pharaoh Narmer approximately 5000 years ago.

■ Ancient Egyptian civilization is divided into four main periods: the Old, Middle, New, and Late kingdoms, the earlier of which were separated by brief intermediate periods of political chaos.

■ The Old Kingdom is notable for its despotic pharaohs and the frenzy of pyramid construction, an activity that may be connected with pragmatic notions of fostering national unity.

■ The Middle Kingdom saw a shift of political and religious power to Thebes and Upper Egypt.

■ New Kingdom pharaohs made Egypt an imperial power with strong interests in Asia and Nubia. These pharaohs were buried in the Valley of Kings near Thebes. The cult of Amun was all-powerful, except for a brief interlude when the heretic pharaoh Akhenaten introduced the worship of the sun god Aten.

- Ancient Egyptian civilization began to decline after 3100 years ago, and the Nile eventually came under the rule of the Assyrians, then the Persians, and finally the Greek pharaohs, the Ptolemies.

- Egypt had few contacts with sub-Saharan Africa, which was widely settled by tropical farmers approximately 2000 years ago. The diffusion of farming coincided with both the introduction of ironworking and the spread of the Bantu-speaking peoples from West Africa over much of east, central, and southern Africa.

- Indigenous African states developed on the southern fringes of the Sahara Desert at the end of the first millennium A.D., owing their initial prosperity to the gold trade across the desert.

- The later prehistory of Africa is marked by continued contacts between Africans and societies living outside the continent. Complex states like that of the Karanga of southern Africa emerged in the last thousand years, several of them trading actively with foreign merchants and voyagers until Africa came into the purview of written history in recent times.

By 5600 years ago, the average Egyptian probably lived much as Upper Nile villagers do today (David, 1975; Johnson, 1978; Ruffle, 1977). Wheat and barley were cultivated in riverside gardens and supplemented by intensive gathering of wild vegetable foods. Cattle, goats, sheep, and pigs were herded. The meat from the herds was supplemented by the rich Nile game population and by fishing. These Amratian (or pre-Dynastic) people were the successors of the Badarians (Chapter 12) (Hoffman, 1979; Trigger, 1968; Trigger et al., 1983). Amratians derive their name from the archaeological site in Upper Egypt, El Amra. Amratian settlements apparently had a material culture somewhat similar to that which flourished in earlier centuries on the same sites of the Nile floodplain (Figure 17.1). The human population of the valley was growing slowly, and there was some cultural fusion and increased interaction between more closely spaced settlements. Pottery was still being made, but elegant stone vessels in alabaster and basalt also were used, probably shaped by specialist craftsworkers and traded widely through the valley. Amratian flintworkers created magnificent knives and daggers, which also were prized possessions. A gradual enrichment of pre-Dynastic culture can be discerned over the centuries, resulting in part from the introduction of copperworking from Asia. Soon metalworkers were making pins, flat axes, and daggers of the new material. The Amratians began to import copper from Sinai, while lead and silver came from Asia. The proportion of luxury goods to functional goods rose steadily; one of the locally manufactured items was *faience*, a form of glass widely traded in prehistoric times. Amratian settlements slowly became larger, and social structure became more elaborate. The archaeological record contains some signs of social classes, in the form of graves of varying opulence.

Chronological Table I

Amratian **5600 B.P.**

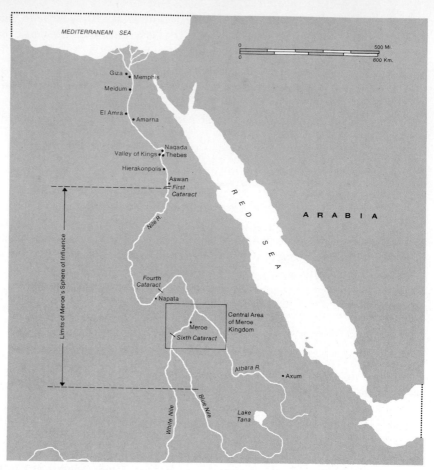

FIGURE 17.1   The Nile Valley.

METALLURGY, WRITING, AND UNIFICATION

The increased volume of trade is reflected in the importation of not only copper but other exotic items found in pre-Dynastic sites. Many of them are of unmistakable west Asian or Mesopotamian origin. The Naqada site, for instance, yielded a cylinder seal of Mesopotamian form. Some of the late pre-Dynastic pottery is painted with dark red colors on a buff background, in Asian style. There are depictions of Mesopotamian boat designs and of fabulous animals and creatures with intertwined necks and other motifs that derive from Asia.

The most important innovation of all, however, was the art of writing, which became fully developed in Egypt. Hieroglyphs (Greek for "sacred carving") are commonly thought to be a form of picture writing. In fact, they constitute a combination pictographic (picture) and phonetic (representing vocal sounds) script, which was not only written on papyrus but also carved on public buildings or painted on clay or wood. It seems most likely that writing was first developed in Mesopotamia and that Egyptian priests developed their own script, which was easier to produce with papyrus reed paper and ink rather than clay.

Ultimately they developed a cursive (running on) hieroglyphic script that was a form of handwriting, much easier to use on documents and other less formal communications. Only the consonants were written in all forms of hieroglyphs; the vowel sounds were omitted, although both were pronounced. With practice, reading this form of script is easy enough, and a smpl tst 'f ths srt shld shw ths qt wll (Figure 17.2) (Diringer, 1962; Pope, 1973).

The acquisition of writing, with all its organizational possibilities, probably was one of the main catalysts of the unification of the whole of Egypt into a single political entity. Unity was not imposed on Egypt from Asia, despite the increase in Asian influences in the material culture of the pre-Dynastic cultures. Rather, it was the culmination of local social and political developments that resulted from centuries of gradual change in economic and social life. Pre-Dynastic villages were autonomous units, each with its local deities. During the fourth millennium B.C., the more important villages became the focal points of different territories, which, in Dynastic times, became the *nomes*, or provinces, through which the pharaohs administered Egypt. The nomarchs (provincial leaders) were responsible for the gradual coalescence of Egypt into larger political and social units. Their deeds are recorded on ceremonial palettes that were used for moistening eye powder. Some of these palettes show alliances of local leaders dismantling conquered villages. Others commemorate the administrative skills of leaders who brought their villages through drought years by skillful management. The unification of Egypt was a gradual process of both voluntary and involuntary amalgamation. Voluntary unification resulted from common needs and economic advantage. Perhaps it was only in the final stages of unification that military force came into play to bring larger and larger political units under single rulers (Hoffman, 1979).

There is little archaeological evidence that documents the long process of unification. Michael Hoffman and a team of Egyptologists (1982) have recently investigated ancient Nekhen, a city called Hierakonpolis, "City of the Falcon," by the Greeks. Pre-Dynastic settlements and cemeteries surround the town. Some 5800 years ago, Nekhen was a village inhabited by a few hundred people.

FIGURE 17.2   Egyptian writing is referred to as hieroglyphs, the familiar symbols that appear on formal inscriptions and on tomb walls. In fact, Egyptian scribes developed cursive hands used in everyday life. These examples show formal hieroglyphic script (top line) and below it both the cursive style and the scribe's shorthand, which was used for rapid writing.

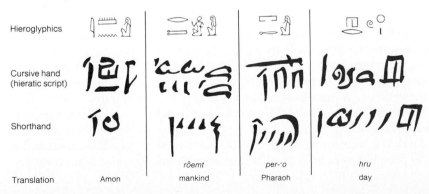

Hieroglyphics			
Cursive hand (hieratic script)			
Shorthand			
	rôemt	*per-'o*	*hru*
Translation	Amon	mankind	Pharaoh	day

During the next three centuries the population mushroomed to perhaps as many as 10,500. People lived in closely clustered mud-brick and plaster dwellings, the more important artisans and traders in larger houses with separate compounds. For the first time, there are signs of social differentiation in Egyptian society. The Abu Suffian cemetery near Nekhen housed important citizens, many of them prosperous traders who had profited from locally made fine-quality "Plum Red" pottery that was used to adorn tombs up and down the river. These people became powerful members of the community, with widespread contacts with settlements near and far.

About 5500 years ago, the fragile ecological balance of desert and grassland collapsed, perhaps as a result of overgrazing by goats and sheep and intensive pottery firing. Hoffman believes that some of the local leaders profited from the disaster by using their wealth to foster irrigation agriculture and settlement closer to the Nile. Their venture was successful and yielded large grain surpluses under the control of the new elite. They used their wealth to increase trade, erect public buildings like temples, and invest in imposing sepulchers. The ambitious leaders of Nekhen were buried in the same Abu Suffian cemetery, which straddled a dry gulch, their graves laid out on either side of the wadi in what Hoffman believes is a symbolic map of a unified Upper and Lower Egypt.

Egypt was finally unified under the pharaoh Narmer at Hierakonpolis about 5050 years ago. In economic terms, the unification may have involved some intensification of agriculture as population densities rose; but, as Karl Butzer (1976) has pointed out, the technology for lifting water was so rudimentary that the early rulers of Egypt were unable to organize any elaborate forms of irrigation. In all probability, most Ancient Egyptian agriculture involved irrigation schemes on a modest scale that merely extended the distribution of seasonal floodwaters from natural flood basins. Still, even these efforts must have required a considerable degree of administrative organization. Also, with a centralized form of administration, the divine leader, the pharaoh himself, was responsible for the success of the harvest. Since the Nile flood fluctuated considerably in cycles of abundant and lean years, and the pharaohs could do little to control the success or failure of irrigation without much more elaborate technology than they possessed, their political position could, theoretically at any rate, be threatened by famine years. If the divine leader could not provide, who could? Perhaps a different leader. Small wonder that some periods of political instability, which may have coincided with poor flood years, saw rapid successions of ineffective pharaohs.

Karl Butzer (1981) argues that episodes of rapid growth in Ancient Egyptian civilization were made possible by a series of important innovations. One was improved irrigation organization in the Old Kingdom, after 4800 years ago. This allowed the development of the delta regions of Lower Egypt, once the bureaucratic structure to organize the work was in place. During the Middle Kingdom (3941 to 3736 years ago), the pharaohs responded to several centuries of repeated low floods by placing closer government controls over food distribution and moving large numbers of people out of the valley into such areas as the Fayum Depression, where they organized huge drainage and irrigation works.

The New Kingdom (3517 to 3035 years ago) saw the introduction of the *shaduf*, a bucket-and-lever lifting device that raised water a yard or so from wells or ditches to gardens and estates. One result of this innovation was a shift of population from the narrow valley to the broad delta. The culmination of agricultural productivity came in the last few centuries B.C., when the last pharaohs undertook the complete drainage of the Fayum, introduced summer crops such as sorghum, and encouraged the development of the animal-drawn waterwheel, known as the *saqiya*. The impact of all these innovations was to increase both the productivity of the state and the size of the labor force. It is probable that the population of Ancient Egypt rose from less than a million 5000 years ago to approximately 5 million by 3500 years ago. These innovations were to continue to support Egyptian agriculture right up to the building of the High Dam at Aswan in the twentieth century A.D. (Fedden, 1977).

Karl Butzer (1981) has pointed out that civilizations can be regarded as ecosystems that emerge in response to sets of ecological opportunities. Over time, a variety of social and environmental adjustments are inevitable, some of them successful, leading to population growth, and others unsuccessful, so that the population shrinks. These demographic adjustments are commonly associated with ups and downs of political power. The political structures of, say, Ancient Egyptian civilization are not nearly as durable as the basic adaptive system they purport to control or the cultural identity of which they were once part. Butzer draws an analogy with the ecological concept of trophic levels among biotic communities, in which organisms with similar feeding habits, such as herbivores and carnivores, define successive tiers interlinked in a vertical chain. Likewise, he hypothesizes, an efficient social hierarchy comprises several levels arranged in what he calls a "low-angle pyramid, supported by a broad base of farmers and linked to the peak of the pyramid by a middle-level bureaucracy. The vertical structures channel food and information through the system, and an efficient energy flow allows each trophic level to flourish in a steady state." In this model, a flatter pyramid with little vertical structure would provide less information flow and limit the potential productivity of the lower levels. Butzer's pyramid would allow growth at the lower levels, with new technologies or organizational devices favoring expanded energy generation at the lower level. A steep, top-heavy pyramid laden with nobles and bureaucrats places excessive burdens on the lowest levels, so much so that external and internal forces can undermine the stability of society.

This model, when applied to the long history of Ancient Egyptian civilization, shows how the Egyptians persisted in adjusting to a floodplain environment for thousands of years. They overcame external and internal crises by reorganizing their state and economic structure. The key variables were the fluctuations of the Nile itself, occasional foreign intervention, the character of the pharaohs' leadership, and a progressively pathological society of elite nonproducers who persisted in exploiting the common farmer, a process that led to eventual social collapse. However, through all these variables the essential components of the sociopolitical system survived more or less intact, right up to the nineteenth century A.D. Indeed, the visitor to rural Egypt still can see farming villages functioning much as they did in Ancient Egyptian times.

PYRAMIDS AND THE OLD KINGDOM: 5050 TO 4131 YEARS AGO

Egyptologists conventionally divide Ancient Egyptian civilization into four broad periods, separated by at least two intermediate periods that were intervals of political change and instability (Table 17.1). The most striking feature of Ancient Egyptian civilization is its conservatism. Many of the artistic, religious, and technological features of early Egyptian civilization survived intact right into Roman times. The political and religious powers of the pharaohs changed somewhat through time, as later rulers became more imperialistic in their ambi-

TABLE 17.1   A much simplified chronology of Ancient Egyptian civilization.

Years B.C./B.P.	Period	Characteristics
30 B.C.	Roman occupation	Egypt an imperial Province of Rome
332 to 30	Ptolemaic Period	The Ptolemies bring Greek influence to Egypt, beginning with conquest of Egypt by Alexander the Great in 332 B.C.
1085 to 332	Late Period	Gradual decline in pharaonic authority culminating in Persian rule (525 to 404 and 343 to 332 B.C.)
3517 to 3035 B.P.	New Kingdom	Great imperial period of Egyptian history, with pharaohs buried in Valley of Kings. Pharaohs include Rameses II, Seti I, and Tutankhamun, as well as Akhenaten, the heretic ruler.
3736 to 3517	Second Intermediate Period	Hyksos rulers in the delta
3941 to 3736	Middle Kingdom	Thebes achieves prominence, also the priesthood of Amun
c. 4131 to 4123	First Intermediate Period	Political chaos and disunity
4636 to 4131	Old Kingdom	Despotic pharaohs build the pyramids and favor conspicuous funerary monuments. Institutions, economic strategies, and artistic traditions of Ancient Egypt established.
5050 to 4036	Archaic Period	Consolidation of state (treated as part of Old Kingdom in this book)
5050	Unification of Egypt under Narmer-Menes	

tions or different gods assumed political supremacy, but the essential continuity was there, in the form of a civilization whose life was governed by the unchanging environment of the Nile Valley, with its annual floods, narrow floodplain, and surrounding desert.

The Old Kingdom (c. 4636 to 4131 years ago) saw four dynasties of pharaohs governing Egypt from a royal capital at Memphis near Cairo. Apparently the country's resources were well organized and controlled by a centralized government. Some of the pharaohs had reputations as cruel despots, notably Cheops and Chephren, who built the pyramids of Giza. The building of pyramids is regarded as the mark of the Old Kingdom pharaohs (Edwards, 1973; Mendelssohn, 1974). The first royal pyramid was built by Djoser approximately 4680 years ago; it was a six-step pyramid that was surrounded by a veritable town of buildings and shrines. The Step Pyramid is a somewhat hesitant structure, its architectural roots in earlier stone-built tombs, but the great pyramids built over the next century show increasing confidence, culminating in the brilliant assurance of the pyramids of Giza, with their perfect pyramid shape (Figure 17.3). The largest of these, the Great Pyramid, covers 13.1 acres (5.3 ha) and is 481 feet (146 m) high. It dates to the Fourth Dynasty reign of Cheops, approximately 4600 years ago. Just under two centuries later, the pharaohs stopped building huge pyramids and diverted their organizational talents to other public works.

There is something megalomaniacal about the pyramids, built as they were with an enormous expenditure of labor and energy. They reflect the culmination of centuries of gradual evolution of the Egyptian state, during which the complexity of the state and the authority of the bureaucracy grew hand in hand. The pyramids were the houses and tombs for the pharaohs in eternity, symbols of the permanence of Egyptian civilization. They reflect the importance that the Egyptians placed on the life of the pharaoh in the afterworld, and in the notion of resurrection, a central belief in their religion for thousands of years.

Kurt Mendelssohn (1974) has argued that the pyramids were built over a relatively short period of time, during which the architects experimented with the pyramid shape. At least one pyramid collapsed during construction, before the builders mastered the correct 52° angles of the Great Pyramid. Every flood season, when agriculture was at a standstill, the pharaohs organized thousands of peasants into construction teams who quarried, transported, and laid the dressed stones of the pyramids. The permanent (year-round) labor force was relatively small, mainly skilled artisans, the fruit of whose work was placed in position on the main structure once a year. As far as is known, the peasants were paid volunteers, fed by the state bureaucracy, whose loyalty to the divine pharaoh provided the motivation for the work. Mendelssohn feels the construction of the pyramids was a practical administrative device designed to organize and institutionalize the state. As construction proceeded from one generation to the next, the villagers became dependent on the central administration for food for three months a year, food obtained from surpluses contributed by the villages themselves in the form of taxation. After a while the pyramids fulfilled their purpose, and the state-directed labor forces could be di-

FIGURE 17.3 The pyramids of Giza.

verted to other, less conspicuous state works. A new form of state organization had been created, one that both fostered and exploited the interdependence of Egyptian villages.

The Egyptian State

Egypt was the first state of its size in history. The pharaohs ruled by their own word, following no written laws, unlike the legislators of Mesopotamian city-states. The pharaoh had power over the Nile flood, rainfall, and all people, including foreigners. He was a god in his own right, respected by all people as a tangible divinity whose being was the personification of *Ma'at*, or "rightness." *Ma'at* was far more than just rightness, it was a "right order," and stood for order and justice. The pharaoh embodied *ma'at* and dispensed justice. *Ma'at* was pharaonic status and eternity itself — the very embodiment of the Egyptian state (Morenz, 1973).

The pharaoh's pronouncements were law, regulated by a massive background of precedent set by earlier pharaohs. Egyptian rulers lived a strictly ordered life. As one Greek writer tells us: "For there was a set time not only for his holding audience or rendering judgment, but even for his taking a walk, bathing, and sleeping with his wife; in short, every act of his life."

A massive, hereditary bureaucracy effectively ruled the kingdom, with rows of officials forming veritable dynasties. Their records tell us that much official energy was devoted to tax collection, harvest yields, and administration of irrigation (Figure 17.4). An army of 20,000 men, many of them mercenaries, was maintained at the height of Egypt's prosperity. The Egyptian Empire was a literate one, that is to say, trained scribes who could read and write were an integral part of the state government. Special schools trained writers for careers in the army, the palace, the treasury, and numerous other callings (Aldred,1986; Johnson, 1978).

Despite the number of scribes and minor clerics, a vast gulf separated one who could read and write from the uneducated peasant worker. The life of an Egyptian peasant, given good harvests, was easier than that of a Greek or a Syrian farmer, although the state required occasional bouts of forced labor to clear irrigation canals or to haul stone, both tasks being essential to maintain Egyp-

FIGURE 17.4 A tomb painting from the tomb of Menena at Thebes showing the harvesting and measuring of fields near the Nile.

tian agriculture. Minor craftsworkers and unskilled laborers lived more regimented lives, working on temples and pharaohs' tombs (Steindorff and Steele, 1954). Many were organized in shifts under foremen. There were strikes, and absenteeism was common. A scale of rations and daily work was imposed. Like many early states, however, the Egyptians depended on slave labor for some public works and much domestic service, but foreign serfs and war prisoners could wield much influence in public affairs. They were allowed to rent and cultivate land.

THE FIRST INTERMEDIATE PERIOD AND MIDDLE KINGDOM: 4131 TO 3736 YEARS AGO

The Old Kingdom ended with the death of Pepi II approximately 4200 years ago (Wilson, 1951). By this time the authority of the monarchy had been weakened by constant expenditure on lavish public works and, perhaps, by a cycle of bad harvest years, which undermined the people's confidence in the abilities of the rulers to provide for them. A period of political instability now known as the First Intermediate ensued, during which there were Asian incursions into the fertile delta country and Egypt was ruled by the local monarchs, even though there was nominal allegiance to a central government.

First Intermediate
Period
4131 to 4123 B.P.

Approximately 4133 years ago, the city of Thebes in Upper Egypt became the center of rebel movements that eventually took over the country under pharaoh Mentuhotep II 3990 years ago. The Middle Kingdom pharaohs who followed were mostly energetic rulers who extended trading contacts throughout the Near East and conquered the desert lands of Nubia south of the First Cataract (see Figure 17.1). The pharaohs became somewhat less despotic and considered themselves more like shepherds of the people, who had some concern for the common welfare. It was during the Middle Kingdom that the city of Thebes came into prominence, especially as a center for the worship of the sun god Amun.

Middle Kingdom
3941 to 3736 B.P.

THE SECOND INTERMEDIATE PERIOD: 3736 TO 3517 YEARS AGO

Second Intermediate
Period
3736 to 3517 B.P.

The Middle Kingdom lasted until approximately 3736 years ago, when another period of political instability and economic disorder ensued. Disputes over the royal succession at Thebes led to a procession of pharaohs who reigned for short periods. Pharaonic control of the Nile Valley as a whole weakened, and Asian intruders managed to penetrate the fertile lands of the delta downstream. Their leaders became known as the Hyksos and formed two dynasties that ruled over much of Egypt between 3625 and 3517 years ago. They probably were nomadic chiefs from the desert, who brought the horse and chariot to Egypt for the first time.

The Hyksos had little control over Upper Egypt, where the pharaohs of Thebes quarreled among themselves. Eventually, though, the Thebans came to realize that they could never control the whole of the country again unless they threw out the Hyksos and paid careful attention to the political realities of Asia. From this point on, the Egyptian pharaohs took an active interest in their Asian neighbors, and there was a constant flow of people and ideas with other nations.

THE NEW KINGDOM: 3517 TO 3085 YEARS AGO

The New Kingdom began when a series of Theban pharaohs fought and won a war of independence from the Hyksos. It was Ahmose the Liberator who finally overcame the foreigners and established a firm hold on Egypt from the delta to Nubia. He was the first of a series of great rulers whose names have become symbolic of the power of Ancient Egypt: Tutmosis, Amenophis, Seti, and Rameses. Rameses was the greatest of Egypt's pharaohs, who extended the Egyptian Empire into deepest Nubia and far into Palestine. The pharaohs campaigned against the Hittites in Syria and tried to keep their eastern boundary secure against raiding Mesopotamian armies. The spiritual center of the empire was at Thebes, where the great temples of Luxor and Karnak housed the priests of Amun. This priesthood was a formidable political force in New Kingdom Egypt.

New Kingdom
3517 to 3085 B.P.

The New Kingdom pharaohs adopted new burial customs and abandoned conspicuous sepulchers. Their mummies were buried in the desolate Valley of Kings on the west bank of the Nile at Thebes (Romer, 1981). An entire community of workers did nothing but prepare the rock-cut tombs of the pharaohs, their queens, and privileged nobles. To date, only one undisturbed royal tomb has come to light in the Valley of Kings, that of the pharaoh Tutankhamun, who died 3296 years ago (H. Carter, 1923; Desroches-Noblecourt, 1963). The world was astounded when Howard Carter and Lord Carnarvon discovered and cleared the tomb of the young pharaoh in the 1920s (Figure 17.5). It gives us an impression of the incredible wealth of the New Kingdom pharaohs' courts.

Tutankhamun died in his late teens but was responsible for restoring religious order after a curious interlude of chaos during the reign of Akhenaten (3313–3300 B.P.) (Aldred, 1986). Like many pharaohs before him, Akhenaten had been worried about the overriding power of the priests of Amun at Thebes, so he espoused the worship of the god Aten, the life-giving disk of the sun. Akhenaten took up the new religion with fanatical zeal and even founded a new capital downstream of Thebes called Akhetaten, near the modern village el-Amarna. After his death 3300 years ago, the regents for Tutankhamun worked hard to restore the power and prestige of Amun, a move apparently supported by the mass of the people, for Akhenaten had produced no viable alternatives to the established political and religious institutions he had abolished.

THE LATE PERIOD: 1085 TO 332 B.C.

With the death of Rameses III in 1085 B.C., Egypt entered on a period of political weakness, when local rulers exercised varying control over the Nile. The pharaohs were threatened by Nubian rulers, who actually ruled over Egypt for a

Late Period
1085 to 332 B.C.

FIGURE 17.5 The antechamber of Tutankhamun's tomb, stacked with priceless royal possessions. Tutankhamun's chariots lie against the left wall, two animal-head funerary beds, stools, storage chests filled with possessions, and other items are to the right.

short time in the eighth century B.C. The Assyrians were a constant hazard after 725 B.C. and actually occupied parts of the country and looted Thebes in 665. After the eclipse of Assyria, the Egyptians enjoyed a few centuries of independence before being conquered by the Persians in 343 B.C. and Alexander the Great in 332 B.C. He in turn was succeeded by the Ptolemies, pharaohs of Greek ancestry, who ruled Egypt until Roman times. It was they who brought much of Egyptian lore and learning into the mainstream of emerging Greek civilization and ensured that the Land of the Pharaohs made a critical contribution to Western civilization.

Ptolemies
332 to 30 B.C.

THE EMERGENCE OF AFRICAN STATES

What were Egypt's relationships with the vast African continent that bordered the Nile? Its influence on southern and Saharan neighbors was surprisingly small, for Egypt's ties were closer to the Mediterranean world than to sub-Saharan Africa. The pharaohs exercised political control only as far south as the

First Cataract, near today's Aswan Dam, but the areas to the south were an important source of ivory for ornaments and of slaves for the divine rulers.

Meroe

Approximately 900 B.C., an unknown governor of the southernmost part of 900 B.C. Egypt founded his own dynasty and ruled a string of small settlements extending far south into the area that is now the Sudan. His capital at Napata began to decline because the fragile grasslands by the Nile were overgrazed. The inhabitants moved south and founded a town called Meroe on a fertile floodplain between the Nile and Atbara rivers. There they built their own thriving urban civilization, which was in contact with peoples living far to the west on the southern edge of the Sahara (Shinnie, 1967). Meroe's inhabitants kept up at 590 B.C. least sporadic contacts with the Classical World. They gained prosperity from extensive trading in such items as copper, gold, iron, ivory, and slaves. Some of Meroe's prosperity may have been based on ironworking, for deposits of this vital material were abundant near Napata. Iron artifacts are, however, fairly rare in the city itself.

In the early centuries after Christ, the empire declined, following raids from the kingdom of Axum centered on the Ethiopian highlands (Oliver and Fage, 1963). Meroe was abandoned, and the stratified society that had ruled it collapsed. A scattered rural population continued to live along the banks of the Nile. The fertile grasslands that had surrounded Meroe were now overgrazed, and the increasingly arid countryside made urban life difficult. A dispersed settlement pattern replaced the centralized city style of Meroe's heyday. Chief- A.D. 300 doms replaced divine kings.

North Africa

The North African coast had long been a staging post for maritime traders from the eastern Mediterranean. During the first millennium B.C., the Phoenicians set up ports (N. K. Sanders, 1977). The colonists came into contact with well-established barter networks that criss-crossed the Sahara (Bovill, 1968). The desert is rich in salt deposits that were controlled by the nomadic peoples who lived there. They came in touch with black tribes living to the south of the desert, who bartered salt for copper, ivory, gold, and the other raw materials that Africa has traditionally given to the world. Soon, long trading routes connected North Africa with tropical regions, well-trodden highways that provided much of the Greek and Roman wealth during the height of their civilizations.

Most of the Saharan trade was in the hands of nomadic tribes, middle agents between sub-Saharan Africa and the bustling markets of the Mediterranean. In Roman times the camel was introduced to the Sahara. These "ships of the des- A.D. 350 ert" enabled merchants to organize sizable camel caravans that crossed the Sahara like clockwork, from the North African coast to West Africa; the caravans increased direct contact between the Mediterranean world and West Africa and built a much greater volume of trade.

Ironworking and African States

Ironworking had reached West Africa by the fourth century B.C., perhaps by the Saharan trade routes (McIntosh and McIntosh, 1988). The new metallurgy, unlike that of copper, spread rapidly over sub-Saharan Africa in a few centuries. Its spread was connected in part with the dispersal of Bantu-speaking peoples over much of east, central, and southern Africa. Bantu languages are now spoken by many inhabitants of tropical Africa. The original area of Bantu tongues may have been north of the Zaire forest (Oliver and Fagan, 1975).

This spread of new language coincides with the arrival of negroid (a racial term) peoples both in the Zaire forest and on the savanna woodlands to the east and south of it. Ironworking farmers were living near the great East African lakes by the third century A.D., by the banks of the Zambezi River at approximately the same time, and crossing the Limpopo into South Africa during the first millennium A.D. They introduced farming and domestic animals into wide areas of Africa, absorbing, eliminating, or pushing out the indigenous hunter-gatherers (Phillipson, 1977).

The Bantu farmers used shifting agriculture and careful soil selection to produce a diet of sorghum, millet, and other cereal crops. They kept cattle and sheep or goats, and relied on hunting and gathering for much of their diet. Their architectural styles and pottery have a clear but indirect relationship with those of many present-day rural black Africans.

West African States

The past 1000 years have seen the proliferation of prosperous African states ruled by leaders whose power was based on religious ability, entrepreneurial skill, and control of vital raw materials (Connah, 1987; McIntosh and McIntosh, 1981). The West African states at the southern edges of the Sahara, such as Ghana, Mali, and Songhay, based their prosperity on the gold trade with North Africa (Figure 17.6). The Saharan trade passed into Islamic hands at the end of the first millennium A.D., and Arab authors began describing the remarkable African kingdoms flourishing south of the desert. The geographer al-Bakri drew a vivid picture of the kingdom of Ghana, whose gold was well known in northern latitudes by the eleventh century. "It is said," he wrote, "that the king owns a nugget as large as a big stone."

Ghana

The Kingdom of Ghana straddled the northern borders of the gold-bearing river valleys of the upper Niger and Senegal (Levetzion, 1973). No one knows when it first came into being, but the kingdom was described by Arab writers in the eighth century A.D. The Ghanians' prosperity depended on the gold trade and the constant demand for ivory in the north. Kola nuts (used as a stimulant), slaves, and swords also crossed the desert, but gold, ivory, and salt were the foundations of their power. Islam was brought to Ghana sometime in the late first millennium and linked the kingdom more closely to the desert trade. The king of Ghana was a powerful ruler who, wrote al-Bakri, "can put 200,000 men in the field, more than 40,000 of whom were bowmen."

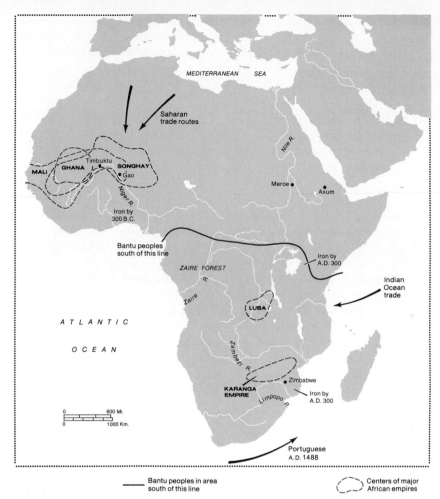

FIGURE 17.6 Map of later African prehistory, showing extent of Bantu Africa and indigenous states.

Ghana was a prime target for Islamic reform movements, whose desert leaders longingly eyed the power and wealth of their southern neighbor. One such group, the Almoravids, attacked Ghana in approximately A.D. 1062, but it was fourteen years before the invaders captured the Ghanian capital. The power of Ghana was fatally weakened, and the kingdom fell into its tribal parts soon after.

A.D. 1062

Mali

The kingdom of Mali appeared two centuries later, after many tribal squabbles (Levetzion, 1973). A group of Kangaba people under the leadership of Sundiata came into prominence in approximately A.D. 1230 and annexed their neighbors' lands. Sundiata built his new capital at Mali on the Niger River. He founded a vast empire that a century later extended over most of sub-Saharan West Africa. The fame of the Malian kings spread all over the Muslim world.

A.D. 1230

Timbuktu became an important center of learning. Malian gold was valued everywhere. When the king of Mali went on a pilgrimage to Mecca in A.D. 1324, the price of gold in Egypt was reduced sharply by the king's liberal spending. Mali appeared on the earliest maps of West Africa as an outside frontier of the literate world, providing gold and other luxuries for Europe and North Africa.

The key to Mali's prosperity was the unifying effect of Islam. Islamic rulers governed with supreme powers granted by Allah and ruled their conquered provinces through religious appointees or wealthy slaves. Islam provided a reservoir of thoroughly trained, literate administrators, too, who owed allegiance to peace, stability, and good trading practices.

Songhay

Approximately A.D. 1325, the greatest of the kings of Mali, Mansa Musa, brought the important trading center of Gao on the Niger under his sway (Hunwick, 1971). Gao was the capital of the Dia kings, who shook off Mali's yoke in approximately A.D. 1340 and founded the kingdom of Songhay. Their state prospered increasingly as Mali's power weakened. The great chieftain Sonni Ali

led the Songhay to new conquests between A.D. 1464 and 1492, expanding the frontiers of his empire deep into Mali country and far north into the Sahara. He monopolized much of the Saharan trade, seeking to impose law and order with his vast armies to increase the volume of trade that passed through Songhay

hands. Sonni Ali was followed by other competent rulers who further expanded Songhay. Its collapse came in the sixteenth century.

Karanga and Zimbabwe

Powerful kingdoms also developed in central and southern Africa. The Luba kingdom of the Congo and the Karanga Empire between the Zambezi and Limpopo rivers were led by powerful chiefs, priests, and ivory traders who also handled such diverse raw materials as copper, gold, seashells, cloth, and porcelain. Their power came from highly centralized political organizations and effective religious powers, which channeled some of their subjects' energies into exploiting raw materials and long-distance trade.

The Karanga peoples lived where the nation of Zimbabwe is today and developed a remarkable kingdom that built its viability on trade in gold, copper, and ivory and on its leaders' religious acumen (Garlake, 1973). The Karanga leaders found their power on being intermediaries between the people and their ancestral spirits, upon whom the people believed the welfare of the nation

depended. Approximately A.D. 1000, the Karanga began to build stone structures, the most famous of which is Zimbabwe, built at the foot of a sacred hill. Zimbabwe became an important commercial and religious center. Its chiefs lived in seclusion on the sacred hill, known to archaeologists as "the Acropolis." In the valley below sprawled a complex of homesteads and stone enclosures, which were dominated in later centuries by the high, freestanding stone walls of the Great Enclosure, or Temple (Figure 17.7).

At least five stages of occupation have been recognized at Zimbabwe, the first of them dating to the fourth century A.D., when a group of farmers camped at the site but built no stone walls. They were followed by later occupants who

FIGURE 17.7 The Zimbabwe ruins, an important trading and religious center of the Karanga peoples of south central Africa in the second millennium A.D. Most of the Great Enclosure, or Temple, was built by A.D. 1500.

constructed the Great Enclosure in stages and built retaining walls on the Acropolis. The heyday of Zimbabwe was between A.D. 1350 and 1450, when imported cloth, china, glass, and porcelain were traded to the site. Gold ornaments, copper, ivory, and elaborate iron tools were in common use. A.D. 1350 to 1450

Zimbabwe declined after A.D. 1450, probably because overpopulation impoverished the environment, where agricultural resources were relatively poor anyway.

Foreign Traders

Most of African history is about exploitation of the peoples and raw materials by foreign traders and explorers. The East African coast was visited by Arabs and Indian merchants who used the monsoon winds of the Indian Ocean to sail to Africa and back within twelve months on prosperous trading ventures. The Portuguese skirted Africa's western and southeastern coasts in the fifteenth century and rounded the Cape of Good Hope in 1488, establishing precarious colonies ruled from Portugal to exploit raw materials (Alpers, 1975). Some parts of Africa, however, had no contact with the outside world until Victorian explorers and missionaries met remote and exotic peoples as they strove toward elusive goals, including such prizes as the source of the Nile (see Brodie, 1957). A.D. 1488

A.D. 1850

GUIDE TO FURTHER READING

Aldred, Cyril. *The Egyptians* (2d ed.). New York: Thames and Hudson, 1986.
> A superb short essay on Ancient Egyptian civilization that is especially good on daily life and society. Exceptional illustrations.

Connah, Graham. *African Civilizations.* Cambridge: Cambridge University Press, 1987.
> A general account of early sub-Saharan African states for the beginning reader.

Fagan, Brian M. *The Rape of the Nile.* New York: Scribner's, 1975.
> A history of Egyptology, complete with tomb robbers, travelers, and the most flamboyant of archaeologists. Concentrates on Giovanni Belzoni, circus performer and grave robber extraordinaire.

Fedden, Robin. *Egypt.* London: Murray, 1977.
> The best book ever written on ancient and modern Egypt for the casual tourist. Gives a striking impression of modern Egyptian life and also of Islamic architecture and the Egyptian personality.

Johnson, Paul. *The Civilization of Ancient Egypt.* London: Weidenfeld and Nicholson, 1978.
> A comprehensive account of Ancient Egyptian civilization from pre-Dynastic times up to the advent of Roman rule. Especially good on religious and economic life and changing political conditions.

Romer, John. *The Valley of Kings.* New York: Morrow, 1981.
> A description in exhaustive detail of centuries of excavations in the royal burial grounds near Thebes. Shows vividly how modern Egyptology is as much detective work as it is excavation.

Trigger, Bruce C., et al. *Ancient Egypt: A Social History.* Cambridge: Cambridge University Press, 1983.
> A series of authoritative essays on the changing face of Ancient Egyptian society. Deservedly a popular college text.

CHAPTER 18

The Harappan Civilization and Southeast Asia

Preview

- The Harappan civilization of the Indus Valley (present-day Pakistan) is thought to have developed from indigenous roots around 4700 years ago.

- The Harappans maintained extensive connections with areas to the north, especially Afghanistan, and are thought to have been in sporadic contact with the Iranian plateau and Mesopotamia.

- Harappan civilization flourished from approximately 4800 to 3900 years ago over an enormous area of the Indus Valley. Harappa and Moenjo-daro were the largest cities, each laid out in an inflexible design dominated by a great citadel. It is assumed that the civilization was ruled by priest-kings who controlled both religious and economic life.

- After 3900 years ago, Harappan civilization declined, perhaps in part because of flooding and deterioration of the environment. The period between the end of the Harappan culture and the beginnings of ironworking is obscure. Ironworking in India, by comparison, is associated with the period of painted gray wares, beginning around 3100 years ago and thriving when the subcontinent was occupied by the Persian King Darius, in 516 B.C.

- Southeast Asian peoples had developed bronzeworking by at least 3500 years ago, possibly very much earlier. The process of local state formation began around the same time, but the first historical records of complex states date to the third century A.D.

- Later southeast Asian prehistory was dominated by the changing fortunes of various empires ruled by divine kings who espoused a strongly centralized economic system, as secular and religious concerns were molded together in a single type of complex society.

Water has always played an important role in Indian life and thought, for India's great rivers are the perennial gift of the snow-clad Himalayas. The Indus River, on the banks of which Indian civilization began, rises in southern Tibet and then descends 1000 miles (1609 km) through Kashmir before debouching onto the Pakistani plains (Figure 18.1). The Indus floodplain landscape now is almost entirely humanly made, a network of irrigation canals and flood embankments used to control the inundation that reaches the plains between June and September of each year. The people plant their wheat and barley on the fertile alluvial plains as the floods recede, then harvest them the following spring. They use the flood-borne silts as a natural fertilizer. The soils are soft enough to be cultivated without the aid of metal artifacts. Five thousand years ago, the Indus farmers were making use of the same flood cycle to irrigate their fields.

THE ROOTS OF INDIAN CIVILIZATION

As in other parts of the world, it seems that the roots of south Asian farming and later civilization were almost entirely indigenous. Most authorities on south Asian archaeology agree that humped cattle, buffalo, and pig were domesticated there from local wild populations (Sharmar et al., 1980). Perhaps sheep and goats were also. The earliest dates for domesticated animals are in the 6500- to 6000-year range, from sites near Quetta in Baluchistan and Rajastan in northwest India. However, it seems likely that farmers and herders have lived in these areas for much longer, for palynologists have found evidence for recurrent fires in the desert savanna of Rajastan starting approximately 10,000 years ago (Jacobson, 1979). These may signal repeated clearance of sour grass to allow lush grazing for cattle, a practice followed in the area to this day. The farmers eventually domesticated not only indigenous Indian cultigens such as rice and dwarf wheat but also peas, barley, lentils, and other west Asian species, but the dates of early domestication still are unknown. In the millennia before the emergence of urban civilization in India, dozens of regional variations of farming culture flourished throughout India and Pakistan; these peasant cultures still are little understood (Allchin and Allchin, 1982; Posselh, 1982).

For six years between 1974 and 1980, French and Pakistani archaeologists excavated a series of agricultural settlements at Mehrgarh south of Quetta, 125 miles (201 km) west of the Indus River (Jarrige and Meadow, 1979). They found traces of farmers who had settled in the area before 8000 years ago. By 7000 years ago, the Mehrgarh people lived in sizable, permanent houses of mud brick, a building material used not only by the Harappan civilization in later times but also by Indus people to this day. They possessed copper tools and imported turquoise from Iran and shells from the Arabian coast. Living as they did on a direct trade route from the Indus Valley to the Iranian highlands, the Mehrgarh people learned of the unique qualities of a new Indian domesticated crop: cotton. This white, fluffy flower turned out to be a priceless asset, for it could be woven into fine cloth, not only for convenient domestic use in a hot climate but also for export to people looking for a light, hard-wearing textile. Cotton was to become a staple of Indian trade for the rest of recorded history.

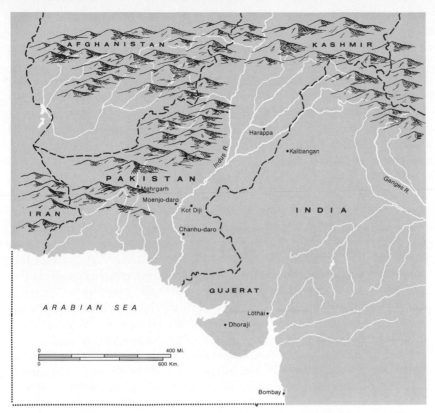

FIGURE 18.1   The Harappan civilization, showing sites mentioned in this chapter.

The Mehrgarh sites include the Nausharo mound, which dates from about 5000 to 4500 years ago, straddling the centuries when the Harappan civilization emerged in the Indus Valley. The villages in this region flourished on the cotton and metal trade until the rise of the Harappan civilization by 4500 years ago. Every year its workshops manufactured millions of beads and hundreds of clay vessels, which were in demand throughout the Indus Valley. The simple technologies used by village artisans in settlements such as Mehrgarh provided all the artifacts needed to create an urban civilization on the Indus floodplains. The ancient trade routes that linked villages from the Indus deep into Afghanistan and Iran became the regular caravan highways monopolized by the Harappans.

The alluvial plains themselves were settled as early as the fourth millennium B.C. Scattered across a vast area of the plains are hundreds of pre-Harappan settlements, many of them boasting fortifications, metallurgy, and planned streets. There are clear signs that many villages and small towns practiced intensive agriculture and were built above the highest flood level but as close to the river as possible. Typical of these settlements is Kot Diji on the left bank of the Indus approximately 20 miles (33.3 km) from the river (Jacobson, 1979; Mughal, 1974). As early as 4000 years ago, the inhabitants were forced to pile boulders to protect themselves against the inundation. They ended up erecting a massive defensive wall that served as both a flood dike and a fortress. The

Kot Diji c. 4000 B.P.

stone and mud-brick houses of the village clustered inside the wall. Nevertheless, Kot Diji was attacked and burned at least twice. The same fate must have awaited many other settlements that became involved in quarrels between ambitious local chieftains vying for control of smaller communities and prime agricultural lands. The increased competition is hardly surprising, for between 5000 and 4500 years ago farming had changed the natural ecology of the Indus Valley beyond all recognition (Agrawal, 1982).

Botanists have chronicled these ecological changes by using the minute pollen grains embedded in the Indus Valley soils. They found that the natural tree and grass cover on the floodplain increased between 4400 and 3000 B.P., perhaps as a result of a period of higher rainfall that lasted at least 2000 years. This thicker tree cover became established just as the farming population was taking advantage of good rains and expanding agricultural production. The pollen counts show not only more trees but dramatic rises in the proportions of cereal grains and cultivated weeds at the expense of the natural vegetation. A complex multiplier effect then linked rapidly rising village populations with corresponding increases in agricultural production, leading to drastic consequences for the plains environment. As the valley population rose, so did pressure on the land. The farmers cleared and burned off more and more riverine forest and grazed ever-growing herds of goats and sheep on watershed meadows. Acres of forest were burned to bake bricks for the houses of growing villages and newly founded cities. Mile after mile of the plains was denuded of natural vegetation, with disastrous consequences for erosion control and the floodplain environment. Deprived of natural controls, the rising floodwaters swept over the plains, carrying everything with them. Confronted with what may have seemed like the wrath of the gods, the people had but one defense — cooperative flood-works and irrigation agriculture that fed more mouths and provided at least a degree of security against the vagaries of the elements. The obvious leaders of these new communal efforts were the chieftains, priests, and kin leaders who acted as intermediaries between the people and the gods. The religious philosophy and motivation that provided the catalyst for these efforts was a simple one, a pervasive belief that humans are part of an ordered cosmos that can be maintained only by unremitting toil and a subordination of individual ambition to the common good.

This is a hypothetical scenario, but one that seems to fit the few archaeological facts available. It accounts for the remarkable drabness and conservatism of the urban civilization that arose in the changing landscape of the Indus Valley. Like the Sumerian and Egyptian civilizations, the Harappan arose from deeply ingrained indigenous roots with cultural traditions that stressed unquestioned allegiance on the part of everyone, whether priest, merchant, artisan, or farmer. The philosophies of the Indus people would have been entirely alien to the ambitious, individualistic Sumerians or to the balanced, intelligent Egyptians. The Harappans suffered a much grimmer, regimented existence, one in which personal wealth and success counted for little. We can only wonder at the remarkable abilities of the anonymous leaders who blended an austere mix of secular and religious authority to secure the loyalty of millions of people for a thousand years.

THE HARAPPAN CIVILIZATION

4700 B.P.

By 4700 years ago, the Indus people had mastered the basic problems of irrigation and flood control, partly by using millions of fired bricks made of river alluvium, baked with firewood cut from the riverine forests. Like the Sumerians, they adopted the city as a means of organizing and controlling their civilization. We know of at least five major Harappan cities: Harappa, after which the civilization is known, Moenjo-daro, Kalibangan, Chanhu-daro, and the recently discovered Dhoraji in Gujerat (Allchin and Allchin, 1983; Posselh, 1982). Harappa and Moenjo-daro were built on artificial mounds above the floods at the cost of Herculean efforts. Moenjo-daro was rebuilt at least nine times, sometimes as a result of disastrous inundations. Yet on each occasion the builders followed a gridlike street pattern that was set by the first city rulers and followed until the end. Sir Mortimer Wheeler (1962, 1968) characterizes both cities as giving an impression of "middle-class prosperity with zealous municipal supervision." The two cities are so similar that they might have been designed by the same architect.

A high citadel lies at the west end of each city, dominating the streets below. Here lived the rulers, protected by great fortifications and flood-works. Nearby rose the granary, under the careful supervision of the municipal authorities. Harappa's citadel is 460 yards (414 m) long and 215 yards (194 m) wide, surrounded by a forbidding brick wall at least 45 feet (13.5 m) high. Moenjo-daro's towering citadel rises 40 feet (12 m) above the plain and is protected by massive flood embankments and a vast perimeter wall with towers. The public buildings on the summit include a pillared hall almost 90 feet (27 m) square, perhaps the precinct where the rulers gave audience to petitioners and visiting officials. Everything is utilitarian, efficient, and unostentatious, for there are no spectacular temples or richly adorned shrines. Religious life was centered on a great lustral bath made of bitumen-sealed brickwork and fed by a well. An imposing colonnade surrounded the pool, which was approached by sets of steps at both ends. We cannot be sure of the exact use of the great bath, but perhaps it was where the devout carried out their ceremonial bathing rituals.

Moenjo-daro's municipal granary lies on the west side of the citadel. The builders erected twenty-seven rectangular brick supports and then built a huge wooden granary on top so that the air could circulate freely under the stored grain. There is no more eloquent testimony to the tight control the rulers exercised over the city than this inaccessible granary. The food surpluses it contained were their ultimate, material instrument of social and economic control, for the grain fed or paid thousands of menial laborers and state employees. Harappa's granary lay to the north of the citadel and formed part of an entire grain-processing complex, including both threshing floors and two rows of barracklike buildings for the laborers who toiled there.

The rulers of each city looked down on the north-south street grid laid out in city blocks. The widest east-west thoroughfares at Moenjo-daro were only 30 feet (9 m) wide, the cross streets only half as wide and unpaved (Figure 18.2). Hundreds of drab, standardized houses presented a blind brick facade to the streets and alleys they lined. The more spacious dwellings, perhaps those of the

FIGURE 18.2 A typical street in Moenjo-daro, Pakistan, uncovered in Sir Mortimer Wheeler's excavations.

nobility and merchants, were laid out around a central courtyard where guests may have been received, where food was prepared, and where servants probably lounged. Staircases and thick ground walls indicate that some houses had two or even three stories, with wooden balconies overlooking the courtyard rather than the street, as was the case at Sumerian Ur. The larger residences owned a well and had bathrooms and toilets that may have been joined to an elaborate system of public drains.

The organizing tentacles of the government extended to every detail of city life. Some areas of Harappa and Moenjo-daro were designated as bazaars, complete with shops (Fairservis, 1976). Archaeologists have inventoried the finds from artisans' quarters where bead makers, coppersmiths, cotton weavers, and other specialists manufactured and sold their wares. The potters' workshops were filled with painted pots decorated with animal figures and everyday plain wheel-made vessels manufactured not only in the cities but also in villages for hundreds of miles around. There were water jars and cooking bowls, storage pots and drinking vessels. Metalworkers cast simple axes in open molds, and manufactured chisels, knives, razors, spears, and fish hooks. Only a few expert artisans made more elaborate objects, such as small figurines or a piece as complicated as a canopied cart. They would make a wax model of the cart and encase it in clay, which was fired to melt the wax. Then molten copper or bronze was poured into the mold. This "lost-wax" method is still employed by Indian artists.

The technologies used in Harappan cities were developed centuries earlier in small villages and transferred to the cities without change. One of the most developed manufactures was the seal, made from steatite and other soft rocks. Seal workshops have yielded not only finished specimens, hardened in a furnace, but the blocks of steatite from which square seals were cut as intaglios. For hours, the seal makers would crouch over the tiny squares, expertly cutting representations of animals in profile. They reserved some of their best efforts for religious scenes. Indian archaeologists working at the Harappan city of Chanhu-daro south of Moenjo-daro found a complete bead maker's shop that gave some idea of the labor needed to produce small ornaments. The bead makers prepared bars of agate and carnelian approximately 3 inches (7.6 cm) long that were then ground and polished into shorter, perforated cylinders and strung in necklaces. To experience the bead-making process, the archaeologists took a Harappan stone-tipped drill and some abrasive powder from the workshop and attempted to drill through one of the bead blanks. It took them 20 minutes to drill a small pit in the end of the bead. At that rate, it would have taken 24 hours to drill a single bead!

The overall impression of Harappan cities is faintly depressing. Perhaps the most striking memory of many visitors might have been the constant thump of grain pounders wielded by hundreds of menial workers laboring at the public granaries. The city authorities provided row after row of standardized, two-room houses for those who labored on this and the many other routine but essential tasks that kept this labor-intensive civilization running. With so many unskilled hands and abundant food supplies, there was no incentive for technological innovation, nor, apparently, did the religious philosophies of the time encourage culture change.

Who Were the Harappans?

Half a century of excavations has revealed a standardized, monotonous civilization that archaeologists named the *Harappan*, simply because they did not know what the Harappans called themselves. Their archives, thoughts, and beliefs elude us. We do not even know the names of the rulers who controlled at least five great cities, and a civilization that extended over a half million square miles of the Punjab and Sind plains, from Baluchistan to the deserts of Rajastan, and from the Himalayan foothills to near Bombay.

The Harappan leaders controlled their own people as well as long-distance trade routes that extended along the Arabian coast, into northern Afghanistan and Turkmenia, and onto the Iranian plateau, through thousands of square miles of mountainous terrain rich in minerals and other natural resources. The cities sent merchants with wheeled carts driven by oxen and water buffalo along regular caravan routes far into the highlands. They exported grain and textiles, carnelian beads, pearls, and sweet-smelling rosewood, and received minerals and other raw materials in exchange. Much of the long-distance trade was conducted by deep-sea vessels coasting the shores of the Indian Ocean into the Persian Gulf. Ever thorough, the authorities controlled even this commerce. During the 1950s and 1960s, Indian archaeologists uncovered a Harappan port at Lothal, a landlocked town on the Gulf of Cambay. The only way to enter the harbor was through a specially dug canal at high tide. Every oceangoing ship had to berth at the official, brick-lined dock surrounded by government warehouses. Probably other similar ports await discovery elsewhere on the Pakistani coastline. We know that Harappan seafarers voyaged as far afield as Sumer and Bahrein, for a scatter of Indus seals dating to between 4300 and 4000 years ago have come from Ur and other Sumerian cities. Perhaps there was a colony of Harappan merchants in Sumer at one time, but we know nothing of its transactions. Few Mesopotamian imports have come from excavations in Indus cities, yet we cannot doubt that there was contact between the two areas, perhaps through such entrepôts (commercial centers, sometimes warehouses) as the walled Sumerian trading port of Dilmun on the island of Bahrein in the Persian Gulf.

The anonymity of the Harappan leaders extends even to their appearance. These were no bombastic rulers, boasting of their achievements on grandiose palace walls. They left almost no portraits. One exception is a limestone figure from Moenjo-daro that depicts a thick-lipped, bearded man staring at the world through slitted eyes, perhaps dazzled by the brilliant Indus sunlight. He seems to be withdrawn in meditation, perhaps detached from worldly affairs. The man wears an embroidered robe that was once inlaid with metal. The only clue to his status is that one shoulder is uncovered, a sign of reverence during the Buddha's lifetime more than 1000 years later. Could it be that the same convention applied to Harappan times and that the portrait is that of a priest or a priest-king? Thus far, the evidence of archaeology reveals leadership by rulers who led unostentatious lives marked by a complete lack of priestly pomp or lavish public display. There is nothing of the ardent militarism of the Assyrian kings, nor of the slavish glorification of the pharaohs.

The secular power of this civilization was based almost completely on bountiful agricultural production. Harappan civilization may have revolved around cities, but most people still were village farmers, cultivating irrigated fields of barley and wheat that lapped the city suburbs. The Harappans ate rice, too, a crop first cultivated somewhere between India and southeast Asia before 7000 years ago. They cultivated cotton and dates and kept cattle and water buffalo. Every farmer turned over a substantial portion of the annual harvest to the state, and indeed the authorities may have controlled the ownership of much of the land. The entire agricultural enterprise was a much larger scale version of the communal village farming that originally had made colonization of the Indus Valley possible.

Both Harappa and Moenjo-daro housed a comfortable and unpretentious middle class of merchants and petty officials who lived in stolid and standardized brick houses along the city streets. They wore finely woven, decorated cotton robes. Judging from clay figurines, the women wore short skirts and headdresses, and perhaps longer robes (Figure 18.3). Dozens of shops sold wire neck bangles, necklaces, and pendants, but there is nothing of the elaboration found in Egyptian or Mycenaean palaces. The more prosperous city dwellers

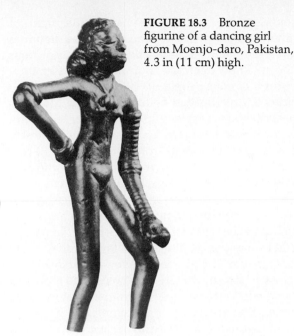

FIGURE 18.3 Bronze figurine of a dancing girl from Moenjo-daro, Pakistan, 4.3 in (11 cm) high.

sometimes owned some ornate carved rosewood furniture, but the life style was far from lavish. Even the wealthiest and most powerful merchants maintained a low profile in public.

The artisans — metalsmiths, potters, weavers, bead makers, seal carvers — formed a distinct class, as did the many petty bureaucrats and priests needed to run the multifarious affairs of government, each with their designated quarters. However, such people were a tiny minority compared with the vast mass of the populace: farmers, laborers, seafarers, and menial workers of every type. They lived in servile dwellings and wore but the simplest of cotton loincloths or robes. Their unquestioning hands kept the Harappan civilization in existence, although in their way they were as deadening a cultural influence as were the armies of slaves that sustained Mesopotamian civilization. To judge from modern Indian life, they had an extended family of several generations, which provided a network of kinship ties and other benefits such as communal ownership of property. Perhaps, too, the Harappan people were organized in a hierarchy of castes that restricted upward mobility and provided a wider identity outside the confines of the family.

Harappan Beliefs

Like the Sumerians, the Harappans lived in an environment that they modified for their own protection, one in which the annual floods meant a renewal of life and food for the coming year. Like the Mesopotamians, they seem to have believed that they lived in the valley to serve the gods, who caused crops to grow and soils to be fertile. The primeval roots of Indian religion may have been age-old fertility cults that served the same function as Inanna among the Sumerians and the mother goddess in many other Near Eastern civilizations —

an assurance that life would continue. The only clues we have to the origins of Indian religion come from minute seal impressions and small clay figurines from Harappan villages and cities that depict a female deity with conspicuous breasts and sexual organs. We do not know her name, but she probably embodied earth and life-giving nature for the Indus people.

A seal from Moenjo-daro bears a three-headed figure who sits in the yogic posture and wears a horned headdress. He is surrounded by a tiger, elephant, rhinoceros, water buffalo, and deer. Some archaeologists believe that the seal represents a forerunner of the great god Shiva in his role of Lord of the Beasts. Many Harappan seals depict cattle that may be symbols of Shiva, who was worshiped in several forms. To judge from later beliefs, he may have had a dual role, serving as a fertility god as well as tamer or destroyer of wild beasts (Wolpert, 1977; D. Miller, 1985). Shiva gave life by planting the seed but also could destroy any creature, including human beings, at a flick of the finger. In part he may symbolize the unpredictable dangers of flood and famine that could threaten a village or a city. Harappa and Moenjo-daro have yielded dozens of carved phallic symbols and circular stones with round holes that represent Shiva's consort Devi's teeming womb. Perhaps these are simple prototypes of the Hindu *lingam* and *yoni* symbols that are found in the temples of Shiva and Devi to this day. If the evidence of figurines and seals is to be believed, the symbolism of early Indus religion bears remarkable similarities to that of modern Hinduism. This similarity highlights the deeply ingrained conservatism of Indian society from the very earliest moments of Harappan civilization.

Writing and Weights

One reason we know so little about the Harappans is that their script still has not been deciphered. Finnish and Russian scholars have used computers to encode and analyze the pictures and signs of the Harappan seals but without success. Almost 400 different pictographic symbols have been identified from their seals. Linguists do not even agree on the language in the script, let alone the ultimate identity of the Harappans. Some authorities believe the seals served not only as religious symbols but also as tags or labels written in Sumerian on bundles of merchandise sent to distant Sumer. Some success has been attained with computer-aided deciphering techniques that have established the script as logo-syllabic; that is to say it is a mixture of sounds and words, just like Egyptian hieroglyphs (Fairservis, 1983). Many scholars believe it is written in a Proto-Dravidian language, for Dravidian exercised a considerable influence on the Sanskrit used widely in India centuries later.

Enough of the Indus script has been deciphered to show how many of the short seal inscriptions designate the names of individuals and their ranks. It seems, too, that some describe major figures of the Harappan cosmos and name the chiefs, as well as identifying scribes and artisan leaders in society. There are certainly close links between the Harappan script and later writings. Many of the Indus symbols are similar to those appearing on Brahmi documents from the Ganges Valley centuries later. Both were written in what is called the *boustrophedon* style. This writing alternates lines going from right to left and left to right. This contrasts with English, which progresses from left to right, and Arabic, which runs in the opposite direction. Many signs and symbols used on Harappan seals are found on pottery and other objects made as late as the ninth century B.C.

Even more striking evidence for cultural continuity comes from the humble half-ounce weight. No government monopoly can survive without weights and measures, so the Harappan authorities developed a standard weight that was close to one-half of a modern ounce. Later, Indian societies used a unit known as the *karsa* for the same purpose. This weighed the equivalent of 32 *rattis*, seeds of the Gunja creeper, a measure that could fluctuate slightly from year to year. Four karsas weighed almost exactly the same as the basic Harappan unit of a half ounce. Similar devices could be found in nineteenth-century bazaars.

The Decline of Harappan Civilization

The Harappan civilization reached its peak approximately 4000 years ago. **4000 B.P.** Moenjo-daro housed at least 40,000 people at that time, but the city was already in trouble from repeated floods that undercut the citadel's defenses and inundated acres of city streets. The authorities deployed more and more laborers to strengthen the flood-control works and to rebuild houses, but there are revealing signs of architectural degeneration after 3900 years ago, as if the constant battle against the Indus was taking its material and psychological toll (Raikes, 1967). At first the serious floods may have resulted from centuries of uncontrolled deforestation and grazing that removed natural barriers for the waters. However, this was not enough to destroy the cities. Approximately 3700 years ago, the Indus changed its course abruptly at both Harappa and **3700 B.P.** Moenjo-daro, perhaps as a result of a series of earthquakes and enormous floods, conceivably inundating the river cities beyond hope of recovery (Dales, 1966; Raikes, 1967).

The effects of the floods were felt throughout the Indus Valley. The great cities of the interior collapsed. Only Lothal and a few coastal centers away from the destructive river continued to flourish as local states, deprived of the authoritative umbrella that had maintained their political and economic stability. They survived unscathed for two centuries more, until Aryan nomads swept down on the Indus Valley and took over the plains. By that time, the Harappans had passed on a priceless legacy of beliefs and philosophies that formed one of the mainstreams of all subsequent Indian history.

From the archaeological point of view, the period between the breakdown of the Harappan cities and the beginning of ironworking is the most obscure in India's later prehistory (Wolpert, 1977). Despite the abandonment of the cities, there were no major disruptions in economy or material culture. Iron tools appeared in India by 3100 years ago and are associated with painted gray wares, **Ironworking** made on a wheel and adorned with simple black painted designs. The advent of **Painted gray wares 3000 B.P.** iron tools enabled farmers to break up the hard, calcareous soils of the Ganges Plain, an area that was to become the heartland of later empires.

Meanwhile, King Darius of Persia invaded the subcontinent in 516 B.C. and **516 B.C.** incorporated part of India into the Persian Empire. Two centuries later, Alexander the Great ventured to the Indus River and brought Greek culture to the area. His incursion also provided a stimulus for cultural developments in the **316 B.C.**

Ganges that culminated in a nationalistic revolt headed by the priest Chandra-gupta. This leader founded an empire which linked the Indus and the Ganges in a single administrative unit that traded as far afield as Malaya and the Near East. The period between approximately 200 B.C. and A.D. 300 saw India linked with lands far to the east and west by regular trading routes that persisted more or less independently of political developments. By this time, the influence of Indian religion in the form of Buddhism and Hinduism was being felt over enormous areas of Asia.

SOUTHEAST ASIAN CIVILIZATIONS

The emergence of complex states in southeast Asia (Figure 18.4) probably is closely connected with the spread of rice cultivation and bronze metallurgy. As we saw in Chapter 13, the early history of rice cultivation is inadequately docu-

FIGURE 18.4 Southeast Asia.

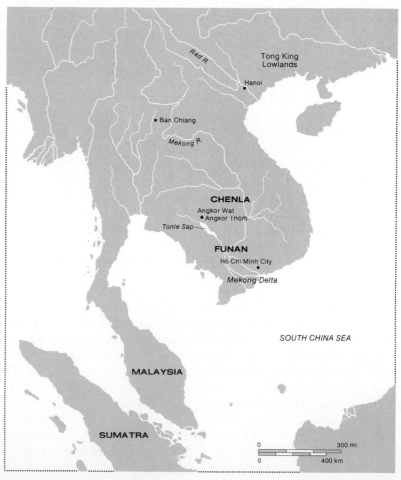

mented, but we do know that the spread of rice agriculture throughout southeast Asia may prove to be connected with southern Chinese farmers. Pottery that shows the influence of their widespread traditions has been found in Thailand and possibly Malaya. The genesis of copper and bronze metallurgy in southeast Asia is even less well documented. The Non Nok Tha cemetery yielded some bronze axes originally dated to about 4100 years ago (Bayard, 1977). However, the contexts from which the dates came have been a matter of controversy. Some authorities believe they date to no earlier than the second millennium B.C. (Higham, 1984a; Higham and Kijngam, 1984; for more discussion, see Bayard, 1984).

More controversy surrounds the emergence of bronzeworking in southeast Asia. Until recently, the Ban Chiang cemetery in northern Thailand was claimed as evidence for very early bronzeworking in the area, with burials dating to a long period between about 5600 years ago and A.D. 300, and bronze artifacts to at least 4500 years ago (Figure 18.5) (White, 1982). But the radiocarbon dates from the burial pits have been questioned by archaeologists digging three other sites nearby (Higham, 1984a). At Ban Nadi, 14 miles (22 km) southwest of Ban Chiang, securely dated occupation levels with bronze equivalent to those at the cemetery dated on average to about 3350 years ago, fully a thousand years later. These later dates are confirmed by excavations elsewhere. A vigorous debate surrounds claims for early bronzeworking in Thailand (see Bayard, 1984, 1986; Higham, 1984a). Only future excavations and further radiocarbon dates can resolve the chronological conundrum.

Charles Higham's shorter chronology receives important support from exca-

Ban Chiang
Date uncertain

FIGURE 18.5   Excavation at Ban Chiang, Thailand, 1975.

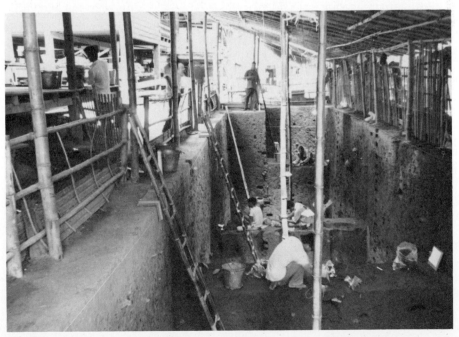

vations in Vietnam's lower Red River Valley. There, bronze appeared by about 3500 years ago in sites of the late Phung Nguyen culture (Huyen, 1984). Unfortunately, only isolated radiocarbon dates are available, so the chronology is still loosely anchored. Bronze metallurgy was also well established on the Vietnamese coast during the late second millennium B.C. One site near Ho Chi Minh City has yielded sandstone molds and bronze artifacts identical to those found in northeast Thailand (Higham, 1984a).

There are two possible interpretations of this dating evidence. The long time scale means that the Ban Chiang people worked bronze at least 1500 years earlier than people elsewhere in southeast Asia. Proponents of the shorter chronology say that bronzeworking was present in coastal Vietnam and the Mekong Valley by 3500 years ago, and that the Ban Chiang metal objects are imports dating to between 500 and 300 B.C. (Higham, 1984a; Higham and Kijngam, 1984).

Vietnam's Dong Son culture represents the culmination of early bronze- and ironworking in prehistoric times. Co Loa, near Hanoi, comprises three sets of ramparts, with moats supplied with water by a tributary of the Red River. At Co Loa's greatest extent, the fortifications enclosed about 1482 acres (600 ha). By this time, rice cultivation was sufficiently productive to support a considerable population density, combined as it was with plow cultivation, double cropping, and water control. According to Chinese records, local chieftains named Lac Lords, keepers of the drums, controlled the rights to rice land. The area was incorporated as a Chinese protectorate in 111 B.C., by which time the Dong Son rulers were in regular contact with Han China (Wheatley, 1979).

Foreign Influences

Although archaeological evidence still is largely lacking, it seems likely that state forms of society were evolving in southeast Asia as early as 3500 years ago (Higham, 1984a). What is uncertain is the extent to which foreign influences played a part in the dissemination of more complex state organizations. Much of our information on early southeast Asian states comes from Chinese and Indian sources (Wheatley, 1975, 1980; Hall, 1985).

Trading systems established

For centuries southeast Asia was dominated, at least tangentially, by two foreign presences. To the north the Chinese imposed their political will on the Lăc peoples on the Tong-king lowlands and extended their tribute systems into the Red River Valley. This was an arbitrary imposition of an entirely different economic system onto trading systems based on reciprocity. It was quite different from the cultural changes going on in the southerly parts of southeast Asia.

Approximately 2000 years ago, the busy sea-trading networks of southeast Asia were being incorporated into the vast oceanic trade routes stretching from China in the east to the shores of the Red Sea and the east coast of Africa in the west. No one people controlled the whole of this vast trade. Most of the Indian Ocean commerce was in the hands of traders, who used monsoon winds to traverse the long sea-lanes from India to Africa and from Arabia to both continents. The trade carried raw materials and luxury goods such as glass beads and cloth. During the heyday of the Roman Empire, the Greeks and Egyptians of Alexandria took some interest in the Indian Ocean trade but rarely ventured farther than the Red Sea.

Beyond India, the trade was held by Indian merchants who penetrated deep into the numerous islands and channels of southeast Asia. The traders themselves were an entirely maritime people, called *Mwani* or *barbarians* by the Chinese of the time. They spoke a polyglot of tongues and were of many lands, some Malays, some Indians, true wanderers who ventured as far east as the South China Sea. The Gulf of Tonkin and South China were served by *Jiwet*, Chinese mariners who brought luxuries to the coast, whence they were transported overland to the Chinese capital.

Indian merchants certainly were active on southeast Asian coasts by the early centuries of the Christian era. They were trading with the tribal societies of both mainland and islands. Voyaging was now accelerated by changing circumstances. First came larger cargo vessels with a more efficient rig that enabled them to sail closer to the wind. No one knows how large these vessels were, but they must have been substantial. The Chinese are known to have transported horses by sea to Indonesia in the third century A.D., and the monk Fa Hsien recorded his sailing trip from Ceylon to China with 200 other passengers in A.D. 414.

Another factor influencing trade was a new demand for gold and other metals. The Emperor Vespasian had prohibited exporting metals from the Roman Empire in approximately A.D. 70, a move that turned Indian merchants' eyes to the southeast, particularly because the Siberian gold mines had been closed to them by nomadic raids on Asian caravans. Metals were not the only attraction; spices could be obtained in abundance. Trade was expanded entirely for commercial profit.

Religions imported

Buddhism had made great strides in India since it appeared in the fourth century B.C. The older religion, Brahmanism, had placed severe and authoritarian restraints on foreign voyages, but Buddhism and Jainism, a form of Hinduism, rejected the notion of racial purity espoused by the predecessor religion. Travel was encouraged; the merchant became a respected part of Buddhist belief. As voyaging increased, especially from southern India to southeast Asia, a strong cultural influence came to be felt. The tribal societies of southeast Asia were introduced to many alien products and some of the foreigners' philosophical, social, and religious beliefs. In a few centuries, kingdoms appeared with governments run according to Hindu or Buddhist ideas of social order.

Chieftains become divine kings

The initial but regular contacts between merchants and tribal societies were seasonal, dictated by the monsoon winds. The chieftains who represented the people of the tribes would have acted as intermediaries between the foreigners and the indigenous people. All exchanges and transactions having to do with the trade were channeled through them. Inevitably, argues Sinologist Paul Wheatley (1975), the chieftains learned a new way of seeing society and the world, perhaps assembling the collection of commodities for trade, acquiring organizational skills alien to their own societies. As principal beneficiaries of the trade, they would gain status, many more possessions, and strong interest in seeing the trade maintained. However, the authority and powers needed to expand and maintain the commerce were not part of the kin-linked society in which the chieftains had lived all their lives. In time, they might come to feel closer sympathy with their visitors, the people who gave them their power and prestige. Philosophically they would come to feel closer to Indian models of authority and leadership. They would become familiar with the Brahman and Buddhist conceptions of divine kingship. There was even a brahmanic rite by which chieftains could be inducted into the ruling class, a group whose authority was vested in an assumption of divine kingship. Wheatley hypothesizes that regular trading contacts, combined with changes in beliefs about the legitimizing of authority, led to the birth of states in southeast Asia.

Divine kingship was a cultural borrowing from India that revolutionized social and political organization in southeast Asia. Numerous city-states arose in strategic parts of this huge region. Many were served by Brahman priests, who, among other functions, consecrated divine kings as they started their reigns. Some of these states became very powerful, with extensive trading connections and large Brahman communities. As early as the third century A.D., Chinese envoys to southeast Asia reported on a state in the northern part of the Malay Peninsula that enjoyed regular trading contacts with Parthia and India as well as southern China.

Funan
c. A.D. 100 to 546 The Chinese visited many small southeast Asian kingdoms that modified Indian civilization to their own purposes, but the most famous was Funan, a mercantile empire that extended along the Mekong Delta in Vietnam and some distance inland into Kampuchea (Briggs, 1951). Funan appears in Chinese histories from approximately the third to seventh centuries A.D., but probably came into being in approximately A.D. 100. Most accounts of Funan extol its "port of a thousand rivers" and its rich trade in gold, silver, bronze, and spices. They tell of the Funan people, who built a drainage and irrigation system that rapidly transformed much of the delta from barren swamps into rich agricultural land. The development of these fields took the communal efforts of hundreds of people living off the fish that teemed in the bayous of the delta. Most Funans lived in large lake cities fortified with great earthworks and moats swarming with crocodiles. Each major settlement was a port connected to the ocean and its neighbors by a network of artificial canals.

Funan prospered greatly from the third to sixth centuries. The ports handled goods from all over the East, even horses brought by sea from central Asia. Large numbers of Chinese merchants and Indian artisans settled in the cities and worked with bronze, ivory, silver, gold, even coral. They brought new skills with them that the local people copied, for they were not creative folk. In the sixth century many more Indian Brahmans arrived in Funan. They brought the cult of Shiva, the god who was to become the focus of all subsequent southeast Asian civilization. He appeared in the temples in the form of a *linga*, a phallic emblem of masculine creative power. The royal linga stood in a temple on the hill that symbolized the center of every capital. Shiva's omnipresent emblem soon was the focus of all Kampuchean civilization, surviving the fall of Funan in the sixth century.

The Rise of the God-Kings

Funan was succeeded by the state of Chenla, the economic hub of which lay around the Great Lake in the central basin of Kampuchea (Briggs, 1951). Most of the year the lake is a shallow series of muddy pools some 40 miles (66.6 km) long, drained by the Tonle Sap River that runs into the Mekong. However, so much water floods into the Mekong Delta from July to January that the Tonle Sap's course is reversed and the pools become a vast lake, 80 to 100 miles (133 to 167 km) long, 15 to 30 miles (25 to 50 km) wide, and up to 50 feet (15.5 m) deep. Late in October the water starts receding, trapping millions of fish in the muddy bayous. The Great Lake provided such favorable opportunities for rice cultivation and fishing that its shores supported a far higher population density than even the irrigated delta downstream. This unique environment enabled the Chenla kings not only to embark on ambitious conquests but also to develop a new political concept of divine kingship that united their far-flung domains in a common purpose — the glorification of the god-king on earth. The earlier Khmer kings were unable to hold the kingdom together, until a dynamic monarch named Jayavarman II was crowned in A.D. 802. He had spent some years in Java, where he had studied a new cult, the worship of the god-king. This *Devaraja* cult taught that the king did not rule by divine authority alone but that he was a god himself to be worshiped and obeyed without question. Jayavarman II adopted the teachings of this powerful cult to consolidate his vast kingdom. His subjects were taught to worship him as a god. All resources were devoted to the preservation of the cult of the god-king. Everyone, whether noble, high priest, or commoner, was expected to subordinate his or her ambitions to the need to perpetuate the existence of the king on earth and his identity with the god in this life and the next. The symbol of the king's authority was the royal linga (Briggs, 1951). Jayavarman II's new strategy was brilliantly successful. He reigned for forty-five years, founded a dynasty that prospered for 600 years, and united the Khmer kingdoms into a colorful, spectacular empire that reached the height of its prosperity between A.D. 900 and 1200, shortly after his death.

Previous monarchs had encouraged the worship of Shiva in the form of this phallic image, but now Jayavarman II presented himself as the reincarnation of Shiva on earth. He was the *varman*, the protector, and his priests were the instruments of practical political power. The high priests were invariably energetic, imposing nobles, who presided over a highly disciplined hierarchy of religious functionaries. They supervised every aspect of Khmer life, from agriculture to warfare and the rituals of the state religion. The custom of building a new majestic and holy temple to house the royal linga of each king was the most important of all the religious rituals. As a result, most of the thirty monarchs who followed Jayavarman II left massive religious edifices to commemorate their reigns. These they built on temple mountains or artificial mounds in the center of their capitals, the hub of the Khmer universe.

Jayavarman II's new policies, based on the assumption that he had no living superior on earth, were brilliantly successful, but only after several decades of brutal suppression and cruelty. The king played one prince off against another, planted spies everywhere, and executed everyone who stood in his way. His

Chenla
A.D. 611 to 802

Khmer
A.D. 802 to 1218

propaganda machine successfully convinced the masses that their individual welfare as well as that of the kingdom depended on the success of the new cult. For the next three centuries, each Khmer king ruled as "great master, king of kings." Inevitably, the despotism overwhelmed them. They surrounded themselves with a brilliant and powerful court that upheld their desire for supreme power, so much so that the kings lost touch with their subjects. Soon they were completely obsessed with life after death and their memorials on earth. Thousands of their subjects toiled to build fabulous temples and palaces such as Angkor Wat purely for the king's pleasure. When the people were admitted, they prostrated themselves not before the gods but before the god-king. The Khmer's unique form of divine kingship produced, instead of an austere civilization like that of the Indus, a society with a blind faith in powerful kings who carried the cult of wealth, luxury, and self-aggrandizement to amazing lengths.

Angkor Wat

Angkor Wat
A.D. 1200 to 1432

The Khmer kings who followed Jayavarman II indulged two passions: warfare and temple building. They surrounded themselves with artists, poets, and sculptors whose sole task it was to embellish and adorn their magnificent capitals. Most of these capitals were built in a fertile area teeming with fish near the Tonle Sap, an area known as *Angkor.* Of all the edifices there, the most famous is Angkor Wat (Figure 18.6). This extraordinary shrine is a spectacle of beauty, wonder, and magnificence, the largest religious building in the world, greater even than Vatican City, 5000 feet (1500 m) by 4000 feet (1200 m) across. The central block measures 717 feet (215 m) by 620 feet (186 m) and rises more than 200 feet (60 m) above the forest. It dwarfs even the largest Sumerian ziggurat and makes Moenjo-daro's citadel look like a village shrine. Angkor Wat took forty years to build and finally was abandoned in 1432.

Angkor Wat is approached through an entrance gallery with a tower by a paved causeway 500 feet (150 m) long that is flanked with balustrades adorned with mythical multiheaded snakes. It opens onto a cruciform terrace in front of a rectangular temple that rises in three imposing tiers to a central cluster of five towers. Each tower bears a lofty pinnacle that, from afar, looks like a giant lotus bud. The causeway leads across a huge moat 600 feet (180 m) wide enclosed by masonry walls 4 miles (6.4 km) in circumference. The engineers built the walls with a total error of less than an inch! The moat still is a beautiful sight, with floating water lilies, wild orchids, and other shimmering blooms. Angkor Wat was built in three great rising squares (Giteau, 1966). A central group of chambers and then long open galleries extend all around each square, with a double square of columns on their outer face. Each terrace is surrounded by a gallery interspersed with corner towers, pavilions, stairways, and other structures. On the highest terrace, the central tower is tied to axial pavilions by galleries supported by pillars that divide it into four paved courts. The towers themselves are without interior windows or staircases and are finished with superb lotus-bud cones.

Every detail of this extraordinary building reproduces part of the heavenly world in a terrestrial mode. The Khmer believed that the world consists of a central continent known as *Jambudvipa,* with the cosmic mountain *Meru* rising

FIGURE 18.6   The temple at Angkor Wat.

from its center. The gods lived at the summit of Meru, represented at Angkor Wat by the highest tower. The remaining four towers depict Meru's lesser peaks; the enclosure wall, the mountain at the edge of the world; and the surrounding moat, the ocean beyond. Angkor Wat was the culminating attempt of the Khmer to reproduce a monument to the Hindu gods: Shiva, the creator; Vishnu, the preserver of the universe; and Brahma, who raised the earth. Everything about Angkor Wat is on a massive and lavish scale, as if expense, time, and slave labor were of little importance.

The galleries of Angkor Wat are adorned with more than 4000 feet (1212 m) of polished sandstone bas-reliefs, each approximately 8 feet (2.42 m) high (Giteau, 1966). Some 2000 temple dancers wearing ropes of pearls dance in graceful, acrobatic poses along the galleries, walls, and pillars. These lovely, smiling, and often seductive creatures soften the dark gray edifice, stretching naked to the waist for hundreds of feet over the walls of the second and third terraces. Most of the bas-reliefs depict religious scenes, popular legends, and wars. Hundreds of soldiers mounted on elephants ride victorious over opposing armies, warriors fight from chariots, and fleets sail to battle. There even are armies of monkeys and men, and victory marches with bands and banners. The sculptures invoke the Hindu Trinity, gods, goddesses, and guardian deities. The god-king rides on a royal elephant surrounded by slaves and soldiers. He is depicted setting forth to fight Angkor's enemies with the blessings of his priests and is seen administering his domains and enjoying the triumphs of his reign.

Angkor Wat taxed the resources of the kingdom so severely that civil war ensued. Undeterred, the rulers used thousands of prisoners of war to erect a huge new capital at Angkor Thom nearby. The sheer size of Angkor Thom is overwhelming. A dark and forbidding 8-mile (12.8-km) wall surrounds the capital.

The five gateways rise 60 feet (18 m) and the crocodile-filled moat is 540 feet (162 m) across. When visitors walked into the capital, they entered a symbolic Hindu world with the king's funerary temple at the center. Great triple-headed elephants guard the flanks of the gates, and four huge Buddha faces adorn the towers above the massive doorways. The Grand Plaza of Angkor Thom was the scene of ceremonies and contests, of vast military reviews and massed bands. Long bas-reliefs of animals and kings walking in procession above seas of snakes and fish lead to the plaza and look down on its wide spaces.

It is said that a million people once lived in or near Angkor Thom. The architectural and artistic legacy they left is mind-boggling, one so large that a single frieze of marching elephants extends over 1200 feet (360 m) of sculpted wall! The task of building the city beggared the state. The temple of the king's father contained no fewer than 430 images, with more than 20,000 in gold, silver, bronze, and stone in the wider precincts. Another inscription in the same temple records that 306,372 people from 13,500 villages worked for the shrine, consuming 38,000 tons of rice a year. An inscription in the nearby temple of Ta Prohm inventories a staff of 18 senior priests, 2740 minor functionaries, 615 female dancers, and a total of 66,625 "men and women who perform the service of the gods." The same temple owned gold and silver dishes, thousands of pearls, 876 Chinese veils, and 2387 sets of clothing for its statues. The result of the ruler's megalomaniacal orgy was a totally centripetal and macabre religious utopia in which every product, every person's labor, and every thought was directed to embellishing the hub of the universe and the men who enjoyed it (Wheatley, 1975).

After A.D. 1218 an exhausted nation built no more stone temples. The seemingly endless pool of prisoners of war dried up once the economy faltered, and there were no longer the resources to support the army or maintain the great irrigation works of Tonle Sap. The only way the Khmer could maintain their strange utopia was through oppression, promiscuous use of slave labor, and the blind obedience of their own subjects. Once the image of the divine king was challenged and the slaves ceased to serve, the empire was doomed. Angkor Thom fell to alien armies in approximately 1430, and the divine kings and their works were soon just a shadowy memory.

GUIDE TO FURTHER READING

Allchin, Bridget, and Allchin, Raymond. *The Rise of Civilization in India and Pakistan.* Cambridge: Cambridge University Press, 1983.
A summary account of the roots of the Indus civilization that is readable and well argued.

Fairservis, Walter A. *The Roots of Ancient India* (2d ed.). New York: Macmillan, 1976.
A popular account of the Harappan that contains an excellent description of the cities.

Wheeler, Sir Mortimer. *The Indus Civilization* (2d ed.). Cambridge: Cambridge University Press, 1962.
Wheeler's classic account is based on his Indus Valley excavations in the late 1940s. Somewhat outdated, but it reads well.

White, Joyce C. *Ban Chiang: Discovery of a Lost Bronze Age Civilization.* Philadelphia: University of Pennsylvania Press, 1982.

A brief but clearly written account of this remarkable site written to accompany a museum exhibition. Gives useful insight into southeast Asian bronzeworking.

Wolpert, Stanley A. *A New History of India.* London: Oxford University Press, 1977.

By far the most lucid account of Indian history for the beginner. A good synthesis of archaeology, legend, and documentary sources.

Southeast Asia is difficult to study in any depth, for books on Khmer civilization are few and far between. However, the following are suggested:

Briggs, L. Cabot. "The Ancient Khmer Empire." *Transactions of the American Philosophical Society* 41 (1951).

Perhaps the standard archaeological and historical source for specialists and lay readers alike. Highly technical, but crammed with useful information, much of it from very obscure sources.

Giteau, M. *Khmer Sculpture and the Angkor Civilization.* London: Thames and Hudson, 1966.

A wonderful lay reader's guide to the elaborate artistry and architecture of the Khmer. Lavishly illustrated.

CHRONOLOGICAL TABLE J

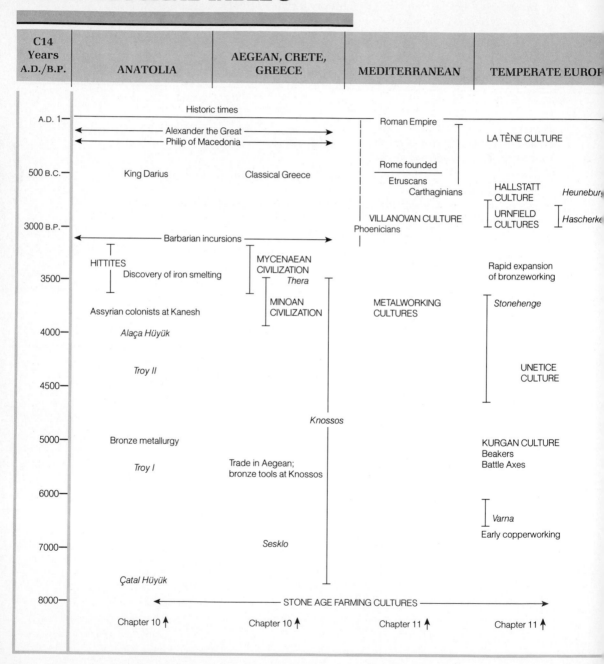

C14 Years A.D./B.P.	ANATOLIA	AEGEAN, CRETE, GREECE	MEDITERRANEAN	TEMPERATE EUROPE
	Historic times			
A.D. 1	←— Alexander the Great —→		Roman Empire	LA TÈNE CULTURE
	←— Philip of Macedonia —→			
500 B.C.	King Darius	Classical Greece	Rome founded	
			Etruscans	HALLSTATT CULTURE Heuneburg
			Carthaginians	
3000 B.P.			VILLANOVAN CULTURE	URNFIELD CULTURES Hascherke
	←— Barbarian incursions —→		Phoenicians	
	HITTITES	MYCENAEAN CIVILIZATION		Rapid expansion of bronzeworking
3500	Discovery of iron smelting	Thera		
		MINOAN CIVILIZATION	METALWORKING CULTURES	Stonehenge
	Assyrian colonists at Kanesh			
4000	Alaça Hüyük			
	Troy II			UNETICE CULTURE
4500				
		Knossos		
5000	Bronze metallurgy			KURGAN CULTURE Beakers Battle Axes
	Troy I	Trade in Aegean; bronze tools at Knossos		
6000				
				Varna Early copperworking
7000		Sesklo		
	Çatal Hüyük			
8000		←— STONE AGE FARMING CULTURES —→		
	Chapter 10 ↑	Chapter 10 ↑	Chapter 11 ↑	Chapter 11 ↑

CHAPTER 19

Anatolia, Greece, and Italy

Preview

- ▪ Anatolia was a major locale for the development of early farming villages, one of which, Çatal Hüyük, became a small town by 7600 years ago. Strangely, however, Çatal Hüyük failed to develop the necessary administrative and social mechanisms to cope with the increased complexity of the settlement and its trading activities. The town failed, and Anatolians of the fifth millennium B.C. reverted to village life.

- ▪ Small fortified villages flourished in the fourth millennium B.C. One of them, Troy I, dates to just after 5500 years ago. Troy II, founded approximately 4300 years ago, was a fortified town with more elaborate architecture and fine gold and bronze metallurgy. By this time the Anatolians were trading widely over the highlands and into the Aegean, and chieftaincies were scattered over mineral-rich areas. About 3900 years ago, the Assyrians set up a trading colony at Kanesh in central Anatolia.

- ▪ The Hittites were a small group of leaders who originated in the north and assumed power in Anatolia approximately 3650 years ago. They held a vital place in contemporary history, for they played the Assyrians off against the Egyptians. Hittite power was based on diplomatic and trading skills and lasted until approximately 3200 years ago. They are associated with the discovery of iron smelting.

- ▪ The Aegean and the Greek mainlands were settled by sedentary farming villages well before 7000 years ago. Painted pottery styles came into widespread use near that time.

- ▪ There were radical changes after 5500 years ago, when the cultivation of the olive and the vine became widespread, and trading of minerals, stone wares, and other products expanded rapidly. Numerous small towns were flourishing throughout the Aegean and eastern Greece by 4500 years ago, linked by regular trading routes.

- ▪ The Minoan civilization of Crete developed as a result of these cultural routes approximately 4000 years ago and lasted until approximately 3400 years ago. The growth of this civilization is known from the ruins of the Palace of Knossos. The Minoans traded as far afield as Egypt and the eastern Mediterranean and were expert metalworkers and potters with a lively artistic tradition.

■ Minoan power apparently was weakened by the great explosion of its satellite island, Thera, about 3500 years ago. The center of civilization passed to the mainland, where the Mycenaeans flourished until 3150 years ago. The Mycenaeans were able to develop some trading connections with temperate Europe as well as continue many Minoan trade routes. They were overthrown by Phrygian peoples at the end of the second millennium B.C.

■ Trading activities continued to expand in the Aegean after the decline of Mycenae. Small city-states flourished, unifying only in the face of a common danger such as the Persian invasions of the fifth century B.C. The Athenians enjoyed a long period of supremacy among city-states, the period of Classical Greek civilization in the fifth century B.C.

■ Alexander the Great built an enormous empire across the Near East, of which Greece was part, in the late fourth century B.C. The Roman Empire, which followed, marks the entry of the entire Mediterranean area into historic times. Developed from Villanovan and Etruscan roots in Italy, the Roman Imperial power was based on the ruins of Alexander's empire.

Chronological
Table J

This chapter begins with a disclaimer: the prehistory of Anatolia, Europe, and the Mediterranean Basin is so complicated, and our knowledge so spotty, that we can touch only the highlights here (Trump, 1980). Interested readers should consult the references in the Bibliography of Archaeology for more information on these areas.

ANATOLIA

Çatal Hüyük
7600 B.P.

During the height of its prosperity over 7600 years ago, the town of Çatal Hüyük controlled trade over huge areas of central Anatolia (Figure 19.1), so much so that it was the focus for villages hundreds of miles around (Mellaart, 1967). This complex settlement was organized by creating ritual and other mechanisms that attempted to retain the close kinship ties of village life while adapting to the new complexities of long-distance trading and growing population. Unlike Mesopotamia, where new mechanisms and organizations evolved to handle social change, the system at Çatal Hüyük broke down. Anatolia's first and largest town was abandoned, and people went back to living in small villages (Mellaart, 1975; Redman, 1978).

The entire plateau of Anatolia seems to have experienced a subsequent gradual population increase after 5000 years ago, as long-distance trading with Mesopotamia in minerals and other materials increased. The evidence for the concentration of power and wealth in major Anatolian settlements is found

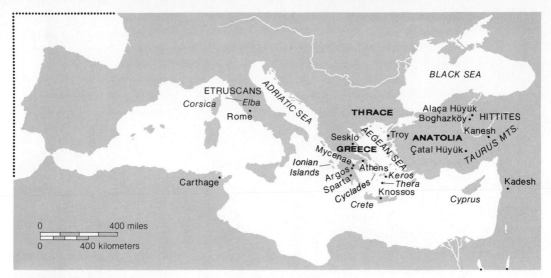

FIGURE 19.1 Sites and cultures mentioned in this chapter.

after 5000 years ago in the walled fortresses of Hissarlik (Troy) and Kultepe (ancient Kanesh) (Blegen, 1971).

Hissarlik was first occupied approximately 5500 years ago, when a small fortress was built on bedrock. Its foundations show it contained a rectangular hall of a basic design that had been in use for centuries. The structure was to become the standard palace design of later centuries and perhaps a prototype for the Classical Greek temple. Approximately 4300 years ago, a new settlement known to archaeologists as Troy II flourished at Hissarlik. This fortified town boasted more elaborate buildings and yielded valuable hoards of gold and bronze ornaments — a clear sign that the rulers of the settlement were supporting skilled craftspeople who designed and executed fine ornaments of rank.

> Troy I (Hissarlik)
> 5500 B.P.

> Troy II
> 4300 B.P.

Thirteen royal tombs were found at the site of the town of Alaça Hüyük in central Anatolia, dating to about 4000 years ago. The tombs contain the bodies of men and their wives accompanied by domestic vessels, weapons, and many metal items (Piggott, 1965). The ornaments include copper figurines with gold breasts and finely wrought cast bronze stags inlaid with silver, which were perhaps mounted on the ends of poles (Figure 19.2).

> Alaça Hüyük
> 4000 B.P.

Both the Alaça Hüyük and Hissarlik finds testify to widespread trade in gold, copper, tin, and other raw materials by 4000 years ago. Major centers like these maintained long-distance trading contacts throughout the Near East. These, along with trading offshore to Cyprus and the Aegean islands, could well have influenced social and political developments.

Toward the end of the third millennium B.C., Indo-European-speaking peoples seem to have infiltrated Anatolia from the northwest, causing considerable political unrest. By this time, central Anatolia was coming into much closer contact with Mesopotamia. By 3900 years ago, there was a sizable Assyrian merchant colony outside the city of Kanesh, one of several important trading centers or *karums* that were staging posts for long-distance commerce in minerals and other commodities (Lloyd, 1967). The karums served as marketplaces

> Kanesh
> 3900 B.P.

FIGURE 19.2 Bronze stag from Alaça Hüyük, inlaid with silver.

and termini for caravans, neutral entrepôts where prices for goods were regulated. Local rulers levied taxes on the caravans, which brought important Assyrian ideas to Anatolia and reinforced the political and economic power of Anatolian kings.

THE HITTITES

Hittites
3650 to 3200 B.P.

The Hittites appear to have been a group of able Indo-European people from the vast steppes north of Anatolia, who infiltrated the plateau and seized power from the leaders of Kanesh and other cities, probably just before 3650 years ago (Lehmann, 1977; MacQueen, 1987).

No historian would be taken in by the Hittites' own extravagant claims for their glorious history. The Hittites seem, in practice, to have been a foreign minority who rose to political power by judiciously melding conquest and astute political maneuvering. The minority soon became acculturated into its new milieu, even though it seems to have preserved its traditional values and outlook on life.

The Hittites were a down-to-earth people, with a talent for political and military administration. They were not intellectuals, but religion was important to them. The king was not deified until after his death, if then. His duties were well defined: to ensure the state's welfare, wage war, and act as high priest under clearly defined circumstances. A hierarchy of officials supported the king. One unusual institution was the *pankush*, a form of assembly that may have had a restricted membership, perhaps open only to those of pure Hittite stock. However, we see no sign that this institution, with its undertones of racial superiority, ever wielded much power.

The Hittites exercised enormous political influence in the Near East from their vast capital at Boghazköy, with its 4 miles (6.4 km) of city walls. They used their wealth and diplomatic skill to play Assyria and Egypt against one another. They were hardened warriors as well, who campaigned as far south as Babylon and fought Rameses II on the outskirts of Kadesh. Their objectives were simple enough: to acquire new spheres of political influence and to control trade routes. Boghazköy

One major achievement of the Hittites was the systematic use of iron, thought to have been smelted first in the middle of the second millennium B.C., in the highlands immediately south of the Black Sea. The military advantages of this metal lay in its relative abundance in a natural state, even if it was hard to smelt. The Hittites seem to have guarded the secrets of ironworking for some time, but eventually foreign mercenaries in their armies carried the new techniques to their homelands. Iron tools soon became commonplace over a wide area of Europe and the Near East, although it was some time before domestic artifacts such as axes and hoes were invariably made of the new metal (Wertime and Muhly, 1980). Ironworking

Hittite rule did not last long in Anatolia. Approximately 3200 years ago, repeated migrations of foreigners flowed into Anatolia from the northwest, whence the Hittites had come only four centuries earlier. These population movements came to a head when the Phrygian peoples from Thrace ravaged the plateau as far as the Taurus Mountains. Anatolia became the homeland of dozens of small city-states, each striving to maintain its independence. Only a few Hittite communities survived, in small states in northern Syria that lasted until they were engulfed in the vast Persian Empire. Phrygians 3200 B.P.

THE AEGEAN AND GREECE

Parts of mainland Greece and the Aegean were settled by farming peoples as early as 8500 years ago, but more intensive settlement of western Greece, the islands, and Crete did not occur until much later. 8500 B.P.

The Sesklo village in Thessaly was occupied approximately 7000 years ago and is typical of northern Greek sites of the time (Warren, 1975). The people lived in stone and mud houses connected by courtyards and passages. Their mixed farming economy depended heavily on cereal cultivation. Somewhat similar villages are found on Crete, where farming settlement dates back to at least 7500 years ago. Sesklo 7000 B.P.

There were radical changes in the settlement pattern after 5500 years ago, when villages were established in the Cyclades, throughout Crete, and on the Ionian islands of the west. In contrast, northern Greece seems to have lagged behind. The reason may have been agriculture, for southern Greece and the islands are ideal environments for the cultivation of olives and vines, with cereal crops interspersed between them (C. Renfrew, 1972). There was a veritable explosion in village crafts as well, in the manufacture of fine painted pottery, mar- 5500 B.P.

ble vessels, and magnificent stone axes (Figure 19.3). Stone vases and fine seals were made by Cretan workers; the seals were used to mark ownership of prized possessions or pots full of oil or other commodities. By 5500 years ago, the peoples of the Aegean and Greece were smelting copper and making bronze artifacts as well as ornaments in gold and silver. These included exquisite gold and silver drinking cups and the elaborate ornaments found at Troy II, which included more than 8700 gold beads, wire ornaments, chain links, and objects of fine gold sheet. The achievements of the Aegean metallurgists were in part owing to the rapid expansion of trading throughout the Aegean, far into Anatolia, and to Cyprus, with its rich copper outcrops (see Renfrew and Wagstaff, 1982).

The Aegean is well endowed with comfortable ports and alternative trading routes that provided easy communication from island to island for most of the year. Even relatively primitive vessels could coast from one end of the Aegean to the other in easy stages. Sailing vessels are depicted on Cretan seals dating to approximately 4000 years ago. The Aegean trade flourished on olive oil and wine, metal tools and ores, marble vessels and figurines, and pottery. The success of the trade led to a constant infusion of new products and ideas to Greece and the Aegean. By 4500 years ago, numerous small towns housed farmers, traders, and skilled craftsworkers on the mainland and the islands.

4500 B.P.

The beginnings of town life created considerable cultural diversity in the Aegean, a diversity fostered by constant trading connections and increased complexity in social and political organization. Nowhere is this better documented than on Crete, where a brilliant civilization flourished in towns and palaces throughout the island. In contrast, mainland Greece lagged somewhat, its many small towns having only occasional contact with the Aegean islands and Crete.

FIGURE 19.3 Harpist in marble, executed by a craftsworker on the island of Keros in the Aegean.

THE MINOANS

The development of the Minoan civilization of Crete was almost certainly the result of many local factors, among them the intensive cultivation of the olive and the vine. Its development is best documented at the famous Palace of Knossos near Heraklion in northern Crete (Figure 19.4) (Hood, 1973; Warren, 1975).

The first prehistoric inhabitants of Knossos settled there approximately 8100 years ago. No fewer than 23 feet (7 m) of early farming occupation underlie the Minoan civilization. The first Knossos settlement was founded at approximately the same time that Çatal Hüyük was first occupied in Anatolia. The Knossos farmers lived in sun-dried mud and brick huts of a rectangular ground plan that provided for storage bins and sleeping platforms. By 5730 years ago, signs of long-distance trading increase in the form of exotic imports such as stone bowls. The first palace at Knossos was built approximately 3930 years ago; it is a large building with many rooms grouped around a rectangular central court.

At least nine periods of Minoan civilization have been distinguished by pottery styles found in the later levels of the Knossos site. Even during the earlier periods of the civilization, the Minoans were trading regularly with Egypt, for their pottery and metal objects have been found in burials there. About 3700 years ago, the earlier palaces were destroyed by an earthquake.

The high point of Minoan civilization followed that destruction, occurring between 3700 and 3450 years ago, when the Palace of Knossos reached its

Knossos
8100 to 3400 B.P.

5730 B.P.

Minoan civilization
c. 4000 to
3400 B.P.

3700 B.P.

FIGURE 19.4 General view of the Palace of Minos at Knossos.

greatest size. This remarkable structure was made mainly of mud-brick and timber beams with occasional limestone blocks and wood columns. Some buildings had two stories; the plaster walls and floors were decorated, initially with geometric designs, and after 3700 years ago with vivid scenes or individual pictures of varying size. Sometimes the decorations were executed in relief; in other cases, colors were applied to the damp plaster (Figure 19.5).

Artistic themes included formal landscapes, dolphins and other sea creatures, and scenes of Minoan life. The most remarkable art depicted dances and religious ceremonies, including acrobats leaping vigorously along the backs of bulls (Figure 19.6). Writer Mary Renault (1963) has vividly reconstructed Cretan life at Knossos in novels that bring Minoan culture to life.

At the height of its prosperity, Crete was self-supporting in food and basic raw materials, exporting foodstuffs, cloth, and painted pottery all over the eastern Mediterranean. The Cretans were renowned mariners. Their large ships transported gold, silver, obsidian, ivory, and ornaments from central Europe, the Aegean, and the Near East, and ostrich eggs probably were traded from North Africa.

We know very little of Minoan religious beliefs, except for some chilling finds made by Peter Warren (1984) in a house on the north side of Knossos. This fine building had collapsed in the great earthquake of 3450 years ago. The first-floor ceiling fell into the basement, taking a magnificent set of ritual vessels with it.

FIGURE 19.5 Reconstruction of the throne room at Knossos, Crete. The wall paintings are modern reconstructions from fragments found at the site; details may be inaccurate.

FIGURE 19.6   A Minoan bull and dancers, as painted on the walls of the Palace of Knossos. The bull, a domesticated form, has a piebald coat. This very fragmentary scene has been reconstructed from rather inadequate original pieces and is somewhat controversial. (After Evans, 1921)

The basement fill also contained the scattered bones of two children in perfect health. A microscopic examination of the limb bones showed that knives had been used to remove flesh from the bone. Warren believes that this may be evidence not only of human sacrifice but, perhaps, of ritual cannibalism as well, and possibly this related to a fertility rite associated with the Cretan Zeus and the Earth Mother.

In 3473 B.P., a volcano on the island of Thera, a Minoan outpost 70 miles (113 km) from Crete, exploded with such violence that it probably caused catastrophic destruction on the north coast of the Minoan kingdom. (Some authorities believe it was about 150 years earlier.) This event is equated by some people with the eternal legend of Atlantis, the mysterious continent said to have sunk to the ocean bottom after a holocaust thousands of years ago (Luce, 1973). The Thera eruption may have accelerated the decline of Minoan civilization, which was already showing signs of weakness. Fifty years later many Minoan sites were destroyed and abandoned. Warrior farmers, perhaps from mainland Greece, established sway over the empire and decorated the walls of Knossos with military scenes. Seventy-five years later the palace finally was destroyed by fire, thought to have been the work of Mycenaeans who razed it. By this time the center of the Aegean world had shifted to the Greek mainland, where Mycenae reached the height of its power.

Thera
3473 B.P.

? 3400 B.P.

3375 to 3350 B.P.

The dramatic flowering of Minoan civilization stemmed from the intensified trading contacts and the impact of olive and vine cultivation on hundreds of Greek and Aegean villages. As agricultural economies became more diversified and local food surpluses could be exchanged both locally and over longer distances, a far-reaching economic interdependence resulted. Eventually this led to redistribution systems for luxuries and basic commodities, systems that were organized and controlled by the inhabitants of Minoan palaces and elsewhere in the Aegean where there were major centers of olive production.

The redistribution networks carried metal objects and other luxury products the length and breadth of the Aegean. Interest in long-distance trading brought about some cultural homogeneity from trade, gift exchange, and perhaps piracy. The skills of craftsworkers were highly valued in village and palace alike.

Specialized artisans practiced their crafts in the major palaces; they lived well, in stone buildings with well-designed drainage systems, and had wooden furniture.

Colin Renfrew (1973) describes both Minoan society and that of its successors, the Mycenaeans of the Greek mainland, as civilizations. He points to their sophisticated art and metalwork, to the complex palaces organized around specialized craftsworkers, and to their developed redistribution networks for foods. The Minoans and Mycenaeans did not build vast temples like those at Tikal in Guatemala (Chapter 22) or those in Egypt. They also did not live in cities. Palaces and elaborate tombs were the major monuments. Renfrew looks for the origins of Minoan and Mycenaean civilization within Greece and the Aegean, and considers them to be the result of local social change and material progress, not external population movements. His theory sharply differs from earlier hypotheses that claimed migration of new peoples into Greece from the north or diffusion of new culture traits from Anatolia or the eastern Mediterranean were responsible (Childe, 1956).

THE MYCENAEANS

Mycenaeans
3600 to 3200 B.P.

The Mycenaean civilization, centered on the fertile plain of Argos on the Greek mainland, began to flourish about 3600 years ago (Taylour, 1969). The chieftains who ruled over the walled fortress of Mycenae (Figure 19.7) were buried in spectacular shaft graves that contained weapons adorned with copper and gold, as well as fine gold face masks modeled in the likeness of their owners (Figure 19.8). Their wealth and economic power came from far-flung trading contacts as well as from their warrior skills (Figure 19.9). The kings were skilled charioteers and horsemen, whose material culture and lifeway are immortalized in the Homeric epics. These epics, however, were written many centuries after the Mycenaeans themselves had become folk memories (Rieu, 1945).

Mycenaean commerce took over where Minoan left off. Much of the rulers' prestige was based on their contacts in the metal trade. Minerals were in constant demand in the central and eastern Mediterranean, especially tin for alloying copper to make bronze. Both copper and tin were abundant in central Cyprus and Anatolia, and the Mycenaeans developed the necessary contacts to obtain regular supplies.

The Mycenaeans also prized Baltic amber, a yellow-brown fossil resin that when rubbed seems to be "electric." Occasional pieces of this precious substance reached Mycenae, and amber is found in the royal graves there (Piggott, 1965). Just how extensive the Mycenaeans' European trading activities were has been much debated. They may well have been minimal (for a discussion, see Harding, 1984).

So complex did their trading transactions become that the Mycenaeans found it necessary to establish a writing system. They refined one that had been developed by the Minoans. The Mycenaeans used a form of script written in the Greek language, known now as Linear B (Chadwick, 1958; Diringer, 1962). Eighty-nine characters make up Linear B, forty-eight of which can be traced back to Minoan writing, Linear A. Linear A probably originated in the simple

FIGURE 19.7   The Lion Gate at Mycenae.

pictographic script of the earliest Minoans (Figure 19.10). The terms Linear A and Linear B were coined by Sir Arthur Evans when he first studied Minoan writing. Linear B was in more widespread use than A, partly because the Mycenaeans exerted greater political and economic power than their Cretan neighbors.

Mycenae continued to dominate eastern Mediterranean trade until about 3150 years ago, when its power was destroyed by warrior peoples from the **3150 B.P.** north. In the same century, other northern barbarians overthrew the Hittite kingdom in Anatolia. These incursions into the Mediterranean world were caused by unsettled political conditions in Europe, at least partly the result of population pressures and tribal warfare (Chapter 20).

THE MEDITERRANEAN AFTER MYCENAE

After Mycenae fell 3200 years ago, small-town merchants on the Greek main-   **3200 B.P.** land continued to trade, monopolizing commerce in the Aegean and Black seas. By the seventh and eighth centuries B.C., small colonies of Greek settlers lived   **700 to 600 B.C.** on the northern and western shores of the Black Sea and along the north coast of Anatolia, and developed trade in gold, copper, iron, salt, and other commod-

FIGURE 19.8 Gold mask of a bearded man, from Shaft Grave V at Mycenae, 3600 B.P.

ities (Bonzek, 1985). Other Greeks voyaged westward and settled in southern France; they soon made a brisk trade in wine and other commodities with central Europe.

The Greek City-States

In Greece many fertile agricultural areas are separated by ranges of mountains. Traders and seafarers of the Aegean islands and the Greek mainland therefore formed a network of small city-states that competed with each other

FIGURE 19.9 Impression of a warrior fighting an enemy with a dagger, from an engraved gold ring, shaft graves, Mycenae, Greece.

for trade and political power. Athens was one of the larger and more prosperous states. The island of Sifnos in the Aegean was another, famous for its gold and silver. Paros marble was known all over the eastern Mediterranean, while Milos provided obsidian for many centuries.

Greek states unified only in times of grave political stress, as when the Persian King Xerxes sought to add Greece to his possessions. Xerxes' defeats at Marathon (490 B.C.) and ten years later in a naval battle at Salamis ensured the security of Greece and made Classical Greek civilization possible. Athens was foremost among the Greek states (Kinley, 1963; Kitto, 1958), becoming head of a league of maritime cities, which was soon turned into an empire. This was the

490 B.C.

FIGURE 19.10 Early forms of writing: (a) Cretan pictographic script; (b) Linear A signs.

Athens that attracted wealthy immigrants, built the Parthenon, and boasted of Aeschylus, Sophocles, and other mighty playwrights. Classical Greek civilization flourished for fifty glorious years.

However, throughout the brilliant decades of Athenian supremacy, bickering with Sparta in Peloponnesus never abated. A deep animosity between the two cities had its roots in radically different social systems. Sparta's government was based on military discipline and a rigid class structure. Athenians enjoyed a more mobile society and democratic government.

The long rivalry culminated in the disastrous Peloponnesian War, from 431 to 404 B.C., which left Sparta a dominant political force on the mainland. The contemporary historian Thucydides documented the war, which was followed by disarray (Livingston, 1943). Greece soon fell under the sway of Philip of
Macedonia, whose rule between 359 and 336 B.C. began to develop political unity. His son Alexander the Great then embarked on a campaign of imperial conquest that took him from Macedonia into Persia and then to Mesopotamia. Alexander was welcomed as a hero and a god in Egypt, where he paused long enough to sacrifice to local deities and have himself proclaimed pharaoh. His continued quests took him as far east as the Indus Valley and back to Babylon,
where he died of fever in 323 B.C. By the time of his death, Alexander had united an enormous area of the ancient world under at least nominal Greek rule. His extraordinary empire fell apart within a generation, but his conquests paved the way for the uniform government of Imperial Rome.

The Phoenicians

While the Greeks were developing their trading endeavors in the Aegean and Black seas, other maritime peoples, too, had turned into vigorous traders.
The Phoenicians of Lebanon first rose to prosperity by acting as middle agents in the growing trade in raw materials and manufactured products (Harden, 1962; N. K. Sanders, 1977). Phoenician ships carried Lebanese cedarwood and
dye to Cyprus and the Aegean area as well as to Egypt. After Mycenae declined, Phoenicians took over much of the copper and iron ore trade of the Mediterranean. Their trading networks later extended far to the west, as they ventured to Spain in search of copper, tin, and the purple dye extracted from seashells and
much used for expensive fabrics. By 800 B.C., Phoenician merchants were everywhere. They were using a fully alphabetical script by the tenth century B.C.

Phoenicians not only traded widely but also set up small colonies that served as their vassals and were marketplaces for the hinterlands of Spain and North Africa. Some settlements won independence from home rule. The greatest was the North African city Carthage, which challenged the power of the Roman Empire.

The Etruscans

The Greeks and Phoenicians were expanding maritime activities at the same time as skilled bronzeworkers and copper miners in northern Italy were developing a distinctive but short-lived urban civilization.

Approximately 3000 years ago, some Urnfield peoples from central Europe (Chapter 20) had settled south of the Alps in the Po Valley (Wells, 1981). They developed a skilled bronzeworking tradition, in which products were traded far into central Europe and throughout Italy. This people evolved into the Villanovan culture, which appeared in the ninth century B.C. and was soon in touch with Greek colonies in southern Italy and perhaps with the Phoenicians (Piggott, 1965). Ironworking was introduced to the Villanovans in approximately the ninth century B.C. Iron tools and extensive trading contacts won the Villanovans political control over much of northern and western Italy. They established colonies on the islands of Elba and Corsica. Several centuries of trade and other contacts culminated in a literate Etruscan civilization.

Like Classical Greece, Etruscan civilization was more a unity of cultural tradition and trade than a political reality (Pallotino, 1977). The Etruscans traded widely in the central Mediterranean and with warrior peoples in central Europe. Etruscan culture was derived from the Villanovan, but it owed much to eastern immigrants and trading contacts that brought Oriental influence to Italian towns.

Etruscan territory was settled by city-states with much independence, each with substantial public buildings and fortifications. Their decentralized political organization made them vulnerable to foreign raiders. Warrior bands from central Europe overran some Etruscan cities in the centuries after 450 B.C., at which time Etruscan prosperity began to crumble.

By the time of Etruscan decline, however, the Mediterranean was a civilized lake. Phoenician colonists had founded Carthage and other cities in North Africa and Spain and controlled the western Mediterranean. The rulers of Greece and Egypt and later Philip of Macedonia controlled the east, and the Etruscans were in control of most of Italy and many central European trade routes.

The Romans

The Etruscans had been the first people to fortify the seven famed hills of Rome. In 509 B.C., a foreign dynasty of rulers was evicted by these native Romans, who began to develop their own distinctive city-state. The next few centuries saw the emergence of Rome from a cluster of simple villages by the Tiber River to the leadership of the Mediterranean and far beyond. The Romans inherited the mantle of Classical Greece and added their own distinctive culture to this foundation. They then carried Greco-Roman civilization to many parts of the world that were still inhabited by preliterate peasant societies. Roman legions campaigned not only in Egypt and Mesopotamia and as far as India but also in central and western Europe and in Britain. If it were not for the Romans, the administrative and linguistic face of Europe would be very different today (Grant, 1960; Vickers, 1977).

By 295 B.C., the power of Rome dominated the whole of Italy. At this time Rome was a form of democracy, governed by a delicate balance of aristocratic and popular authority. This type of governance was appropriate for a large city-state but was hopelessly inadequate for the complexities of a huge empire.

Eventually, civil strife led to autocratic rule of the empire under the emperors, the first of whom was Julius Caesar, familiar to every student of Roman history for his epic conquest of Gaul (France). (His great-nephew Augustus was the first ruler actually to claim the title of emperor.)

200 to 133 B.C.

After two vicious wars with their rich rival, Carthage, the Romans achieved mastery over the western Mediterranean by 200 B.C., and by 133 B.C. much of Asia was under uneasy Roman domination. Unfortunately, the Romans lacked the mechanisms to administer their empire successfully until the Emperor Augustus reorganized the civil service and established the Pax Romana over his vast domains. There ensued a period of great material prosperity and political stability, at the price of political freedom of speech.

The stresses that led to the collapse of the Roman Empire first began to appear on the European frontiers in the second and third centuries A.D. Roman power began to decline as ambition and sophistication grew among the Iron Age tribes living on the edges of Roman territory. The "barbarians" on the fringes of the empire were mainly peasant farmers who had obtained iron by trading and intermarriage with La Tène peoples (Chapter 20). Many served as mercenaries in the Roman armies, acquiring wealth and sophistication, and perhaps most important of all, an insight into Roman military tactics.

A.D. 395

A.D. 410

Shortage of farming land and increasing disrespect for Rome caused many Germanic tribes to raid Rome's European provinces. The raids were so successful that the imperial armies were constantly campaigning in the north. In A.D. 395, after Emperor Theodosius died, the Roman Empire was split into eastern and western divisions. Large barbarian invasions from northern Europe ensued. Fifteen years later, a horde of Germanic tribesmen from central Europe sacked Rome itself; then the European provinces were completely overrun by warrior peoples. Other Germanic hordes disturbed North Africa and crossed much of Asia Minor but left little lasting mark on history there.

What was the legacy of Rome? Its material legacy can be seen in the road system, which still provides a basis for many of Europe's and the Near East's communications, and in the towns, like London, which are still flourishing modern cities. In cultural terms, its principal legacy was the legal system, which lies at the core of most Western law codes. Roman literature and art dominated European culture for centuries after the Renaissance. Their spoken and written language, Latin, survived for centuries as the language of the educated person and as the principal means of business communication between nations. Latin lies at the base of many modern European languages and was only recently abandoned as the liturgical language of the Roman Catholic Church. The Romans and their culture lie at the foundations of our Western civilization.

GUIDE TO FURTHER READING

Hood, Sinclair. *The Minoans.* London: Thames and Hudson, 1973.
> A superb summary of the origins, history, and decline of the Minoan civilization for the informed layperson. Excellent illustrations.

Luce, J. V. *Atlantis.* New York: McGraw-Hill, 1973.
A convincing account of the Atlantis legend and a possible explanation for it in the eruption and explosion at Santorini (Thera) in the Aegean.

MacQueen, J. G. *The Hittites.* London: Thames and Hudson, 1987.
An admirable summary of Hittite civilization that is lavishly illustrated.

Renfrew, Colin. *The Emergence of Civilization.* London: Methuen, 1972.
A study containing a mass of information about Aegean civilization and trade that adopts a systems approach. Technical, but invaluable to the general reader.

Taylour, Lord William. *The Mycenaeans.* London: Thames and Hudson, 1969.
Mycenaean civilization described by a leading authority; a companion volume to Hood on the Minoans. Lavishly illustrated.

Warren, Peter. *The Aegean Civilizations.* Oxford: Elsevier Phaidon, 1975.
A synthesis of Bronze Age Greece and its antecedents for the beginner. Excellent illustrations and thoughtful text.

CHAPTER 20

Temperate Europe Before the Romans

Preview

■ In contrast to earlier hypotheses, archaeologists now believe that copper-working was developed independently in southeast Europe about 6800 years ago. The Varna Cemetery in Bulgaria shows just how elaborate the gold and copper metallurgy of the area became. The industry flourished because of a demand for the fine metal ornaments. Copperworking also developed early in southern Spain and northern Italy.

■ Copperworking was a logical outgrowth of earlier stone and ceramic technologies. Its more widespread use coincides with the spread of Beaker and Battle Ax artifacts throughout much of Europe.

■ Bronzeworking began at an unknown date but was widespread in what is now Czechoslovakia by 4500 years ago, as part of the Unetice culture. The trading networks of earlier times expanded to meet increased indigenous demand for metal artifacts during a period of rapid technological change after 3700 years ago. Some rich chieftaincies developed in the temperate zones.

■ The Urnfield peoples of central Europe began to expand from their homeland approximately 800 B.C. Armed with new slashing swords, they settled all over Europe, bringing their more effective agricultural techniques with them.

■ After 1000 B.C., ironworking techniques diffused into temperate Europe and spread through the Hallstatt and La Tène cultural traditions during the first millennium B.C.

The fundamental question about the emergence of complex societies in temperate Europe is simple: did they emerge as a result of indigenous cultural evolution, or because of diffusion of people and ideas from the Near East?

V. Gordon Childe (1956), Stuart Piggott (1965), and others have argued that the constant demands by Near Eastern societies for copper, tin, and other metals led to cultural development in the backwater that was temperate Europe. However, this traditional viewpoint has been challenged by the calibrated radiocarbon chronologies that place the appearance of copperworking in the Balkans earlier than in Greece or the Aegean. Many people now believe that Europeans were just as innovative as their eastern neighbors (Champion et al., 1984; Melisauskas, 1978).

EARLY COPPERWORKING

Colin Renfrew (1978) and Ruth Tringham (1971) have argued that the farmers of southeast Europe developed copper smelting independently, partly because they already used improved pottery firing techniques that were very suitable for copper smelting (Figure 20.1). They cite as proof of the early development the finds at the Varna Cemetery near the Black Sea in Bulgaria.

The Varna Cemetery

At the Varna Cemetery, more than 130 richly decorated graves have yielded dozens of fine copper and gold tools and ornaments. Colin Renfrew (1978) has described the Varna finds as "the earliest major assemblage of gold artifacts to be unearthed anywhere in the world," for they date to approximately 6600 to 6200 years ago. Both the copper and the gold are of Balkan origin; indeed both metals were being worked here earlier than they were in the Near East. (Such a statement reflects findings thus far; it does not preclude future discoveries of earlier metals in the Near East.) The Balkan copper industry was quite sophisticated and was organized to serve trading networks over a wide area. At Rudna Glava in Yugoslavia fissures mark the places where early miners followed ore veins deep into the ground. One mine in Bulgaria has ancient shafts more than 32 feet (10 m) deep. These copper mines are the earliest so far discovered in the world and show that metallurgy developed rapidly into a considerable industry in the Balkans during the fifth millennium B.C. (Jovanovic, 1980).

The Varna burials provide striking evidence for differential wealth; some of the graves are richly decorated with gold ornaments while others contain few artifacts. Unfortunately, the settlement associated with the Varna Cemetery has yet to be found, but Renfrew (1978) has suggested that the users of the burial ground were part of a chiefdom in which the leaders used gold and copper ornaments to fulfill the social need for conspicuous display. As he points out, the problem with explaining the rise of metallurgy is not a technical but a social one — defining the social conditions under which metal objects first came into widespread use. The earliest copper artifacts had few practical advantages over stone axes. Both copper and gold were used mainly for ornamental purposes

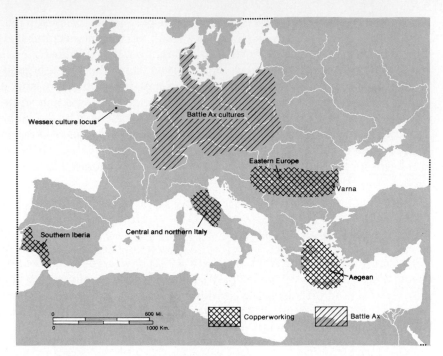

FIGURE 20.1 Major centers of early metallurgy in temperate Europe and the distribution of Battle Ax cultures.

(Figure 20.2). Perhaps it was no coincidence that the first metallurgists in temperate Europe developed a wide range of ornaments, luxury items traded through exchange networks that accelerated the spread of copperworking to other parts of temperate Europe.

BATTLE AXES AND BEAKERS

The technology of copperworking is really an outgrowth of that used for pottery manufacture and probably arose after many experiments with fire, clay, and stone. The beginnings of copper metallurgy in temperate Europe were probably almost imperceptible, since a handful of simple, hammered copper artifacts date to as early as 5500 years ago. At least two possible areas of indigenous copperworking have been identified in southern Europe, both near copper outcrops. One is in southern Spain (Iberia) the other in northern Italy. In both regions, the copper workers started smelting approximately 4000 years ago. Britain is also rich in copper ores, and the metal was exploited early there, too. Wherever it developed, copper smithing was probably a seasonal, or at best a part-time occupation, and it was not until much later that tougher bronze artifacts came into daily use in the field and the chase.

The archaeological record of the period between 5500 and 4000 years ago is incredibly complicated, but we can discern two broad groupings of societies, the so-called Battle Ax and Beaker peoples, who ultimately mingled.

5500 B.P.

In east Europe, settled farming societies had lived on the edge of the huge Russian steppe for hundreds of years. Like the peoples of Anatolia and Greece, they had sporadic contacts with the nomads who roamed the plains to the east; about these we know little. In the southern Russian region, a widespread population of copper-using agriculturalists lived in rectangular, thatched huts, cultivated many crops, and also tamed domestic animals, possibly including the horse. This loosely defined Kurgan culture was remarkable for its burial customs, depositing each corpse under a small mound (Piggott, 1965). The Kurgans used wheeled vehicles and made the copper or stone battle ax a very important part of their armory. The wheeled cart and the battle ax had spread widely over central and parts of northern Europe by 5000 years ago. The globular pots associated with these characteristic artifacts, many of them bearing characteristic cord-impressed decorations, have been found at hundreds of sites. The same artifacts have often been found in megalithic tombs. These new cultural traits were absorbed into the millennia-old European cultural tradition, and many experts feel that Indo-European language spread into Europe at about this time. (Indo-European speech is thought to have originated in the region between the Carpathian and Caucasus mountains.)

Kurgan culture
5000 B.P.

It was at about this time that new house forms appeared in temperate zones. Smaller timber dwellings, just large enough to house a single family, replaced the Danubian longhouse. Warriors were buried with their battle axes under small mounds, a reflection of new cultural traditions that were to persist in Europe for thousands of years. The warrior leaders who descended from Bronze Age chieftains were the German tribesmen that the Romans encountered on the frontiers of their European empire.

Between 4700 and 4000 years ago, a series of highly characteristic artifacts came into fashion over a large region of Europe: coastal Spain, southern France, Sardinia, northern Italy, east and central Europe, the Low Countries, and Brit-

Beakers
4700 to 4000 B.P.

FIGURE 20.2 Copper ax heads from Czechoslovakia (one-third actual size).

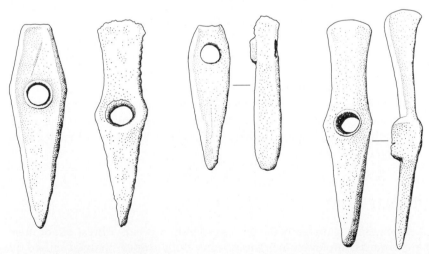

FIGURE 20.3 Beaker vessels and other artifacts, including arrowheads, from various localities in south central Britain.

ain (Figure 20.3) (Harrison, 1980). These include finely made bell-shaped beakers found in hundreds of graves and burial mounds. Archaeologists like V. Gordon Childe thought in terms of tribes of "Beaker Folk," who spread the length and breadth of Europe bringing a new culture and copperworking with them. But it seems more likely that these vessels spread widely not as a result of itinerant merchants or great population movements but simply because beakers, as well as other trinkets like metal brooches, became prized status symbols throughout Europe. Perhaps they became valued heirlooms, priceless grave furniture, and artifacts exchanged as bride wealth or displayed at tribal gatherings. Beakers were but one of several innovations that were changing the face of European society. Another was the plow, which came into widespread use about 4200 years ago, opening the way for the cultivation of heavier soils and much larger acreages.

THE BRONZE AGE

In the Aegean, there was steady development from this early threshold of metalworking toward complex state organizations, but Europe remained settled by small village societies. The temperate zones were densely occupied and exploited, and vast acreages of forest had been cleared and brought under cultivation by 4000 years ago. The villagers managed woodland carefully, engaged in hunting to supplement their diet, and mined both hard ax stone and soft copper ore. They also panned for gold. Communal burials and individual internments were part of tribal tradition. If ambitious community works were needed, the basic metal technologies were known, and both boats and wheeled transport were available, as well as the humanpower and resources. European village society was stable and self-sufficient, with thousands of communities connected by ties of kin and family, and by long-established paths that led from valley to valley along well-drained ridges. Above all, European society enjoyed assured and reliable food supplies that helped bind the communities together.

The European Bronze Age began not as a result of dramatic events and military conquest, nor because of some startling invention (Coles, 1982; Coles and Harding, 1979). It was merely a gradual, and inevitable, quickening of responses to a number of new opportunities. Many of these changes were in material culture and settlement patterns. A series of landscape surveys in southern Britain, for example, have revealed vast networks of fields and land boundaries joining river valleys, ridges, and watersheds into a managed landscape, in which different communities now owned closely defined agricultural land. One Dorsetshire, England, Bronze Age agricultural system encompassed 494 acres (200 ha), with settlements of four to five huts linked to enclosures with sunken herd paths. There were fields, hoe plots, stock corrals, and homesteads, all joined in single managed agricultural units. By 900 B.C., Bronze Age food production was sophisticated. It relied heavily on plow agriculture and field fallowing, as well as manuring, and it was based on the rotation of many different cereal and root crops.

From about 4000 years ago, metallurgy was a growth industry throughout temperate Europe. A series of local bronze industries developed in different parts of Europe, bringing with them a whole range of related activities: trading of ores and finished artifacts from major mining centers and the barter of both prosaic and prestigious artifacts and ornaments over considerable distances. For the first time, a major European industry was practiced in areas where supplies of raw materials were scarce. For instance, Bronze Age communities in Scandinavia, which had no metals, went to considerable trouble to acquire metal ore and finished tools both from tribes in Britain and from central European sources. European smiths produced some of the finest bronze artifacts ever made in the ancient world: axes and adzes, battle axes, daggers, swords, spearheads, shields, and an enormous range of brooches, pins, and other ornaments. They also made delicate, prestigious gold ornaments that were highly prized and buried with important chieftains.

For all these metallurgical innovations, the basic tenor of agricultural life remained unchanged, except for gradual evolution in the structure of European society — the emergence of social ranking. Just what form this ranking took is a matter of lively controversy (Coles, 1982), since it is reflected only in a differentiation of grave goods between a few individuals and the rest of society. In Denmark, for example, excavations on the island of Fyn have revealed rich Bronze Age burials and a nearby settlement with a wealth of gold and bronze. This is clear evidence that there was a powerful community there, having extensive trading connections with metal-rich regions to the south. The evidence from Bronze Age graves across Europe shows that the rich and the poor were buried side by side, the former with substantial quantities of valuable metal artifacts that were thus lost to the people burying them. This can only mean that some members of society, perhaps important traders, more probably influential kin leaders, were aggrandized at the expense of others and became a new elite in European society (Coles and Harding, 1979).

Although the first occurrence of bronze may one day be shown to date to some 6000 years ago in southeast Europe, the earliest widespread use of tin-copper alloys was approximately 4500 years ago in what is now Czechoslovakia (Coles and Harding, 1979). The new bronze implements with tougher working edges (Figure 20.4) were initially in short supply, but their use spread gradually as new trade routes were opened across central and west Europe. The earliest bronzeworking was centered in Unetice, an industry manufacturing axes, knife blades, halberds, and many types of ornament (Piggott, 1965). The bronzeworkers themselves obviously belonged to cultural traditions long es-

Unetice culture
4500 B.P.

FIGURE 20.4 Copper and bronze implements from Britain: simple flat axes and flanged and socketed axes (left, one-third actual size); a dagger and sword blades (right, one-fourth actual size).

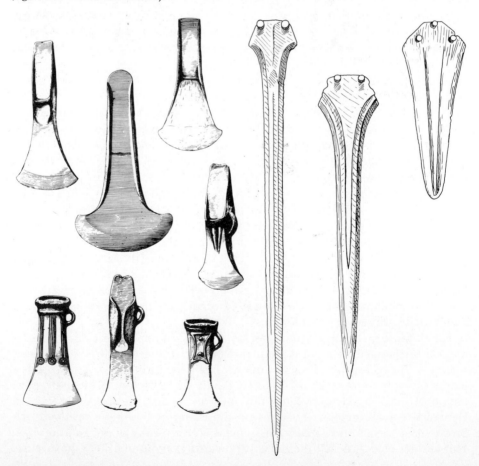

478   *Old World Civilizations*

tablished in the area, for their burial customs are identical to those of earlier centuries. Some believe that the art of alloying tin with copper, as well as casting techniques, came to Europe from Syria. Most people now argue, however, that bronzeworking developed independently in Europe, for the calibrated C14 dates from the Unetice industry are earlier than those for the Near Eastern prototypes from which the other school of thought assumes Unetice to have evolved.

Bronzeworking soon appeared in southern Germany and Switzerland as well, where deposits of copper and tin were to be found. Other places with copper outcrops were soon using the new methods, including Brittany, the British Isles, and northern Italy, all more remote from the initial centers of bronzeworking. The period between approximately 3700 and 3300 years ago was one of rapid technological progress and considerable social change, generated in large part by the reinforcing effects on the local centers of bronzeworking of persistent demand for critical raw materials and finished tools. **3700 to 3300 B.P.**

By this time, European trading networks carried far more than bronze artifacts and metal ores. The amber trade went from the shores of the Baltic to the Mediterranean, following well-established routes (Figure 20.5) (P. Phillips, 1980). Seashells, perhaps faience (glass) beads, and other exotic luxuries were dispersed northward into the temperate zones in exchange for raw materials. Some centers of bronze production became major places for redistributing other goods as well. The salt miners of Austria also were very active in the long-distance trade.

FIGURE 20.5 Amber trade routes in Europe and to Mycenae. The northern coastlines were the primary sources of Baltic amber. Amber was being passed southward to the Mediterranean by the time the Mycenaeans came to power.

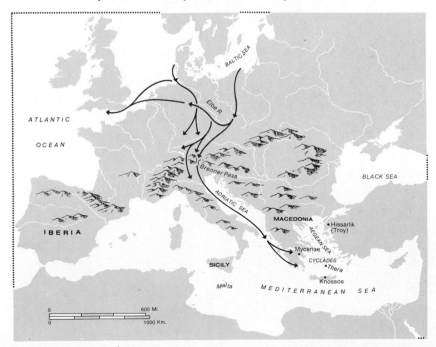

By 3300 years ago, even societies remote from metal outcrops were engaged in metallurgy, but the archaeological record tells little of increased specialization, although many richly adorned burials testify that the trade was concentrated among wealthy chieftains. The surplus food and energy were not devoted to generating additional surpluses and extra production, but, in some societies, were channeled into erecting majestic religious monuments, of which Stonehenge in southern Britain probably is the most celebrated (Figure 20.6).

Stonehenge

Shrouded in fantasy and speculation, associated by many people with the ancient Druids' cult, Stonehenge is in fact a fantastically old religious temple (Chippindale, 1983). It began as a simple circle of ritual pits approximately 4700 years ago and went through vigorous reconstructions, reaching the zenith of its expansion in the late second millennium B.C. That Stonehenge was associated with some form of astronomical activity seems unquestionable, although the details are much debated.

The inhabitants of southern Britain also erected enormous earthwork enclo-

FIGURE 20.6 Stonehenge as seen from the air. This photograph was taken before modern tourism caused development at the site.

sures and huge circles of timber uprights known as *henges* (see Chapter 11 and C. Renfrew, 1983). Doubtless special priests were needed to maintain these spectacular monuments and to perform the rituals in their precincts. Religious activity was supported by the food surplus, not the increased productivity that generated spectacular social evolution in the Near East. Thus, during the third and part of the second millennia B.C., little social evolution went on in Europe; political power and wealth belonged to the chieftains and warriors rather than to divine kings and a hierarchic society.

BRONZE AGE WARRIORS

European societies became more socially ranked as time went on. As trade intensified, local monopolies over salt and other supplies became concentrated in the hands of comparatively few individuals. Population growth and perhaps some climatic deterioration put new pressure on agricultural land (P. Phillips, 1980; Piggott, 1965). All of this may have led to considerable political instability in Europe, to alliances of small tribes under the rule of powerful and ambitious chieftains, themselves once minor village leaders. Some warrior groups even began to strike at the fringes of the Mediterranean world, destroying Mycenae and the Hittite Empire.

As time went on, many more copper and bronze artifacts became available for domestic consumption. Some new tool forms were introduced by central European smiths, including socketed axes, varied woodworking tools, and the *ard* (a scraping plow drawn by oxen). The ard was a particularly important innovation, for it allowed deeper plowing, more advanced agricultural methods, and higher productivity. The new farming techniques were vital to feed the many new mouths, and prime farming land was harder to find than ever before.

Between 3200 and 2800 years ago, the population movements associated with central European peoples introduced a more consolidated system of agriculture to much of Europe, which allowed exploitation of much heavier soils, as well as stock breeding (J. G. D. Clark, 1952; Dennell, 1983). For the first time, stock were fully integrated into the food-producing economy, and cattle were used for meat, milk, and draft work, though sheep were bred as much for wool as for their flesh. Improved technology for new implements of tillage was fully exploited to achieve a truly effective economic symbiosis between flora and fauna, carefully balancing forest clearance with cultivation and pasturage.

One powerful group of warrior tribes in west Hungary is known to archaeologists as the Urnfield people because of their burial customs: their dead were cremated and their ashes deposited in urns; huge cemeteries of urn burials are associated with fortified villages, sometimes built near lakes. Urnfield people began to make full use of horse-drawn vehicles and new weaponry. Skilled bronzesmiths produced sheet-metal helmets and shields. The Urnfield people also used the slashing sword, a devastating weapon far more effective than the cutting swords of earlier times.

Urnfield culture
?1000 B.C

Approximately 800 B.C., the Urnfield people began to expand from their Hungarian homeland. Within a couple of centuries, characteristic slashing swords and other central European tools had been deposited in sites in Italy, the

Balkans, and the Aegean. By 750 B.C., Urnfield peoples had settled in southern France and moved from there into Spain (Figure 20.7). Soon Urnfield miners were exploiting the rich copper mines of the Tyrol in Austria. Bands of miners used bronze-tipped picks to dig deep in the ground for copper ore. Their efforts increased the supplies of copper and tin available to central Europeans (J. G. D. Clark, 1952; Coles and Harding, 1979).

The Scythians and Other Steppe Peoples

The vast rolling grasslands and steppes from China to the Ukraine were not settled by farming peoples until they had a culture enabling them to survive in an environment with extreme contrasts of climate and relatively infertile soils. The carrying capacity of the land is such that only a vast territory can support herds of domestic stock. The prehistory of this huge area is obscure until the first millennium B.C., when the Scythians (from Scythia, an area in southeast Europe) and other steppe peoples first appeared in the historical record. No one should doubt, however, the importance of nomads in the prehistory of Europe in earlier millennia (E. D. Phillips, 1972). The Kurgan people and other possible Indo-European speakers were familiar with the vast open spaces of the steppes,

FIGURE 20.7 Approximate distribution of Urnfield cultures in Europe.

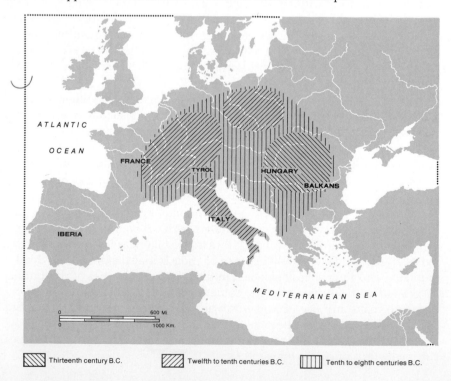

Thirteenth century B.C.   Twelfth to tenth centuries B.C.   Tenth to eighth centuries B.C.

where domestication of the horse ultimately made the nomadic life a potent force in frontier politics. For centuries before the Scythians came out of history's shadows, people had roamed the steppes, relying on the horse and wagon for mobility, living in stout felt tents, and subsisting mostly on horse's milk and cheese, as well as on food from hunting and fishing. The nomadic life, though, leaves few traces in the archaeological record, except when permafrost has preserved burials in a refrigerated state.

We are fortunate in having extensive data about the vigorous society of nomad peoples from the spectacular frozen tombs of Siberia. Russian archaeologist Sergei Rudenko (1970) has excavated several nomad burial mounds erected in 400 B.C. at Pazyryk in northeast Siberia. The chiefs of Pazyryk were elaborately tattooed, wore woollen and leather clothes, and employed skillful artists to adorn their horse trappings and harnesses with exuberant, elaborate, stylized animal art. A powerful chief was accompanied to the next world by his wife and servants, horses and chariots, and many of his smaller possessions. The Pazyryk burials contain fragments of woven rugs, the earliest examples of such art in the world.

400 B.C.

The steppe peoples lived to the north of the well-traveled trade routes of Greek merchants, but their territory was constantly being explored and sometimes colonized by farmers whose lands were becoming overpopulated or overgrazed. Enormous areas of steppe were needed to support even a small band of horsemen, for just a slight increase in population could drastically affect the food supplies of the original inhabitants. The result was constant displacement of populations as the nomads sought to expand their shrinking territory to accommodate their own population pressures. The nomads menaced the northern frontiers of the Mediterranean world throughout Classical and more recent times.

The Eurasian nomad population flourished during the closing millennia of prehistory. The Pazyryk finds let us glimpse a prehistoric way of life that in some areas survived unchanged right into historic times.

THE EMERGENCE OF IRONWORKING

The Urnfield people were effective agriculturalists as well as traders and metallurgists, capable of exploiting Europe's forested environment far more efficiently than their predecessors could. They lived amid a complicated network of trade that carried not only metals but also salt, grain, gold, pottery, and many other commodities. Their economic organization probably included community smiths, specialists supported by the community, but still no centralized state system of the Near Eastern type.

The secrets of ironworking, guarded carefully by Hittite kings, were slow to reach Europe, but sometime after 3000 years ago, ironworking techniques were introduced into temperate Europe, presumably via existing trade routes. Ironworking is much more difficult than bronzeworking, for the technology is harder to acquire and takes much longer, but once it is learned, the advantages of the new metal are obvious. Because the ore is found in many more places, the

Ironworking
3000 B.P.

metal is much cheaper and can be used for weapons and utilitarian artifacts as well. These would, of course, include both axes and hoes, as well as plow shares, all of which contributed much to agricultural efficiency, higher crop yields, and greater food surpluses. The population increases and intensified trading activities of the centuries immediately preceding the Roman Empire are partly attributed to the success of iron technology in changing European agriculture and craftsmanship (Collis, 1984).

As iron technology spread into the country north of the Alps, new societies arose whose leaders exploited the metal's artistic and economic potentials. The tribal chieftaincy was the structure of government; the most coherent broader political unit was a loose confederacy of tribes formed in time of war or temporarily under the aegis of a charismatic chieftain. Despite the onslaught of Roman colonization and exploitation, culture beyond the frontiers retained its essentially European cast, an indigenous slant to cultural traditions that began when farming did (Wells, 1981).

For all the technological changes, farming life continued much as before. Peter Wells (1984) has excavated an Iron Age farming community near Hascherkeller in lower Bavaria, Germany, where he found three enclosed farmsteads. The farmstead complexes included dwellings, barns, sheds, and workshops, with between fifteen and thirty people living in each settlement. Occupied between 3000 and 2800 years ago, they were self-sufficient communities without iron tools that traded foodstuffs for such items as imported bronze scraps, beads, and graphite, which were used for pottery decoration. Hascherkeller was apparently without iron, which was still a new metal. But it was occupied at a time when the first towns were emerging in central Europe, communities like the Heuneburg, a significant cluster of timber houses occupied between 800 and 400 B.C. by about 200 people. The Heuneburg was a market town, one of many such local centers that were the forerunners of much later medieval communities of the same type.

Hascherkeller
3000 to 2800 B.P.

Heuneburg
800 to 400 B.C.

The Hallstatt Culture

Hallstatt 730 B.C.

One strong culture was the Hallstatt, named after a site near Salzburg, Austria (Rowlett, 1967; Wells, 1981). Hallstatt culture began in the seventh and sixth centuries B.C. and owed much to Urnfield practices, for the skillful bronzeworking of earlier times was still practiced, although some immigrants from the east may have achieved political dominance over earlier inhabitants. Bronze, however, was still the dominant metal for horse trappings, weapons, and ornaments. Chiefs were buried in large mounds within wooden chambers, some in wagons (Figure 20.8).

The Hallstatt people and their culture spread through former Urnfield territories as far north as Belgium and the Netherlands and into France and parts of Spain (Figure 20.9). Many Hallstatt sites are particularly notable for their fortifications. The Hallstatt people traded with the Mediterraneans along well-traveled routes up the Rhone River and through the Alps into central Europe. A significant import was the serving vessel for wine; containers of Mediterranean wine were carried far into central Europe, as Hallstatt chieftains discovered wine drinking.

FIGURE 20.8 Bronze ritual cart from a Hallstatt grave in Austria, approximately 1 ft (0.3 m) long.

The La Tène People

By the last quarter of the fifth century B.C., a new and highly distinctive technology, La Tène, had developed in the Rhine and Danube valleys (Jacobsthal, 1944; Megaw, 1970). An aristocratic clique of chieftains in the Danube Valley enjoyed implements and weapons elaborately worked in bronze and gold. Much of their sophisticated art had roots in Classical Greek and Mediterranean traditions, for La Tène craftsworkers were quick to adopt new motifs and ideas from the centers of higher civilization to the south (Figure 20.10). The La Tène people spoke Celtic, a language that spread widely through Europe from perhaps as early as the ninth century B.C. Greek and Roman writers referred to these people as Celts, a term that has survived in their linguistic label.

La Tène technology was a specific adaptation of ironworking to woodland Europe. The culture extended north into the Low Countries and Britain in the fourth century B.C. La Tène art is justly famous, and the hill forts and defensive settlements of this Iron Age culture are widespead in west Europe. The superior military tactics of the La Tène people introduced the Romans to the short sword, for La Tène peoples survived long after France and southern Britain had

La Tène **450 B.C.**

350 B.C.

FIGURE 20.9 Distribution of Hallstatt Iron Age cultures (shaded area) in Europe during the seventh to fifth centuries B.C. The trade routes in southern France are also shown.

FIGURE 20.10 Iron Age helmet from the bed of the River Thames in London, 8.07 in (205 cm) at the base.

been conquered by Rome in 55 B.C. (Cunliffe, 1974). Much territory in the temperate zones came under Roman domination, an uneasy frontier province that eventually crumbled before the inexorable pressure of the warlike tribes on its boundaries. The illiterate peoples who eventually sacked Rome and ravaged its provinces were the descendants of prehistoric Europeans whose cultural traditions had been evolving ever since the first farming cultures developed north of the Mediterranean Basin.

Roman conquest
55 B.C.

GUIDE TO FURTHER READING

Champion, Timothy G., et al. *Prehistoric Europe*. New York: Academic Press, 1984.
    A textbook on European prehistory that goes from the earliest times up to the expansion of the Roman Empire. Major emphasis on subsistence, trade, and social organization.

Coles, J. M., and Harding, A. F. *The Bronze Age in Europe*. London: Methuen, 1979.
    An authoritative account of the complexities of the European Bronze Age that covers the topic far more fully than we can in this book.

Collis, John. *The European Iron Age*. London: Batsford, 1984.
    A useful introduction to European ironmaking cultures.

Cunliffe, Barry. *Iron Age Communities in Britain*. London: Routledge and Kegan Paul, 1974.
    The literature on the European Iron Age is scattered and is published in many different languages. Cunliffe's account of Iron Age hill forts and other settlements in Britain will give you a general impression of the archaeology of the period.

Phillips, Patricia. *The Prehistory of Europe*. Bloomington: Indiana University Press, 1980.
    A detailed synthesis of west European prehistory from the earliest times. Particularly good on the later periods.

Piggott, Stuart. *Ancient Europe*. Chicago: Aldine, 1965.
    Somewhat outdated, an account of prehistoric Europe that is closer to Childe than to current evolutionary thinking but is still authoritative, with excellent illustrations.

CHRONOLOGICAL TABLE K

Calibrated Dates a.d./b.c.	C14 Years A.D./B.C./B.P.	CULTURE	PHASE
		Historic times	
420-5 b.c. —	A.D. 1 —		
	221 B.C. —	Unification of China	
820-400 b.c. —	2500 B.P. —	ZHOU	
1530-905 b.c. —	3000 B.P. —		
		SHANG	Late Shang
			Middle Shang
			Early Shang
4830 -4305 b.p. —	4000 B.P. —	XIA	
		LONGSHAN	
5950 -5640 b.p. —	5000 B.P. —		

C I V I L I Z A T I O N*

S H A N G

Chapter 13 ↑

*SHANG CIVILIZATION refers to a civilization that survived the changing of ruling dynasties.

CHAPTER 21

Shang Civilization in East Asia

Preview

- Early Chinese civilization emerged independently from state-organized societies in the West. By 4500 years ago, population densities were rising in farming communities throughout China. By this time, there are signs of social differentiation in village cemeteries. Exchange networks linked thousands of small communities by 6000 years ago, spurring social and technological changes that included copper metallurgy and the widespread use of earthen fortifications. A new cosmology based on animals and the use of divination to communicate with the dead came into widespread use. These Longshan cultures are found in at least three major variants throughout China.

- The Shang civilization of the Yellow Valley is the best-known early Chinese state, flourishing from approximately 3766 to 3122 years ago. It probably was the dominant state among several throughout northern China. Shang origins are partly from Longshan roots and partly from influences that came to the Shang from the east.

- There were at least three stages of Shang civilization, associated with distinctive writing and bronze metallurgy. Shang society was organized along class lines, with the rulers and nobles living in segregated precincts while the mass of the people were scattered in townships and villages in the surrounding countryside.

- Shang civilization ended with the overthrow of the Shang dynasty by Zhou rulers, who reigned over a wide area of northern China from 3122 to 2221 years ago.

The origins of Chinese civilization were known only from legend until the late 1920s, when Tung Tso-pin and, later, Li Chi began digging in the Anyang area of Henan province in northern China. Their excavations resulted in the discovery of the Shang civilization, which flourished in the Yellow Valley more than 3500 years ago (Chang, 1980, 1986; Keightley, 1983).

THE EMERGENCE OF CHINESE CIVILIZATION

4500 B.P.

By 4500 years ago, agriculture had taken such hold in China that population densities rose throughout the country. The farmers took more and more land into cultivation until there was little new acreage available for planting. Some pollen analyses from northern villages show how the trees that once surrounded many settlements were felled as the fields lapped right up to the houses (Chang, 1986). This population growth also coincided with an expansion of rice farming in lowland areas, on moist floodplains, and in lush water meadows where irrigation was easy (Figure 21.1). Those villages fortunate enough to possess lands that could be irrigated, especially in the Yellow and Yangtze valleys, soon turned into much more permanent settlements, often protected with earthen walls to guard against floods and marauding neighbors. Even these larger communities were part of a self-regulating folk society in

FIGURE 21.1 (Left) Distribution of farming cultures that immediately preceded Shang civilization in China (commonly called Longshan). Each shaded area represents a different regional variant of Longshan (not discussed in detail in the text). Compare with the second map (right), which shows the approximate distribution of Shang culture about 3400 years ago. (Xiao-tun and other royal sites are close to Anyang.)

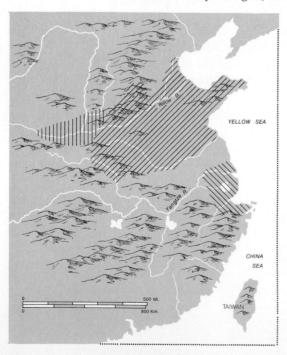

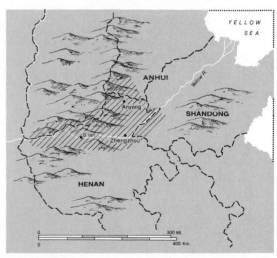

which kinship loyalties and the extended family were all-important, and age was deeply revered. The family ancestors were the conduit to the gods who controlled the harmony of the world.

However, there are signs that a new order existed, for some settlements of 5000 years ago contain elaborate burials adorned with jade ornaments and ceremonial weapons. Village artisans created fine clay vessels exclusively for the use of these privileged people. These were important leaders who are known to have raided their neighbors, for the corpses of their enemies have been found buried in village wells. In both the north and south, a few peasant villages became important centers ruled by new generations of kin leaders who became the nobles of more sophisticated societies. They probably were expert warriors and certainly were people of great spiritual authority, who were experts at predicting the future and communicating with the ancestors.

These developments would never have been possible without the unswerving conservatism of the country farmer. The village crops might change from rice to cereals, the fertility of the soils depend on radically different rainfall patterns, and building materials alter from brick and tile to bamboo, but what never varied was the unquestioning acceptance by the peasants of an emerging social order that imposed an almost alien wealthy, privileged society. The viability of this aristocratic civilization depended on simple loyalties that persisted from the earliest centuries of farming life right into modern times. Every Chinese noble, however unimportant, cashed in on this loyalty.

About 6000 years ago, the several regional farming cultures of north and south China became interlinked in what Chang (1986) calls an "interaction sphere," trading raw materials, luxury goods, and other commodities over long distances. This interdependence spurred similar developments in more complex social organization as well as technological changes that spilled over from narrow territorial boundaries to affect much of China. These innovations included copper metallurgy, construction of stamped-earth town walls, and the first widespread use of earthen fortifications. There is far more evidence for warfare and violence, including the decapitation of prisoners. New, powerful rituals emerged, among them a cosmology based on animals and birds, and the use of divination to communicate with the ancestors. These Longshan cultures, found in at least three major variants throughout China, show clear evidence of marked social stratification, with sharp economic and political distinctions between the elite and the mass of the common people.

These many changes were the result of constant interaction between many different farming societies, a kind of relationship between complex chiefdoms that inevitably drew them into a larger system (H. T. Wright, 1977). This interaction developed over a period of 2000 years after 6000 years ago, culminating in the emergence of Chinese civilization about 4000 years B.P. (for a full discussion, see Chang, 1986).

Shoulder Blades and Oracles

When archaeologists dug into a village named Longshan on the Yellow River in Shando province in 1930 to 1931, they found not only the remains of a farming village but also dozens of cracked ox shoulder blades that they identified as

Longshan
?4700 B.P.

oracle bones used in divination ceremonies (Figure 21.2) (Keightley, 1983). The cracks were made by applying hot metal to the bone and then were interpreted as messages from the ancestors. None of the Longshan bones bore written inscriptions, but the hundreds of shoulder blades found in pits near Anyang farther upstream are a mine of information about the origins of Chinese civilization, a unique written archive of official deliberations by the very first kings of northern China. One scholar has suggested that Chinese writing may have originated from the need to interpret the cracks on the bones, with the new writing symbols resembling persistent crack patterns found on oracle bones. Clearly some Chinese ideographs originated as pictograms, such as that for the hill, originally shown with three humps and now written as a horizontal line with three vertical strokes (Fitzgerald, 1978).

Perhaps as early as 4500 years ago, divination rituals were a vital part of village government. All official divinations were addressed to the royal ancestors, who acted as intermediaries between the living and the ultimate ancestor and supreme being, the ruler of heaven and the creator, Shang Di. This deity served as the ancestor not only of the royal line but also of the "multitude of the people." The king was the head of all family lines that radiated from his person to the nobility and then to the common people. These actual and imputed kinship ties were the core of early Chinese civilization, for they obligated the peasants to provide food and labor for their rulers.

In addition to shoulder blades from oxen and water buffalo, the diviners used tortoiseshell for their ceremonies. The term *scapulimancy*, meaning "shoulder blade divination," refers to the bones used most frequently in the ceremonies. The bones and shells were smoothed and cleaned and perhaps soaked in liquid to soften them. Rows of hollows were then produced on the underside to make the substance thinner and the surface more susceptible to being cracked. When a question was posed, the diviner would apply a metal point to the base of the hollow, causing the surface to crack. The response of the ancestors was "read" from the fissures. A skillful diviner could control the extent and direction of the cracks. Thus, divination provided an authoritative leader with a useful and highly effective way of giving advice; a leader could regard disagreement as treason.

Xia and Shang: ?4700 to 3100 B.P.

The obvious starting point in the study of Chinese civilization is Chinese legends, which tell us that the celebrated Yellow Emperor Huang Di founded civilization in the north approximately 4698 years ago. This great legendary warlord set the tone for centuries of the repressive harsh government that was the hallmark of early Chinese civilization. About 4200 years ago, a Xia ruler named Yu the Great gained power through his military prowess and his knowledge of flood control, by which he could protect the valley people from catastrophic inundations.

What exactly do these legends mean? Who were the Xia and the Shang? In all probability they were dynasties of local rulers who achieved lasting prominence among their many neighbors after generations of bitter strife (Chang,

Xia and Shang
dynasties
?4700 to 3100 B.P.

FIGURE 21.2 Shang oracle bones.

1980, 1986). Every chieftain lived in a walled town and enjoyed much the same level of material prosperity, but each ruler came from a different lineage and was related to his competitors by intricate and closely woven allegiances and kin ties. Each dynasty assumed political dominance in the north in turn, but, for all these political changes, Shang civilization itself continued more or less untouched, a loosely unified confederacy of competing small kingdoms that quarreled and warred incessantly.

The archaeological record reveals that Shang-type remains are found stratified on top of Longshan occupation levels at many places in northern China, and they represent a dramatic increase in the complexity of material culture and social organization (Chang, 1986). The same trends toward increasing complexity are thought to have occurred elsewhere in China at approximately the same time, for literate states may have emerged from a Longshan base in the south and east as well. In form they probably resembled the Shang closely, but few details of the others are known. It seems likely that the Shang dynasty was dominant from approximately 3766 to 3122 years ago, but that other states continued to grow at the same time. The larger area of Chinese civilization ultimately extended from the north into the middle and lower courses of the Yellow and Yangtze rivers. In this account, we concentrate on northern Chinese civilization, simply because more is known about the archaeology of the Shang than about any other early Chinese state.

Shang
3766 to 3122 B.P.

Capitals and Sepulchers

The oracle bones and other historical sources provide but a sketchy outline of the early dynasties and the ways the Shang kings went about their business. The bones inform us that they lived in at least seven capitals, situated near the middle reaches of the Yellow River in the modern provinces of Henan, Shandong, and Anhui. The sites of all these towns are still uncertain, but approximately 3557 years ago the Shang kings moved their capital to a place named Ao, which archaeologists have found under the modern industrial city of Zhengzhou, some 95 miles (153 km) south of Anyang close to the Yellow River (Wheatley, 1971). Unfortunately, the royal compound lies underneath the modern downtown area, so only limited excavations have been possible. However, the diggers have found traces of a vast precinct surrounded by an earthen wall more than 33 feet (9.9 m) high, enclosing an area of 2 square miles (5.18 sq km). It would have taken 10,000 workers laboring 330 days a year for no fewer than eighteen years to erect the fortifications alone. This walled compound housed the rulers, the temples, and the nobles. Some foundations of their large houses and ancestral altars have come from excavations inside the compound. The residential quarters and craft workshops lay outside the Shang walls. These include two bronze factories, one of them covering more than an acre. The metalworkers lived in substantial houses near their furnaces. There were bone workshops, too, places where animal and human bones were fashioned into arrowheads, pins, and awls. Zhengzhou's potters lived in a satellite village close to the kilns where they fired hundreds of fine vessels. The excavations revealed dozens of unfired and incomplete vessels.

The capital moved to the Anyang area approximately 3400 years ago (the beginning of the Late Shang phase), where it remained until the fall of the Shang more than 250 years later. This new royal domain was known as *Yin* and may in fact have encompassed a network of compounds, palaces, villages, and cemeteries extending over an area some 120 square miles (310 sq km) on the northern bank of the Yellow River. The core of this "capital" was near the hamlet of Xiao-tun, 1.5 miles (2.4 km) northwest of the modern city of Anyang. Years of excavations at Xiao-tun have revealed fifty-three rectangular foundations of stamped earth up to 120 feet (36 m) long, 65 feet (19.5 m) wide, and as

Early Shang
?3750 to 3650 B.P.

Zhengzhou

Middle Shang
3650 to 3400 B.P.

Late Shang
3400 to 3100 B.P.

much as 5 feet (1.5 m) high, many of them associated with sacrificial burials of both animals and humans (Chang, 1980, 1986). One group of fifteen foundations on the north side of the excavated area supported timber houses with mud and stick walls, devoid of sacrificial victims. These are believed to be the royal residences that housed extended families of nobles living in large halls and smaller rooms closed off with doors (Figure 21.3). Twenty-one massive foundations on an elevated area in the center of the excavations formed two rows of temples associated with a series of five ceremonial gates. The builders buried animals, humans, and even chariots in this vicinity, perhaps to dedicate the temples. Nearby lay semisubterranean houses where the royal servants and artisans lived. The service areas included bronze foundries, workshops, and pottery kilns.

The Shang Royal Burials

The Shang rulers at first buried their dead among the compound houses but later moved their cemetery to a location just more than a mile northeast. Eleven royal graves from this cemetery were excavated during the 1930s (Chang, 1986). They were furnished on a lavish scale and date to between 3500 and 3200 years ago. The best-known grave is in the shape of a crosslike pit approximately 33 feet (9.9 m) deep with slightly sloping walls. Four ramps lead from the surface to each side of the pit (Chang, 1960). The coffin of the ruler, which was placed inside a wooden chamber erected in the burial pit, was accompanied by superb bronze vessels and shell, bone, and stone ornaments. One ceremonial halberd has an engraved jade blade set in a bronze shaft adorned with dragons and inlaid with malachite. The rulers were accompanied in death by slaves and sacrificial victims buried both in the chamber itself and on the approach ramps. Many were decapitated, so their bodies were found in one place and their heads in another.

The Shang kings surrounded their sepulchers with hundreds of lesser burials. No fewer than 1221 small graves have been dug up nearby, many of them burials of between two and eleven people in a single tomb. Some of the skeletons are associated with pottery, weapons, or bronze vessels, but most are devoid of all adornment. In 1976 archaeologists uncovered nearly 200 of these

FIGURE 21.3 Reconstruction of a structure from the ceremonial area at Xiao-tun, Anyang, in Henan province.

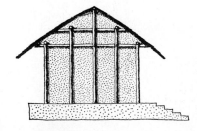
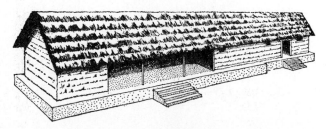

graves. Most of them contained decapitated, dismembered, or mutilated bodies. Some of the victims had been bound before death. These can only have been sacrificial offerings consecrated when the kings and their relatives died.

The Bronzesmiths

The Shang people are justly famous for their bronzework, best known to us from ceremonial artifacts found in royal tombs. The prestigious metal was not gold, which was in short supply, but bronze. Most Shang bronzes are food or drinking vessels, some are weapons, a few are musical instruments, and many are chariot and horse fittings. Bronzeworking was the guarded monopoly of the rulers, a complex art that the Chinese developed quite independently from the West before 4000 years ago. Their smiths produced some of the most sophisticated and elegant bronze objects ever crafted (Figure 21.4).

The Shang people discovered bronzeworking on their own, perhaps as a result of their long experience with kiln-fired pottery baked at high temperatures (Barnard, 1961). The smaller objects, such as spear- and arrowheads and halberds were made by pouring a mixture of copper and tin into a single- or two-piece mold. Much more complex procedures had to be employed to manufacture large ceremonial vessels. These elaborate display pieces were copies of clay prototypes carefully sculpted around a baked clay core and encased in a segmented mold. Once the clay version was completed, the baked outer mold was removed, the model broken away from the core, and the two parts reassembled to receive the molten bronze. This complex technique remained in use for at least five centuries. An alternative would have been the "lost-wax" method, in which a single-piece mold encases a wax mold that is heated and then poured out to be replaced with metal.

FIGURE 21.4 Shang ceremonial bronze vessels, from approximately 3300 years ago.

THE WARLORDS: 1122 TO 221 B.C.

Every early Chinese ruler stayed in power by virtue of a strong army. Shang society was organized on what might be called military lines, so that the royal standing army could be supplemented with thousands of conscripts on very short notice. The kings frequently were at war, protecting their frontiers, suppressing rebellious rivals, or raiding for as many as 30,000 sacrificial victims at one time. In a sense, every early Chinese state was an armed garrison that could call on armies of more than 10,000 men. The secret was a sophisticated, permanent military establishment and a kin organization through which people were obligated to serve the king when called upon. The same basic organization persisted long after the fall of the Shang dynasty in 1100 B.C.

The Anyang graves reveal that every foot soldier carried a set of weapons: a bow and arrows, halberd, shield, small knife, and sharpening stone. The bows were made of horn and ox sinew and were approximately a man's height. They propelled stone-, bone-, or bronze-tipped arrows equipped with feathers (Kiernan and Fairbank, 1974). The Shang soldiers used a small leather or basketry shield for chariot warfare and a longer one on foot, both painted with tiger designs. Most surviving Shang weapons come from sacrificial chariot burials, such as the one excavated near Anyang in 1973. The archaeologists did not uncover the wooden chariot itself but a cast of the wooden parts preserved in the soil (Figure 21.5). They brushed away the surrounding soil with great care until they reached the hardened particles of fine sand that had replaced the wooden structure of the buried chariot. They were able to photograph not only the "ghost" of the chariot but also the skeletons of the two horses. The charioteer had been killed at the funeral and his body placed behind the vehicle. The yokes of the chariot rested on the horses' necks. Even the reins were marked by lines of bronze roundels in the grave. The charioteer rode on a wicker and leather car measuring between 3 and 4 feet (0.9 and 1.2 m) across and borne on a stout axle and two spoked wheels with large hubs adorned with bronze caps. In all probability, the nailless chariot was held together with sinew lashings, adorned with bronze and turquoise ornaments, and perhaps painted in bright colors.

The Shang dynasty fell about 3100 years ago at the hands of the neighboring Zhou. The conquerors did not create a new civilization; rather, they took over the existing network of towns and officials and incorporated them into their own state organization, thus shifting the focus of political and economic power to the south and west, away from Anyang into the fertile Wei Valley near the modern city of S'ian. By this time, the influence of what may loosely be called Shang civilization extended far beyond the north, into the rice-growing areas of the south and along the eastern coasts. The Zhou divided their domains into various almost independent provinces, which warred with one another for centuries (Fitzgerald, 1978). It was not until 221 B.C. that the great emperor Xuang Ti unified China into a single empire. By Roman times, Chinese civilization had been flourishing for more than 2000 years, a distinctive and highly nationalistic culture that differed sharply from its Western contemporaries in its ability to assimilate conquerors and the conquered into its own traditions. In contrast, the Roman Empire was built on the groaning backs of slaves and collapsed into the

FIGURE 21.5 Chariot burial from the royal Shang tombs near Anyang. The wooden parts of the chariot were excavated by following discolorations made by the decaying wood in the ground.

Dark Ages when attacked by barbarian nomads. The ability of the Chinese people simply to assimilate these same nomadic conquerors explains why the essential fabric of their civilization survives to this day.

GUIDE TO FURTHER READING

Chang Kwang-Chih. *The Shang Civilization.* New Haven: Yale University Press, 1980.
  A detailed reconstruction of Shang civilization derived not only from archaeological data but also from a complicated palimpsest of legends, oracle bone inscriptions, and documentary records. An impressive, meticulous book that is an ultimate source on this remarkable society.

Chang Kwang-Chih. *The Archaeology of Ancient China* (4th ed.). New Haven: Yale University Press, 1986.

The fundamental account of prehistoric China for all serious students, with the priceless advantage that it is regularly updated. Lavishly illustrated. Major emphasis on chronology and artifacts.

Fitzgerald, Patrick. *Ancient China.* Oxford: Elsevier Phaidon, 1978.

A well-illustrated history (and prehistory) of China for the lay reader which concentrates on the period after the Shang dynasty. Clearly written and a good starting point.

Keightley, David N. (ed.). *The Origins of Chinese Civilization.* Berkeley and Los Angeles: University of California Press, 1983.

An up-to-date and authoritative description of early Chinese civilization, with a strong historical emphasis. Useful to read in conjunction with Chang's works.

Wheatley, Paul. *The Pivot of the Four Quarters.* Chicago: Aldine, 1971.

A learned book that will daunt many casual readers but is a crucial source for understanding early Chinese civilization. Concentrates on the early Chinese city.

New World Civilizations

(3550 Years Ago to A.D. 1530)

What, then, must have been the emotions of the Spaniards, when, after working their toilsome way into the open air, the cloudy tabernacle parted before their eyes, and they beheld these fair scenes in all their pristine magnificence and beauty. It was like the spectacle which greeted the eyes of Moses from the summit of Pisgah, and, in the warm glow of their feelings, they cried out, "It is the promised land!"

— W. H. Prescott, *The Conquest of Mexico*, 1843

Part VI contains descriptions of the great and complex states of the New World. The theoretical literature surrounding the emergence of states in Mesoamerica and Peru is enormous, and interested readers are referred to Chapter 15 for some of the principal arguments surrounding the subject.

CHRONOLOGICAL TABLE L

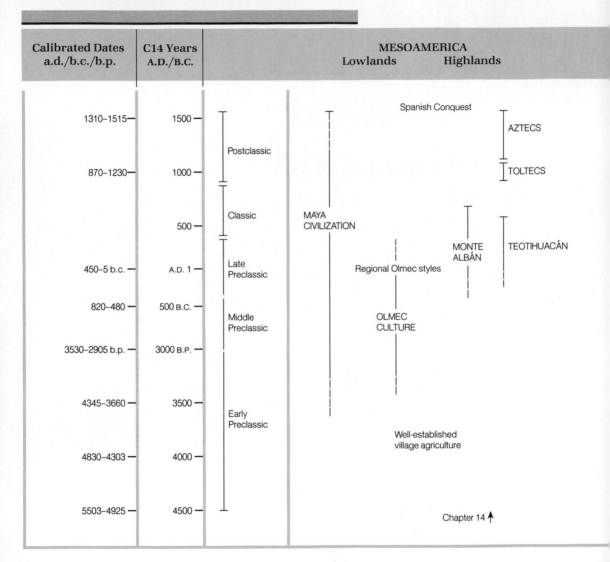

Calibrated Dates a.d./b.c./b.p.	C14 Years A.D./B.C.		MESOAMERICA Lowlands Highlands	
1310–1515	1500	Postclassic	Spanish Conquest	AZTECS
870–1230	1000			TOLTECS
	500	Classic	MAYA CIVILIZATION	TEOTIHUACÁN
450–5 b.c.	A.D. 1	Late Preclassic	Regional Olmec styles	MONTE ALBÁN
820–480	500 B.C.	Middle Preclassic	OLMEC CULTURE	
3530–2905 b.p.	3000 B.P.			
4345–3660	3500	Early Preclassic		
			Well-established village agriculture	
4830–4303	4000			
5503–4925	4500		Chapter 14 ↑	

CHAPTER 22

Mesoamerican Civilizations

Preview

- The Preclassic period of Mesoamerican prehistory lasted from approximately 4000 years ago to A.D. 250, a period of major cultural change in both lowlands and highlands. Sedentary villages traded with each other in raw materials and exotic objects. These exchange networks became increasingly complex and eventually came under the monopolistic control of larger villages. Increasing social complexity went hand in hand with the appearance of the first public buildings and evidence of social stratification.

- These developments are well chronicled in the Valley of Oaxaca and in the Olmec culture of the lowlands, which flourished from approximately 3500 to 2500 years ago. Olmec art styles and religious beliefs were among those that spread widely over lowlands and highlands during the late Preclassic period.

- The complex societies that developed in the Mesoamerican lowlands and highlands depended on diverse agricultural techniques. In the lowlands, Maya farmers used not only slash-and-burn methods, but also raised swamp gardens. Some of the largest areas of the latter are close to major Maya centers, where highly organized food production was necessary. In the highlands, agricultural environments were very diverse. Many early communities relied on simple "pot irrigation." Later farmers used dry farming, slash-and-burn methods, and cultivated slopes, occasionally using terracing. Valley of Mexico societies used raised fields known as *chinampas*, reclaimed swamps, to feed large urban and rural populations.

- The Preclassic cultural developments culminated in the highlands in a number of great cities, among them Monte Albán and Teotihuacán. The latter housed more than 120,000 people and covered more than 8 square miles (20.7 sq km) at the height of its prosperity. Teotihuacán collapsed approximately A.D. 700, probably as a result of warfare with other rival states in the highlands.

- Maya civilization arose in the lowlands after 3000 years ago. Religious ideologies, ritual organization, and extensive trading networks were key factors in the development of Maya society. The late Preclassic city of El Mirador endured more than 900 years. It covered about 10 square miles (25.9 sq km), most of its temples and pyramids being built between 150 B.C. and A.D. 50. The city was controlled by a highly organized elite.

- Classic Maya civilization flourished from A.D. 250 to 900 and was remarkable for its sophisticated trade networks, great ceremonial centers, and elaborate ceremonies, known to us through sculptures, murals, and hieroglyphs. Maya rulers sought to appease their many gods with the aid of an elaborate sacred calendar based on astronomical events.

- Maya glyphs have recently been deciphered. They show Maya civilization was far from uniform. Emblem glyphs identify individual rulers and ruling dynasties. Each center developed its own cultural traditions. The Maya were unified more by religious beliefs than by political or economic interests. Their political mechanisms include warfare, diplomacy, and arranged marriages to create alliances between neighboring centers.

- Maya political history is known through deciphered glyphs. Until about A.D. 600, the largest states were in northeast Petén, with a multicenter polity headed by the "Sky" rulers of Tikal. Maya civilization reached its height in the southern lowlands after the seventh century. By A.D. 800, Maya populations were declining rapidly.

- Maya civilization collapsed suddenly in the Yucatán after A.D. 900; the reasons for the collapse are still uncertain, but pressure on the labor force and food shortages doubtless were among them.

- Teotihuacán's collapse in the highlands resulted in a political vacuum for some centuries, which eventually was filled by the Toltecs and then the Aztecs, whose bloodthirsty civilization was dominant in the Valley of Mexico at the time of the Spanish conquest in A.D. 1519.

- Aztec civilization was unable to resist the Spanish and collapsed suddenly, partly as a result of serious internal stresses and rebellion by subject tribes.

Chronological
Table L

Few topics are surrounded by more fantasy, myth, and archaeological lunacy than the origins of pre-Columbian civilization in the Americas. Ever since Columbus first set foot in the Bahamas, scholars and others have speculated about the origins of the American Indians. The discovery of the Aztec and Inca civilizations fueled speculation and mythmaking to new and even more frenzied heights. The Ten Lost Tribes of Israel, the Canaanites, and all manner of other strange candidates have been invoked as the first civilized peoples to settle in the Americas. The survivors of the Lost Continents of Atlantis and Mu have been prime candidates for generations (Wauchope, 1962). Nineteenth-century readers were entranced by stories of a great Mound Builder Civilization that flourished in the Midwest, only to perish under attack from savage hordes (Silverberg, 1968). Today, we are treated to sagas about ancient astronauts who colonized the Americas from space and then departed, leaving the roots of civilization behind them (von Däniken, 1970).

In the latest attack of incredible speculation, a respected Harvard zoologist tells us that America was settled by colonists from Europe and North Africa in the first millennium B.C., long before the Vikings or Columbus (Fell, 1976, 1980). His evidence consists of a comparison of alleged ancient American inscriptions and "timeworn" ruins in the lands from which the "Colonists" came. According to Barry Fell's theories, the settled civilizations of America, which were founded by Old World colonists, were subjected to upheaval and disaster in approximately A.D. 1000, just as the Vikings arrived. Hundreds of people have written to him, he claims, some of them American Indians trying to relate his fables to their own cultural traditions of people who arrived across the water centuries before. In other words, the inspiration for pre-Columbian civilization came from the Old World, perhaps only 3000 years ago.

What are we to make of these centuries of fantasy? Why is American archaeology so surrounded by crazy myth with no basis in scientific reality? One obvious explanation is people's appetite for a good adventure story, for epic heroes and transoceanic voyages. Another is that stories such as Barry Fell's or Erich von Däniken's are based on a haphazard collection of facts strung together into a convincing pattern without the rigor of systematic scientific analysis: this approach makes an adventure story easy to compile and to enjoy. Third, unlike Europeans, most Americans, because they are immigrants, feel no cultural identity with the Indians or their history. They feel more comfortable believing stories of age-old colonization by familiar peoples from the world of Egypt and the Near East. For many people, history is a faith, too, something to cling to and to believe against all scientific odds. Most of the strange works that purport to describe early civilization in the Americas play on such faith. They invite the reader to join in the group who knows the "truth," and either attack scientists as frauds or simply ignore their work. It is significant, for example, that Fell cites no works of archeological scholarship in his *Saga America* (1980) except some descriptions of American Indian rock art. One can conclude only that scientific archaeological research is irrelevant to his tale, or that he is unfamiliar with it, or that it challenges the "faith."

The account of early American civilization that follows is based on scientific archeological excavations and surveys by which evidence has been accumulating for the indigenous origins of New World civilization for more than a century. The cumulative scientific evidence is overwhelming and impressive in its consistency. No one can dismantle a sincerely held faith, and so I shall make no attempt to destroy the illusions of those who believe that America was settled by Atlanteans, Ancient Egyptians, or anyone else: to do so is a waste of time. The irony is that the unfolding story of New World civilization revealed by science is far more fascinating and intellectually stimulating than any outer-space adventure story, however well conceived or marketed. (For more serious accounts of transoceanic voyaging, see Carter, 1981; Davies, 1979.)

PRECLASSIC PEOPLES IN MESOAMERICA

Preclassic
c. 4000 B.P. to
A.D. 250

By 4000 years ago, sedentary farming villages were common in most of Meso-america (R. E. W. Adams, 1977a; Sanders and Price, 1968; Weaver, 1981). In their agriculture, people relied on many plant species, and slash-and-burn farming methods were in wide use in the lowlands. With such methods people could clear small gardens in the forest by cutting tree trunks and brush, and carefully burning branches to fertilize the soil with a layer of wood ash. Then, using pointed digging sticks, they planted maize and other crops. A few seasons later they abandoned the land, planting less important crops on older plots or leaving them to the forest. The search for new lands was constant, even when slash-and-burn was combined with irrigation or riverside agriculture.

Early Preclassic

Many centuries elapsed between the beginnings of village life and that of Mesoamerican civilization. Mesoamericans began to live in larger settlements and to build elaborate ceremonial centers at the beginning of an era named the *Preclassic* or *Formative* period, approximately 4000 years ago to A.D. 250 (N. Hammond, 1987). The earliest centuries of the Preclassic witnessed the appearance of pottery and the first ceremonial centers. One such site is Cuello in lowland northern Belize, which is radiocarbon dated to between c. 3000 years ago and A.D. 300 (Figure 22.1) (N. Hammond, 1980a, 1982). The inhabitants of this site were cultivating maize and probably relied heavily on wild plants for their diet. The Middle Preclassic period is known for the Olmec culture, appearing from 3000 to 300 B.C.. The Late Preclassic period has various regional centers, some with Olmeclike artistic and cultural characteristics (Willey, 1966).

Cuello
c. 3000 B.P. to
A.D. 300

Middle Preclassic: The Olmecs

The first major ceremonial centers appeared in the Middle Preclassic period, marking the transformation of village society into a wider social order with more complex social and economic organizations (Coe, 1962). Signs of social stratification began to appear when food surpluses were achieved; the extra food was used to support certain individuals, probably religious leaders, whose contribution to the society was to organize the production and distribution of food on a new scale. The first ceremonial centers probably developed as a response to population increase and the desire to maintain and symbolize kinship and religious unity. These revered centers became the foci of political and religious power, as their new priest-leaders engaged in trading, employed increasing numbers of specialized craftspeople, and manipulated labor forces and food surpluses.

Olmec
3500 to 2500 B.P.

The best-known Preclassic culture is that of the Olmec, centered in the lowland regions of southern Veracruz and western Tabasco (Bernal, 1969; Coe, 1965, 1968; Coe and Diehl, 1980). There, ceremonial centers achieved remarkable complexity at an early date. *Olmec* means "rubber people," and the region was long important for rubber production. Although the Olmec homeland is

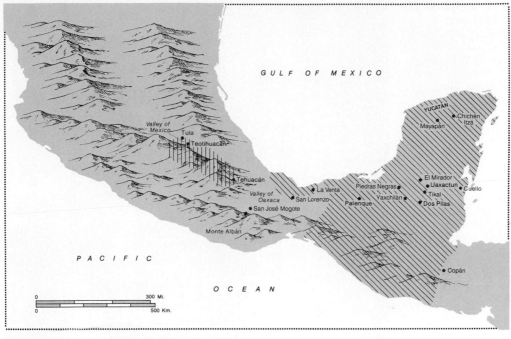

Olmec
1500–500 B.C.

Teotihuacán
100 B.C.–A.D. 700

FIGURE 22.1 Mesoamerican archaeological sites mentioned in this chapter. Approximate distributions of various traditions are shown.

low-lying, tropical, and humid, its soil is fertile, and the swamps, lakes, and rivers are rich in fish, birds, and other animals. Olmec societies prospered in this region for 1000 years from approximately 3500 years ago and created a highly distinctive art style.

San Lorenzo

The earliest traces of Olmec occupation are best documented at San Lorenzo, where Olmec people lived on a platform in the midst of frequently inundated woodland plains. They erected ridges and mounds around their platform, upon which they built pyramids and possibly ball courts and placed elaborate monumental carvings overlooking the site. The earliest occupation of San Lorenzo shows few Olmec features, but by 3250 years ago, the inhabitants were beginning to build some raised fields, a task that required organized labor forces. By that time, too, distinctive Olmec sculpture began to appear. A century later, magnificent monumental carvings adorned San Lorenzo (Figure 22.2), distinctive and often mutilated by the Olmec themselves (Coe and Diehl, 1980).

San Lorenzo
3250 B.P.

One archaeologist has estimated the population of San Lorenzo at 2500 (Coe and Diehl, 1980). The inhabitants enjoyed extensive trade, especially in obsidian and other semiprecious materials obtained from many parts of Mesoamerica. San Lorenzo fell into decline after 2900 years ago and was surpassed by La Venta, the most famous Olmec site, nearer the Gulf of Mexico.

FIGURE 22.2 Giant stone head from San Lorenzo made from basalt, approximately 8 ft (2.4 m) high. Michael Coe (1965) has suggested that these heads are portraits of rulers, while David Grove (1973) has identified what he thinks are name glyphs on the "helmets."

La Venta

La Venta
800 to 400 B.C.

The La Venta ceremonial center was built on a small island in the middle of a swamp (Drucker, 1959). A rectangular earth mound, 393 feet long by 229 feet wide and 105 feet high (120 m by 70 m by 32 m), dominates the island. Long low mounds surround a rectangular plaza in front of the large mound, faced by walls and terraced mounds at the other end of the plaza (Figure 22.3). Vast monumental stone sculptures litter the site, including some Olmec heads bear-

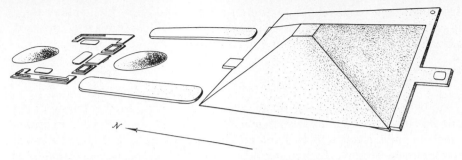

FIGURE 22.3 La Venta, site 4: layout of the major structures.

ing expressions of contempt and savagery. Caches of jade objects, figurines, and a dull green rock (serpentine) are common, too (Figure 22.4). Every stone for sculptures and temples had to be brought from at least 60 miles (96 km) away, a vast undertaking, for some sculptured blocks weigh more than 40 tons. The people traded ceremonial jade and serpentine from as far away as Costa Rica. La Venta flourished for approximately 400 years from 800 B.C. After approximately 400 B.C., the site probably was destroyed; we deduce this from signs that many of its finest monuments were intentionally defaced.

La Venta is perhaps most renowned for its distinctive Olmec art style, executed both as sculptured objects and in relief. Olmec sculpture concentrated on natural and supernatural beings and its dominant motif was the "were-jaguar," or humanlike jaguar. Many jaguars were given infantile faces, drooping lips, and large swollen eyes, a style also applied to human figures; some have almost negroid faces; others resemble snarling demons. The Olmec contributions to

FIGURE 22.4 An Olmec altar or throne sculpture from La Venta. The sculpture is approximately 6 ft (2 m) high. At least one of these thrones shows the ruler in front connected to his parents on the side by umbilical cords.

Mesoamerican art and religion was enormously significant. Elements of their art style and imagery were diffused during the first millennium B.C. southward to Guatemala and San Salvador and northward into the Valley of Mexico.

Late Preclassic

Late Preclassic
300 B.C. to A.D. 250

We believe that the spread of the Olmec art style and the beginning of the Late Preclassic period in approximately 300 to 250 B.C. signal the period during which a common religious system and ideology began to unify large areas of Mesoamerica. A powerful priesthood congregated in spectacular ceremonial centers, commemorating potent and widely recognized deities. Distinctive art and architecture went with the new religion, the practice of which required precise measurements of calendar years and of longer cycles of time. Writing and mathematical calculations were developed to affirm religious practices, a unifying political force in the sense that they welded scattered village communities into larger political units. By the time the Classic Mesoamerican civilizations arose, dynasties of priests and aristocrats had been ruling parts of Mesoamerica along well-established lines for nearly 1000 years.

THE RISE OF COMPLEX SOCIETY IN OAXACA

The Preclassic cultures of the Valley of Oaxaca have been studied intensively by Kent Flannery and his students, using highly sophisticated systems approaches to document changing settlement patterns and economic and demographic trends (Flannery, 1976; Flannery and Marcus, 1983). Something like 90 percent of the Preclassic Oaxaca villages were little more than hamlets of 50 to 60 people, while the remainder were much larger settlements of 1000 to 1200 souls, with populations of priests and craftspeople.

The evolution of larger settlements in Oaxaca and elsewhere was closely connected with the development of long-distance trade in obsidian and other luxuries such as seashells and stingray spines from the Gulf of Mexico. The simple barter networks for obsidian of earlier times evolved into sophisticated regional trading organizations in which village leaders controlled monopolies over sources of obsidian and its distribution. Magnetite mirrors, seashells, feathers, and ceramics all were traded on the highlands, and from the highlands to the lowlands as well. Olmec pottery and other ritual objects began to appear in highland settlements between 3150 and 2650 years ago, many of them bearing the distinctive were-jaguar motif of the lowlands, which had an important place in Olmec cosmology.

Public buildings began to appear in villages such as San José Mogote between 3400 and 3150 years ago. Many of them were oriented 8° west of north; they were built on adobe and earth platforms. Conch shell trumpets and turtle shell drums from the Gulf of Mexico are associated with these buildings, as are clay figurines of dancers wearing costumes and masks (Figure 22.5). There were marine fish spines, too, probably used in personal bloodletting ceremonies that were still practiced even in Aztec times. [The Spanish described how Aztec nobles would gash themselves with knives or with the spines of fish or stingray

FIGURE 22.5 Four clay figurines shaped and posed deliberately to form a scene, buried beneath an Early Preclassic house at San José Mogote, Oaxaca.

in acts of mutilation before the gods, penances required of the devout (Valliant, 1941).] It has been suggested that the diffusion of the Olmec art style through Mesoamerica resulted both from an increased need for religious rituals to bring the various elements of society together and because the Oaxacan elite, aspiring to the status of their Olmec neighbors, took to the new beliefs in slavish conformity (Flannery, 1976; Flannery and Marcus, 1983). This diffusion took place after long-distance trading had been in existence for centuries and probably signaled an increase in larger villages such as San José Mogote.

Monte Albán

By 400 B.C., there were at least seven small states in the Valley of Oaxaca, of which the one centered at Monte Albán soon became dominant. Although massive population growth and increased economic power were among the interacting factors that aided in the rise of Monte Albán, its special terrain may have been of vital importance in its ascendancy (Blanton, 1978, 1983). Richard Blanton has surveyed more than 2000 terraces on the slopes of Monte Albán, terraces used for agriculture and housing areas. Monte Albán commanded the best terrain in the valley, sloping land that was organized for agriculture and dense settlement by a population of several thousand people, far larger than

Monte Albán
400 B.C.

that of most major settlements in Mesoamerica at the time. Even as early as 400 B.C., some of the terraces were in use by a highly organized population whose leaders resided in a ceremonial and civic center built on the summit of the Monte Albán ridge. Although the large-scale buildings of later times have contoured the summit beyond recognition, it is clear that the first leaders to live there undertook major public works, many of them wood and thatch buildings which had incised sculptures of what may be dead and tortured enemies set into the walls.

Monte Albán went on to develop into a vast ceremonial center with splendid public architecture; its settlement area included public buildings, terraces, and housing zones that extended over approximately 15 square miles (40 sq km) (Figure 22.6). The more than 2000 terraces all held one or two houses, while small ravines were dammed to pond valuable water supplies. Blanton suggests that between 30,000 and 50,000 people lived at Monte Albán between A.D. 200 and 700. Many very large villages and smaller hamlets lay within easy distance of the city. The enormous platforms on the ridge of Monte Albán supported complex layouts of temples and pyramid-temples, palaces, patios, and tombs. A hereditary elite seems to have ruled Monte Albán, the leaders of a state that had emerged in the Valley of Oaxaca by A.D. 200. Their religious power was based on ancestor worship, a pantheon of at least thirty-nine gods, grouped around major themes of ritual life. The rain god and lightning were associated with the jaguar motif; another group of deities are linked with the maize god Pitao Cozabi. Nearly all these gods were still worshiped at the time of Spanish contact, although Monte Albán itself was abandoned after A.D. 700, at approximately the same time as another great ceremonial center, Teotihuacán, in the Valley of Mexico, began to eclipse.

MESOAMERICAN STATES SHAPED BY AGRICULTURAL TECHNIQUES

Everyone agrees that the emergence of unifying artistic traditions (such as the Olmec), religious ideologies, ritual organization, and extensive trading networks were key factors in the development of Mesoamerican civilization (N. Hammond, 1982). But it is only in recent years that people have begun to study early Mesoamerican agriculture in an attempt to understand how the Maya and other peoples were able to support the enormous urban populations that built and organized the ceremonial centers of both highland and lowland Mesoamerica (R. E. W. Adams, 1977b).

Long-held views of Mesoamerican agriculture, specifically those concerning the Maya, have always assumed that the populations lived in dispersed villages and used only slash-and-burn agriculture, which, as we have seen, cannot support a high population density (R. E. W. Adams, 1977a). This viewpoint is now discarded, for it has been shown that raised fields and terracing were important in lowland cultivation, not only of maize but of other subsistence crops as well. One popular hypothesis argued that the breadnut (ramon) tree, which grows on land not otherwise used for cultivation, was cultivated because of its high-

FIGURE 22.6 Monte Albán, Valley of Oaxaca — Zapotec ruins, 1951.

protein nuts (Puleston, 1971). However, there is no evidence that the Maya ever cultivated the ramon.

Some fascinating experiments involving scanning the Maya lowlands with imaging radar have shown that areas of wet-season swamp near known Maya sites often have irregular grids of gray lines, multitudes of ladder, lattice, and curvilinear patterns. These have been compared with known ancient canal systems and are thought to represent long-forgotten raised field systems built in swamps (Adams, Brown, and Culbert, 1981). The investigators believe that many swamp edges in the Petén, the rain-forest lowlands of northern Guatemala, once were extensively canalized for agriculture and communication purposes. Thus, the swamps became assets rather than liabilities, artificial environments wherein large food surpluses could be grown and goods be readily transported by canoe. Such swamp areas constitute as much as 50 percent of the land in some lowland areas, land that could not be cultivated by slash-and-burn techniques.

While there is no question that raised fields were important, the real issue is whether there was *intensification* of such cultivation, organization of food production by some centralized authority. As Patrick Culbert points out (1988b), the preparation and maintenance of raised fields was well within the capabilities of individual households and small hamlets. It is significant that some of the largest areas of raised fields are close to major Maya centers, places where highly organized food production was probably necessary and large labor forces would have been needed to maintain canals and fields, especially after damage caused by heavy rains. Most Maya agricultural techniques did not require large numbers of people, except, perhaps, the most extensive field systems near major centers.

The Mesoamerican highlands are highly diverse agricultural environments, as we have seen in Tehuacán (Chapter 14). The earliest farming villages in

Oaxaca are concentrated in the valley floors, where water is within easy reach of the surface. Modern farmers choose similar villages for simple "pot" irrigation, where they plant their maize and other crops near small shallow wells. They simply dip pots into the wells and water surrounding plants from the shallow water table. Flannery (1968b) has argued that the Oaxacans used the same technique in prehistoric times.

Pot irrigation does not require large numbers of people or complex social organization. From approximately 3300 to 2350 years ago, Oaxaca was inhabited by widely spaced larger villages with small villages dependent on them. The changing settlement pattern was accompanied by population growth that led to the taking up of less desirable agricultural land on slopes and the development of new agricultural techniques to work this land. The Oaxaca environment was so diverse that the people were able to build on their simple and highly effective original techniques, which remained part of their repertoire. They expanded to the slopes, and then even cultivated the arid lands. Eventually the economic power generated by these rising populations gave highland areas such as Oaxaca a decided edge in cultural evolution.

Similar diversity of agricultural techniques is found in the Valley of Mexico, where slash-and-burn methods, dry farming, and irrigation agriculture all were in use. The farmers used both floodwaters and canals to bring water to dry gardens. The most famous of all raised field techniques, however, is the *chinampa* or floating garden technique, a highly intensive and productive agricultural system based on the reclaiming of swamps. The farmers piled up natural vegetation and lake mud to form huge grids of naturally irrigated gardens. The chinampas were used very systematically to grow a variety of crops, so timed that different crops came into harvest throughout the year (Sanders et al., 1970). This system is amazingly productive and is estimated to have supported approximately 100,000 people from 25,000 acres (10,117 ha) in 1519, the time of Spanish contact. Each chinampa produced large food surpluses that could be used to feed thousands of nonagricultural workers and specialists. William Sanders has argued that these 25,000 acres (10,117 ha) of chinampas actually could have supported approximately 180,000 people. That this highly effective agricultural system was the basis of early civilization and urban life in the valley of Mexico is beyond question.

The agricultural system of the Valley of Mexico may seem complicated, but it supported and was part of a far more elaborate system of food marketing, which provided not only tribute for taxes but also opportunities for the trading of special foodstuffs from one area of the highlands to another. The highland peoples relied on elaborate markets that were strictly regulated by the state and conducted on a barter system. The Valley of Mexico was an economic unit before Teotihuacán made it a political one as well. It was the great agricultural productivity of the valley and the sophisticated market economy of the emerging city that made the prodigious social and religious, as well as material, developments of later centuries possible. This economic system fostered the development of specialist crafts that were sold in the city markets and exported over wide areas.

The sequence of events in the highlands may have begun with the buildup of agricultural populations in diverse environments such as the Valley of Oaxaca in the first and second millennia B.C. This population growth led to the development of more intensive agricultural methods, including both irrigation and chinampa systems. At the same time, different areas were linked by increasingly sophisticated trading networks and by an emerging market economy, with, perhaps, some specialized merchants.

Religious activity was stimulated by the introduction of beliefs and sacred objects from the lowlands. Trade in exotic luxuries increased as ceremonial centers and stratified societies were founded. By 200 B.C., the effects of increased religious activity, intensified trading, and the production of huge food surpluses from the diverse environment had led to the founding of at least two major cities in the Valley of Mexico. One of these, Teotihuacán, reached an enormous size and enjoyed vast political, economic, and religious power in the centuries that followed. In the Valley of Oaxaca, Monte Albán achieved a similar dominance. The two great states probably enjoyed an uneasy alliance.

Teotihuacán

Teotihuacán lies northeast of Mexico City and is now one of the great archaeological tourist attractions of the world. It was one of the dominant political and cultural centers of all Mesoamerica in approximately A.D. 500, the culmination of centuries of vigorous cultural development in the Valley of Mexico (Millon, Drewitt, and Cowgill, 1974).

The first buildings appeared at Teotihuacán in approximately 200 B.C., comprising a handful of villages, at least one of which may have specialized in obsidian manufacture. By 100 B.C., Teotihuacán had begun to expand rapidly, and the scattered villages became a settlement covering more than 3.5 square miles (9.06 sq km). Much of this early settlement is covered by the vast structures of later times. It is estimated that 600 people inhabited this early town. There were several public buildings. *Teotihuacán 200 B.C. to A.D. 700*

René Millon, who carried out a systematic survey of Teotihuacán, found that by A.D. 150 the city extended over 5 square miles (12.9 sq km) and housed more than 20,000 people. Obsidian trade and manufacture were expanding fast (Parsons and Price, 1971). There were two major religious complexes for which, among other structures, the Pyramids of the Sun and Moon were first built at this time.

Between A.D. 150 and 750, Teotihuacán exploded in size. Anyone traversing the Valley of Mexico had to pass through the city with its diverse population of priests, merchants, craftspeople, and other specialists. The rulers of the city erected hundreds of standardized apartment complexes and continued a master plan that laid out the city on a north-south axis, centered on the Avenue of the Dead (Figure 22.7), with another great avenue oriented east-west. The 8 square miles (20.7 sq km) of Teotihuacán consisted of avenues and plazas, markets, temples, palaces, apartment buildings, and complex drainage and agricultural works. The entire city was dominated by the Pyramid of the Sun (an Aztec name), a vast structure of earth, adobe, and piled rubble. The pyramid, faced with stone, is 210 feet (64 m) high and 650 feet (198 m) square. A wooden tem- *City layout*

FIGURE 22.7 Aerial view of the ceremonial precincts at Teotihuacán, with the Pyramid of the Moon in the foreground. At left in the background (to the left of the Avenue of the Dead) is the Pyramid of the Sun. (From *Urbanization at Teotihuacán, Mexico,* I, Part 1, 1973. © 1973 by René Millon.)

ple probably sat on the summit of the terraced pyramid. The long Avenue of the Dead passes the west face of the pyramid, leading to the Pyramid of the Moon, the second largest structure at the site (Figure 22.7). The avenue is lined with civic, palace, and religious buildings, and the side streets lead to residential areas. A large palace and temple complex dedicated to the Plumed Serpent (Quetzalcóatl), with platform and stairways around the central court, lies south of the middle of Teotihuacán, across from a central marketplace.

The Avenue of the Dead and the pyramids lie amid a sprawling mass of small houses. Priests and craftsworkers lived in dwellings around small courtyards; the less privileged lived in large compounds of rooms connected by narrow alleyways and patios. By any standard, Teotihuacán was a city, and it once housed up to 120,000 people. Although some farmers probably lived within the city, we know that rural villages flourished nearby. These were compact, expertly planned, and administered by city rulers.

The comprehensive settlement pattern data from the Millon survey enables us to say something about the structure of Teotihuacán society. The food surpluses to support the city were produced by farmers who lived both in the city and in satellite villages nearby. Tribute from neighboring states also helped feed the city, and control of large areas of the plateau ensured that adequate food supplies came to Teotihuacán's huge market. Most of the people lived in the city. It is not known how important chinampa agriculture was for Teotihuacán, but irrigation farming was a key element in subsistence. Craftspeople accounted for perhaps 25 percent of the urban population; they lived in compounds of apartments near the more than 500 workshops that produced everything from obsidian tools to clay vessels. Merchants probably were an important class in the city, as were civil servants, who carried out the routine administration of Teotihuacán. There were even foreign quarters, one of which housed Oaxacans. The elite included priests, warriors, and secular leaders, who controlled the vast city and its many dealings through a strictly class society. Religious beliefs continued the rituals of earlier times, but it appears that cannibalism and human sacrifice became increasingly important in later centuries, as the leaders of the city became more and more militaristic, a trend that was to continue into Aztec times.

Agriculture

Teotihuacán ruled the Valley of Mexico and parts of Puebla, but its influence through alliance, tribute, and warfare, as well as trading, extended over a far larger area of Mesoamerica. As in later times, the rulers of Teotihuacán probably controlled some highly strategic and economically important zones, but there were large areas where their influence was minimal. In the final analysis, Teotihuacán probably was a huge city-state bound to other city-states by uneasy alliances and tribute exchanges.

By A.D. 600, Teotihuacán probably was ruled by a secular ruler who was looked upon as a divine king of some kind — a person with formidable military powers. A class of nobles controlled the kinship groups that organized the bulk of the city's huge population. In approximately A.D. 650, Teotihuacán was deliberately burned down. Only fifty years later its population was scattered in a few villages. Much of the former urban population settled in neighboring regions, which thereby reaped the benefit of Teotihuacán's misfortunes. No one knows exactly why this great city collapsed so suddenly. Its rapid development may have resulted in serious internal weaknesses which made Teotihuacán vulnerable to easy overthrow. A drought may also have weakened the city and provided an opportunity for jealous rivals to attempt an attack.

The very success of Teotihuacán may have accelerated its downfall. The new orders of society and politics spawned by the city may have been copied by other leaders, perhaps more aggressive and less tradition bound than those of the mother city. Teotihuacán was not the only sophisticated city-state in the highlands between A.D. 500 and 700. William Sanders (1965) has argued that Teotihuacán was overthrown by a coalition of city-states that included Tula to the northwest, Xochicalco in the southwest, and Cholula to the southeast. All these expanded after the downfall of Teotihuacán, and all had been powerful regional states at the time of the former's collapse. Whatever the causes of Teotihuacán's downfall, its end resulted in a dispersal of specialist craftsworkers, priests, and other functionaries throughout Mesoamerica, as a period of political and military competition among rival states ensued.

THE CLASSIC PERIOD IN FULL FLOWER: THE MAYA

The Maya civilization probably is the best known of all early American civilizations, one that has excited the imagination of scholars for more than a century. Maya civilization took shape slowly. It was centered on lowland rain-forest areas that provided a relatively uniform environment in which people grew maize and other crops, as well as harvested trees such as the ramon. Traces of primordial Maya culture are discernible in the Yucatán and Belize many centuries before the brilliant Maya civilization flourished in the lowlands. Norman Hammond has found platforms and other structures at Cuello in Belize that date to the second millennium B.C. (N. Hammond, 1978, 1980a; Henderson, 1981). The associated pottery styles can be traced through the first millennium B.C. and appear to be ancestral to Classic Maya ceramics.

In the early second millennium B.C., the farmers of northern Belize were growing at least three kinds of maize, probably in small forest gardens. By the late second millennium, pollen analyses at Cuello show that the forest cover was considerably reduced, with a corresponding increase in grassland, probably as a result of more forest clearance and possibly also owing to a decrease in the length of time fields lay fallow. The trend toward more forest clearance appears to have continued until the late first millennium B.C., when there was a massive increase in the lowland population. Preliminary investigations at Cuello reveal that maize was still the staple crop, together with a range of as yet unidentified root crops. Norman Hammond points out that large numbers of an edible snail called *Pomacea* come from these particular Cuello layers (Hammond and Miksicek, 1981). This species flourishes in shallow water and swampland and strongly suggests that raised fields and irrigated swamps were then in use near the settlement (see also Turner and Harrison, 1981). At the same time, the Maya may have grown tree crops, carefully tended fruit trees nurtured in house gardens and mulched with domestic waste. This new reliance on swamp agriculture and tree crops was essential to support the large populations of Classic Maya times.

Maya Origins

Although the roots of Maya culture go back far into the Preclassic period, considerable debate surrounds the origins of Maya civilization, partly because until recently virtually nothing was known about Maya subsistence patterns (R. E. W. Adams, 1977a; N. Hammond, 1982). Perhaps the initial Maya settlement pattern was dispersed, with villages scattered through the rain forest, in situations that seemed to militate against political or economic unity. They flourished in a fundamentally empty landscape, where there was plenty of room for slash-and-burn agriculture and little incentive for cooperation between neighboring communities.

Debate about the origins of the Maya civilization centers on the dramatic population growth of the mid–first millennium B.C. and the changes in subsistence and settlement patterns that led to the closer economic and social cooperation of dispersed Maya villages and eventually to the concentration of tens of thousands of people into huge urban centers. William Rathje (1972) has provided one possible explanation: the Maya environment was very deficient in many vital resources, including stone for grinding maize, salt (always vital for agriculturalists), obsidian for knives and weapons, and many luxury materials. All these could be obtained from the highlands in the north, from the Valley of Mexico as well as from Guatemala and other regions, if the necessary long-distance trading networks and mechanisms could be set up. Such connections, and the trading expeditions to maintain them, could not be organized by individual villages alone. The Maya lived in a uniform environment where the rain forest provided similarly deficient resources for every settlement. Long networks therefore were developed through the authority of the ceremonial centers and their leaders. The integrative organization needed must have been considerable, for communications in the rain forest, especially in areas remote from the highlands, were extremely difficult to maintain.

Rathje carries his arguments a stage further. Obviously, peoples living on the border between the lowlands and the highlands had the best opportunities for trade. Those who lived farther away, such as the Maya, were at a disadvantage. They offered the same agricultural commodities and craft exports as their more fortunate border neighbors but were farther from markets. They had one competitive advantage, however — a complex and properly functioning state organization and the knowledge to keep it going. This knowledge itself was very exportable. Along with pottery, feathers, specialized stone materials, and lime plaster, they exported their political and social organization, as well as their religious beliefs.

The Rathje hypothesis (1971) highlights the importance of trade and long-distance exchange in the emergence of the complex Maya civilization. Long trading networks did connect the lowlands and the highlands. A well-defined cosmology with roots in Olmec beliefs, a strongly centralized economic and religious system based on ceremonial centers, and sophisticated and highly competitive commercial opportunities all contributed to a complex system that caused the dramatic rise of Classic Mesoamerican civilization. It should be pointed out, however, that Rathje's hypothesis suffers from the objection that suitable alternative raw materials for metates (grindstones) and other imported objects do exist in the lowlands. It could be, too, that warfare became a competitive response to population growth and the disappearance of prime agricultural land.

Recent excavations in Guatemala's Petén promise to throw new light on the development of Maya civilization. The late Preclassic city of El Mirador flourished long before the great later Classic Maya cities of A.D. 600 to 850. Most of El Mirador's public buildings were built in the Late Preclassic, between 150 B.C. and A.D. 50. The city covered about 6 square miles (16 sq km), lying on low, undulating land; parts of the area flooded during the rainy season. Archaeologists from Brigham Young University have uncovered more than 200 buildings; among them are great complexes of pyramids, plazas, causeways, and buildings.

El Mirador c. 150 B.C. to A.D. 150 and later

The Danta pyramid at the east end of the site dominates El Mirador. It rises from a natural hill more than 210 feet (70 m) high. The western face of the hill is sculpted into large platforms that are surmounted by buildings and temples. A little over a mile (2 km) west rises the Tigre complex, a pyramid 182 feet (55 m) high surrounded by a plaza, a small temple, and several smaller buildings (Figure 22.8). The Tigre complex covers about 58,000 square meters — an area a little larger than the base of Teotihuacán's Pyramid of the Sun. Three buildings, with the largest in the center, are on a truncated landing on the pyramid. This "triad" theme is also found at later sites such as Tikal.

El Mirador is unique because it was not altered in any significant way after the Preclassic. As excavations proceed, it should be possible to compare Preclassic with Classic occupation and to study the evolution of Maya architecture, city planning, and social and political organization. El Mirador is yielding some of the earliest examples of Maya writing. They appear on an inscribed potsherd, and some symbols are inscribed on the Tigre sculpture. El Mirador itself was an elaborate city and was probably controlled by a highly organized elite. They used artisans, priests, architects, and engineers, as well as traders and thousands of unskilled villagers. This stupendous city, together with some other

FIGURE 22.8 Archaeologists at work on the east stucco mask on the Tigre Temple, El Mirador. The building and mask date to the late Preclassic. *Inset:* El Mirador, Petén: Reconstruction of the Tigre complex of buildings and platforms. The entire complex dates to the late Preclassic period, c. 100 B.C. to A.D. 50.

Preclassic centers, flourished successfully for centuries before it suddenly collapsed in the early Christian era. It was to be centuries before Maya civilization recovered, only to collapse again in the eighth century A.D. And the Classic Maya collapse (see p. 526) may have been a replay of the unknown forces that had destroyed El Mirador centuries earlier.

Major Centers

Classic Maya civilization had been in existence for centuries when such centers as Copán and Tikal were founded in the fourth century A.D. (for Tikal, see Coe and Haviland, 1982). Their rubble-filled pyramids were topped with temples ornamented with sculptured stucco (Figure 22.9) (Coe, 1984). The pyramids were faced with cemented stone blocks and covered with a high-quality plaster to protect against the rains. The large temples on top had small, dark rooms because the builders did not know how to construct arches and were forced to corbel their roofs, supporting them with external braces. Tikal was an

FIGURE 22.9   Temple I at Tikal, Guatemala, which dates to about A.D. 700.

important trade center and, like others, attracted specialized craftsworkers who served the priests and the gods.

Maya rulers constantly sought to appease their numerous gods (some benevolent, some evil) at the correct moments in the elaborate sacred calendar. Each sacred year, as well as each cycle of years, had its destiny controlled by a different deity. The state's continued survival was ensured by pleasing the gods with sacrificial offerings, some of them human.

Astronomy The Maya were remarkable astronomers who predicted most astronomical events, including eclipses of the sun and moon (Figure 22.10). Religious events were regulated according to a sacred year (*tzolkin*) with thirteen months of twenty days each. The 260 days of the sacred year were unrelated to any astronomical phenomenon, being closely tied to ritual and divination. The length of this year was arbitrary and probably established by long tradition. Tzolkins were, however, closely intermeshed with a secular year (*haab*) of 365 days, an astronomical calendar based on the solar cycle. The *haab* was used to regulate state affairs, but the connections between sacred and secular years were of great importance in Maya life. Every fifty-two years a complete cycle of all the variations of the day and month names of the two calendars occurred, an occasion for intense religious activity.

The Maya developed a hieroglyphic script used for calculating calendars and regulating religious observances (Coe, 1984; Jones, 1984; Thompson, 1950). The script was also much used for recording genealogies, king lists, conquests, and dynastic histories. Partly because of the Spanish bishop Diego de Landa, who recorded Maya dialects surviving in the mid–sixteenth century, scholars have been able to decipher part of the script that was written on temple walls and modeled in stucco. The symbols are fantastically grotesque, consisting mostly of humans, monsters, or gods' heads (Figure 22.10).

Copán Copán, founded in the fifth century A.D., was one of the major astronomical centers of Mesoamerica. Its pyramids, temples, and pillars are a remarkable monument to Maya skill. Copán, like Tikal, preserves the essential architectural features of Maya ceremonial centers. These include platforms, pyramids, and causeways, grouped around open concourses and plazas presumably for religious effect and also to handle the large numbers of spectators who flocked to the religious ceremonies.

Ball courts were built at some late centers. They were used for an elaborate ceremonial contest, perhaps connected with the fertility of crops, between competing teams using a solid rubber ball. The details of the game remain obscure, but it is known that the players hit the balls so as to strike stone markers shaped like parrot heads.

Political Organization

Maya civilization was far from uniform, as recent advances in the decipherment of its glyphs have shown. It appears to have been a mosaic of independent political units, large and small. "Emblem glyphs," symbols associated with different sites, have been identified at dozens of diverse Maya centers. Some Mayanists believe that these reflect autonomous sites. There are cases where two or more sites, often a larger site and one or more smaller neighbors, share

Emblem glyphs

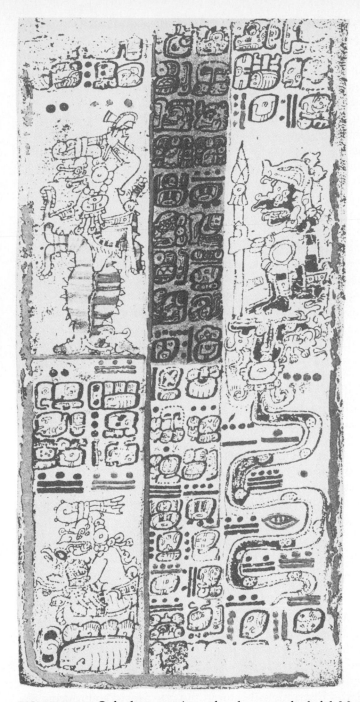

FIGURE 22.10 Only three certain, and perhaps one doubtful, Maya codices (books of picture writing) are known to have survived destruction by the Spanish. Here is a page from the so-called Dresden Codex, which records astronomical calculations, ritual detail, and tables of eclipses.

the same glyph; perhaps all were part of the same political unit (for a summary, see Culbert, 1988b; Marcus, 1973).

It is very difficult to be specific about the political relationships between Maya settlements, divided as the people were into a myriad of small and multi-center polities. Sometimes, however, the leader of a small settlement without its own emblem glyph acknowledged the overlordship of a ruler at another. He was invariably a member of the *cahal* class, subordinate to that of the elite *ahau*, who governed larger centers. Even some ahaus acknowledged the overlordship of others of their class, so it appears there was some form of hierarchical political organization within Maya domains, even if most of the details elude us.

There were many elements common to all Maya polities, among them the calendar and hieroglyphic script, essential to the regulation of religious life and the worship of the gods. Architectural and artistic styles in ceramics and small artifacts varied from center to center as each developed its own characteristics and cultural traditions (Coe, 1984). The Maya were unified more by religion than by political or economic interests, in much the same way, perhaps, as the spread of Islam unified diverse cultures.

Political mechanisms

The political mechanisms used by the Maya included warfare, but it is questionable just how important this was in territorial expansion. The art and inscriptions concentrate on the ceremonial and ideological aspects of war — the capture and sacrifice of prisoners as a way of validating political authority (Schele and Miller, 1986). Whether this was the primary purpose of going to war is uncertain. However, judging from emblem glyphs, most wars were between immediate neighbors, with the capture and sacrifice of a ruler sometimes leading to dominance of one center by another for generations, at others apparently having little effect. Intermarriage between ruling families of neighboring sites was also a significant political device among the Maya. The marrying of women into other dynasties even allowed some sites to acquire lasting political control over others. The inscriptions tell us that visits by rulers or their representatives to other centers were important occurrences, usually commemorating significant political events such as accession or occasions when a ruler designated his heir (Culbert, 1988b; Schele and Miller, 1986).

Political History

The decipherment of Maya hieroglyphs has thrown important new light on Maya political history (Schele and Miller, 1986). The great Mayanist Tatiana Proskouriakoff revolutionized Maya studies when she identified seven successive groups of rulers' monuments at Piedras Negras, each erected on the fifth anniversary of the ruler's ascent to the throne (for key references and a summary description, see N. Hammond, 1982). A small group of experts has expanded her pioneering research through Maya country in recent years, with dramatic results. Carved inscriptions began in the northeast Petén during the early third century A.D. and were confined to that area for about a century. Then they spread rapidly throughout the lowlands. By the mid–fifth century, most major sites had established ruling dynasties that can be at least partially identified from their inscriptions. For example, the Tikal rulers are known not only from inscriptions but from iconographic studies as well. The Sky dynasty

Ruling dynasties

at Tikal has been traced from the late fourth to the late eighth century A.D. The first identified ruler is Jaguar Paw, who died in A.D. 376. Three celebrated but anonymous rulers, known to Mayanists as Rulers A, B, and C, revitalized and expanded Tikal between A.D. 682 and the late eighth century.

Palenque yielded an exciting discovery in 1952, when Alberto Ruz cleared a stairway below the pyramid of the inscriptions. The stairs led to a rock-cut chamber containing a great sarcophagus with a finely carved lid. The inscriptions on the coffin revealed that the elderly man buried within was named Pacal ("Shield"). The hieroglyphs tell us that he was born on March 24, A.D. 603, ascended to the throne of Palenque on July 27, A.D. 615, and died on September 29, A.D. 684, at age eighty-one. Pacal commissioned texts to record the history of the rulers who preceded him, and his successors kept up the records on wall panels until around A.D. 799.

In 1983, the burial of an Early Classic ruler dating to A.D. 450 came to light at the 500-acre (202 ha) center at Río Azul in northern Guatemala, 50 miles (80.4 km) north of Tikal. The body was buried in a shroud atop a wooden bier. The remains of a jade necklace lay among the bones, which were surrounded by fine clay vessels, including tripod jars and a unique screw-topped container, made by dovetailing clay spirals in the lid and on the neck of the pot. The walls of the rock-cut burial chamber are decorated with hieroglyphs that should tell experts much about Early Classic life.

Throughout the Early Classic, until about A.D. 600, the northeast Petén had the largest states, with an important multicenter polity headed by the rulers of Tikal (for summary see Culbert, 1988b). The Sky dynasty extended their influence not only by conquest and long-distance trade but also by judicious political marriages that gave neighboring rulers maternal kin ties to the great center. In A.D. 378, Tikal conquered its important neighbor Uaxactún, 12.4 miles (20 km) to the north, installing a ruler named Smoking Frog on the throne. Eventually Tikal's territory covered 965 square miles (2500 sq km), with an estimated population of more than 360,000. The city enjoyed regular trading and political contacts with distant Teotihuacán in the highlands. After a period of apparent political trouble between A.D. 534 and 593, Tikal continued to prosper into the Late Classic.

The Late Classic was the apogee of Maya civilization in the southern lowlands, with high population densities, many competing rulers, and a great flowering of art and architecture. The west and the southeast were the realm of numerous small and independent polities, each with its own dynasties. In the central Pasión region, the Dos Pilas center established a multicenter polity that lasted for a century. The ruler Flint Sky came to the throne at Dos Pilas in A.D. 645. Perhaps he was an outsider from Tikal, but he was an astute political operator by any standards, establishing his authority over neighbors through marriage and conquest. His successors expanded his conquests, but their influence declined sharply until the polity vanished in about A.D. 791. At its maximum, the Dos Pilas polity was probably about 49 by 31 miles (80 by 50 km), but it lasted only about forty years.

During the very Late Classic, after A.D. 771, a new political pattern emerged, indicative of changed conditions and stressful times. Carved inscriptions began to appear in the houses of local nobles at Copán and other sites, as if the rulers were now granting the privilege of using inscriptions to important individuals, perhaps as a way of gaining their continued support in times of trouble. This proliferation of inscriptions in the Petén and elsewhere may also reflect minor nobles taking advantage of confused times and a disintegrating political authority to claim their own brief independence. The confusion accelerated. By A.D. 800, Maya populations were declining sharply, and both monument carving and major construction soon came to an end.

Maya polities

Most Maya polities were small-scale, independent units that rarely interfered with their neighbors. The lowlands were never unified politically during the Classic period. What the elite did share was a set of highly complex traditions and a network of contacts between rulers that transcended the local interests of individual polities and considerable local cultural diversity. Maya civilization was a local phenomenon. Only when a few aggressive, successful leaders emerged at places like Tikal did larger, multicenter polities emerge. These tended to disintegrate within a few generations.

As Norman Yoffee (quoted by Culbert, 1988b) points out, there are some parallels between the Classic Maya and early Mesopotamian civilizations. The Sumerians were governed by independent rulers with strong ritual powers, presiding over independent polities that were in a constant state of change and interaction. The city-state remained the practical political unit long after Sargon created a theoretically unified Mesopotamia about 4400 years ago (Chapter 16). Just as in the Maya lowlands, larger political units forged by leaders of exceptional ability soon fragmented back into their city-state parts. Perhaps the most aggressive Maya leaders had ambitions of widespread conquest, but a combination of powerful local cultural traditions and the limitations of the rain-forest environment prevented wider political unification in the Maya lowlands.

Originally, people thought of the Maya as a civilization ruled by priests, who interpreted the heavens for thousands of village farmers (Figure 22.11). In fact, Classic Maya society was much more complex, consisting of a series of social layers, position within society being determined by birth. The ruling elite were an exclusive, self-perpetuating group. Below them were various specialists — administrators who supervised public works projects and ran the complex affairs of state, priests, architects, artisans like potters and stoneworkers, and also performers, laborers, and common farmers (Figure 22.12). This type of social organization is typical of many early civilizations, among them the Sumerians and Ancient Egyptians. Like the ens and pharaohs of the Near East, the Maya rulers extracted labor and food from those they ruled, but the means by which they did so are still unknown (N. Hammond, 1982).

The Maya civilization flourished until about A.D. 900, when it suddenly, and inexplicably, collapsed.

THE COLLAPSE OF CLASSIC MAYA CIVILIZATION

Collapse hypotheses

Maya civilization reached its peak after A.D. 600. Then, at the end of the eighth century, the great ceremonial centers of the Petén and the southern lowlands were abandoned, the calendar was discontinued, and the structure of religious life and the state decayed. No one has been able to explain this sudden and dra-

FIGURE 22.11 A richly clad Maya ruler wears the mask of the long-nosed god. His name is Bird-Jaguar. Three people, probably prisoners about to be sacrificed, kneel before him. From Yaxchilán, c. A.D. 750 (From J. Eric S. Thompson, *The Rise and Fall of Maya Civilization*. Copyright 1954, 1966, by the University of Oklahoma Press)

matic collapse of Maya civilization, which is the subject of a prolonged debate in American archaeology (Culbert, 1973; 1988a).

The Classic Maya collapse has fostered varied traditional explanations, most of them unilinear and monocausal. They have included catastrophes, such as earthquakes, hurricanes, and disease. Ecological theories mention exhausted soils, water loss, and erosion. Internal social revolt might have led the peasants to rebel against cruel rule by their elitist overlords. Each of these hypotheses has been rejected because either the evidence is insufficient or the explanation is oversimplified. Another popular hypothesis is that there was a disruptive invasion of Maya territory by peoples from the highlands. Certainly evidence reports Toltec intrusions into the lowlands, although it is hard to say how broad the effects of the invasions were or what damage they did to the fabric of Maya society.

The Late Classic was a period of great activity and rapid population growth at almost all major sites in the Maya lowlands. The collapse began at some sites early in the ninth century. Major centers were abandoned, monumental inscriptions and major public building ceased, populations declined rapidly. The effects were most strongly felt in the south. Within a century, huge sections of the southern lowlands were abandoned, never to be reoccupied (Culbert, 1988a). At Tikal, perhaps the greatest Maya center, the elite vanished and the

FIGURE 22.12 A portion of the famous Bonampak murals at Chiapas, Mexico. This segment is in Room 4, showing Maya ruler, warriors, and war captives.

population declined to a third of its earlier level. The commoner survivors clustered in the remains of great masonry structures and tried to retain a semblance of earlier life. But within a century, even they were gone. All this is not to say that Maya civilization vanished completely, for new centers may have emerged in neighboring areas, with some of the displaced population moving to them. Maya civilization continued to flourish in the northern Yucatán (Sabloff and Friedel, 1984).

Multiple factors
Everyone studying the Maya collapse agrees that a multiplicity of factors led to catastrophe in the southern lowlands (Culbert, 1973). The theories of the 1970s argued that the collapse of Teotihuacán gave the Maya a chance to enlarge their managerial functions in Mesoamerican trade. The elite became increasingly involved in warfare, trade, and competition between regions. The Late Classic saw a frenzy of public building and increased pressure on commoners, the source of both food and labor for prestige projects. Agricultural

productivity fell, disease may have reached epidemic proportions, and population densities plummeted, making recovery impossible.

These theories have been subjected to exhaustive analysis in recent years, by researches that involve both simulation studies and examination of trading patterns and demographic and ecological stresses that could have affected population densities (for a detailed discussion, see Culbert, 1988a). Patrick Culbert has examined population densities and the potential for agricultural production in the southern lowlands. He shows that population densities rose as high as 77 persons per square mile (200 per km) during the Late Classic over an area so large that it was impossible for people to adapt to bad times by moving to new land or emigrating. He believes that the magnitude of the population loss during the two centuries after A.D. 800 was such that social malfunction alone cannot account for it. Failure of the agricultural base must have been an important component in the collapse equation.

Maya agriculture became increasingly intense as populations rose, with both terrace and raised-field systems covering large areas in many parts of the lowlands. At some of the larger sites like Tikal, the people may have been transporting great quantities of foodstuffs from distances of between 31 and 62 miles (50 and 100 km) away. In the short term, the intensification strategies worked, but they carried the seeds of collapse. The risks of climatic change, plant disease, erosion, and long-term declines in soil fertility were ever present in such enterprises. To continue functioning efficiently, the newly intensified systems would have to be managed constantly. Just the repair of field systems after floods and rains would have required watchful effort on a large scale. But there are no signs that the Maya made any social changes that enabled them to achieve such a level of management, especially when so many people were engaged in public construction projects and, apparently, in military activity (perhaps the Maya were under pressure from the north).

Agricultural collapse

There is so little data that we can reconstruct almost any scenario of agricultural collapse. Culbert believes that long-term environmental degradation was an important element in the scenario, where short-term gains in productivity were followed by catastrophic declines. For example, as populations rose, fallow cycles may have been shortened, leading to increased competition between crop plants and weeds, a problem that can only be solved by constant weeding, a very labor-intensive activity. Shortened fallow cycles also lead to lower levels of plant nutrients and declining crop yields. We do not know if the Maya counteracted these trends by systematic mulching or by planting of soil-restoring crops. The problem of erosion may have been even more acute. There are signs that the people lost much soil to runoff in the lowlands, for they did not build the terraces needed to retain soil in time. Some of this erosion may have resulted from extensive deforestation.

The Maya collapse may have had many interlocking causes, but Culbert makes a convincing case for a major demographic and subsistence disaster. He draws an interesting parallel with Mesopotamia, where at Ur an abundance of water from an expanded canal system led to overirrigation, shortened fallow cycles, and high levels of salt coming into the soil (R. M. Adams, 1981). To quote Robert Adams, "long-term agricultural decline was in some ways a direct consequence of its earlier apparent success.'' The expanding Maya population was dependent on an agricultural system that made no allowance for long-term problems. Eventually the system could produce no further riches, could not expand, and could only decline — with catastrophic results.

This model has many gaps, of course, especially in not showing how the collapse affected the lowland population and why the Maya did not simply adopt several useful technological devices known to them that could have dramatically enhanced agricultural productivity, but we can be fairly sure that varied interacting pressures helped overthrow the Maya civilization. To test all the hypotheses in this comprehensive model will require much new field data and many new excavations.

THE TOLTECS

Although by A.D. 900 the Classic period had ended, Maya religious and social orders continued in northern Yucatán (Figure 22.13). The continuity of the ancient Mesoamerican tradition survived unscathed. Basic economic patterns and technological traditions were retained, although religious and ideological patterns and priorities were disarranged. New ceremonial centers were built, but war and violence became primary as militaristic rulers achieved dominance in Mesoamerica (Davies, 1973, 1977, 1980). (See McVicker, 1985, for a discussion of Maya roles in the highlands.)

FIGURE 22.13 Distribution of Classic Maya, Toltec, and Aztec civilizations.

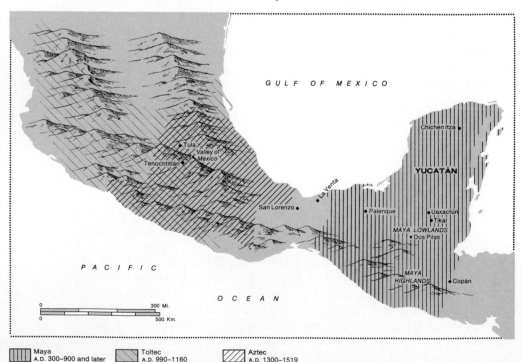

We have mentioned the unsettled Postclassic political conditions caused by population movements and tribal warfare. Many groups of invaders vied for political power in central Mexico until the Toltecs achieved dominance in the tenth century. The oral legends of the Aztec rulers, who followed the Toltecs, describe how the Toltecs came into Mesoamerica from the northwest frontiers beyond the civilized world. They settled at Tula, 37 miles (57 km) north of the Valley of Mexico, where they built a ceremonial center dedicated to their serpent god, Quetzalcóatl (Figure 22.14) (Davies, 1977; Diehl, 1984; Wolfe, 1959). Tula is notable for its animal sculpture and pottery styles, but it did not have a long life, for in approximately A.D. 1160 some newcomers with a less developed religious organization arrived from the north and destroyed the temples.

Chichén Itzá in northern Yucatán was an important Maya ceremonial center in Postclassic times (Figure 22.15). In the ninth century A.D., Chichén Itzá came under Toltec influence (Coggins, 1985; Roys, 1972; Weaver, 1981). The extent of this influence is much debated, but it probably represented a new political order, a complex mixing of Mexican and Maya factions among the elite. They developed new artistic and political styles that separated political functions from the personality of an individual ruler. The Chichén Toltecs developed a

Postclassic
A.D. 900 to 1521

Toltecs

Tula
A.D. 900

A.D. 1160

Chichén Itzá

FIGURE 22.14 Tula. The summit of its pyramid bears statues of richly adorned warriors with elaborate breastplates. These once supported the roof of the temple of the feathered serpent god Quetzalcóatl.

FIGURE 22.15 Chichén Itzá, Temple of the Warriors.

flexibility and a resilience that enabled them to be far more adaptive to changing political conditions than their southern neighbors had been. The leaders of Chichén Itzá developed a truly regional state. They controlled the two great resources of the northern Yucatán: a talented, well-organized population and massive salt fields along the coast. The site was abandoned in the thirteenth century, but the city of Mayapán, a walled settlement clustered around a ceremonial center, rose to prominence elsewhere in northern Yucatán. At least 12,000 people lived in this Maya city, which was ruled by the Cocom family. Maya civilization enjoyed a resurgence in this area, although Mayapán declined during the civil wars of the fifteenth century. A century later, the Spanish found Yucatán ruled by numerous petty chiefs.

Mayapán

The militaristic Toltecs were the leading military and political force in Mesoamerica for such a short time that their influence evaporated rapidly when Tula was destroyed. Another period of political chaos in the Valley of Mexico ensued, as more barbarians from the north (Chichimecs) maneuvered for political power (Davies, 1980).

THE AZTECS AND THE SPANISH CONQUEST

When the first Spanish conquistadors arrived in highland Mexico in 1519, they were astounded by the rich civilization they found. The capital city of Tenochtitlán was the headquarters of a series of militaristic Aztec kings, who ruled over a wide area by religious decree, constant human sacrifice, and bloodthirsty campaigning. Within a few years of Spanish contact, Aztec civilization literally ceased to exist. Tenochtitlán was reduced to rubble after a siege that lasted ninety-one days.

The Aztecs were one of several nomadic, semicivilized Chichimeca groups who settled in the Valley of Mexico after the fall of Tula (Davies, 1973). They arrived during the early twelfth century, a politically weak but aggressive group who barely retained their own identity. After years of military harassment, the Aztecs fled into the swamps of Lake Texcoco in about 1325. There they founded a small hamlet named Tenochtitlán (now Mexico City). Less than two centuries later, this village had become the largest city in pre-Columbian America (Conrad and Demarest, 1984).

At first the Aztecs lived peaceably with their neighbors, and Tenochtitlán flourished as an important market center. But by judicious diplomacy, discreet military alliance, and well-timed royal marriages, the Aztecs quietly advanced their cause until they were a force to be reckoned with in local politics. Then, in the early fifteenth century, they changed their foreign policy abruptly and embarked on a ruthless campaign of long-term military and economic conquest. Soon they controlled a loosely connected network of minor states and cities that extended right across Mesoamerica. The real leader behind this change was a counselor and general named Tlacaelel, who was adviser to a series of aggressive Aztec rulers. It was he who encouraged the use of terror and human sacrifice as means of controlling conquered territory. The rich tribute from conquered states and cities made Tenochtitlán the center of the Mesoamerican world, the hub of a political and economic confederacy that extended from the Pacific Ocean to the Gulf of Mexico, and from northern Mexico as far south as Guatemala.

Tenochtitlán was a spectacular sight in the sixteenth century, with markets where more than 60,000 people are said to have assembled every day (Diaz, 1963; Morris, 1962). The market sold every form of foodstuff and provided every luxury and service. The principal streets of Tenochtitlán were of beaten earth, and there were at least forty pyramids adorned with fine decorated stonework (Moctezuma, 1984). Tenochtitlán certainly was larger, and probably cleaner, than many European cities of the time (Figure 22.16).

Large residential areas surrounded the central precincts, while houses with chinampa gardens lay on the outskirts of the city. Six major canals ran through Tenochtitlán, and there were three causeways that connected the city with the mainland. At least 200,000 canoes provided convenient transport for the people of the city, which was divided into sixty or seventy well-organized wards. Tenochtitlán was a magnificent city set in a green swath of country near a clear lake, with a superb backdrop of snow-capped volcanoes (Fagan, 1984b).

Aztec society was moving closer and closer to a rigid, highly stratified class system at the time of Spanish contact. No commoner was allowed to enter a waiting room in the palace used by nobles. The king was revered as a semigod and had virtually despotic powers. He was elected from a limited class group of *pipiltin*, or nobles. There were full-time professional merchants called *pochteca*, and also a class of warriors whose ranks were determined by the number of people they had killed in battle. Groups of lineages called *calpulli* (big house) were the most significant factor in most people's religious, social, and political life. Many of them coincided with wards in the city. The great mass of the peo-

FIGURE 22.16 A general view of the excavations and restoration at the Aztec Temple of Huitzilopochtli and Tlaloc, the Templo Major, Tenochtitlán.

ple were free people or *macehualtin,* while serfs, landless peasants, and slaves made up the bottom strata of society.

Much of Aztec society's efforts went toward placating the formidable war and rain gods, Huitzilopochtli and Tlaloc, whose benevolence was assured by constant human sacrifices. These sacrifices reached their peak at the end of each fifty-two-year cycle, like those of the Maya, when the continuity of the world would be secured by bloodthirsty rites.

By the time of the Spanish conquest in 1519, Aztec society seems to have been functioning in a state of frenetic and bloody terrorism that flourished at the behest of arrogant, imperial rulers. The Aztecs had learned the fine art of terror as a political instrument and regularly staged elaborate public displays in Tenochtitlán to which subject leaders were invited. The Spaniards estimated that at least 20,000 people were sacrificed to the gods throughout the Aztec empire each year. This figure may be an exaggeration, but there is no doubt that a considerable number of prisoners of war and slaves perished by having their hearts ripped out in the presence of the gods. There was also a steady flow of sacrificial victims from the Aztecs' constant military campaigns. Indeed, the finest death for an Aztec warrior was to perish under the sacrificial knife after honorable capture in battle. Such a fate was known as the "flowery death."

The Aztecs have acquired a formidable reputation from historians — and, it must be confessed, from some archaeologists — because of their penchant for human sacrifice and cannibalism. That they were addicted to human sacrifice is certain, the cannibalism less so. Some believe that the Aztec nobles ate human flesh to compensate for a lack of meat in their diet, but the beans they ate as a staple were more than sufficient as a source of protein. It seems more likely that the Aztec nobles and priests engaged in occasional ritual cannibalism as part of their intensely symbolic religious beliefs (for a discussion, see Fagan, 1984b).

By the time the Spaniards landed on the Mexican lowlands, Aztec civilization was in danger of being torn apart. The society was becoming top-heavy with nobles, because they were allowed to marry commoners and their children automatically became aristocrats. The demands for tribute both from subject states and from the free people of the city became ever larger and more exacting. There may well have been intense philosophical disagreements between the militant priests and warriors, who increasingly encouraged conquest and human sacrifice, and those more sophisticated and educated Aztecs who believed in a gentler, less aggressive world. It is fascinating to speculate what would have happened had Cortés not landed in Mexico. Given the past history of Mexico, it seems likely that Aztec civilization would have collapsed suddenly, to be replaced in due time by another society much like it. In truth, Aztec civilization had reached a point of complexity that was beyond the capacity of its rulers to control and administer, a complexity that Old World civilizations had brought under control, and we can be certain that the Aztecs' successors would have eventually done so as well.

The Aztecs were one of the most important groups in Mesoamerica when the Spaniards first explored the New World. From coastal villagers in the lowlands they heard stories of the fabled rich kingdoms in the high interior. Soon the conquistadors pressed inland. Hernán Cortés was the first Spaniard to come into contact with the Aztecs, now ruled by Moctezuma II, a despotic ruler who assassinated most of his predecessor's counselors and had himself deified. Moctezuma's reign was disturbed by constant omens of impending doom and predictions that the god Quetzalcóatl would return to reclaim his homeland (Anderson and Dibble, 1978). The king was deeply alarmed by the reports of Spanish ships on the coast. There were, then, considerable internal psychological stresses on Moctezuma and his followers before the Spaniards arrived.

It took Cortés only two years to reduce the Aztecs to slaves and their marvelous capital to rubble. A handful of explorers on imported horses, armed with a few muskets, were able to overthrow one of the most powerful tribute states in the history of America. Without question, Cortés's task was made easier by both rebellious subjects of the Aztecs and the extraordinary stresses the Aztecs had placed on themselves.

By 1680, the Indian population of the Aztec heartland was reduced from approximately 1.2 million to some 70,000 — a decimation resulting from war, slavery, disease, overwork and exploitation, famine, and malnutrition. Mesoamerica as a whole lost between 85 and 95 percent of its indigenous population during that 160-year period. Only a few fragments of the fabulous Mesoamerican cultural tradition survived into modern times, as the Indian population faced a new and uncertain chapter in their long history (Gibson, 1964).

GUIDE TO FURTHER READING

Adams, R. E. W. *Prehistoric Mesoamerica*. Boston: Little, Brown, 1977.
  A college text that is readable and very thoroughly illustrated. Particularly good on environmental background. Covers all aspects of Mesoamerican prehistory.

Coe, Michael D. *The Maya* (3d ed.). London: Thames and Hudson, 1984.
  Regarded by many as the definitive account of the Maya civilization. With an emphasis on art styles, chronology, and culture history.

Davies, Nigel. *The Aztecs*. Norman: University of Oklahoma Press, 1973.
  A skillfully assembled narrative of the rise of the Aztecs, largely compiled from oral histories and codices as well as archaeological evidence. Complicated but authoritative.

Fagan, Brian M. *The Aztecs*. New York: Freeman, 1984.
  A straightforward description of the Aztecs written for the general public. Strong description and narrative, little theoretical argument.

Hammond, Norman. *Ancient Maya Civilization*. New Brunswick, N.J.: Rutgers University Press, 1982.
  Authoritative synthesis of the Maya civilization by an expert on the lowlands and on Maya ecology. A good starting point, with an excellent theoretical underpinning.

Schele, Linda, and Miller, E. *The Blood of Kings*. Austin: University of Texas Press, 1986.
  A brilliant, definitive account of Maya civilization and political history based on inscriptions and glyphs. An exemplary piece of long-term research.

Weaver, Muriel Porter. *The Aztecs, Maya, and Their Predecessors* (2d ed.). New York: Academic Press, 1981.
  A culture history that has been a standard reference for a decade, and the second edition is even more thorough than the first. Strongly recommended for detailed reading. Comprehensive illustrations of sites and artifacts.

CHRONOLOGICAL TABLE M

Calibrated Dates a.d./b.c./b.p.	C14 Years A.D./B.C.		PERU	
			Highlands	Lowlands (Coast)
	1532 —	Colonial Period		Spanish conquest
a.d. 1310–1515 —	1500 —	⊤Late Horizon	INCA	INCA
		Late Intermediate Period		
870–1230 —	1000 —	Middle Horizon	WARI TIWANAKU	CHIMU
265–640 —	500 —			NASCA
		Early Intermediate Period		MOCHE
450–5 b.c. —	A.D. 1 —			
820–480 —	500 B.C. —	Early Horizon	CHAVÍN	
3530–2905 b.p. —	3000 B.P. —			
		Initial Period		
4345–3660 —	3500 —		Large settled communities on the coast (well-established agriculture)	
4830–4305 —	4000 —			
5503–4925 —	4500 —		Chapter 14 ⬆	

CHAPTER 23

Early Civilization in Peru

Preview

■ The earliest complex societies of coastal Peru may have developed as a result of intensive exploitation of maritime resources, especially small fish easily netted from canoes. In time, abundant food surpluses, growing population densities, and larger settlements may have preadapted coastal people for adopting intensive irrigation agriculture. These societies were organized in increasingly complex ways.

■ During the so-called Initial Period of Peruvian prehistory, large monumental structures appeared, many of them U-shaped, just before and during the transition toward greater dependence on maize agriculture. This was also a period of continuous interaction and extensive trade between coast and highlands.

■ This efflorescence of social complexity, new art traditions, and monumental architecture coincided with the emergence of several small polities in river valleys on the coast. The culmination of this trend is seen in various local traditions, among them the famous Chavín style. This central Peruvian style, once thought to have been the source of Peruvian civilization, is now known to be a late manifestation of cultural trends that began as early as 3800 years ago.

■ After the Early Period ended in about 200 B.C., a series of coastal kingdoms developed, the political and economic influence of which spread beyond their immediate valley homelands. These states included the Moche, Nasca, and Recuay, which were remarkable for their fine pottery styles and expert alloy and gold metallurgy. They flourished in the first millennium A.D.

■ The Middle Horizon lasted from A.D. 600 to 1000 and saw the rise of numerous small states that traded with one another and depended heavily on irrigation agriculture. We describe the highland empires of Tiwanaku and Wari, in which an acceleration of the process of broader unification took place.

- Approximately A.D. 1000, Chimu, with its great capital at Chan Chan on the northern coast, dominated a wide area of the coast. Its compounds reflect a stratified state, with many expert craftspeople and a complex material culture.

- During the Late Horizon of Peruvian prehistory, there was unification of highlands and lowlands under the Inca Empire, which may have emerged as early as A.D. 1200 and lasted until the Spanish conquest in A.D. 1534. The Inca rulers were masters of bureaucracy and military organization and governed a highly structured state — one, however, that was so weakened by civil war and disease that it fell easily to the conquistador Francisco Pizarro and his small army of adventurers.

Chronological Table M

The rugged central Andean mountains are second only to the Himalayas in height, but only 10 percent of the rainfall on them descends the Pacific watershed. The foothill slopes and plains at the western foot of the mountains are mantled by the world's driest desert, which extends virtually from the equator to 30° south, much of it along the Peruvian coast. Yet, ironically, the richest fishery in the Americas hugs the Pacific shore, yielding millions of small schooling fish like anchovies. These easily netted shoals support millions of people today, and supported dense prehistoric populations. In contrast, the cultivation of this dry landscape requires controlling runoff from the Andes with large irrigation systems that use long canals built by the coordinated labors of hundreds of people. Only 10 percent of this desert can be farmed, so its inhabitants rely heavily on the incredible bounty of the Pacific. Surprisingly, perhaps, this apparently inhospitable desert was a major center of complex early states, states that traded with neighbors in the highlands and built large ceremonial centers.

How did such complex states arise in the Andean area, in such a dry environment? Recent archaeological researches have generated some sophisticated hypotheses to account for them.

THE MARITIME FOUNDATIONS OF ANDEAN CIVILIZATION

The mechanisms by which complex states arose on the Peruvian coast are still little understood, partly because research has tended to concentrate on larger, more spectacular sites (Haas et al., 1987; Moseley, 1975b, 1986; D. J. Wilson, 1983). Such researches tell us little about the relative size of different communities or about population densities, which are critical measures of an evolving state society. It is only recently that larger scale river valley surveys have collected such data, researches like Gordon Willey's classic work on the Virú

(1963) and Donald Proulx's field work in the Nepeña Valley (1973, 1985). These investigations have shown that there were major changes in site clustering through time, especially after the introduction of maize agriculture and irrigation to the coast after 4500 years ago.

In the 1970s, archaeologist Michael Moseley (1975b) proposed what he called the "maritime foundations of Andean civilization" hypothesis. He argued that the unique maritime resources of the Pacific coast provided sufficient calories to support rapidly growing, sedentary populations, which clustered in large communities. Not only that but the same food source produced sufficient surplus to free up time and people to erect large public monuments and temples, work organized by the leaders of newly complex coastal societies. This scenario runs contrary to conventional archaeological thinking, which regards agriculture as the economic basis for state-organized societies. In the Andes, argued Moseley, it was fishing. For thousands of years coastal populations rose, and their rise "preadapted" them to later circumstances, under which they would adopt large-scale irrigation and maize agriculture.

Maritime foundations theory

Moseley implied that mollusks and large fish were vital resources on the coast, but marine biologists drew his attention to the incredible potential of anchoveta and other small schooling fish. Anchoveta can be easily netted throughout the year from small canoes. The fish offer predictable food supplies that can be dried or ground into fine meal. Such harvests would provide an abundance of protein. Judging from modern yields, if prehistoric coastal populations had lived at 60 percent of the carrying capacity of the fisheries and eaten nothing but small fish, the coast could have supported more than 6.5 million people. That is not to say that it did, but the figures make the point that the exploitation of small fish would have provided a more than adequate economic base for the emergence of complex societies on the coast. It is interesting that small mesh nets and floats have come from earlier coastal sites like Paloma (Chapter 14).

Several critiques of the maritime foundations hypothesis have appeared, all of them based on the assumption that large coastal settlements could not have been supported by maritime resources alone (see, for example, D. J. Wilson, 1983). Most of these critiques have tended to ignore the potential of anchovetas. Another argument revolves around the famous El Niño phenomenon, the periodic changes in Pacific currents that reduce the fisheries to a shadow of their normal selves for several years at a time. In fact, as Moseley (1986) points out, the El Niño brings unfamiliar fish species to the coast, as well as violent rainfall that has the potential to disrupt irrigation systems with catastrophic results, some of which are now being identified in the archaeological record. Overall, the maritime foundations hypothesis has stood the test of time well, provided it is seen as a component in a much broader evolutionary process, which also took place inland, in the highlands, and in areas where the width of the coastal shelf precluded extensive anchoveta fishing.

Critiques of maritime foundations

Richard Burger (1985) argues that changing dietary patterns in the highlands, where agriculture became increasingly important, would have created a demand among farmers for lowland products — salt, fish, and seaweed. Seaweed is rich in marine iodine and could have been an important medicine in the highlands, used to combat endemic goiter and other conditions. By the same token, carbohydrate foods like oca, ullucu, and white potatoes that could not be grown on the coast have been found in preceramic sites in the Ancón-Chillón area of the Pacific lowlands. Thus, the formation of states in both lowlands and highlands may have been fostered by continuous, often highly localized interchange between coast and interior.

Michael Moseley believes that this reliance on maritime resources led to a "preadaptation" in the form of large, densely concentrated populations, whose leaders were able to organize the labor forces needed not only for building large ceremonial centers but also for transforming river valleys with sizable irrigation schemes. Under this scenario, irrigation farming was in the hands of a well-defined group of authority figures, who took advantage of existing simple technology and local populations to create new economies. And this transformation, based as it was on trade, maize agriculture, and a maritime diet, acted as a "kick" for radical changes in Andean society (for discussion, see Moseley, 1986). But the transformation was based on ancient fishing traditions, which can be documented thousands of years earlier at Paloma and other early coastal villages.

Moseley's key point is that Andean civilization evolved in many ways, in a wide variety of ecological zones, from highland, tropical rain-forest, and lowland strategies that were all of great antiquity, some dating to the earliest millennia of human settlement. Thus, the maritime foundations hypothesis may help explain the development of states on the Peruvian coast, but it cannot account for parallel developments elsewhere in South America.

COASTAL FOUNDATIONS: THE INITIAL PERIOD

Initial Period
3900 to 2900 B.P.

Sometime between 4500 and 3800 years ago, maize agriculture came to the Peruvian coast, and many villages moved inland. By this time, the coastal fishing villages were much larger communities with highly organized social structures, as reflected in the first signs of communal structures, such as an 80-foot- (24-m-) high temple mount at Salinas de Chao. The people may have cooperated in fishing and food gathering, but the cooperative effort in erecting large earthen platforms for temples or other public buildings satisfied entirely different needs and requires explanation.

Architecture

One of the persistent themes of ceremonial architecture in the Andes and on the coast has been the habit of artificially raising or lowering sacred spaces relative to one another in what Michael Moseley (1985) calls "complementary opposition arranged linearly along a horizontal axis." On the coast, early ceremonial sites feature rectangular platform mounds fronting on a circular, sunken court that is usually housed in a rectangular forecourt (for discussion, see Donnan, 1985). This form of architecture appeared at least 4000 years ago. It had people enter the forecourt of the sacred complex at ground level, descend into the sunken court, and then climb the temple platform.

After 4000 years ago, coastal ceremonial buildings were greatly elaborated, with new architectural devices being adopted, among them a distinctive U-shaped platform, often associated with elaborate adobe friezes. This arrangement is found in the great Río Rímac complex of Huaca Florida, built about 3700 years ago. Huaca Florida 3700 B.P.

El Paraíso, close to the mouth of the Chillón River near Lima, is the oldest of these U-shaped ceremonial complexes, and the closest one to the Pacific (Figure 23.1) (Bankes, 1977; Engel, 1957; Quilter, 1985). This vast site consists of at least six huge square buildings constructed of roughly shaped stone blocks cemented with unfired clay. The people painted the polished clay-faced outer walls in brilliant hues. Each complex consisted of a square building surrounded by tiers of platforms reached by stone and clay staircases. The largest is more than 830 feet (250 m) long and 166 feet (50 m) wide, standing more than 30 feet (10 m) above the plain. The rooms apparently were covered with matting roofs supported by willow posts. Perhaps as much as 100,000 tons of rock excavated from the nearby hills was needed to build the El Paraíso buildings. There are few signs of occupation around them, though, as if they were shrines and public precincts rather than residential quarters. The two largest mounds of collapsed masonry lie parallel to one another, defining a vast, elongated patio covering more than 6 acres (2.5 ha). This U-shaped layout is thought to be the precursor of this intrusive architectural style on the coast after 4000 years ago.

What is most surprising is that these huge structures were erected by people from dozens of scattered villages. For reasons not yet understood, they united in a building project that channeled most of their surplus energies into a vast

FIGURE 23.1 El Paraíso.

monumental center, a place where few people lived but where everyone apparently congregated for major public ceremonies. The people themselves lived a life of seeming simplicity. They owned but the simplest of stone and wooden artifacts and wore cotton clothing decorated with basic geometric patterns and stylized animallike motifs. They buried their dead in several layers of garments, nets, or looped sacks. Why should such an unsophisticated society build such enormous structures, and who were the leaders who organized these massive public works?

El Paraíso is thought to have been built by people who subsisted off a fish meal diet from the incredibly rich fisheries close offshore and who traded extensively with communities inland. Its U-shaped layout coincides with the florescence of similarly shaped ceremonial centers in the interior, at a time when coastal people began to consume much larger amounts of root crops, to make pottery, and to shift their settlements inland to river valleys. Some scholars believe that this move coincided with the introduction of large-scale canal irrigation (for discussion see Moseley, 1985). Perhaps the spread of U-shaped ceremonial centers reflects a radical restructuring of society that coincided with

FIGURE 23.2 Peruvian archaeological sites mentioned in this chapter. Approximate distributions of various traditions are also shown.

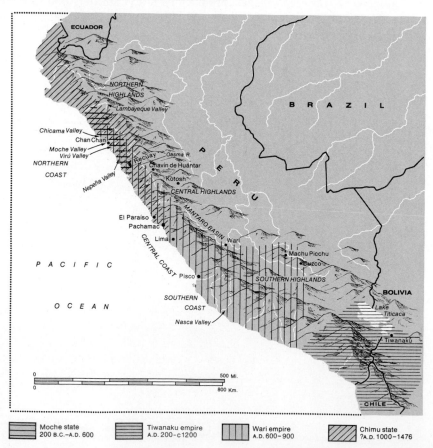

major economic change. Moseley argues that the introduction of irrigation technology required a major reorganization of labor, which coincided with the appearance of new artistic traditions and architectural devices.

What does this mean in ritual terms? In many parts of the Americas the ritual manipulation of smoke and water served as a way of bridging stratified layers of air, earth, and bodies of water in the cosmos (Lathrap, 1985). Thus, it is argued, the early ceremonial centers of the coast and highlands (Figure 23.2) reflect an ancient tradition of using these substances to maintain communication with the cosmos. Burnt offerings are found at some Andean sites, among them Kotosh. Water was caused to flow through masonry channels and cut stone ways at many highland sites and also at the famous ritual center at Chavín de Húantar. There, galleries and ritual waterways flowed through the ceremonial platform and beneath a circular, sunken court, connections that allowed the water to resonate under the ground, so that the temple "roared." The vast, open courts of coastal U-shaped ceremonial complexes may have housed sacred orchards and gardens irrigated with specially manipulated water supplies. These ritual waterways were to reach their greatest elaboration with the Chimu state of the coast and the great imperial Inca capital at Cuzco thousands of years later (for discussion see Donnan, 1985).

THE EARLY HORIZON, CHAVÍN, AND THE INITIAL PERIOD

In 1943, archaeologist Julio Tello identified a distinctive art style in stone, ceramics, and precious metals over a wide area of Peru, a style he named *Chavín* after a famous prehistoric ceremonial center at Chavín de Húantar in central Peru. Tello's research led to a long-held belief among Peruvianists that the widespread Chavín art style was a "mother culture" for all later Andean civilizations, somewhat equivalent to the Olmec phenomenon in Mesoamerican prehistory (Pozorski and Pozorski, 1987). This became a distinctive "Early Horizon" in Peruvian prehistory, dating to about 900 B.C., a period when there was a great expansion of indigenous religious belief by conquest, trade, and colonization, the time when civilization began.

There is no doubt that Chavín de Húantar is testimony to an elaborate, well-developed iconography. The temple area is terraced with an impressive truncated pyramid on the uppermost level. The 32-foot- (10-m-) high pyramid appears solid but is in fact hollow, a honeycomb of stone passages and rooms. The galleries are ventilated by special rectangular tubes. The temple housed a remarkable carving of a jaguarlike human with hair in the form of serpents (Figure 23.3) (Burger, 1984; Rowe, 1962). Chavín art, like this carving, is dominated by animal and human forms: jaguar motifs predominate; humans, gods, and animals have jaguarlike fangs or limbs; snakes flow from the bodies of many figures. The art has a grace that is grotesque and slightly sinister. Many figures were carved in stone, others in clay or bone.

Chavín de Húantar
900 B.C.

With its tangled animal and human motifs, Chavín art has all the flamboyance and exotic touches of the tropical forest. The animals depicted — cayman, jaguar, and snake — are all forest animals. The art may have originated in

FIGURE 23.3 A Chavín wall insert (approximately 7.8 in [20 cm] high) showing feline features, from Chavín de Huántar and a Chavín carving on a pillar in the temple interior at Chavín de Huántar. Stone insets such as these are common on the walls of the Chavín ceremonial buildings.

the tropical forests to the east of the Andes, but the Early Horizon Chavín temple has a U shape with a sunken central plaza, an architectural design documented centuries earlier at other coastal and highland sites (Burger, 1981, 1985; Pozorski and Pozorski, 1987).

But Chavín de Huántar is far more than just a temple. Richard Burger has recently excavated areas outside the well-known ceremonial precincts and established that the site was occupied between about 850 and 200 B.C. At first the population was small, perhaps little more than 100 people. But it seems to have expanded considerably by the fourth century B.C., at which point as many as 2000 to 3000 people may have been living near the temple precincts. Chavín de Huántar was certainly a large center, probably an influential place within its local area, and one of the largest settlements in Peru at the time of its occupation. It failed to expand into a fully developed urban center, however, and the nascent civilization that worshiped there collapsed, leaving nothing more than a small town and a persistent art style and iconography (Burger, 1981).

The Chavín style may have influenced artistic traditions over a wide area of

Peru, and it may also be that the religious beliefs behind the motifs were more important than the art itself. Settlements like Chavín de Huántar were important ceremonial centers that unified surrounding farming villages with a common religious belief, but Chavín de Huántar was not unique. There were many other, and often much earlier centers with the same general architectural and iconographic style.

For example, from about 4000 to 2200 years ago, the small ceremonial center at Huaricoto in the highlands, only 34 miles (55 km) from Chavín de Huántar, was the home of a religious ideology (Burger and Salazar-Burger, 1985). This "Kotosh Religious Tradition" is known to us by sacrificial hearths in which ceremonial offerings were burnt. These included animal bones and grain. The ritual hearth was sunk into the floor with a ventilator leading to the outside. Once the sacrifice was complete, the hearth was filled in. At first the rituals were performed in the open, but by late Initial Period times the hearths were surrounded by larger superstructures. The rituals may have been performed sporadically at certain times of the year, with the audience watching in the open. The Kotosh religious tradition appears to have flourished over an area of at least 155 miles (250 km) north to south in the highlands, in the region where the Chavín cult with its wild and extravagant animal motifs was to gain strength.

Huaricoto
4000 to 2200 B.P.

The so-called Early Horizon associated with Chavín has often been assumed to have been a period of unification and coalescence of early Peruvian culture under the rubric of a single theology. In fact, state formation occurred far earlier, during the Initial Period among the north and central ports of the coast, where a set of interacting polities arose after 3800 years ago. Political units centered on the Moche, Casma, Chillón, and other river valleys where irrigation agriculture developed. Centuries before, when pottery was unknown on the coast but cotton was already widely cultivated, communication networks had arisen that linked not only neighboring coastal river valleys but lowlands and highlands as well. These trade routes helped spread technology, ideology, pottery making, and architectural styles over large areas, giving a superficial sense of unity, reflected in the widespread use of common art motifs.

Initial Period sites are known from many coastal river valleys (see Haas et al., 1987, for details). For example, Huaca Florida is an imposing mound of boulders and adobe lying approximately 8 miles (12.8 km) inland of El Paraíso. Built somewhat later, about 3700 years ago, and on an even larger scale, the great platform is more than 840 feet (252 m) long, 180 feet (54 m) wide, and towers 100 feet (30 m) above the valley. A rectangular court lies close to the north side of the platform, but here the landscape is revealing, for Huaca Florida lies in the midst of an artificial environment created by irrigation. The focus of human settlement had now moved inland, and the subsistence base changed from fishing to large-scale irrigation agriculture.

This was by no means the earliest irrigation in Peru, for even the first farmers probably made some limited use of canals to water their riverside gardens. However, the new works were on a far larger scale, spurred by the availability of an army of workers fed by abundant Pacific fish, and by the presence of gentle, cultivable slopes inland, and the expertise of the local people in farming cotton, gourds, and many lesser crops such as squashes and beans. Huaca Florida's leaders organized the reclamation of the desert by building canals along the steeper areas of the coastal valleys, in places where the gradients made the diversion of river water an easy task. This earliest of irrigation works may seem straightforward, but considerable organization was required to coordinate and develop it, and many people were needed to supervise the digging, to mediate land ownership disputes, and to maintain canals.

At first, each family may have worked together to irrigate its own sloping gardens, but gradually each community grew so much that essential irrigation works could be handled only by cooperative effort. Organized irrigation perhaps began as many minor cooperative works between individual families and neighboring villages. These simple projects eventually evolved into elaborate public works that embraced entire inland valleys, controlled by a corporate authority who held a monopoly over both the water and the land it irrigated. The process of organization, which may have taken centuries, was the result of many complex interacting factors, among them population growth and the emergence of increasing numbers of nonfarming society members such as priests and artisans, whose food needs had to be met by other people. By the time El Paraíso and Huaca Florida were built, it is possible that public works such as irrigation canals and temples were constructed using a form of taxation by labor. Perhaps the rulers devised a forerunner of the *mita* tax employed 2000 years later by the Inca, by which people worked a certain number of days per year for the state, as either construction laborers or farmers. When one worked for the state, pay was given in food and shelter, sometimes in the form of a share of the yield from the land allocated to the state (Donnan, 1985).

As for Chavín itself, it is a late manifestation of a primeval Andean architectural style, a coalescence of traits and ideas from both the coast and the forest that formed a flamboyant cultural manifestation over a local area of the highlands. The Early Horizon itself, rather than being a catalytic time of unification, may well have been a long period of disruption of age-old communication networks and well-established small polities on the coast. For instance, the Casma polity was invaded by foreigners from the highlands, who forged the coastal valley and neighboring highlands into a single political unit for the first time in prehistory. This development was the precursor of far larger states. Perhaps it is better to refer to the Early Horizon as the Early Period, a prolonged time of cultural change and political adjustment.

Textiles and Coastal Prehistory

Initial and Early Period sites are remarkable for their fine textiles. Few prehistoric societies rivaled the textile artistry of the coastal Peruvians. They lived in an environment in which both animal and plant (especially cotton) fibers were plentiful, and were able to create fine and complex fabrics adorned with colorful, intricate patterns (Figure 23.4). The textiles have survived remarkably well in the dry coastal environment, in huge cemeteries where the dead were wrapped in fabric burial shrouds. The most spectacular textile finds come from huge cemeteries of mummified Indians on the sandy, desolate Paracas Peninsula south of the modern town of Pisco. The (Early Horizon) Paracas people lie

FIGURE 23.4 A border motif from a Paracas mantle showing an anthropomorphic figure wearing a tunic and skirt similar to those found on Paracas mummy bundles.

in bottle-shaped chambers or stone-lined subterranean vaults with wooden roofs approximately 16 feet (4.87 m) high and 13 feet (3.90 m) across cut through sand into soft rock. The sepulchers were divided into small chambers where dozens of mummy bundles were placed. The Indians did not practice mummification in the formal Ancient Egyptian sense. They simply took advantage of the exceptionally dry climate. Each corpse was disemboweled and then allowed to dry out in the hot sand in a fetal position with the knees at the chin. Eventually, the bodies were wrapped in brightly colored cotton, wool, or both. Sometimes the dead wore decorated mantles, shirts, turbans, or loincloths tailored to the size of the mummy bundle rather than the living person. Occasionally, the mourners attached small gold ornaments to the mummies, or buried tools, food, or even pet monkeys or parrots with the deceased (Figure 23.5).

It is from these mummies that we learn the most minute details of Peruvian textiles, for the wrapping cloths often are almost perfectly preserved. The earliest textiles preserved on the coast date to approximately 6500 years ago, soon after cotton was first cultivated. The weavers were expert dyers and used more than 190 hues from plant dyes. The earliest dye in common use was blue, followed by red and then a multitude of bright colors. Decorative motifs included simple checkerboards, filled squares, and stylized depictions of birds, felines, and other animals. The oldest textiles had rather coarse and uneven yarns produced by twisting untreated yarn. After 4000 years ago, however, the weavers began to use delicate wood and thorn spindles mounted in a special pottery, gourd, or wooden cup that minimized vibration. Thus they could produce much finer cloth. Most of the textiles found in coastal tombs were made on

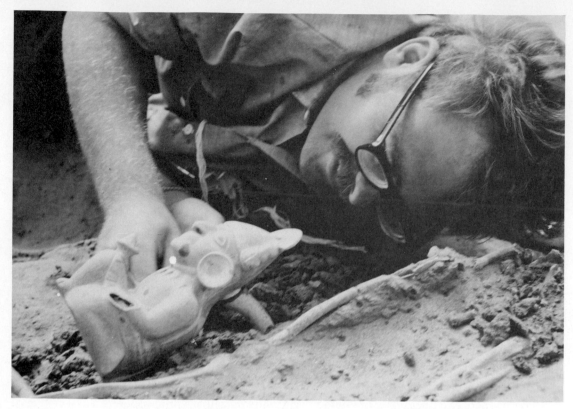

FIGURE 23.5 Archaeologist excavating an effigy pot of a kneeling warrior at a burial site at the Pyramid of the Sun and the Moon, Chan Chan, Peru.

backstrap looms just like those still in use in Peru today. Two sticks carry the lengthwise threads, the upper one suspended from a post and the lower tied to a belt around the weaver's back. As the work proceeds, the fabric is unrolled from the upper bar and the finished cloth is rolled onto the lower stick. The yarn is wound with a figure-eight motion between the two stakes and is laced fast to the loom sticks so that the edges of the fabric are uniformly finished off. The disadvantage of this type of loom is that the width of the cloth is limited by the span of the weaver's arms. The Indians sometimes combined several backstrap looms to create wider cloths.

From the Initial Period onward, the Andean region witnessed an extraordinary array of state-organized societies that displayed a remarkable diversity of culture, art, organization, and religious belief. At the same time, there were broad similarities in cosmology and culture that distinguish these societies from states elsewhere in the prehistoric world. As Michael Moseley and many others have pointed out, we are only now beginning to understand just how diverse and complicated the evolution of state-organized societies was in this region (see Haas et al., 1987). In the pages that follow, we survey some of the major states that emerged in the Andean area after 200 B.C.

THE EARLY INTERMEDIATE PERIOD

By 200 B.C., irrigation agriculture had developed on a very large scale on the coast, so much so that some settlements, such as Cerro Arena in the Moche Valley, covered more than a square mile. Excavations during the 1970s revealed more than 2000 separate structures, some with as many as twenty rooms (Bankes, 1977). A small group of twenty-five finely finished houses may have formed the administrative and residential quarters of Cerro Arena. There were considerable variations between these quarters and the humbler dwellings that surrounded them, as if Cerro Arena society was more complex than that of earlier settlements. This and other large settlements were supported by irrigation systems that required not only organized labor to construct and maintain but strict water controls as well. Most of the cultivated land lay along the terraced edges of the valleys, where the soils were better drained and easily planted with simple wooden digging sticks, just as they are to this day. Even today the local people divert the seasonal river water into side canals by building dams of stakes and boulders into the streams. There is no reason to suppose that the same simple but effective technique was not used in antiquity. The ancient irrigation canals wound along the sides of the valleys, a series of narrow channels approximately 4 feet (1.2 m) wide, set in loops and S-shaped curves, watering plots approximately 70 feet (21.3 m) square. The surplus flowed off into the Pacific.

Moche

By 200 B.C., the Moche state had begun in northern coastal Peru. It flourished for 800 years. Its origins lay in the Chicama and Moche valleys, with great ceremonial centers and huge irrigation works (Donnan and McClelland, 1979). Information about the Moche peoples of 2000 years ago comes not only from irrigation systems and spectacular monuments but also from hundreds of finely modeled clay pots and human burials preserved in the dry desert sand of their cemeteries. Unfortunately, these burials are a prime target of commercial grave robbers. Many Moche cemeteries look like battlefields after heavy bombardment, for their pots fetch astronomical prices on the international art market. What little we know about Moche society comes from undisturbed burials, and from museum studies of looted pots. They show that Moche society consisted of farmers and fisherfolk, as well as skilled artisans and priests, who are depicted on pots with felinelike fangs set in their mouths and wearing puma-skin headdresses. A few expert craft potters created superb modeled vessels with striking portraits of arrogant, handsome men who can only have been the leaders of Moche society (Figure 23.6). The potters modeled warriors, too, complete with shields and war clubs, well-padded helmets and colorful cotton uniforms. Moche burials show that some members of society were much richer than others, lying in graves filled with as many as fifty vessels or with weapons or staffs of rank. We do not know exactly how Moche society was organized, but we can assume that the ruler wielded authority over a hierarchical state of warriors, priest-doctors, artisans, and the mass of the agricultural population.

Moche
200 B.C. to A.D. 600

FIGURE 23.6 Moche portrait vessel approximately 11.4 in (29 cm) high.

For instance, there was at least one Moche-style settlement in each subject valley.

Fortunately, the Moche artists and artisans gave us some more intimate glances at their society than do many civilizations (Figure 23.7). Their paintings show the ruler with fine feather headdress seated on a pyramid, while a line of naked prisoners parades before him. A decapitated sacrifice at the base of one painting reminds us that human sacrifice may have been the fate of some prisoners of war. We see Moche soldiers in battle, charging their opponents with raised clubs. The defenders raise their feather-decked shields in defiance as the battle is fought to the death. The potters modeled maize-beer befuddled drunks being supported by their solicitous friends, women giving birth with the midwife in attendance, and wives carrying babies on their backs in shawls and in wooden cradles suspended by nets. The women carried out all domestic activities, while the men served as warriors, farmers, and fishermen. We see them on a seal hunt, clubbing young seals on the rocky coast as their prey scurries in every direction. A clay llama strains reluctantly under its load, and a mouse eats a maize cob.

The pots also depict vividly what the Moche people wore. The men worked in short loincloths or cotton breeches and short sleeveless shirts underneath tunics that ended above the knee, fastened around the waist with colorful woven belts. More important people wore large mantles and headdresses made from puma heads or feathers from highland jungles. Nearly everyone donned some form of headgear: brightly decorated cotton turbans wound around small caps and held in place with fabric chin straps were in common use. A small cloth protected the back of the neck from the burning sun. Moche women dressed in loose tunics that reached the knee, and went bareheaded or draped a piece of cloth around the head. Many men painted their lower legs and feet in bright colors and tattooed or daubed their faces with lines and other motifs. They often wore disk or crescent nose ornaments and cylindrical bar earrings, sometimes modeled in gold. Their necks bore large collars of stone beads or

FIGURE 23.7 Moche vessel depicting an owl-woman healer.

precious metal, while bracelets covered arms and legs. Many people wore fiber sandals to protect their feet against the hot sand.

By this time the coastal people were expert metalworkers (Benson, 1979). They had discovered the properties of gold ore and extracted it by panning in streambeds rather than by mining. Soon they had developed ways of hammering it into fine sheets and had learned how to emboss it to make raised designs (Figure 23.8). They also had worked out the technique of annealing, making it possible to soften the metal and then hammer it into more elaborate forms, and they joined sheets with fine solder. The smiths used gold as a setting for turquoise and shell ornaments, crafted crowns, circlets, necklaces, pins, and tweezers. Gold was in such short supply in prehistoric times that the metalworkers became expert at depletion gilding, an annealing technique which oxidizes the metal in an alloy of copper and gold to give the finished product a goldlike appearance even when the gold content is as low as 12 percent by weight. Many of the large gold objects such as animals and plate decorations seized from the Inca by Pizarro's soldiers were, in fact, manufactured of an elaborate alloy of some gold, silver, and copper.

The greatest efforts of the Moche people were devoted not to irrigation systems or elaborate burials but to the erection of vast monumental platforms and temples on the southern edge of the cultivated land in the Moche Valley, approximately 4 miles (6.4 km) southeast of the modern city of Trujillo. They used

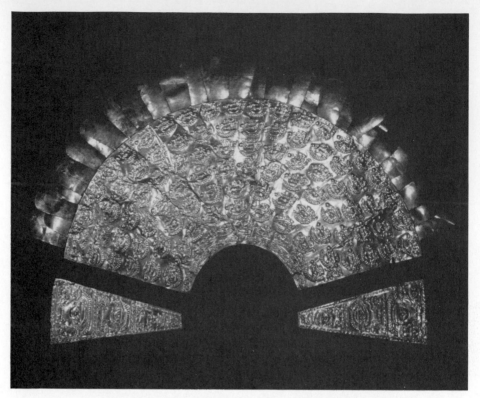

FIGURE 23.8 Moche hammered gold breastplate.

tax labor to build a huge adobe temple platform rising 76 feet (23 m) above the plain at the foot of a conical hill named Cerro Blanco. The Spaniards called this complex *Huaca de la Luna*, the Temple of the Moon. *Huaca del Sol* (Temple of the Sun) stands close to the west, a confused mass of mud brick that once consisted of a ramp that gave access to five temple platforms, the highest, to the south, towering 135 feet (41 m) above the ground. The sides of the pyramid were steeply terraced and have been badly damaged by erosion and looters. Both platforms once supported courts, corridors, and room complexes, perhaps roofed with matting. Huaca del Sol may have been a palace, for there are deep rubbish heaps on the summit of the platform. In contrast Huaca de la Luna is spotlessly clean, its temple buildings painted with brightly colored murals.

The Moche was a multivalley state that may have consisted of a series of satellite centers that ruled over individual valleys yet owed allegiance to the great centers of the Moche Valley. At one time the Moche Valley presided over the coast as far south as the Nepeña Valley. Where possible, the Moche extended their ambitious irrigation systems to link several neighboring river valleys, and then constructed lesser copies of their capital as a basis for secure administration of their new domains. Their traders were in contact with the north and with the Nasca people on the south coast as well (Proulx, 1983a). In approximately A.D. 600, the Moche people moved their center of administrative activity north to the Pampa Grande in the Lambayeque Valley. By this time the southern centers were abandoned, as the political and economic influence of the southern highlands and coast began to rise. The agricultural system of the southern valleys may have collapsed, perhaps as a result of major droughts. So the people moved north to an area where there was more water. They may also have been under pressure from Wari people inland.

THE MIDDLE HORIZON: THE FIRST EMPIRES

A series of brilliant states had flourished on the coast and in the highlands during the Early Intermediate Period — Moche on the north coast, Nasca in the south, and Recuay in the northern highlands, to mention only a few. The same period also saw the beginnings of monumental building at a highland site that would influence much of the Peruvian world — Tiwanaku (Proulx, 1985).

Between A.D. 600 and 1000 (the so-called Middle Horizon), the wealthiest highland districts lay at the southern end of the central Andes, in the high flat country surrounding Lake Titicaca. This was fine llama country. The local people maintained enormous herds of these beasts of burden. The *altiplano* supported the densest population in the highlands, and, almost inevitably, the Titicaca region became an economic and demographic pole to the prosperous northern coast. By A.D. 200 Tiwanaku, on the eastern side of the lake, was becoming a major population center as well as an important economic and religious focus for the region (Kolata, 1982, 1986). The arid lands on which the site lies were irrigated and supported a population of perhaps 20,000 around the monumental structures near the center of the site. By A.D. 600 Tiwanaku was acquiring much of its prosperity from trade around the lake's southern shores. Copperworking was especially important and probably developed independently of the well-established copper technology on the northern coast.

Middle Horizon
A.D. 600 TO 1000

Tiwanaku
? A.D 200 to c. A.D. 1200

Tiwanaku was not only an economic force, it was a very important religious one as well. The great enclosure of Kalasasaya is dominated by a large earth platform faced with stones. Nearby, a rectangular enclosure is bounded with a row of upright stones and there is a doorway carved with an anthropomorphic god, believed to be the creator deity, Viracocha (Figure 23.9). Smaller buildings, enclosures, and huge statues are also near the ceremonial structures.

But it is the Tiwanaku art style that is most striking. Like Chavín, this tradition probably represents a powerful iconography. Tiwanaku's art motifs include jaguars and eagles as well as anthropomorphic gods being attended to by lesser deities or messengers. They occur over much of southern Peru, as well as in Bolivia, the southern Andes, and perhaps as far afield as northwest Argentina. So powerful was the iconography, and, presumably, the political and economic forces behind Tiwanaku, that there was a serious political vacuum in the south after A.D. 1200, when Tiwanaku inexplicably collapsed into obscurity.

The influence of Tiwanaku can be seen at Wari in the Mantaro Valley, an important ceremonial center that stands on a hill (Isbell and Schreiber, 1978; Rowe, Collier, and Willey, 1950). It is associated with huge stone walls and many dwellings that cover several square miles. The Wari art styles show some Tiwanaku influence, especially in anthropomorphic, feline, eagle, and serpent

FIGURE 23.9 Gateway of the Sun at Tiwanaku, made from one block of lava. The central figure is known as the Gateway god; notice its jaguar mouth and serpent-ray headdress. The running figures flanking the god often are called messengers.

Wari
? A.D. 600 to
A.D. 900

beings depicted on ceramic vessels. Like their southern neighbors, the Wari people seem to have revered a Viracochalike being. By A.D. 800, their domains extended from Moche country in the Lambayeque Valley on the northern coast to south of Nasca territory, and into the highlands south of Cuzco. They were expert traders, who probably expanded their domain through conquest, commercial enterprise, and perhaps religious conversion. Storehouses and roads probably were maintained by the state. As with the Inca of later centuries, the state controlled food supplies and labor (Schreiber, 1987).

Wari itself was abandoned in the ninth century A.D., but its art styles persisted on the coast for at least two more centuries. Both Wari and Tiwanaku were a turning point in Peruvian prehistory, a stage when small, regional states became integrated into much larger political units. This unification may have been achieved by conquest and other coercive means, but the iconography shared by many coastal and highland Peruvians at the time must have been a powerful catalyst for closer political unity.

These two great polities collapsed toward the end of the first millennium, leaving a vast political vacuum of small, competing tribes that was filled by the Inca after a period of conflict and warfare.

THE LATE INTERMEDIATE PERIOD: LATE COASTAL STATES

Chimu

The highland states traded regularly with several emerging polities on the coast, each of them founded on extensive irrigation systems. Of these, the most famous is the Chimu kingdom, centered on the Moche Valley of the northern coast, the same area inhabited 400 years earlier by the Moche peoples. The Moche Valley had long been densely cultivated, but the Chimu people now embarked on much more ambitious irrigation schemes; they built large storage reservoirs and terraced hundreds of miles of hillside to control the flow of water down steep slopes. One channel extended nearly 20 miles (32 km) from the Chicama Valley to the capital, Chan Chan, designed to supplement the relatively limited water supplies that came from the nearby Moche Valley (Figure 23.10). Even in periods of extreme drought these canals carried water from the deep-cut riverbed to terraces long distances away. Thus, the Chimu created thousands of acres of new fields and used water from great distances to harvest two or three crops a year from plots where only one crop had been possible before, and that at the time of the annual flood. So effective were these irrigation techniques that the Chimu controlled more than twelve river valleys with at least 125,000 cultivable acres, all of it farmed with hoes or digging sticks. Today, the local Indians water their maize crops approximately every ten days, and this probably was the practice in Chimu times as well (Bankes, 1977).

Chimu
? A.D. 1000 to 1476

FIGURE 23.10 Chan Chan. Oblique air photograph of a walled enclosure or compound.

According to seventeenth-century Spanish chroniclers, the Chimu always maintained that their domains were originally ruled over by petty chiefs, but when the Inca conquered them between 1462 and 1470 they were led by a ruler named Michancamán, who governed through a network of hereditary local nobility. His courtiers held specific ranks, such as "Blower of the Shell Trumpet," "Master of the Litter and Thrones," and "Preparer of the Way," the official who scattered powdered shell dust wherever the ruler was about to walk. An archaeologist working at Chan Chan in 1969–70 found a layer of powdered shell dust on a bench in a forecourt, perhaps evidence that the Preparer of the Way had been at work. The various provinces of the kingdom were ruled by loyal local leaders. They enjoyed not only tribute privileges but also rights to crops and land and to agricultural labor by commoners. Perhaps the most privileged members of society were the *Oquetlupec,* herb curers paid by the state to look after the sick. This was a hierarchical, highly organized society with strict social classes of nobles and commoners, but one in which women's rights were nearly equal to those of men. Perhaps to enforce the social hierarchy, the legal system was very strict (Rowe, 1946).

The focus of the Chimu state was Chan Chan, a huge complex of walled compounds lying near the Pacific at the mouth of the Moche Valley. Chan Chan covers nearly 4 square miles (10.3 sq km), the central part consisting of nine large enclosures laid out in a sort of broken rectangle. Each enclosure probably functioned as the palace for the current ruler of Chan Chan, who probably built himself a new headquarters near those of his predecessors (Lanning, 1967; Moseley, 1975a; Moseley and Day, 1982). The adobe walls of these compounds once stood as high as 33 feet (9.9 m) and covered areas as large as 670 by 2000 feet (201 by 600 m). The walls were not constructed to defend the rulers but to provide privacy and some shelter against the ocean winds. Each enclosure had its own water supply, a burial platform, and lavishly decorated residential rooms roofed with cane frames covered with earth and grass. The same enclosure that served as a palace during life became the ruler's burial place in death. The common people lived in tracts of small adobe and reed-mat houses on the western side of the city. Similar dwellings can be seen on the coast to this day.

Oral traditions tell us that when a Chimu ruler died, his successor inherited the office of supreme leader, but the lands, revenues, and wealth of the deceased went to junior members of the family, who were responsible for venerating the memory of the dead man. Consequently, the new ruler had to build his own palace and raise new revenues to finance his reign. He had only one resource to achieve such goals: control of a huge labor pool. The Chimu rulers employed laborers to expand and maintain irrigation works, in addition to their serving as military levies to acquire new lands and expand the tax base. Rulers soon learned the value of efficient communications, of officially maintained roadways that enabled them to move their armies from one place to the next with rapid dispatch. They constructed roads that connected each valley in their domain with the capital. The rural routes were little more than tracks between low adobe walls or widely spaced posts, mostly following centuries-old paths through the fields. In the densely populated valleys, Chimu roads were between 15 and 25 feet (4.5 and 7.5 m) across. In some places the roadway widened dramatically to 80 feet (24 m) or more. These were the roads that carried gold ornaments and fine hammered vessels to Chan Chan and textiles and fine black painted vessels throughout the empire. The traveler occasionally would encounter heavily laden llamas carrying goods to market, but most loads were carried on people's backs, for the Chimu had never heard of the wheeled cart. All revenues and tribute passed along the official roadways, as did newly conquered peoples being resettled in some area far from their original homeland. This draconian resettlement tactic was so successful that the Inca adopted it. The ruler then would install his own appointee in the new lands, in a compound-palace that was a smaller version of Chan Chan itself.

The Chimu Empire extended far south, at least to Casma, perhaps reaching to the vicinity of modern Lima, for the main focus of civilization lay on the northern Peruvian littoral, where the soils were fertile and large-scale irrigation was a practical reality. Chimu armies fought with powerful neighbors to the south, among them the chief of Pachácamac, who controlled some narrow valleys south of Lima. Pachácamac had long been a venerated shrine and already boasted a terraced temple covering two-thirds of an acre (0.3 ha). Pachácamac has been a grave robbers' paradise for centuries. Later, the Inca built a vast Temple of the Sun at Pachácamac, an irregular trapezoid in a commanding position on a rocky hill.

For all its wide-ranging military activities and material wealth, the Chimu Empire was very vulnerable to attack from outside. The massive irrigation works of the northern river valleys were easily disrupted by an aggressive conqueror, for no leader, however powerful, could hope to fortify the entire frontier of the empire. We know little of the defenses, except for Paramonga in the Fortaleza Valley, a massive terraced structure built of rectangular adobes that overlooks the probable southern limits of Chimu territory. The Chimu were vulnerable to prolonged drought, too, for the storage capacity of their great irrigation works was only sufficient to carry them over one or two lean seasons. Perhaps, too, the irrigated desert soils became too saline for agriculture, so that crop yields fell drastically at a time when population densities were rising sharply. Since the Chimu depended on a highly specialized agricultural system, once that system was disrupted — whether by natural or artificial causes — military conquest and control of the irrigation network was easy, especially for aggressive and skillful conquerors such as the Inca, who pounced on the Chimu in the 1460s.

THE LATE HORIZON: THE INCA STATE

The Late Horizon of Peruvian archaeology was also the shortest, dating from A.D. 1476 to 1534. It is the period of the Inca Empire, when those mighty Andean rulers held sway over an enormous area of highland and lowland country (Bankes, 1977; Rowe, 1946).

Late Horizon
A.D. 1476 to 1534

The Inca were born into an intensely competitive world, their homeland lying to the northwest of the Titicaca basin, in the area around Cuzco (for an extended description, see Conrad and Demarest, 1984). They were a small-scale farming society living in small villages, organized in kin groups known as *ayllu*, groups claiming a common ancestry and also owning land in common. The Inca were a self-sufficient people, and their ayllu leaders contributed labor to one another as a means of organizing and distributing labor on a reciprocal basis. The ayllu was legitimized in its land ownership and protected by the ancestors. It was small wonder that the Inca always took good care of their ancestral mummies. The bodies of the dead, their tombs, and their fetishes, as well as numerous other sacred places and phenomena, were known as *huaca*.

The later Inca rulers clothed their origins in a glorious panoply of heroic deeds. It is likely, however, that the Inca were a fractious, constantly quarreling petty chiefdom. The chronicles of early conquest reflect the constant bickering of village headmen, and the earliest Inca rulers were probably petty war leaders *(sinchi)*, elected officials whose success was measured by their victories and booty. But to stay in office, they had to be politically and militarily adept so that they could both defeat and appease their many potential rivals. The official Inca histories spoke of at least eight Inca rulers between 1200 and 1438, but these genealogies are hardly reliable (Rowe, 1946). They probably depict little more than legendary figures. During the fourteenth century, a number of small tribal groups in the southern highlands began to develop a more powerful military confederacy, but the Inca flourished in this competitive atmosphere because their leaders were expert politicians as well as warriors. A leader named Viracocha Inca rose to power at the beginning of the fifteenth century. Unlike his raiding predecessors, however, he turned to permanent conquest and soon presided over a small kingdom centered in Cuzco. Viracocha Inca became the living god, the first in a series of constant religious changes that kept the new kingdom under tight control. At about the same time a new religious cult emerged, that of Inti, a celestial divine ancestor who was part of the sky god. (We say *part* because Inti was more of a cluster of solar aspects than the sun god).

Around 1438, a brilliant warrior named Cusi Inca Yupanqui was crowned Inca after a memorable victory over the neighboring Chanca tribe. He immediately took the name Pachakuti ("He Who Remakes the World") and set about transforming the Inca state. In particular, he and his henchmen developed a form of royal ancestor cult. This in itself was not especially significant, since Pachakuti simply reworked an age-old Andean tradition, but the law of split inheritance that went along with it had a lasting and profound significance. A dead ruler was mummified. His palace, servants, and possessions were still considered his property and were maintained by all his male descendants *except* his successor, normally one of his sons. The deceased was not considered dead, however. His mummy attended great ceremonies and would even visit the houses of the living. Those entrusted to look after the king ate and talked with him, just as if his life were still going on. This element of continuity was extremely important, because it made the royal mummies some of the holiest artifacts in the empire. Dead rulers were living sons of Inti, visible links with the gods, the very embodiment of the Inca state and of the fertility of nature. Meanwhile the ascending ruler was rich in prestige but poor in possessions. The new king had to acquire wealth, so he could both live in royal splendor and provide for his mummy in the future — and the only wealth in the highland kingdom was taxable labor.

Therefore, every adult in Inca country had to render a certain amount of labor to the state each year after providing for the basic subsistence needs of his own ayllu. This *mita* system repaired bridges and roads, cultivated state-owned lands, manned the armies, and carried out public works. It was a reciprocal system. The state, or those benefiting from the work, had to feed and entertain those doing it. But the split inheritance of the Inca rulers meant that all taxes levied by their predecessors went to them and not to the newcomer. He had to develop a new tax base and could do this in only two ways: by levying more labor from existing taxpayers or by conquering new lands. Since the Inca rulers needed land to provide food for those who worked for them and the earlier kings owned most of the land near Cuzco, the only way a new ruler could obtain his own royal estates was by expansion into new territory. This expansion could not take the form of temporary raids. The conquest had to be permanent, the conquered territory had to be controlled and taxed, and the ruler's subjects had to be convinced of the value of a policy of long-term conquest.

The Inca rulers turned into brilliant propagandists, reminding everyone that they were gods and that the welfare of all depended on the prosperity of all rulers, past and present, and on constant military conquest. There were initial economic advantages, too, in the form of better protection against famine. Also, the rulers were careful to reward prowess in battle. Nobles were promoted to new posts and awarded insignia that brought their life style ever closer to that of the king, and even a brave commoner could become a member of the secondary nobility. A highly complicated set of benefits, economic incentives, rewards, and justifications fueled and nourished the Inca conquests. Their successful ideology provided them with a crucial advantage over their neighbors, and within a decade of Pachakuti's accession they were masters of the southern highlands. Their army had become an invincible juggernaut, and in less than a century the tiny kingdom taken over by Pachakuti had become a vast empire. Topa Yupanqui (1471–1493) extended the Inca Empire into Ecuador, northern Argentina, parts of Bolivia, and Chile. His armies also conquered the Chimu state, whose water supplies Topa already controlled. The best Chimu craftsworkers were carried off to work for the court of the Incas. Another king, Huanya Capac, ruled for thirty-four years after Topa Inca and pushed the empire deeper into Ecuador.

The Inca rulers developed an efficient administrative system to run their empire, one based firmly on the precedents of earlier societies. *Tawantinsuyu*, "The Land of the Four Quarters," was divided into four large provinces known as *suyu* (quarters), each subdivided into smaller provinces, some of them coinciding with older, conquered kingdoms. The conquered peoples in the Inca empire were usually ruled by a leading member of a local family, known as a *curaca*. These hereditary chiefs were a form of secondary non-Inca nobility who governed a taxpaying population of 100 people or more, but all the really important government posts were held by Inca nobles. The Inca rulers realized, however, that the essence of efficient government in such varied topography was efficient communications, so the road builders commandeered a vast network of age-old Indian highways from the states they conquered. They linked them in a coordinated system with regular rest houses so that they could move armies, trade goods, and messengers from one end of the kingdom to the other in short order (Hyslop, 1984).

The Incas' passion for organization impinged on everyone's life. Their society was organized into twelve age divisions for the purposes of census and tax assessment, divisions based on both physical changes like puberty and major social events like marriage. The most important stage was adulthood, which lasted as long as one could do a day's work. All the census and other data of the empire were recorded not on tablets but on knotted strings. The *quipu* were a complex and sophisticated record-keeping system that seems to have been so efficient that it more than made up for the lack of writing (Ascher and Ascher, 1981). They also were a powerful instrument for enforcing social conformity, codifying laws, and providing data for the inspectors, who regularly visited each household to check that everyone was engaged in productive work and living in sanitary conditions. No one could travel without official permission. Everything about the Inca lifeway stressed conformity, and the need to respect and obey the central government.

At the time of the Spanish conquest, the Inca controlled the lives of as many as 6 million people, most of them living in small villages dispersed around religious and political centers. It was here that Inca artisans labored, producing major works of art in gold and silver. Bronze was widely used also, mostly for agricultural implements and weapons. Brightly painted Inca pottery is found throughout the empire; it is decorated with black, white, and red geometric designs. Despite the widespread distribution of Inca pots and artifacts, however,

FIGURE 23.11 Inca masonry from the fortress of Sacsahuaman, near Cuzco.

regional pottery styles flourished because the village potters, many of whom were conquered subjects, continued the cultural traditions of earlier centuries.

Inca political and religious power was centered on major urban complexes like Cuzco in the Andes, where the ceremonial center was built of carefully fitted stones (Figure 23.11) (Protzen, 1986). Such locations as Machu Picchu, high in the Andes (Figure 23.12), are famous for their fine masonry structures (Gasparini and Margolies, 1980). The Inca himself held court in Cuzco, surrounded by plotting factions and ever-changing political tides. One villain was the very institution of split inheritance that fueled Inca military conquest. Every ruler faced increasingly complex governance problems as a result. The need for more and more conquests caused great military, economic, and administrative stress. The logistics of long-distance military campaigns were horrendous, and the soldiers had to be fed from state-owned land, not royal estates. Moreover, while their tactics were well adapted to open country, where their armies were invincible, the rulers eventually had to start fighting in forest country, where they fared badly. Meanwhile the empire had grown so large that communication became a lengthier and lengthier process, compounded by the great diversity of people living within the Inca domain. Also, the increasing number of high-ranking nobles devoted to the interests of dead rulers led to chronic

Cuzco

Machu Picchu

FIGURE 23.12 Machu Picchu. Forgotten for 400 years after the Spanish conquest, it was rediscovered by the American explorer Hiram Bingham in 1911.

factionalism in Cuzco. Under its glittering facade, *Tawantinsuyu* was becoming a rotten apple. In the end, the Inca Empire was overthrown not by Peruvians but by a tiny band of foreigners with firearms who could exploit the inherent vulnerability of such a hierarchical, conforming society.

THE SPANISH CONQUEST: 1532–1534

This vulnerability came home to roost in 1532, when a small party of rapacious Spanish conquistadors landed in northern Peru. When Francisco Pizarro arrived, the Inca state was in some political chaos, its people already decimated by smallpox and other diseases introduced by the first conquistadors. Inca Huayna Capac had died in an epidemic in A.D. 1525. The empire was plunged into a civil war between his son Huascar and another son, Atahuallpa, half-brother to Huascar. Atahuallpa eventually prevailed, but, as he moved south from Ecuador to consolidate his territory, he learned that Pizarro had landed in Peru.

A.D. 1533
A.D. 1536

The Spaniards had vowed to make Peru part of Spain and were bent on plunder and conquest. Pizarro arrived in the guise of a diplomat, captured Atahuallpa by treachery, ransomed him for a huge quantity of gold, and then brutally murdered him. A year later the Spaniards captured the Inca capital with a tiny army. They took over the state bureaucracy and appointed Manco Inca as puppet ruler. Three years later, Manco Inca turned on his masters in a bloody revolt. Its suppression finally destroyed the greatest of the Peruvian empires.

The Spanish conquest of Mexico and Peru saw the first major confrontation between the forces of an expanding Europe emerging from centuries of feudalism and complex non-Western societies that were still living with the full legacy of prehistoric times.

THE END OF PREHISTORY

The four and a half centuries since the Spanish conquests of Mexico and Peru have seen European settlement in all corners of the globe, the emergence of the industrial state, and the acting out of the last, tragic chapter of human prehistory: the clash between the Western and non-Western worlds (Fagan, 1984b). The basic scenario was relived again and again. A small party of European explorers arrived, like Captain James Cook in Tahiti or the French voyager Marion du Fresne in Tasmania. The first encounter was a fleeting kaleidoscope of curiosity, sometimes horrified fascination, and often romantic excitement. Sometimes even experts like Cook had trouble understanding peoples like the Tasmanians or Australian aborigines. "They wander about in small parties from place to place in search of food," he wrote. "They are all together an ignorant, wretched race of mortals, though at the same time the natives of a country capable of producing every necessity of life." Right from the beginning there was incomprehension.

Even in paradisal areas like the South Seas, initial romance soon turned to bitter disillusionment on both sides. Sometimes the people thought their strange visitors were gods, as the Aztec did Hernán Cortés. An elderly Maori chief in New Zealand told a nineteenth-century official that the priests had told them the whites were goblins with eyes in the back of their heads, an apparent reference to their oarsmen facing the stern in their boats. Soon, the strangers proved to be aggressive, warlike, and acquisitive, all too human in their ambitions and goals. And their exotic diseases decimated tens of thousands of people, in California alone millions of Indians within a few generations.

At first the contacts were brief ones, with Europeans coming to trade furs, refit their ships, or search for gold. Then the missionaries arrived, seeking to convert the heathen and save their souls. They were followed by colonists, often impoverished, land-hungry farmers who saw a better life in the fertile soils of Tasmania, New Zealand, British Columbia, and the African interior. It was then that the process of catastrophic culture change began, and indigenous hunters, foragers, fisherfolk, and farmers started competing for land with the newcomers. Inevitably, the strangers with their iron tools and firearms won, and the indigenous population retreated into marginal areas and enclaves, where they preserved a shadow of their former culture and lifeway, if they were able to survive at all.

Today, the clash of cultures is still in inexorable progress, deep in the Amazon rain forest and in highland New Guinea, where rain forests are felled and age-old lifeways destroyed forever. The world lives with a tragic legacy of misunderstanding as we face what will probably be the question of questions for the twenty-first century: How do we bridge the great gulf of incomprehension that exists between the Western and non-Western worlds, between the rich and the poor? How can we begin to understand human biological and cultural diversity in all its bewildering complexity? Our journey through 2 million years of human prehistory has shown you just how similar humans are in their general behavior and their responses to a multitude of environmental challenges. We are all part of the same human family, and archaeology is just about the only way we have to understand many of the forces that shaped today's world. We hope *People of the Earth* has given you some understanding of the compelling biological and cultural forces that have shaped our past and will help shape our future.

GUIDE TO FURTHER READING

Bankes, George. *Peru Before Pizarro.* Oxford: Phaidon, 1977.
    A useful introduction to Peruvian archaeology that examines different aspects of prehistoric life. Good for the beginner.

Conrad, Geoffrey W., and Demarest, Arthur A. *Religion and Empire: The Dynamics of Aztec and Inca Expansionism.* Cambridge: Cambridge University Press, 1984.
    A clear and succinct analysis of two imperial, preindustrial civilizations. A sophisticated, well-argued book. Strongly recommended.

Jennings, Jesse D. (ed.). *Ancient Native Americans.* San Francisco: Freeman, 1983.
    Summary essays on Peruvian archaeology that are admirable introductions to a complex subject.

Keatinge, Richard (ed.). *Peruvian Prehistory*. Cambridge: Cambridge University Press, 1988.

Essays reviewing the current state of Peruvian archaeology.

Moseley, Michael E. *The Maritime Foundations of Andean Civilization*. Menlo Park, Calif.: Cummings, 1975.

A short essay that argues that the foundations of Peruvian civilization lay on the coast, in subsistence patterns that relied heavily on maritime resources. Controversial but convincing for the most part.

Rowe, John H. *Inca Culture at the Time of the Spanish Conquest. Handbook of South American Indians*, vol. 2. Washington, D.C.: Smithsonian Institution, 1946.

The classic account of Inca culture reconstructed from historical documents and limited archaeological investigations.

Willey, Gordon R. *An Introduction to American Archaeology: South America*, vol. 2. Englewood Cliffs, N.J.: Prentice Hall, 1971.

A culture history of South America that still is the ultimate source for all basic research conducted in Peru up to the 1970s. Especially strong on the coast. Very much for the advanced student.

The Calibration of Radiocarbon Dates

IMPORTANT NOTE

It has been apparent for some time that the ages provided by most radiocarbon samples suffer from considerable inaccuracies owing to variations in cosmic ray bombardment of the earth. As is explained in Chapter 1, dates from sites to about 7250 years old (about 5300 B.C.) can be calibrated by using tree rings to provide absolutely accurate ages.

These calibrations place me in somewhat of a chronological dilemma. Calibrated radiocarbon dates are used regularly only in a few parts of the world, noticeably in Europe, whereas many American archaeologists ignore them. Should we use calibrated dates in *People of the Earth*?

I have set up the text in such a way that you can use calibrated dates if you wish. Each chronological table has a column giving radiocarbon ages, another giving the calibrated dates. You can read from whichever column you wish.

The dates in the margins are uncalibrated except in the European chapters, where such dates are commonly used. You can convert them to C14 ages by referring to the requisite chronological table. The following conventions are used:

> *Radiocarbon ages and dates established by historical chronologies, tree-ring dating, and other methods* are expressed as follows: A.D. 1225 or 3250 B.C., with the A.D./B.C. convention in *Roman* letters.
>
> *Calibrated dates* are expressed in tables as follows: a.d. 1225 or 3250 b.c., with lowercase letters.

This procedure follows common European practice. It should be noted that dates *earlier* than about 7250 years ago are at present beyond the range of calibration tables and must be treated as radiocarbon ages.

Until recently, there were several different calibration tables. However, the major laboratories have got together and produced an agreed-upon calibration chart, which is used in this book. The tables can be consulted in Jeffrey Klein, J. C. Lerman, P. E. Damon, and E. K. Ralph, "Calibration of Radiocarbon Dates: Tables Based on the Consensus Data of the Workshop on Calibrating the Radiocarbon Time Scale," *Radiocarbon*, 1982, 24(2):103–149.

CALIBRATION TABLE

The following are the calibrations for 500-year intervals from A.D. 1500 to 7250 years ago.*

Radiocarbon age A.D./B.C./B.P.	Calibrated age range a.d./b.c./b.p.
1500	1300 to 1515
1000	870 to 1230
500	265 to 640
A.D. 1	a.d. 420 to 5 b.c.
500 B.C.	820 to 400
3000 B.P.	3530 to 2905 b.p.
3500	4345 to 3660
4000	4830 to 4305
4500	5505 to 4925
5000	5950 to 5640
5500	6545 to 5960
6000	7235 to 6575
6500	7705 to 7205
7000	8285 to 7445
7300	8585 to 8595
Before 7500	Outside calibration range

* Calibrated dates are based on an assumed standard deviation of 100 years. Date range varies with standard deviation (see tables).

Bibliography
of Archaeology

The chapters on the basic methods and theory of archaeology in this book are necessarily sketchy. To supplement these, here is an annotated bibliography of primary sources on aspects of archaeology itself.

WORLD PREHISTORIES

J. G. D. Clark's *World Prehistory: A New Outline,* Cambridge University Press, Cambridge, 1977, is the third edition of a global culture history that is strong on later prehistory and gives little consideration to theoretical controversies. Robert Wenke's *Patterns in Prehistory,* second edition, Oxford University Press, New York, 1984, is an authoritative account, with a strong ecological and evolutionary emphasis. Ronald L. Wallace's *Those Who Have Vanished*, Dorsey Press, Homewood, Illinois, 1983, is a basic college text that covers most major culture areas of the world.

GENERAL BOOKS ON METHOD AND THEORY IN ARCHAEOLOGY

A good starting point is my own *Archaeology: A Brief Introduction*, third edition, Scott, Foresman/Little Brown, Boston, 1988, or, if you want a more detailed treatment, any of the following: Brian M. Fagan, *In the Beginning,* sixth edition, Scott, Foresman/Little, Brown, Boston, 1988; Frank Hole and Robert F. Heizer, *An Introduction to Prehistoric Archaeology,* third edition, Holt, Rinehart and Winston, New York, 1973; the same authors' *Prehistoric Archaeology: A Brief Introduction,* Holt, Rinehart and Winston, New York, 1977; and Robert J. Sharer and Wendy Ashmore, *Archeology: Discovering the Past,* Mayfield Publishing Company, Palo Alto, Calif., 1987. All these works will lead the reader to the major controversies in the field.

HISTORY OF ARCHAEOLOGY

Brian M. Fagan, *The Adventure of Archaeology*, National Geographic Society, Washington, D.C., 1985, is a lavishly illustrated account of early archaeology for the layperson. You can amplify it with Glyn E. Daniel's *A Short History of Archaeology*, Thames and Hudson, London, 1981, and the same author's *A Hundred and Fifty Years of Archaeology*, Duckworth, London, 1976. American archaeology is described by Gordon R. Willey and Jeremy A. Sabloff in *A History of American Archaeology*, second edition, W. H. Freeman, San Francisco, 1980. The history of archaeological theory has been poorly served by archaeological writers, but Marvin Harris, *The Rise of Anthropological Theory*, Crowell, New York, 1968, is an invaluable if polemical source. W. W. Taylor, *A Study of Archaeology*, American Anthropological Association, Menasha, Wisconsin, 1948, also is a landmark monograph.

TIME

How archaeologists date their finds has been summarized by Joseph W. Michels, *Dating Methods in Archaeology*, Seminar Press, New York, 1973. H. N. Michael and E. K. Ralph, editors, *Dating Techniques for the Archaeologist*, MIT Press, Cambridge, 1971, also is useful. So is Stuart Fleming, *Dating in Archaeology*, St. Martin's Press, London, 1977. Karl Butzer's *Environment and Archaeology*, third edition, Aldine Press, Chicago, 1974, is a good source on Pleistocene geochronology. Andrew Goudie, *Environmental Change*, second edition, Clarendon Press, Oxford, 1983, is an admirable introduction. David Q. Bowen's *Quaternary Geology*, Oxford University Press, Oxford, 1978, describes the subject with clear eloquence. V. Gordon Childe's *Piecing Together the Past*, Routledge and Kegan Paul, London, 1956, contains an interesting and cogent section on chronology and dating. Stratigraphy is well summarized by Sir Mortimer Wheeler, *Archaeology from the Earth*, Clarendon Press, Oxford, 1954; and Edward Pydokke, *Stratification for the Archaeologist*, Phoenix, London, 1961, is a useful source.

ARCHAEOLOGICAL SURVEY

A good survey of preservation conditions is to be found in J. G. D. Clark, *Archaeology and Society*, Barnes and Noble, New York, 1965. S. J. de Laet, *Archaeology and Its Problems*, Macmillan, New York, 1957, is also useful. Remote sensing is a burgeoning field. Try Robert N. Colwell, editor, *Manual of Remote Sensing*, second edition, Society of Photogrammetry, Falls Church, Virginia, 1983. Thomas N. Hester, J. Sharer, and R. F. Heizer's *Field Methods in Archaeology*, Mayfield Publishing Company, Palo Alto, California, 1988, contains much of value on archaeological survey.

EXCAVATION

Really good excavation manuals are few and far between. I think H. S. Dancey, *Archaeological Field Methods: An Introduction*, Burgess Publishing Company, Minneapolis, 1981, is the best one on American conditions. Martha Joukowsky, *A Complete Manual of Field Archaeology*, Prentice-Hall, Englewood Cliffs, New Jersey, 1981, and Hester, Sharer, and Heizer's *Field Methods*, already mentioned, are widely used. Phillip Barker, *Techniques of Archaeological Excavation*, second edition, Batsford, London, 1983, gives a more international perspective. On conservation, see Elizabeth A. Dowman, *Conservation in Field Archaeology*, Methuen, London, 1970, and for photography see V. M. Conlon, *Camera Techniques in Archaeology*, John Baker, London, 1973. See also Elmer Harp, *Photography for Archaeologists*, Academic Press, New York, 1978.

Historical archaeology is most ably covered by Ivor Noël Hume, *Historical Archaeology*, Knopf, New York, 1968, and underwater archaeology is summarized by George Bass, *Archaeology Underwater*, Praeger, New York, 1966. The same author's *A History of Seafaring Based on Underwater Archaeology*, Thames and Hudson, London, 1972, is a beautiful summary of the results of underwater research. Paul L. MacKendrick, *The Greek Stones Speak*, St. Martin's Press, New York, 1962, and *The Mute Stones Speak*, St. Martin's Press, New York, 1961, are two surveys of Classical archaeology. On industrial archaeology, see Kenneth Hudson, *World Industrial Archaeology*, Cambridge University Press, Cambridge, 1979. Last, Warwick Bray and David Trump, *A Dictionary of Archaeology*, Penguin Press, London, 1970, is a useful tool.

ENVIRONMENT AND SUBSISTENCE

There is no one comprehensive volume on economic archaeology, but the following are widely used and cited: bones are covered by Richard G. Klein and Kathryn Cruz-Uribe, *The Analysis of Animal Bones from Archaeological Sites*, University of Chicago Press, Chicago, 1984. Lewis R. Binford, *Bones*, Academic Press, New York, 1981, is a provocative essay on the problems of interpreting faunal remains. Seeds and vegetal remains are covered by Jane M. Renfrew, *Palaeoethnobotany: The Prehistoric Plants of the Near East*, Methuen, London, 1973; also by Richard I. Ford, editor, *Prehistoric Food Production in North America*, Museum of Anthropology, University of Michigan, Ann Arbor, 1985. This volume of essays takes into account flotation research. Michael Jochim's *Strategies for Survival: Cultural Behavior in Ecological Context*, Academic Press, New York, 1981, focuses on the relationship between culture, behavior, and the environment.

TECHNOLOGY

The literature on ancient technology is enormous, but the following are useful introductions. Stone technology is summarized by J. Bordaz, *Tools of the Old and New Stone Age*, American Museum of Natural History, New York, 1971. François Bordes, *The Old Stone Age*, McGraw-Hill, New York, 1968, contains much information on stone tool types. Earl Swanson's edited *Lithic Technology*, Mouton, The Hague, 1975, surveys the techniques. Anna O. Shepard, *Ceramics for the Archaeologist*, Smithsonian Institution, Washington, D.C., 1956, is still a definitive work on pottery. The literature on metallurgy is enormous, but Theodore A. Wertime and James D. Mulhy, editors, *The Coming of the Age of Iron*, Yale University Press, New Haven, 1980, surveys the major issues. David L. Clarke's *Analytical Archaeology*, revised edition, Methuen, London, 1978, Chapters 11–14, has a lengthy analysis of advanced taxonomic methods.

ORDERING AND INTERPRETATION

Gordon R. Willey and Philip Phillips, *Method and Theory in American Archaeology*, University of Chicago Press, Chicago, 1958, contains fundamental reading on archaeological units. V. Gordon Childe, *Piecing Together the Past*, cited earlier, is another thought-provoking source. The principles of diffusion, migration, and independent invention are well described by Bruce G. Trigger, *Beyond History: The Methods of Prehistory*, Holt, Rinehart and Winston, New York, 1968, and by V. Gordon Childe, *Piecing Together the Past*. Colin Renfrew has edited a large volume of papers, *The Explanation of Culture Change: Models in Prehistory*, Duckworth, London, 1973, which contain much provocative and theoretical discussion on cultural process. See also W. W. Taylor, *A Study of Archaeology*, American Anthropological Association, Menasha, Wisconsin, 1948; and Fred T. Plog, *The Study of Prehistoric Change*, Academic Press, New York, 1974. A good volume on typology is Robert Whallon and James A. Brown, *Essays on Archaeological Typology*, Center for American Archaeology, Evanston, Illinois, 1982.

PROCESSUAL ARCHAEOLOGY

Patty Jo Watson, Steven LeBlanc, and Charles L. Redman, *Archeological Explanation: The Scientific Method in Archeology*, Columbia University Press, New York, 1984, is a useful starting point. Then try Lewis R. Binford, *An Archaeological Perspective*, Academic Press, New York, 1972, which has a very personal essay on the development of processual archaeology and reprints Binford's major papers. The same author's *In Pursuit of the Past*, Thames and Hudson, New York, 1983, summarizes his basic viewpoints, while *Working at Archaeology*, Academic Press, New York, 1983, is a collection of his papers. Guy Gibbon, *Anthropological Archaeology*, Columbia University Press, New York, 1984, highlights the confusion at the cutting edge of theoretical research. Ian Hodder, editor, *Symbolic and Structural Archaeology*, Cambridge University Press, Cambridge, 1982, contains essays on a "structural" approach to prehistory.

SETTLEMENT ARCHAEOLOGY

Karl Butzer, *Archaeology as Human Ecology: Method and Theory for a Contextual Approach*, Cambridge University Press, Cambridge, 1982, describes basic spatial and environmental concepts in archaeology. This is a fundamental source, as is Kent V. Flannery's edited *The Early Mesoamerican Village*, Academic Press, New York, 1976, which talks more common sense about contemporary archaeology than any other source known to me. For trade in prehistory, see Jeremy A. Sabloff and C. C. Lamberg-Karlovsky, editors, *Early Civilization and Trade*, University of New Mexico Press, Albuquerque, 1975. Perhaps the most comprehensive settlement study to date is William T. Sanders, Jeffrey R. Parsons, and Robert S. Santley, *The Basin of Mexico: Ecological Processes in the Evolution of a Civilization*, Academic Press, New York, 1979.

ETHNOARCHAEOLOGY, EXPERIMENTAL ARCHAEOLOGY

Much of this literature is in periodical form, but the following will be of help in finding references. Richard A. Gould, editor, *Explorations in Ethnoarchaeology*, University of New Mexico Press, Albuquerque, 1978. Also see John E. Yellen, *Archaeological Approaches to the Present*, Academic Press, New York, 1977. Lewis R. Binford, *Nunamiut Ethnoarchaeology*, Academic Press, New York, 1978, is a much-quoted case study. Another aspect of living archaeology is ably summarized by John Coles, *Archaeology by Experiment*, Hutchinson University Library, London, 1973. Also see D. Ingersoll and colleagues, *Experimental Archeology*, Columbia University Press, New York, 1977.

DESTRUCTION OF ARCHAEOLOGICAL SITES

Karl Meyer, *The Plundered Past*, Atheneum Press, New York, 1973, is a fascinating and shocking account of the illegal traffic in antiquities. C. R. McGimsey, *Public Archaeology*, Seminar Press, New York, 1973, is fundamental reading for all American archaeologists. Massimo Pallotino, *The Meaning of Archaeology*, Thames and Hudson, London, 1968, is a thoughtful analysis of archaeology in the modern world. For American archaeology and cultural resource management, the most authoritative source is David J. Meltzer, Don D. Fowler, and Jeremy A. Sabloff, editors, *American Archaeology Past and Future*, Smithsonian Institution Press, Washington, D.C., 1986. The essays in this volume represent a wide cross section of state-of-the-art thinking about American archaeology and its problems and challenges.

Bibliography
of World Prehistory

The literature of world prehistory proliferates more and more every year, to the point that it is now beyond the ability of any one scholar to keep abreast of it. This bibliography is not intended as a comprehensive reference guide to world prehistory. Rather it is a compilation of both the majority of sources used to write this book and a cross section of the most important monographs and papers relating to all parts of the world. Readers interested in probing more deeply into the literature should pursue the references given in the publications listed here or consult a specialist.

Adams, R. E. W., ed. 1977a. *The Origins of the Classic Maya.* Albuquerque: University of New Mexico Press.
———. 1977b. *Prehistoric Mesoamerica.* Boston: Little, Brown.
Adams, R. E. W., Brown, W. E., and Culbert, T. Patrick. 1981. "Radar Mapping, Archeology, and Ancient Maya Land Use." *Science* 213 (4515):1457–1462.
Adams, Robert M. 1966. *The Evolution of Urban Society.* Chicago: Aldine.
———. 1981. *Heartland of Cities.* Chicago: University of Chicago Press.
Adams, Robert M., and Nissen, Hans J. 1972. *The Uruk Landscape.* Chicago: University of Chicago Press.
Adovasio, James M., et al. 1981. *Meadowcroft Rockshelter and the Archaeology of the Cross Creek Drainage.* Pittsburgh: University of Pittsburgh Press.
———. 1984. "Meadowcroft Rockshelter and the Pleistocene/Holocene Transition in South-West Pennsylvania." In Hugh Genoways and Mary Dawson, eds., *Contributions in Quaternary Vertebrate Paleontology.* New York: Carnegie Museum of Natural History. Pp. 1–56.
———. 1986. "Who Are Those Guys? An Examination of the Pre-Clovis Flintworking Complex from Meadowcroft Rockshelter and the Cross Creek Drainage." *American Antiquity* 62: 117–124.
Agrawal, D. P. 1982. "The Indian Bronze Age Cultures and Their Metal Technology." *Advances in World Archaeology* 1:213–264.
Aigner, Jean S. 1970. "The Unifacial, Core, and Blade Site on Anagula Island, Aleutians." *Arctic Anthropology* 7 (2):59–88.
Aikens, C. Melvin. 1970. *Hogup Cave.* Salt Lake City: University of Utah Press.

Aikens, C. Melvin, and Higuchi, Takayasu. 1981. *Prehistory of Japan*. New York: Academic.

Aitken, M. J. 1985. *Thermoluminescence Dating*. Orlando: Academic.

Akazawa, Takeru. 1982. "Cultural Change in Prehistoric Japan." *Advances in World Archaeology* 1:151–212.

Aldred, Cyril. 1968. *Akhenaten*. London: Thames and Hudson.

———. 1986. *The Egyptians*. 2d ed. New York: Thames and Hudson.

Allan, William. 1965. *The African Husbandman*. Edinburgh: Oliver and Boyd.

Allchin, Bridget. 1966. *The Stone Tipped Arrow*. New York: Barnes and Noble.

Allchin, Bridget, and Allchin, Raymond. 1983. *The Rise of Civilization in India and Pakistan*. Cambridge: Cambridge University Press.

Allen, J. 1969. "The Hunting Neolithic: Adaptations to the Food Quest in Prehistoric Papua, New Guinea." In J. V. S. Megaw, ed., *Hunters, Gatherers, and First Farmers Beyond Europe*. Atlantic Highlands, N.J.: Humanities. Pp. 167–188.

———. 1977. "Sea Traffic, Trade and Expanding Horizons." In J. Allen, J. Golson, and Rhys Jones, eds., *Sunda and Sahel*. New York: Academic. Pp. 387–414.

Allen, J., Golson, J., and Jones, Rhys, eds. 1977. *Sunda and Sahel: Prehistoric Studies in Southeast Asia, Melanesia, and Australia*. New York: Academic.

Alpers, Edward A. 1975. *Ivory and Slaves in East Central Africa*. Berkeley and Los Angeles: University of California Press.

Ambrose, Stanley H. 1984. "The Introduction of Pastoral Adaptations to the Highlands of East Africa." In J. Desmond Clark and Steven A. Brandt, eds., *From Hunters to Farmers*. Berkeley and Los Angeles: University of California Press. Pp. 212–239.

Ammerman, A., and Cavalli-Sforza, L. 1973. "Measuring the Rate of Early Farming in Europe." In Colin Renfrew, ed., *The Explanation of Culture Change*. London: Duckworth. Pp. 343–357.

Anderson, Arthur O. and Dibble, Charles, eds. 1978. *The Florentine Codex*. Salt Lake City: University of Utah Press.

Anderson, Atholl. 1987. "Recent Developments in Japanese Prehistory: A Review." *American Antiquity* 61 (232):270–281.

Anderson, Douglas. 1970. "Akmak." *Acta Arctica* 15:1–25.

———. 1979. "Archaeology and the Evidence for the Prehistoric Development of Eskimo Culture." *Arctic Anthropologist* 16 (1):16–26.

Anderson, J. E. 1969. *The Human Skeleton: A Manual for Archaeologists*. Ottawa: National Museum of Canada.

Asch, David L., and Asch, Nancy E. 1985. "Prehistoric Plant Cultivation in West Central Illinois." In Richard I. Ford, ed., *Prehistoric Food Production in North America*. Ann Arbor: University of Michigan Museum of Anthropology. Pp. 149–204.

Ascher, Marcia, and Ascher, Robert. 1981. *The Code of the Quipu*. Ann Arbor: University of Michigan Press.

Bada, Jeffrey L., and Helfman, Patricia Masters. 1975. "Amino Acid Racemization Dating of Fossil Bones." *World Archaeology* 7 (2):160–173.

Bailey, G. N. 1978. "Shell Middens as Indicators of Postglacial Economies: A Territorial Perspective." In Paul Mellars, ed., *The Early Post Glacial Settlement of Northern Europe*. London: Duckworth. Pp. 235–261.

Bailey, G. N., ed. 1983. *Hunter-Gatherer Economy in Prehistory*. Cambridge: Cambridge University Press.

Baillie, M. G. L. 1982. *Tree Ring Dating and Archaeology*. New York: Columbia University Press.

Bankes, George. 1977. *Peru Before Pizarro*. Oxford: Phaidon.

Bannister, Bryant, and Robinson, William J. 1975. "Tree-Ring Dating in Archaeology." *World Archaeology* 7 (2):210–225.

Barker, Phillip. 1983. *Techniques of Archaeological Excavation*. 2d ed. London: Batsford.

Barnard, Noel. 1961. *Bronze Casting and Bronze Alloys in Ancient China*. Canberra: Australian National University.

Barry, John C., et al. 1985. "Neogene Mammalian Faunal Change in Southern Asia: Correlations with Climatic, Tectonic, and Eustatic Events." *Geology* 13:637–640.

Bar-Yosef, O. 1975. "Archaeological Occurrences in the Middle Pleistocene of Israel." In Karl Butzer and Glynn Ll. Isaac, eds., *After the Australopithecines*. Chicago: Aldine. Pp. 571–604.

———. 1986. "The Walls of Jericho." *Current Anthropology* 27 (2):157–162.

———. 1987. "Late Pleistocene Adaptations in the Levant." In Olga Soffer, ed., *The Pleistocene Old World: Regional Perspectives*. New York: Plenum. Pp. 219–236.

Bayard, Donn T. 1970. "Excavations at Non Nok Tha, Northeast Thailand, 1968: An Interim Report." *Asian Perspectives* 13:109–144.

———. 1972. "Early Thai Bronze: Analysis and New Dates." *Science* 176:1411–1421.

———. 1977. "Phu Wiang Pottery and the Prehistory of Northeastern Thailand." In G. Bartstra et al., eds., *Modern Quaternary Research in South East Asia*. Rotterdam: Balkema. Pp. 57–102.

———, ed. 1984. *The Origins of Agriculture, Metallurgy, and the State in Mainland Southeast Asia*. Dunedin, New Zealand: University of Otago Press.

———. 1986. "Agriculture, Metallurgy, and State Formation in Southeast Asia." *Current Anthropology* 25 (1):103–105.

Beadle, George. 1981. "The Ancestor of Corn." *Scientific American* 242 (1):96–103.

Beaumont, Peter. 1980. "On the Age of Border Cave Hominids 1–5." *Palaeontologica Africana* 23:21–33.

Bellwood, Peter. 1970. "Fortifications and Economy in Prehistoric New Zealand." *Proceedings of the Prehistoric Society* 37 (1):56–95.

———. 1979. *Man's Conquest of the Pacific*. Oxford: Oxford University Press.

———. 1985. *The Prehistory of the Indo-Malaysian Archipelago*. North Ryde, NSW: Academic.

———. 1987a. *The Polynesians*. London: Thames and Hudson.

———. 1987b. "The Prehistory of Island Southeast Asia: A Multidisciplinary Review of Recent Research." *Advances in World Archaeology* 1 (2):171–224.

Bender, Barbara. 1985. "Emergent Tribal Formations in the American Midcontinent." *American Antiquity* 50 (1):52–62.

Benfer, Robert. 1982. "The Lomas Site of Paloma (5000 to 7500 B.P.), Chilca Valley, Peru." In Ramerio Matos, ed., *Andean Archaeology*. New York: Academic Press. Pp. 27–54.

Benson, Elizabeth, ed. 1971. *Dumbarton Oaks Conference on Chavín*. Washington, D.C.: Dumbarton Oaks.

———. 1979. *Pre-Columbian Metallurgy of South America*. Washington, D.C.: Dumbarton Oaks.

Bernal, Ignacio. 1969. *The Olmec World*. Berkeley and Los Angeles: University of California Press.

Berry, Michael S. 1985. "The Age of Maize in the Greater Southwest: A Critical Review." In Richard I. Ford, ed., *Prehistoric Food Production in North America*. Ann Arbor: University of Michigan Museum of Anthropology. Pp. 279–308.

Binford, Lewis R. 1964. "A Consideration of Archaeological Research Design." *American Antiquity* 29:425–441.

———. 1965. "Archaeological Systematics and the Study of Cultural Process." *American Antiquity* 31:203–210.

————. 1968. "Post-Pleistocene Adaptations." In Lewis R. Binford and Sally Binford, eds., *New Perspectives in Archaeology*. New York: Academic. Pp. 313–341.

————. 1972. *An Archaeological Perspective*. New York: Academic.

————. 1978. *Nunamiut Ethnoarchaeology*. New York: Academic.

————. 1979. "Organization and Formation Processes: Looking at Curated Technologies." *Journal of Anthropological Research* 35 (3):225–273.

————. 1980. "Willow Smoke and Dog's Tails: Hunter-Gatherer Settlement Systems and Archaeological Formation Processes." *American Antiquity* 45(1):4–20.

————. 1981. *Bones*. New York: Academic.

————. 1983. *In Pursuit of the Past*. New York: Thames and Hudson.

————. 1984. *Faunal Remains from Klasies River Mouth*. New York: Academic.

Binford, Lewis R., and Binford, Sally. 1966. "A Preliminary Analysis of Functional Variability in the Mousterian of Levallois Facies." *American Anthropologist* 68 (2):238–295.

Binford, Lewis R., and Chuan Kun Ho. 1986. "Taphonomy at a Distance." *Current Anthropology* 26 (4):413–442.

Binford, Lewis R., and Stone, Nancy. 1986. "Zhoukoudien: A Closer Look." *Current Anthropology* 27 (5):453–475.

Bishop, W. W. 1976. "Pliocene Problems Relating to Human Evolution." In Glynn Ll. Isaac and Elizabeth McCown, eds., *Human Origins: Louis Leakey and the East African Evidence*. Menlo Park, Calif.: Benjamin. Pp. 36–74.

Blanc, Alberto C. 1961. "Some Evidence for the Ideologies of Early Man." In S. L. Washburn, ed., *The Social Life of Early Man*. New York: Viking Fund. Pp. 119–136.

Blanton, Richard E. 1978. *Monte Albán: Settlement Patterns at the Ancient Zapotec Capital*. New York: Academic.

————. 1983. "Advances in the Study of Cultural Evolution in Prehispanic Highland Mesoamerica." *Advances in World Archaeology* 2:245–288.

Blegen, Carl. 1971. *Troy*. London: Thames and Hudson.

Bogucki, Peter, and Grygiel, Ryszard. 1983. "Early Farmers of the North European Plain." *Scientific American* 248 (4):105–115.

Bonzek, Jan, ed. 1985. *The Aegean, Anatolia, and Europe in the 2nd Millenium B.C.* New York: Academic.

————. 1988. *Forest Farmers and Stockherders*. Cambridge: Cambridge University Press.

Bordes, François. 1968. *The Old Stone Age*. New York: McGraw-Hill.

Boserup, Ester. 1965. *The Conditions of Agricultural Growth: The Economics of Agrarian Change Under Population Pressure*. Chicago: Aldine.

Boule, Marcellin, and Vallois, H. 1957. *Fossil Men*. London: Thames and Hudson.

Bovill, E. W. 1968. *The Golden Trade of the Moors*. London: Heinemann.

Bowdler, J. M., Jones, R., and Thorne, A. G. 1970. "Pleistocene Human Remains from Australia: A Living Site and Human Cremation from Lake Mungo, Western New South Wales." *World Archaeology* 2:39–60.

Bowdler, S. 1977. "The Coastal Colonization of Australia." In J. Allen, J. Golson, and Rhys Jones, eds., *Sunda and Sahul*. New York: Academic. Pp. 233–248.

————. 1984. "Hunter Hill, Hunter Island," *Terra Australis* 8:1–21.

Bowen, David Q. 1978. *Quaternary Geology*. Oxford University Press.

Bower, John R. F. 1984. "Settlement Behavior of Pastoral Cultures in East Africa." In J. Desmond Clark and Steven A. Brandt, eds., *From Hunters to Farmers*. Berkeley and Los Angeles: University of California Press. Pp. 252–259.

Braidwood, L. S., ed. 1982. *Prehistoric Village Archaeology in South-eastern Turkey*. Oxford: British Archaeological Reports, International Series, no. 138.

Braidwood, R. J., and Braidwood, L. S., eds. 1983. *Prehistoric Archaeology Along the Zagros Flanks*. Chicago: Oriental Institute.

Braidwood, R. J., and Cambel, H. 1980. *Prehistoric Research in Southeastern Anatolia.* Istanbul: Edebiyat Facultesi Basimevi.

Brain, C. K. 1981. *The Hunters or the Hunted: An Introduction to African Cave Taphonomy.* Chicago: University of Chicago Press.

Brauwer, Günter. 1984. "A Craniological Approach to the Origin of Anatomically Modern *Homo sapiens* in Africa and Implications for the Appearance of Modern Europeans." In Fred Smith and Frank Spencer, eds., *The Origins of Modern Humans.* New York: Liss. Pp. 327–410.

Breuil, Henri. 1908. *La Caverne d'Altamira.* Paris: Payot.

———. 1952. *Four Hundred Centuries of Cave Art.* Montignac: Centre d'Etudes et de Documentation.

Briggs, L. Cabot. 1951. "The Ancient Khmer Empire." *Transactions of the American Philosophical Society,* no. 41.

Brodie, Fawn. 1957. *The Devil Drives.* London: Eyre and Spottiswoode.

Brose, David C. 1980. "A Speculative Model of the Role of Exchange in the Prehistory of the Eastern Woodlands." In David C. Brose and N'omi Greber, eds., *Hopewellian Archaeology.* Kent, Ohio: Kent State University Press. Pp. 3–8.

Brose, David C., and Greber, N'omi. 1980. *Hopewellian Archaeology.* Kent, Ohio: Kent State University Press.

Brothwell, Don R. 1985. *Digging Up Bones.* London: British Museum.

Browman, David L. 1978. "Toward the Development of the Tiahuanaco (Tiwanaku) State." In David L. Browman, ed., *Advances in Andean Archaeology.* The Hague: Mouton. Pp. 327–349.

Brown J., and Phillips, J., eds. 1983. *Late Archaic Hunter-Gatherers in the Midwest.* New York: Academic.

Brumfiel, Elizabeth. 1983. "Aztec State Making: Ecology, Structure, and the Origin of the State." *American Anthropologist* 85 (2):261–284.

Bryan, Alan Lyle, ed. 1978. *Early Man in America from a Circum-Pacific Perspective.* Edmonton: University of Alberta.

———. 1983. "South America." In Richard Shutler, Jr., ed., *Early Man in the New World.* Beverly Hills: Sage. Pp. 137–146.

———. 1986. *New Evidence for the Pleistocene Peopling of the Americas.* Orono, Maine: Center for the Study of Early Man.

Bryant, Vaughn. 1974. "Prehistoric Diet in South Texas: The Coprolite Evidence." *American Antiquity* 39:100–109.

Buckley, W., ed. 1968. *Modern Systems Research for the Behavioral Sciences.* Chicago: Aldine.

Buikstra, Jane, et al. 1986. "Fertility and the Development of Agriculture in the Prehistoric Midwest." *American Antiquity* 51 (3):528–546.

Bunn, Henry, et al. 1980. "FxJj50: An Early Pleistocene Site in Northern Kenya." *World Archaeology* 12 (2):109–136.

Bunn, Henry, and Kroll, J. 1986. "Systematic Butchery by Plio/Pleistocene Hominids at Olduvai Gorge, Tanzania." *Current Anthropology* 27 (5):431–451.

Burch, Ernest S. 1972. "The Caribou/Wild Reindeer as a Human Resource." *American Antiquity* 37 (3):339–368.

Burger, Richard L. 1981. "The Radiocarbon Evidence for the Temporal Priority of Chavín de Huántar." *American Antiquity* 46:592–602.

———. 1984. *The Prehistoric Occupation of Chavín de Huántar.* Berkeley and Los Angeles: University of California Press.

———. 1985. "Prehistoric Stylistic Change and Cultural Development at Huaricoto, Peru." *National Geographic Research* 1 (4):505–534.

Burger, Richard L., and Burger, Lucy Salazar. 1980. "Ritual and Religion at Huaricoto." *Archaeology* 33 (6):26–32.

Burger, Richard L., and Salazar-Burger, Lucy. 1985. "The Early Ceremonial Center of Huaricoto." In Christopher Donnan, ed., *Early Ceremonial Architecture in the Andes.* Washington, D.C.: Dumbarton Oaks. Pp. 111–138.

Butzer, Karl. 1974. *Environment and Archaeology.* 3d ed. Chicago: Aldine.

———. 1976. *Early Hydraulic Civilization in Egypt.* Chicago: University of Chicago Press.

———. 1981. "Civilizations: Organisms or Systems?" *American Scientist* 68:517–524.

———. 1982. *Archaeology as Human Ecology: Method and Theory for a Contextual Approach.* Cambridge: Cambridge University Press.

Butzer, Karl, and Isaac, Glynn Ll., eds. 1975. *After the Australopithecines.* Chicago: Aldine.

Caldwell, Joseph R. 1958. *Trend and Tradition in the Prehistory of the Eastern United States.* Washington, D.C.: American Anthropological Association Memoir 88.

Campbell, Bernard. 1974. *Human Evolution.* 2d ed. Chicago: Aldine.

———. 1985. *Humankind Emerging.* 3d ed. Boston: Little, Brown.

Canby, Thomas. 1979. "The Search for the First Americans." *National Geographic Magazine* September, 1979:330–363.

Cann, R. L., et al. 1987. "Mitochrondrial DNA and Human Evolution." *Nature* 325:31–36.

Capitan, L., and Peyrony, Denis. 1928. *La Madeleine, son gisement, son industrie, ses oeuvres d'art.* Paris: Librairie Emile Nourry.

Carneiro, Robert L. 1972. "A Theory of the Origin of the State." *Science* 169:733–738.

Carter, George F. 1981. *Earlier Than You Think.* College Station: Texas A & M University Press.

Carter, Howard. 1923. *The Tomb of Tut-ankh-Amun.* London: Macmillan.

Caton-Thompson, G., and Gardner, E. W. 1934. *The Desert Fayum.* 2 vols. London: Royal Anthropological Institute.

Ceram, C. W. 1953. *Gods, Graves and Scholars.* New York: Knopf.

Chadwick, John. 1958. *The Decipherment of Linear B.* Cambridge: Cambridge University Press.

Chagnon, Napoleon, and Irons, J., eds. 1979. *Evolutionary Biology and Social Behavior.* North Scituate, Mass.: Duxbury.

Champion, Timothy G., et al. 1984. *Prehistoric Europe.* New York: Academic.

Chang Kwang-Chih. 1980. *The Shang Civilization.* New Haven: Yale University Press.

———. 1981. "In Search of China's Beginnings: New Light on an Old Civilization." *American Scientist* 60:148–160.

———. 1986. *The Archaeology of Ancient China.* 4th ed. New Haven: Yale University Press.

Chapman, Jefferson, et al. 1982. "Man-Land Interaction: 10,000 Years of American Indian Impact on Native Ecosystems in the Lower Little Tennessee Valley, Eastern Tennessee." *Southeastern Archeology* 1:115–121.

Chard, Chester S. 1969. *Man in Prehistory.* New York: McGraw-Hill.

———. 1971. *Northeast Asia in Prehistory.* Madison: University of Wisconsin Press.

Cheng Te-k'un. 1960. *Shang China.* Vol. 2, Archaeology in China. Cambridge: Heffers.

Childe, V. Gordon. 1925. *The Dawn of European Civilization.* London: Routledge and Kegan Paul.

———. 1936. *Man Makes Himself.* London: Watts.

———. 1942. *What Happened in History.* London: Routledge and Kegan Paul.

————. 1952. *New Light on the Most Ancient East.* London: Routledge and Kegan Paul.

————. 1956. *Piecing Together the Past.* London: Routledge and Kegan Paul.

————. 1958. "Retrospect." *Antiquity* 32:69–74.

Chippindale, Christopher. 1983. *Stonehenge Complete.* London: Thames and Hudson.

Chung Tang and Pei Gai. 1986. "Upper Palaeolithic Cultural Traditions in North China." *Advances in World Archaeology* 5:339–364.

Cinq-Mars, Jacques. 1979. "Bluefish Cave I: A Late Pleistocene Eastern Beringian Cave Deposit in the Northern Yukon." *Canadian Journal of Anthropology* 3:1–32.

Clark, Geoffrey, and Yi Seonbok. 1983. "Niche-Width Variation in Cantabrian Archaeofaunas." In Juliet Clutton-Brock and Caroline Grigson, eds., *Hunters and Their Prey.* Vol. 1, Animals and Archaeology. Oxford: British Archaeological Reports, International Series no. 163. Pp. 183–208.

Clark, J. Desmond. 1959. *The Prehistory of Southern Africa.* Baltimore: Pelican.

————. 1967. "The Problem of Neolithic Culture in Sub-Saharan Africa." In W. W. Bishop and J. Desmond Clark, eds., *Background to Evolution in Africa.* Chicago: University of Chicago Press. Pp. 601–628.

————. 1970. *The Prehistory of Africa.* London: Thames and Hudson.

————. 1971. "A Re-examination of the Evidence for Agricultural Origins in the Nile Valley." *Proceedings of the Prehistoric Society* 37 (2):34–79.

————. 1983. "The Significance of Culture Change in the Early Later Pleistocene in Northern and Southern Africa." In Erik Trinkhaus, ed., *The Mousterian Legacy.* Oxford: British Archaeological Reports International Series, No. 151. Pp. 1–12.

————. 1984. "Prehistoric Cultural Continuity and Economic Change in the Central Sudan in the Early Holocene." In J. Desmond Clark and Steven A. Brandt, eds., *From Hunters to Farmers.* Berkeley and Los Angeles: University of California Press. Pp. 113–126.

Clark, J. D., and Brandt, Steven A., eds. 1984. *From Hunters to Farmers.* Berkeley: University of California Press.

Clark, J. Desmond, and Harris, J. W. K. 1985. "Fire and Its Roles in Early Hominid Lifeways." *African Archaeological Review* 3:3–28.

Clark, J. G. D. 1952. *Prehistoric Europe: The Economic Basis.* Palo Alto, Calif.: Stanford University Press.

————. 1954. *Star Carr.* Cambridge: Cambridge University Press.

————. 1958. "Blade and Trapeze Industries of the European Stone Age." *Proceedings of the Prehistoric Society* 24:24–42.

————. 1965. *Archaeology and Society.* New York: Barnes and Noble.

————. 1970. *Aspects of Prehistory.* Berkeley and Los Angeles: University of California Press.

————. 1975. *The Earlier Stone Age Settlement of Scandinavia.* Cambridge: Cambridge University Press.

————. 1977. *World Prehistory: A New Outline.* 3d ed. Cambridge: Cambridge University Press.

————. 1979. *Mesolithic Prelude.* Edinburgh: Edinburgh University Press.

Clarke, David L. 1976. "Mesolithic Europe: The Economic Basis." In G. de Sieveking et al., eds. *Problems in Economic and Social Archaeology.* London: Duckworth. Pp. 449–481.

CLIMAP Project Members. 1976. "The Surface of the Ice Age Earth." *Science* 191:1126–1131.

Clutton-Brock, Juliet. 1981. *Domesticated Animals from Early Times.* Austin: University of Texas Press.

Coe, Michael D. 1962. *Mexico.* New York: Praeger.

————. 1965. *The Jaguar's Children.* New York: Museum of Primitive Art.

————. 1968. *America's First Civilization: Discovering the Olmec.* New York: American Heritage.

————. 1984. *The Maya.* 3d ed. London: Thames and Hudson.

Coe, Michael D., and Diehl, Richard. 1980. *In the Land of the Olmec.* 2 vols. Austin: University of Texas Press.

Coe, William, and Haviland, William A. 1982. *Introduction to the Archaeology of Tikal, Guatemala.* Philadelphia: University Museum, University of Pennsylvania. (The first of a projected 39 reports on Tikal.)

Coggins, Clemency. 1985. *The Sacred Cenote of Sacrifice.* Austin: University of Texas Press.

Cohen, Mark, 1977. *The Food Crisis in Prehistory.* New Haven: Yale University Press.

Cohen, Mark N., and Armelagos, George J., eds. 1984. *Paleopathology and the Origins of Agriculture.* New York: Academic.

Coles, J. M. 1962. "European Bronze Age Shields." *Proceedings of the Prehistoric Society* 28:156–190.

————. 1973. *Archaeology by Experiment.* London: Heinemann.

————. 1982. "The Bronze Age in North West Europe: Problems and Advances." *Advances in World Archaeology* 1:266–321.

Coles, J. M., and Harding, A. F. 1979. *The Bronze Age in Europe.* London: Methuen.

Collis, John. 1984. *The European Iron Age.* London: Batsford.

Conkey, Margaret W. 1981. "A Century of Paleolithic Cave Art." *Archaeology* 34 (4):20–28.

————. 1983. "On the Origins of Paleolithic Art: A Review and Some Critical Thoughts." In Erik Trinkhaus, ed., *The Mousterian Legacy.* Oxford: British Archaeological Reports International Series, No. 151. Pp. 201–227.

Connah, Graham. 1987. *African Civilizations.* Cambridge: Cambridge University Press.

Conrad, Geoffrey W., and Demarest, Arthur A. 1984. *Religion and Empire: The Dynamics of Aztec and Inca Expansionism.* Cambridge: Cambridge University Press.

Cordell, Linda. 1984a. *The Archaeology of the Southwest.* New York: Academic.

————. 1984b. "Southwestern Archaeology." *Annual Review of Anthropology* 13:130–132.

Cotter, John. 1981. "The Upper Paleolithic: However It Got Here, It's Here." *American Antiquity* 46:926–928.

Cotterell, Arthur. 1981. *The First Emperor of China.* New York: Holt, Rinehart and Winston.

Courand, Claude. 1985. *L'Art Azilien.* Paris: Gallia Prehistoire.

Covey, Curt. 1984. "The Earth's Orbit and the Ice Ages." *Scientific American* 280 (2):58–77.

Cranstone, B. A. L. 1972. "The Tifalmin: A Neolithic People in New Guinea." *World Archaeology* 3 (2):132–142.

Crawford, O. G. S. 1953. *Archaeology in the Field.* New York: Praeger.

Creamer, Winifred, and Haas, Jonathan. 1985. "Tribes versus Chiefdoms in Lower Central America." *American Antiquity* 50 (4):738–754.

Culbert, T. Patrick, ed. 1973. *The Classic Maya Collapse.* Albuquerque: University of New Mexico Press.

————. 1988a. "The Collapse of Classic Maya Civilization." In Norman Yoffee and George Cowgill, eds., *The Collapse of Ancient States and Civilizations.* Tucson: University of Arizona Press. In press.

————. 1988b. "Political History and the Decipherment of Maya Glyphs." *Antiquity.* In press.

Cunliffe, Barry. 1974. *Iron Age Communities in Britain.* London: Routledge and Kegan Paul.

Dales, George F. 1966. "The Decline of the Harappans." *Scientific American* 26 (5):210–216.

Dalrymple, C. Brent, and Lamphere, Mason. 1970. *Potassium Argon Dating: Principles, Techniques and Applications in Geochronology.* San Francisco: Freeman.

Daniel, Glyn E. 1973. *Megaliths in History.* London: Thames and Hudson.

———. 1981. *A Short History of Archaeology.* London: Thames and Hudson.

Dart, Raymond A. 1925. *"Australopithecus africanus:* The Man-Ape of Southern Africa." *Nature* 115:195.

———. 1957. *The Osteodontokeratic Culture of Australopithecus prometheus.* Pretoria: Transvaal Museum.

David, A. Rosalie. 1975. *The Egyptian Kingdoms.* Oxford: Elsevier Phaidon.

Davidson, Janet. 1985. "New Zealand Prehistory." *Advances in World Archaeology* 4:239–292.

Davies, Nigel. 1973. *The Aztecs.* Norman: University of Oklahoma Press.

———. 1977. *The Toltecs.* Norman: University of Oklahoma Press.

———. 1979. *Voyages to the New World: Fact or Fantasy.* London: Macmillan.

———. 1980. *The Toltec Heritage.* Norman: University of Oklahoma Press.

Davis, Richard S. 1987. "Regional Perspectives on the Soviet Central Asian Paleolithic." In Olga Soffer, ed., *The Pleistocene Old World: Regional Perspectives.* New York: Plenum. Pp. 121–134.

Deacon, Hilary. 1979. "Excavations at Boomplas Cave: A Sequence Through the Upper Pleistocene and Holocene in South Africa." *World Archaeology* 10:241–257.

Deetz, James. 1967. *Invitation to Archaeology.* Garden City, N.Y.: Natural History Press.

Delcourt, P. A., and Delcourt, H. R. 1981. "Vegetation Maps for Eastern North America." *Geobotany* 2:123–165.

Dennell, Robin C. 1983. *European Economic Prehistory: A New Approach.* New York: Academic.

Dennell, R. W., et al. 1988. "Early Tool-making in Asia: Two-Million-Year-Old Artifacts in Pakistan." *Antiquity* 62 (234):98–105.

de Selincourt, Aubrey, trans. 1966. *Livy's Early History of Rome.* Baltimore: Pelican.

Desroches-Noblecourt, G. 1963. *Tutankhamun.* New York: New York Graphic Society.

Diaz, Bernal. 1963. *The True History of the Conquest of New Spain.* Translated by A. P. Maudslay. Baltimore: Pelican.

Dibble, Charles E., and Anderson, Arthur J. O. 1978. *Florentine Codex,* vol. 14. Salt Lake City: University of Utah Press.

Dibble, Harold. 1987. "Reduction Sequences in the Manufacture of Mousterian Implements of France." In Olga Soffer, ed., *The Pleistocene Old World: Regional Perspectives.* New York: Plenum. Pp. 33–46.

Diehl, Richard A. 1984. *Tula.* London: Thames and Hudson.

Dillehey, Tom D. 1984. "A Late Ice Age Settlement in Southern Chile." *Scientific American* 254 (4):100–109.

Dincauze, Dena. 1983. "An Archaeo-Logical Evaluation of the Case for Pre-Clovis Occupations." *Advances in World Archaeology* 3:275–324.

Di Peso, C. C., et al. 1974. *Casas Grandes: A Fallen Trading Center of the Gran Chichimeca.* Flagstaff, Ariz.: AmerInd Foundation.

Diringer, David. 1962. *Writing.* New York: Praeger.

Dolukhanov, Paul H. 1982. "Upper Pleistocene and Holocene Cultures of the Russian Plain and Caucasus." *Advances in World Archaeology* 1:323–358.

———. 1986. "The Late Mesolithic and the Transition to Food Production in Eastern Europe." In Marek Zvelebil, ed., *Hunters in Transition.* Cambridge: Cambridge University Press. Pp. 109–120.

Donnan, Christopher B., ed. 1985. *Early Ceremonial Architecture in the Andes.* Washington, D.C.: Dumbarton Oaks.

Donnan, Christopher B., and McClelland, Donna. 1979. *The Burial Theme in Moche Iconography.* Washington, D.C.: Dumbarton Oaks.

Dortch, Charles. 1977. "Early and Late Stone Industrial Phases in Western Australia." In R. V. S. Wright, ed., *Stone Tools as Cultural Markers.* Canberra: Australian Institute of Aboriginal Studies. Pp. 104–132.

Dortch, Charles, and Merrilees, Duncan. 1973. "Human Occupation of Devil's Lair, Western Australia, during the Pleistocene." *Archaeology and Physical Anthropology in Oceania* 8:89–115.

Dragoo, Don W. 1976. "Some Aspects of Eastern North American Prehistory: A Review 1975." *American Antiquity* 41 (1):3–27.

Drucker, Phillip. 1959. *La Venta, Tabasco: A Study of Olmec Ceramics and Art.* Washington, D.C.: Smithsonian Institution.

Dumond, Don. 1987a. *The Eskimos and Aleuts.* London: Thames and Hudson.

———. 1987b. "A Reexamination of Eskimo-Aleut Prehistory." *American Anthropologist* 89 (1):32–56.

Dunnell, Robert C. 1971. *Systematics in Prehistory.* New York: Free Press.

———. 1980. "Evolutionary Theory and Archaeology." *Advances in Archaeological Method and Theory* 3:35–99.

Earle, Timothy. 1978. *Economic and Social Organization of a Complex Chiefdom: The Halelea District, Kaua'i, Hawaii.* Ann Arbor: Museum of Anthropology, University of Michigan.

Edwards, I. E. S. 1973. *The Pyramids.* New York: Viking.

Eisenberg, J. F. 1981. *The Mammalian Radiation.* London: Athlone.

Eliade, Mircea. 1954. *The Myth of the Eternal Return.* New York: Pantheon.

———. 1959. *The Sacred and the Profane.* New York: Harcourt, Brace.

Elphick, Richard. 1977. *Kraal and Castle.* New Haven: Yale University Press.

Emory, Kenneth P. 1972. "Easter Island's Position in the Prehistory of Polynesia." *Journal of the Polynesian Society* 81:57–69.

Engel, Frederic. 1957. "Early Sites on the Peruvian Coast." *Southwestern Journal of Anthropology* 13:54–68.

———. 1966a. *Geografía Humana Prehistorica y Agricultura Precolumbina de la Quebrada de Chilca.* Lima: Universidad Agraria.

———. 1966b. *Paracas.* Lima: Librería Juan Megia Base.

Evans, Sir Arthur J. 1921. *The Palace of Minos at Knossos.* 4 vols. Oxford: Clarendon.

Evans, Robert K., and Rasson, Judith A. 1984. "*Ex Balkanis Lux?* Recent Developments in Neolithic and Chalcolithic Research in Southeastern Europe." *American Antiquity* 49:713–741.

Fagan, Brian M. 1975. *The Rape of the Nile.* New York: Scribners.

———. 1979. *Return to Babylon.* Boston: Little, Brown.

———. 1984a. *The Aztecs.* New York: Freeman.

———. 1984b. *Clash of Cultures.* New York: Freeman.

———. 1985. *The Adventure of Archaeology.* Washington, D.C.: National Geographic Society.

———. 1987. *The Great Journey.* London: Thames and Hudson.

————. 1988a. *Archaeology: A Brief Introduction*. 3d. ed. Boston: Scott, Foresman/Little, Brown.

————. 1988b. *In the Beginning*. 6th ed. Boston: Scott, Foresman/Little, Brown.

Fagan, Brian M., and van Noten, F. 1971. *The Hunter-Gatherers of Gwisho*. Tervuren: Musée Royal de l'Afrique Centrale.

Fairservis, Walter A. 1976. *The Roots of Ancient India*. 2d ed. New York: Macmillan.

————. 1983. "The Script of the Indus Valley Civilization." *Scientific American* 243 (3):58–77.

Falk, Dean. 1984. "The Petrified Brain." *Natural History* 93 (9):36–39.

Farnsworth, Paul, et al. 1985. "A Re-evaluation of the Isotopic and Archaeological Reconstruction of Diet in the Tehuacán Valley." *American Antiquity* 50 (1):102–116.

Fedden, Robin. 1977. *Egypt*. London: Murray.

Fedigan, L. M. 1986. "The Changing Role of Women in Models of Human Evolution." *Annual Review of Anthropology* 15:25–66.

Fell, Barry. 1976. *America B.C.* New York: Times.

————. 1980. *Saga America*. New York: Times.

Finney, Ben R. 1967. "New Perspectives on Pacific Voyaging." In Genevieve Highland et al., eds., *Polynesian Culture History*. Honolulu: Bishop Museum. Pp. 141–166.

Fish, P. R., and Fish, S. R. 1977. *Verde Valley Archaeology: Review and Perspective*. Flagstaff: Museum of Northern Arizona.

Fitzgerald, Patrick. 1978. *Ancient China*. Oxford: Elsevier Phaidon.

Fladmark, Knud. 1978. *A Palaeoecological Model for Northwest Coast Prehistory*. Ottawa: National Museums of Canada.

Flannery, Kent V. 1965. "The Ecology of Early Food Production in Mesopotamia." *Science* 147:1247–1256.

————. 1968a. "Archaeological Systems Theory and Early Mesoamerica." In Betty Meggers, ed., *Anthropological Archaeology in the Americas*. Washington, D.C.: Anthropological Society of Washington. Pp. 67–87.

————. 1968b. "The Olmec and the Valley of Oaxaca: A Model for Interregional Interaction in Formative Times." In Elizabeth Benson, ed., *Dumbarton Oaks Conference on the Olmec*. Washington, D.C.: Dumbarton Oaks. Pp. 79–110.

————. 1969. "Origins and Ecological Effects of Early Domestication in Animals." In Peter J. Ucko and G. W. Dimbleby, eds., *The Domestication and Exploitation of Plants and Animals*. London: Duckworth. Pp. 207–218.

————. 1972. "The Cultural Evolution of Civilizations." *Annual Review of Ecology and Systematics*. 4:399–426.

————. 1973. "The Origins of Agriculture." *Annual Review of Anthropology* 2:271–310.

————, ed. 1976. *The Early Mesoamerican Village*. New York: Academic.

————, ed. 1982. *Maya Subsistence*. New York: Academic.

————. 1983. "Settlement, Subsistence, and Social Organization of the Proto-Otomangueans." In Kent V. Flannery and Joyce Marcus, eds., *The Cloud People*. New York: Academic Press. Pp. 32–36.

Flannery, Kent V., et al. 1981. "The Preceramic and Formative of the Valley of Oaxaca." In Jeremy A. Sabloff, ed., *Archeology*. Vol. 1, Supplement to the Handbook of American Indians. Austin: University of Texas Press. Pp. 48–93.

Flannery, Kent V., and Marcus, Joyce, eds. 1983. *The Cloud People*. New York: Academic.

Flannery, Kent V., et al. 1985. *Gila Niguel*. New York: Academic.

Fleischer, Robert L. 1975. "Advances in Fission Track Dating." *World Archaeology* 7 (2):136–150.

Flenniken, Jeffrey. 1988. "Morphological Projectile Point Typology: Replication Experimentation and Technological Analysis." *American Antiquity*. In press.

Flint, R. F. 1965. "The Plio-Pleistocene Boundary." In H. E. Wright and D. G. Frey, eds.,

International Studies in the Quaternary. Washington, D.C.: Geological Society of America. Pp. 497–533.

———. 1971. *Glacial and Quaternary Geology.* New York: Wiley.

Folan, William J., et al. 1983. *Coba: A Classic Maya Metropolis.* New York: Academic.

Foley, Robert. 1981. *Off-site Archaeology and Human Adaptation in Eastern Africa.* Oxford: British Archaeological Reports International Series, no. 97.

———. 1984a. "Early Man and the Red Queen." In Robert Foley, ed., *Hominid Evolution and Community Ecology.* London: Academic. Pp. 85–110.

———, ed. 1984b. *Hominid Evolution and Community Ecology: Prehistoric Human Adaptation in Biological Perspective.* London: Academic.

———. 1984c. "Putting People into Perspective." In Robert Foley, ed., *Hominid Evolution and Community Ecology.* London: Academic. Pp. 1–24.

———. 1987. "Hominid Species and Stone-Tool Assemblages: How Are They Related?" *Antiquity* 61:380–392.

Ford, Richard I., ed. 1985. *Prehistoric Food Production in North America.* Ann Arbor: University of Michigan Museum of Anthropology.

Fowler, Don D. 1987. "Uses of the Past: Archaeology in the Service of the State." *American Antiquity* 52(2):229–248.

Fowler, Melvin L. 1958. *Modoc Rockshelter.* Springfield: Illinois State Museum.

———. 1969. "The Cahokia Site." In Melvin L. Fowler, ed., *Investigations in Cahokia Archaeology.* Urbana: Illinois Archaeological Survey. Pp. 1–14.

———. 1978. "Cahokia and the American Bottom: Settlement Archaeology." In Bruce D. Smith, ed., *Mississippian Settlement Patterns.* New York: Academic. Pp. 455–478.

Freeman, Leslie, and Echegaray, Jesús. 1981. "El Juyo: A 14,000-Year-Old Sanctuary from Northern Spain." *History of Religions* 21:1–19.

Frison, George C. 1978. *Prehistoric Hunters of the High Plains.* New York: Academic.

Gabel, Creighton. 1983. "The Search for Human Origins: Facts and Questions." *Journal of Field Archaeology* 10:193–211.

Galinat, Walter C. 1985. "Domestication and Diffusion of Maize." In Richard I. Ford, ed., *Prehistoric Food Production in North America.* Ann Arbor: University of Michigan Museum of Anthropology. Pp. 245–278.

Gamble, Clive. 1986a. "The Mesolithic Sandwich." In Marek Zvelebil, ed., *Hunters in Transition.* Cambridge: Cambridge University Press. Pp. 33–42.

———. 1986b. *The Palaeolithic Settlement of Europe.* Cambridge: Cambridge University Press.

Gardner, R. Allen, and Gardner, Beatrice A. 1969. "Teaching Sign Language to a Chimpanzee." *Science* 163:664–672.

Garlake, Peter. 1973. *Great Zimbabwe.* New York: McGraw-Hill.

Garrod, D. A. E. 1951. "A Transitional Industry from the Base of the Upper Palaeolithic in Palestine and Syria." *Journal of the Royal Anthropological Institute* 81:121–129.

———. 1957. "The Natufian Culture: The Life and Economy of a Mesolithic People in the Near East." *Proceedings of the British Academy* 43:211–237.

Garrod, D. A. E., and Bate, Dorothea. 1937. *The Stone Age of Mount Carmel.* Cambridge: Cambridge University Press.

Gasparini, Graziano, and Margolies, Luise. 1980. *Inca Architecture.* Bloomington: Indiana University Press.

Geddes, D. 1983. "Neolithic Transhumance in the Mediterranean Pyrenees." *World Archaeology* 15:51–66.

———. 1985. "Mesolithic Domesticated Sheep in West Mediterranean Europe." *Journal of Archaeological Science* 12:25–48.

Gerasimov, M. M. 1958. "The Paleolithic Site of Ma'lta (1956–57 Excavations)." *So-vyetskayen Etnografiya* 3:28–52.

Gibson, Charles. 1964. *The Aztecs Under Spanish Rule.* Palo Alto, Calif.: Stanford University Press.

Giddings, J. L. 1967. *Ancient Men of the Arctic.* New York: Knopf.

Gifford, Diane P. 1981. "Taphonomy and Paleoecology: A Critical Review of Archaeology's Sister Discipline." *Advances in Archaeological Method and Theory* 4:365–437.

Gingerich, Phillip D. 1985. "Nonlinear Molecular Clocks and Ape-Human Divergence Times." In Philip V. Tobias, ed., *Hominid Evolution: Past, Present, and Future.* New York: Liss. Pp. 441–466.

Giteau, M. 1966. *Khmer Sculpture and the Angkor Civilization.* London: Thames and Hudson.

Glover, Ian G. 1977. "The Hoabhinian: Hunter-Gatherers or Early Agriculturalists in Southeast Asia?" In J. V. S. Megaw, ed., *Hunters, Gatherers, and First Farmers Beyond Europe.* Atlantic Highlands, N.J.: Humanities. Pp. 145–166.

Golson, Jack. 1977. "No Room at the Top: Agricultural Intensification in the New Guinea Highlands." In J. Allen, J. Golson, and Rhys Jones, eds., *Sunda and Sahel.* New York: Academic. Pp. 602–638.

Goodall, Jane. 1973. *In the Shadow of Man.* Boston: Houghton Mifflin.

———. 1986. *The Chimpanzees of Gombe.* Cambridge: Harvard University Press.

Goodman, Jeffrey. 1980. *American Genesis.* New York: Summit.

Gorman, Chester A. 1969. "Hoabhinian: A Pebble-Tool Complex with Early Plant Associations in Southeast Asia." *Science* 163:671–673.

———. 1971. "Hoabhinian and After: Subsistence Patterns in Southeast Asia During the Late Pleistocene and Early Recent Periods." *World Archaeology* 2 (3):300–320.

———. 1977. "A Priori Models and Thai Prehistory: A Reconsideration of the Beginnings of Agriculture in Southeast Asia." In Charles A. Reed, ed., *Origins of Agriculture.* The Hague: Mouton. Pp. 321–355.

Goudie, Andrew. 1983. *Environmental Change.* 2d ed. Oxford: Clarendon Press.

Gould, Richard A. 1977. *Puntutjarpa Rockshelter and Australian Desert Culture.* New York: American Museum of Natural History.

———, ed. 1978. *Explorations in Ethnoarchaeology.* Albuquerque: University of New Mexico Press.

———. 1980. *Living Archaeology.* Cambridge: Cambridge University Press.

Gould, S. J. 1977. *Ever Since Darwin: Reflections in Natural History.* Baltimore: Penguin.

Gowlett, John. 1978. "Culture and Conceptualization: The Oldowan-Acheulian Gradient." In G. N. Bailey and P. Callow, eds., *Stone Age Prehistory.* Cambridge: Cambridge University Press. Pp. 243–260.

———. 1984. "Mental Abilities of Early Man." In Robert Foley, ed., *Hominid Evolution and Community Ecology.* London: Academic. Pp. 167–192.

———. 1986. "Culture and Conceptualization." *In* G. N. Bailey and P. Callow, eds., *Stone Age Prehistory.* Cambridge: Cambridge University Press. Pp. 243–260.

Gowlett, John. 1987. "The Archaeology of Radiocarbon Accelerator Dating." *Journal of World Prehistory* 1(2):127–170.

Grant, Michael. 1960. *The Romans.* London: Weidenfeld and Nicholson.

Grasiosi, Paolo. 1960. *Palaeolithic Art.* New York: Abrams.

Grayson, Donald K. 1983. *The Search for Human Antiquity.* New York: Academic.

Green, R. C. 1969. "Lapita." In Jesse D. Jennings, ed., *The Prehistory of Polynesia.* Cambridge: Harvard University Press. Pp. 27–60.

Greenberg, Joseph. 1987. *Language in the Americas.* Palo Alto, Calif.: Stanford University Press.

Gribben, J., ed. 1978. *Climatic Change.* Cambridge: Cambridge University Press.

Griffin, J. B. 1967. "Eastern North American Prehistory: A Summary." *Science* 156:175–191.

Grootes, P. M. 1978. "Carbon-14 Time Scale Extended: Comparison of Chronologies." *Science* 200 (4337):11–15.

Groube, L. M. 1970. "The Origins and Development of Earthwork Fortifications in the Pacific." In R. C. Green and M. Kelly, eds., *Studies in Oceanic Culture History*. Hawaii: Bishop Museum. Pp. 133–164.

———. 1971. "Tonga, Lapita Pottery, and Polynesian Origins." *Journal of the Polynesian Society* 80:278–316.

Groube, L., et al. 1986. "40,000-Year-Old Human Occupation Site at Huon Peninsula, Papua, New Guinea." *Nature* 324:453–455.

Grove, David. 1973. "Olmec Altars and Myths." *Archaeology* 26:128–135.

Gryziel, Ryszard, and Boguchi, T. 1986. "Early Neolithic Sites at Brzesc Kujawski, Poland." *Journal of Field Archaeology* 13 (2):121–138.

Guidon, Niede, and Delibrias, G. 1986. "Carbon 14 Dates Point to Man in the Americas 32,000 Years Ago." *Nature* 321:769–771.

Haas, Jonathan, et al., eds. 1987. *The Origins and Development of the Andean State*. Cambridge: Cambridge University Press.

Haland, Randi, and Shinnie, Peter. 1985. *African Iron Working—Ancient and Traditional*. Bergen: Norwegian University Press.

Hall, Kenneth R. 1985. *Maritime Trade and State Development in Early Southeast Asia*. Honolulu: University of Hawaii Press.

Hallam, Sylvia. 1975. *Fire and Hearth*. Canberra: Australian Institute of Aboriginal Studies.

Hamden, G. 1961. "The Evolution of Irrigation Agriculture in Egypt." *Arid Zone Research* 17:119–142.

Hammond, F. 1981. "The Colonization of Europe: The Analysis of Settlement Process." In Ian Hodder et al., eds., *Pattern of the Past*. Cambridge: Cambridge University Press. Pp. 211–248.

Hammond, Norman, ed. 1973. *South Asian Archaeology*. London: Duckworth.

———. 1974. "Palaeolithic Mammalian Faunas and Parietal Art in Cantabria: A Comment on Freeman." *American Antiquity* 39:618–619.

———. 1978. *Cuello Project 1978: Interim Report*. New Brunswick, N.J.: Archaeological Research Program.

———. 1980a. "Early Maya Ceremonial at Cuello, Belize." *Antiquity* 54:176–190.

———. 1980b. "Prehistoric Human Utilization of the Savanna Environments of Middle and South America." In David R. Harris, ed., *Human Ecology in Savanna Environments*. New York: Academic. Pp. 73–106.

———. 1982. *Ancient Maya Civilization*. New Brunswick, N.J.: Rutgers University Press.

———. 1986. "New Light on the Most Ancient Maya." *Man* 21:299–413.

Hammond, Norman, and Miksicek, Charles H. 1981. "Ecology and Economy of a Formative Maya Site at Cuello, Belize." *Journal of Field Archaeology* 8:259–269.

Haq, J., et al. 1977. "Corrected Age of the Pliocene Boundary." *Nature* 269:483–488.

Harden, Donald. 1962. *The Phoenicians*. London: Thames and Hudson.

Harding, A. F. 1983. "The Bronze Age in Central and Eastern Europe: Advances and Prospects." *Advances in World Prehistory* 2:1–50.

———.1984. *The Mycenaeans and Europe*. New York: Academic.

Harlan, Jack. 1967. "A Wild Wheat Harvest in Turkey." *Archaeology* 19(3):197–201.

Harlan, Jack, DeWet, John, and Stemler, Ann, eds. 1976. *Origins of African Plant Domestication*. The Hague: Mouton.

Harris, David R. 1978. "Alternative Pathways Toward Agriculture." In Charles A. Reed, ed., *The Origins of Agriculture*. The Hague: Mouton.

———, ed. 1980. *Human Ecology in Savanna Environments*. New York: Academic.

Harris, Marvin. 1968. *The Rise of Anthropological Theory*. New York: Crowell.

Harrison, Richard J. 1980. *The Beaker Folk*. London: Thames and Hudson.

Harrisson, Tom. 1957. "The Great Cave of Neah." *Man* 211:223–224.

Hassan, Fekri. 1986. "Desert Environment and Origins of Agriculture in Egypt." *Norwegian Archaeological Review* 19 (2):63–76.

———. 1987. "High Precision Radiocarbon Chronology of Ancient Egypt, and Comparisons with Nubia, Palestine, and Mesopotamia." *Antiquity* 61 (231):119–135.

Hatch, Elvin. 1973. *Theories of Man and Culture*. New York: Columbia University Press.

Haury, Emil. 1936. *The Mogollon Culture of Southwestern New Mexico*. Globe, Ariz.: Gila Pueblo.

———. 1976. *Hohokam, Desert Farmers and Craftsmen: Excavations at Snaketown*. Tucson: University of Arizona Press.

Haven, Samuel. 1856. *The Archaeology of the United States*. Washington, D.C.: Smithsonian Institution.

Haynes, C. Vance. 1964. "Fluted Projectile Points: Their Age and Dispersion." *Science* 145:1408–1413.

———. 1980. "Paleoindian Charcoal from Meadowcroft Rockshelter: Is Contamination a Problem?" *American Antiquity* 45:582–587.

———.1982. "Were Clovis Progenitors in Beringia?" In David M. Hopkins et al., eds., *Paleoecology of Beringia*. New York: Academic. Pp. 383–398.

Hays, T. R. 1984. "A Reappraisal of the Egyptian Predynastic." In J. Desmond Clark and Steven A. Brandt, eds., *From Hunters to Farmers*. Berkeley and Los Angeles: University of California Press. Pp 65–73.

Heizer, R. F., and Berger, Rainer. 1970. "Radiocarbon Age of the Gypsum Cave." *Contributions of the University of California Archaeological Research Facility* 7:1–12.

Henderson, John S. 1981. *The World of the Ancient Maya*. Ithaca: Cornell University Press.

Hey, Richard L. 1975. *Geology of the Olduvai Gorge*. Berkeley and Los Angeles: University of California Press.

Higgs, Eric S., and Jarman, P. 1969. "Origins of Agriculture." *Antiquity* 43:31–41.

Higham, Charles F. W. 1972. "Initial Model Formation in Terra Incognita." In David L. Clarke, ed., *Models in Prehistory*. London: Methuen. Pp. 453–476.

———. 1984a. "The Ban Chiang Culture in Wider Perspective." *Proceedings of the British Academy* 110:1–30.

———. 1984b. "Prehistoric Rice Cultivation in Southeast Asia." *Scientific American* 84:138–146.

Higham, Charles F. W., and Kijngam, Amphan. 1984. *Prehistoric Investigations in Northeast Thailand*. Oxford: British Archaeological Reports, International Series, No. 156.

Higham, Charles. 1988. *The Archaeology of Mainland Southeast Asia*. Cambridge: Cambridge University Press.

Hill, Andrew. 1984. "Hyaenas and Hominids." In Robert Foley, ed., *Hominid Evolution and Community Ecology*. London: Academic. Pp. 111–128.

Ho Ping-Ti. 1969. "Loess and the Origins of Chinese Agriculture." *American Historical Review* 75:1–36.

Hockett, Charles F., and Ascher, Robert. 1964. "The Human Revolution." *Current Anthropology* 5 (3):135–168.

Hodder, Ian, ed. 1982. *Symbolic and Structural Archaeology*. Cambridge: Cambridge University Press.

Hoffman, Michael A. 1979. *Egypt Before the Pharaohs.* New York: Knopf.

Hoffman, Michael A., et al. 1982. *The Predynastic of Hierakonpolis.* Cairo: Egyptian Studies Association.

Hole, Frank, Flannery, Kent V., and Neely, J. A. 1969. *The Prehistory and Human Ecology of the Deh Luran Plain.* Ann Arbor: University of Michigan Museum of Anthropology.

Hole, Frank, and Heizer, Robert F. 1973. *An Introduction to Prehistoric Archaeology.* 3d ed. New York: Holt, Rinehart and Winston.

Holmes, Charles. 1987. "Prehistoric Maritime Adaptations in Southeast Alaska and Adjacent Canada." Paper presented at symposium, Prehistoric Maritime Adaptations Around the North Pacific Rim, October 15–17, 1986. Hokkaido: Sapporo Abashiri.

Hood, Sinclair. 1973. *The Minoans.* London: Thames and Hudson.

Hooton, E. A. 1948. *Up from the Ape.* New York: Macmillan.

Hopkins, David M., et al., eds. 1982. *Paleoecology of Beringia.* New York: Academic.

Horton, D. R. 1978. "The Extinction of the Australian Megafauna." *Australian Institute of Aboriginal Studies Newsletter* 9:72–75.

Howell, F. Clark. 1957a. "The Evolutionary Significance of Variation and Varieties of 'Neanderthal' Man." *Quarterly Review of Biology* 32:330–347.

———. 1957b. "Pleistocene Glacial Ecology and the Evolution of 'Classic' Neanderthal Man." *Southwestern Journal of Anthropology* 8:377–410.

———. 1966. "Observations on the Earlier Phases of the European Lower Palaeolithic." *American Anthropologist* 68 (2):111–140.

———. 1974. *Early Man.* Chicago: Time-Life.

Howell, F. Clark, and Clark, J. Desmond. 1963. "Acheulian Hunter-Gatherers of Sub-Saharan Africa." *Viking Fund Publications in Anthropology* 36:458–533.

Howell, John M. 1987. "Early Farming in Northwestern Europe." *Scientific American* 237(11): 118–126.

Hunwick, John D. 1971. "Songhay, Bornu and Hausaland in the Sixteenth Century." In Jacob F. Ajayi and Michael Crowder, eds., *History of West Africa*, vol. 1. London: Longmans. Pp. 120–157.

Huxley, Thomas H. 1863. *Man's Place in Nature.* London: Macmillan.

Huyen Pham Minh. 1984. "Various Phases of the Development of Primitive Metallurgy in Viet Nam." In Donn T. Bayard, ed., *The Origins of Agriculture, Metallurgy, and the State in Mainland Southeast Asia.* Dunedin, New Zealand: University of Otago Press. Pp. 173–182.

Hyslop, John. 1984. *The Inca Road System.* New York: Academic.

Hyslop, John, et al. 1987. *Huaca Prieta.* New York: American Museum of Natural History.

Ikawa-Smith, Fumio. 1978. "Lithic Assemblages from the Early and Middle Upper Pleistocene Formations in Japan." In Alan Lyle Bryan, ed., *Early Man in America from a Circum-Pacific Perspective.* Edmonton: University of Alberta.

———. 1980. "Current Issues in Japanese Archaeology." *American Scientist* 68 (2):134–145.

Imbrie, J., and Imbrie, K. P. 1979. *Ice Ages.* Short Hills, N.J.: Enslow.

Institute of Vertebrate Paleontology and Paleoanthropology, Chinese Academy of Sciences. 1981. *Atlas of Primitive Man in China.* New York: Van Nostrand Reinhold.

Irwin, H. T., and Wormington, H. M. 1970. "Paleo-Indian Tool Types in the Great Plains." *American Antiquity* 325:24–34.

Irwin-Williams, Cynthia. 1968. *Early Man in North America.* Portales: Eastern New Mexico University Press.

———. 1973. "The Oshara Tradition: Origins of Anasazi Culture." *University of New Mexico Contributions in Anthropology,* no. 4.

———. 1978. "Summary of Archaeological Evidence from the Valsequillo Region, Puebla, Mexico." In David L. Browman, ed., *Cultural Continuity in Mesoamerica.* The Hague: Mouton. Pp. 7–22.

Irwin-Williams, Cynthia, and Haynes, C. Vance. 1970. "Climatic Change and Early Population Dynamics in the Southwestern United States." *Quaternary Research* 1 (1):59–71.

Isaac, Glynn Ll. 1977. *Olorgesaillie.* Chicago: University of Chicago Press.

———.1978. "The Food-sharing Behavior of Protohuman Hominids." *Scientific American* No. 238:90–110.

———. 1981a. "Emergence of Human Behavior Patterns." *Philosophical Transactions of the Royal Society of London* 292:177–188.

———. 1981b. "The Origin of Man." *Quarterly Review of Archaeology* 2:16.

———. 1984. "The Archaeology of Human Origins: Studies of the Lower Palaeolithic in East Africa, 1971–1981." *Advances in World Archaeology* 3:1–89.

Isaac, Glynn Ll., and Harris, J. W. K. 1978. "Archaeology." In M. D. Leakey and Richard E. Leakey, eds., *The Fossil Hominids and an Introduction to Their Context, 1968–1974.* Vol. 1, Koobi Fora Research Project. Oxford: Clarendon. Pp. 47–76.

Isaac, Glynn Ll., and McCown, Elizabeth, eds. 1976. *Human Origins: Louis Leakey and the East African Evidence.* Menlo Park, Calif.: Benjamin.

Isbell, William, and Schreiber, Katharina J. 1978. "Was Huari a State?" *American Antiquity* 43:372–389.

Jacobsen, Thomas W. 1981. "Franchthi Cave and the Beginning of Village Settled Life in Greece." *Hesperia* 50:303–319.

Jacobson, Jerome. 1979. "Recent Developments in South Asian Prehistory and Protohistory." *Annual Review of Anthropology* 8:467–502.

Jacobsthal, P. 1944. *Early Celtic Art.* Oxford University Press.

Jarrige, J., and Meadow, R. 1979. "The Antecedents of Civilization in the Indus Valley." *Scientific American* 240 (1):122–133.

Jeffries, R. W. 1987. *The Archaeology of Carrier Mills.* Carbondale: Southern Illinois University Press.

Jelenik, Arthur. 1981. "The Middle Paleolithic of the Levant." In J. Cauvin and P. Sanlaville, eds., *Prehistoire de Levant.* Paris: CRNS Publications. Pp. 299–302.

Jennings, Jesse D. 1957. *Danger Cave.* Salt Lake City: University of Utah Press.

———. 1975. *The Prehistory of North America.* 2d ed. New York: McGraw-Hill.

———, ed. 1979. *The Prehistory of Polynesia.* Cambridge: Harvard University Press.

———, ed. 1983. *Ancient Native Americans.* 2d ed. 2 vols. New York: Freeman.

Jochim, Michael. 1976. *Hunter-Gatherer Subsistence and Settlement.* New York: Academic.

———. 1981. *Strategies for Survival: Cultural Behavior in Ecological Context.* New York: Academic.

———. 1983. "Paleolithic Cave Art in Ecological Perspective." In G. N. Bailey, ed., *Hunter-Gatherer Economy in Prehistory.* Cambridge: Cambridge University Press. Pp. 212–219.

Johanson, Donald C., and Edey, Maitland A. 1981. *Lucy: The Beginnings of Humankind.* New York: Simon and Schuster.

Johanson, Donald C., and White, Tim. 1979. "A Systematic Assessment of Early African Hominids." *Science* 202:321–330.

Johanson, Donald C., et al. 1987. "New Partial Skeleton of *Homo habilis* from Olduvai Gorge, Tanzania." *Nature* 327:205–211.

Johnson, Paul. 1978. *The Civilization of Ancient Egypt.* London: Weidenfeld and Nicholson.

Jolly, Clifford. 1970. "The Seed-Eaters: A New Model of Hominid Differentiation Based on Baboon Analogy." *Man* 5:5–26.

Jones, Christopher. 1984. *Deciphering Maya Hieroglyphs.* Philadelphia: University Museum, University of Pennsylvania.

Jones, Peter R. 1980. "Experimental Butchery with Modern Stone Tools and Its Relevance for Palaeolithic Archaeology." *World Archaeology* 12 (2):153–165.

Joukowsky, Martha. 1981. *A Complete Manual of Field Archaeology.* Englewood Cliffs, N.J.: Prentice-Hall.

Jovanovic, Borislav. 1980. "The Origins of Copper Mining in Europe." *Scientific American* 242 (5):152–168.

Judd, Neil M. 1954. *The Material Culture of Pueblo Bonito.* Washington, D.C.: Smithsonian Institution.

———. 1964. *The Agriculture of Pueblo Bonito.* Washington D.C.: Smithsonian Institution.

Kalb, J. F., et al. 1984. "Early Hominid Habitation of Ethiopia." *American Scientist* 72:168–178.

Kano, Chiaki. 1979. *The Origins of the Chavín Culture.* Washington, D.C.: Dumbarton Oaks.

Keatinge, Richard, ed. 1988. *Peruvian Prehistory.* Cambridge: Cambridge University Press.

Keightley, David N. 1978. *Sources of Shang History: The Oracle Bone Inscriptions of Bronze Age China.* Berkeley and Los Angeles: University of California Press.

———, (ed.) 1983. *The Origins of Chinese Civilization.* Berkeley and Los Angeles: University of California Press.

Kenyon, Kathleen. 1961. *Archaeology in the Holy Land.* London: Edward Benn.

———. 1981. *Excavations of Jericho,* vol. 3. Jerusalem: British School of Archaeology.

Kidder, A. V. 1927. *An Introduction to the Study of Southwestern Archaeology, with a Preliminary Account of the Excavations at Pecos.* New Haven: Yale University Press.

Kiernan, F. A., and Fairbank, J. K. 1974. *Chinese Ways of Warfare.* Cambridge: Harvard University Press.

Kinley, M. I. 1963. *The Ancient Greeks.* London: Chatto and Windus.

Kinnes, Ian. 1982. "Les Fouaillages and Megalithic Origins." *Antiquity* 56:24–30.

Kirch, Patrick V. 1982. "Advances in Polynesian Prehistory: Three Decades in Review." *Advances in World Archaeology* 2:52–102.

———. 1984. *The Evolution of the Polynesian Chiefdoms.* Cambridge: Cambridge University Press.

———. 1985. *Feathered Gods and Fishhooks.* Honolulu: University of Hawaii Press.

———, ed. 1986. *Island Societies.* Cambridge: Cambridge University Press.

Kirk, Ruth. 1975. *Hunters of the Whale.* New York: Morrow.

Kirkbride, Diana. 1968. "Beidha: Early Neolithic Village Life South of the Dead Sea." *Antiquity* 42:263–274.

———. 1975. "Umm Dabaghiyah 1974: A Fourth Preliminary Report." *Iraq* 37:3–10.

Kirkby, Anne V. T. 1973. *The Use of Land and Water Resources in the Past and Present Valley of Oaxaca.* Ann Arbor: University of Michigan Museum of Anthropology.

Kitto, H. D. F. 1958. *The Greeks.* Baltimore: Pelican.

Klein, Jeffrey, et al. 1982. "Calibration of Radiocarbon Dates." *Radiocarbon* 24 (2):103–150.

Klein, Richard G. 1969. *Man and Culture in the Late Pleistocene.* San Francisco: Chandler.

———. 1971. "The Pleistocene Prehistory of Siberia." *Quaternary Research* 2 (1):131–161.

———. 1979. "Stone Age Exploitation of Animals in Southern Africa." *American Scientist* 67:23–32.

———. 1984. "The Prehistory of Stone Age Herders in South Africa." In J. Desmond Clark and Steven A. Brandt, eds., *From Hunters to Farmers.* Berkeley and Los Angeles: University of California Press. Pp. 281–289.

Klein, Richard G., and Cruz-Uribe, Kathryn. 1984. *The Analysis of Animal Bones from Archaeological Sites.* Chicago: University of Chicago Press.

Knudsen, Ruthann. 1986. "Contemporary Cultural Resource Management." In David Meltzer, Don D. Fowler, and Jeremy Sabloff, eds., *American Archaeology Past and Future.* Washington, D.C.: Smithsonian Institution Press. Pp. 395–413.

Kohl, P. 1975. "Carved Chlorite Vessels: A Trade in Finished Commodities in the Mid–Third Millenium." *Expedition* (Fall): 18–31.

———. 1978. "The Balance of Trade in Southwestern Asia in the Mid–Third Millenium B.C." *Current Anthropology* 19:463–492.

Kolata, Alan L. 1982. "Tiwanaku: Portrait of an Andean Civilization." *Field Museum of Natural History Bulletin* 53 (8):13–28.

———. 1986. "The Agricultural Foundations of the Tiwanaku State: A View from the Heartland." *American Antiquity* 51 (4):748–762.

Kornietz, Ninelj L., and Soffer, Olga. 1984. "Mammoth Bone Dwellings on the North Russian Plain." *Scientific American* 251 (5):164–175.

Kramer, Samuel. 1963. *The Sumerians.* Chicago: University of Chicago Press.

Kristiansen, K. 1981. "A Social History of Danish Archaeology." In Glyn E. Daniel, ed., *Towards a History of Archaeology.* London: Thames and Hudson, Pp. 20–44.

Kroeber, A. L., and Kluckhohn, Clyde. 1952. *Culture: A Critical Review of Concepts and Definitions.* Cambridge, Mass.: Peabody Museum.

Kukla, G. J. 1977. "Pleistocene Land Correlations, I. Europe." *Earth Science Review* 13:307–374.

Kurtén, Björn. 1968. *Pleistocene Mammals in Europe.* Chicago: Aldine.

Kurtén, Björn, and Anderson, E. 1980. *Pleistocene Mammals of North America.* New York: Columbia University Press.

Laitman, Jeffrey T. 1984. "The Anatomy of Human Speech." *Natural History* 93 (9):20–27.

Lamberg-Karlovsky, C. C. 1973. "Urban Interactions on the Iranian Plateau: Excavations at Tepe Yahya, 1967–1973." *Proceedings of the British Academy* 59:5–43.

———. 1978. "The Proto-Elamites and the Iranian Plateau." *Antiquity* 52:114–120.

Lancaster, Jane, and Whitten, Phillip. 1980. "Family Matters." *The Sciences* 1:10–15.

Lanning, Eric P. 1967. *Peru Before the Incas.* Englewood Cliffs, N.J.: Prentice-Hall.

Larichev, Vitaliy, et al. 1987. "Lower and Middle Paleolithic of Northern Asia: Achievements, Problems, and Perspectives." *Journal of World Prehistory* 1 (4):415–464.

Lathrap, Donald W. 1985. "Jaws: The Control of Power in the Early Nuclear American Ceremonial Center." In Christopher Donnan, ed., *Early Ceremonial Architecture in the Andes.* Washington, D.C.: Dumbarton Oaks. Pp. 241–268.

Laughlin, William S. 1980. *Aleuts, Survivors of the Bering Land Bridge.* New York: Holt, Rinehart and Winston.

Laughlin, William S., and Marsh, G. H. 1954. "The Lamellar Flake Manufacturing Site on Anangula Island in the Aleutians." *American Antiquity* 20:27–39.

Laughlin, William S., Marsh, G. H., and Harper, A. B., eds. 1979. *The First Americans: Origins, Affinities and Adaptations*. New York: Fisher.

Laville, Henri, Rigaud, Jean-Philippe, and Sackett, James. 1980. *Rock Shelters of the Perigord*. New York: Academic.

Leakey, L. S. B. 1951. *Olduvai Gorge, 1931–1951*. Cambridge: Cambridge University Press.

Leakey, M. D. 1971. *Olduvai Gorge*, vol. 3. Cambridge: Cambridge University Press.

———. 1978. "Pliocene Footprints at Laetoli, Tanzania." *Antiquity* 52:133.

Leakey, M. D., et al. 1976. "Fossil Hominids from the Laetoli Beds." *Nature* 262:460–466.

Leakey, Richard, and Lewin, Roger. 1977. *Origins*. New York: Dutton.

Lee, J. E. 1866. *The Lake Dwellings of Switzerland and Other Parts of Europe*. London: Murray.

Lee, Richard B. 1979. *The !Kung San*. Cambridge: Cambridge University Press.

Lee, Richard B., and DeVore, Irven, eds. 1976. *Kalahari Hunter-Gatherers*. Cambridge: Harvard University Press.

Legge, A. J., and Rowley-Conwy, Peter. 1987. "Gazelle Hunting in Stone Age Syria." *Scientific American* 238 (8):88–95.

Lehmann, Johannes. 1977. *The Hittites: People of the Thousand Gods*. London: Collins.

Leroi-Gourhan, Andre. 1965. *Treasures of Palaeolithic Art*. New York: Abrams.

———. 1984. *The Dawn of European Art: An Introduction to Palaeolithic Cave Painting*. Cambridge: Cambridge University Press.

Leveque, François, and Vandermeersch, Bernard. 1982. "Les découvertes de restes humains dans un horizon Castelperronien de Saint-Césaire (Charente-Maritime)." *Bulletin de la Société Préhistorique Française* 77:35.

Levetzion, Nehemiah. 1973. *Ancient Ghana and Mali*. London: Methuen.

Lewin, Roger. 1987. *Bones of Contention*. New York: Simon and Schuster.

———. 1988a. *Human Evolution*. 2d ed. Oxford: Blackwell.

———. 1988b. "A Revolution of Ideas in Agricultural Origins." *Science* 240:984–986.

Lewis, David. 1972. *We the Navigators*. Honolulu: University of Hawaii Press.

Lewis-Williams, David. 1981. *Believing and Seeing: Symbolic Meanings in Southern San Rock Art*. New York: Academic.

Lhote, Henri. 1959. *The Search for the Tassili Frescoes*. London: Hutchinson University Library.

Lipe, William D. 1983. "The Southwest." In Jesse D. Jennings, ed., *Ancient Native Americans*. 2d ed. San Francisco: Freeman. Pp. 403–454.

Livingstone, Sir R., trans. 1943. *Thucydides' History of the Peloponnesian War*. Cambridge: Oxford University Press.

Lloyd, Seton. 1963. *Mounds of the Near East*. Chicago: Aldine.

———. 1967. *Early Highland Peoples of Anatolia*. New York: McGraw-Hill.

———. 1980. *Foundations in the Dust*. London: Thames and Hudson.

———. 1983. *The Archaeology of Mesopotamia*. 2d ed. London: Thames and Hudson.

Lourandos, Henry. 1987. "Pleistocene Australia: Peopling a Continent." In Olga Soffer, ed., *The Pleistocene Old World: Regional Perspectives*. New York: Plenum. Pp. 147–166.

Lovejoy, G. O. 1981. "The Origin of Man." *Science* 211:341–350.

———. 1984. "The Natural Detective." *Natural History* 93 (10):24–28.

Luce, J. V. 1973. *Atlantis*. New York: McGraw-Hill.

Lumley, Henry de. 1969. "A Paleolithic Camp near Nice." *Scientific American* 87:23–32.

Lynch, Thomas F. 1983. "The South American Paleo-Indians." In Jesse D. Jennings, ed., *Ancient Native Americans*. 2d ed. San Francisco: Freeman. Pp. 455–490.

———, ed. 1980. *Guitarrero Cave*. New York: Academic.

Lyons, Thomas R., and Avery, Thomas. 1977. *Remote Sensing: A Handbook for Archaeologists and Cultural Resource Managers*. Washington, D.C.: National Park Service.

McBurney, C. B. M. 1976. *Early Man in the Soviet Union.* London: British Academy.

McGimsey, Charles R. 1973. *Public Archaeology.* New York: Academic.

McIntosh, Susan Keech, and McIntosh, Roderick J. 1981. "West African Prehistory." *American Scientist* 69:602–613.

McIntosh, S. K., and McIntosh, R. J. 1988. "From Stone to Metal: New Perspectives on the Later Prehistory of West Africa." *Journal of World Prehistory* 2 (1):89–131.

MacNeish, Richard, ed. 1970. *The Prehistory of the Tehuacán Valley.* Austin: University of Texas Press.

———. 1971. "Early Man in the Andes." *Scientific American* (4):36–46.

———. 1978. *The Science of Archaeology.* North Scituate, Mass.: Duxbury.

———. 1979. "Earliest Man in the New World and Its Implications for Soviet-American Archaeology." *Arctic Anthropology* 16 (1):2–15.

———. 1983. "Mesoamerica." In Richard Shutler, Jr., ed., *Early Man in the New World.* Beverly Hills: Sage. Pp. 125–136.

———. 1986. "The Preceramic of Middle America." *Advances in World Archaeology* 5:93–130.

MacNeish, Richard, and Nelken-Terner, Antoinette. 1983. "The Pre-Ceramic of Mesoamerica." *Journal of Field Archaeology* 10 (1):71–84.

MacNeish, Richard, et al. 1980. *The Prehistory of the Ayacucho Basin, Peru.* Ann Arbor: University of Michigan Press.

MacNeish, Richard, et al. 1980, 1981. *The Prehistory of the Ayacucho Basin, Peru.* University of Michigan: Ann Arbor. Vol. 2: Excavations and Chronology (1981); Vol. 3: Nonceramic Artifacts (1980).

MacQueen, J. G. 1987. *The Hittites.* London: Thames and Hudson.

McVicker, Donald. 1985. "The 'Mayanized' Mexican." *American Antiquity* 50 (1):82–101.

Malinowski, Bronislaw. 1922. *Argonauts of the Western Pacific.* London: Routledge and Kegan Paul.

Malthus, Thomas Henry. 1798. *An Essay on the Principle of Population.* London: Johnson.

Marcus, Joyce. 1973. "Territorial Organization of the Lowland Maya." *Science* 180:911–916.

Maringer, J., and Bandi, H. G. 1953. *Art in the Ice Age.* New York: Praeger.

Marks, Anthony E. 1983. "The Middle to Upper Palaeolithic Transition in the Levant." *Advances in World Prehistory* 2:51–98.

Marquardt, William H. 1978. "Advances in Archaeological Seriation." *Advances in Archaeological Method and Theory* 1:1–26.

Marshack, Alexander. 1972. *The Roots of Civilization.* New York: McGraw-Hill.

———. 1975. "Exploring the Mind of Ice Age Man." *National Geographic* 154:62–89.

Martin, Kay, and Voorhies, Barbara. 1975. *The Female of the Species.* New York: Columbia University Press.

Martin, Paul. 1973. "The Discovery of America." *Science* 179:969–974.

Martin, Paul, and Klein, Richard, eds. 1984. *A Pleistocene Revolution.* Tucson: University of Arizona Press.

Martin, Paul, and Plog, Fred T. 1973. *The Archaeology of Arizona.* Garden City, N.Y.: Natural History Press.

Martin, Paul, and Wright, H. E. 1967. *Pleistocene Extinctions: The Search for a Cause.* New Haven: Yale University Press.

Mason, Ronald J. 1981. *Great Lakes Archaeology.* New York: Academic.

Maxwell, Moreau S. 1985. *Prehistory of the Eastern Arctic.* New York: Academic.

Meacham, William. 1977. "Continuity and Local Evolution in the Neolithic of South China: A Non-nuclear Approach." *Current Anthropology* 18:419–440.

Megaw, J. V. S. 1970. *Art of the European Iron Age.* Bath: Baker.

Meggers, Betty. 1973. *Prehistoric America*. Chicago: Aldine.

Melisauskas, Saraunas. 1978. *European Prehistory*. New York: Academic.

Mellaart, James. 1967. *Çatal Hüyük*. New York: McGraw-Hill.

———. 1975. *The Neolithic of the Near East*. London: Thames and Hudson.

Mellars, Paul. 1973. "The Character of the Middle-Upper Palaeolithic in Southwestern France." In Colin Renfrew, ed., *The Explanation of Culture Change*. London: Duckworth. Pp. 255–276.

———. 1985. "The Ecological Basis of Social Complexity in the Upper Palaeolithic of Southwestern France." In T. Douglas Price and James Brown, eds., *Complexity Among Prehistoric Hunter-Gatherers*. Orlando: Academic. Pp. 271–297.

Meltzer, David J., Fowler, Don D., and Sabloff, Jeremy A., eds. 1986. *American Archaeology Past and Future*. Washington, D.C.: Smithsonian Institution Press.

Mendelssohn, Kurt. 1974. *The Riddle of the Pyramids*. New York: Praeger.

Menozzi, P., Piazza, A., and Cavalli-Sforza, L. 1978. "Synthetic Maps of Human Gene Frequencies in Europeans." *Science* 201 (4358):786–792.

Menzel, Dorothy, et al. 1964. "The Paracas Pottery of Inca." *University of California Bulletins in American Archaeology and Ethnology* 50.

Michels, Joseph W. 1973. *Dating Methods in Archaeology*. New York: Seminar.

Miller, Daniel. 1985. "Ideology and the Harappan Civilization." *Journal of Anthropological Archaeology* 4:1–38.

Millon, R., Drewitt, R. Bruce, and Cowgill, George. 1974. *Urbanization at Teotihuacán, Mexico*. Austin: University of Texas Press.

Minnis, Paul. 1985. "Domesticating People and Plants in the Greater Southwest." In Richard I. Ford, ed., *Prehistoric Food Production in North America*. Ann Arbor: University of Michigan Museum of Anthropology. Pp. 309–339.

Mochanov, Yuri A. 1978. "Stratigraphy and Chronology of the Paleolithic of Northeast Asia." In Alan L. Bryan, ed., *Early Man in America from a Circum-Pacific Perspective*. Edmonton: University of Alberta. Pp. 67–68.

Moctezuma, Eduardo Matos. 1984. "The Great Temple of Tenochtitlán." *Scientific American* 251 (2):80–89.

Moore, Andrew, T. 1979. "A Pre-Neolithic Farming Village on the Euphrates." *Scientific American* 241 (2): 62–70.

———. 1985. "The Development of Neolithic Societies in the Near East." *Advances in World Archaeology* 4:1–70.

Moorehead, Alan. 1966. *The Fatal Impact*. London: Hamish Hamilton.

Moratto, Michael. 1985. *California Archaeology*. New York: Academic.

Morenz, Siegfried. 1973. *Egyptian Religion*. London: Macmillan.

Morison, Samuel Eliot. 1971. *The Northern Voyages*. Vol. 1, The European Discovery of America. New York: Oxford University Press.

Morlan, Richard E. 1983. "Pre-Clovis Occupation North of the Ice Sheets." In Richard Shutler, Jr., ed., *Early Man in the New World*. Beverly Hills: Sage. Pp. 47–66.

Morlan, Richard E., and Cinq-Mars, Jacques. 1982. "Ancient Beringians: Human Occupation in the Late Pleistocene of Alaska and the Yukon Territory." In David M. Hopkins et al., eds., *Paleoecology of Beringia*. New York: Academic. Pp. 353–382.

Morris, J. Bayard, ed. 1962. *Five Letters of Cortes to the Emperor, 1519–26*. New York: Norton.

Morse, Dan, and Morse, P. A. 1983. *Archaeology of the Central Mississippi Valley*. New York: Academic.

Moseley, Michael E. 1975a. "Chan Chan: Andean Alternative to the Preindustrial City." *Science* 187:219–225.

———. 1975b. *The Maritime Foundations of Andean Civilization*. Menlo Park, Calif.: Cummings.

————. 1983. "The Evolution of Andean Civilization." In Jesse D. Jennings, ed., *Ancient Native Americans.* 2d ed. San Francisco: Freeman. Pp. 491–542.

Moseley, Michael E. 1985. "The Exploration and Explanation of Early Monumental Architecture in the Andes." In Christopher Donnan, ed., *Early Ceremonial Architecture in the Andes.* Washington, D.C.: Dumbarton Oaks. Pp. 28–58.

Moseley, Michael E. 1986. "Maritime Foundations in Retrospect: A Fishy Hypothesis." Paper to the Society for American Archaeology, New Orleans.

Moseley, Michael, and Day, Kent C., eds. 1982. *Chan Chan: Andean Desert City.* Albuquerque: University of New Mexico Press.

Movius, Hallam L. 1944. "Early Man and Pleistocene Stratigraphy in South and East Asia." *Papers of the Peabody Museum* 19:3.

————. 1973. "Quelques commentaires supplémentaires sur les sagaies d'Isturitz: données de l'Abri Pataud." *Bulletin de la Société Prehistorique Française* 70:85–89.

————. 1977. *Excavation of the Abri Pataud, Les Eyziés (Dordogne).* Cambridge, Mass.: Peabody Museum.

Mueller, James A., ed. 1975. *Sampling in Archaeology.* Tucson: University of Arizona Press.

Mughal, R. M. 1974. "New Evidence of the Early Harappan Culture from Jalipur, Pakistan." *Archaeology* 27 (2):106–113.

Muhly, James D. 1985. "Tin and Bronze." *American Journal of Archaeology* 89 (2):275–291.

Muller, Jon D. 1983. "The Southeast." In Jesse D. Jennings, ed., *Ancient Native Americans.* 2d ed. San Francisco: Freeman. Pp. 222–326.

————. 1986. *Archaeology of the Lower Ohio River Valley.* New York: Academic.

Muller-Beck, Hansjurgen. 1961. "Prehistoric Lake Dwellings." *Scientific American* 211(4):36–44.

————. 1982. "Late Pleistocene Man in Northern Eurasia and the Mammoth-Steppe Biome." In David M. Hopkins et al., eds. *Paleoecology of Beringia.* New York: Academic. Pp. 329–352.

Mulvaney, Derek. 1975. *The Prehistory of Australia.* 2d ed. Baltimore: Pelican.

Murdock, George Peter. 1968. "The Current Status of the World's Hunting and Gathering Peoples." In Richard B. Lee and Irven DeVore, eds., *Man the Hunter.* Chicago: Aldine. Pp. 13–20.

Murrill, Rupert Ivan. 1981. *Petralona Man.* Springfield, Ill.: Thomas.

Napier, J. R. 1980. *Hands.* Cambridge: Cambridge University Press.

Nelson, Sarah. 1982. "Recent Progress in Korean Archaeology." *Advances in World Archaeology* 1:103–150.

Niederberger, C. 1979. "Early Sedentary Economy in the Basin of Mexico." *Science* 203:131–146.

Oakley, K. P. 1955. "Fire as a Palaeolithic Tool and Weapon." *Proceedings of the Prehistoric Society* 21:36–48.

————. 1964. *Frameworks for Dating Fossil Man.* Chicago: Aldine.

Oates, David, and Oates, Joan. 1976. *The Rise of Civilization.* Oxford: Elsevier Phaidon.

Oates, Joan. 1973. "The Background and Development of Early Farming Communities in Mesopotamia and the Zagros." *Proceedings of the Prehistoric Society* 39:147–181.

O'Brien, Eileen. 1984. "What Was the Acheulian Hand Ax?" *Natural History* 93 (3):23–28.

Ohel, Milla Y. 1979. "The Clactonian: An Independent Complex or an Integral Part of the Acheulian?" *Current Anthropology* 20 (2):685–726.

Oliver, Douglas. 1977. *Ancient Tahitian Society.* Honolulu: University of Hawaii Press.

Oliver, Roland, and Fagan, Brian M. 1975. *Africa in the Iron Age.* Cambridge: Cambridge University Press.

Oliver, Roland, and Fage, John D. 1963. *A Short History of Africa.* Baltimore: Pelican.

Olivier, Robert C. D. 1982. "Ecology and Behavior of Living Elephants: Bases for Assumptions Concerning the Extinct Woolly Mammoth." In David M. Hopkins et al., eds., *Paleoecology of Beringia.* New York: Academic. Pp. 291–306.

Olsen, S. J. 1987. "The Practice of Archaeology in China Today." *Antiquity* 61, (232):282–290.

Otto, Martha Potter. 1980. "Hopewell Antecedents in the Adena Heartland." In David C. Brose and N'omi Greber, eds. *Hopewellian Archaeology.* Kent, Ohio: Kent State University Press. Pp. 9–14.

Ovey, C. D., ed. 1964. *The Swanscombe Skull: A Survey of Research on a Pleistocene Site.* London: Royal Anthropological Institute.

Pallotino, Massimo. 1977. *The Etruscans.* Translated by David Ridgeway. Harmondsworth: Lane.

Parkington, John. 1987. "Prehistory and Paleoenvironments at the Pleistocene-Holocene Boundary in the Western Cape." In Olga Soffer, ed., *The Pleistocene Old World: Regional Perspectives.* New York: Plenum. Pp. 349–364.

Parsons, Lee, and Price, Barbara. 1971. "Mesoamerican Trade and Its Role in the Emergence of Civilization." *Contributions of the University of California Archaeological Research Facility* 11:169–195.

Patterson, Thomas C. 1985. "The Huaca La Florida, Rímac Valley, Peru." In Christopher Donnan, ed., *Early Ceremonial Architecture in the Andes.* Washington, D.C.: Dumbarton Oaks. Pp. 59–70.

Peake, Harold, and Fleure, Herbert J. 1927. *Peasants and Potters.* Oxford: Oxford University Press.

Pearson, Richard. 1981. "Social Complexity in Chinese Coastal Neolithic Sites." *Science* 213:1078–1088.

Pearson, Richard J., et al., eds. 1986. *Window on the Japanese Past: Studies in Archaeology and Prehistory.* Ann Arbor: Center for Japanese Studies, University of Michigan.

Pelto, Peter J. 1966. *The Nature of Anthropology.* Columbus, Ohio: Merrill.

Penck, Albrecht, and Brückner, Edward. 1909. *Die Alpen im Eiszeitalter.* Leipzig: Tauchnitz.

Penniman, T. K. 1965. *A Hundred Years of Anthropology.* New York: Humanities.

Peringuey, Louis. 1911. *The Stone Age in South Africa.* Capetown: South African Museum.

Perkins, Dexter. 1964. "The Prehistoric Fauna from Shanidar, Iraq." *Science* 144:1565–1566.

Peyrony, Denis. 1934. "La Ferrassie." *Prehistoire* 3:1–54.

Pfeiffer, John E. 1982. *The Creative Explosion.* New York: Harper and Row.

———. 1985. *The Emergence of Man.* 4th ed. New York: Harper and Row.

Phillips, E. D. 1972. "The Scythian Domination in Western Asia." *World Archaeology* 4:129–138.

Phillips, Patricia. 1980. *The Prehistory of Europe.* Bloomington: Indiana University Press.

Phillipson, David. 1977. *The Later Prehistory of Eastern and South Africa.* London: Heinemann.

———. 1984. *African Archaeology.* Cambridge: Cambridge University Press.

Pickersgill, Barbara. 1972. "Cultivated Plants as Evidence for Cultural Contacts." *American Antiquity* 37 (1):97–103.

Piggott, Stuart. 1965. *Ancient Europe*. Chicago: Aldine.

Pilbeam, David. 1985. "Patterns of Human Evolution." In Eric Delson, ed., *Ancestors*. New York: Liss. Pp. 51–59.

———. 1986. "Distinguished Lecture: Hominoid Evolution and Hominoid Origins." *American Anthropologist* 88 (2):295–312.

Plog, Fred T., and Upham, Steadman. 1983. "Analysis of Prehistoric Political Organization." In Elizabeth Tooker, ed., *The Development of Political Organization in Native North America*. Washington, D.C.: American Ethnological Society. Pp. 199–213.

Plomley, N. J. B. 1969. *An Annotated Bibliography of the Tasmanian Aborigines*. London: Royal Anthropological Institute.

Polyani, Karl. 1975. "Traders and Trade." In Jeremy A. Sabloff and C. C. Lamberg-Karlovsky, eds., *Ancient Civilization and Trade*. Albuquerque: University of New Mexico Press. Pp. 133–154.

Pope, Geoffrey G. 1984. "The Antiquity and Paleoenvironment of the Asian Hominidae." In R. O. I. Whyte, ed., *The Evolution of the East Asian Environment*. Hong Kong: Center of Asian Studies, University of Hong Kong. Pp. 922–947.

Pope, Geoffrey G., et al. 1986. "Earliest Radiometrically Dated Artifacts from Southeast Asia." *Current Anthropology* 27, (3):275–279.

Pope, Michael. 1973. *Decipherment*. London: Thames and Hudson.

Posselh, Gregory L., ed. 1979. *Ancient Cities of the Indus*. Durham: University of North Carolina Press.

———, ed. 1982, *The Harappan Civilisation*. London: Aris and Phillips.

Postgate, Nicholas. 1977. *The First Empires*. Oxford: Elsevier Phaidon.

Potts, Richard. 1984a. "Home Bases and Early Hominids." *American Scientist* 72:338–347.

———.1984b. "Hominid Hunters? Problems of Identifying the Earliest Hunter-Gatherers." In Robert Foley, ed., *Hominid Evolution and Community Ecology*. London: Academic. Pp. 129–166.

Powers, William R., and Hamilton, Thomas D. 1978. "Dry Creek: A Late Pleistocene Human Occupation in Central Alaska." In Alan L. Bryan, ed., *Early Man in America from a Circum-Pacific Perspective*. Edmonton: University of Alberta. Pp. 72–78.

Pozorski, Thomas. 1983. "The Caballo Muerto Complex and Its Place in the Andean Chronological Sequence." *Annals of the Carnegie Museum* 52:1–40.

———. 1987. "Changing Priorities within the Chimu State: The Role of Irrigation Agriculture." In Jonathan Haas et al., eds., *The Origins and Development of the Andean State*. Cambridge: Cambridge University Press. Pp. 111–120.

Pozorski, Thomas, and Pozorski, Sheila. 1987. "Chavín, the Early Horizon, and the Initial Period." In Jonathan Haas et al., eds., *The Origins and Development of the Andean State*. Cambridge: Cambridge University Press. Pp. 36–46.

Premack, Ann James, and Premack, David. 1972. "Teaching Language to an Ape." *Scientific American* 241 (1):92–99.

Prescott, William H. 1847. *History of the Conquest of Peru*. New York: Everyman's.

Price, T. Douglas. 1983. "The European Mesolithic." *American Antiquity* 48:761–778.

———. 1985. "Foragers of Southern Scandinavia." In T. Douglas Price and James Brown, eds., *Complex Hunter-Gatherers*. New York: Academic. Pp. 212–236.

———. 1987. "The Mesolithic of Western Europe." *Journal of World Prehistory* 1, (3):225–305.

Price, T. Douglas, and Brown, James, eds. 1985. *Complexity Among Prehistoric Hunter-Gatherers*. New York: Academic.

Price, T. Douglas, et al. 1982. "Thermal Alteration in Mesolithic Assemblages." *Proceedings of the Prehistoric Society* 48:467–485.

Protzen, Jean-Pierre. 1986. "Inca Stonemasonry." *Scientific American* 254 (2):94–105.

Prickett, Nigel, ed. 1983. *The First 1000 Years: Regional Perspectives in New Zealand Archaeology.* Palmerston North: New Zealand Archaeological Association.

Proulx, Donald. 1973. *Archaeological Investigations in the Nepeña Valley, Peru.* Amherst: University of Massachusetts Press.

———. 1983a. "The Nasca Style." In Lois Katz, ed., *Art of the Andes: Pre-Columbian Sculptured and Painted Ceramics from the Arthur M. Sackler Collection.* Washington, D. C.: Arthur M. Sackler Foundation. Pp. 87–104.

———. 1983b. "Tiahuanaco and Huari." In Lois Katz, ed., *Art of the Andes: Pre-Columbian Sculptured and Painted Ceramics from the Arthur M. Sackler Collection.* Washington, D.C.: Arthur M. Sackler Foundation. Pp. 107–114.

———. 1985. "An Analysis of the Early Cultural Sequence in the Nepeña Valley, Peru." *Research Report of Department of Anthropology, University of Massachusetts, Amherst,* no. 25.

Puleston, Dennis. 1971. "An Experimental Approach to the Function of Maya Chultuns." *American Antiquity* 36:322–335.

Quilter, Jeffrey. 1985. "Architecture and Chronology at El Paraíso, Peru." *Journal of Field Archaeology* 12 (3):274–298.

Raab, Mark L., and Goodyear, Albert C. 1984. "Middle Range Theory in Archaeology: A Critical Review of Origins and Applications." *American Antiquity* 49:255–268.

Raikes, Robert. 1967. *Water, Weather, and Prehistory.* London: Baker.

Rak, Yoel. 1983. *The Australopithecine Face.* New York: Academic.

Ranov, V. A., and Davis, R. S. 1979. "Toward a New Outline of the Soviet Central Asian Paleolithic." *Current Anthropology* 20 (2):249–270.

Rathje, William L. 1971. "The Origin and Development of Classic Maya Civilization." *American Antiquity* 36:275–285.

———. 1972. "Praise the Gods and Pass the Metates: A Hypothesis of the Development of Lowland and Rainforest Civilizations in Mesoamerica." In Mark P. Leone, ed., *Contemporary Archaeology.* Carbondale: Southern Illinois University Press. Pp. 365–392.

Raymond, J. Scott. 1981. "The Maritime Foundations of Andean Civilization: A Reconsideration of the Evidence." *American Antiquity* 46:806–820.

Redman, Charles L., ed. 1973. *Research and Theory in Current Archaeology.* New York: Wiley Interscience.

———. 1978. *The Rise of Civilization: From Early Farmers to Urban Society in the Ancient Near East.* San Francisco: Freeman.

———. 1987. "Surface Collection, Sampling, and Research Design: A Retrospective." *American Antiquity* 52 (2):249–265.

Reidhead, V. A. 1980. "The Economics of Subsistence Change: A Test of an Optimization Model." In T. K. Earle and A. L. Christianson, eds., *Modelling Change in Prehistoric Subsistence Economies.* New York: Academic. Pp. 141–186.

Renault, Mary. 1963. *The King Must Die.* New York: Random House.

Renfrew, Colin. 1967. "Colonialism and Megalithismus." *Antiquity* 41:276–288.

———. 1970. "The Tree-Ring Calibration of Radiocarbon: An Archaeological Evaluation." *Proceedings of the Prehistoric Society* 36:280–311.

———. 1972. *The Emergence of Civilization.* London: Methuen.

———. 1973. *Before Civilization.* New York: Knopf.

———. 1978. "Varna and the Social Context of Early Metallurgy." *Antiquity* 52:199–203.

———. 1983. "The Social Archaeology of Megaliths." *Scientific American* 249:152–163.

———, ed. 1984. *The Megalithic Monuments of Western Europe.* London: Thames and Hudson.

Renfrew, Colin, and Dixon, J. E. 1976. "Obsidian in Western Asia: A review." In Ian Longworth and K. E. Wilson, eds., *Problems in Economic and Social Archaeology.* London: Duckworth. Pp. 137–150.

Renfrew, Colin, Dixon, J. E., and Cann, J. R. 1966. "Obsidian and Early Cultural Contact in the Near East." *Proceedings of the Prehistoric Society* 32:1–29.

Renfrew, Colin, and Wagstaff, J. M., eds. 1982. *An Island Polity: The Archaeology of Exploitation in Melos.* Cambridge: Cambridge University Press.

Renfrew, Jane. 1973. *Palaeoethnobotany: The Prehistoric Food Plants of the Near East.* London: Methuen.

Reynolds, T. E. G., and Barnes, G. L. 1984. "The Japanese Palaeolithic: A Review." *Proceedings of the Prehistoric Society* 50:49–62.

Rick, John W. 1980. *Prehistoric Hunters of the High Andes.* New York: Academic.

Rieu, E. V., trans. 1945. *Homer's Iliad.* Baltimore: Pelican.

Rightmire, G. Philip. 1984. "*Homo sapiens* in Sub-Saharan Africa." In Fred Smith and Frank Spencer, eds., *The Origins of Modern Humans.* New York: Liss. Pp. 295–326.

Rindos, David. 1984. *The Origins of Agriculture: An Evolutionary Perspective.* New York: Academic.

Roberts, Neil. 1984. "Pleistocene Environments in Time and Space." In Robert Foley, ed., *Hominid Evolution and Community Ecology.* London: Academic. Pp. 25–54.

Rodden, Robert J. 1962. "Excavations at the Early Neolithic Site at Nea Nikomedeia, Greek Macedonia (1961 Season)." *Proceedings of the Prehistoric Society* 28:267–288.

Roe, Derek, 1981. *The Lower and Middle Palaeolithic Periods in Britain.* London: Routledge and Kegan Paul.

Rognon, Pierre. 1981. "Interprétation paleoclimatique des changements d'environments en Afrique du Nord et au Moyen Orient durant les 20 derniers millénaires." *Palaeoecology of Africa* 13:21–44.

Romer, John. 1981. *The Valley of Kings.* New York: Morrow.

Ronen, Avraham, ed. 1982. *The Transition from Lower to Middle Paleolithic and the Origins of Modern Man.* Oxford: British Archaeological Reports, International Series, no. 151.

Rose, M. D. 1984. "Food Acquisition and the Evolution of Primate Behavior: The Case of Bipedalism." In D. J. Chivers et al., eds., *Food Acquisition and Processing in Primates.* New York: Plenum. Pp. 509–524.

Roth, H. Ling. 1887. "On the Origins of Agriculture." *Journal of the Royal Anthropological Institute* 16:102–136.

Rowe, John H. 1946. *Inca Culture at the Time of the Spanish Conquest.* Handbook of South American Indians, Vol. 2. Washington, D.C.: Smithsonian Institution.

———. 1948. "The Kingdom of Chimor." *Acta Americana* 6:26–59.

———. 1962. *Chavín Art: An Inquiry into Its Form and Meaning.* New York: Museum of Primitive Art.

Rowe, John H., Collier, John, and Willey, Gordon R. 1950. "Reconnaissance Notes on the Site of Huari, near Ayacuchu, Peru." *American Antiquity* 16:120–137.

Rowlett, Ralph. 1967. "The Iron Age North of the Alps." *Science* 161:123–134.

Rowley-Conwy, Peter. 1986. "Between Cave Painters and Crop Planters: Aspects of the Temperate European Mesolithic." In Marek Zvelebil, ed., *Hunters in Transition.* Cambridge: Cambridge University Press. Pp. 17–32.

Roys, R. 1972. *The Indian Background of Colonial Yucatán.* Norman: University of Oklahoma Press.

Rudenko, Sergei. 1970. *The Frozen Tombs of Siberia: The Pazyryk Burials of Iron Age Horsemen.* Translated by M. W. Thompson. Berkeley and Los Angeles: University of California Press.

Ruffle, John. 1977. *Heritage of the Pharaohs.* Oxford: Phaidon.

Rukang, Wu, and Shenglong, Liu. 1983. "Peking Man." *Scientific American* 248 (6):80–95.

Sabloff, Jeremy A., and Friedel, David A. 1984. *Cozumel: Late Maya Settlement Patterns.* New York: Academic.

Sabloff, Jeremy A., and Lamberg-Karlovsky, C. C., eds. 1975. *Ancient Civilization and Trade.* Albuquerque: University of New Mexico Press.

Sahlins, Marshall, and Service, Elman, eds. 1960. *Evolution and Culture.* Ann Arbor: University of Michigan Press.

Salmon, M. 1982. *The Philosophy of Archaeology.* New York: Academic.

Sanders, N. K. 1977. *The Sea People.* London: Thames and Hudson.

Sanders, William T. 1965. *The Cultural Ecology of the Tehuacán Valley.* University Park: Pennsylvania State University Press.

Sanders, William T., Parsons, Jeffrey R., and Santley, Robert S. 1979. *The Basin of Mexico: Ecological Processes in the Evolution of a Civilization.* New York: Academic.

Sanders, William T., and Price, Barbara J. 1968. *Mesoamerica: The Evolution of a Civilization.* New York: Random House.

Sanders, William T., and Webster, David. 1978. "Unilinealism, Multilinealism, and the Evolution of Complex Societies." In Charles L. Redman et al., eds., *Social Archaeology.* New York: Academic. Pp. 249–302.

Sanders, William T., et al. 1970. *The Natural Environment: Contemporary Occupation and Sixteenth Century Population of the Valley: Teotihuacán Valley Project Final Report.* University Park: Pennsylvania State University Press.

Sarich, Vincent. 1971. "A Molecular Approach to the Problem of Human Origins." In Phyllis Dolhinow and Vincent Sarich, eds., *Background for Man.* Boston: Little, Brown. Pp. 60–81.

———. 1983. "Retrospective on Hominoid Macromolecular Systematics." In R. L. Ciochon and R. S. Corrucini, eds., *New Interpretations of Ape and Human Ancestry.* New York: Plenum. Pp. 137–150.

Sauer, Carl O. 1952. *Agricultural Origins and Dispersals.* New York: American Geographical Society.

Schaller, George B. 1971. *Serengeti: A Kingdom of Predators.* New York: Knopf.

———. 1972. *The Serengeti Lion.* Chicago: University of Chicago Press.

Schapera, Isaac. 1930. *The Khoisan Peoples of South Africa.* New York: Humanities.

Schele, Linda, and Miller, E. 1986. *The Blood of Kings.* Austin: University of Texas Press.

Schiffer, Michael. 1976. *Behavioral Archaeology.* New York: Academic.

———. 1983. "Towards the Identification of Site Formation Processes." *American Antiquity* 48:675–706.

Schiffer, Michael, and House, John. 1977. *The Cache River Archaeological Project.* Fayetteville: Arkansas Archaeological Survey.

Schmandt-Besserat, D. 1978. "The Earliest Precursor of Writing." *Scientific American* 238 (6):50–59.

Schreiber, Katharina J. 1987. "Conquest and Consolidation: A Comparison of the Wari and Inka Occupation of a Highland Peruvian Valley." *American Antiquity* 52 (2):266–284.

Schrire, Carmel, ed. 1984. *Past and Present in Hunter-Gatherer Studies.* New York: Academic.

Scudder, Thayer. 1962. *The Ecology of the Gwembe Tonga*. Manchester: Manchester University Press.

———. 1971. *Gathering Among African Woodland Savannah Cultivators*. Lusaka: University of Zambia.

Serge, Aldo, and Asconzi, Antonio. 1984. "Italy's Earliest Middle Pleistocene Hominid Site." *Current Anthropology* 25 (2):230–235.

Service, Elman. 1962. *Primitive Social Organization*. New York: Random House.

———. 1975. *The Origins of the State and Civilization*. New York: Norton.

Shackleton, N. J., and Opdyke, N. D. 1973. "Oxygen Isotope and Paleomagnetic Stratigraphy of Equatorial Pacific Ocean Core V28-238." *Quarternary Research* 3:38–55.

Sharer, Robert J., and Ashmore, Wendy. 1987. *Archaeology: Discovering Our Past*. Palo Alto, Calif.: Mayfield.

Sharman, G. R., et al. 1980. *Beginning of Agriculture*. Allahabad: University of Allahabad.

Sharp, Andrew. 1957. *Ancient Voyagers in the Pacific*. Baltimore: Pelican.

Shawcross, Kathleen. 1967. "Fern Root and Eighteenth-Century Maori Food Production in Agricultural Areas." *Journal of the Polynesian Society* 76:330–352.

Shennan, S. J. 1982. "Ideology, Change, and the European Early Bronze Age." In Ian Hodder, ed., *Symbolic and Structural Archaeology*. Cambridge: Cambridge University Press. Pp. 235–247.

Sherratt, Andrew G. 1981. "Plough and Pasture." In Ian Hodder et al., eds., *Patterns of the Past*. Cambridge: Cambridge University Press. Pp. 344–361.

Shinnie, Peter. 1967. *Meroe*. London: Thames and Hudson.

Shipman, Pat. 1984. "Scavenger Hunt." *Natural History* 93 (4):20–28.

Shipman, Pat, and Rose, J. 1983. "Evidence of Butchery and Hominid Activities at Torralba and Ambrona." *Journal of Archaeological Studies* 10 (5):475–482.

Shutler, Richard, Jr., ed. 1983. *Early Man in the New World*. Beverly Hills: Sage.

Silverberg, Robert. 1968. *The Mound Builders of Ancient America*. New York: New York Graphic Society.

Simons, Elwyn. 1984. "Dawn Ape of the Fayum." *Natural History* 93 (5):18–20.

Singer, C. 1988. "The Dates of Eden." *Nature* 331 (6157):565–566.

Singer, Ronald, and Wymer, John. 1982. *The Middle Stone Age at Klasies River Mouth in South Africa*. Chicago: University of Chicago Press.

Singer, Ronald, et al. 1973. "Clacton-on-Sea, Essex: Report on Excavations 1969–1970." *Proceedings of the Prehistoric Society* 39:6–74.

Smith, Andrew B. 1984. "Origins of the Neolithic in the Sahara." In J. Desmond Clark and Steven A. Brandt, eds., *From Hunters to Farmers*. Berkeley and Los Angeles: University of California Press. Pp. 84–92.

Smith, Bruce D. 1975. *Middle Mississippian Exploitation of Animal Populations*. Ann Arbor: University of Michigan Museum of Anthropology.

———, ed., 1978a. *Mississippian Settlement Patterns*. New York: Academic.

———. 1978b. "Variations in Mississippian Settlement Patterns." In Bruce D. Smith, ed., *Mississippian Settlement Patterns*. New York: Academic. Pp. 479–503.

———. 1986. "The Archaeology of the Southeastern United States: From Dalton to De Soto, 10,500–500 B.P." *Advances in World Archaeology* 5:1–92.

Smith, P. E. L. 1978. "An Interim Report on Ganj Dareh Tepe, Iran." *American Journal of Archaeology* 82:538–540.

Snow, Dean. 1980. *Archaeology of New England*. New York: Academic.

Soffer, Olga. 1985. *The Upper Palaeolithic of the Central Russian Plains*. New York: Academic.

Solecki, Ralph. 1972. *Shanidar: The Humanity of Neanderthal Man*. Baltimore: Pelican.

Solheim, William. 1971. "An Earlier Agricultural Revolution." *Scientific American* 133 (11):34–51.

Sollas, W. J. 1910. *Ancient Hunters.* London: Macmillan.

Spaulding, Albert C. 1968. "Explanation in Archaeology." In S. R. Binford and Lewis R. Binford, eds., *New Perspectives in Archaeology.* Chicago: Aldine. Pp. 33–39.

Spencer, Herbert. 1855. *Social Statistics.* London: Macmillan.

Speth, John. 1983. *Bone Kills and Bone Counts: Decision Making by Ancient Hunters.* Chicago: University of Chicago Press.

Spooner, Brian, ed. 1972. *Population Growth: An Anthropological Perspective.* Cambridge: MIT Press.

Stahl, Ann Bower. 1984. "Hominid Dietary Selection Before Fire." *Current Anthropology* 25 (2): 151–168.

Stanford, Dennis. 1983. "Pre-Clovis Occupation South of the Ice Sheets." In Richard Shutler, Jr., ed. *Early Man in the New World.* Beverly Hills: Sage. Pp. 65–72.

Stark, Barbara. 1986. "Origins of Food Production in the New World." In David Meltzer et al., eds., *American Archaeology Past and Future.* Washington, D.C.: Smithsonian. Pp. 277–322.

Starling, N. J. 1985. "Colonization and Success: The Earlier Neolithic of Central Europe." *Proceedings of the Prehistoric Society* 51:41–57.

Starling, N. J., and Barreis, C. 1983. "The Evolution of Human Ecosystems in the Eastern United States." In H. E. Wright, Jr., ed., *The Holocene.* Vol. 2, Late Quaternary Environments of the United States. Minneapolis: University of Minnesota Press. Pp. 252–268.

Steindorff, George, and Steele, Keith. 1954. *When Egypt Ruled the East.* Chicago: University of Chicago Press.

Steward, Julian. 1970. *A Theory of Culture Change.* Urbana: University of Illinois Press.

Steward, Julian, et al. 1955. *Irrigation Civilizations: A Comparative Study.* Washington, D.C.: Pan American Union.

Stoltman, James B. 1978. "Temporal Models in Prehistory: An Example from Eastern North America." *Current Anthropology* 19:703–746.

Stoltman, J. B., and Barreis, D. A. 1983. "The Evolution of Human Ecosystems in the Eastern and Central United States." In H. E. Wright, ed., *Late-Quaternary Environments of the United States, Vol 2: The Holocene.* Minneapolis: University of Minnesota Press. Pp. 252–268.

Street, F. Alayne. 1980. "Ice Age Environments." In Andrew G. Sherratt, ed., *The Cambridge Encyclopaedia of Archaeology.* New York: Cambridge University Press and Crown Publishers. Pp. 52–56.

Stringer, Chris. 1984. "Human Evolution and Biological Adaptation in the Pleistocene." In Robert Foley, ed., *Human Evolution and Community Ecology.* London: Academic. Pp. 55–84.

———. 1988. *The Neanderthals.* London: Thames and Hudson.

Stringer, Chris, et al. 1979. "The Significance of the Fossil Hominid from Petralona, Greece." *Journal of Archaeological Science* 6:235–253.

———. 1984. "The Origin of Anatomically Modern Humans in Western Europe." In Fred Smith and Frank Spencer, eds., *The Origins of Modern Humans.* New York: Liss. Pp. 51–136.

Struever, Stuart, ed. 1971. *Prehistoric Agriculture.* Garden City, N.Y.: Natural History Press.

Struever, Stuart, and Holton, Felicia Antonelli. 1979. *Koster: Americans in Search of Their Past.* New York: Anchor Press/Doubleday.

Struever, Stuart, and Houart, Gail. 1968. "An Analysis of the Hopewell Interaction

Sphere." In Edwin Wilmsen, ed., *Social Exchange and Interaction*. Ann Arbor: University of Michigan Museum of Anthropology. Pp. 47–49.

Suess, Hans. 1965. "Secular Variations of the Cosmic-Ray-Produced Carbon 14 in the Atmosphere." *Journal of Geophysical Research* 70:23–31.

Symons, Becky A., and Cybulski, Jerome, eds. 1981. *Homo erectus*. Toronto: University of Toronto Press.

Tanner, Nancy M. 1981. *On Becoming Human*. London: Cambridge University Press.

Taylor, R. E., and Meighan, C. W., eds. 1978. *Chronologies in New World Archaeology*. New York: Academic.

Taylour, Lord William. 1969. *The Mycenaeans*. London: Thames and Hudson.

Telegin, D. J. 1987. "Neolithic Cultures of the Ukraine and Adjacent Areas and Their Chronology." *Journal of World Prehistory* 1 (3):307–331.

Tello, Julio C. 1943. "Discovery of the Chavín Culture in Peru." *American Antiquity* 9:135–160.

Terrace, H., Petitto, L., Sanders, R., and Bever, T. 1979. "Can an Ape Create a Sentence?" *Science* 206:891–902.

Terrell, John E. 1986. *Prehistory in the Pacific Islands*. Cambridge: Cambridge University Press.

Thomas, David. 1973. *Archaeology*. New York: Holt, Rinehart and Winston.

———. 1983. *The Archaeology of Monitor Valley 2: Gatecliff Shelter*. New York: American Museum of Natural History.

Thomas, David, and Bettinger, Robert. 1983. *The Archaeology of the Monitor Valley*. New York: American Museum of Natural History.

Thomas, Julian. 1987. "Relations of Production and Social Change in the Neolithic of Northwestern Europe." *Man* 22 (3):405–430.

Thompson, J. Eric S. 1950. *Maya Hieroglyphic Writing: Introduction*. Washington, D.C.: Carnegie Institution.

Tobias, Philip V. 1967. *Olduvai Gorge*, vol. 2. Cambridge: Cambridge University Press.

Torrance, Robin. 1986. *Production and Exchange*. Cambridge: Cambridge University Press.

Toth, Nicholas. 1985. "The Oldowan Reconsidered: A Close Look at Early Stone Artifacts." *Journal of Archaeological Science* 12:101–120.

Trigger, Bruce G. 1968. *Beyond History: The Methods of Prehistory*. New York: Holt, Rinehart and Winston.

———. 1980. *Gordon Childe: Revolutions in Archaeology*. London: Thames and Hudson.

———. 1981. "Anglo-American Archaeology." *World Archaeology* 13:138–145.

Trigger, Bruce G., et al. 1983. *Ancient Egypt: A Social History*. Cambridge: Cambridge University Press.

Tringham, Ruth. 1971. *Hunters, Fishers, and Farmers of Eastern Europe: 6000–3000 B.C.* London: Hutchinson University Library.

Tringham, Ruth. 1983. "V. Gordon Childe 25 Years After." *Journal of Field Archaeology* 10 (1):85–100.

Tringham, Ruth, et al. 1980. "The Early Agricultural Site of Selevac, Yugoslavia." *Archaeology* 33 (2):24–32.

Trinkhaus, Erik. 1982. "Evolutionary Continuity Among Archaic *Homo sapiens*." In Avraham Ronen, ed., *The Transition from Lower to Middle Paleolithic and the Origins of Modern Man*. Oxford: British Archaeological Reports, International Series, no. 151. Pp. 301–320.

———, ed. 1983a. *The Mousterian Legacy*. Oxford: British Archaeological Reports, International Series, no. 151.

————. 1983b. *The Shanidar Neanderthals.* New York: Academic.

————. 1984. "Western Asia." In Fred Smith and Frank Spencer, eds., *The Origins of Modern Humans.* New York: Liss. Pp. 251–294.

Trinkhaus, Erik, and Howells, W. W. 1979. "The Neanderthals." *Scientific American* 241:118–133.

Trump, David. 1980. *The Prehistory of the Mediterranean.* New Haven: Yale University Press.

Turekian, K. K., ed. 1971. *Late Cenozoic Glacial Ages.* New Haven: Yale University Press.

Turner, Alan. 1984. "Hominids and Fellow Travelers." In Robert Foley, ed., *Hominid Evolution and Community Ecology.* London: Academic. Pp. 193–218.

Turner, B. L., II, and Harrison, Peter D. 1981. "Prehistoric Raised-Field Agriculture in the Maya Lowlands." *Science* 213 (4506):399–405.

Turner, Christy. 1984. "Advances in the Dental Search for Native American Origins." *Acta Anthropogenetica* 8:23–78.

Tuttle, Russell. 1969. "Knuckle-Walking and the Problem of Human Origins." *Science* 166:953.

————, ed. 1972. *The Functional and Evolutionary Biology of Primates.* Chicago: Aldine-Atherton.

Tylecote, R. F. 1987. *The Early History of Metallurgy in Europe.* London: Longmans.

Tylor, Edward. 1871. *Anthropology.* London: Macmillan.

Ucko, Peter J., and Dimbleby, G. W., eds. 1969. *The Domestication and Exploitation of Plants and Animals.* London: Duckworth.

Ucko, Peter J., and Rosenfeld, A. 1967. *Prehistoric Art.* London: Thames and Hudson.

Vadya, Andrew P. 1959. "Polynesian Cultural Distribution in New Perspective." *American Anthropologist* 61:817–828.

Valliant, G. C. 1941. *The Aztecs of Mexico.* New York: Doubleday.

Vavilov, N. I. 1951. "Phytogeographic Basis of Plant Breeding." *Chronica Botanica* 13:14–54.

Vickers, Michael. 1977. *The Roman World.* Oxford: Elsevier Phaidon.

Villa, Paola. 1983. *Terra Amata and the Middle Pleistocene Archaeological Record of Southern France.* Berkeley and Los Angeles: University of California Press.

Vinnecombe, Patricia. 1976. *People of the Eland.* Pietermaritzburg: Natal University Press.

von Däniken, Erich. 1970. *Chariots of the Gods.* New York: Bantam.

Wahlgren, Erik. 1986. *The Vikings and America.* London: Thames and Hudson.

Walker, Alan. 1981. "Dietary Hypotheses and Human Evolution." *Philosophical Transactions of the Royal Society of London* 292:56–64.

Walker, Alan, et al. 1986. "*Australopithecus* Finds from West of Lake Turkana." *Nature* 322:517.

Ward, S. C., and Kimbel, W. H. 1983. "Subnasal Alveolar Morphology and the Systematic Position of *Sivapithecus.*" *American Journal of Physical Anthropology* 61:157–171.

Warren, Peter. 1975. *The Aegean Civilizations.* Oxford: Elsevier Phaidon.

————. 1984. "Knossos: New Excavations and Discoveries." *Archaeology* 37 (4):48–57.

Washburn, Sherwood. 1967. "Behavior and the Origin of Man." *Proceedings of the Royal Anthropological Institute* 97:21–27.

Washburn, Sherwood, and Moore, Ruth. 1987. *Ape into Man.* Boston: Little, Brown.

Watson, Patty Jo, LeBlanc, Steven, and Redman, Charles L. 1971. *Explanation in Archeology: An Explicit Scientific Approach.* New York: Columbia University Press.

———. 1984. *Archeological Explanation: The Scientific Method in Archeology.* New York: Columbia University Press.

Wauchope, Robert. 1962. *Lost Tribes and Sunken Continents.* Chicago: University of Chicago Press.

Weaver, Muriel Porter. 1981. *The Aztecs, Maya, and Their Predecessors.* 2d ed. New York: Academic.

Webb, Clarence H. 1968. "The Extent and Content of Poverty Point Culture." *American Antiquity* 33:297–331.

Webb, W. S. 1974. *Indian Knoll.* New ed. Knoxville: University of Tennessee Press.

Weidenreich, Franz. 1946. *Apes, Giants, and Men.* Chicago: University of Chicago Press.

Weiss, Mark L., and Mann, Alan E. 1988. *Human Biology and Behavior.* 5th ed. Boston: Scott, Foresman/Little, Brown.

Wells, Peter. 1981. *Culture Contact and Culture Change.* Cambridge: Cambridge University Press.

———. 1984. "Early Iron Age Community in Central Europe." *Scientific American* 249 (6):68–93.

Wendorf, Fred, ed. 1968. *The Prehistory of Nubia.* Dallas: Southern Methodist University Press.

Wendorf, Fred, and Schild, Romuald. 1980. *Prehistory of the Eastern Sahara.* New York: Academic.

———. 1981. "The Earliest Food Producers." *Archaeology* 34 (5):30–36

Wendorf, Fred, et al., eds. 1984. *Cattle Keepers of the Eastern Sahara: The Neolithic of Bir Kiseiba.* Dallas: Southern Methodist University Press.

Wertime, Theodore A., and Muhly, James D., eds. 1980. *The Coming of the Age of Iron.* New Haven: Yale University Press.

Wheat, Joe Ben. 1972. *The Olsen-Chubbock Site.* Washington, D.C.: Society for American Archaeology.

Wheatley, Paul. 1971. *The Pivot of the Four Quarters.* Chicago: Aldine.

———. 1975. "Satyarta in Suvarnadvīpa: From Reciprocity to Redistribution in Ancient Southeast Asia." In Jeremy A. Sabloff and C. C. Lamberg-Karlovsky, eds., *Ancient Civilization and Trade.* Albuquerque: University of New Mexico Press. Pp. 227–284.

———. 1979. "Urban Genesis in Mainland Southeast Asia." In R. B. Smith and W. Watson, eds., *Early Southeast Asia.* Oxford: Oxford University Press. Pp. 288–303.

———. 1980. *Kings of the Mountain.* Kuala Lumpur: University of Malaysia Press.

Wheeler, Sir Mortimer. 1954. *Archaeology from the Earth.* Oxford: Clarendon Press.

———. 1962. *The Indus Civilization.* 2d ed. Cambridge: Cambridge University Press.

———. 1968. *Early India and Pakistan.* New York: Praeger.

White, Joyce C. 1982. *Ban Chiang: The Discovery of a Lost Bronze Age Civilization.* Philadelphia: University of Pennsylvania Press.

White, J. Peter, and O'Connell, James. 1982. *A Prehistory of Australia, New Guinea, and Sahul.* Sydney: Academic.

White, Leslie. 1949. *The Science of Culture.* New York: Grove.

White, Randall. 1982. "Rethinking the Middle/Upper Paleolithic Transition." *Current Anthropology* 23 (2):169–191.

———. 1986. *Dark Caves and Bright Visions.* New York: American Museum of Natural History.

Whittle, Alasdair. 1985. *Neolithic Europe: A Survey.* Cambridge: Cambridge University Press.

Whyte, R. O. I. 1983. "The Evolution of the Chinese Environment." In David N. Keightley, ed., *The Origins of Chinese Civilization*. Berkeley and Los Angeles: University of California Press. Pp. 3–20.

Wilcox, David R. 1980. "The Current Status of the Hohokam Concept." In D. E. Doyel and Fred T. Plog, eds., *Current Issues in Hohokam Prehistory: Proceedings of a Symposium*. Tempe: Arizona State Museum. Pp. 236–243.

———. 1985. "The Tepiman Connection: A Model of Mesoamerican-Southwestern Interaction." In Randall H. McGuire and Francis Joan Mathier, eds., *Ripples in the Chichimec Sea*. Carbondale: Southern Illinois University Press. Pp. 86–94.

Wilk, R. R., and Ashmore, Wendy, eds. 1987. *House and Household in the Mesoamerican Past*. Albuquerque: University of New Mexico Press.

Willey, Gordon R. 1953. *Prehistoric Settlement in the Virú Valley, Peru*. Washington, D.C.: Smithsonian Institution.

———. 1963. *The Archaeology of the Virú Valley, Peru*. Cambridge: Peabody Museum.

———. 1966. *North and Middle America*. Vol. 1, An Introduction to American Archaeology. Englewood Cliffs, N.J.: Prentice-Hall.

———. 1971. *South America*. Vol. 2, An Introduction to American Archaeology. Englewood Cliffs, N.J.: Prentice-Hall.

Willey, Gordon R., and Sabloff, Jeremy A. 1980. *A History of American Archaeology*. 2d ed. San Francisco: Freeman.

Williams, Elizabeth. 1987. "Complex Hunter-Gatherers in Australia." *Antiquity* 61 (232):310–321.

Williams, Leon Carlos. 1978–80. "Complejas de pirámides con planta en U." *Revista del Museo Nacional* 44:95–110.

Williams, M. A. J. 1984. "Late Quaternary Prehistoric Environments in the Sahara." In J. D. Clark and Steven A. Brandt, eds., *From Hunters to Farmers*. Berkeley and Los Angeles: University of California Press. Pp. 74–83.

Wilson, David J. 1981. "Of Maize and Men: A Critique of the Maritime Hypothesis of State Origins on the Coast of Peru." *American Anthropologist* 83:931–940.

———. 1983. "The Origins and Development of Complex Prehispanic Society in the Lower Santa Valley, Peru: Implications for Theories of State Origins." *Journal of Anthropological Archaeology* 2:209–276.

Wilson, Edward O. 1980. *Sociobiology: The Abridged Edition*. Cambridge: Harvard University Press.

Wilson, J. A. 1951. *The Burden of Egypt*. Chicago: University of Chicago Press.

Windels, Ferdinand. 1965. *The Lascaux Cave Paintings*. London: Faber and Faber.

Winters, Howard. 1967. *The Riverton Culture*. Springfield: Illinois State Museum.

Wittfogel, Karl W. 1957. *Oriental Despotism: A Comparative Study of Total Power*. New Haven: Yale University Press.

Wobst, Martin. 1976. "Locational Relationships in Palaeolithic Society." *Journal of Human Evolution* 5:49–58.

———. 1978. "The Archaeo-ethnology of Hunter-Gatherers or the Tyranny of the Ethnographic Record in Archaeology." *American Antiquity* 43:303–309.

Wolfe, Eric. 1959. *Sons of the Shaking Earth*. Chicago: University of Chicago Press.

Wolpert, Stanley A. 1977. *A New History of India*. London: Oxford University Press.

Wolpoff, Milford H., et al. 1984. "Modern *Homo sapiens* Origins: A General Theory of Hominid Evolution Involving the Fossil Evidence from East Asia." In Fred Smith and Frank Spencer, eds., *The Origins of Modern Humans*. New York: Liss. Pp. 411–484.

Woolley, Sir Leonard. 1934. *The Royal Cemetery*. Vol. 2, Ur Excavations. London: British Museum.

Worsaae, J. J. A. 1849. *The Primeval Antiquities of Denmark*. London: Murray.

Wright, Gary. 1971. "Origins of Food Production in Southwestern Asia: A Survey of Ideas." *Current Anthropology* 12:447–478.

Wright, Henry T. 1977. "Recent Researches on the Origin of the State." *Annual Review of Anthropology* 6:355–370.

Wright, Henry T., and Johnson, G. 1978. "Population, Exchange, and Early State Formation in Southwestern Iran." *American Anthropologist* 77:267–289

Wright, R. V. S. 1971. *Archaeology of the Gallus Site, Koonalda Cave.* Canberra: Australian Institute of Aboriginal Studies.

———. 1977. *Stone Tools as Cultural Markers.* Canberra: Australian Institute of Aboriginal Studies.

Wylie, Alison. 1985. "The Reaction Against Analogy." *Advances in Archaeological Method and Theory* 8:63–111.

Yellen, John E. 1977. *Archaeological Approaches to the Present.* New York: Academic.

Yen, Douglas E. 1977. "Hoabhinian Horticulture: The Evidence and Questions from Northwest Thailand." In J. Allen, J. Golson, and Rhys Jones, eds., *Sunda and Sahel.* New York: Academic. Pp. 567–600.

Yesner, David K. 1980. "Maritime Hunter-Gatherers: Ecology and Prehistory." *Current Anthropology* 21:727–750.

———. 1987. "Life in the Garden of Eden: Causes and Consequences of the Adoption of Marine Diets by Human Societies." In Marvin Harris and Eric B. Ross, eds., *Food and Evolution.* Philadelphia: Temple University Press. Pp. 111–131.

Zohary, Daniel. 1969. "The Progenitors of Wheat and Barley in Relation to Domestication and Agricultural Dispersal in the Old World." In Peter J. Ucko and G. W. Dimbleby, eds., *The Domestication and Exploitation of Plants and Animals.* London: Duckworth. Pp. 47–66.

Zubrow, Ezra. 1971. "Carrying Capacity and Dynamic Equilibrium in the Prehistoric Southwest." *American Antiquity* 36:127–138.

Zvelebil, Marek, ed. 1986. *Hunters in Transition.* Cambridge: Cambridge University Press.

———, and Rowley-Conwy, Peter, eds. 1984. "Transition to Farming in Northern Europe: A Hunter-Gatherer Perspective." *Norwegian Archaeological Records* 17:104–128.

Figure 1.3, page 19: From *Invitation to Archaeology* by James Deetz. Copyright © 1967 by James Deetz. Reprinted by permission of Doubleday, a division of Bantam, Doubleday, Dell Publishing Group, Inc. *Figure 1.4, page 26. Left:* Vida Freeman/Earthwatch; *right:* Courtesy of the Society of Antiquaries of London. *Figure 1.5, page 28:* From *Invitation to Archaeology* by James Deetz. Copyright © 1967 by James Deetz. Reprinted by permission of Doubleday, a division of Bantam, Doubleday, Dell Publishing Group, Inc.

CHAPTER 2

Figure 2.1, page 45: From Karl W. Butzer *Archaeology as Human Ecology* (New York: Cambridge University Press), 1982, p. 16. Reprinted by permission. *Figure 2.2, page 46:* From Karl W. Butzer *Archaeology as Human Ecology* (New York: Cambridge University Press), 1982, p. 31. Reprinted by permission. *Figure 2.3, page 48:* From Karl W. Butzer *Archaeology as Human Ecology* (New York: Cambridge University Press, 1982, p. 83. Reprinted by permission. *Figure 2.4, page 53:* From Richard B. Lee and Irven De Vore (eds.) *Kalahari Hunter-Gatherers* (Cambridge: Harvard University Press), 1976. Reprinted by permission.

CHAPTER 3

Table 3.1, page 66: Adapted from *Glacial and Quaternary Geology* by R.F. Flint, © 1971, by permission of John Wiley & Sons. *Figure 3.1, page 70:* From N.J. Shackleton and N.D. Opdyke, "Oxygen Isotope and Paleomagnetic Stratigraphy of Equatorial Pacific Ocean Core V28-238," in *Quaternary Research* 3:38-55. Reprinted by permission. *Figure 3.2, page 73, and Figure 3.3, page 75:* From Karl W. Butzer, *Environment and Archaeology*, 2nd edition (Hawthorn, N.Y.: Aldine Publishing Company), 1971. Reprinted by permission of the author.

CHAPTER 4

Figure 4.1, page 84: By permission of Elwyn L. Simons, Center for the Study of Primate Biology and History, Duke University, Durham, North Carolina. *Figure 4.2, page 85, and Figure 4.3 a) and b), page 87:* Redrawn with permission of Macmillan Publishing Co., Inc. from *The Ascent of Man* by David Pilbeam. Copyright © 1972 by David Pilbeam. *Figure 4.3 c), page 87:* Redrawn with permission of Bantam Books, Inc. from *Monkeys and Apes* by Prudence Napier, copyright © 1972. All rights reserved. *Figure 4.5, page 93:* Photograph by courtesy of the Transvaal Museum, South Africa. *Figure 4.6, page 94:* Courtesy of Alan R. Hughes, University of the Witwatersrand. *Figure 4.7, page 96:* Reprinted courtesy of the Institute of Human Origins, Berkeley, California. *Figure 4.8, page 97:* Photograph by John Reader, courtesy of Mary Leakey. *Figure 4.9, page 98:* © Copyright held by The National Museums of Kenya, P.O. Box 40658, Nairobi, Kenya. Reprinted with permission. *Figure 4.10, page 99:* Anthro-Photo/Cannon-Bonventre photographer. *Figure 4.11, page 101:* From Mark L. Weiss and Alan E. Mann, *Human Biology and Behavior: An Anthropological Perspective*, 4th ed. Copyright © 1986 by Little, Brown and Company (Inc.). Reprinted by permission. *Figure 4.12, page 104:* Robert Foley/Antiquity Publications Ltd. *Figure 4.13, page 106:* Henry T. Bunn. *Figure 4.14, page 111:* Photographed by Hugo van Lawick © National Geographic Society. *Figure 4.15, page 113, and Figure 4.16 top, page 114:* From *Life Nature Library/Early Man.* Redrawn from Lowell Hess © 1980 Time-Life Books Inc. *Figure 4.16 bottom, page 114:* Adapted by permission from *Olduvai Gorge: Excavations in Beds I and II* by M.D. Leakey, © 1971, Cambridge University Press. *Figure 4.17, page 115:* From John Gowlett in Robert Foley, ed., *Hominid Evolution and Community Ecology* (New York: Academic Press), 1984, p. 176, Fig. 7.1.

CHAPTER 5

Figure 5.1, page 125: © Copyright held by The National Museums of Kenya, P.O. Box 40658, Nairobi, Kenya. Reprinted with permission. *Figure 5.2, page 126:* Cambridge Museum of Archaeology and Anthropology. *Figure 5.3, page 131:* From H.L. Movius, Jr., "The Lower Paleolithic Structures of Southern and Eastern Asia," *Transactions of the American Philosophical Society*, Vol. 38, Pt. 4 (1948). Reprinted by permission of the Society and the author. *Figure 5.4, page 134. Top:* From Grahame Clark, *Aspects of Prehistory.* Copyright © 1970 by The Regents of the University of California. Reprinted by permission of the University of California Press. *Bottom:* Redrawn by permission for Ronald Singer et al., "Excavation of the Clactonian Industry," *Proceedings of the Prehistoric Society*, by permission of the Society. *Figures 5.5, page 135, 5.6, page 136, & 5.7, page 137:* Robert Foley/Antiquity Publications Ltd. *Figure 5.8, page 139. Top:* From John Gowlett in Robert Foley, ed., *Hominid Evolution and Community Ecology* (New York: Academic Press), 1984, Figs. 7.3, 7.5, & 7.6. *Figure 5.8, page 141. Middle:* From Jacques Bordaz *Tools of the Old and New Stone Age*, Copyright 1970 by Jacques Bordaz. Reprinted by permission. *Figure 5.8, page 141. Bottom:* From M.D. Leakey *Olduvai Gorge: Excavations in Beds I & II*, Cambridge University Press, 1971. Reprinted by permission of Cambridge University Press. *Figure 5.9 top and bottom, page 141. Top:* Acheulian hand ax from Figure 26 *The Swanscombe Skull: A Survey of Research on Pleistocene Site* (Occasional Paper No. 20, Royal Anthropological Institute of Great Britain and Ireland), by permission of the Society. *Bottom left:* From *The Distribution of Prehistoric Culture in Angola* by J.D. Clark, Companhia de Diamantes de Angola, Africa, 1966. *Bottom right:* Adapted from *Prehistory of Africa* by J.D. Clark, Thames and Hudson, Ltd., London. *Figure 5.11, page 142:* From John Gowlett in Robert Foley, ed., *Hominid Evolution and Community Ecology* (New York: Academic Press), 1984, p. 176, Fig. 7.1. *Figure 5.12, page 145:* Courtesy of F. Clark Howell. *Figure 5.13, page 146:* Karl Butzer *Environment and Archaeology*, Cambridge University Press, 1982. Reprinted with permission of Cambridge University Press. *Figure 5.14, page 147:* By permission of Henry de Lumley, Laboratoire de Paléontologie Humaine et de Préhistoire, Marseilles. *Figure 5.15, page 150, and 5.16, page 156:* Drawings by Janis Cirulis from *Mankind in the Making* by William Howells. Copyright © 1959, 1967 by William Howells. Reprinted by permission of Doubleday, a division of Bantam, Doubleday, Dell Publishing Group, Inc. *Figure 5.17 top, page 159:* From Jacques Bordaz *Tools of the Old and New Stone Age,* copyright 1970 by Jacques Bordaz. Copyright © 1958 by the American Museum of Natural History. Reprinted by permission of the author. *Figure 5.17 bottom, page 159. Left:* Redrawn from J.M. Coles and E.S. Higgs *The Archaeology of Early Man* by permission of Faber and Faber Ltd. *Bottom right:* Redrawn from *Prehistory* by Derek Roe. Courtesy of the British Museum (Natural History). *Figure 5.18, page 160. Top, middle left and center, bottom center:* Adapted from *The Old Stone Age* by F. Bordes. Copyright © 1968 by McGraw-Hill, Inc. Used by permission of McGraw-Hill Book Company and Weidenfeld & Nicolson Ltd. *Figure 5.18, page 160. Middle right:* Redrawn from *The Stone Age of Mt Carmel* by D.A.E. Garrod and D.M.A. Bate by permission of Oxford University Press. *Figure 5.18, page 160. Bottom left:* Adapted from *Prehistory of Africa* by J.D. Clark, Thames and Hudson Ltd., London. *Figure 5.18, page 160. Bottom right:* Redrawn from J.M. Coles and E. S. Higgs, *The Archaeology of Early Man* by permission of Faber and Faber Ltd. *Figure 5.19, page 162:* From A.C. Blanc, "Torre in Pietra Saccopastore, Monte Circeo: On the Position of the Mousterian in the Pleistocene Sequence of the Rome Area," in *Hundert Jahre Neanderthaler* (Cologne: Bohlau Verlag, 1958).

CHAPTER 6

Figure 6.2, page 171: Anthro-Photo/M. Shostak photographer. *Figure 6.3, page 173:* Courtesy of Milford Wolpoff. *Figure 6.4, page 174. Top b):* From Jacques Bordaz *Tools of the Old and New Stone Age,* Copyright 1970 by Jacques Bordaz. Reprinted by permission. *Figure 6.4, page 174. Top a) and bottom left:* Adapted from *The Old Stone Age* by F. Bordes. Copyright © 1968 by McGraw-Hill, Inc. Used with permission of McGraw-Hill Book Company and Weidenfeld & Nicholson Ltd. *Figure 6.4, page 174. Bottom right:* Adapted by permission from *Le paléolithique supérieur en Périgord* by Denise de Sonneville-Bordes, Directeur de recherches au Centre national de la Recherche scientifique, Institut du Quaternaire, Université de Bordeaux. *Table 6.1, pages 180 and 181. Left page bottom and right page bottom left:* H. Breuil. *Right page top and middle left:* Adapted by permission from *Le paléolithique supérieur en Périgord* by Denise de Sonneville-Bordes, Directeur de recherches au Centre national de la Recherche scientifique, Institut du Quaternaire, Université de Bordeaux. *Middle right:* After Lowell Hess *Early Man,* Life Nature Library, © 1965 Time Inc. by permission of the publisher, Time-Life Books Inc. *Bottom right:* Adapted from *The Old Stone Age* by F. Bordes. Copyright © 1968 by McGraw-Hill Book Company and Weidenfeld & Nicolson Ltd. *Figures 6.5, page 184, Figure 6.6, page 185, & Figure 6.7, page 186:* Collection Musée de l'Homme. *Figure 6.8, page 187:* © Alexander Marshack, 1972. *Figure 6.9, page 190:* From O. Soffer *The Upper Paleolithic of the Central Russian Plain,* Academic Press, 1985, Fig. 2.67. Reprinted with permission of Academic Press and the author. *Figure 6.10, page 191. Top:* From Richard G. Klein *Man and Culture in the Late Pleistocene,* © 1969 by Chandler Publishing Company. By permission of Dun-Donnelley Publishing Corporation. *Figure 6.10, page 191. Bottom:* From *The Archeology of the USSR* by A.L. Mongait, Mir Publishers, Moscow. *Figure 6.11, page 193:* From C.B.M. McBurney *Early Man in the Soviet Union,* Fig. 6. p. 44. Published by Oxford University Press for The British Academy; from the Proceedings of the British Academy, Volume LXI, 1975. *Figure 6.12, page 194:* Reprinted by permission of Faber and Faber Ltd. From: J.M. Coles and E.S. Higgs *The Archaeology of Early Man.*

CHAPTER 7

Figure 7.2, page 203: Redrawn with permission of the Glencoe Press from *Foundations of Archeology* by Jason W. Smith. Copyright © 1976 by Jason W. Smith *Figure 7.3, page 207:* From Brian M. Fagan *The Great Journey* (London: Thames and Hudson), 1987, p. 93. Julie M. Longhill, artist. *Figure 7.4, page 212:* Redrawn from Gordon R. Willey *An Introduction to American Archaeology, Vol. I: North and Middle America,* © 1966. Reprinted by permission of the author and Prentice Hall Inc., Englewood Cliffs, N.J. *Figure 7.5, page 220:* Courtesy of University of Colorado Museum, Joe Ben Wheat photo. *Figure 7.6, page 222:* Redrawn by permission of McGraw-Hill Book Company from *Prehistory of North America* by Jesse D. Jennings. Copyright © 1968 by McGraw-Hill, Inc. *Figure 7.7, page 224:* From Brian M. Fagan *The Great Journey* (London: Thames and Hudson), 1987, p. 162. *Figure 7.8, page 228:* Field Museum of Natural History (Neg. #953.5.73.6), Chicago. *Figure 7.9, page 230:* U.S. Information Agency No. 111-SC-33831 in National Archives Building. *Figure 7.10, page 231:* University of Alaska Museum.

CHAPTER 8

Figure 8.1, page 238: From Jacques Bordaz *Tools of the Old and New Stone Age.* Copyright 1970 by Jacques Bordaz. Reprinted by permission. *Figure 8.2, page 240:* South African Archeological Bulletin and Professor v. Riet Lowe. *Figure 8.3, page 241: South African Archeological Bulletin* and Murray Schoonraal. *Figure 8.4, page 241:* Courtesy of the University of Witwatersrand/D.S. Whitley. *Figure 8.5, page 242:* Marshall/!Kung San Foundation. *Figure 8.6, page 244:* F. Peron. *Figure 8.7, page 245:* Reproduced with permission of the publishers from Bellwood, P., *Prehistory of the Indo-Malaysian Archipelago,* Academic Press, Sydney, Australia, 1985. *Figure 8.8, page 247:* Courtesy Robert Edwards, Aboriginal Arts Board. *Figure 8.9, page 248:* Redrawn by permission from Richard A. Gould, "The Archaeologist as Ethnographer," *World Archaeology* 3, 2 (1971), 143–177, Fig. 18.

CHAPTER 9

Figure 9.1, page 255: Adapted by permission from *The Material Culture of the People of the Gwembe Valley* by Dr. Barrie Reynolds, published by Manchester University Press for the Livingstone Museum, Zambia. *Figure 9.2, page 260:* From Roger Lewin *Human Evolution,* Blackwell Scientific Publications Ltd., 1984. Reprinted by permission. *Figure 9.3, page 266:* S. von Herbenstain. *Figure 9.4, page 267:* From Sonia Coles *The Neolithic Revolution,* by permission of the Trustees of the British Museum (Natural History). *Figure 9.5, page 269. Top:* Wyatt Davis, Courtesy Museum of New Mexico, (Neg. 44191); *Bottom left:* Tyler Dingee, Courtesy of Museum of New Mexico, (Neg 73453); *Bottom right:* Tyler Dingee, Courtesy of Museum of New Mexico, (Neg. 73449). *Figure 9.6, page 270:* Reproduced courtesy of the Trustees of the British Museum.

CHAPTER 10

Figure 10.2, page 278. Left: Redrawn from D.A.E. Garrod and D.M.A. Bate *The Stone Age of M. Carmel* by permission of Oxford University Press. *Right:* From James Mellaart *The Earliest Civilizations of the Near East.* Reprinted by permission of Thames and Hudson Ltd., London. *Figure 10.3, page 280:* British School of Archaeology in Jerusalem. *Figure 10.4, page 281:* Courtesy of Tell Abu Hureyra excavation. *Figure 10.5, page 282:* British School of Archaeology in Jerusalem. *Figure 10.6, page 283:* Peter Dorrell & Stuart Laidlaw, Institute of Archaeology, University of London. *Figure 10.7, page 287:* Redrawn from James Mellaart, *Catal Huyuk* by permission of Thames and Hudson Ltd., London. *Figure 10.8, page 288:* Redrawn from James Mellaart, *Catal Huyuk* by permission of Thames and Hudson, Ltd., London.

CHAPTER 11

Figure 11.1, page 298: From *Proceedings of the Prehistoric Society* by permission of the Society. *Figure 11.3, page 302:* From *Prehistory* by Derek Roe, with permission of the Biologisch-Archaeologisch Institut der Rijksuniversiteit, Groningen, the Netherlands. *Figure 11.4, page 303:* From Grahame Clark *World Prehistory,* 3rd ed., p. 140: © 1977 Cambridge University Press. *Figure 11.6, page 308:* From *Prehistory* by Derek Roe, with permission of Presses Universitaires de France. *Figure 11.7, page 309:* Neg #39604, Courtesy Department of Library Services, American Museum of Natural History. *Figure 11.8, page 311:* Redrawn from *Ancient Europe* by Stuart Piggott, with permission of Edinburgh University Press. Copyright © Stuart Piggott, 1965.

CHAPTER 12

Figure 12.1, page 315: Photo by John S. Shelton.

CHAPTER 13

Figure 13.3, page 331, 13.4, page 332, and 13.6, page 334: Reprinted by permission from *The Archaeology of Ancient China,* 3rd ed. by Kwang-chih Chang (New Haven: Yale University Press, 1977). *Figure 13.7, page 335:* Scala/Art Resource, N.Y. *Figure 13.9, page 340:* Courtesy of Professor R.C. Green. *Figure 13.10, page 341:* Field Museum of Natural History (Neg. #100629), Chicago. *Figure 13.11, page 342:* Courtesy of The British Library.

CHAPTER 14

Figure 14.1, page 350: Reprinted by permission from *Prehistoric Food Production in North America,* ed. by Richard Ford, University of Michigan Museum of Anthropology. *Figure 14.3, page 355:* From Gordon R. Willey *An Introduction to American Archaeology Vol. II: South America,* © 1971. Reprinted by permission of Prentice Hall Inc., Englewood Cliffs, N.J. *Figure 14.4, page 356:* Drawing by Junius Bird. Courtesy of The American Museum of Natural History. *Figure 14.5, page 358:* Photo by Thomas F. Lynch. *Figure 14.7, page 363:* Photograph taken by Jonathan E. Reyman. *Figure 14.8, page 366:* Courtesy of the Louisiana Office of State Parks. *Figure 14.9, page 368:* Redrawn by permission of McGraw-Hill Book Company from *Prehistory of North America* by Jesse D. Jennings. Copyright © 1968 by McGraw-Hill, Inc. Used with permission of McGraw-Hill Book Company. After W.S. Webb, *University of Kentucky Reports in Anthropology and Archaeology,* Vol. 5, no. 2. *Figure 14.10, page 369, a) and c):* Courtesy of the Werner Forman Archive Limited. *Figure 14.10, page 369, b):* Field Museum of Natural History (Neg. #90925), Chicago. *Figure 14.11, page 371:* Artist's reconstruction by William Iseminger. Photograph courtesy of Cahokia Mounds State Historic Site. *Figure 14.12, page 372:* Courtesy of Cahokia Mounds State Historic Site.

CHAPTER 15

Figure 15.1, page 388: Adapted from *Physical Anthropology and Archaeology* by Clifford J. Jolly and Fred Plog. Copyright © 1976 by Alfred A. Knopf, Inc. Reprinted by permission of Alfred A. Knopf, Inc. *Figure 15.2, page 390:* From *The Rise of Civilization: From Early Farmers to Urban Society in the Ancient Near East* by Charles Redman. W.H. Freeman and Company. Copyright © 1978. Reprinted by permission.

CHAPTER 16

Figure 16.2, page 400: Courtesy of the Oriental Institute, University of Chicago. *Figure 16.3, page 402 and Figure 16.4, page 104, bottom:* Fotoarchiv Hirmer Verlag München. *Figure 16.4, page 404. Top:* From *Early Mesopotamia and Iran* by Max E. Mallowan. Thames and Hudson Ltd., London. *Figure 16.5, page 406:* From Samuel Noah Kramer, "The Sumerians," *Scientific American,* October 1957. Reprinted with permission of W.H. Freeman and Company. Copyright © 1957 by Scientific American, Inc. All rights reserved. *Figure 16.6, page 411:* Courtesy of The University Museum, University of Pennsylvania.

CHAPTER 17

Figure 17.3, page 422: © George Holton, Photo Researchers. *Figure 17.4, page 423:* Michael Holford, London. *Figure 17.5, page 426:* All rights reserved, The Metropolitan Museum of Art. *Figure 17.7, page 431:* Courtesy of the Rhodesian National Tourist Board.

CHAPTER 18

Figure 18.2, page 438: Roger-Viollet Documentation Générale Photographique, Paris. *Figure 18.5, page 445:* Courtesy of the University Museum, The University of Pennsylvania. *Figure 18.6, page 451:* Magnum Photos, Inc./Mark Riboud.

CHAPTER 19

Figure 19.2, page 458. Left: From *Ancient Europe* by Stuart Piggott, with permission of Edinburgh University Press. Copyright © Stuart Piggott, 1965. *Figure 19.2, page 458. Right:* Reproduced by Courtesy of the Trustees of the British Museum. *Figure 19.3, page 460:* Ekdotike Athenon S. A. Athens. *Figure 19.4, page 461:* Fotoarchiv Hirmer Verlag München. *Figure 19.9, page 467:* From *Ancient Europe* by Stuart Piggott, with permission of Edinburgh University Press. Copyright © Stuart Piggott, 1965. *Figure 19.10, page 467:* Adapted from *Writing* by David Diringer, with permission of Thames and Hudson Ltd., London © David Diringer, 1962.

CHAPTER 20

Figure 20.1, page 474, and Figure 20.2, page 475: From *Ancient Europe* by Stuart Piggott, with permission of Edinburgh University Press. Copyright © Stuart Piggott, 1965. *Figure 20.3, page 476:* Courtesy of the Ashmolean Museum. *Figure 20.4, page 478:* From R.F. Tylecote, in *The Prehistory of Metallurgy in the British Isles*, 1986. Reprinted by permission of R.F. Tylecote. *Figure 20.6, page 480:* Aerofilms Library, London. *Figure 20.7, page 482:* From *Ancient Europe* by Stuart Piggott, with permission of Edinburgh University Press. Copyright © Stuart Piggott, 1965. *Figure 20.10, page 486:* Reproduced courtesy of the Trustees of The British Museum.

CHAPTER 21

Figure 21.2, page 508: Peabody Museum, Harvard University © President & Fellows of Harvard College. Photo by Hillel Burger #N28172 © 1978. *Figure 21.4, page 496:* Courtesy of Smithsonian Institution. *Figure 21.5, page 498:* The China Friendship Society: from Grahame Clark, *World Prehistory*, 3rd edition, p. 306, © 1977 Cambridge University Press.

CHAPTER 22

Figure 22.2, page 508: Courtesy of Franklin Graham. *Figure 22.3 and Figure 22.4, page 509:* From Gordon Willey, *An Introduction to American Archaeology, Vol. I: North and Middle America.* © 1966. Reprinted by permission of the author and Prentice Hall, Inc., Englewood Cliffs, N.J. *Figure 22.5, page 511:* From Robert D. Drennan "Contextual Analysis of Ritual Paraphernalia from Formative Oaxaca," in Kent V. Flannery (ed.) *The Early Mesoamerican Village* (Orlando, Fla.: Academic Press, 1976). Reprinted by permission of the author and the publisher. *Figure 22.6, page 513:* Arizona State Museum, The University of Arizona, E.B. Sayles, photographer. *Figure 22.7, page 516:* From *Urbanization at Teotihuacan, Mexico*, I, Pt. 1, 1973. © 1973 by Rene Millon. *Figure 22.8, page 520. Photo:* Copyright © Project El Mirador; *drawing:* Copyright © Richard Hansen. *Figure 22.9, page 521:* Photo Researchers/Carl Frank. *Figure 22.10, page 523:* Courtesy of Smithsonian Institution, National Anthropological Archives. *Figure 22.11, page 527:* From J. Eric S. Thompson *The Rise and Fall of Maya Civilization*, Copyright 1954, 1966, by the University of Oklahoma Press. *Figure 22.12, page 528:* Peabody Museum, Harvard University © President & Fellows of Harvard College. Neg #21622 F.P. Orchard © 1953. *Figure 22.13, page 530:* Courtesy of Smithsonian Institution. *Figure 22.14, page 531:* Lesley Newhart. *Figure 22.15, page 532:* Courtesy of Franklin C. Graham. *Figure 22.16, page 534:* Lesley Newhart.

CHAPTER 23

Figure 23.1, page 543: Photo by Jeffrey Quilter. *Figure 23.3, page 546. Left:* Courtesy Gordon Willey. *Figure 23.3, page 546. Right:* Courtesy of Franklin Graham. *Figure 23.4, page 549:* Anne Paul/Earthwatch. *Figure 23.5, page 550:* M. Moseley/Anthrophoto. *Figure 23.6, page 552:* Peabody Museum, Harvard University © President & Fellows of Harvard College. David de Harpoort © 1958. *Figure 23.7, page 553:* Peabody Museum, Harvard University © President & Fellows of Harvard College. Hillel Burger © 1982. *Figure 23.8, page 554:* Lee Boltin. *Figure 23.9, page 556:* Bettman Archive, Inc. *Figure 23.10, page 557:* M. Moseley/Anthrophoto. *Figure 23.11, page 562:* Courtesy of Franklin C. Graham. *Figure 23.12, page 563:* George Holton/Photo Researchers, Inc.

Index

es-Skhūl, 155
Ethiopia, 92–94, 96
Ethnoarchaeology, 52–54
Ethnographic analogy, 36, 50–51
Etruscans, 469
et-Tabūn, 155, 175
Europe, 472–487
　agriculture in, 276, 297–312
　archaeological sites in, 300. See
　　also names of specific sites
　art in, 183–188, 458, 459–460,
　　462, 463, 485
　bronzeworking in, 458, 464,
　　476–479, 485
　burials in, 296, 304–305, 310,
　　311–312, 464, 473, 475, 484
　chronology of, 298
　copperworking in, 473–474, 475,
　　478
　earliest human settlement in, 129
　hunter-gatherers in, 41, 144–148,
　　157, 176–183
　ironworking in, 483–486
　religions in, 161–163
　technology in, 180, 181
　vegetation in, 73, 75, 76–77
　warrior tribes in, 481–483
European Century, 34–35
Evans, Arthur, 465
Evolution, 85
　biological, 83–86, 91–100
　cladistic theory of, 103–104
　cladogram of, 135
　cultural, 35–36, 56–57
　diagram of, 104
　fossil evidence for, 91–100
　molecular biology and, 86–87
　multilinear, 56–57
Excavation, 6, 24–27
Experimental archaeology, 51

Faience, 415
Falk, Dean, 117
Farming. See Agriculture; Food
　production
Fayum Depression, 317, 418
Features, 15
Fell, Barry, 505
Fertile Crescent theory, 379–380
Finney, Ben, 339
Fire, 127–128
Fishing, 38, 170, 227, 296, 309,
　355–356
Fission track dating, 23
Flakes, 106, 112, 113, 114, 115, 116,
　127, 130, 134, 135, 137, 138,
　139, 142, 144, 147–148, 159, 160,
　175, 195
Flannery, Kent, 58, 229, 257–258,
　261, 265, 353, 389, 391, 392,
　402, 510
Flenniken, Jeffrey, 58
Foley, Robert, 55, 135–137,
　152–153

Food production. See also
　Agriculture
　in Africa, 255, 268, 316–320, 415,
　　418–419, 428
　in the Americas, 5, 56, 58,
　　257–258, 348–374, 506, 511,
　　512–515, 529, 547–548, 551
　in Asia, 324–338
　consequences of, 254–256
　drought and, 255–256
　in Europe, 276, 297–312
　in Near East, 4, 40, 258, 265,
　　276–289, 381–383, 398–399,
　　401, 402, 408, 413
　nutrition and, 263–264
　origins of, 256–263
　in Pacific Islands, 337–343
Food remains, 43
Foraging. See Gathering;
　Hunter-gatherers
Fossil pollens, 42–43
Fossils, 42–43, 99–100
　of animals, 71
　of skulls, 93, 94, 97, 98, 99,
　　117–118, 124, 125, 126, 127,
　　149, 150, 155, 156, 282, 283
Franchthi Cave, 300
Fried, Morton, 56
Frison, George, 215
Fuegian Indians, 229
Funan, 448

Gamble, Clive, 34, 49, 50, 54,
　132–133, 157, 293
Gaming sticks, 222
Ganj Dareh, 285
Garnsey site, 219, 221
Garrod, Dorothy, 175
Gatecliff Rock Shelter, 221, 223
Gateway of the Sun, 556
Gathering, 110–111, 145, 147. See
　also Hunter-gatherers
Geoarchaeology, 46–49
Geological record, 67–71
Ghana, 428–429
Gibbons, 86
Giza, 9, 15, 23, 421, 422
Glacial periods, 65
Glaciations, 67, 72–74, 76–77
　Elster, 73
　Mindel, 67
　Saale, 74
　Weichsel, 75, 155, 200, 236, 243,
　　277
　Wisconsin, 200, 201, 202,
　　208–214
Gold, 411, 457, 460, 466, 553
Golson, Jack, 336
Gorillas, 86, 87
Gorman, Chester, 324, 326
Gould, Richard, 248–249
Gould, Stephen J., 103
Gowlett, John, 142, 144

Grasses, 299
Gravettian art, 183–184
Great Basin, 52, 221, 359
Great Bison Belt, 218
Great Enclosure, 430, 431
Great Plains, 26, 218–221
Great Pyramid, 421
Greece, 5, 8, 18, 71, 299–300,
　459–460, 466–468
Green, R. C., 339
Greenberg, Joseph, 208
Grotte Gazel, 308
Grove, David, 508
Growth cycles, 56
Guattari Cave, 162–163
Guidon, Niede, 212–213
Guitarrero Cave, 357, 358
Gwisho, 239–240
Gypsum Cave, 221

Habitats, 45
Hacilar, 286
Hadar, 93–94, 96, 100, 105
Halafian culture, 401, 402
Hallstatt culture, 484, 485, 486
Hammerstone, 113
Hammond, Norman, 518
Hammurabi, 412
Hand ax, 131, 134, 137–138, 139,
　140, 141, 142, 143, 144
Harappan civilization, 377, 409,
　435, 437–444
Harpoons, 181
Harris, David, 262
Hascherkeller, 484
Hassan, Fekri, 316, 317
Hassuna, 399, 400
Haury, Emil, 360
Haven, Samuel, 200
Haynes, Vance, 359
Herds. See Domestication of
　animals
Heuneburg, 484
Hieroglyphic writing, 416–417, 522,
　523, 524
Higham, Charles, 326, 327,
　445–446
Hillman, Gordon, 282
Hinduism, 447, 451
Hissarlik, 3, 457
Historical archaeology, 10
Historical records, 23
History, 10
Hittites, 458–459
Hoabhinian tools, 324
Hodge, A. W., 371
Hoffman, Michael, 417, 418
Hogup Cave, 221
Hohokam tradition, 360–361
Hole, Frank, 258
Holstein interglacial, 73
Home bases, 105–108
Hominidae, 33, 81–116